Women and Mass Communications in the 1990's

Women and Mass Communications in the 1990's

An International, Annotated Bibliography

Compiled by
JOHN A. LENT

Bibliographies and Indexes in Women's Studies, Number 29

GREENWOOD PRESS
Westport, Connecticut • London

Barnard

Library of Congress Cataloging-in-Publication Data

Lent, John A.
   Women and mass communications in the 1990's : an international,
annotated bibliography / compiled by John A. Lent.
      p.   cm.—(Bibliographies and indexes in women's studies,
   ISSN 0742–6941 ; no. 29)
   Includes bibliographical references and index.
   ISBN 0–313–30209–X (alk. paper)
   1. Mass media and women—Bibliography. I. Title.   II. Series.
Z5633.W65L45   1999
[P94.5.W65]
016.30223'082—dc21   99–21787

British Library Cataloguing in Publication Data is available.

Library of Congress Catalog Card Number: 99–21787
ISBN: 0–313–30209–X
ISSN: 0742–6941

First published in 1999

Greenwood Press, 88 Post Road West, Westport, CT 06881
An imprint of Greenwood Publishing Group, Inc.
www.greenwood.com

Printed in the United States of America

Contents

Preface

In the predecessor volume to this book, *Women and Mass Communications: An International Annotated Bibliography* (Greenwood, 1991), I elaborated on the omission of women from the printed discourse in mass communications studies well into the 1970s, and the progress made to redress that neglect since then. In the 1990s, women figure even more frequently and prominently in mass communication literature, with book series, special issues of journals, and sections of academic conferences devoted to their advancements and sometimes to lingering problems of discrimination and stereotyping.

Women and Mass Communications in the 1990s: An International, Annotated Bibliography follows the pattern of the earlier bibliography in that it is an international survey of all types of literature on women and mass communications for the 1990s. Included are all mass media, such as publishing, radio, television, film, magazines, newspapers, video, and computerized systems, and affiliates, such as advertising, public relations, and wire services. Omitted are speech communication, language and communication, and interpersonal communication, except for the few items that relate specifically to mass media.

The book is organized by continents and regions: Africa and the Middle East; Asia, Australia, and Oceania; Europe; Latin America and the Caribbean; and North America. An attempt has been made to include items on a wide range of countries, and this has meant including some "fugitive" and ephemeral items if not much else has been written about a country's media and women.

The first chapter takes a global perspective and subsumes comparative analyses, non-country specific material, special issues of journals, long-run representations of journals' contents, edited volumes, and conference proceedings. Topically, all chapters are divided into general studies, historical studies, images of women, women as audience, women practitioners, and women's media. The "images of women" category encompasses sex roles; sex stereotyping; representation, portrayal, and coverage of women in media; and pornography. The "women practitioners" category includes women working in mass media -- their experiences, anecdotes, successes, and struggles for job equality. Categories under the much larger United States section were expanded to include advertising and public relations, broadcasting, film, and print media under each of the six main topics.

The emphasis in this volume is on the 1990s, as the previous volume was made up of materials through December 1989. However, some pre-1990 works missed in the earlier book are picked up here.

A serious effort was made to compile a bibliography that would cover the most important literature on women in mass communications, a careful representation of the types of materials and a comprehensive overview of the field and its significant literature. The bibliography is representative in covering all genres of publications (books, periodicals, dissertations, theses, conference papers, etc.), writing formats and styles, time period, geographical areas, and languages. Although the compilation consists mainly of English-language publications, hundreds of citations appear from other languages. In the compiler's estimation, this book provides an overall survey of the most important (sometimes even the less important) materials on women and mass communications.

Many of the citations are annotated, descriptively and succinctly, without evaluative comments. Fuller annotations are provided for edited volumes, listing the contributors and their chapters, and for topics or countries about which not much is otherwise known. The citations are arranged alphabetically by author, or by article title when an author is not listed, and are numbered consecutively.

Search Process

The gathering of sources was both manual and electronic, the former because much literature is not in computerized databases yet and because that is how the compiler works. Keywords such as "woman/women" and "media," "communication," "journalism," "mass media," "broadcasting," etc., were searched in Sociofile, PsycLIT, and ERIC (Educational Resources Information Clearinghouse) through December 1997, and ABI/Inform through December 1995.

Many bibliographies, indices, bibliographic periodicals, and runs of hundreds of periodicals were used -- too numerous to list here. These included journals and other works in at least the fields of mass communications, popular culture, women's studies, sex research, social psychology, marketing, advertising, sociology, history, area studies, anthropology, critical studies, cultural studies, and others. The literature was published on every continent.

As before, "fugitive" materials, such as dissertations not indexed through the University of Michigan program, theses, conference papers, and pamphlets, make up part of the bibliography for a few reasons. First, although conference papers presented between 1996 and 1998 have probably not yet been published, they contain valuable information that should be available to researchers willing to contact the association where they were given. Second, "fugitive" documents are sometimes the only sources on women and mass communications in certain countries. Third, unpublished dissertations and theses, if properly supervised, are often some of the best work on a topic. There are not very many times in an academician's life -- especially given the increasing demands of bureaucratized universities -- when virtually all of her/his time and energy are concentrated on a single project guided by at least three-to-five other professionals.

Besides the usual methods of gathering citations, I also employed other means. A flyer calling for women (and men) to send me lists of their writings on women and mass communications was distributed at annual conferences of Asian Cinema Studies Society (1997), Association for Asian Studies (1997), International Association for Media and Communication Research (1996), and Popular Culture Association (1997). Although only a half dozen individuals responded (Louis Bosshart, Linda K. Fuller, Nora R. Roberts, Karen Ross, Dulcilia H. Schroeder Buitoni, and Annabelle Sreberny-Mohammadi), the materials they provided were valuable because of their stature in the field and the quality of their work. I thank them for their participation.

Others to whom I am indebted are the librarians and bibliographers who continue to carry out this tedious work and keep us abreast of the literature; Greenwood Press (particularly Alicia Merritt and Pamela St. Clair), which continues to believe that printed bibliographies are relevant in a time when many publishers (and scholars and students) are myopically focussed on computer databases; and Temple University graduate students who have worked with me. Concerning the latter, I wish to single out Nandini Sen, Daiwon Hyun, and Asli Tunç, who helped with computer searches; Asli also typed and formatted this book.

Women and Mass Communications in the 1990's

CHAPTER 1

Women and Mass Communications: Global and Comparative Perspectives

GENERAL STUDIES

1.   Allen, Donna, Ramona R. Rush, and Susan J. Kaufman, eds. *Women Transforming Communications: Global Intersections*. Newbury Park, California: Sage, 1996. 378 pp.
      Pulls together work of 39 women media practitioners, teachers, and researchers from around the world; shows how they and other women used strategies for liberating communication systems from gender and cultural biases; the 34 chapters are divided into communication visions, chasms, and transformative communications.

2.   Anand, Anita. "Moving from the Alternative to the Mainstream for a New Gender Perspective." *Intermedia*. June/July 1993, pp. 54-56.

3.   Anderson, Karen. "Engineering Gender Parity: Not Just a Problem of Technical Support." *Intermedia*. June/July 1993, pp. 58-60.

4.   Andsager, Julie L. and Robert O. Wyatt. "More Than a Matter of Sex: Gender Differences in Support for Various Media Rights in Four Cultures." Paper presented at Association for Education in Journalism and Mass Communication, April 1996. 20 pp.
      Examines men and women's support for the media's advertising, entertainment, and journalism rights in the US, Russia, and Israel, both among Jews and Arabs.

5.   Antrobus, Peggy and Judith Bizot. "Women's Perspectives: Towards an Ethical, Equitable, Just and Sustainable Livelihood in the 21st Century." *Women in Action*. 4/1992 and 1/1993, pp. 28-35.

6.   Association for Education in Journalism and Mass Communication. Annual Meeting, Minneapolis, Minnesota, August 1-4, 1990.

Includes Dru Riley Evarts, "Newspaper Headlines About the Possibility of Having a Woman President: A Descriptive Study"; Jennifer Swanson, "News Coverage of the Abortion Issue: Framing Changes in the 1980s"; Brenda Cooper and Glenda Jenkins," Depictions of Men and Women in Advertising in *Time* and the *Ladies' Home Journal*, 1930-1980s"; Carole Eberly, "The Journalists' Bible: Bad News for Women"; Elizabeth L. Toth, "Public Relations Practitioner Attitudes Toward Gender Issues"; Ramona R. Rush and Sonia Gutierrez-Villalobos, "From Making of Myths into Hardening of Realities: Media Images and Employment of Women--Case in Point, Latin America"; Phyllis Miller and Elizabeth R. Hall, "Television News Coverage of Women's Sports"; Frankie Hutton, "Free Women and the Antebellum Black Press: The Gender Oppression View Reconsidered"; Helen Benedict, "Virgins and Vamps: Sex Crimes in the Press"; Sue A. Lafky, "The Role of Gender in the Professional Values and Orientation of Journalists: A Cross-Cultural Comparison"; Mark D. Harmon, "Who Will Meet the Press? A Content Analysis of Program Guests"; Lee Jolliffe, "Liberal Feminism: The Strategies of an Activist Audience"; Judith A. Cramer, "The Invisible Female Athlete: Gender Issues in the Promotion of Women's Sports"; Catherine Pratt, "Gender Implications in Public Relations Ethics"; Larissa A. Grunig, "Communication and Subculture: The Case of Women in the Foreign Service"; Gay Wakefield, "Career Goals and Perceptions of Self-Worth and Organizational Power Among Female and Male Public Relations Practitioners: A Pilot Study"; Robert Jensen, "The Epistemology of Pornography"; Catherine Van Horn," Flynt and Feminism in Court"; Jane Rhodes, "Ida B. Wells as Prototype: Race and Gender in Journalism History"; Robert Abelman, "Portrayal of a Housewife: The Depiction of Women in Religious Television"; Sarah Evans, "Non-Sexist Visual Symbolism: A Guide for Photographers"; Paula Horvath-Neimeyer and Kurt Kent, "Stereotypes and News Gathering: Biases that Guide Reporters"; Dominic Lasorsa, "Women on the Front Page: A Study of News Roles Over 100 Years"; David Atkin and Jay Moorman, "Portrayals of Women on Television in the 1980s"; Barbara S. Reed, "The Link Between Mobilizing Information and Service Journalism as Applied to Women's Magazines Coverage of Eating Disorders"; Julia Hedgepeth, "A Quiet Revolution, 1739-1748: How America's First Three Women Newspaper Editors Treated the Topic of Women"; Agnes Hooper Gottlieb, "Feminism and Femininity: An Analysis of *The Washington Post*'s Women's Page, 1940-1970"; Rodger Streitmatter, "Alice Allison Dunnigan: Pioneer Black Woman Journalist"; Ann E. Presten, "The Invisible Woman: Two Decades of Magazine Images of Nurses"; Marilyn S. Greenwald," All Brides Are Not Beautiful: The Influence of Charlotte Curtis on Women's News in *The New York Times*"; Carolyn M. Byerly, "Through a Lens Clearly: Women and the Evolution of World News"; Mary M. Cronin, "An Analysis of a Wartime Agenda: The Korean War Reporting of Marguerite Higgins," and Judith Knelman, "Lucrezia Borgia in Albion: Images of Female Criminals c.1850."

7.   Association for Education in Journalism and Mass Communication. Annual Meeting, Boston, Massachusettes, August 1991.

Includes Katherine T. Frith and Subir Sengupta, "Individualism: A Cross-Cultural Analysis of Print Advertisement from the U.S. and India"; Liz Watts, "Bess Furman: Nebraska's Front Page Girl"; Rose M. Kundanis, "Child Care for

Rosie the Riveter and the United Nations: Images of Innovations and Visions for the Future in Popular Magazines 1941-1949"; Dianne Lynch-Paley, "Covering the Capitol: Is Gender an Issue?"; Margaret Duffy, "A Critical Review of Studies of Women's Portrayal in Advertising"; Fiona A. E. McQuarrie, "The Experiences of Female Journalism Graduates in the Canadian Labor Market: A Longitudinal Assessment"; Georgia Ne-Smith, "Feminist Historiography and Journalism History: Time for Conceptual Change"; Donna M. Bertazzoni, "Gender-Based Differences in Attitudes Towards Stories: An Examination of Maryland Editors"; Aralynn Abare McMane, "Hello, Handsome, Get Me Rewrite: Toward an Understanding of the Portrayal of the Female Journalist in Film and on Television"; Robert Jensen, "The Ideology of Pornography: Portrayals of Female Sexuality in Pornographic Novels"; Maurine H. Beasley, "Mary Marvin Breckinridge Patterson: Case Study of One of 'Murrow's Boys'"; Samuel P. Winch,"On Naming Rape Victims: How Editors Stand on the Issue"; Wendy Gibbons, "Pretty Housewives and World-Famous Physicians: Coverage of Abortion in General Interest Magazines between 1951 and 1969"; Daniel A. Stout,"Resolving Conflicts of Worldviews: Women, Television and Religious Community"; Agnes H. Gottlieb, "Rethinking the Questions: An Essay on Writing Journalism History from a Feminist Perspective"; Carmen Luke, "A View of One's Own: Rural Women and TV"; Kimberly K. Burks and Vernon A. Stone, "Differences at Home and at Work: Factors in Career Advancement by Male and Female News Directors"; Joe S. Foote, "Women's Network News Visibility"; Roger C. Saathoff and Julie Ann Moellering, "Down the Path of Domesticity: A Content Analysis of Three Women's Service Magazines: 1905-1985"; Barbara S. Reed, "Trude Weiss-Rosmarin: Rebel with a Cause"; William G. Christ and Sammye Johnson, "From Ethel Merman to Barbara Bush: 50 Years of Women's Images Through Time"; Russell J. Cook, "Dorothy Fuldheim's Activist Journalism and the Kent State Shootings"; B. Lee Becker, "Finding Work and Getting Paid: Predictors of Success in the Mass Communications Job Market."

8. Association for Education in Journalism and Mass Communication. Annual Meeting, Montreal, Canada, August 1992.
    Includes Lisa Barr, "Re-visioning the Role and Effects of Women as Gatekeepers: A Pilot Study"; Paul Belgrade, "Talian Pie: The Life of a Retarded Man"; Terri Catlett, "Effects of Staff Gender on Newspaper Content"; Judith A. Cramer, "Missing in Action: Women Sports Journalists"; David R. Spencer, "Unequal Partners: Gender Relationships in Victorian Radical Journalism"; Elizabeth V. Burt, "Mixed Messages in a Progressive Newspaper: The Milwaukee Journal and Woman Suffrage, 1911-1912"; Haejung Paik, "Gender and the Effects of Television Violence: A Meta-Analysis"; Ted Pease, "Race, Gender and White Male Backlash in Newsrooms"; M. Mark Miller, Julie L. Andsager and Robert O. Wyatt, "How Gender and Select Demographics Relate to Support for Expressive Rights"; Venise T. Berry, "Limited Vision: Realism, The New Ghetto Aesthetic, and Black Female Representation in Today's Popular Black Films"; Kathleen Endres and Ann Shierhorn, "Closing the Gap: An Analysis of Gender-based Differences and Similarities in Magazine Writing Instruction"; Leah Grant, "'You've Gone All The Way, Baby.' The Portrayal of Women in Playboy Cartoons"; David Abrahamson, "A Quantitative Analysis of U.S. Consumer Magazines: Baseline Study and Gender Determinants"; J. Steven Smethers and

Lee Jolliffe, "Radio Homemaker Programming: Old Time Radio's Ingredient for Attracting Women Listeners"; Sandra D. Scott, "Beyond Reason: A Feminist Theory of Ethics for Journalists"; Brenda Cooper and David Descurtner, 'Through the Eyes of Gender and Hollywood: Conflicting Visions of Isak Dinesen's Africa"; Sonya F. Duhé and Vernon A. Stone, "Sexual Harassment in Television Newsrooms"; Hazel Warlaumont, "The Gaze and Psychoanalytic Theory: Ideology and Female Images in Advertisements"; Elizabeth Fakazis, "Get Thee to the Kitchen! The First Wave of the Women's Movement in the 19th Century Political Cartoons of *Puck, Punchinello* and *Harper's Weekly*"; Barbara M. Freeman, "Her Amplified Voice: Gender, War and Canadian Motherhood, 1939-1943"; Evelyn Trapp Goodrick, "Different Voices: Selected Women Editorial Page Editors Discuss Their Work"; Marilyn Greenwald and Joseph Bernt, "Newspaper Coverage of Gays and Lesbians: Editors' Views of Its Longterm Effects"; Mark Harmon, "Larry Agran: Victim of Agenda Setting"; Therese Lueck, "The Effect of Gender on Course Evaluations in Mass Communications: A Pilot Study"; Linda Lumsden, "The 'Nasty' Truth: Press Shortcomings in Commentary on the 2 Live Crew Obscenity Ruling"; Carolyn Martindale, "Significant Silences: Selected Newspaper Coverage of Problems Facing Black Americans, 1950-1989"; Katherine C. McAdams and Maurine H. Beasley, "Sexual Harassment of Washington Women Journalists: An Initial Study"; Aralynn Abare McMane, "A Comparative Study of Journalism and Gender in France"; Marian Meyers, "Television News Coverage of Violence Against Women"; Virginia Ordman and Dolf Zillmann, "Women Sports Reporters: Have They Caught Up?"; Lana F. Rakow, "Remote Mothering and the Parallel Shift: Women Meet the Cellular Telephone"; Jawahara K. Saidullah, "Children of the Himalayas: The Message of Chipko"; Orly Shachar, "'What Did You Do During the War, Mother?' Propagandistic Communications in Crisis Situations: Press Images of Israeli Women in Wartime"; Richard Shafer and Susanna Hornig, "The Role of Women Journalists in Philippine Political Change"; Kevin R. Stoner, "Rape Survivors' Perceptions of the Effect of Newspaper Stories About Sexual Assault: Listening to Other Voices"; Jane Twomey, "May Craig as Liberal Feminist: Studying Women Journalists from a New Perspective"; Mary Ann Weston, "Native Americans in the News: Symbol, Stereotype or Substance"; Pamela Creedon, "Babes in Toyland: Sports Reporting Classes in U.S. Colleges and Universities"; Barbara Diggs-Brown, "Philippa Duke Schuyler: African-American Journalist," and Jack Glascock and Robert LaRose, "Dial-a-Porn Recordings: Confessions of a Jilted Lady."

9.   Association for Education in Journalism and Mass Communication. Annual Meeting, Kansas City, Missouri, August 11-14, 1993.
       Includes Bonnie Brennen, "Newsworkers During the Interwar Era: A Critique of Traditional Media History"; Lisa Barr, "The Next Step: Showing a Common History of Treatment for Minorities, Women and Gays in Media Content, Newsroom and Journalism Schools; A Proposal for Further Research and Suggestions for a Curriculum"; Kathryn S. Egan, "Constructivists' Use of Mentoring for Success in Broadcast Academe"; Therese L. Lueck, "Mass Communication Course Evaluations: An Exploratory Study on the Effect of Gender"; Nancy Worthington," Constructing the Post-Colonial Woman in Kenya: A Textual Analysis of Nairobi's 'Daily Nation'" Kate Peirce, "Socialization of

Teenage Girls Through Teen-Magazine Fiction: The Making of a New Woman or an Old Lady?"

10.   Association for Education in Journalism and Mass Communication. Annual Meeting, Atlanta, Georgia, August 10-14, 1994.
       Includes Albert Talbott, "Men and Women Journalists in the Movies: Exploration of Some Sexism and Gender Issues in Their Portrayals in Eleven Films"; Teresa L. Thompson and Eugenia Zerbinos, "Television Cartoons: Do Children Notice It's a Boy's World?"; Virginia Whitehouse and Caryl Cooper, "To Name or Not to Name: Yes, No, Maybe Some Questions to Ask When the Story Is Rape"; Nancy Worthington, "The Nairobi Women's Conference, the World Bank, and *The Weekly Review*: Defining Development in a Kenyan Newsmagazine"; Jana Frederick-Collins,"'He Kept Pressing Me For Details!': A Critical Cultural Analysis of Domestic Narratives in Post-World War II Pinup Advertising Calenders"; Fakhri Haghani, "Female Archetypes in the Late '80s Film"; Robert Jensen and Elvia R. Arriola, "Feminism and Free Expression: Silence and Voice"; Kim E. Karloff, "To Know Her Name: *Wisconsin v. Evjue* and the Origins of the Rape Victim Identification Debate"; Susan V. Lockwood, "The Power of the Tobacco Industry to Negatively Influence Women's Health"; Katherine McAdams, "Women Journalism Students and MANagement: Slow Climb or No Climb?"; Marian Meyers, "Justify Your Coverage: Reporters and Crimes Against Women"; Radhika E. Parameswaran, "Romance Reading in the Third World: A Postcolonial Intersection of Gender, Ethnicity, and Sexuality"; Melinda Robins, "Women in the Media: The Case of Tanzania"; Norma M. Schulman, "Wrinkling the Fabric of the Press: Newspaper Opinion Columns in a Different Voice"; David Shaw and Lynn S. Clark, "The Removal of Gender from the News Agenda: A Case Study"; E. E. Adams and J. V. Bodle, "Scholarship and AEJMC: How Well Represented Are Women in Divisional Paper Competition?"; Julie L. Andsager, Jean Nagy, and Jennifer L. Bailey, "Sexual Harassment in Communications: Manifestations of Power Between Graduate Students and Faculty"; Diane Borden, "Reputational Assault: A Critical and Historical Analysis of Gender and the Law of Defamation"; Michelle Bowen and Suzanne Laurion, "Incidence Rates of Sexual Harassment in Mass Communications Internship Programs: An Initial Study Comparing Intern, Student, and Professional Rates"; Matthew D. Bunker, "Sexual Harassment and Vicarious Liability of Media Organizations"; Linda Steiner, "Vocational Guidance Books' Assessment of the Social Responsibility of the Press"; Fred Fedler, "Will More Diversified Staffs Diversify Newspaper Content? A Pilot Study"; Elizabeth V. Burt, "Reform Allies: The Temperance and Prohibition Press and Woman Suffrage, Wisconsin, 1910-1920"; Beverly G. Merrick, "Mary Margaret McBride, Talkshow Host: The Perfect Proxy for Radio Listeners"; Beverly G Merrick, "From Ghosting to Free-lancing: Mary Margaret McBride Covers Royalty and Radio Rex," and Beverly G. Merrick, "Sponsors Court Mary Margaret McBride, Talkshow Host: 'All about Life in a Biscuit Factory, on the Radio."

11.   Association for Education in Journalism and Mass Communication. Annual Meeting, Washington, D.C., August 9-12, 1995.
       Includes Anne Cooper-Chen, "The Second Giant: Portrayals of Women in Japanese Advertising"; Ann M. Colbert, "Women's Editions of Newspapers:

Marketing Baking Powder to the New Woman"; Nilanjana R. Bardhan, "Portrayal of Women in the Advertisements in 'India Today'-- India's Leading Current Affairs Magazine: 1984-1994"; Jon Bekken, "Dusting with a Ballot: The Portrayal of Women in the *Milwaukee Leader*"; Janet M. Cramer, "Woman as Citizen: An Ideological Analysis of Three Women's Publications, 1900-1910," and Carolyn Kitch, "'The Courage to Call Things by Their Right Names': Fanny Fern, Feminine Sympathy, and Feminist Journalism in the Nineteenth-Century American Popular Press."

12.   Association for Education in Journalism and Mass Communication. Annual Meeting, Anaheim, California, August 1996.
        Includes Kathy B. McKee, Berry and Carol J. Pardun, "Face-ism Reconsidered: Facial Prominence and Body Emphasis of Males and Females in Magazine Advertising"; Nancy J. Nentl and Ronald J. Faber, "Where the Boys Are: Ad-Inspired Social Comparisons Among Male and Female Teens"; Lauren Danner and Susan Walsh, "'Radical' Feminists and 'Bickering' Women: Backlash in U.S. Media Coverage of the United Nations Fourth World Conference on Women"; Lois A. Boynton and W. Joseph Campbell, "Does It Matter Who Asks? A Study of Regional Affiliation and Gender in the Interviewer-Respondent Interaction in Public Opinion Telephone Surveys"; Kristine Kay Johnson, Tracy Lee Clarke and Erica W. Austin, "Let's Talk About What We're Watching: Parental Behavior Towards Children's Gender and Age Regarding Television Viewing"; Erica Scharrer and Jacqueline Arnold, "First Ladies; A Look at Coverage in Two Major Newspapers"; Janet M. Cramer, "Womanliness Is an Attribute Not a Condition: Conceptions of Civic Womanhood in the *Woman's Era*, 1894-1897"; Robert Huesca and Jamie Newmeyer, "Rethinking Media Reforms To Improve Treatment of Women and Minorities"; Julie L. Andsager and Robert O. Wyatt, "More Than a Matter of Sex: Gender Differences in Support for Various Media Rights in Four Cultures"; Linda Aldoory, "The Stories of Women Public Relations Campaign Planners Revealed Through Feminist Theory and Feminist Scholarship"; Esther Thorson and Andrew Mendelson, "Perceptions of News Stories and News Photos of Hillary Rodham Clinton"; Cecelia Baldwin, "The Distorted Reflection: The Adaptation of Social Reproduction Theory in the Cultural Analysis of Young Women's Perception of Sexuality as Power in Advertising Images"; Laurie A. Lattimore, "Let's Go to the Videotape: Gender Bias in Local Television Sports Coverage"; Beverly G. Merrick, "Mary Margaret McBride, the Conquering Talk Show Host Wears a Mink: City Editor Broadcasts Her Own Triumphant Return to the Mexico Ledger"; Debashis Aikat, "The First Lady: Newspaper Portrayal of Presidential Candidates' Wives: 1988-1992"; Dan Berkowitz, Joanne Fritz, Radhika Parameswaran, and Sue Lafky, "Gender and News Source Use: A University Case Study"; Sue Carter, "Riding the Airwaves: Three Models of Women's Access to Broadcasting"; Chingching Chang, "Viewers' Responses to Female Candidates' Political Advertising"; Diana Cornelius, "The Road Less Traveled: Ms. and Advertising-Free Publishing"; Dru R. Evarts, "Coverage of Men's and Women's Basketball in Four Midwestern Newspapers"; Anat First and Donald L. Shaw, "Not There Yet: Coverage of Women in Foreign News: A 1995 Multi-National Study"; Margot Hardenbergh, "Women and Front Page News"; Therese L. Lueck, Richard E. Caplan, and Kathleen L. Endres, "How Women are Faring as the Dust Settles: The Effect of

Gender on Journalism/Mass Communication Context"; Sally McMillan and Debra Merskin, "Personal Comfort and Personal Care Products: A Survey of Women's Dependency on Advertising"; Beverly G. Merrick, "Mary Margaret McBride, The College and Cub Reporting Years: An Early Graduate Makes the Most of Missouri Journalism Schooling"; Merrill Morris, "Feminists as Fans: Women Watching Men's Basketball"; Maggie J. Patterson and Megan W. Hall, "Abortion, Moral Maturity, and Civic Journalism"; Sarah W. Plaster, "The Spiral of Silence and Its Impact on Feminist Voices in Public Opinion"; James V. Pokrywczynski and John H. Crowley, "Job Satisfaction in Advertising: A Gender Perspective"; Shirley A. Serini, Angela A. Powers, and Susan Johnson, "Of Horse Race and Policy Issues: A Case Study of Gender of a Gubernatorial Election by Two Major Metropolitan Newspapers"; Lynn Silverstein, "Full-Court Press? *The New York Times*' Coverage of the 1995 Women's NCAA Basketball Tournament"; Susan Snyder, "'Somewhere Between Average and Perfect': Women's Magazines and the Construction of Sexuality"; Kim Walsh-Childers, Jean Chance and Kristin Herzog, "Who Harasses Women Journalists? A Qualitative Look at Sexual Harassment Among U.S. Newswomen"; Zhou He, "Pornography, Perception of Sex, and Sexual Callousness in China"; Elizabeth V. Burt, "A Bid for Legitimacy: The Woman's Press Club Movement, 1881-1900"; Carolyn L. Kitch, "Domestic Images in the Age of the Girl: The Work of Jessie Willcox Smith and Other Women Artists in Early-Twentieth Century Magazine Illustration"; Dan Alinange, "Who Reports the Hard/Soft News? A Study of Differences in Story Assignments to Male and Female Journalists at *Newsweek*"; Chiung Hwang Chen, "Feminization of Asian (American) Men in U.S. Society and the Mass Media: Analysis of *The Ballad of Little Jo*"; David T.Z. Mindich, "A 'Slanderous and Nasty-Minded Mulattress,' Ida B. Wells Confronts 'Objectivity' in the 1890s."

13.   Association for Education in Journalism and Mass Communication. Annual Meeting, Chicago, Illinois, July 30-August 2, 1997.

Includes U-Ryong Kim, In-Suk Chung, Hongsung-Up and Cheong-Yi Park, "Running Head: Newscaster Gender and Viewing Satisfaction -- The Effects of Audience's Gender-based Expectations About Newscasters on News Viewing Satisfaction in a Collective Culture: South Korea"; Seung Hyun Park and Ho-kyu Lee, "The Consumption of Korean Television Viewing, Gender, and Power"; Jocelyn Steinke, "Connecting Theory and Practice: Are Counterstereotypes Effective in Changing Girls' Perceptions of Science and Scientists?"; Ed Adams and John Bodle, "Gender, Scholarship and AEJMC: How Well Are Women Doing? A Ten-Year Study"; Steve Weinberg, "The Greatest Work of Investigative Journalism Ever Published: Ida Tarbell and Her Expose of Standard Oil Company"; Alan Fried, "A Time Out of Mind: When the *Chicago Tribune* Rescued Trapped Suburban Women"; Cecelia Baldwin, "The Development of Self Efficacy in Young Women in Relation to the Perception of Attention to Sexuality as Power in Advertising Images"; Jimmy L. Reeves, "Re-Covering the Homeless: Hindsights on the Joyce Brown Story"; Jack Lule, "News, Myth and Society: Mother Teresa as Exemplary Model"; Ann Haugland, "Oprah's Book Club Radical Reading and Talk Show Literature"; Carolyn Bronstein, "After the Second Wave: Toward an Interpretation of the American Feminist Antipornography Movement"; Shirley Serini, Elizabeth Toth, Donald Wright, and Arthur Emig, "Sexual Harassment and Public Relations: Confusion and the Need for Leadership in the Workplace"; Carolina Acosta-Alzuru, "Scratching the Surface: *The New York Times* Coverage of the Mothers of Plaza De Mayo, 1977-1997"; Mara H. Huberlie, "Women in Public Relations: How Their Career Path Decisions Are Shaping the Future of the Profession"; B. Carol Eaton, "Beyond Sex; The Political Gender Gap in the 1996 Presidential Election"; Renee A. Botta, "Interacting with Thin Media Images: Mass Communication Theories Predict Adolescent Girls' Body Image Disturbance and the Internalization of a Thin Ideal"; Lisa Hynd, Patricia Stout, and Joan Schleuder, "Gender Response to Sexual Appeals in Ads Featuring Male Models"; Agnes H. Gottlieb, "More than Angels: Women and Reform as a Topic in American Magazines, 1890-1910"; Ann Mason, "Martha Stewart Media: Revisiting Domesticity"; Linda Aldoory, "Published Feminist Research at a Crossroads: A Critical Analysis of Mass Communications Studies in Scholarly Journals"; Melanie Laverman, "Images of Older Women in Magazine Advertisements: A Content Analysis and an Analysis of Content"; Beverly G. Merrick, "Jane Grant, *The New Yorker*, and Ross: A Lucy Stoner Practices Her Own Style of Journalism"; Sarah W. Plaster, "How the Nineteenth Amendment Was Framed in the Pages of the *Ladies' Home Journal*"; Isaac Abeku Blankson, "Representation of Women in African News Magazines"; C. Anthony Giffard, "International News Agency Coverage of the Fourth World Conference on Women"; Sheila Webb, "Dorothy Day and the Early Days of the Catholic Worker -- Social Action Through the Pages of the Press"; Jan Whitt, "A 'Labor From the Heart': Lesbian Magazines from 1947-1994"; Janice Hume, "Private Lives, Public Virtues: Remembered Values of Women's Lives in Suffrage-ERA Obituaries"; Patrick M. Jablonski, "Murphy Brown Sets the Agenda: A Time Series Analysis of the Family Values Issues, 1988-1996"; Lillie M. Fears, "An Investigation of Colorism of Black Women in News"; Linda Aldoory, "Content Analysis of Popular Songs Sung by Female Performers from 1965 to 1995"; Michelle Johnson, "The Effect of Rape Victim Identification on Readers' Perceptions of Victims and News Stories"; Melinda D. Hawley, "Is the Women's Section an Anachronism? Affinity for Ambivalence about the *Chicago Tribune*'s WomaNews"; Michael G. Elasmar, Mary Brain, and Kazumi Hasegawa, "The Portarayal of Women on Prime Time TV Programs Broadcast in the United States"; Julie Andsager and Leiott Smiley, "Evaluating the Public Informations Function: How Media Agents Framed the Silicone Breast Implant Controversy"; Marie Myers Hardin, "Julie Collier Harris at the Columbus *Enquirer Sun*: Contributions Toward, and Consequences of, The Pulitzer Prize"; Lisa M. Weidman, "Of Sports Pages and Bad Attitudes: An Investigation of the Relationship between Attention to Sports Media and Attitudes Toward Women's Sports"; Elizabeth V. Burt, "'Upholding the Womanhood of Woman' by Opposing the Vote: The Countermovement Rhetoric of the Remonstrance, 1890-1920"; Linda Steiner, "Why Did They Leave the Newsroom? Stories of Quitting by Twentieth Century Women Journalists"; Janet M. Cramer, "Of Heathens and Heroines: Constructions of Gender and Empire in the Women's Foreign Missionary Press, 1869-1895"; Joey Senat, "From Pretty Blondes and Perky Girls to Competent Journalists: *Editor & Publisher's* Evolving Depiction of Women from 1967 to 1974"; Carol B. Gardner, "Are You Letting Your Mental Health Problems Hurt Him?: Advice to Women about Mental Health & Illness in Women's Magazines, 1960-1990"; Catherine L. Marston, "Hand-Ling Media Research on Disability: Toward Including a Feminist 'Exile' Perspective on

Theory and Practice"; Gail Synder, "Children's Television Commercials and Gender-Stereotyped Messages"; James Stewart, "One Paper's Coverage of a Retreat for Women: A Case Study in the Media's Role in Providing a Forum for Examination of Public Issues"; Eliza Tanner, "Mexican Journalist Elena Poniatowska: 'Angel's Wings and a Smile'"; Lynn M. Zoch, "Women as Sources: Gender Patterns in Framing the News"; Maurine H. Beasley, "New Directions for Historical Study of Women Journalists"; W. Joseph Campbell and Robert L. Stevenson,"Women as Global Newsmakers and Correspondents: Does Press Freedom Matter?"; Carolyn Dale, "Uncommon Roles and Common Routes: Narrative in Obituaries of Prominent Women, 1994-1995"; B. Carol Eaton, "Cyber-Wimmin: Co-opting the Dominant Discourse"; Barbara M. Freeman, "'North or South, It's All the Same...' The Media and Aboriginal Women in the Canadian North, 1968"; Ana C. Garner, "Negotiating Our Positions in Culture: Popular Adolescent Fiction and the Self Images of Professional Women"; Kim E. Karloff, "You Be the Editor: A Three-Year Study of Student-Journalists and the Rape Victim Identification Debate"; Katherine N. Kinnick, "Gender Bias in Newspaper Coverage of the 1996 Olympic Games: A Content Analysis of Five Major Dailies"; Angela Powers, "Breast Implants: Newspaper Coverage of a Women's Health Care Controversy"; Betsy Robertson, "How Do Our Daughters Grow? Adolescent Socialization Messages in Selected Print and Electronic Media."

4.   Baehr, Helen and Ann Gray. *Turning It On: A Reader in Women and the Media.* London: Arnold and St. Martin's, 1995. 256 pp.
       Charts the main issues in the study of women and media; sectionalized according to representation, genre, audience, and industry working practices; includes Noreene Janus, "Research on Sex-Roles: A Critical Approach"; Gaye Tuchman, "Women's Depiction by the Mass Media"; Jo Spence, "What Do People Do All Day? Class and Gender in Images of Women"; Tessa Perkins, "Rethinking Stereotypes"; Judith Williamson, "Woman Is an Island: Femininity and Colonization"; E. Ann Kaplan, "Feminism/Oedipus/Postmodernism: The Case of MTV"; Susan Bordo, "'Material Girl': The Effacemants of Postmodern Culture"; Annette Kuhn, "Women's Genres"; Christine Geraghty, "A Women's Space"; Kathleen Rowe, "Roseanne: Unruly Woman as Domestic Goddess"; Ros Ballaster et al., "Critical Analysis of Women's Magazines"; Ellen McCracken, "The Cover: Window to the Future Self"; Tania Modleski, "The Rhythms of Reception: Daytime Television and Women's Work"; Dorothy Hobson, "Behind Closed Doors: Video Recorders in the Home"; Elizabeth Frazer, "Teenage Girls Reading Jackie"; Ellen Seiter et al., "'Don't Treat Us Like We're Stupid and Naive': Towards an Ethnography of Soap Opera Viewers"; Evelyn Cauleta Reid, "Viewdata: The Television Viewing Habits of Young Black Women in London"; Charlotte Brunsdon, "Identity in Feminist Television Criticism"; Jacqueline Bobo and Ellen Seiter, "Black Feminism and Media Criticism"; Helen Baehr and Angela Spindler-Brown, "Firing a Broadside: A Feminist Intervention into Mainstream TV"; Hilary Hinds, "Fruitful Investigations: The Case of the Successful Lesbian Text"; Patricia Holland, "When a Woman Reads the News"; Brigitte Jalov, "Woman on the Air: Community Radio as a Tool for Feminist Messages", Ros Gill, "Ideology, Gender and popular Radio: A Discourse Analytic Approach."

15.   "The Bangkok Declaration." *Media Development*. 41:2 (1994), pp. 25-26.
        Final statement of "Women Empowering Communication" conference in Bangkok, February 1994, with recommendations and goals; conference attended by more than 400 women communicators from more than 80 countries.

16.   "Beijing Declaration: Woman Need Greater Access to Communications." *The Democratic Communique*. February 1996, pp. 1-2.
        Excerpts the NGO Communications Strategy Proposal drafted by the Fourth World Conference on Women in Beijing.

17.   Biernatzki, William E., ed. "A Latin Perspective on the Media: Gender, Law and Ethics, the Environment and Media Education." *Communication Research Trends*. 15:3 (1995), pp. 1-42.
        Includes Mercedes C. Creel, "Women and Men in the Latin American Media," pp. 3-10; Vicente Baca Lagos, "Public Communication and Gender: Research in Spain," pp. 16-19.

18.   Bolinder, Vibeke. "Who Calls the Shots: Impressions and Experiences from a Week in Manila." *Gender and Mass Media Newsletter*. November 1991, pp. 11-14.
        Reports on an international conference on women, media, and advertising, held in Manila, May 12-17, 1991, including reports from delegates from around the world and resolutions to media leaders, legislators, consumers, media outlets, advertisers, the conference secretariat and delegates, and women in media.

19.   Brown, Mary Ellen, ed. *Television and Women's Culture: The Politics of the Popular*. Newbury Park, California: Sage, 1990. 248 pp.
        Examines the profound role television plays in defining women's culture; addresses women as audience, rock videos, feminist criticism of television, and consumerism. Includes: M. E. Brown, "Feminist Culturalist Television Criticism: Culture, Theory and Practice"; V. Nightingale, "Women as Audiences"; C. J. Deming, "For Television-Centred Television Criticism: Lessons from Feminism"; I. Ang, "Melodramatic Identifications: Television Fiction and Women's Fantasy"; L. A. Lewis, "Consumer Girl Culture: How Music Video Appeals to Girls"; S. Stockbridge, "Rock Video: Pleasure and Resistance"; D. Clark, "*Cagney & Lacey*: Feminine Strategies of Detection"; J. Fiske, "Women and Quiz Shows: Consumerism, Patriarchy, and Resisting Pleasures"; B. Poynton and J. Hartley, "Male Gazing: Australian Rules Football, Gender and Television"; A. L. Press, "Class, Gender and the Female Viewer: Women's Responses to *Dynasty*"; M. E. Brown, "Motley Moments: Soap Opera, Carnival, Gossip and the Power of the Utterance"; M. E. Brown, "Consumption and Resistance: The Problem of Pleasure."

20.   *Camera Obscura*.
        No. 22 -- Thematic issue on "Feminism and Film" includes: Patrice Petro, "Feminism and Film History"; Lea Jacobs, "Reformers and Spectators: The Film Education Movement in the Thirties"; Miriam Hansen, "Adventures of Goldilocks: Spectatorship, Consumerism, and Public Life"; Heide Schlüpmann,

"Melodrama and Social Drama in the Early German Cinema"; Ben Singer, "Female Power in the Serial-Queen Melodrama: The Etiology of an Anomaly."

No. 23 -- Thematic issue on "Popular Culture and Reception Studies" includes: Robert C. Allen, "'The Leg Business': Transgression and Containment in American Burlesque," pp. 43-60; Lauren Rabinowitz, "Temptations of Pleasure: Nickelodeons, Amusement Parks, and the Sights of Female Sexuality," pp. 61-90, and Tricia Rose, "Never Trust a Big Butt and a Smile," pp. 109-132.

No. 24 -- Thematic issue on "Unspeakable Images" includes: Elisabeth Lyon, "The Unspeakable," pp. 5-6, and Raymond Bellour, "The Film Stilled," pp. 99-124.

No. 26 -- Thematic issue on "Male Trouble" includes: Alexander Doty, "The Sissy Boy, the Fat Ladies, and the Dykes: Queerness and/as Gender in Pee-Wee's World," pp. 125-144; Christine Holmlund, "When Is a Lesbian Not a Lesbian? The Lesbian Continuum and the Mainstream Femme Film," pp. 145-180; Danac Clark, "Commodity Lesbianism," pp. 181-202; Henry Jenkins, "'Don't Become Too Intimate with That Terrible Woman!': Unruly Wives, Female Comic Performance and *So Long Letty*," pp. 203-224; Edward B. Turk, "Deriding the Voice of Jeanette MacDonald: Notes on Psychoanalysis and the American Film Musical," pp. 225-250; Vicky Lebeau, "'You're My Friend': *River's Edge* and Social Spectatorship," pp. 251-274; Sharon Willis, "Special Effects: Sexual and Social Difference in *Wild at Heart*," pp. 275-296, and Amelia Jones, "'She Was Bad News': Male Paranoia and the Contemporary New Woman," pp. 297-320.

No. 27 -- Elizabeth Young, "*The Silence of the Lambs* and the Flaying of Feminist Theory," pp. 5-36; Judith Halberstam, "Skin-Flick: Posthuman Gender in Jonathan Demme's *The Silence of the Lambs*," pp. 37-54; Laura Marks, "Tie a Yellow Ribbon Around Me: Masochism, Militarism and the Gulf War on TV," pp. 55-76, and Elissa Marder, "*Blade Runner*'s Moving Still," pp. 89-108.

No. 28 -- Thematic issue on "Imaging Technologies, Inscribing Science" includes: Paula A. Treichler, "Beyond *Cosmo*: AIDS, Identity, and Inscriptions of Gender"; Alexandra Juhasz, "WAVE in the Media Environment: Camcorder Activism and the Making of *HIV TV*"; Juanita Mohammed, "WAVE in the Media Environment: Camcorder Activism in AIDS Education," and Carol Stabile, "Shooting the Mother: Fetal Photography and the Politics of Disappearance."

No: 29 -- Thematic issue on "Imaging Technologies, Inscribing Cultures 2" includes: Stacie Colwell, "The End of the Road: Gender, the Dissemination of Knowledge, and the American Campaign Against Venereal Disease During World War I" and Ann B. Flood, "Empowering Patients: Using Interactive Media Programs for Patients Facing Difficult Choices."

No. 30 -- Rebecca Egger, "Deaf Ears and Dark Continents: Dorothy Richardson's Cinematic Epistemology," pp. 5-30; Marty Roth, "Hitchcock's Secret Agency," pp. 35-50; Rajani Sudan, "Company Loves *Misery*," pp. 59-76; Lesley Stern, "The Oblivious Transfer: Analyzing *Blue Velvet*," pp. 77-92; Phillip B. Harper, "Playing in the Dark: Privacy, Public Sex, and the Erotics of the Cinema Venue," pp. 93-112.

No: 31 -- Erin Addison, "Saving Other Women from Other Men: Disney's *Aladdin*," pp. 5-26; Edith P. Thornton, "On the Landing: High Art, Low Art, and *Upstairs, Downstairs*," pp. 27-48; Laura Mulvey, "*Xala*, Ousmane Sembene 1974: The Carapace That Failed," pp. 49-72; John Mowitt, "Sembene Ousmane's *Xala*: Postcoloniality and Foreign Film Languages," pp. 73-96; Anna Williams,

"Domesticity and the Aetiology of Crime in *America's Most Wanted*," pp. 97-120, and Lea Jacobs, "The Woman's Picture and the Poetics of Melodrama," pp. 121-147.

No. 32 -- Robert Miklitsch, "*Total Recall*: Production, Revolution, Simulation - Alienation Effect," pp. 5-40; Sharon Willis, "The Fathers Watch the Boys' Room," pp. 41-74; David L. Eng, "Love at Last Site: Waiting for Oedipus in Stanley Kwan's *Rouge*," pp. 75-102; Tara McPherson, "Disregarding Romance and Refashioning Femininity: Getting Down and Dirty with the *Designing Women*," pp. 103-124, and Timothy Murray, "Televisual Fears and Warrior Myths: Mary Kelly Meets Dawn Dedeaux," pp. 125-160.

Nos. 33/34 -- Thematic issue on "Lifetime: A Cable Network 'For Women'" includes: Julie D'Acci, "Introduction," pp. 7-12; Jackie Byars and Eileen R. Meehan, "Once in a Lifetime: Constructing the 'Working Woman' Through Cable Narrowcasting," pp. 13-42; Eithne Johnson, "Lifetime's Feminine Psychographic Space and the 'Mystery Loves Company' Series," pp. 43-76; Susan White, "*Veronica Clare* and the New *Film Noir*," pp. 77-102; Pamela Wilson, "Upscale Feminine Angst: *Molly Dodd*, the Lifetime Cable Network and Gender Marketing," pp. 103-132; Jane Feuer, "Feminism on Lifetime: Yuppie TV for the Nineties," pp. 133-146; Sasha Torres, "War and Remembrance: Televisual Narrative, National Memory, and *China Beach*," pp. 147-166; Laura S. Mumford, "Stripping on the Girl Channel: Lifetime, *thirtysomething*, and Television Form," pp. 167-192; Joe Wlodarz, "Smokin' Tokens: *thirtysomething*, and TV's Queer Dilemma," pp. 193-212; Carolyn Bronstein, "Mission Accomplished? Profits and Programming at the Network for Women," pp. 213-242; Thomas Streeter and Wendy Wahl, "Audience Theory and Feminism: Property, Gender, and the Televisual Audience," pp. 243-261.

No. 35 -- Amy Zilliax, "The Scorpion and the Frog: Agency and Identity in Neil Jordan's *The Crying Game*"; Caryl Flinn, "The Deaths of Camp"; Julia Erhart, "'She Could Hardly Invent Them!' From Epistemological Uncertainty to Discursive Production: Lesbianism in *The Children's Hour*"; Robert von Dassanowsky, "'Wherever You May Run, You Cannot Escape Him'; Leni Riefenstahl's Self-Reflection and Romantic Trancendence of Nazism in *Tiefland*"; Catherine Russell, "'Overcoming Modernity': Gender and the Pathos of History in Japanese Film Melodrama"; Amanda Howell, "Reproducing the Past: Popular History and Family Melodrama on *China Beach*," and Scott MacDonald, "Interview with Sally Porter."

No. 36 -- Thematic issue on "Black Women Spectatorship and Visual Culture" includes: Joy James, "Black Femmes Fatales and Sexual Abuse in Progressive 'White' Cinema: Neil Jordan's *Mona Lisa* and *The Crying Game*"; Noliwe Rooks, "The African Americans in Question: Cicely Tyson, *Sweet Justice*, and the Consequences of Class"; Lisabeth G. Stevenson, "African Women: A View from the Inside Out"; Elizabeth H. Freydberg, "Wham, Bam, Thank You, Ma'am: Gratuitous Violence Against Black Women in Film"; Scott MacDonald, "An Interview with Cauleen Smith," and Marla Shelton, "Whitney Is Everywoman? Contextualizing the Cultural Politics of Blackness and Black Womanhood."

Nos. 37/38 -- Mary Conway, "Inhabiting the Phallus: DeCerteau and the Jeff Stryker Dildo in the Lesbian Safe Sex Video, 'She Is Desire'"; Elena del Rio, "The Body as Foundation of the Screen: Allegories of Technology in Atom

Egoyan's *Speaking Parts*"; Bill Nericcio, "Autopsy of a Rat: Odd, Sundry Parables of Speedy Gonzales and Other Latino Marionettes in the First World Visual Emporium"; Bill Nichols and Gerald Peary, "Children, Art, Sex, Pornography: Jennifer Montgomery's *Art for Teachers of Children*"; Aviva Briefel and Sianne Ngai, "'How Much Did You Pay for This Place?' Fear, Entitlement, and Urban Space in Bernard Rose's *Candyman*"; Keya Ganguly, "Carnal Knowledge: Visuality and the Modern in *Charulata*"; Scott Paulin, "Sex and the Singled Girl: Queer Representation and Containment in *Single White Female*," and Kaja Silverman and Harun Faroki, "In Her Place."

21.   Campbell, Patrick, ed. *Analyzing Performance: Issues and Interpretations.* Manchester: Manchester University Press, 1996. 413 pp.

        Includes Elaine Aston, "Gender as Sign-System: The Feminist Spectator as Subject"; E. Ann Kaplan, "Feminisms / Postmodernisms: MTV and Alternative Women' Videos and Performance Art."

22.   Caputi, Jane. "Men's Violence Against Women: An International Overview." *Current World Leaders.* December 1991, pp. 847-878.

        Summarizes literature on types of violence commited against women worldwide; covers issues such as rape, incest, battery, sexual slavery, femicide, denial of contraception and abortion, pornography, sexual murder, gorenography (sexually violent and objectifying media depictions).

23.   *Communication Research Trends.*

        12:1 (1992) -- Thematic issue on "Women and Men in the Media," edited by Margaret Gallagher, includes "Feminist Theory, Communication and Politics," pp. 1-3; "Content, Image, Representation," pp. 4-7; "Audience, Reception, Consumption," pp. 7-11; "Production of Media Content: Making a Differerence," pp. 11-15; "Current Research on Gender and Mass Media," pp. 16-20; "Resources," p. 21; "Annotated Bibliography on Gender and Mass Media," pp. 22-35.

        15:3 (1995) -- Thematic issue on "A Latin Perspective on the Media: Gender, Law and Ethics, the Environment and Media Education," edited by William E. Biernatzki and José L. Piñuel Raigada, includes Mercedes C. Creel, "Women and Men in the Latin American Media," pp. 3-10; Vicente B. Lagos, "Publication Communication and Gender: Research in Spain," pp. 10-19; "New Work on Gender and Communication in English," pp. 19-20.

24.   Corredorova, Milada. "The Letter of the Law Is Not Enough." *Democratic Journalist.* January 1991, p. 19.

25.   De Lauretis, Teresa. *Technologies of Gender: Essays on Theory, Film, and Fiction.* Bloomington: Indiana University Press, 1987. 166 pp.

26.   *Development Communication Report.*

        3/1990 -- Thematic issue on women, development, and communication includes Mallica Vajrathon, "Communicating With Women," pp. 1-3; H. Leslie Steeves, "Agricultural Extension and African Women," pp. 4-5; May Yaacob, "Women and Water: The Bucket Stops Here," pp. 6, 17; Marcia Griffiths, "How

To Improve Child Well-Being? First, Increase Mothers' Self-Confidence," pp. 7-8, 18; Suzanne Kindervatter, "Making Training Effective and Empowering for Women," pp. 9-11, 18; Kathy B. Stewart, "Community Publishing as a Strategy for Women's Development: A Zimbabwean Experience," pp. 12-13; Anne F. Murray and Gretchen Sutphen, "Funding Communication for Women in Development," pp. 14-16; "New Books," p. 16; "Resources," p. 19; Heather Royes, "Have Women Missed the Boat on Communication Technology?" p. 20.

27.   "Empowering Women Through Media." *Gender and Mass Media Newsletter.* November 1992, pp. 17-18.
Reports on conference of this title, held in Bangalore, India, August 16-28, 1991; quotes at length from speech, "Alternatives in Empowering Women in Communication," given by Desmond A. D. Abreo.

28.   "Feminist Theories and Methodologies: The State of the Art; Current Research." *Gender and Mass Media Newsletter.* November 1992, pp. 7-10.
Includes abstracts of papers dealing with The U.S., Netherlands, Norway, Finland, Mexico, and Malaysia.

29.   "Feminist Theory and Political Economy." *Gender and Mass Media Newsletter.* November 1992, pp. 10-11.
Abstracts of IAMCR papers on gender and media in U.S., Canada, and India.

30.   Florence, Penny and Dee Reynolds, eds. *Feminist Subjects, Multi-Media: Cultural Methodologies.* Manchester: Manchester University Press, 1995. 256 pp.
Addresses feminist question: how do we represent ourselves? Looks at range of media, from paintings and family photography, through opera, TV, and film, to novels and poetry.

31.   Gallagher, Margaret. "Communication and Human Dignity: A Women's Right Perspective." *Media Development.* 3, 1995, pp. 6-9, 13.
Claims that the legal framework within which societies are run has a "powerful male bias"; discusses how this situation evolved in the context of mass media, advertising, pornography, and violence.

32.   Gallagher, Margaret and L. Quindoza-Santiago, eds. *Women Empowering Communication: A Research Book on Women and the Globalisation of Media* (4th ed.). London/Manila/New York: World Association for Christian Communication / ISIS / International Women's Tribune Centre, 1994.

33.   "A Gathering at Portoroz: Conference Report." *Gender and Communication Section IAMCR Newsletter.* November 1995, p. 3.
Reports on gender and communication section activities at International Association for Mass Communication Research conference in Slovenia.

34.   *Gender and Mass Media Newsletter.*
March 1991 -- Includes abstracts of papers presented at Working Group on Gender and Mass Communication, International Association for Mass

Communication Research, Bled, 1990; Working Group on Gender and New Information Technologies, IAMCR, Bled, 1990; reports on International Association of Women in Radio and Television, New York and Washington, 1990; International Communication Association, Dublin, 1990; Association for Education in Journalism and Mass Communications, Minneapolis, 1990; European Broadcasting Union, Athens, Greece, 1990; "Draft Legislation To Prohibit Gender Discrimination in Advertising in Sweden; Waithira L. Gikonyo, "Kenya: Strategies and Action for Change in the 1990s"; Prabha Krishnan and Anita Dighe, "Affirmation and Denial"; "Nari Tu Narayani"; "Dissertations on Women in Korea. 1975-1985"; Marian Flick, "The Advertisement as the Generalized Other"; "Three Reports on Women and News in USA"; Linda Jeffery and Kevin Durkin, "Children's Reactions to Televised Counter-Stereotyped Male Sex Roles"; "Are We Nearing the Top of the Hill? (Sweden)"; "Women and the New World Information and Communication Order." "A Petition Advocating Equality for Women and Men in Broadcasting (Japan)"; "Into Focus. Changing Media Images of Women. An Asian Resource Kit"; "Institute for the Study of Media and the Family (Israel)."

November 1991 -- Includes brief abstracts of papers presented at International Association for Mass Communication Research, Istanbul, 1991; Haruko K. Watanabe, "UNESCO Seminar on the Role of Asian Women Journalists in Economic Reporting"; Zhao Ning, "Women and Development -- The Role of the Media"; Vibeke Bolinder, "Who Calls the Shots?"; abstracts of papers on gender at 10th Nordic Conference on Mass Communication Research in Reykjavik, Iceland; Ulla B. Abrahamsson, "Start for Equality Work in Finnish Media"; "Articles, Books, Papers, Reports"; "Efforts to Improve Equality."

November 1992 -- Includes "Forthcoming Events," "Reports from Conferences" (IAMCR, GRANITE, "Empowering Women Through Media," "Gender, Technology and Ethics"), "Articles, Books, Papers, Reports," Margaret Gallagher, "Perspective"; "Efforts to Improve Equality."

35.   Hermano, Teresita. "Women Empowering Communication: The Conference Experience." *Media Development*. 41:2 (1994), p. 3.
Summarizes World Association for Christian Communication Conference, held in Bangkok, February 12-17, 1994.

36.   International Communication Association Conference. Montréal, Canada, May 22-26, 1997.
Includes Debra L. Merskin, "It'll Be Our Little Secret: Adolescence, Advertising, and the Menstrual Taboo"; Meenakshi G. Durham, "Dilemmas of Desire: Representations of Adolescent Sexuality in Two Teen Magazines"; Laurie Ouellette, "The Upwardly Mobile Self: Class, Sex, Identity and the 'Cosmo Girl'"; Janna Jones, "The Distance From Home: The Domestication of Desire in Interior Design Manuals"; Janet M. Cramer, "Exporting Gender Ideology: The Woman's Foreign Missionary Press 1869-1895"; Kathleen M. Torrens, "I Can Get *Any* Job and Feel Like a Butterfly! Symbolic Violence in the TV Advertising of Jenny Craig"; Chen Yanru, "In Search of the Essential Woman -- China's First TV Drama Serial *On* Woman, *By* Women, *For* Women"; Alissa Sklar, "Unflinching Gazes: Re-Articulations of Desire in Woman - Authored Erotic Fiction"; Emilie Falc, "Unifying Rhetoric and the Politics of Difference of the Fourth World

Conference on Women"; B. Carol Eaton, "Reformatory or Revolutionary? The Public Identity of the Women's Movement in Contemporary US Newspapers"; Michael Real, "Motivation and Ideals in Shaping the Gendered Body: Why We Sweat It"; Margaret MacNeil and Margaret Ptolemy, "Codes of Instruction: Female Aerobic Instructors, Professional Development, and the Multi-Mediated Expression of Body Cultures"; Lisa Weidman, "Coverage of Women's Sports in the Media: Economics or Hegemony?"; Debra L. Merskin, "Constructing the Real Body"; Sarah Banet-Weiser, "Miss America / Miss Universe: Gender, Race and Nation in Televised Beauty Pageants"; Marie-Helene Cosineau, "Inuit Women's Media Use and Identity Construction at the Local, National and Global Levels"; E. Anne Laffoon, "The Rhetorical Construction of the Battered Body"; Patricia L. Dooley, "Intersections or Dead-Ends: Women's Stories of Abuse, Journalism, and Public Policy"; Karen Lee Ashcraft, "Negotiating SAFE: Interactions of Meaning and Doing at a Feminist Shelter"; Mia Consalvo, "*Cosmopolitan* and the Construction of Domestic Violence: A Preliminary Study"; Radhika E. Parameswaran, "Reading as a Cultural Practice in the Lives of Urban Women: An Ethnography of Romance Readers in a South Indian City"; Vickie Rutledge Shields, "If the Male Gaze Is No Longer My Master, Whose Gaze Is Disciplining My Body?"; Jennifer Lynn Bailey, "Race vs. Gender: African-American Women Interpret Anita Hill"; Kathleen D. Clark, "A Communication-As-Procedure Methodological Perspective: An Etnographic and Sense-Making Study of a Women's Spirituality Group"; Charlene Melcher, Barbara J. Walkosz, Michael Burgoon and Xin Chen, "The Weigh It Is II: Men's and Women's Comparisons to People on Television"; Jennifer H. Meadows, "Body Image, Women, and Media: A Media System Dependency Theory Perspective"; Eleanor Novek, "Service-Learning Is a Feminist Issue: The Ethic of Care in Communication Pedagogy"; Michelle L. Rodino, "The Intellectual and the Boom: Understanding and Contributing to Feminist Media Studies"; Nicole M. Keating, "Stars in Her Eyes: An Intertextual Approach to Cinematic Identification and the Female Spectator"; JoAnn M. Valenti and Daniel A. Stout, "Women Talk, Men Talk: Risk, Religion and Gender"; Shannon S. Kaml, "The Creation of Meaning in the Visual Texts of the Guerrilla Girls"; Daniel R. Nicholson, "Advertising and Generation X: Problematics and Potentials"; B. Carol Eaton, "The Image of Males in Women's Magazine Advertisements: Trends over the Past Thirty-Five Years"; Tien-tsung Lee and Hsiao-Fang Hwang, "The Feminist Movement and Female Gender Roles in Movie Advertisements: 1963 to 1993"; Poonam Pillai, "Imagining International Communities: Feminism and the Discourse of Global Agricultural Trade"; Lisa L. Barley, "Speaking Themselves: Palestininian Women's Views on Feminism and Their Movement"; Dafna Lemish and Chava E. Tidhar, "Still Marginal: Women in Israel's 1996 Television Election Campaign"; Denice Yanni, "Women's Indigenous Knowledge Societies and an Epistemology of Everyday Life"; Karin G. Wilkins, "The Role of Gender in the Globalization of Development Communication Praxis"; Lisa Holderman, "When Father Knew Best: The Influence of 'Classic' Television on Gender Schema Activation"; Myoung-Hye Kim and Hoonsoon Kim, "The Patriarchal Narrative Strategies of Korean Television Dramas"; Richard Butsch, "Women's Voice: Gender and the Construction of Radio Listening in the 1920s"; Susan Kray, "Mothers, Movies, Mirror Moments, and Origins of Self in the Feminist Mind, or: If They Can Make Myths, Why Can't We? Intercultural Considerations and Male Myth"; Katherine

A. Jackson, "Feminism and Sexuality: Further Double Binds Facing Women in Politics"; Julie L. Andsager and M. Mark Miller, "Engendering Conflicts: Themes in Newspaper Coverage of RU-486"; Martha M. Lauzen and David M. Dozier, "Making a Difference in Prime Time: Women on Screen and Behind the Scenes in the 1995-1996 Season"; Bernadette Barker-Plummer, "'Policing' the Public Sphere: NOW, the *New York Times* and the Processing of Feminism, 1966-1980"; Roya Akhava-Majid, Jyotika Ramaprasad, and Melissa Boyster, "Framing Beijing: US Daily Newspaper Coverage of the Fourth UN Conference on Women and the NGO Forum"; Jo Ellen Fair, "Mapping Power and Marking Difference: Examples of News Coverage of Africa"; Cheryl Renee Gooch, "Reconciling Traditional and New Communication Strategies to Empower African Women"; Clemencia Rodriguez, "Mafia Women, Guerrilla Women: A Discourse of Women and Violence in Colombia"; Bella Mody, Ho-Chen Hung, "Women, Work and Patriarchy: The Facts and Television Fiction in Taiwan."

37.   International Conference on Women, Media and Advertising, Manila, Philippines, May 12-17, 1991.

Thematic conference on "Who Calls the Shots?" includes: Donna Allen, "Who Owns the Media?" Sally Cloninger, "The Necessity of a Female Ethic"; Maria V. Montelibano, "Breaking out of the Mold"; Teresa M. Otondo, "Control of Media and Politics Are Essential"; Inge von Bonninghausen, "Commercial Media or Public Media: How Much Do Women Matter?"

38.   "It Matters Who Makes It." *Gender and Mass Media Newsletter*. November 1992, pp. 22, 18.

Discusses roundtable in Montréal, Canada, September 7-8, 1992, at which 50 women from 17 countries agreed that women are losing ground in the mass media.

39.   Jensen, Jens F. "Powerplay -- Gender, Power and Violence in Video Games." Paper presented at International Association for Mass Communication Research, Sydney, Australia, August 20, 1996.

Contends that video games are a form of pleasure and of symbolic resistance that uses popular texts and contexts to produce meanings of the world and the self; says that computer games are powerplay, a symbolic fight for power.

40.   Jogan, Maca. "The Mass Media as (Re)Producers of the Women's (In)Visibility." Paper presented at IAMCR, Bled, Yugoslavia, August 26-30, 1990.

Contends that a gender asymmetric division of social power exists in both the public and private media spheres.

41.   Jouet, J. "Femmes: Sujet et Objet dans les Nouvelles Technologies de Communication." In *Les Femmes Vivent la Technique*. II, pp. 36-38. Paris: Cité des Sciences et de l'Industrie, Association FEM, 1987.

42.   Joyrich, L. "Going Through the Emotions: Gender, Post Modernism, and Affect Television Studies." *Discourse*. Winter 1991/1992, pp. 23-40.

43.   Kaplan, E. Ann. "Televisions Forskning og Feministisk Kritik" (Television Research and Feminist Criticism). *Kvinnovetenskaplig Tidskrift.* 9:3 (1988), pp. 4-15.

44.   Kember, S. "Feminism, Technology and Representation." In *Cultural Studies and Communications*, edited by James Curran, David Morley, and Valerie Walkerdine, pp. 229-247. New York: St. Martin's Press, 1996.
       Examines the production of science and technology, a subject of intense feminist debate similar to feminist analysis of the media.

45.   Kleberg, Madeleine. "Gender and Communications." *Gender and Mass Media Newsletter.* November 1992, pp. 5-6.
       Reports on 15 papers presented to Gender Section, International Association for Mass Communication Research, Sao Paulo, Brazil, 1992.

46.   Kuhn, Annette, ed., with Susannah Redstone. *The Women's Companion to International Film.* Berkeley: University of California Press, 1994. 480 pp.
       Provides comprehensive feminist guide to cinema worldwide.

47.   Mahoney, Eileen. "Women, Development and Media: An Assessment for the 1990s." *Journal of Development Communication.* December 1991, pp. 26-40.

48.   Mahoney, Eileen. "Women, Development and Media." *Media Development.* 38:2 (1991), pp. 13-17.
       Covers topics of "Women, Media, Development and Power," "Academe: Media and Cultural Studies," "Feminism and the Study of Media," and "Media Organisations."

49.   Mattelart, Michèle. "Las Mujeres y el Orden de la Crisis" (Women and the Order of the Crisis). In Comunicación e Ideologia de la Seguridad (Communication and the Ideology of Security), by Michèle Mattelart and Armand Mattelart. Barcelona: Anagrama, 1978.

50.   Mattelart, Michèle. "Women, Media and Power: A Time of Crisis." *Media Development.* 41:2 (1994), pp. 8-11.
       Focuses on internal debates within feminism as they relate to critical media theory.

51.   *Media, Culture and Society.*
       January 1992 -- Thematic issue on "Gender and Technology" includes Liesbet van Zoonen, "Feminist Theory and Information Technology," pp. 9-30; Valerie Frissen, "Trapped in Electronic Cages? Gender and New Information Technologies in the Public and Private Domain: An Overview of Research," pp. 31-50; Ann Moyal, "The Gendered Use of the Telephone: An Australian Case Study," pp. 51-72, and Chantal Rogerat, "The Case of Elletel," pp. 73-88.

52.   *Media Development.*
       38:2 (1992) -- Thematic issue on "Women's Perspectives on Communication" includes "Women's Values Could Liberate Public

Communication," p.1; Colleen Roach, "Feminist Peace Researchers, Culture and Communications," pp. 3-6; Michèle Mattelart, "Où en Est l'Ordre de la Représentation Sexiste Aujourd'hui?" pp. 7-9; Elizabeth Lozano, "Rhetorical Constructions of Time: Feminine Taste, Melodramatic Hours," pp. 10-12; Eileen Mahoney, "Women, Development and Media," pp. 13-17; Janice J. McFarlane, "The Cultural Censorship of Women," pp. 18-19; Pilar Riano, "Myths of the Silenced: Women and Grassroots Communication," pp. 20-22; Mary E. Brown, "Soap Opera as a Site of Struggle -- The Politics of Interpretation," pp. 23-25; Béatrice Damiba, "Le Pari de l'Information Face au Défi du Progrès," pp. 26-27; Anne-Lieke Nol, "Experimenting with Home Language Instruction for Moroccan Women via Interactive Cable," pp. 28-29; John A. Lent, "Women and Mass Communications: A Selected International Bibliography," pp. 30-32.

   41:2 (1994) -- Thematic issue on "Women Empowering Communication," based on 1994 Bangkok conference that name, includes Teresita Hermano, "Women Empowering Communication: The Conference Experience," p. 3; Kamla Bhasin, "Women and Communication Alternatives: Hope for the Next Century," pp. 4-7; Michèle Mattelart, "Women, Media and Power: A Time of Crisis," pp. 8-11; Noeleen Heyzer, "Women, Communication and Development: Changing Dominant Cultures," pp. 12-14; Brigalia Bam, "Women, Communication and Socio-Cultural Identity: Creating a Common Vision," pp. 15-17; "Women Organize for Alternative Media," pp. 18-24; "The Bangkok Declaration," pp. 25-26; Alison Gillwald, "Women, Democracy and Media in South Africa," pp. 27-32; Melanie A. May, "Replacing False Images," pp. 33-37; George Gerbner, "Women and Minorities on TV: A Study in Casting and Fate," pp. 38-44; "The Warsaw Statement on 'Free Media,'" p. 45; "The Honolulu Statement of the MacBride Round Table," pp. 46-47.

53.   *Media Studies Journal.*
   Winter - Spring 1993 -- Thematic issue on "The Media and Women Without Apology" includes: Caryl Rivers, "Bandwagons, Women and Cultural Mythology," pp. 1-18; Kay Mills, "The Media and the Year of the Woman," pp. 19-32; Marion T. Marzolf, "Deciding What's 'Women's News,'" pp. 33-48; "Symposium -- In the Media, a Woman's Place," pp. 49-68; Pamela J. Creedon, "Framing Feminism -- A Feminist Primer for the Mass Media," pp. 69-80; "A Field Guide for Women in Media Industries," pp. 81-98; Maureen Dowd, "Requiem for the Boys on the Bus," pp. 99-104; Betsy Wade, "Surviving Being a Survivor or, Whatever Became of What's Her Name?" pp. 105-116; Suzanne B. Levine, "News-speak and 'Genderlect' -- (It's Only News If You Can Sell It)," pp. 117-124; Jane O'Reilly, "The Pale Males of Punditry," pp. 125-133; "Who's Covering What in the Year of the Woman," pp. 134-140; Linda M. Scott, "Fresh Lipstick -- Rethinking Images of Women in Advertising," pp. 141-156; Jean Otto, "A Matter of Opinion," pp. 157-166; Susan Miller, "Opportunity Squandered -- Newspapers and Women's News," pp. 167-182; Jean Ward, "Talking (Fairly) about the World-- A Reprise on Journalistic Language," pp. 183-196; Deborah Howell, "True Confessions -- My Life as a White Male," pp. 197-204; Andrew Merton, "The Evolution of a Male Feminist Journalist," pp. 205-214; Audrey Edwards, "From Aunt Jemima to Anita Hill: Media's Split Image of Black Women," pp. 215-222; Mary Thom, "The Personal Is Political -- Publishable, Too," pp. 223-230; Lucía Castellón and and Alejandro Guillier, "Chile -- The

Emerging Influence of Women in Journalism," pp. 231-240; Maurine H. Beasley, "Myths, Media and Women," pp. 241-254; "For Further Readings," pp. 255-256.

54. *Median Journal*.
     16:3 (1992) -- Thematic issue on "Gender" includes Marie-Luise Angerer, "Prolog. Gender als Soziale und Denk-Kategorie"; Marie-Luise Angerer and Karin Stockinger, "Feministische Theorien in der Medien-und Kommunikations-wißenschaft"; Irene Neverla, "Von der Frauenforschung zur Geschlechten-forschung. Ziemlich am Rande und Nicht zu Übersehen"; Monika Bernold, "'Let's Talk about Clips': Feministische Analysen von MTV. Ein Blick auf die Anglo-Amerikanische Diskussion"; Andrea Ellmeier, "Special British Mix. Feminismus und Cultural Studies"; Andrea Prenner, "Frauen und Nachrichten. Kurzmeldungen zu Einem 'Nicht-Thema'"; ANISS Projektgruppe, "'Looking Good and Feeling Great'. Methodische Anmerkungen zur Bildanalyse"; Susanna Lummerding, "'A Movie without the Picture'"; Marie-Luise Angerer, "Über Ängstliche und Angstvolle. Weibliche und Männliche Arbeitnehmer in der Öffentlichkeit"; Brigitte Geiger, "Feministische Öffentlichkeit. Anmerkungen zu ihrer Theorie und Praxis aus Anlaß Einer Aktuellen Veröffentlichung"; Sieglinde Rosenberger, "Feminism and Multiculturalism. Gedanken zur 'Verschiedenheit'"; Monika Bernold and Andrea Ellmeier, "'Zur Geschichte des Senders.' Ein Projektbericht."

55. Nava, Mica. *Changing Cultures: Feminism, Youth and Consumerism*. Thousand Oaks, California: Sage, 1992. 218 pp.
     Assesses feminist theory, its transformations, and its ability to highlight issues and practices; includes "Outrage and Anxiety in the Reporting of Child Sexual Abuse: Cleveland and the Press" and three chapters on consumerism, including "Discriminating or Duped? Young People as Consumers of Advertising/Art."

56. Nordberg, Karin. "Gender, Technology and Ethics." *Gender and Mass Media Newsletter*. November 1992, pp. 19-21.
     Reports on mass communication papers presented at conference in Lulea, Sweden, July 1-2, 1992; included U.S., England, Norway, Sweden, Denmark, Netherlands, and Canada.

57. Paletz, David L., ed. *Political Communication in Action: States, Institutions, Movements, Audiences*. Cresskill, New Jersey: Hampton Press, 1996. 352 pp.
     Offers a theoretical overview and numerous case studies, including Liesbet van Zoonen, "New Social Movement and Mass Media" in Netherlands and Tamar Liebes and Roni Grissek, "Television News and the Politicisation of Women."

58. Pietropaolo, Laura and Ada Testaferri, eds. *Feminisms in the Cinema*. Bloomington: Indiana University Press, 1995. 248 pp.
     Well-known feminist theorists juxtapose their work with that of women filmmakers; each writer addresses an aspect of marginality.

59. Popular Culture Association Conference. Orlando, Florida, April 8-12, 1998.
     Includes Mary E. Strunk, "Ma Barker: Film Star and Public Enemy No.1"; Dawn F. Thomsen, "Adventure for Women Readers: The World of Women in the

Detective Novels of *The New York Weekly Story Teller* 1875-1877"; Jennifer J. Algoe, "Shattered Glass Ceilings: The Female Role Portrayal in *ER* and *Chicago Hope*"; Steve Craig, "Cigarettes as Women's Liberation: The Marketing of Virginia Slims"; Tamara K. Baldwin, "Eliza Haywood and Emily Faithful: Two British Female Pioneer Journalists"; J. P. Williams, "I've Got You Where I Want You: Female Subjectivity in Golden Age Superman Comics"; Jan Todd, "Bring on the Amazons: The Media and Muscular Womanhood"; Juliann Sivulka, "Soap, Sex, and Stereotypes: A Case Study of Soap Ads in the *Ladies Home Journal*, 1920-1930"; Batya Weinbaum, "Sex Role Reversals in *Star Trek*'s Planets of Women, 1968 and 1988"; Vanessa Brantley, "Fashion and Race: A Comparison of Models in *Vogue*"; Therese L. Lueck, "Women's Pages = Woman's Place: A Preliminary Analysis of the Daily Paper"; Peter Seely, "The Portrayal of Women in the Dick Van Dyke Television Series"; Doug Highsmith, "The Long Strange Trip of Barbara Gordon: Depictions of Librarians in Comics"; Olga Abella, "Comics in the Movie Tank Girl: Making Violence Less Violent"; Mark C. Rogers, "From Femme Fatales to Ninja Hookers: Crime Comics and the Influence of Film Noir"; James Britton, "X-ing out the Rational Woman: Female Logic and Male Intuition in *The X-Files*"; Helen M. Lewis, "The Women Behind -- and in Front of -- the Badge: Women and Law Enforcement in Westerns"; Judy Kutulas, "Liberated Women and New, Sensitive Men: The Courting of the Baby Boomer Audience with 1970s Television"; Leah Lowe, "Radio Screwball: Gracie Allen and Her 1940 Presidential Campaign"; Lisa M. Ortiz, "Selling Womanhood: An Ideological Interpretation of Breasts in Magazine Advertisements"; Donna Casella, "The Moll in Recent American Gangster Films"; Liahna Babener, "Julia Ormond Between Men"; Mailin Barlow, "Xena and Nikita: Women Warriors on the Margins of TV"; Kathryn Lasky, "Pleasure, Eroticism and Identification: Brad Pitt and Female Spectatorship"; Jessica Bertini, "Returning the Stare"; Michael Simon, "Imitation of Wife: The Hollywood Melodrama and the Dildonic Woman"; Victoria Amador, "The 'Charming One of Evil Intent': Olivia de Havilland in *Hush, Hush, Sweet Charlotte*"; Andrew Jefchak, "She Could've Been a Tragic Heroine"; Nicole Ames, "Gaye Tuchmann's 'Modeling Concept' and Television's Presentation of Women"; Joyce Y. Karpay, "Immortality and the Feminine: Blurring Gender Boundaries in *Tin Cup*"; Ellen Weber, "Text as Heroine: *The Color Purple*"; Patrick White, "Holding Together: Women as Leaders in Contemporary Film"; Susan Swift, "Film, Feminism, and the Sacred: Transformation in Sorceress"; Eric Leatherwood, "Photographs, Mirrors, and Convertibles: Frames of Containment in *Thelma and Louise*"; Denise Lowe, "The Classical Archetype: Hollywood Style Zena and Buffy as Her-O"; Brenda Brandt, "Images of Women in Western Film: Myth Versus Reality?"

60. Rakow, Lana F. "Gendered Technology." *Critical Studies in Mass Communication*. March 1988.

61. Rakow, Lana F., ed. *Women Making Meaning: New Feminist Directions in Communication*. New York: Routledge, 1992. 302 pp.

    Contains three sections: "The Politics of Making Meaning," "Beyond the Field's Boundaries," and "Case Studies in Making Meaning" with contributions by Cheris Kramarae, Angharad N. Valdivia, Victoria Chen, Lourdes Torres, Nina Gregg, Linda Steiner, Jane Rhodes, Elspeth Probyn, and Rakow.

62.   "Resolutions of the Delegates to 'Who Calls the Shots?'" *ISIS Women in Action.* No.2, 1991, pp. 34-36.

　　Gives resolutions of 1991 International Conference on Women, Media and Advertising, Manila, Philippines, May 12-17.

63.   Riaño, Pilar. "Myths of the Silenced: Women and Grassroots Communication." *Media Development.* No.2, 1991, pp. 20-22.

　　Outlines the analytical dimensions involved in looking at women as active communicative subjects: their access to communication resources, as producers of communication, and as consumers; concludes that "far greater integration" in these areas is needed in Third World.

64.   Riaño, Pilar, ed. *Women in Grassroots Communication: Furthering Social Change.* Thousand Oaks, California: Sage, 1994. 318 pp.

　　Brings together contributors from Africa, Asia, Latin America, and North America to focus on women bringing about change at grassroots levels; looks at ways women have been perceived, the social roles of women in their communities, their ability to communicate, media production, and issues of media competency, identity, representation, evaluation, and group process.

　　Includes P. Riaño, "Women's Participation in Communication: Elements for a Framework"; P. Riaño, "Gender in Communication: Women's Contributions"; P. Mlama, "Reinforcing Existing Indigenous Communication Skills: The Use of Dance in Tanzania"; S. Y. Dyer-Bennem, "Cultural Distinctions in Communication Patterns of African-American Women: A Sampler"; S. Muñoz, "Notes for Reflection: Popular Women and Uses of Mass Media"; M. Protz, "Understanding Women's Grassroots Experiences in Producing and Manipulating Media"; J. Kawaja, "Process Video: Self-Reference and Social Change"; C. Rodríguez, "A Process of Identity Deconstruction: Latin American Women Producing Video Stories"; C. Ruíz, "Losing Fear: Video and Radio Productions of Native Aymara Women in Bolivia"; D. Kidd, "Shards of Remembrance: One Woman's Archeology of Community Video"; M. Mata, "Being Women in the Radio"; R. Mensah-Kutin, "The WEDNET Initiative: A Sharing Experience Between Researchers and Rural Women"; S. Taylor, "Communicating for Empowerment: Women's Initiatives To Overcome Poverty in Rural Thailand and Newfoundland"; L. Lloyd, "*Speak* Magazine: Breaking Barriers and Silence"; R. M. Alfaro, "Women as Social Agents of Communication: Social Maternity and Leadership."

65.   Roach, Colleen. "Feminist Peace Researchers, Culture and Communication." *Media Development.* 38:2 (1991), pp. 3-6.

　　Explores "feminist critiques of society, particularly the militarism engrained in its culture"; concludes that the type of cultural transformation needed to bring about peace can be achieved only through solidarity between women of the South and North.

66.   Roach, Colleen. "Women and Communications Technology: What Are the Issues?" In *The Democratization of Communication*, edited by Philip Lee, pp. 130-142. Cardiff: University of Wales Press, 1996.

Examines key issues involved in women and communications technology; highlights some feminist and gender-focused perspectives.

67.   Roth, Nancy and Linda K. Fuller, eds. *Women's Ways of Acknowledging AIDS: Communication Perspectives.* Binghamton, New York: Haworth Press, 1997.

Includes Fuller's "To Desire or To Direct Differently: Women Producers / Directors of AIDS Films."

68.   Scannell, Paddy, Philip Schlesinger, and Colin Sparks, eds. *Culture and Power: A Media, Culture and Society Reader.* Newbury Park, California: Sage, 1992. 357 pp.

Includes Sarah Franklin, Celia Lury, and Jackie Stacey, "Feminism and Cultural Studies"; Elizabeth Frazer, "Teenage Girls Reading Jackie"; Susan Kippax, "Women as Audience: The Experience of Unwaged Women of the Performing Arts."

69.   Sharma, Kalpana. "The Media and Women." *Media Digest.* May 1988.

70.   Sklar, Robert. *Film: An International History of the Medium.* New York: Harry N. Abrams, 1993.

Includes "Women's Film Genre," pp. 116-117, 210-211, 361; film noir influences, pp. 304, 310; cinematic treatment of, pp. 87, 149, 206, 229-230, 372, 474, 490; as filmgoers, p. 28; filmmakers and directors, 104-106, 136, 373, 397, 444, 447, 452, 457-458, 474-475, 476-477, 482-484, 489, 491-493, 498-499, 501, 506-507, 514; films dealing with situation or condition of, pp. 328-329, 447, 457, 497; screenwriters, pp. 104-105, 109; stars, p. 72; feminist movement, pp. 374, 415, 457, 474, 476, 488-492.

71.   Sreberny-Mohammadi, Annabelle. "Who Is (Not) Critical Now? On Engendering Critical Approaches in International Communication." In *A Different Road Taken,* edited by John A. Lent, pp. 202-228. Boulder, Colorado: Westview Press, 1995.

72.   Steeves, H. Leslie. "Gender and Mass Communication in a Global Context." In *Women in Mass Communication.* Second Edition, edited by Pamela Creedon, pp. 32-60. Newbury Park, California: Sage, 1993.

73.   Steinberg, Deborah L., Debbie Epstein, and Richard Johnson, eds. *Border Patrols: Policing the Boundaries of Heterosexuality.* London: Cassell Academic, 1997. 256 pp.

Looks at nexus of heterosexuality and contemporary "gender troubles"; explores through media, scientific discourse, etc. the ways sexual divisions are constructed, regulated, and transgressed.

74.   Tannen, Deborah. *You Just Don't Understand. Women and Men in Conversation.* New York and London: Random House, 1991.

75.   Tasker, Yvonne. *Spectacular Bodies: Gender, Genre and the Action Cinema.* London: Routledge, 1993.

76.   Tierney, Helen, ed. *Women's Studies Encyclopedia.* Westport, Connecticut: Greenwood Press, 1990. 400 pp.
Volume II, which deals with literature, arts, and learning, includes media.

77.   "Towards 'Women Empowering Communication'...." *Action.* January 1994, p.1.

78.   Türkoglu, Nurcay. "The News Media, the War, the Opera, and the Spectators." Paper presented at International Association for Mass Communication Research, Istanbul, Turkey, June 19-20, 1991.
Compares the reporting of the Gulf War with the soap opera mode, stating, "Today, the 'take it easy' form of the soap opera is not only directed to women viewers but to the mass media audience completely, removing all the gender identifications." She contends this easy comprehensiveness was applied to the war.

79.   United States Information Agency. *A Media Guidebook for Women.* Washington, D.C.: USIA, n.d. 49 pp.
Represents effort to help women globally to tell their stories.

80.   Valdivia, Angharad N. "Is Modern to Male as Traditional Is to Female? Is There Room for Women in Current Scholarship and Mainstream Press Coverage?" *Gender and Mass Media Newsletter.* November 1992, p. 7.
Analyzes gender in international communications scholarship and concludes that the "use of the generic 'he' was much more than a discursive strategy."

81.   Valdivia, Angharad N., ed. *Feminism, Multiculturalism, and the Media: Global Diversities.* Thousand Oaks, California: Sage, 1995. 332 pp.
Illustrates through case studies how issues of gender, race, class, sexual orientation, global origin, and ethnicity affect the coverage, portrayal, media production, and reception of human beings.

82.   Van Zoonen, Liesbet. *Feminist Media Studies.* Thousand Oaks, California: Sage, 1994. 182 pp.
Explores how feminist theory / research contribute to an understanding of the media's multiple roles in the construction of gender; includes topics such as "'New' Themes," "A 'New' Paradigm," "Media Production and the Encoding of Gender," "Media Texts and Gender," "Spectatorship and the Gaze," "Gender and Media Reception," and "Research Methods."

83.   Van Zoonen, Liesbet. "Feminist Perspectives on the Media." In *Mass Communication and Society*, Second Edition, edited by James Curran and Michael Gurevitch. London: Edward Arnold, 1991.

84.   Van Zoonen, Liesbet. "Feminist Theory and Information Technology." *Media, Culture and Society.* January 1992, pp. 9-29.
Reveals research of three cases of women and new information technologies: introduction of telephone in U.S., gender-based adaptation of French Teletel, and the use of VCRs in the domestic sphere; shows how both

technology and gender have been constructed by social relations and how both can be seen to have been changed in relation one to another.

85.   Van Zoonen, Liesbet. "Moeten Strijdende Vrouwen zo Grof Zijn? De Vrouwenbeweging en de Media" (Do Militant Women Have To Be So Rough? The Women's Movement and the Media). *Tijdschrift voor Vrouwenstudies*. 12:2 (1991), pp. 249-253.

86.   Van Zoonen, Liesbet. "One of the Girls? The Incipient Feminization of News." In *News, Gender and Power*, edited by C. Carter, G. Branston, and S. Allen. London: Routledge, 1998.

87.   Van Zoonen, Liesbet. "Rethinking Women and the News." *European Journal of Communication*. March 1988, pp. 35-53.

88.   "WACC's Study and Action Programme (Part 4)." *Action*. December 1991, pp. 4-5.
          Includes women's empowerment, portrayal of women in media, women's networks.

89.   "Women and the New World Information and Communication Order." *Gender and Mass Media Newsletter*. March 1991, p. 27.
          Points out that in its report, *Many Voices, One World* (1980), the Mac-Bride Commission spent two of its 250 pages and one of its 82 recommendations on women's issues.

90.   "Women and the Pace of Development." *Action*. February / March 1992, pp. 4-5.
          Includes women and media and women and development support communication.

91.   Women Institute for Freedom of the Press. *Media Report to Women. Annotated Index of Media Activities and Research*. Washington, D.C.: WIFP, 1977. 32 pp.
          Covers years 1972 through 1976.

92.   Women Institute for Freedom of the Press. *Media Report to Women. Annotated Index of Media Activities and Research*. Washington, D.C.: WIFP, 1987. 10 pp.
          Covers 1987 issues.

93.   Women Institute for Freedom of the Press. *The Second Five-Year Index to Media Report to Women. An Annotated Index of Women's Media Activities and Research*. Washington, D.C.: WIFP, 1981. 52 pp.
          Covers 1977 through 1981.

94.   Women Institute for Freedom of the Press. *Third Five-Year Index of Media Report to Women. Annotated Index of Media Activities and Research*. Washington, D.C.: WIFP, 1986. 52 pp.
          Covers 1982 through 1986.

HISTORICAL STUDIES

95. Hunter, Ian, David Saunders and Dugald Williamson. *On Pornography: Literature, Sexuality and Obscenity Law.* New York: St. Martin's, 1993. 290 pp.
     Maps history of obscenity across five centuries in England and two in the U.S. and documents the fluidity that allows pornography to be many things in many forms -- an "eroticizing instrument, a saleable commodity, a crime, an object of governmental concern and medical regulation, an ethical occasion... an[d] aesthetic phenomenon."

IMAGES OF WOMEN

96. Anderson, Arnold E. and Lisa DiDominico. "Diet vs. Shape Content of Popular Male and Female Magazines: A Dose-Response Relationship to the Incidence of Eating Disorders." *International Journal of Eating Disorders.* 11:3 (1992), pp. 283-287.

97. Arcand, Bernard. *The Jaguar and the Anteater: Pornography Degree Zero.* London: Verso, 1993. 286 pp.
     Argues against pornography because it encourages masturbation; recognizes that much pornography is degrading to women.

98. Baker, Roger, with Peter Burton and Richard Smith. *Drag: A History of Female Impersonation in the Performing Arts.* London: Cassell Academic, 1995. 304 pp.
     Presents a spectacle of drag performers from ancient times and from around the world; includes "Hollywood and Bust."

99. Bakøy, Eva. "Feminism and Images of Children in Film." Paper presented at International Association for Mass Communication Research, Bled, Yugoslavia, August 26-31, 1990.
     Argues that a feminist strategy of social change has to include a deeper understanding of children's role in a culture; provides approaches of studying children in film texts.

100. Ballinero Cohen, Colleen, Richard Wilk, and Beverly J. Stoeltje, eds. *Beauty Queens on the Global Stage: Gender, Contests, and Power.* New York: Routledge, 1995. 250 pp.
     Brings together studies of beauty pageants in 14 different cultures; looks at how each is local and unique, and "simultaneously global and remarkably repetitious."

101. Caputi, Mary. *Voluptuous Yearning: A Feminist Theory of the Obscene.* Lanham, Maryland: Rowman and Littlefield, 1994. 114 pp.
     Argues that obscenity frees humans from cultural constraints, from the "intelligible, orderly world of rationality, progress, technology."

102. Carol, A. and Mary Hayward. "Letters." *Index on Censorship.* January 1991, p. 32.

Women and pornography issue discussed by representatives of Campaign Against Censorship and Feminists Against Censorship.

103. Carson, Diane, Linda Dittmar, and Janice R. Welsch, eds. *Multiple Voices in Feminist Film Criticism*. Minneapolis: University of Minnesota Press, 1994. 547 pp.
    Strives to find the blindspots in feminist film theory, offer textual analyses of several films, and make available course files on how to teach feminist films; includes essays by Judith Mayne, B. Ruby Rich, Janet Walker, Laura Mulvey, Jackie Byars, Nancy Chodorow, Carol Gilligan, Lisa Cartright, Christine Gledhill, Janice R. Welsch, Patrice Petro, Jane Gaines, Janet Staiger, Diane Carson, Judith E. Smith, Gina Marchetti, Ana López, Julianne Burton-Carvajal, Poonam Arora, and Esther C. M. Yau; deals with U.S., Cuba, China, India, Mexico.

104. Cook, Pam and Philip Dodd, eds. *Women and Film: A Sight and Sound Reader*. Philadelphia, Pennsylvania: Temple University Press, 1993. 320 pp.
    Reflects various directions that the representations of women in film have taken; contributors are: Karen Alexander, Carole Angier, Stephen Bourne, Stella Brooks, Carol Clover, Jenny Diski, Richard Dyer, Thomas Elsaesser, Lizzie Franke, Julia Knight, Gertrud Koch, Irene Kollatz, Alison Light, Angela McRobbie, Berenice Reynaud, B. Ruby Rich, Cherry Smyth, Andrea Stuart, Amy Taubin, Ginette Vincendeau, Linda Ruth Williams, Elizabeth Wilson, Jeanette Winterson, and the editors.

105. *Critical Arts* (South Africa)
    5:2 (1989) -- Thematic issue on "Women Represented" includes: Mikki van Zyl and Tammy Shefer, "Editorial"; Mikki van Zyl, "Rape Mythology"; Tammy Shefer, "Feminist Theories of the Role of the Body within Women's Oppression"; "The Political Application of Ideologies of Femininity: The Case of Marion Spang"; Hilary Janks, "Language, Myth and Disempowerment"; Michelle Friedman, "The Social Construction of Gender: Historically Changing Meanings of (White) Femininity and Masculinity."

106. Czernis, L. "Media Constructions of Feminine Mystery." Paper presented at International Sociological Association, 1994.
    Shows how early and recent cinematic images, along with news depictions, of women in Central and South America and the Middle East have been used to create a highly marketable fantasy of the mysterious and dangerous woman.

107. Dahlgren, Peter and Colin Sparks, eds. *Communication and Citizenship. Journalism and the Public Sphere in the Media Age*. New York: Routledge, 1991. 256 pp.
    Concentrates on the role and future of the public sphere in the U.S. and Europe; one of topics discussed is feminist perspectives on the public sphere.

108. "Day for Monitoring Women in the Media Will Record Data on Portrayal." *Action*. July 1994, p.3.

109.   De Camargo, Nelly. "Nurse and Nursing Profession as Depicted by the Mass Media: An Image Study." Paper presented at International Association for Mass Communication Research, Bled, Yugoslavia, August 26-31, 1990.

Studies the image of nurse and nursing in mass media; states that in TV films and series, their characterization is based on deviant behavior within the profession.

110.   De Roubaix, Marie-Jeanne. "Gender Differences in the Transfer of Meaning Through Juxtaposition of Persons and Products in Advertising." Paper presented at International Association for Mass Communication Research, Bled, Yugoslavia, August 26-31, 1990.

111.   De Roubaix, Marie-Jeanne. "Sex Differences in the Transfer of Meaning Through Juxtaposition of Persons and Products in Advertising." Paper presented at International Association for Mass Communication Research, Bled, Yugoslavia, August 26-31, 1990.

Tries to understand how women and men depicted in advertising are used to give meaning to objects; claims gender differences and similarities are found when considering the kind of products for which the juxtaposing of persons and objects is used.

112.   Doutreligne, Bernadette. "Women and the Media." *Unda News*. June 1995, p. 11.

Account of 1995 symposium on women's representation in the media, held in Toronto.

113.   Dowell, Pat. "Demystifying Traditional Notions of Gender." *Cineaste*. 20:1 (1993), pp. 16-17.

In film.

114.   Duby, Georges and Michelle Perrot. *Power and Beauty: Images of Women in Art.* New York: St. Martin's and Tauris Parke, 1995. 192 pp.

Includes self-portraits by Frida Kahlo and cartoons by Claire Bretécher.

115.   Field, David, Jenny Hockey, and Neil Small, eds. *Death, Gender and Ethnicity.* New York: Routledge, 1997. 256 pp.

Examines the ways in which gender and ethnicity shape the experiences of dying and bereavement; includes media treatment of the violent death of young women and minorities.

116.   Flórez, Florentino. "Mujeres de Tebeo." *El Wendigo*. No. 64, 1994, pp. 8-10.

Discusses women in the comics of Italy, Spain, and the United States.

117.   Gibbs, Liz, ed. *Daring to Dissent: Lesbian Culture from Margin to Mainstream.* London: Cassell Academic, 1996. 256 pp.

Includes perspectives on lesbians in TV, radio, journalism, film, theater, and poetry of U.S. and Europe.

118.   Gibson, Pamela C. and Roma Gibson, eds. *Dirty Looks: Women, Pornography, Power.* Bloomington: Indiana University Press, 1993. 248 pp.

Looks at the eclectic variety of porn available and explores sexual identities that offer treats and alternatives to normative models of sexuality; includes chapter on changes in Asian pornographic cinema.

119.   Giffard, C. Anthony. "International News Agency Coverage of the Fourth World Conference on Women." Paper presented at Association for Education in Journalism and Mass Communication, Chicago, Illinois, July 31-August 2, 1997.
        Studies coverage by Associated Press, Reuters, and Inter Press Service; finds little to substantiate that women were depicted in a condescending or degrading manner.

120.   Gilly, Mary C. "Sex Roles in Advertising: A Comparison of Television Advertisements in Australia, Mexico, and the United States." *Southwest Journal of Business and Economics*. Spring 1990, pp. 27-37.
        Examines sex role portrayals in television advertising of Australia, Mexico, and the U.S. to determine effects of different cultural values on advertising's depiction of women.

121.   Giri, Ram Ashish. "The Image of Women in the American and Indian TV Commercials: A Comparative Analysis." *EDRS*, 1990. 22 pp.
        Reveals that while U.S. television commercials continue to depict women only in relationship to men, Indian commercials imitate Western traditions and increase the abuse of women daily.

122.   Goodrich, Norma L. *Heroines, Demigoddess, Prima Donna, Movie Star*. New York: HarperCollins, 1993. 282 pp.
        Celebrates heroic icons throughout history from Eurydice and Electra to "Thelma and Louise."

123.   Griffin, Michael, K. Viswanath, and Dona Schwartz. "Gender Advertising in the US and India: Exporting Cultural Stereotypes." *Media, Culture and Society*. July 1994, pp. 487-507.
        Samples ads from *Life*, *Newsweek*, *India Today*, and *Illustrated Weekly of India* to examine gender displays; of attributes found, feminine touch/self touching was the most comon; concludes that Western advertising conventions are transferred cross-culturally.

124.   Hall, Stuart, ed. *Representation. Cultural Representations and Signifying Practices*. Thousand Oaks, California: Sage, 1997. 368 pp.
        Brings a variety of approaches to representation; includes work on gendering of narratives in television soap operas.

125.   Heine-Wiedenmann, Dagmar. "Between Sexual Emancipation and Violence: New Works on Pornography" (Zwischen Sexueller Emanzipation und Gewaltverhaltnis: Neuere Arbeiten zur Pornographie). *Soziologische Revue*. October 1992, pp. 360-367.
        Analyzes books by Bettina Bremme, Andrea Dworkin, Henner Ertel, and Rudiger Lautman and Michael Schetsche.

126.   Heyzer, Noeleen. "Women, Communication and Development: Changing Dominant Cultures." *Media Development.* 41:2 (1994), pp. 12-14.
       Stresses need to counter gender stereotypes and western male domination of global media.

127.   Huang, J.-H. "National Character and Sex Roles in Advertising." *Journal of International Consumer Marketing.* 7:4 (1995), pp. 81-96.
       Employs the concept of national character to explain differences in sex-roles portrayed in television advertising of Taiwan and U.S.; claims the more masculine a society, the more sex-role stereotyping in advertising.

128.   ISIS International. *Powerful Images: A Woman's Guide to Audiovisual Resources.* Rome: ISIS International, 1986.

129.   Itzin, Catherine. "Pornography and Civil Liberties." *Index on Censorship.* October 1990, pp. 12-13.
       In U.S. and England.

130.   Itzin, Catherine, ed. *Pornography: Women, Violence, and Civil Liberties: A Radical View.* New York: Oxford University Press, 1992, 1993.
       Uses 26 articles designed to show that pornography is a "crucial element" causing violence against women and children and a major element in male dominance.

131.   Janks, Hilary. "Language, Myth and Disempowerment." *Critical Arts.* 5:2 (1990), pp. 58-66.
       Use of periodicals and advertisement to discuss myths about menstruation.

132.   Jimenez-David, Rina, ed. *Women's Experiences in Media.* Manila: ISIS-International Manila and World Association for Christian Communication, 1997.
       Presents results from 1994 Bangkok Conference, "Women Empowering Communication"; collects 25 stories of women in mass media worldwide.

133.   Jogan, Maca. "The Mass Media as (Re)producers of the Women's Social (In)visibility." Paper presented at International Association for Mass Communication Research, Bled, Yugoslavia, August 26-31, 1990.

134.   *Journal of Film and Video.*
       Winter 1993 -- Thematic issue on "Women in Film," includes Walter C. Metz, "Pomp(ous) Sirk-umstance: Intertextuality, Adaptation, and *All That Heaven Allows*," pp. 3-21; Ruth D. Johnston, "Committed: Feminist Spectatorship and the Logic of the Supplement," pp. 22-39; Cynthia Erb, "The Madonna's Reproduction(s): Miéville, Godard, and the Figure of Mary," pp. 40-56; Steve Fore, "Tales of Recombinant Femininity: *The Reincarnation of Golden Lotus*, the *Chin P'ing Mei*, and the Politics of Melodrama in Hong Kong," pp. 57-70, and Jon Lewis' review of *Men, Women, and Chain Saws: Gender in the Modern Horror Film*, by Carol Clover.

135. Kersten, Joachim. "Culture, Masculinities and Violence Against Women." *British Journal of Criminology.* 36:3 (1996), pp. 381-395.
     Compares official crime statistics, victim survey data, and media coverage of rape in Australia, Germany, and Japan to show differences in visibility of male assaultive crimes against women.

136. Klein, M. L. "Women in the Discourse of Sports Reports." *International Review for the Sociology of Sport.* 23:2 (1988), pp. 139-152.

137. Lageschulte, Melanie. "Media Distorts [sic] China Women's Conference." *Iowa Journalist.* Spring 1996, p. 20.
     Feels U.S. media distorted the Fourth UN Women's Conference in Beijing (1995) by emphasizing China interference and security, the weather, and Hillary Clinton.

138. Laurent, Jean-Fernand, ed. *La Femme, l'Enfant et les Medias.* Fribourg, Switzerland: Delval, 1989. 230 pp.
     Presents papers of 1987 Unesco Seminar on images of women that children obtain from the media.

139. Lee, J. "Media Portrayals of Male and Female Olympic Athletes: Analyses of Newspaper Accounts of the 1984 and 1988 Summer Games." *International Review for the Sociology of Sport.* 27:3 (1992), pp. 197-218.

140. Leong, W.-T. "The Pornography 'Problem': Disciplining Women and Young Girls." *Media, Culture and Society.* January 1991, pp. 91-117.
     Examines how radical feminists and other women have constructed pornography as a social problem, through cognitive claims about pornography as a mass medium and moral claims about the sexuality of men and women.

141. Liebes, T. and S. M. Livingstone. "Mothers and Lovers: Managing Women's Role Conflicts in American and British Soap Operas." In *Comparatively Speaking: Communication and Culture Across Space and Time,* edited by J. G. Blumler, J. M. McLeod, and K. E. Rosengren, pp. 94-120. Newbury Park, California: Sage, 1992.
     Focuses on the expression of conflict between mother, lover, and career woman in four popular British ("Coronation Street" and "East Enders") and American ("The Guiding Light" and "As the World Turns") soap operas.

142. Liestøl, Eva. *Femme Fatale. En Idehistorisk Analyse av Kvinnestereotypien, fra Maleri Til Film* (Femme Fatale: An Historical Analysis of a Female Stereotype, from Painting to the Cinema). Rapport om pågående prosjekt til NAVF, Oslo, 1993.
     Analyzes development of femmes fatales beginning with fin-de-siècle painting and literature and proceeding to contemporary film and television.

143. *Literature / Film Quarterly*
     24:4 (1996) -- Includes George Tseo, "Joy Luck: The Perils of Transcultural 'Translation'"; Rodney Farnsworth, "An Australian Cultural

Synthesis: *Wayang*, the Hollywood Romance, and *The Year of Living Dangerously*"; Kathy Howlett, "'Are You Trying To Make Me Commit Suicide?': Gender, Identity, and Spatial Arrangements on Kurosawa's *Ran*"; Christopher J. Knight, "Woody Allen's *Hannah and Her Sisters*: Domesticity and Its Discontents"; David Malone II, "A Linguistic Approach to the Bakhtinian Hero in Steve Martin's *Roxanne*," and Suzanne Diamond, "Who's Afraid of George and Martha's Parlour? Domestic F(r)ictions and the Stir-Crazy Gaze of Hollywood"; Suzanne Ferriss, "The Other in Woody Allen's *Other Woman*," and William P. Helling, "Rita Hayworth's *The Loves of Carmen* as Literary Criticism."

144.   MacDonald, Myra. *Representing Women: Myths of Femininity in the Popular Media*. London: Edward Arnold, 1995. 224 pp.
        Assesses how women are talked about and constructed visually across a range of popular media; includes "Discourse, Consumerism, Femininity: Discipline Approaches -- Redefining Femininity," "Voices Off: Women, Discourse and Media," "From Mrs. Happyman to Kissing Chaps Goodbye: Advertising Reconstructs Femininity," "Feminine Myths: Replay or Fast Forward?" "Caring and Sharing," "Sex 'n Spice," and "Refashioning the Body."

145.   McEntee, Joy. "Ladies, Bring a Poisoned Plate: Cinematic Representations of the Vengeful Woman." *Media Information Australia*. May 1994, pp. 41-48.
        Looks at the revival of revenge films through "The Cook, the Thief, His Wife and Her Lover" from Europe and "The War of the Rose" from the U.S.

146.   McKee, Neill and Christian Clark. "Meena and Sara: Two Characters in Search of a Brighter Future for Girls." *Animation World*. May 1996, 5 pp.
        Describes UNICEF project to use animation characters ("Meena" in Asia, "Sara" in Africa) to point out problems girls have in Asia and Africa and how they can be solved.

147.   McKie, David and Emily Robertson. "Expanding Generic Possibilities: Female Private Eyes and Public Bodies of Evidence." *Australian Journal of Communication*. 21:1 (1994), pp. 21-32.
        Discusses women police and private detectives in crime novels, film, and TV of three countries.

148.   McLaughlin, Lisa. "Feminism, the Public Sphere, Media and Democracy." *Media, Culture and Society*. October 1993, pp. 599-620.
        Elaborates on three essays by Nancy Fraser who criticizes the Habermasian public sphere as a point of departure for feminist scholarship extending it; Fraser suggests that the role of democracy is crucial for consideration in a feminist critique of the public sphere.

149.   McNair, Brian. *Mediated Sex: Pornography and Postmodern Culture*. London: Arnold, 1996. 208 pp.
        Shows that images of sexuality and debate about their significance are in all media; with many examples from the U.S. and England, attempts to make sense of the many contradictory claims about the impact of sexual representation upon individuals and societies.

150. Masavisut, Nataya, George Simson, and Larry E. Smith, eds. *Gender and Culture in Literature and Film East and West: Issues of Perception and Interpretation.* Honolulu: University of Hawaii Press, 1994. 197 pp.

    Volume of conference papers by individuals such as Chetana Nagavajara, Wimal Dissanayake, Rosalind Morris, Shirley Geok-lin Lim, William A. Callahan, etc.

151. "The Media Must Advance the Cause of Women." *Media Development.* 1/1996, pp. 47-48.

    Excerpts the Platform for Action from the Fourth World Conference on Women, Beijing, China, September 4-15, 1995.

152. Mendus, Susan. "Legal Rights Can Threaten Freedoms." *Index on Censorship.* October 1990, pp. 11-12.

    Argues about free speech and the restrictions on pornographic material.

153. Michel, Andree. *Down with Stereotypes! Eliminating Sexism from Children's Literature and School Textbooks.* Paris: UNESCO, 1986. 105 pp.

    Discusses extent of sexism in textbooks and children's literature in China, Peru, Zambia, France, Norway, the Ukraine, and seven Arab nations; second section focuses on eliminating sexism, providing guidelines for recognizing sex bias and how to develop non-sexist materials.

154. Ndalianis, Angela. "Muscle, Excess & Rupture: Female Bodybuilding and Gender Construction." *Media Information Australia.* February 1995, pp. 13-23.

    Articulates and names contradictions and confusions associated with the growing emphasis on muscle mass and the representation and marketing of the female bodybuilder in bodybuilding competitions and magazines.

155. Newson, Doug A. and Bob J. Carrell. *Silent Voices.* Lanham, Maryland: University Press of America, 1995. 256 pp.

    Examines a number of issues concerning the second-class status of women globally -- development, work, media perception, etc.

156. Parameswaran, Radhika. "Media Representations of Third World Women." *Peace Review.* March 1996, pp. 127-133.

    Claims that Third World women are represented in mass media as homogeneous category, as passive victims of patriarchal cultures, and as exoticized icons that stand for an entire culture.

157. Pillai, Poonam. "Gendering the International: Media and the Discourse of Global Agricultural Trade." Paper presented at International Association for Mass Communication Research, Sydney, Australia, August 20, 1996.

    Examines the signifying practices through which media discourses construct people as part of an international community; specifically traces the gendering of the notion of internationalism as it is produced within media discourses of global agriculture, and critiques the ideological work performed by these representations.

158. Riggs, Larry W. "Desire, Substitution, and Violence in the Contracting Space of Gender." In *Significant Others: Gender and Culture in Film and Literature East*

and West: Selected Conference Papers, edited by William Burgwinkle, Glenn May, and Valerie Wayne, pp. 53-62. Honolulu: University of Hawaii and East-West Center, 1993.

Deals with gender, representation, and the films, "Tie Me Up! Tie Me Down!" by Pedro Almodóvar and "In the Realm of the Senses" by Naoisa Oshima.

159.   Robinson, Doug. *No Less a Man: Masculist Art in a Feminist Age*. Bowling Green, Ohio: Popular Press, 1994. 323 pp.

Develops a three-stage transformation myth and applies it to three male heroes -- Spenser, Rambo, Springsteen.

160.   Rodgerson, G. and E. Wilson. *Pornography and Feminism*. London: Lawrence and Wishart, 1991.

161.   Rodowick, D. N. *The Difficulty of Difference. Psychoanalysis, Sexual Difference and Film Theory*. New York: Routledge, 1991. 200 pp.

Argues that misreadings of Freud and Lacan on sexual difference have characterized models of psychoanalytical film criticism.

162.   Ronai, Carol R., Barbara A. Zsembik, and Joe F. Feagin, eds. *Everyday Sexism in the Third Millennium*. New York: Routledge, 1997. 264 pp.

Shows that despite rumors of its demise, sexism is still rampant in many places, including the Internet.

163.   Schneider, Hans J. "Violence in the Mass Media." *Studies on Crime and Crime Prevention*. 5:1 (1996), pp. 59-71.

Argues that media violence is partly responsible for brutalization of Western society; contends a connection exists between violence in media and in reality concerning pornography and the treatment of women and other topics.

164.   Sengupta, Subir. "The Influence of Culture on Portrayals of Women in Television Commercials: A Comparison Between the United States and Japan." *International Journal of Advertising*. 14:4 (1995), pp. 314-333.

Examines influence of culture on portrayals of women in advertising by analyzing TV commercials from U.S. and Japan; finds that in both, there is a significant relationship between the model's sex and the type of role portrayed.

165.   Sengupta, Subir. "Role Portrayals of Women in Magazine Advertisements: A Cross-Cultural Study." *Media Asia*. 19:3 (1992), pp. 145-149, 155.

Compares the role women portray in advertisements from Eastern and Western cultures; propounds that because women's roles in society are changing constantly, it is plausible that role portrayals of women in ads perceived appropriate in one culture may not be in another.

166.   Shefer, Tammy. "Feminist Theories of the Role of the Body Within Women's Oppression." *Critical Arts*. 5:2 (1990), pp. 37-54.

Deals in part with images of women's bodies in culture, including advertising messages.

167. Springer, Claudia. "Reporters, Women, and the Third World in 1980s Film." *Phoebe*. October 1989, pp. 88-92.
     Claims films such as "Under Fire," "The Year of Living Dangerously," "Last Plane Out," "Salvador," or "Deadline" uphold male dominance.

168. Thompson, Bill. *Soft Core: Moral Crusades Against Pornography in Britain and America*. London: Cassell Academic, 1994. 320 pp.
     Challenges pressure groups seeking to outlaw soft-core pornography, which raises difficult questions about parts of the women's movement, media coverage of the debate, and major political parties' involvement in promoting censorship.

169. Tuchmann, Gaye. "Die Verbannung von Frauen in die Symbolische Nichtexistenz durch die Massenmedien." In *Fernsehen und Bildung*, 14: 1/2 (1980), pp. 10-43.

170. Van Zyl, Mikki. "Rape Mythology." *Critical Arts*. 5:2 (1990), pp. 10-36.
     Includes role of mass media.

171. Van Zyl, Mikki and Tammy Shefer. "Editorial." *Critical Arts*. 5:2 (1990), pp. 1-9.
     Gives an overview of the representation of women in Western male-dominated culture.

172. Varto, Petteri. "Representations of Alcohol in Finnish and American Films: A Comparison." *Alkoholipolitiikka*. 61:1 (1996), pp. 9-17.
     Examines gender aspects of alcohol consumption in Finnish and U.S. films; shows female alcohol abuse is shown less frequently and differently than that of male abuse; in Finnish films, women often are shown trying to restrain the drinking of men.

173. Vitell, Scott J., Kumar C. Rallapalli, and Rene Desborde. "Role Portrayal of Women in Indian Versus American Magazine Advertisements: A Comparative Study." *Journal of Marketing Management*. Fall/Winter 1994, pp. 37-45.

174. Wigmore, Sheila. "Gender and Sports: The Last 5 Years." *Sports Science Review*. 5:2 (1996), pp. 53-71.
     Reviews literature on women in sports; claims it has grown in scope and depth of study and analysis.

175. Wiles, Charles R. and Anders Tjernlund. "A Comparison of Role Portrayal of Men and Women in Magazine Advertising in the USA and Sweden." *International Journal of Advertising*. 10:3 (1991), pp. 259-267.
     Finds a major difference to be the treatment of the sexes in ads depicting nonworking activities -- Swedish magazines more often showed women and men in recreational roles, U.S. magazines, in decorative roles; Swedish women's magazines were more likely to portray women in working and recreational roles and far less likely to depict them in decorative roles than U.S. magazine advertisers.

176.   Williams, C., G. Lawrence, and D. Rowe. "Patriarchy, Media and Sport." In *Power Play*, edited by G. Lawrence and D. Rowe. Sydney: Hale & Iremonger, 1986.

177.   Williams, Eric and Lawrence F. Glatz. "Cinema and the Feminine Threat: The Lost Honor of *Katharina Blum* and *A Taxing Woman*." In *Significant Others: Gender and Culture in Film and Literature East and West: Selected Conference Papers*, edited by William Burgwinkle, Glenn May, and Valerie Wayne, pp. 75-86. Honolulu: University of Hawaii and East-West Center, 1993.

   Analyzes, contrasts how the German film, "Katharina Blum," and the Japanese movie, "A Taxing Woman," make use of their "debt to the psychological underpinnings of classical Hollywood cinema."

178.   Wingate, Maeve. "We Taught Our Data Entry System to Speak a New Language: Dumb Blond." Paper presented at International Association for Mass Communication Research, Sydney, Australia, August 20, 1996.

   Argues that investigation of the material and representational position of women in the transnationalization of information offers an insight to the political economy of racism, sexism, and neo-colonialism.

179.   "Women Don't Buy the Soap in South Africa...and They Don't Sell It in the UK." *Action*. November/December 1997, p.3.

   Reports that South African media, such as South African Broadcasting Corporation, *Cape Times*, *Argus*, still carry sexist advertising despite in-house policies against it; in England, advertisers using provocative images of women and the notion of girl power to sell products were recently given the blessing of the Advertising Standards Authority.

WOMEN AS AUDIENCE

180.   Alcala, Pilar Riaño. *Empowering through Communication: Women's Experiences with Participatory Communication in Development Processes*. Ottawa: IDRC, 1990. 55 pp.

   Discusses role that media such as video, radio, or theatre might play in strengthening participatory processes among women's group in the Third World; reviews characteristics, outcomes, constraints, and limitations of these programs.

181.   Ang, Ien and Joke Hermes. "Gender and/in Media Consumption." In *Mass Media and Society*, edited by James Curran and Michael Gurevitch, pp. 307-328. London: Edward Arnold, 1991.

   Claims mass communication research on gender and media consumption reinforce static, monolithic, oversimplified notion of the feminine, patriarchy, and sexism.

182.   Beverley, Jack. "Women Turning to Magazines, Government Report Finds." *Panpa Bulletin*. September 1993, pp. 47, 49-50.

183.   Bloom, Clive. *Cult Fiction: The Popular Reading Cultures of America and Britain*. New York: St. Martin's Press, 1996. 256 pp.

Provides history of pulp literature in U.S. and England, looking at a new set of coordinates for questions regarding publishing and readership.

184. Brown, Mary E. "Soap Opera as a Site of Struggle -- The Politics of Interpretation." *Media Development*. 38:2 (1991), pp. 23-26.
     Analyzes discursive position of soap opera fans of American, British, and Australian serials.

185. Brunsdon, Charlotte. *Screen Tastes. Soap Opera to Satellite Dishes*. New York: Routledge, 1997. 256 pp.
     Analyzes a number of contemporary U.S. and British films and television shows to show the meanings and pleasures they offer women viewers; also deals with feminine criticism.

186. Cartmell, Deborah, I. Q. Hunter, Heidi Kaye, and Imelda Whelehan, eds. *Trash Aesthetics: Popular Culture and Its Audience*. London: Pluto Press, 1997. 160 pp.
     Takes the audience as its starting point in analyzing response, interaction, and manipulation to/of various film genres of U.S. and England.

187. "Communications for Women in Development." Papers presented at International Consultative Meeting, October 24-28, 1988. Santo Domingo; Dominican Republic: United Nations International Research and Training Institute for the Advancement of Women, 1988.
     Series of 29 papers from conference; includes three overviews, 12 case studies of communication projects or approaches, and separate reports from 10 UN agencies and six international NGOs, case studies on use of radio in Zimbabwe, TV in Nigeria, and TV in China for objectives related to women's development.

188. D'Acci, Julie. "Looking at the Female Spectator." *Media Information Australia*. August 1990, pp. 52-56.

189. Geraghty, Christine. "Feminism and Media Consumption." In *Cultural Studies and Communications*, edited by James Curran, David Morley, and Valerie Walkerdine, pp. 306-322. New York: St. Martin's Press, 1996.
     Focuses on modes of film and television consumption with gender and feminist perspectives on film and television theory.

190. Goetz, A. M. "From Feminist Knowledge to Data for Development: The Bureaucratic Management of Information on Women and Development." *IDS Bulletin*. April 1994, pp. 27-36.
     Argues that the dominant economistic paradigm for information classification, valuation, and analysis institutionalizes interpretations of the meaning of women's experience of development.

191. Gray, Ann. *Video Playtime. The Gendering of a Leisure Technology*. New York: Routledge, Comedia, 1992. 176 pp.
     Investigates what women felt about the VCR, its use within their households, kinds of films and programs they enjoyed.

192. International Women's Tribune Centre. *Women Using Media for Social Change*. New York: IWTC, 1984.

193. *La Información y las Comunicaciones como Recursos de Desarrollo para el Adelanto de la Mujer, Conferencia Mundial del Decenio de las Naciones Unidas para la Mujer* (Information and Communication as Resources of Development for the Advancement of the Woman: World Conference for the United Nations Decade for the Woman). Copenhagen (July. A/CONF. 94/27), 1980.

194. Murray, Anne F. and Gretchen Sutphen. "Funding Communication for Women in Development." *Development Communication Report*. 3/1990, pp. 14-16.
      Describes Global Fund for Women, a grant-making agency that provides funds for women's development, and its emphasis on communication as a program area; deals with Africa, Latin America, Asia, and other regions. In Asia, many groups seek Global Fund money to promote non-sexist mass media.

195. Schlesinger, Philip, R. Emerson Dobash, Russell P. Dobash, and C. Kay Weaver. *Women Viewing Violence*. London: British Film Institute, 1992. 224 pp.
      Provides women's responses to violence in the media -- soap operas, true crime shows, TV dramas, feature films, etc.

196. Seiter, Ellen, Hans Borchers, Gabriele Kreutzner, and Eva-Maria Warth, eds. *Remote Control: Televison Audiences and Cultural Power*. New York: Routledge, 1991. 272 pp.
      Looks at how people view television and their impressions about programs; contributors from Western Europe, Australia, U.S., and Israel offer various perspectives, including feminism.

197. Sreberny-Mohammadi, Annabelle. *Women, Media and Development in a Global Context*. Paris: UNESCO, 1994.

198. Steeves, H. Leslie. "Creating Imagined Communities: Development Communication and the Challenge of Feminism." *Journal of Communication*. Summer 1993, pp. 218-229.
      Contends that for development communication to work, it must liberate and proceed from the perspective of women; further states that women's perspective can only be understood in context, context is understood in dialogue, and dialogue must engage many levels of power.

199. Steeves, H. Leslie and R. A. Arbogast. "Feminism and Communication in Development: Ideology, Law, Ethics, Practice." In *Progress in Communication Sciences*, Vol. II, edited by Brenda Dervin and U. Harihara, pp. 229-277. Norwood, New Jersey: Ablex, 1993.

200. Talbot, Mary and Maggie Andrews, eds. *"All the World and Her Husband": Women in Twentieth-Century Consumer Culture*. London: Cassell Academic, 1997. 320 pp.
      Provides a wide perspective on women and consumerism; explores notion of consumption as empowering for women; includes "Purchasing Power: Women,

Community and Authority in American Shop-by-Television Discourse," "Advertising: Menstruation in Visual Culture," "Consuming Personal Relationships: The Promotion of Family Values in Singapore," "Pampers in Poland: The Globalization of Mothering," "Advertising Difference: Women and Consumer Citizenship in Western Europe," "The Acceptable Face of Feminism in Advertising," "Popular Media and Female Audiences -- 'All the World and Her Husband': *The Daily Mail* 1896-1936," and others.

201.   Vajrathon, Mallica. "Communicating with Women." *Development Communication Report.* 3/1990, pp. 1-3.
        Argues development communicators and educators must consider Third World women because they are economic agents, farmers, agents of environmental protection, and agents of human development; states the challenge for development communicators is to "counter the negative reactions when 'women's issues' are brought up at national or international development sessions."

202.   Vajrathon, Mallica. "Communicating with Women Is Communicating Development." *Gender and Mass Media Newsletter.* November 1991, pp. 33-34.
        Tells why and how development communicators must think about women.

203.   Vajrathon, Mallica. "Women and the Pace of Development." *Action.* February / March 1992, pp. 4-5.
        States that "when development communicators ignore women, they consciously or unconsciously slow down the pace of development and perpetuate the vicious cycles of poverty, illiteracy, starvation and human suffering."

WOMEN PRACTITIONERS

204.   Agarwal, Sumegha. "Women in Media: A Visible and Invisible Story." *Reportage.* Winter 1996, pp. 20-21.
        Reports on worldwide study by Media Watch Canada which stated that women make up 43 percent of journalists and presenters but only 17 percent of interviewees in world news coverage.

205.   Barreca, Regina, ed. *The Penguin Book of Women's Humor.* New York: Penguin, 1996. 658 pp.
        Includes cartoonists Lynda Barry, pp. 56-58; Clare Bretecher, pp. 103-106; Roz Chast, pp. 141-143; Cathy Guisewite, p. 245; Nicole Hollander, pp. 202-204; Libby Reid, pp. 447-449.

206.   Bobo, Jacqueline, ed. *Black Women Film and Video Artists.* New York: Routledge and American Film Institute, 1998. 288 pp.
        Provides history and analysis of genre of film produced by black women since earliest part of twentieth century; includes Madeline Anderson, Monica Freeman, Jacqueline Shearer, Kathleen Collins, Julie Dash, Camille Billops, Zeinabu Davis, Michelle Parkerson.

207.   Brunsdon, Charlotte. "Identity in Feminist Television Criticism." *Media, Culture and Society.* April 1993, pp. 309-320.

Argues that the formative stage of feminist television criticism extends from 1976 to the mid-1980s, and that the key feature of that stage was the move from outside to inside the academy.

208. Campbell, Loretta. "Reinventing Our Image: Eleven Black Women Filmmakers." *Heresies*. 16 (1983), pp. 58-62.

209. Campbell, W. Joseph, Robert L. Stevenson, and Stephen P. Jackson. "Women As Correspondents and Newsmakers in a 37-Nation Study of Foreign and International News Flow." Paper presented at International Association for Mass Communication Research, Sydney, Australia, August 21, 1996.

Extracts information on women from a larger study, showing in a survey of 125 media in 37 countries, over a two day period in May 1995, that women correspondents made up 14 percent of the total, that women were the main actors in the news 18 percent of the time.

210. Chadwick, Whitney and Isabelle de Courtivron, eds. *Significant Others: Creativity and Intimate Partnership*. London: Thames and Hudson, 1993.

Discusses women filmmakers who were closely tied to a male (usually husband) director; among them were Faith Hubley, Penny Marshall, Yoko Ono, Julia Solntseva, Elizaveta Svilova.

211. *Cine and Media* (Brussels). November 1990.

Includes Daniel Van Espen, "Women in the Place of Honour," pp. 4-5; "Women Filmmakers" (including Tanja Rizk of Lebanon, Attiat El-Abnoudi of Egypt, Néjia Ben Mabrouk of Tunisia, Mónica Vasquez of Ecuador, Mercedes Ramirez of Costa Rica, Suzana Amaral of Brazil), pp. 9-13; Deepa Dhanraj, "Women and Film: The Example of India," p. 13.

212. Cole, Janis and Holly Dale. *Calling the Shots: Profiles of Women Filmmakers*. Ontario: Quarry Press, 1993.

213. Foster, Gwendolyn A. *Women Film Directors: An International Bio-Critical Dictionary*. Westport, Connecticut: Greenwood, 1995. 443 pp.

Compiles biographical data on more than 200 women filmmakers from every continent, including filmographies and bibliographies for each.

214. *Frontiers*.

15:1 (1994) -- Thematic issue on "Women Filmakers [sic] and the Politics of Gender in Third Cinema" includes Diana Robin and Ira Jaffe, "Introduction," pp. 1-19; Diane Sippl, "Al Cine de las Mexicanas: Lola in the Limelight," pp. 20-50; Catherine Benamou, "Cuban Cinema: On the Threshold of Gender," pp. 51-75; Patricia Mellencamp, "Making History: Julie Dash," pp. 76-101; N. Frank Ukadike, "Reclaiming Images of Women in Films from Africa and the Black Diaspora," pp. 102-122; Elena Feder, "In the Shadow of Race: Forging Images of Women in Bolivian Film and Video," pp. 123-140; Karen Schwartzman," The Seen of the Crime," pp. 141-182; "Selected Bibliography," pp. 183-186.

215. Fuller, Linda K. "Olympic Access for Women: Athletes, Organizers, and Sports Journalists." In *The Olympic Movement and the Mass Media, Past, Present, and Future Issues.* International Conference Proceedings, The University of Calgary. Calgary, Canada: Hurford Enterprises, 1987.

216. Fuller, Linda K. "Reporters' Rights in the Locker Room." *Feminist Issues.* Spring 1992, pp. 39-45.

217. Gallagher, Margaret. *Gender Patterns in Media Employment.* Paris: UNESCO, 1995.
	Reports that women's share of media jobs is below 25 percent in Africa, Asia, and Latin America, 30 percent in European press and 36 percent in European broadcasting and that of 300 national media studied in 43 countries on four continents, only eight were headed by women (and these were small radio stations or news magazines, mainly in Latin America).

218. Gallagher, Margaret. "Women in the Media -- Making a Difference." *Gender and Communication Section International Association for Mass Communication Research Newsletter.* November 1995, p. 4.
	States women "must still struggle to achieve recognition and respect as media professionals"; includes tables on women's employment in media of Asia, Africa, and Latin America in 1993-1994.

219. *Index on Censorship.* October 1990.
	Thematic issue on "Women and Censorship" includes articles on women in journalism and literature and their problems with censorship, in U.S., England, Canada, Israel, Egypt, Ghana, Namibia, Somalia, India, Sri Lanka, China, Guatemala, USSR, Switzerland, and Yugoslavia.

220. "IOJ and Women Journalists." *IOJ Newsletter.* August 1992, p.2
	Interviews Adriana Nuñez, entrusted with drafting a plan to give priority to the work of women in journalism.

221. Jayamanne, Laleen. *Kiss Me Deadly. Feminism and Cinema for the Moment.* Bloomington: Indiana University Press, 1995. 286 pp.
	Examines directors "outside the canon," such as Kathryn Bigelow, Jane Campion, Rainer Werner Fassbinder, and Martin Scorsese.

222. Kivikuru, Ullamaija. "Survey of International Association for Mass Communication Research Women Members: Glass Ceiling Found in Academy: Big-Boy Games in the Association." *International Association for Mass Communication Research Newsletter.* November 1996, pp. 23-24.

223. Kuhn, Annette, with Susannah Radstone, eds. *The Women's Companion to International Film.* Berkeley: University of California Press, 1994. 480 pp.
	Claims distinction of first comprehensive feminist guide to cinema, presenting women and men worldwide, historically and presently, involved in filmmaking: 79 contributors deal with more than 600 entries on women directors and actresses.

224.   MacDonald, Scott. *A Critical Cinema 3: Interviews with Independent Filmmakers*. Berkeley: University of California Press, 1998. 456 pp.
        Interviews filmmakers of Asia, Europe, and North America, including women.

225.   McFarlane, Janice. "Women and Censorship: An Introduction." *Index on Censorship*. October 1990, pp. 7-8.
        Claims "insistent cultural sexualisation of women which occurs everywhere also contributes a great deal to the silencing of women."

226.   Pilling, Jayne, ed. *Women and Animation*. London: British Film Institute Publications, 1992. 144 pp.
        Aims to document women in animation for art's sake or as a means of expression; covers partnerships, American independents, and animators from Europe, India, UK, Australia, and USSR/Russia.

227.   Rodríguez Calderón, Mirta. "Tania, la Guerrillera." *UPEC*. March-April 1968, pp. 15-17.

228.   Rush, Ramona, Elizabeth Buck, and Christine Ogan. "Women and the Communications Revolution: Can We Get There From Here?" *Chasqui*. July-September, 1982.

229.   Saperstein, Patricia. "Women Filmers See Int'l Action." *Variety*. May 9-15, 1994, p. C-83.

230.   Scott, Barbara A. "Empowering Women in the Global Media." *Peace Review*. June 1996, pp. 289-294.
        Argues that women have been denied significant roles in global media; recommends changes.

231.   Skeggs, Beverly. *Feminist Cultural Theory: Process and Production*. Manchester: Manchester University Press, 1995. 256 pp.
        Brings together leading writers on feminism who describe how they work; draws from different areas, including film and TV.

232.   Spender, Dale. *Nattering on the Net: Women, Power and Cyberspace*. Spinifex Press, 1995. 278 pp.
        Calls for women to be computer-competent; traces women's contemporary status to when printing presses were introduced throughout Europe.

233.   Streitmatter, Rodger. "American-Soviet Women Journalists." *Editor & Publisher*. August 3, 1991, p. 48.
        Reports on meeting of a few Soviet and U.S. women; states the most obvious similarity was the dual responsibilities they had of being journalists and mothers.

234.   Torrijos, Delia. "New Communication Technologies, Women and Democracy." *Media Asia*. November-December 1995, pp. 12-13.

Encourages women to play roles in new information technologies in keynote address before "New Communications Technologies, Women and Democracy" seminar, Bangkok, Thailand, October 19, 1995.

235. "Training Women in Broadcast Management." *Combroad.* No. 89, 1990, pp. 11-15.

236. Wells, Alan. "Women on the Pop Charts: A Comparison of Britain and the United States, 1960-88." *Popular Music and Society.* Spring 1991, pp. 25-32.
        Shows that in Britain, of top 40 singles, women averaged between 5.4 and 9.1 hits during the periods; in the U.S., the average was 10 of *Billboard*'s top 50 since 1955.

237. "Women Are Laying Claim to International Reporting Beats." *Media Report to Women.* Winter 1997, pp. 5-7.
        Interviews women journalists of Canada, Mali, Lebanon, Chile, France, Russia, and U.S. about women's careers in international news.

238. "Women in Animation." Special issue. *Animation World.* May 1996.
        Articles about animators Aleksandra Korejwo, Stephanie Graziano, Clare Kitson, Rose Bond, Linda Simensky, Mary Ellen Bute, Claire Parker; the group, "Women in Animation"; and women animators of Central and East Europe.

239. "Women in Broadcasting." *InterMedia.* June-July 1993, pp. 54-60.
        Deals with three articles: Anita Anand, "Moving from the Alternative to the Mainstream"; Rita Gurha, "India: Telling It Like It Isn't"; Karen Anderson, "Engineering Gender Parity."

240. "Women in Commonwealth Broadcasting: A Status Report." *Combroad.* March 1993, pp. 2-14.

WOMEN'S MEDIA

241. Allen, Donna. "Women Are Creating Their Own Communications Systems." *Media Report to Women.* Winter 1997, p. 9.
        Shows how women worldwide are building their own communications networks through Internet, etc.

242. Allen, Robert C., ed. *To Be Continued...Soap Operas and Global Media Culture.* New York and London: Routledge and Comedia, 1995. 408 pp.
        Scans soap opera as a global media phenomenon, in Asia, Australia, Europe, Latin America and the U.S.; considers the soap opera as a media text, the history of the serial narrative, and the role of soaps in the development of feminist media criticism.

243. Anand, Anita. "Communications for Women in Development: The Experience of Inter Press Service." *Development.* 2, 1990, pp. 77-78.

Surveys successes and future needs of the Women's Feature Service of Inter Press Service; notes progress in international efforts to address women's issues in the media since the UN Decade for Women.

244.   Anand, Anita. "The Women's Feature Service: A News Alternative." Paper presented at the Women Empowering Communications Conference, Bangkok, Thailand, February 1994.

245.   Bhasin, Kamla. "Women and Communication Alternatives: Hope for the Next Century." *Media Development.* 41:2 (1994), pp. 4-7.
Challenges prevailing dominant structures of media and society; warns against trends of globalization, centralization, and monopolization; gives examples of Tanzania Media Women's Association and Kali for Women Publishers (India) as examples of alternative media.

246.   Butalia, Urvashi and Rita Menon. *Making a Difference: Feminist Publishing in the South.* Chestnut Hill, Massachusetts: Bellagio Publishing Network, August 1995.

247.   Darren, Alison. *The Lesbian Film Guide.* London: Cassell Academic, 1997. 244 pp.
Covers "A-Z" "lesbian films" such as "Desert Hearts," "Go Fish," and "I Heard the Mermaids Singing," as well as films with a lesbian character, theme, or subplot; includes 200 reviews from all over the world.

248.   Downing, John, Ali Mohammadi, and Annabelle Sreberny-Mohammadi, eds. *Questioning the Media: A Critical Introduction.* Thousand Oaks, California: Sage, 1995. 514 pp.
Includes new chapters from previous three printings; deals also with feminist media theories.

249.   Drucker, Susan J. and Gary Gumpert, eds. *Voices in the Street: Explorations in Gender, Media, and Public Space.* Cresskill, New Jersey: Hampton Press, 1996. 384 pp.
Includes Gary Gumpert and Susan J. Drucker, "Mediated Communication, Public Space and Gender in Greece and a Greek Community in New York"; Lana Rakow, "The Telephone and Women's Place"; Jonathan Tankel and Jane Banks, "A Tube of One's Own: *Lifetime* as Electronic Space for Women"; Sara F. Luther, "Feminist International Radio Endeavor: Shortwave Radio for Women"; Michele Hunkele and Karen Cornwell, "The Cyberspace Curtain: Hidden Gender Issues."

250.   Frissen, Valerie. "Toys for the Boys? Research on Gender and New Information Technologies: Main Currents in Research and Literature." Paper presented at International Association for Mass Communication Research, Bled; Yugoslavia, August 26-31, 1990.

251.   Frissen, Valerie. "Trapped in Electronic Cages? Gender and New Information Technologies in the Public and Private Domain: An Overview of Research." *Media, Culture and Society.* January 1992, pp. 31-49.

Reviews literature on new information technologies and concludes that production and design of the technology is a male practice, that the boundaries between work and leisure for women are not clearly defined, and that research on the topic does not focus on communication technology in the home.

252. Frissen, Valerie, *et al. For Business Only? Gender and New Information Technologies*. Amsterdam: SISWO, 1990.

253. *Frontiers.*

10:3 (1989) -- Thematic issue on "Women and Words" includes Elizabeth Young, "The Business of Feminism -- Issues in London Feminist Publishing," pp. 1-5; Barbara Smith, "A Press of Our Own -- Kitchen Table: Women of Color Press," pp. 11-13; Mickey Spencer and Polly Taylor, "Journey on a Broom: Some Adventures of Two Over-Forty Editing Feminists," pp. 14-15; Anita D. McClellan, "An 'Unpaid-for-Education' -- A Feminist Labor Organizer in Boston Publishing," pp. 16-21; Carol Ascher, "On Becoming Carol Ascher," pp. 32-35; Nancy Mairs, "Reading Houses, Writing Lives," pp. 73-79.

254. Gever, Martha, John Greyson, and Pratibha Parmar, eds. *Queer Looks: Perspectives on Lesbian and Gay Film and Video*. New York: Routledge, 1993.

255. Inoue, Teruko, *et al. Josei Zasshi o Kaidoku Suru: Comparepolitan -- Nichi, Bei, Mekishiko Hikaku Kenkyo* (Reading Women's Magazines: *Comparepolitan* -- A Comparative Study of Japan, USA, Mexico). Tokyo: Kakiuchi Shuppan, 1989.

256. "International Women's Tribute Centre: Information Repackaging and Communications Skill Building." *Media Development*. 3/1996, pp. 14-15.
Relates 20-year history of this center that, through its information resources and communication skill-building activities, supports efforts by women's groups to improve the lives of women in their countries.

257. Kabir, Shameen. *Daughters of Desire: Lesbian Representations in Film*. London: Cassell Academic, 1997. 256 pp.
Explores lesbian films, from early representations to contemporary ones, spanning 25 films over 60 years and from U.S., Europe, and Asia.

258. *La Comunicación al Servicio de la Mujer: Informe Sober los Programas de Acción e Investigación: 1980-1985* (Communication at the Service of the Woman: Report on the Action and Research Programs). London/Paris: City University/Unesco, 1986.

259. Liebes, Tamar and S. M. Livingstone. "Mothers and Lovers: Managing Women's Role Conflicts in American and British Soap Operas." In *Communication and Culture Across Space and Time: Prospects of Comparative Analysis*, edited by J. Blumler, J. M. McLeod, and K. E. Rosengren, pp. 94-120. Newbury Park, California: Sage, 1992.

260. Luther, Sara F. "Can We Talk? Women's Voices on Shortwave Radio Worldwide." *Gender and Mass Media Newsletter*. November 1992, pp. 13-14.

Examines Feminist International Radio Endeavor (FIRE), which broadcasts three hours daily from the University for Peace in Costa Rica, and Women's International News Gathering Service (WINGS), which produces/distributes audiotapes to small community radio stations in the U.S.

261.   McRobbie, Angela. *Feminism and Youth Culture: From "Jackie" to "Just Seventeen."* London: Macmillan, 1991.

262.   McRobbie, Angela. "More! New Sexualities in Girls' and Women's Magazines." In *Cultural Studies and Communications*, edited by James Curran, David Morley, and Valerie Walkerdine, pp. 172-194. New York: St. Martin's Press, 1996.

Points out new women's and girls' magazines have come onto the scene that both reflect and reinforce women's liberation.

263.   Pedersen, Vibeke. "Bad Girls in Bad TV?" *Gender and Communication Section International Association for Mass Communication Research Newsletter.* November 1995, p. 8.

Analyzes U.S. talk shows, "Oprah Winfrey" and "Ricky Lake" and Danish talk show, "Synnove Sue," to show their "carnival style."

264.   Pleasance, Helen. "Open or Closed: Popular Magazines and Dominant Culture." In *Off Centre: Feminism and Cultural Studies*, edited by S. Franklin, C. Lury, and J. Stacey, pp. 69-84. London: Harper / Collins Academic, 1991.

265.   Smelik, Anneke. *And the Mirror Cracked: Feminist Cinema and Film Theory.* New York: St. Martin's Press, 1998. 232 p.

Explores politics and pleasures of contemporary feminist cinema; highlights cinematic issues central to feminist films -- authorship, point of view, metaphor, montage, and the excessive image.

266.   "Women Organize for Alternative Media." *Media Development.* 41:2 (1994), pp. 18-24.

Describes communication projects/programs by and for women, including The Women's Feature Service of New Delhi, The Development Through Radio Project (Harare, Zimbabwe), Kali for Women (New Delhi), The Friends of Women Foundation (Bangkok), Women Living Under Muslim Laws (France), Feminist International Radio Endeavour (Colón City, Costa Rica), Tanzania Media Women's Association (Dar es Salaam), and women's communication networks in Brazil.

267.   Wong, Tina. "Global PR Campaign Publicised Women's Legal Rights." *Asian Advertising & Marketing.* December 1987, pp. 36-37.

268.   Ziegler, Dhyana and Bette J. Dickerson. "Breaking Through the Barriers: Using Video as a Tool for Intercultural Communication." *Journal of Black Studies.* December 1993, pp. 159-177.

Describes a video letter exchange project used to augment intercultural communications between two groups of women in the U.S. and Senegal.

CHAPTER 2

Africa and the Middle East

AFRICA

General Studies

269. Bam, Brigalia. "Women, Communication and Socio-Cultural Identity: Creating a Common Vision." *Media Development*. 41:2 (1994), pp. 15-17.

 Urges women to develop a common identity; challenges them to seek communication between people, not machines; talks from perspectives of South Africa.

270. Bryce, Jane. "Women in Popular Culture: Women and Modern African Popular Fiction." In *Readings in African Popular Culture*, edited by Karin Barber, pp. 118-125. Bloomington: Indiana University Press, 1997.

 Deals with "The Construction of Gender and Sexuality: Critical Responses," "Women's Writing: Love and Romance," and "Other Readings of 'Popular.'"

271. Dawitt, T. "Media et Femmes en Afrique." *Assignment Children* (Geneva). No. 38, 1997.

272. Efrat, Roni Ben. "Censorship by the Mob." *Index on Censorship*. October 1990, pp. 14, 26.

 Rails against Israeli press and group, Women in Black, that reminds public that the occupation exists.

273. *Estrategias de Nairobi Orientadas Hacia el Futuro para el Adelanto de la Mujer* (Strategies of Nairobi Oriented Towards the Future for the Advancement of the Woman). Conferencia Mundial para el Examen y la Evaluación de los Logros del Decenio de las Naciones Unidas para la Mujer: Igualdad, Desarrollo y Paz (Nairobi, Kenya, July 15-26, 1985). Madrid: Ministry of Culture, Institute of the Woman, Serie Documentos, No. 4, 1987.

274. Gikonyo, Waithira. "Kenya: Strategies and Action for Change in the 1990s." Paper presented at National Seminar on Women in the Development Process, Nairobi, Kenya, July 30-August 1, 1990.

      Focuses on representation of women in the media, women's role in mainstream media organization, and women's resistance to global media opppression.

275. Ngechu, Mary. "Gender Sensitive Communication Research among Male and Female Farmers." In *Communication Research in Africa: Issues and Perspectives*, edited by S.T.K. Boafo and N.A. George, pp. 53-68. Nairobi: African Council for Communication Education, 1992.

276. "Nigerian Media Women To Expand Their Media Positions, Influence Image of Women." *Media Report to Women*. October 1, 1981, pp. 1, 6.

      Expounds on these goals at first workshop for women in Nigerian mass media, May 1981.

277. Nuttall, Sarah. "Reading in the Lives and Writing of Black South African Women." *Journal of Southern African Studies*. 1994, pp. 85-98.

278. Pate, Umaru A. "Status of Women in Nigerian Broadcasting Media: A Case for Representation and Upward Mobilitty." *Journal of Development Communication*. June 1994, pp. 75-85.

      Examines representation and status of women in radio and television stations in three states in the Northeast zone of Nigeria; reveals a number of women are rising in the Nigerian broadcast media but at a slow rate.

279. Various authors. *The Influence of Women and Media on the Issues of Development in the Egyptian Countryside*. Cairo: Faculty of Mass Communication and IDRC, 1994. Unpublished report.

Historical Studies

280. Baron, Beth. *The Women's Awakening in Egypt: Culture, Society and the Press*. New Haven, Connecticut: Yale University Press, 1994. 269.

      Focuses on women's press in Egypt from late 19th century through first two decades of the 20th, a time when at least 30 women's magazines were published in Egypt; claims the early women's press provoked change by establishing a women's network and by initiating discussion of women's rights.

Images of Women

281. Abd-el-Kader, Soha. "The Image of Women in Drama and Women's Programmes in Egyptian TV." Ph.D. dissertation, Cairo University, 1982.

282. Adeleye-Fayemi, Bisi. "Either One or the Other: Images of Women in Nigerian Television." In *Readings in African Popular Culture*, edited by Karin Barber, pp. 125-131. Bloomington: Indiana University Press, 1997.

Emphasizes influence of the traveling theater and modern Yorùbá drama on television; representation of Yorùbá women in theater and televison.

283. Adeleye-Fayemi, Bisi. "Representations of Women in Popular Culture: Women in Nigerian Print Media." Master's thesis, University of Middlesex, 1992.

284. Akpan, Emmanual D. "News Photos and Stories: Men's and Women's Roles in Two Nigerian Newspapers." Ph.D. dissertation, Ohio State University, 1979.

    Shows representation of women in *Daily Times* and *New Nigerian*; Nigerian women were minority in the national press.

285. Blankson, Isaac Abeku. "Representation of Women in African News Magazines." Paper presented at Association for Education in Journalism and Mass Communication, Chicago, Illinois, July 31-August 2, 1997.

    Analyzes African news magazines to determine coverage of women and to understand the importance African media give to roles played by African women.

286. Boateng, A. B. "Equality, Development, Peace and Inverted Pyramids: A Study of West Africa Magazine and the United Nations Decade for Women." M.A. thesis, University of Leicester, 1989.

287. "A Broad Approach, and a Variety of Media Combat Female Genital Mutilation." *Action*. April 1994, p. 6.

288. *Critical Arts* (South Africa). 5:2 (1990).

    Thematic issue on "Women Represented" includes, Mikki Van Zyl and Tammy Shefer, "Editorial," pp. 1-9; Mikki Van Zyl, "Rape Mythologies," pp. 10-36; Tammy Shefer, "Feminist Theories of the Role of the Body within Women's Oppression," pp. 37-54; "The Political Application of Ideologies of Femininity: The Case of Marion Sparg," pp. 55-57; Hilary Janks, "Language, Myth and Disempowerment," pp. 58-66; Michele Friedman, "The Social Construction of Gender: Historically Changing Meanings of (White) Feminity [sic] and Masculinity," pp. 67-111.

289. Fair, Jo Ellen. "The Body Politic, the Bodies of Women, and the Politics of Feminine in U.S. Television Coverage of Famine in the Horn of Africa." *Journalism Monographs*. No. 158, April 1996.

290. Fair, Jo Ellen. "The Women of South Africa Weep: Explorations of Gender and Race in U.S. Television News." *Howard Journal of Communications*. Summer 1993, pp. 283-294.

    Analyzes 72 news stories of violence among blacks in South Africa that included images of women; claims U.S. TV images further marginalize South African women.

291. Friedman, Michelle. "The Social Construction of Gender: Historically Changing Meanings of (White) Femininity and Masculinity 1910-1980." *Critical Arts*. 5:2 (1990), pp. 67-111.

    Studies gender portrayal in advertisements of *Natal Mercury*, 1910-1980.

292. "Gender Stereotyping by Media Combated in South Africa." *Action*. March 1994, p. 6.

293. Gillwald, Alison. "Women, Democracy and Media in South Africa." *Media Development*. 41:2 (1994), pp. 27-32.
       States that women's absence from public politics and political reporting do not bode well for South Africa's so-called democracy.

294. Goro, V. N. and S. A. Muluka-Lutta. "An Analysis of the Roles Portrayed by Women in Television Advertising: Nature and Extent of Sexism Present." Unpublished research paper, School of Journalism, University of Nairobi, 1991.
       Examines representations of women in advertisements on Kenya Broadcasting Corporation and KTN television; finds that 63 percent of female characters had no function beyond "decorating" the product, another 34 percent represented as wives/mothers.

295. Harrow, Kenneth, ed. "Africa Cinema." Special issue of *Research in African Literatures*. 26:3. 220 pp.
       Includes Robert Cancel, "Nadine Gordimer Meets Ngugi wa Thiong'o: Text into Film in Oral History" and Laura De Luca and Shadrack Kamenya, "Representation of Female Circumcision in *Finzan, a Dance for the Heroes*."

296. Hill, Michael. "Abandoned to Difference: Identity, Opposition and Trinh T. Minh-ha's *Reassemblage*." *Surfaces*. 3:2 (1993), pp. 1-29.
       Analyzes Trinh T. Minh-ha's film about women in Senegal that challenges the role of the colonized "other."

297. "In Top Form: Ever Been Called a Humourless Feminist?" *Media and Gender Monitor*. Autumn 1997, p. 9.
       Reports on activities of Cape Town Mediawatch Group in reacting to racism and sexism at South African Broadcasting Corporation

298. "Interview: Women in Development in Cameroon." *Action*. October 1997, p.3.
       Interviews Glory Bhala K. Esene, who states mass media doing better job covering women.

299. King'ori, M.W.A. "Editorial Practices, Attitudes and Treatment of Women and Development Issues in Rural Newspapers in Kenya." Unpublished research paper, School of Journalism, University of Nairobi, July 1991.
       Claims not a positive picture as all 11 rural newspapers of Kenya funded by UNESCO are edited by men.

300. Lancaster, Roger and Micaela di Leonardo, eds. *The Gender / Sexuality Reader, Culture, History, Political Economy*. New York: Routledge, 1997. 550 pp.
       Shows how gender, sexuality, and power are inter-related; includes topic of media representations of Africa.

301. Mwangi, Mary W. "Assessment of the Portrayal of Women in the Kenyan Print Media, Before, During and After the United Nations Decade for Women."

Unpublished research paper, School of Journalism, University of Nairobi, July 1991.

Analyzes samples of stories on the front and back pages of three Nairobi dailies in 1970, 1980, and 1990; finds that even after the Decade of Women, only 10 percent of the stories were about women and the dominant images in each of the years were of sports (often foreign) women, victims, and mothers.

302. Mwangi, Mary W. "Gender Roles Portrayed in Kenyan Television Commercials." *Sex Roles*. February 1996, pp. 205-214.

Examines 105 TV advertisements in Kenya to see their portrayal of gender roles; finds no significant differences in number of males and females as major characters, although both were in traditional roles.

303. Mwendamseke, Nancy. "The Female Image in the Mass Media: The Reality and Possible Remedies." *Africa Media Review*. 4:2 (1990), pp. 64-71.

304. Obura, A. *Changing Images: Portrayal of Girls and Women in Kenyan Textbooks*. Nairobi: Acts Press, 1991.

Finds that males appeared far more often than females and that women were depicted in traditional roles.

305. Revah, Suzan. "Shedding Light on Female Circumcision." *American Journalism Review*. June 1996.

Winner of 1995 Pulitzer Prize in photography, Stephanie Welsh, and her story of female circumcision rites in Kenya.

306. Steeves, H. Leslie. "Gender Violence and the Press: Public Discussion of the St. Kizito Tragedy." Paper presented to Association for Education in Journalism and Mass Communication, Atlanta, Georgia, August 1994.

Analyzes print media coverage of July 1991 St. Kizito school tragedy in Kenya where scores of girls were raped / gang raped; finds abundance of "harmful rape myths and stereotypes, the frequent identification of victims (but not assailants), and a failure to report on the larger context of gender violence in society."

307. Worthington, Nancy. "Constructing the Post-Colonial Woman in Kenya: A Textual Analysis of Nairobi's 'Daily Nation.'" Paper presented at Association for Education in Journalism and Mass Communication, Kansas City, Missouri, August 11-14, 1993.

Women as Audience

308. Arthur, Alexina. "Family Planning Communication and the Africa Women's Liberation: A Ghana Case Study." *Africa Media Review*. 2:1 (1987), pp. 38-51.

309. Axinn, George H. and Nancy W. Axinn. "Rural Communications: Preliminary Findings of a Nigerian Study." *Rural Africana*. No.8, 1968, pp. 19-21.

Claims men read more; women talk more.

310.   Bankole, A., G. Rodriguez, and C.F. Westoff. "Mass Media Messages and Reproductive Behaviour in Nigeria." *Journal of Biosocial Science*. April 1996, pp. 227-239.
    Examines effects of exposure to mass media family planning messages on reproductive behavior of 6,696 married Nigerian women; finds results favorable to use of condoms and smaller families.

311.   "Federation of African Media Women -- Southern African Development Community." *Gender and Mass Media Newsletter*. November 1992, pp. 39-40.
    Presents group's "Plan of Action," adopted November 16, 1992.

312.   Hindin, Michelle J., Lawrence D. Kincaid, Opia Mensah Kumah, Winthrop Morgan, Young-Mi Kim, and J.K. Ofori. "Gender Differences in Media Exposure and Action During a Family Planning Campaign in Ghana." *Health Communication*. 6:2 (1994), pp. 117-135.
    Reveals that men were exposed to an average of 8.8 media sources, women to 8.3; that men were more likely to talk to a partner and begin using contraceptives while women were more likely to talk to service providers.

313.   Ismail, E. "Sudanese Women and Mass Media: A Survey of Urban Middle Class Women." Khartoum: DSRC Seminar No. 53, University of Khartoum, 1984.

314.   Mlama, Penina M. "Women and Communication for Development: The Popular Theatre Alternative." Dar es Salaam: The Namionga Child Survival and Development Project, UNICEF, 1989.
    Describes efforts to increase women's participation in popular theater as an alternative stategy for communication for African development; the theater has been successful in getting more women involved in development and in obtaining exposure for women's issues. Also by same author, "Women's Participation in 'Communication for Development': The Popular Theater Alternative in Africa," *Research in African Literatures*, Fall 1991, pp. 41-53.

315.   Mol, Annelieke. "An Experiment with Home Language Instruction for Moroccan Women Via the Interactive Cable Network." Paper presented at International Association for Mass Communication Research, Bled, Yugoslavia, August 26-31, 1990.
    Shows that technological interests were the driving force behind the experiment with home language instruction, resulting in the socio-cultural and domestic context of Moroccan women being slighted.

316.   Mol, Annelieke. "Experimenting with Language Instruction for Moroccan Women via Interactive Cable." *Media Development*. 38:2 (1991), pp. 28-29.
    Based on case study of the introduction process of an interactive cable network in Zalthommel, The Netherlands, to serve as home instruction for Moroccan women living there.

317.   Moyo, Mavis. "Development Through Radio." *Community Development Journal*. July 1991, pp. 227-232.

Reports on pilot development-through-radio project in Zimbabwe, initiated 1985 to reach illiterate women in rural areas; discusses listening clubs.

318.   Ogbodu, J. O. "Marketing Communication as a Startegy for Creating Scientific and Technological Awareness in Rural Women." Paper presented at 7th Conference of the African Council for Communication Education on "Science for Technology: Implications for Communication Development in Africa," Ouagadougou, Burkina Faso, October 22-26, 1990.

319.   Okunna, Chinyere S. "Communication for Self-Reliance Among Women in Nigeria." *Media Development.* 1/1992, pp. 46-48.
   Discusses Better Life for Rural Women program and appropriate media to use for development purposes, including oramedia and participatory media, radio, and video.

320.   Okunna, Chinyere S. "Small Participatory Media Technology as an Agent of Social Change in Nigeria: A Non-Existent Option?" *Media, Culture and Society.* October 1995, pp. 615-627.
   Addresses communication and development, particularly for women, in rural Nigeria; suggests development workers use interpersonal communication to reach these women.

321.   Okunna, Chinyere S. "Sources of Development Information among Rural Women in Nigeria: A Case Study." *Africa Media Review.* 6:3 (1992), pp. 65-77.

322.   Olaleye, David O. and Akinrinola Bankole. "The Impact of Mass Media Family Planning Promotion on Contraceptive Behavior of Women in Ghana." *Population Research and Policy Review.* June 1994, pp. 161-177.
   Examines influence of media campaigns for family planning on the contraceptive behavior of married women of Ghana; claims high positive impact.

323.   Snyder, Leslie B. "Channel Effectiveness over Time and Knowledge and Behavior Gaps." *Journalism Quarterly.* Winter 1990, pp. 875-886.
   Results of study in 20 Gambian villages where women were target of radio, print, and interpersonal efforts to get them to use oral rehydration solution.

324.   Steeves, H. Leslie. "Agricultural Extension and African Women." *Development Communication Report.* 3/1990, pp. 4-5.
   States that women grow 80 percent of the food of sub-Saharan Africa, yet the primary channel for transmitting information on agriculture -- extension workers -- still largely "ignores the needs and situations" of African women farmers.

325.   Steeves, H. Leslie. "Sharing Information in Kenya: Communication and Information Policy Considerations and Consequences for Rural Women." *Gazette.* 56:3 (1995/1996), pp. 157-181.
   Examines communication and information policy considerations from the standpoint of Kenyan rural women; reviews present policy and historical and political context in which discussions have been taking place; suggests four areas

that must be addressed: 1. Women's employment in media and information, 2. Women's access to useful information through media and information technologies and other forms of communication, 3. Representations of women in media and information content, and 4. Gender-sensitive criteria in choices of media and in the acquisition of technologies.

Women Practitioners

326.   "African Women Communicators Challenge Church Leadership." *Action*. February 1993, p. 4.

327.   Blankson-Mills, Maud. "Women in Broadcasting in Ghana." *Combroad*. January-March 1988, pp. 15-18.

328.   "Broadcaster Annette Mbaye Is Woman's Affair Activist in Senegal; Produces Women's Programs." *Media Report to Women*. July 1, 1976, p. 5.
       Reprints article from April-May 1976 *Africa Woman*.

329.   Carty, James W. "Women in East Africa Media Were 1% of Total; Now Are 5% to 10%." *Media Report to Women*. January 1, 1980, p. 6.
       Surveys women in journalism education, news agencies, and broadcasting; looks at women's magazines expansion.

330.   de Villiers, Trish and Gaby Cheminais. "Investigating the Relationship Between Women, Media, and Violence: A CAP Media Project Course." *Critical Arts*. 8:1/2 (1994), pp. 110-124.
       Describes South African course that trains women and gives support in community media projects.

331.   Domatob, Jerry K. "Sub-Saharan African Media Women: Social Status and Structural Challenges." Paper presented at 6th Biennial Conference of ACCE, Jos, Nigeria, October 1988.

332.   Emenyeonu, Nnamdi B. "Motivations for Choice of Course and Career Preferences of Nigerian Female Students: Implications for the Status of Media Women in a Developing Nation." *Africa Media Review*. 5:2 (1991), pp. 71-83.

333.   Harvey, Sylvia. "Third World Perspectives: Focus on Sarah Maldoror." *Women and Film*. 1:5-6 (1974), pp. 71-75, 110.
       Deals with African/Caribbean filmmaker.

334.   Hornig, Susanna, Marilyn Kern-Foxworth, and Cari Zall. "New Media and Old Inequities: Gender and Media Use in Nigeria." *Gazette*. 52:2 (1993), pp. 159-163.
       Surveys Nigerian college students and finds that the introduction of new media technology does not solve problems of gender inequality.

335.   Ibie, Nosa O. "Media / Cultural Imperialism and Nigerian Women: Whose Culture, Which Imperialism?" *Journal of Social Development in Africa*. 7:2 (1992), pp. 39-52.

Discusses Nigerian women's growing and active role in the emerging, post-colonial, elite structure of Nigeria; claims it has become difficult to see imperialism strictly as an external imposition.

336. Kdagala, E. and W. Kiai. "Folk, Impersonal and Mass Media: The Experience of Women in Africa." In *Women Empowering Communication*, edited by Margaret Gallagher and L. Quindoza-Santiago, pp. 11-35. London: World Association for Christian Communication, 1994.

Reports that fewer than 25 females are among 250 journalists in daily newspapers of Kenya, and only two women editors.

337. Martin, Angela. "Four Filmmakers from West Africa." *Framework*. 11 (1979), pp. 16-21.

Includes Safi Faye of Senegal.

338. Mgbemena, Nwabu N. "Nigerian Journalists: A Study of Their Demographic Characteristics and Professional Orientation." Ph.D. dissertation, University of Texas, 1980.

Shows that men outnumbered women nine to one in Nigerian journalism.

339. "More Media Opportunities for Women in Zaire." *Action*. July 1993, p. 1.

340. Moyo, Mavis. "Development of Women in Broadcasting in Zimbabwe." *Combroad*. December 1987, pp. 15-17.

341. Nanjii, Meena. "Pratibha Parmar." *High Performance*. Summer-Fall 1992, pp. 28-29.

About Kenya-born, British lesbian activist/writer/filmmaker.

342. Newell, Stephanie, ed. *Writing African Women: Gender, Popular Culture and Literature in West Africa*. New York: St. Martin's Press, 1997. 224 pp.

Explores links between literature, popular culture, and theories of gender; sections deal with interaction of sexual politics and other polemics of postcolonial Africa and African women's writing in context of how writers approached, appropriated, and subverted issues of female creativity and stereotyping.

343. Ogundipe-Leslie, Molara. "Beyond Heresay and Academic Journalism: The Black Woman and Ali Mazrui." *Research in African Literatures*. Spring 1993, pp. 105-112.

344. Okigbo, Charles. "Nigerian High School Students Evaluate Journalism Careers." *Journalism Quarterly*. 61:4 (1984), pp. 907-909.

Suggests that more Nigerian women will enter journalism careers.

345. Okunna, Chinyere S. "Female Faculty in Journalism Education in Nigeria: Implications for the Status of Women in the Society." *Africa Media Review*. 6:1 (1992), pp. 47-58.

Addresses gender issues in the training of journalists in Nigeria; criticizes absence of women teachers in journalism/mass communications schools and institutes. Also by Okunna, "The Changing Patterns of Journalism Education and Recruitment in Nigeria." Paper presented at 3rd Biennial NIMCA Conference, Enugu, April 1987.

346. Onyekwere, Evelyn C. "Relationship Between Gender and Self-Perceived Communicator Style in the Nigerian Cultural Context: An Empirical Investigation." *Africa Media Review.* 4:2 (1990), pp. 26-36.

347. Pinnock, Don. "Writing Left: The Journalism of Ruth First and the *Guardian* in the 1950s." In *South Africa's Alternative Press: Voices of Protest and Resistance, 1880-1960,* edited by Les Switzer, pp. 308-330. New York: Cambridge University Press, 1997.
    Looks at journalism of Ruth First of the *Guardian* in the context of resistance politics of the 1950s. An activist/journalist, First fought apartheid, poverty, repression against women, and irresponsible capitalism before being silenced by a letter bomb planted by South African security agents.

348. "Profiles of Women in Commonwealth Broadcasting." *Combroad.* March 1990, pp. 19-20.
    Includes Dr. Victoria Ezeokoli, director of programs, Nigerian Television Authority.

349. Stewart, Kathy B. "Community Publishing as a Strategy for Women's Development: A Zimbabwean Experience." *Development Communication Report.* 3/1990, pp. 12-13.
    Describes the Community Publishing Program established in the mid-1980s by the Zimbabwe government to promote development; assesses major role played by women at all levels.

350. Switzer, Les, ed. *South Africa's Alternative Press: Voices of Protest and Resistance, 1880-1960.* New York: Cambridge University Press, 1997. 400 pp.
    Mentions role of women in various resistance press capacities on pp. 43, 110, 117, 198-200, 234, 236, 257-258, 289-290, 308-330.

351. Van der Wijngaard, R. "Women as Journalists: Incompatability of Roles?" *African Media Review.* 6:2 (1992), pp. 47-56.

Women's Media

352. "'Africa Woman' Shares Its Media To Encourage Women's Communication." *Media Report to Women.* March 1, 1977, p. 11.
    Excerpts from January-February 1977 issue of *Africa Woman,* giving editorial philosophy of the periodical; also interview with founder of *Africa Woman* on why it was started.

353. "African Media Women Launch FAMW at 2-Week Workshop of Features Service." *Media Report to Women.* February 1, 1982, pp. 1, 11.

Announces start of the Federation of African Media Women in October 1981; accompanied by article, "AWFS Workshop Plans Team of Women Correspondents from Each Country," p. 11.

354.   "Cameroon Radio Features Women's Media Issues." *Action*. June/July 1990, p. 5.

355.   Data Research Africa. "*Agenda* Research Survey: Volume I." Durban: Data Research Africa, 1994.

A limited and perhaps unrepresentative readership survey of alternative feminist periodical *Agenda* suggested that four of five readers are university educated, half are academics, two-thirds are white.

356.   Jeyifo, B. *The Yorùbá Professional Itinerant Theatre: Oral Documentation*. Lagos: Division of Culture, Federal Ministry of Social Development, Youth, Sports and Culture, 1981.

By the same author: *The Yorùbá Popular Travelling Theatre of Nigeria*. Lagos: Nigeria Magazine Publications, 1984.

357.   Johnson, Angela and Carol A. Douglas. "African Women Publish: South Africa." *Off Our Backs*. March 1992, pp. 2-3, 17.

Spotlights *Speak*, a feminist magazine, through an interview with its editor, "Karen."

358.   Johnson, Angela and Carol A. Douglas. "African Women Publish: Uganda." *Off Our Backs*. March 1992, pp. 4-5, 17.

Interviews Rebecca Musoke, who worked for *Arise*, a women's periodical in Uganda; also discusses ACFODE (Action for Development), publisher of *Arise*.

359.   Morrison, J. F. "Feminist Theater in Africa: Will It Play in Ouagadougou?" *Howard Journal of Communications*. Spring 1995, pp. 245-253.

Combines theater for development, the plight of rural women in Africa, Asia, and Latin America, and feminist theory and practice; discusses political theater and feminist theater as its subcategory.

360.   Moyo, Mavis. "Development of Women in Broadcasting in Zimbabwe." *Combroad*. December 1987, pp. 15-17.

361.   Waterman, Peter. "Holding Mirrors Out of Windows: Part II: A Feminist Agenda and the Creation of a Global Solidarity Culture in the New South Africa." *The Democratic Communique*. October 1995, pp. 9-16.

Discusses *Agenda*, an alternative feminist publication of South Africa, as well as other projects and organizations involved in creating a global solidarity culture.

THE MIDDLE EAST

General Studies

362.   "Israel: Institute for the Study of Media and the Family." *Gender and Mass Media Newsletter*. March 1991, p. 30.
Describes the Israeli institute, a non-profit organization devoted to raising public awareness to the media's role in forming people's perceptions and behavior towards women.

363.   Rizg, Hoda. "Women and Social Change: Methodological Observations." Paper presented at symposium on the Modern Arab Woman, Qar Yunus University, Lidya, 1989.

Images of Women

364.   Abd-el-Rahman, Awatef. "Gender and Media in the Arab World." Paper presented at International Association for Mass Communication Research, Sydney, Australia, August 21, 1996.
Discusses current situation of Arab women, relative to employment, political participation, and personal status laws; contends that Arab media are "far away from covering the real progress and achievements done by women in various sectors."

365.   Abd-el-Rahman, Awatef. "The Image of the Arab Woman in Media." In *Studies in the Modern Arab Press*, pp. 145-149. Beirut: Dar Alfarabi Publishing House, 1989.

366.   Gertz, Nurith. "Woman -- The Image of the 'Other' in Israeli Society." *Literature / Film Quarterly*. 26:1 (1996).

367.   Naficy, Hamid. "The Averted Gaze in Iranian Postrevolutionary Cinema." *Public Culture*. Spring 1991, pp. 29-40.
Concludes that "The presence of women in postrevolutionary cinema -- structurally absent, relegated to the background, limited to domestic space, and governed by codes of modesty and strategies of veiling and unveiling -- may construct a representation of women as modest and chaste ... however, such a representation also tends to replicate the dominant / subordinate relations of power that exist between men and women in society at large."

Women as Audience

368.   "Group of Media and Rural Women in Arab World." *Gender and Mass Newsletter*. November 1992, p. 33.
Describes activities and purposes of this Egypt-based group.

Women Practitioners

369. Allen, Donna. "Women Use Communication To Fight Iranian Repression." *Media Report to Women*. Spring 1997, p. 15.

    Shows how Iranian Resistance Movement is dominated by women who use communication as weapon against repression.

370. Amiri, Noushabeh. "Daughters of the Revolution." *Cinemaya*. Autumn / Winter 1994-1995, pp. 36-40.

    Tells how women have become among the most prominent personalities in Iranian cinema; discusses pioneers Shahla Riahi, Farough Farokhzahd, Marva Nabili, Kobra Sa'eedi, Marzieh Boroomand, Tahmineh Milani, Rakhshan Bani'etemad, Pooran Derakhshandeh, and Ferial Behzad.

371. Amiri, Noushabeh. "Rakhshan Bani'etemad." *Cinemaya*. Autumn / Winter 1994-1995, pp. 42-43.

    Profiles Iranian film director.

372. Creedon, P. J., M. A. W. Al-Khaja, and J. Kruckeberg. "Women and Public Relations Education and Practice in the United Arab Emirates." *Public Relations Review*. 21:1 (1995), pp. 3-26.

373. "Dictionary of Women Directors." *Cinemaya*. Autumn / Winter 1994-1995, p. 41.

    Lists 11 women filmmakers of Iran according to pre- and post-revolutionary eras.

374. Dönmez-Colin, Gönül. "Sema Poyraz: Contending with an Alien Land." *Cinemaya*. Autumn / Winter 1994-1995, pp. 60-62.

    Discusses difficulties of a Turkish woman to go into the film business of Germany; Poyraz talks about her projects.

375. Dorsay, Atilla. "Before Tomorrow, After Yesterday." *Cinemaya*. Autumn / Winter 1994-1995, pp. 56-58.

    Traces history of Turkish women film directors; includes Feyturiye Esen, Fahriye Tamkan Fer, Bilge Olgaç, Lale Oraloglu, Türkan Soray, Nisan Akman, Mahinur Ergun, and others.

376. Dorsay, Atilla. "The Stubborn Ambition of Bilge Olgaç." *Cinemaya*. Autumn / Winter 1994-1995, pp. 59-60.

    Deals with one of Turkey's most famous film directors, Bilge Olgaç, discussing her career and film themes; states that her early works were men's films but later, she added feminine emotions and sensitivities to her works.

377. "A Gentle Look at a Harsh World: Puran Derakhshandeh." *Cinemaya*. Winter 1990-1991, pp. 14-16.

    Iranian filmmaker.

378. Jacob-Arzooni, Ora G. *The Israeli Film*. New York: Garland, 1983.

    Includes women such as Michal Bat Adam.

379.   Leon, Masha. "Israeli Film Star Gila Almagor Wrestles with Her Mother's Demonic Past." *Lilith*. September 1991, pp. 21-24.
       During the Holocaust.

380.   "Mageda al-Batsh: A Journalist on the Face of It." *Index on Censorship*. October 1990, pp. 15, 26.
       Highlights experiences of woman journalist on Palestinian newspaper, *al-Usbu'a al-Jadid*, in Jerusalem.

381.   Maghsoudlou, Bahman. *Iranian Cinema*. New York: New York University Press, 1987.
       Includes women filmmakers such as Rakhshan Bani'etemaad.

382.   "Nawal el Saadawi: Defying Submission." *Index on Censorship*. October 1990, p. 16.
       Details story of a "disobedient woman writer" in Egypt.

383.   Thoraval, Yves. "Jocelyne Saab's Beirut: A World in Microcosm." *Cinemaya*. Autumn / Winter 1994-1995, pp. 14-16.
       Profiles more than 20-year career of Jocelyne Saab, called the most important woman film director of the Arab world; discusses her straddling Paris and Beirut bases while doing more than 30 documentaries.

CHAPTER 3

Asia, Australia, and Oceania

ASIA

General Studies

384. Allison, Tony, Angela Jeffs, and Joyce Moy. "Figure It Out." In *Asia Magazine*. January 7-9, 1994, pp. 8-13.

385. "Amic Hosts Seminar on New Communication Technologies, Democracy and Women in Asia." *Asian Mass Communication Bulletin*. September / October 1997, p. 20.

386. Anand, Anita. "Changing Women, Changing Communication." *Development*. No. 3, 1993, pp. 51-53.

387. "Antipolo Declaration on Gender and Media." *Media and Gender Monitor*. Autumn 1997, pp. 5-6.
      Gives platform, issues, and strategies of declaration issued by women at World Association for Christian Communication conference, Manila, July-August 1997.

388. Appadurai, Arjun, *et al. Gender, Genre and Power in South Asian Expressive Traditions*. Philadelphia: University of Pennsylvania Press, 1991, 486 pp.
      Looks at women's tales, literary traditions, and communications in India. Result of proceedings of University of Pennsylvania seminar. Later republished by Motilal, 1994.

389. Asiah Sarji. "Wanita dan Komunikasi: Satu Persoalan Semasa." *Jurnal Antropologi dan Sosiologi*. 15 (1987), pp. 63-73.
      In Malaysia.

390.   *Asian Forum on Strategies of Networking: Making Networking a Reality.* New Delhi, 1993. New Delhi: Asian Network of Women in Communication, 1994. 107 pp.

Reports on forum of women from 10 different countries who met to compare successes and failures in their attempts to reform the media.

391.   Asian Mass Communication Research and Information Centre. *Impact of New Communication Technologies on Women as Producers and Consumers of Communication in Asia: Case Studies of India and Singapore.* Singapore: AMIC, 1993. Various pagings.

392.   Association for Asian Studies conference, Washington, D.C., March 26-29, 1998.

Includes Isolde Standish, "Gendered Television: Feminine Inflection of the Male Hero in the Samurai Drama and Detective Series, Discourses of Female Powerlesness"; Barbara Mittler, "Cooking, Cleaning, Caring: To Be or Not To Be a 'New Woman' in Women's Magazines of the Later Qing"; Constance Orliski, "The Health of the Body Politic: Jiating Weisheng, Household Sanitation, and Family Hygiene"; Nicole Huang, "Fashioning Public Intellectuals: Popular Journals for Women in Wartime Occupied Shanghai (1941-1945)"; Laikwan Pang, "Reconfiguring Stardom: The Suicides of Two Actresses in Shanghai in the 1930s"; Zhen Zhang, "Embodiment of Excess?: The Proliferation of the 'Martial Arts' Film and the Image of the Female Knight-Errant in Shanghai Cinema, 1920-1930s."

393.   Balakrishnan, Vijayalakshimi, comp. *Lens Eye: Women's Resource Directory on the Electronic Media.* New Delhi: New Concept, n.d. 68 pp.

Divided into five sections: list of filmmakers, lists of 70 films, and three sections on series of audiotapes.

394.   Balasubrahmanyan, Vimal. *Mirror Image: The Media and the Women's Question.* Bombay: Centre for Education and Documentation, 1988. 157 pp.

Covers the legitimization of the women's question in the media in recent years, media distortion of this issue, interactions between media and the movement, audienec responses to feminist message, media cashing in on women's question, and suggestions for initiating change concerning media sexism and distortion of the women's question.

395.   Bhasin, Kamla. "Women Empowering Communication: From Bangkok to Beijing." *Media Development.* 1/1996, pp. 13-17.

Speech before 1995 World Association of Christian Communication Congress '95.

396.   Cooper-Chen, Anne. *Mass Communication in Japan.* Ames: Iowa State University Press, 1997.

Includes women and advertising, 131-132, 139-140, 147-148, 171; women in commercials, 137; erotic *manga* and women, 101; magazines of women, 89-94, 102, 139, 162, 170; media gender differentiation, 20-21, 101-103, 141, 211-212; newspaper hiring practices and women, 203, 210; obscenity and pornography,

176-179; "Oshin" television novel and women, 118, 128-129; women in PR, 157; women and television, 116, 118, 123-124, 127, 168-169, 210.

397. "Fledgling Media Monitoring Effort by Chinese Women Raises Awareness." *Media Report to Women*. Fall 1995, pp. 3-4.

Reports from survey results of 10 major Chinese dailies that only 3.45 percent of front page coverage included women; their bylines represented 12.2 percent of the total.

398. Hermano, Teresita. "Conference Participants Pledge Commitment to Media and Gender Activism." *Media and Gender Monitor*. Autumn 1997, pp. 1, 12.

Reports on Asian conference on "Gender and Communication Policy," Manila, July / August 1997.

399. Inoue, Teruko. "The Role of Modern Journalism." In *Women in a Changing Society: Views from Japan*, pp. 79-93. Geneva: UNESCO, 1985.

400. Jain, Nisha. "Patriarchy Status of Women and Role of Media: A Study of Media Role in Cultural Reproduction in India." Ph.D. dissertation, University of Jammu, 1997.

401. Japanese Popular Culture Conference, Victoria, British Columbia, Canada, April 9-11, 1997.

Includes Anne Allison, "Sailor Moon: Japanese Superheroes for Global Girls"; Karen Kelsky, "White Desire: White Men and Women in Japanese Television Commercials"; Jackie Hogan, "The Geisha and the Ironman: Gendered National Identities in the Television Advertisements of Japan and Australia"; James Stanlaw, "Open Your File, Open Your Mind: Women, English, and Changing Roles and Voices in Japanese Popular Music"; Robert Hamilton, "Synthetic Girls: The Seduction of Artifice in Anime, 'Kisekae' Dolls, and Kyoko Date"; William Lee, "From Sazae-san to Crayon Shin-chan: Family Anime and Social Change in Japan"; Mariko Yamaguchi, "The Generation Gap Between Sazae-san and Crayon Shin-chan"; Maki Takahashi, "Two Different Generations of Japanese Females: Their Gender Role Representations in Two Popular Cultures"; Tamae Pringle, "In the Lacuna of Identities: Girls in Japanese Cinema"; Maia Tsurumi, "Gender and Girls' Comics in Japan"; Hilaria Goessmann, "Changing Attitudes Toward Gender Roles in Popular Japanese TV Dramas of the 1990s."

402. Jha, Rama. *Women and the Indian Print Media: Portrayal and Performance*. Delhi: Chanakya Publications, 1992. 208 pp.

Deals with portraits of women in Indian newspapers, women journalists handling women's issues, women journalists' struggles against cultural bias, journalists as part of women's network, recommendations and appendices that include a brief questionnaire on women and the print media, and writing samples of 15 women journalists. Error prone.

403. Kato, H. and T. Tsuganesawa, eds. *Josei to Media* (Women and Media). Tokyo: Sekai Shisosha, 1992.

404.   Kaur, Kiranjit. "Malaysian Media and the Malaysian Woman." Paper presented at International Association for Mass Communication Research, São Paulo, Brazil, August 16-21, 1992. 22 pp.

Profiles Malaysian mass media and discusses media policies related to gender issues, women in Malaysian media as employees and images, women in advertising, studies on portrayal of women in Malaysian media, and women in TV dramas. Published in *Media Asia* (20:2, 1993, pp. 82-89).

405.   Kipnis, Andrew. "Anti-Maoist Gender: *Hibiscus Town*'s Naturalization of a Dengist Sex / Gender / Kinship System." *Asian Cinema*. Winter 1996/1997, pp. 66-75.

Concludes that in this Chinese film, Maoist politics leads to inverted or deficient masculinities and femininities, absurd, perverted, or unsatisfying sex, and sonless families.

406.   Mananzan, Mary J., Ma. Asuncio Azcuna, and Fe Mangahas, eds. *Sarilaya: Women in Arts and Media*. Manila: Institute of Women's Studies, St. Scholastica's College, 1989. 257 pp.

Includes essay by Leonora C. Angeles, where she argues for media criticism to "extend beyond a content analysis of the portrayal of women in Philippine media, to a reflection of how such portrayal fits in with the prevailing cultural ideology." Maria M. Fajardo, in her essay about broadcast media, contends that women journalists show concern for women's issues but can not put these into action because of discrimination within the profession.

407.   Marran, Christine. "Cinematic Sexualities: The Two Faces of Abe Sada in Japanese 'Poruno' Film." *Asian Cinema*. Winter 1996/1997, pp. 81-90.

Analyzes two Japanese films, "Ai no Koriida" and "Jitsuroku Abe Sada," based on the famous murder case of 1936.

408.   Masterton, Murray and Anita Anand. "Roundtable." *Media Asia*. 18:4 (1992), pp. 210-211.

409.   Mittal, Mukta, ed. *Women in India. Today and Tomorrow*. n.p.: Anmol, 1995. 366 pp.

Includes essays from an interdisciplinary seminar -- women and media, television, communication issues among topics.

410.   Muramatsu, Yasuko. "Of Women, By Women, For Women? -- Toward New Hopes for Television in Japan." Paper presented at International Association for Mass Communication Research, Bled, Yugoslavia, August 26-31, 1990.

411.   Nicolas, Fort Olicia, Jojo de Leon, and M. Juris Aledia Luna, eds. *Women and Media in the Asian Context*. Quezon City: World Association for Christian Communication and People in Communication, 1990. 138 pp.

Case studies on Hong Kong, Indonesia, Japan, Korea, Malaysia, and Philippines; looks at women and images, journalists, and media.

412. Pandian, Hannah. "Yellow Butterflies and Mischief Makers: The State of Gender Policy in Asian Media Today." *Media and Gender Monitor.* Autumn 1997, pp. 1-4, 6.

    Reports on first World Association for Christian Communication regional gender and communication policy meeting, Manila, July-August 1997; treats women and media topics in a number of Asian countries.

413. Polestico, Rachel V. "Systematizing Gender-Based Interventions: The Mindanao Experience." *Adult Education and Development.* No. 40, 1993, pp. 323-331.

414. Prasad, Nandini. *A Pressing Matter: Women in Press.* New Delhi: Friedrich-Ebert-Stiftung, 1992. 100 pp.

415. Prasad, Nandini. *Vision Unveiled: Women on Television.* Delhi: Har-Anand, 1994.

416. Rai, Usha. "Women in the Media: Struggle and Progress." *Span.* March 1987, pp. 32-34.

    In India.

417. Sangari, Kumkum and Sudesh Vaid, eds. *Recasting Women: Essays in Colonial History.* N.p.: Kali for Women, 1989. 372 pp.

    Among 11 essays of women in recent Indian history are those on women's roles in popular culture and feminist consciousness in women's journals.

418. Shimamori, Michiko. *Kokoku no Naka no Onnatachi* (Women in Advertising). Tokyo: Daiwa Shobo, 1984.

419. Shimamura, M. *Fanshii no Kenkyu: Kawaii Ga Hito, Mono, Kane o Shohai Suru* (Research into 'Fancy': Cute Controls People, Objects and Money). Tokyo: Nesco, 1990.

420. Shrivastava, K. M. *Media Issues.* New Delhi: Sterling, 1992. 168 pp.

    Women is one of the issues, along with terrorism, religious controversy, multilingualism, and elections.

421. Singh, Premlata. "Communication Behaviour of Women Scientists." *Communicator.* October-December 1995, pp. 44-45.

    Shows that in a survey of 163 women scientists of India, information was sought for research, followed by "updating knowledge," "working on research reports."

422. Skov, Lise and Brian Moeran, eds. *Women, Media and Consumption in Japan.* Honolulu: University of Hawaii Press, 1995. 318 pp.

    Includes Lise Skov and Brian Moeran, "Introduction: Hiding the Light: From Oshin to Yoshimoto Banana," pp. 1-74; Paul A. S. Harvey, "Interpreting Oshin -- War, History and Women in Modern Japan," pp. 75-110; Brian Moeran, "Reading Japanese in *Katei Gaho*: The Art of Being an Upperclass Woman," pp. 111-142; Nancy Rosenberger, "Antiphonal Performances? Japanese Women's Magazines and Women's Voices," pp. 143-169; Lise Skov, "Environmentalism

Seen Through Japanese Women's Magazines," pp. 170-196; John Clammer, "Consuming Bodies: Constructing and Representing the Female Body in Contemporary Japanese Print Media," pp. 197-219; Sharon Kinsella, "Cuties in Japan," pp. 220-254; Merry White, "The Marketing of Adolescence in Japan: Buying and Dreaming," pp. 255-273; John Whittier Treat, "Yoshimoto Banana's *Kitchen*, or the Cultural Logic of Japanese Consumerism," pp. 274-298.

423.   *Women and Media in the Asian Context.* Quezon City: People in Communication, Inc., 1992. 138 pp.

   Divides into two parts -- women as media practitioners and portrayal of women in media.

424.   "Women and the Media in the Asian Context." *Action.* February / March 1992, p. 7.

425.   "Women in Asia Seek Influence, Access." *Media Report to Women.* January-February 1991, p. 7.

426.   "Women's Conference Plans Media Strategies." *Action.* April 1994, pp. 1, 4-5.

   In Bangkok, February 12-17, 1994.

427.   World Association for Christian Communication. *The Mass Media and Women in the 90's.* Hong Kong: Hong Kong Christian Service Communications Centre, 1993. 187 pp. English, Chinese.

428.   Yau, Esther C. M. "Is China the End of Hermeneutics? Or, Political and Cultural Usage of Non-Han Women in Mainland Chinese Films." *Discourse.* Spring-Summer 1989, pp. 115-136.

Historical Studies

429.   Bandyopadhyay, Samik, ed. *Indian Cinema: Contemporary Perceptions from the Thirties.* Jamshedpur: Celluloid Chapter, 1993. 159 pp.

   Includes Shila Devi Kumid, "Choice of 'Heroes' from a Lady's Standpoint," pp. 61-63; A Lady Artiste, "Should Respectable Ladies Join the Films," pp. 108-110; Sabita Devi, "Why Shouldn't Respectable Ladies Join the Films," pp. 111-113.

430.   Fan, Ruijuan. "An Actress' Life in Old China." In *When They Were Young,* edited by Women of China and New World Press, pp. 156-164. Beijing: New World Press, 1983.

431.   Huang, Nicole. "Fashioning Public Intellectuals: Popular Journals for Women in Wartime Occupied Shanghai (1941-1945)." Paper presented at Association for Asian Studies, Washington, D.C., March 28, 1998.

   Analyzes women as portrayed in popular women's journals, 1940-1945.

432. Kimura, Ryoko. "Historical Research into the Microcosm of Women's Magazines." *Kyoiku Shakaigaku Kenkyu* (Journal of Educational Sociology). October 1995, pp. 100-103.

    Discusses previous research data on gender images found in pre-World II Japanese women's magazines; states the ideal image of women changed considerably between Taisho and early Showa (1920s) eras.

433. Lee, Sang Jin. "Discussions on Women's Education in the 'Independent Newspaper.'" Master's thesis, Hanyang University (Seoul), 1985. 32 pp.

434. McDonald, Keiko I. "Whatever Happened to Passive Suffering? Women on Screen." In *The Confusion Era: Art and Culture of Japan During the Allied Occupation, 1945-1952*, edited by Mark Sandler, pp. 53-71. Washington, D.C.: Arthur M. Sackler Gallery, Smithsonian Institution, in association with University of Washington Press, 1997.

435. Mitter, Partha. "Cartoons of the Raj." *History Today*. September 1997, pp. 16-21.

    Spends considerable space on how nineteenth and early twentieth century Indian cartoon magazines caricatured women -- as "dominating and domineering."

436. Mittler, Barbara. "Cooking, Cleaning, Caring: To Be or Not To Be a 'New Woman' in Women's Magazines of the Later Qing." Paper presented at Association for Asian Studies, Washington, D.C., March 28, 1998.

    Looks at top women's magazines of Shanghai in 1904, 1911; claims some "new women" early on were made to appear as men.

437. Muta, Kazue. "The Family of Modern Japan in General Magazines -- The Paradox of 'Home' in the Meiji Era." *Shakaigaku Hyoron*. June 1990, pp. 12-25.

    Looks at family portrayal in seven Meiji (1867-1912) magazines; reveals shifting definitions of the domestic home, the role of women, and family-state relationship.

438. Orliski, Constance. "The Health of the Body Politic: Jiating Weisheng, Household Sanitation, and Family Hygiene." Paper presented at Association for Asian Studies, Washington, D.C., March 28, 1998.

    Examines "germ theory," household sanitation issues as reflected in Shanghai women's magazines of the 1910s.

439. Ramakrisna, V. "Women's Journals in Andhra During the Late 19th Century: A Study of the Reflection of Reform Issues." *Indian Historical Congress Proceedings 48th* (1987), pp. 524-531.

440. St. André, James. "'Getting Down Off a Tiger Isn't Easy': Editing Wuxia Fiction, 1870-1900." Paper presented at Association for Asian Studies, Washington, D.C., March 29, 1998.

441. Thorsten, Marie. "A Few Bad Women: Manufacturing 'Educating Mamas' in Postwar Japan." *International Journal of Politics, Culture and Society*. Fall 1996, pp. 51-71.

Examines the emergence of the mother role in post-World War II Japan, drawing on popular media texts and fieldwork.

442.   Zhang Yingjin. "Engendering Chinese Filmic Discourse of the 1930s: Configurations of Modern Women in Shanghai in Three Silent Films." *positions: east asia cultures critique*. 2:3 (1994), pp. 603-628.

443.   Zhen Zhang. "Embodiment of Excess?: The Proliferation of the 'Martial Arts' Film and the Image of the Female Knight-Errant in Shanghai Cinema, 1920s-1930s." Paper presented at Association for Asian Studies, Washington, D.C., March 29, 1998.

Images of Women

444.   Abeyesekera, Sunila. "Women, Sexuality, the City and the Village." *Cinemaya*. Spring 1996, pp. 8-13.
Examines the attitudes towards the city, the village, and sexuality as represented in three Sri Lankan films: "Mee Haraka," "Seilama," and "Maruthaya."

445.   Ahn Byung-Sup. "Gender and Sexuality." *Cinemaya*. Winter 1990-1991, pp. 17-19.
In South Korean film.

446.   Aishah Ali. "Portraying Women's Rights in the Media." *Sasaran*. July 1993, pp. 83-85.
In Malaysia.

447.   Allison, Anne. *A Male Gaze in Japanese Children's Cartoons, or Are Naked Female Bodies Always Sexual?* Durham, North Carolina: Duke University Press, Asian / Pacific Studies Institute, 1993.

448.   Allison, Anne. "Sailor Moon: Japanese Superheroes for Global Girls." Paper presented at Japanese Popular Culture Conference, University of British Columbia, April 10, 1997.
Discusses popular Japanese animation series, *Sailor Moon*.

449.   Anuar, Mustafa K. and Wang Lay Kim. "Aspects of Ethnicity and Gender in Malaysian Television." In *Contemporary Television: Eastern Perspectives*, edited by David French and Michael Richards, pp. 262-281. New Delhi: Sage, 1996.
Makes the point that "programmes show that women are being marginalised and trivialised and, in some instances, undergoing a media process of,... symbolic annihilation."

450.   "Bachchan and Bachchan Unlimited." *Asiaweek*. September 20, 1996, pp. 50-51.
Reports on Indian feminists' and Muslim radicals' complaints about this company hosting the 1996 Miss World Contest.

451. Bai Fan. "Wang Jin and His Films on Women's Themes." *China Screen*. 1/1993, pp. 12-13.

452. Baker, David. "Ophelia's Travels." In *Gender and Culture in Literature and Film East and West: Issues of Perception and Interpretation*, edited by Nitaya Masavisut, George Simson, and Larry E. Smith, pp. 3-8. Honolulu: University of Hawaii and East-West Center, 1994.
     Examines Pankaj Butalia's film, "When Hamlet Came to Mizoram."

453. Banakar, Bharathi R. and K. Saroja. *Front Page Coverage of Women's Issues in Regional Newspaper of Karnatka*. 18 pp. Available through AMIC, Nanyang Technological University, Jurong Point P.O. Box 360, Singapore.
     Finds that of 600 front pages of five Indian papers, only three carried three items on women's issues.

454. Banerjee, Arundhat. "The Indian Woman's Dilemma: A Study of Formations in Gender Construct Through Mediation of Western Culture in Tagore's *Ghare Baire* and Ray's Film Version." In *Gender and Culture in Literature and Film East and West: Issues of Perception and Interpretation*, edited by Nitaya Masavisut, George Simson, and Larry E. Smith, pp. 207-224. Honolulu: University of Hawaii and East-West Center, 1994.
     Compares novel and film versions of this Tagore work, where the central theme concentrates on an Indian woman's forced entrance into society.

455. Bansal, Kiron and Gita Bamezai. "Crimes Against Women and the Indian Press." *Media Asia*. 18:4 (1992), pp. 204-207.

456. Baxamusa, Ramola, ed. *Media Reflections on Women's Movement*. Bombay: SNDT Women's University, Readings on Women's Studies Series 2, n.d.

457. Berndt, Caroline M. "Popular Culture as Political Protest: Writing the Reality of Sexual Slavery." *Journal of Popular Culture*. Fall 1997, pp. 177-187.
     Describes a Japanese *manga* (comic book) that depicts sexual slavery that a Korean woman endured in World War II.

458. Bhushan, Madhu. "Images of Women: A Subversive Strength." *Deep Focus* (Bangalore). December 1987.

459. Binford, Mira R. "Alternative Images -- Women in Recent Indian Film." *Media Development*. 1, 1993, pp. 27-29.

460. Bornoff, Nicholas. *Pink Samurai: Love, Marriage and Sex in Contemporary Japan*. New York: Simon and Schuster Pocket Books, 1991. 479 pp.
     Details much on women in porno, film, television, video, comics, and magazines in Japan.

461. Byun Eun-mi. "Female Journalists Rap Sexism in Media Reports." *Korea Newsreview*. March 12, 1994, p. 29.

462.   Callahan, William A. "Comm-fucian-ism, Patriarchal Politics in *Judou*." In *Gender and Culture in Literature and Film East and West: Issues of Perception and Interpretation*, edited by Nitaya Masavisut, George Simson, and Larry E. Smith, pp. 157-179. Honolulu: University of Hawaii and East-West Center, 1994.

   Considers how gender, culture, and nationalism interact and overlap in China, looking at Zhang's film, "Judou."

463.   Chan, Yatsen. "A Discussion of Male/Female Roles in Traditional Chinese Theater and the Shaw Bros. Classic, *Love Eterne*." *Hong Kong Film Connection*. November 1994, pp. 7-8.

   Provides synopses of "Love Eterne" and "Liang Shanbo and Zhu Yingtai."

464.   Chang, Jui-shan. "Refashioning Womanhood in 1990s Taiwan: An Analysis of the Taiwan Edition of *Cosmopolitan* Magazine." Paper presented at Asian Popular Culture Conference, Victoria, British Columbia, Canada, April 16, 1998.

   Points out that *Cosmopolitan* Taiwan promotes an image of a "new woman" not very different from that pushed in the U.S.

465.   "Changing Asian Media Images of Women." *Her World Magazine* (Malaysia). Part I, March 1990; Part II, April 1990.

466.   Chatterji, Shoma A. "From Hunterwalli to Bandit Queen: A Study of the Strong Women in Indian Cinema." In book to celebrate 100 years of Indian Cinema, edited by Nirmalya Acharya. Calcutta: Ananda Publishers, 1996.

467.   Chaudhry, Lubna and Saba Khattak. "Images of White Women and Indian Nationalism: Ambivalent Representations in *Shakespeare Wallah* and *Junoon*." In *Gender and Culture in Literature and Film East and West: Issues of Perception and Interpretation*, edited by Nitaya Masavisut, George Simson, and Larry E. Smith, pp. 19-28. Honolulu: University of Hawaii and East-West Center, 1994.

   Highlights themes of two films in relationship to Indian nationalism, British colonialism, and the "characterization of two white women in love with Indian men."

468.   Chow, Rey. *Primitive Passions: Visuality, Sexuality, Ethnography, and Contemporary Chinese Cinema*. New York: Columbia University Press, 1995. 252 pp.

   Reaches beyond boundaries of any one discipline to include questions of film, literature, postcolonial history, women's studies, cultural studies, and ethnography; argues that Chinese cinema belongs to a history of visuality that has been repressed.

469.   Chu, Donna and Bryce T. McIntyre. "Sex Role Stereotypes on Children's TV in Asia: A Content Analysis of Gender Role Portrayals in Children's Cartoons in Hong Kong." *Communication Research Reports*. Forthcoming.

470.   Cohn, Joel. "Where Two Ways Meet: Women/Warriors in Edo-Period Japan." In *Significant Others: Gender and Culture in Film and Literature East and West: Selected Conference Papers*, edited by William Burgwinkle, Glenn May, and

Valerie Wayne, pp. 20-30. Honolulu: University of Hawaii and East-West Center, 1993.

Discusses representations of male and female members of *bushi* (samurai) class in Kurosawa's film, "Sanjuro" (1962).

471. Consumers Association of Penang. *Why Barbie Dolls Should Be Banned.* Penang: Consumers Association of Penang, 1995. 39 pp.

Tells of CAP's campaign to ban "Barbie" dolls in Malaysia because of possible negative impacts on the molding of children's personalities; uses interviews with "cross-section" of public who agree with CAP.

472. Cooper, Darius. "The Indian Woman in the Bengali/Hindu Dollhouse: Satyajit Ray's Charulata (1964)." *Women's Studies.* January 1996, pp. 189-200.

Analyzes director Satyajit Ray's film, "Charulata"; finds that Ray rescues his woman character "by making her live in a state of authenticity."

473. Cooper-Chen, Anne, Eva Leung, and Sung-Ho Cho. "Sex Roles in East Asian Magazine Advertising." *Gazette.* 55:3 (1995), pp. 207-223.

Looks at 3,016 models in 1,972 ads from 12 magazines; finds most men and women were not shown in occupational roles, and almost no Asian women over 50 years old appeared in the ads.

474. Crist, Marshall. "Space Women in the Kaiju Eiga." *Kaiju Review.* 1:8 (1995), pp. 12-14.

In Japanese monster movies.

475. Da Grossa, Pamela S. "The King and I: East and West, Men and Women." In *Gender and Culture in Literature and Film East and West: Issues of Perception and Interpretation,* edited by Nitaya Masavisut, George Simson, and Larry E. Smith, pp. 90-94. Honolulu: University of Hawaii and East-West Center, 1994.

476. Das, Udita. "Dominant Gender Related Myths: Print Media Advertisements in India and America." Paper presented at International Association for Mass Communication Research, Sydney, Australia, August 21, 1996.

Examines certain universal myths that cut through cultures, related to women and emanating from the U.S. through satellite television.

477. Dasgupta, Shamita D. "Feminist Consciousness in Woman-Centered Hindi Films." *Journal of Popular Culture.* Summer 1996, pp. 173-189.

Analyzes 16 Hindi films with "overt feminist themes, "produced between 1975-1990 and finds almost all (14) deal with Hindu families and their lifestyles, and portray women revolting against the patriarchal system, but ultimately giving into the "anguish of a lonely and discontented life."

478. Dasgupta, Shamita D. and Radha S. Hegde. "The Eternal Receptacle: A Study of Mistreatment of Women in Hindi Films." In *Women in Indian Society: A Reader,* edited by Rehana Ghadially. New Delhi: Sage, 1988.

479.   Dipak, D. E. and A. K. Singh. "Gender and Print Media Coverage of Environmental Issues." Paper presented at International Association for Mass Communication Research, Sydney, Australia, August 20, 1996.

480.   Dissanayake, Wimal, ed. *Cinema and Cultural Identity: Reflections on Films from Japan, India, and China.* Lanham, Maryland: University Press of America, 1988.
        Includes Tadao Sato, "Change in the Image of Mother in Japanese Cinema and Television," Aruna Vasudev, "The Woman: Myth and Reality in the Indian Cinema," Tony Rayns, "The Position of Women in New Chinese Cinema."

481.   Donald, Stephanie. "Women Reading Chinese Films: Between Orientalism and Science." *Screen.* Winter 1995, pp. 325-340.
        Analyzes Chinese films of 1980s, "Yellow Earth" and "Sacrifice of Youth," using theories of Esther Yau, Rey Chow, and Trinh Minh-ha.

482.   Dong Xinyu. "Keeping Silent or Siloloquizing -- Female Figures in New China Films." *Contemporary Cinema.* September 1996.

483.   Dua, M. R. "Covering Women's Issues." *Communicator.* July-September 1995, pp. 45-46.
        Reviews book, *Whose News? The Media and Women's Issues,* edited by Ammu Joseph and Kalpana Sharma (New Delhi: Sage).

484.   Evans, Harriet. "Which Half of the Sky?: Women, Bodies and Spaces in Cultural Revolution Posters." Paper presented at Association for Asian Studies, Washington, D.C., March 28, 1998.
        Argues that despite Mao's dictum that men and women are equal, Cultural Revolution posters show that women did not hold up half of the sky, that the society was still patriarchal.

485.   Fernando, Vijita. "Setting a Watchdog on Sexist Ads." *Impact.* April 1993, pp. 6-7.

486.   Fore, Steve. "Tales of Recombinant Femininity: *The Reincarnation of Golden Lotus,* The *Chin P'ing Mei,* and the Politics of Melodrama in Hong Kong." *Journal of Film and Video.* Winter 1993, pp. 57-70.
        Analyzes Hong Kong-produced film, "The Reincarnation of Golden Lotus," which "quite explicitly wrestles with the dilemmas and contradictions facing women in contemporary Chinese societies"; backgrounds Hong Kong cinema and the "women's film" of Hong Kong.

487.   Freedman, Alisa. "Glorifying Moving Parts: Symphonies of Modern Girls and Mass Transportation in 1930s Chinese City Films." Paper presented at Association for Asian Studies, Chicago, Illinois, March 13, 1997.

488.   Friberg, Freda. "Rape, Race and Religion: Ways of Speaking About Enforced Military Prostitution in World War 2." *Metro Magazine.* No. 104, 1995, pp. 20-24.

Describes "The Murmuring," a Korean film about Japanese use of Korean comfort women during World War II; as well as others on the same subject: "A Half-Century of Homesickness," "50 Years of Silence," and "Senso Daughters."

489. Fujimura-Fanselow, Kumiko and Atsuko Kameda, eds. *Japanese Women: New Feminist Perspectives on the Past, Present, and Future*. New York: The Feminist Press at The City University of New York, 1995. 422 pp.
Includes "Women and Television" and "Pornographic Culture and Sexual Violence."

490. Fuller, Linda K. "Beauty/Body Media Messages Aimed at Singaporean Women." *Awareness: A Journal of the Association of Women for Action and Research*. June 1996.

491. Funabashi, Kuniko. "Pornographic Culture and Sexual Violence." In *Japanese Women: New Feminist Perspectives on the Past, Present and Future*, edited by Kumiko Fujimura-Fanselo and Atsuko Kameda. New York: The Feminist Press, 1995.

492. Garcellano, Rosario, Elizabeth Lolarga, and Anna Leah Sarabia, eds. *Sisterhood Is Global: Dialogues in the Philippines*. Quezon City: Circle Publications, 1992. 307 pp.
Transcript of women's movement meetings in Philippines, October 1988, built around theme in this book's title. "Session on Media," pp. 49-88, includes remarks by Pennie de la Cruz, Madhu Kishwar, Evangeline Valbuena, and Marilyn Waring, dealing with media images of women in Philippines, India, and New Zealand.

493. Gargan, Edward A. "In 'Bollywood,' Women Are Wronged or Revered." *New York Times*. January 17, 1993, pp. 11-12.
In Indian film.

494. "Gender and Communication Policy in Asia." *Media and Gender Monitor*. Autumn 1997, pp. i-iv.
Presents data on communication policies and images/roles of women in media of Australia, Cambodia, China, India, Indonesia, Japan, Korea, Malaysia, Mongolia, The Philippines, Sri Lanka, and Thailand.

495. "The Gender Debate." *Action*. July-August 1995, pp. 4-5.
Reviews first ever seminar in Vietnam on gender and mass media.

496. Goessmann, Hilaria. "Changing Attitudes Toward Gender Roles in Popular Japanese TV Dramas of the 1990s." Paper presented at Japanese Popular Culture Conference, University of British Columbia, April 12, 1997.

497. Gopalan, Lalitha. "The Avenging Women in Indian Cinema." *Screen*. Spring 1997, pp. 42-59.

498.   Gupta, Arun K. and Nisha Jain. "Gender, Mass Media and Social Change: A Case Study of TV Commercials." *Media Asia.* 25:1 (1998), pp. 33-36.
Claims Indian television commercials perpetuate patriarchal values.

499.   Guru, B. P. Mahesh Chandra. "Women and Mass Media: The Indian Scenario." *Communicator.* January-March 1996, pp. 5-10.
Surveys Indian press, broadcasting, and film and concludes: "There is indeed, a 'symbolic annihilation' the consequence of a combination of condemnation, trivialization and absence as far as communication support to women's development in India is concerned."

500.   Hagadorn, Jessica. "Asian Women in Film: No Joy, No Luck." *Ms.* January / February 1994, pp. 74-79.
Critiques 1990's portrayals of Asian women on screen.

501.   Hammond, Stefan and Mike Wilkins. *Sex and Zen and a Bullet in the Head. The Essential Guide to Hong Kong's Mind-Bending Films.* New York: Simon and Schuster Fireside Books, 1996. 272 pp.
Includes "Nail-Polished Fists," pp. 49-67, a chapter about female warriors in Hong Kong cinema.

502.   Hedge, Radha S. and Shamita Das Dasgupta. "Convergence and Divergence from 'Devi,' the Model of Ideal Woman on the Indian Screen." Paper presented at Western Speech and Communication Association, Seattle, Washington, February 18-21, 1984.

503.   Heung, Marina. "Small Triumphs: The New Asian Woman in American Cinema." *Cinemaya.* January-March 1997, pp. 29-32.
Shows that the early 1990s offered an "impressive range of roles featuring strong, independent" Asian and Asian-American women.

504.   Ho, Suk-ching. "Sex Role Portrayals in Print Advertisement: The Case of Hong Kong." *Equal Opportunities International.* 2:4 (1983), pp. 1-4.

505.   Hogan, Jackie. "The Geisha and the Ironman: Gendered National Identities in the Television Advertisements of Japan and Australia." Paper presented at Japanese Popular Culture Conference, University of British Columbia, Victoria, Canada, April 10, 1997.

506.   Hong, Eun Hee. "Imagery of Women in the Children's Dramas." Master's thesis, Yonsei University (Seoul), 1985. 63 pp.

507.   Ibrahim, Faridah and Rahmah Hashim. "Images of Women and Human Rights: A Content Analysis of Malaysian Print Media During the Fourth World Conference on Women in Beijing." Paper presented at International Association for Mass Communication Research, Sydney, Australia, August 20, 1996.
Focuses on images of women's groups as portrayed by print media of Malaysia.

508.   "Images of Women in Indian Films." *ISIS International Bulletin.* 18, 1981, pp. 14-15.

509.   "Into Focus: Changing Media Images of Women. An Asian Resource Kit." *Gender and Mass Media Newsletter.* March 1991, p. 29.
        Describes Into Focus, a multi-media kit on how women are covered in media; deals with media, family, health, violence, and work.

510.   Ito, Kinko. "Images of Women in Weekly Male Comic Magazines in Japan." *Journal of Popular Culture.* Spring 1994, pp. 81-95.

511.   Iwamura, Rosemary. "Blue Haired Girls with Eyes So Deep, You Could Fall into Them. The Success of the Heroine in Japanese Animation." In *Kaboom! Explosive Animation in America and Japan*, pp. 66-75. Sydney: Museum of Contemporary Art, 1994.
        Emphasizes TV anime, "Sailor Moon."

512.   Iwamura, Rosemary. "Letter from Japan: From Girls Who Dress up Like Boys to Trussed-up Porn Stars -- Some of the Contemporary Heroines on the Japanese Screen." *Continuum.* 7:2 (1994), pp. 109-130.

513.   Iwao, Sumiko. *The Japanese Woman: Traditional Image and Changing Reality.* New York: Free Press, 1993.

514.   Jiwani, Yasmin. "The Exotic, the Erotic and the Dangerous: South Asian Women in Popular Film." *Canadian Woman Studies.* Fall 1992, pp. 42-46.
        Claims contemporary images of South Asian women in U.S. and British films have their origins in the literature and imagination of colonizers during colonial times.

515.   Johansson, Perry. "Consuming the Other: White Women and Fetishness in Chinese Advertising." Paper presented at Association for Asian Studies, Chicago, Illinois, March 14, 1997. 9 pp.
        Addresses issue of representation of women in advertising in Chinese women's magazines; questions the assumption that female images in advertising are always structured by a male gaze.

516.   Johnson, Ian. "Breaking Silence." *Far Eastern Economic Review.* August 24, 1995, pp. 40-41.
        Discusses Wu Ziniu's film, "Rape of Nanjing," in light of the silence that has existed concerning the Japanese soldiers' rape of thousands of Chinese women in 1937-1938.

517.   Jones, Sumie, ed. *Imaging / Reading Eros: Proceedings for the Conference, Sexuality and Eros Culture, 1750-1850, Indiana University, Bloomington, August 17-20, 1995.* Bloomington: Indiana University, East Asian Studies Center, 1996. 161 pp.
        Deals with sex, art, media, and Tokyo culture for that period. Particularly appropriate are David Pollock, "Marketing Desire: Advertising and Sexuality in

Edo Literature, Drama and Art," pp. 47-62, and Ueno Chizuko, "Lusty Pregnant Women and Erotic Mothers: Representations of Female Sexuality in Erotic Art in Edo," pp. 110-114.

518.   Joseph, Ammu and Kalpana Sharma, eds. *Whose News? The Media and Women's Issues*. New Delhi: Sage, 1994. 335 pp.

Analyzes five issues related to Indian women; critiques portrayal of women on primetime television, 1979-1988; divides press by English and Indian languages. Includes A. Joseph & K. Sharma, "Introduction"; "Daily Newspapers: Dowry Deaths"; "Daily Newspapers: Rape"; "Daily Newspapers: The Shah Bano Controversy"; "Daily Newspapers: Female Foeticide"; "Daily Newspapers: The Roop Kanwar Tragedy"; K. Sharma, "General Interest Periodicals"; A. Joseph, "Women's Magazines"; K. Sharma & A. Joseph, "Introduction"; S. Gupta, "The Hindi Press"; P. Ramaswamy & V. Surya, "The Tamil Press"; M. Chatterjee, "The Bengali Press"; S. Shukla, "The Gujarati Press"; D. Dhanraj, "Television: A Critical Lens."

519.   Judge, Joan E. "Citizens or Mothers of Citizens?: Reimagining Femininity in Late Qing Women's Textbooks." Paper presented at Association for Asian Studies, Chicago, Illinois, March 14, 1997.

520.   Kaewthep, Kanjana. "'East' Meet 'West': The Confrontation of Different Cultures in Thai TV Dramas and Films." In *Gender and Culture in Literature and Film East and West: Issues of Perception and Interpretation*, edited by Nitaya Masavisut, George Simson, and Larry E. Smith, pp. 180-196. Honolulu: University of Hawaii and East-West Center, 1994.

Uses gender analysis approach to look at character roles played by women as employees, housewives, and sex objects in Thai film and TV scripts.

521.   Kaplan, E. Ann. "Problematising Cross-Cultural Analysis: The Case of Woman in the Recent Chinese Cinema." In *Perspectives on Chinese Cinema*, edited by Chris Berry, pp. 141-154. London: British Film Institute, 1991.

522.   Kelsky, Karen. "White Desire: White Men and Women in Japanese Television Commercials." Paper presented at Japanese Popular Culture Conference, University of British Columbia, Victoria, Canada, April 10, 1997.

523.   Kim Ha-Il. "The Representation of Women in Contemporary Cinema." *Korea Culture*. Fall 1989, pp. 23-32.

524.   Kim, Myung Keum. "Content Analysis of Crime Reports on Womanhood Delinquency by Korean Newspapers." Master's thesis, Ewha Womans University (Seoul), 1977. 110 pp.

525.   Kim, S. *Sex, Pornography and Eroticism*. Seoul: HyunShil-Munwha Yeongu, 1994.

526. Kishwar, Madhu and Ruth Vanita. "The Labouring Woman in Hindi Films." *Manushi: A Journal about Women and Society.* September-December 1987, pp. 62-74, 76.

      Asserts that Hindi film female characters are stripped of all realistic human and social characteristics, thus, ending up on screen as stereotypes.

527. Ko, Suk Joo. "A Study of Attitudes of Consumers Toward Sexism in Advertising: From a Feminist Viewpoint." Master's thesis, Ewha Woman's University (Seoul), 1985. 176 pp.

528. Kodama, Miiko. "Women in Modern Journalism in Japan." *Gender and Mass Media Newsletter.* November 1991, pp. 24-26.

      Reports on author's 1978 survey of Japanese evening news programs on NHK-TV; states that most women appearing in the news were either victims of events or uninvolved bystanders selected for on-the-street interviews. In other surveys, author found that the number of women communicating events on television had increased.

529. Kodama, Tomiko. "Rhetoric of the Image of Women in a Japanese Television Advertisement: A Semiotic Analysis." *Australian Journal of Communication.* 18:2 (1991), pp. 42-65.

530. Krishnan, Prabha and Anita Dighe. *Affirmation and Denial. Construction of Femininity on Indian Television.* New Delhi: Sage Publications India, 1990. 128 pp.

      Discusses women's images on Indian television, as well as the quality of TV programs, and their influence on children. Sample of Doordarshan (Delhi) for July 1986.

531. Lanot, Marra P. L. "In a Macho Society, Gender Makes a Difference." *Cinemaya.* Autumn / Winter 1994-1995, pp. 72-77.

      Claims that woman in Philippine cinema is "either mother or moll, sister or streetwalker, housewife or whore, saint or sinner, virgin or vamp"; contends this is so because of the macho belief that women are shaped according to "male need, male perspective, male-fantasy."

532. Lee, Changhyun and Seungchan Yang. "Third-Person Perception and Support for Censorship of Sexually Explicit Visual Content: A Korean Case Study." Paper presented at Association for Education in Journalism and Mass Communication, Anaheim, California, August 1996. 34 pp.

      Aims to further third-person effect research; examines how the "linkage between third-person perception and pro-censorship attitudes may vary according to the characteristics of different visual media through which sexual content is delivered."

533. Lee, Joann. "Scents of Asian Women: Perception and Reality on American Screens." *CineVue.* July 1994.

534. Lee, Joann. "Zhang Yimou's *Raise the Red Lantern*: Contextual Analysis of Film Through a Confucian / Feminist Matrix." *Asian Cinema*. Spring 1996, pp. 120-127.
      Discusses film, "Raise the Red Lantern," set primarily from the point of view of a woman, with a female as mover of the narrative.

535. Lee, S. K. Jean and Tan Hwee Hoon. "Rhetorical Vision of Men and Women Managers in Singapore." *Human Relations*. April 1993, pp. 527-542.
      Attempts to uncover rhetorical visions of women and men managers portrayed by Singapore mass media; finds women were portrayed facing dilemmas and role conflicts, whereas the vision emphasized for male managers was their managerial abilities.

536. Lee, William. "From Sazae-san to Crayon Shin-chan: Family Anime and Social Change in Japan." Paper presented at Popular Culture Conference, University of British Columbia, Victoria, Canada, April 11, 1997.

537. Leims, Thomas. "Sensational Journalism, Sex and Violence in Japanese Televison -- Japan Specialists Comment on a Current Topic." *Communications*. 18:3 (1993), pp. 355-379.
      Examines sex and violence in Japanese media treatments of crime and disaster.

538. Lent, John A., ed. *Assorted Themes and Issues of Asian Cartooning: Cute, Cheap, Mad, and Sexy.* Bowling Green, Ohio: Bowling Green State University Popular Press, 1999.
      Includes Kanako Shiokawa, "Cute, but Deadly: Women and Violence in Japanese Comics"; Setsu Shigematsu, "Dimensions of Desire: Sex, Fantasy and Fetish in Japanese Comics"; Aruna Rao, "Goddess / Demon, Warrior / Victim: The Representation of Women in Indian Comics"; Mary Grigsby, "The Social Production of Gender as Reflected in Two Japanese Culture Industry Products: *Sailormoon* and *Crayon Shin-Chan*."

539. Lent, John A., ed. *Illustrating Asia: Comics, Humor Magazines, and Picture Books*. Hong Kong and London: ConsumAsiaN and Curzon, 1999.
      Includes section on "Representations and Portrayals," consisting in part of Fusami Ogi, "Gender Insubordination in Japanese Comics (Manga) for Girls," and Ronald Provencher, "Female Images and Feminist Issues: The Play of Tropes in Malaysian Humor Magazines."

540. Leung, Louis. "Appraising Sex-Role Portrayal in Korean Television Commercials." *Media Asia*. 22:2 (1995), pp. 111-116.
      Reveals patterns of stereotyping "very similar" to those reported in U.S. and elsewhere -- men in higher-status occupations, women as parents, homemakers, or sex objects with low occupational authority.

541. Li Haoming. "Dalu Huangchao Gungun Lai" (The Rolling Waves of Pornography in Mainland China). *The Nineties*. June 1993.

542. Liao, Binghui. "Shikong yu Zingbie de Cuoluan: Lun *Bawang Bieji*" (Temporal, Spatial, and Gender Disorder: On *Farewell My Concubine*). *Chung-wai Literary Monthly*. 22:1 (1993), pp. 6-18.

543. Lo, Kwai-cheung. "Feminizing Technology: The *Objet A* in *Black Cannon Incident*." In *Significant Others: Gender and Culture in Film and Literature East and West: Selected Conference Papers*, edited by William Burgwinkle, Glenn May, and Valerie Wayne, pp. 88-95. Honolulu: University of Hawaii and East-West Center, 1993.

Looks at the Chinese film, "Black Cannon Incident," about the modernization movement of the 1980s, in terms of Lacanian psychoanalysis.

544. Lower, Lucy. "Rape, Murder, Impersonation, Metaphor: Appropriation or Annihilation of the Other?" In *Significant Others: Gender and Culture in Film and Literature East and West: Selected Conference Papers*, edited by William Burgwinkle, Glenn May, and Valerie Wayne, pp. 96-104. Honolulu: University of Hawaii and East-West Center, 1993.

Analyzes the play, "Atashi no Biitoruzu," and Oshima Nagisa's film, "Koshikei," to show how gender, race, and culture are manipulated and transposed in the construction of self and other.

545. Lu, Sheldon Hsiao-peng, ed. *Transnational Chinese Cinema: Identity, Nationhood, Gender*. Honolulu: University of Hawaii Press, 1997. 414 pp.

Includes E. Ann Kaplan, "Reading Formations and Chen Kaige's *Farewell My Concubine*," pp. 265-275; Kristine Harris, "*The New Woman* Incident: Cinema, Scandal, and Spectacle in 1935 Shanghai," pp. 277-302; Shuqin Cui, "Gendered Perspective: The Construction and Representation of Subjectivity and Sexuality in *Ju Dou*," pp. 303-329; Wendy Larson, "The Concubine and the Figure of History: Chen Kaige's *Farewell My Concubine*," pp. 334-346; Yi Zheng, "Narrative Images of the Historical Passion: Those *Other* Women -- On the Alterity in the New Wave of Chinese Cinema," pp. 347-359.

546. Lu, Tonglin. "How Do You Tell a Girl from a Boy? Uncertain Sexual Boundaries in *The Price of Frenzy*." In *Significant Others: Gender and Culture in Film and Literature East and West: Selected Conference Papers*, edited by William Burgwinkle, Glenn May, and Valerie Wayne, pp. 63-74. Honolulu: University of Hawaii and East-West Center, 1993.

Analyzes the problem of gender in the post-Cultural Revolution film, "The Price of Frenzy," directed by Zhou Xiaowen in 1989; shows failure to reinforce sexual boundaries through the imitation of Hollywood commercial cinema.

547. Lutz, Helma. "Invisible Shadows? The 'Oriental' Woman in Western Discourses -- On the Conceptualization of a Victim." *Peripherie*. 37, 1989, pp. 51-65.

Describes stereotyping of "Oriental" women in Western society; claims, for example, all "Eastern" women are lumped together as Muslim.

548. Mahajan, Kamlesh. "Portrayal of Women on Television in India." *Comparative Social Research*. 2 (1996), pp. 53-67.

Analyzes 16 broadcast serials over a six-month period in 1991-1992, looking at TV's possibilities for helping women's development in India; finds programs use a double morality standard and are stereotyped according to prevailing standards.

549.   Makita, Tetsuo. "NHK Renzoku Terebi Shosetsu no Kosatsu" (The Concept Behind NHK Serialized Television Novels). In *NHK Hoso Bunka Kenkyo Nenpo*21, pp. 79-94. Tokyo: NHK Shuppankai, 1976.

550.   Mankekar, Purnima. "Television Tales and Woman's Rage: A Nationalist Recasting of Draupadi's 'Disrobing.'" *Public Culture*. Spring 1993, pp. 459-492.

551.   Marchetti, Gina. "Excess and Understatement -- War, Romance, and the Melodrama in Contemporary Vietnamese Cinema." *Genders*. Spring 1991, pp. 47-74.
        Discusses three Vietnamese films ("Karma," "When the Tenth Month Comes," and "Fairytale for Seventeen-Year-Olds") and shows how they are about female subjectivity, gender inequality, and problems of being a woman in an oppressive world of colonialism, feudalism, and war.

552.   Marchetti, Gina. *Romance and the "Yellow Peril": Race, Sex, and Discursive Strategies in Hollywood Fiction*. Berkeley: University of California Press, 1994. 258 pp.
        Looks at Hollywood's depictions of Asia and Asians, beginning with D. W. Griffith's "Broken Blossoms" through "Shanghai Express" and recurring geisha films.

553.   Marchetti, Gina. "White Knights in Hong Kong: Race, Gender, and the Exotic in *Love Is a Many-Splendored Thing* and *The World of Suzie Wong*." *Post Script*. Winter 1991, pp. 36-49.

554.   Masood, Iqbal. "The *Sherni*, the Superintendent, and the Other Woman." *Manushi*. July-August 1988, pp. 43-44.
        Discusses female characters in Doordarshan (India) television serials.

555.   *Mass Media Awareness Seminar, "Mass Media and Women in the 90's," Hong Kong, December 10-12, 1990*. Hong Kong: Tien Dao Christian Media Association, 1991. 187 pp.

556.   Matsumoto, Yoshiko. "Generation and Gender in Media Representation of Young Japanese Women's Speech." Paper presented at Association for Asian Studies, Chicago, Illinois, March 14, 1997.

557.   Mazumdar, Ranjani. "Is There a Type Beyond the Stereotype? Women in Hindi Cinema." *Voices*. 4:2 (1996), pp. 29-32.

558.   Miller, Laura. "Images of Unsatisfactory Women in Japanese Print Media." Paper presented at Association for Asian Studies, Chicago, Illinois, March 16, 1997.

559. Misra, Kalpana and Debasmita Roychowdhury. "Vigilantes, Virgins, and Long Suffering Wives: The Limitations of Contemporary Indian Television's Reconstructions of Femininity." *Contemporary South Asia.* November 1997, pp. 247-258.

Argues that the impact of new television programming on the Indian women's cause has been subversive, that the power of the visual image and broad reach of television threatens to undermine progress the print media and women's groups have made.

560. Mittler, Barbara. "Circumscribing the Reader: Depiction and Prescription of a 'New' Female Audience in Late Qing Newspapers and Magazines." Paper presented at Association for Asian Studies, Chicago, Illinois, March 14, 1997.

561. Moeran, Brian and Lise Skov. "Japanese Advertising Nature: Ecology, Fashion, Women, and Art." In *Asian Perceptions of Nature*, edited by O. Bruun and A. Kalland, pp. 215-243. London: Curzon Press, 1995.

562. Moeslem, Shima. "Bangladesh: Distorted Image." *OANA Newsletter.* July / September 1990, pp. 10-12.

563. Mojumdar, Modhumita. "Medium and the Message: Spreading Stereotyped Images of the Indian Woman." *Indian Express.* July 7, 1993, p. 6.

Claims India's radio and television use two faces in dealing with women; on one hand, they treat women and girls as equal in development oriented messages, but on the other hand, they show women and girls in educative short films and advertisements as domestic drudges.

564. Molony, Barbara. "Japan's 1986 Equal Employment Opportunity Law and The Changing Discourse on Gender." *Signs.* Winter 1995, pp. 268-302.

Examines gender and employment in Japan through analyses of media images of women and men, among other factors.

565. Morimoto, Marie T. "A Woman's Place Is in the Kitchen of Knowledge: Premodern and Postmodern Representations of Food (for Thought) in Japanese Film." In *Gender and Culture in Literature and Film East and West: Issues of Perception and Interpretations,* edited by Nitaya Masavisut, George Simson, and Larry E. Smith, pp. 260-272. Honolulu: University of Hawaii and East-West Center, 1994.

Analyzes two films of Japan depicting scarce resources -- food and knowledge -- and the role of women in conducting the harmony of the social body.

566. Muramatsu, Yasuko. "Of Women, by Women, for Women? -- Toward New Hopes for Television in Japan." Paper presented at International Association for Mass Communication Research, Bled, Yugoslavia, August 26-31, 1990.

Describes importance of Japanese housewives as targets of television, their underrepresentation in programming, and the stereotyping and abundance of sexual content on TV.

567.   Muramatsu, Yasuko. *Terebi Dorama no Joseigaku* (The Study of Women in Television Drama). Tokyo: Ontaimu Shuppan, 1979.

568.   Nag, Dulali. "Fashion, Gender and the Bengali Middle Class." *Public Culture.* Spring 1991, pp. 93-112.
        Includes section on "Tradition, Modernity and Femininity in *Anandalok* Texts."

569.   Napier, Susan J. "From Shojo to 'Ladies' to 'Ghosts': Problems of Female Empowerment in Manga and Animation." Paper presented at Association for Asian Studies, Chicago, Illinois, March 14, 1997.

570.   Nasri Abdullah. "Wanita Dalam Media Massa: Siapa Kata Kami Kurang Kebolehan." *Sasaran.* 1 (1983), pp. 8-9.
        Women in Malaysian mass media.

571.   *New Feminism Review: Pornography.* Vol. 3 Tokyo: Gakuyo Shobo, 1993.
        Includes Akira Akagi, "Bishojo Shokogun Rorikon to Iuu Yokubo"; Yukari Fujiwara, "Onna no Yokubou no Katachi: Ledeezu Komikusu ni Miru Onna no Sei Gensou" (The Contours of Women's Desire: The Sexual Fantasies Found in Ladies Comics); Emai Komotada, "Jissaku Onna no Erochika" (Actual Work: Women's Eroticism).

572.   Ng, Daisy Sheung-Yuen. "When the Woman Looks: Female Desire in Three Chinese Films Directed by Zhang Yimou." *Papers on Chinese Literature.* Fall 1994.

573.   Nightingale, Virginia. "Bewitched Women, Power and Media Magic." Paper presented at International Association for Mass Communication Research, Sydney, Australia, August 21, 1996.
        Begins with a transcript of a discussion between author and two young Japanese women about television programs remembered from childhood; examines the relationship between discourses on women's power and the representation of modernity as magic in children's television.

574.   Ninan, Sevanti. "Treatment of Women in the Print Media." *Gender and Mass Media Newsletter.* November 1991, p. 28.
        Looks at how two leading North and South India dailies, the top English-language newsmagazine, and three other magazines (one English, two Hindi) portray women; only *Saptahik Hindustan* of the magazines covered women intelligently.

575.   Ogi, Fusami. "Gender Insubordination in Japanese Comics (Manga) for Girls." Paper presented at Association for Asian Studies, Chicago, Illinois, March 14, 1997.

576.   "Over the Manga Moon." *Asiaweek.* July 20, 1994, p. 33.
        Covers popular Japanese comics heroine, "Sailor Moon."

577.   "Pageant Protests: For India, They Underscore the Challenges of Change." *Asiaweek*. December 6, 1996, p. 15.

Editorial that takes issue with protests against "Miss World" beauty pageant staged in India.

578.   Pandian, Hannah. "Clean Up the Press!" *Action*. May 1997, p. 8.

Describes effort by women's and media groups to change images of women in Cambodian media. A study of 46 newspapers and magazines found that only 4.5 percent of the articles covered women and 90 percent of all illustrations presented women as sexual objects or in stereotyped roles.

579.   Pandian, Hannah. "(Hypo) Critical Mass: Do Women Make a Difference?" *Media and Gender Monitor*. Autumn 1997, pp. 10-11.

Reports on gender and communication policy meeting in Manila, where speakers complained that the increased number of women in the media was not resulting in a dramatic increase in feminist coverage.

580.   Pandian, M. S. S. *The Image Trap: M. G. Ramachandran in Film and Politics*. New Delhi: Sage, 1992.

Includes sections on women as represented in the films of film star / politician M. G. Ramachandran, pp. 51-52, 70, 79-91, and women in his life, pp. 119-120.

581.   Paranjpye, Sai. "Women in Indian Cinema." *Cinema in India*. January-April 1988.

582.   Patel, Ila. *Representation of Women in Mass Media*. Gujarat: Institute of Rural Management Anand, 1995. 30 pp. [Working Paper 95]

Attempts a global picture of representation of women in the mass media -- films, television and print media--on the basis of available Indian and international research literature on women and mass media; argues that women and their concerns are no longer invisible in the mass media.

583.   Pattanaik, Bharti Bala and Dasarathi Mishra. "Press Coverage of Violence Against Women." *Communicator*. July-September 1995, pp. 15-17.

Reports from analysis of four newspapers of Orissa that although coverage of women is minimal (1 to 2 percent), issues related to women are reported, especially those related to violence.

584.   Pellicono, Katherin. "Gender, Family and Society Through Chinese Film." *China Screen*. 2/1991, p. 35.

585.   Prindle, Tamae K. "In the Lacuna of Identities: Girls in Japanese Cinema." Paper presented at Japanese Popular Culture Conference, University of British Columbia, Victoria, Canada, April 11, 1997.

586.   Prindle, Tamae K. "Money, Sex and Power: A Socialist Feminist Analysis of Mori Ogai's *The Wild Geese* and Toyoda Shiro's *The Mistress*." Paper presented at Association for Asian Studies, Chicago, Illinois, March 16, 1997.

587.   Qian Youjue. "Women in the Contemporary Chinese and TV Series." *Journal of Asian Women's Studies*. No.3, 1996, pp. 92-94.
        Traces some of the women portrayed in Chinese films and television, ranging from China's first empress to women living in rural areas.

588.   Rahman, M. "Hindi Films: Women Strike Back." *India Today*. July 15, 1988, pp. 80-82.

589.   Rana, Kusum and Manju Gupta. "Media Image of Women." *Communicator*. July-September 1995, pp. 5, 28.
        States that in India, "the image of the educated woman is typecast as insensitive, self-centered and uncaring. The economically independent woman is shown as domineering and ruthless. The woman is considered ideal only when she is in her nurturing roles and as a supportive supplement to man."

590.   Rao, Kavita. "Reflections of Women in Indian Film: Depictions in a Changing Cultural Context." 1993. 11 pp. Available through Asian Mass Communication Research and Information Centre, Singapore.

591.   Rao, Leila. "The New Woman Image on Indian Television -- Marketing Strategies for Selling Products and Ideas." *Gender and Mass Media Newsletter*. November 1992, pp. 11-12.
        Analyzes trends in the portrayal of women in the commercials and public service announcements of Indian television.

592.   "Recent Research on TV Shows Women Underrepresented in Realistic Roles." *Media Report to Women*. January-February 1991, pp. 5-6.
        In Asia. See also "Women in Asia Fighting Same Battles with Media Over Access and Influence," pp. 7-9.

593.   Reuter, James B. "Encounter with Faces." *Unda News*. December 1995, p. 3.
        Gives accounts of depictions of women in Asian cinema from an Unda-OCIC/Asia meeting.

594.   Rolandelli, D. R. "Gender Role Portrayal Analysis of Children's Television Programming in Japan." *Human Relations*. December 1991, pp. 1273-1301.
        Analyzes gender-role portrayals of 279 characters from Japanese children's programs; finds programs highly sex typed -- males were overrepresented, shown in professional jobs; females were shown as weak, younger, less mature.

595.   Said, Salid. "Man and Revolutionary Crisis in Indonesian Films." *East-West Film Journal*. June 1990, pp. 111-129.
        Briefly discusses women in Indonesian films.

596.   Saidullah, Jawahara K. "Shakti -- The Power of the Mother: The Violent Nurturer in Indian Mythology and Commercial Cinema." *Canadian Woman Studies*. Fall 1992, pp. 37-41.

Discusses recent Indian films with the traditional image of Hindu women as "shakti," a symbol of energy and power; claims one message emerges: do not take woman for granted.

597. Sasidharan, Rekha M. "Visibility of Women in Indian Magazines, Content Analytical Study of Five English Magazines." Paper presented at International Association for Mass Communication Research, Bled, Yugoslavia, August 26-31, 1990.

Finds that in each of the five Indian magazines, less than 10 percent of the total news was devoted to female portrayal, women were shown in more professional than family roles but not in very positive ways, and women's problems were not treated very seriously.

598. Sears, Laurie, ed. *Fantasizing the Feminine in Indonesia*. Durham, North Carolina: Duke University Press, 1996. 349 pp.

Includes Saraswati Sunindyo, "Murder, Gender, and the Media: Sexualizing Politics and Violence," pp. 120-139; Jean G. Taylor, "*Nyai Dasima*: Portrait of a Mistress in Literature and Film," pp. 225-239; Sita Aripurnami, "A Feminist Comment on the Sinetron Presentation of Indonesian Women," pp. 249-258.

599. Seaton, Kathleen. "Images of Gender in Recent Chinese Films: An Analysis of Three Gong Li Films." Paper presented at New York Conference on Asian Studies, Buffalo, New York, September 15-16, 1995.

600. Sharma, Kalpana. "The Media and Women." *Indian Express*. April 10, 1988. In India.

601. Shrivastava, K. M. *Media Issues*. New Delhi: Sterling Publishers, 1992. 168 pp.

Includes chapter on "Women and Media," pages 60-63; provides some information on images of women on Indian television; claims "bias against women" is slowly decreasing with increasing numbers of women obtaining employment in mass media.

602. Singh, Jija S. Hari. "Domestic Violence: The Police Role and Media Response." *Gender and Mass Media Newsletter*. November 1992, p. 15.

Analyzes the trauma a woman undergoes in a situation of domestic disharmony in India, the role of the police, and how the media handle it.

603. Snehid Group, Madras. "Abusing Women -- The Pornographic Intent of Tamil Magazines." *Manushi*. January-February 1991, pp. 27-31.

604. Srivatsan, R. "Looking at Film Hoardings: Labour, Gender, Subjectivity and Everyday Life in India." *Public Culture*. Fall 1991, pp. 1-23.

605. Staab, Joachim F., Heidi Buchmüller, Martina Gilges, Gisela Winterling. "Dissonate Stereotypisierung Eine Verleichende Inhaltsanalyse der Frauendarstellung in 'Brigitte,' 'Neue Post,' 'Emma,' and 'Playboy.'" *Pulizistik*. 32:4 (1987), pp. 468-479.

606.   Standish, Isolde. "Gendered Television: Feminine Inflection of the Male Hero in the Samurai Drama and Detective Series, Discourses of Female Powerlessness." Paper presented at Association for Asian Studies, Washington, D.C., March 26, 1998.

607.   Standish, Isolde. "Japan: Visual Representations of Women." *Cinemaya*. Winter 1990-1991, pp. 26-31.

608.   State Press and Publication Bureau. "Guanyu Rending Yinhui Ji Seqing Chubanwu de Xanxing Guiding" (Temporary Rules on the Identification of Pornographic and Obscene Material). In *Chu Liuhai Shiyong Fagui Shouce* (A Practical Handbook on Laws and Regulations Concerning the Elimination of Six Evils). Beijing: Police Officers Education Publishing House, 1990.

609.   Subramanayan, Vimal. *Mirror Image: Media and the Women's Question.* Bombay: Centre for Education and Documentation, 1986.
        In India.

610.   Tajima, Renee. "Lotus Blossoms Don't Bleed: Images of Asian Women." In *Making Waves: An Anthology of Writings by and About Asian American Women*, pp. 308-317. Boston: Beacon Press, 1989.

611.   Takahashi, Maki. "Two Different Generations of Japanese Females: Their Gender Role Representations in Two Popular Cultures." Paper presented at Japanese Popular Culture Conference, University of British Columbia, Victoria, Canada, April 11, 1997.

612.   Tamiya, Takeshi. "Masu Komi Hyogen Ni Miru Josei Sabetsu" (Women's Discrimination as Seen in the Language of the Mass Media). In *Josei to Media* (Women and Media), edited by H. Kato and T. Tsuganesawa, pp. 92-110. Tokyo: Sekai Shisosha, 1992.

613.   Tanaka, Keiko. "Intelligent Elegance: Women in Japanese Advertising." In *Unwrapping Japan*, edited by E. Benari, et al., pp. 78-97. Manchester: Manchester University Press, 1990.

614.   Todeschini, Maya M. "'Death and the Maiden': Female *Hibakusha* as Cultural Heroines, and the Politics of A-bomb Memory." In *Hibakusha Cinema: Hiroshima, Nagasaki, and the Nuclear Image in Japanese Film*, edited by Mick Broderick, pp. 222-252. London: Kegan Paul, 1996.
        Insists on the inseparability of gender from the issue of A-bomb suffering, memory, and representation; examines images of young female viewers of two Japanese films, "The Diary of Yumechiyo" and "Black Rain."

615.   Tokita, A. *Representation of Women in Japanese Culture*. Monash: Monash University Asia Institute, 1995.

616.   Tong Xing. "Woguo Yinhui Wupin de Shehui Weihai" (The Social Harms of Pornography in Our Country). *Sociological Research*. 2 (1993).

In China.

617. Toyama, Jean. "To Other or To Be Othered: De Beauvoir / Tanizaki Where Is *The Key?*" In *Significant Others: Gender and Culture in Film and Literature East and West: Selected Conference Papers*, edited by William Burgwinkle, Glenn May, and Valerie Wayne, pp. 105-112. Honolulu: University of Hawaii and East-West Center, 1993.

Uses Simone de Beauvoir's analysis of the other in "The Second Sex" to look at Tanizaki Jun'ichir⊥'s "The Key."

618. Tsurumi, Maia. "Gender and Girls' Comics in Japan." Paper presented at Japanese Popular Culture Conference, University of British Columbia, Victoria, Canada, April 11, 1997.

619. Valaskivi, Katja. *Wataru Seken Wa Oni Bakari: Mothers-in-law and Daughters-in-law in a Japanese Television Family Drama*. Jyväskylä: University of Jyväskylä, 1995. 112 pp.

Textually analyzes representations of mothers-in-law and daughters-in-law in Japanese TV family drama; serial appears as a space where changes in the sex-gender system and family ideology are discussed.

620. Valentine, James. "Skirting and Suiting Stereotypes: Representations of Marginalized Sexualities in Japan." *Theory, Culture and Society*. August 1997, pp. 57-85.

Describes portrayal of lesbians and gays on Japanese television over five months of 1992-1993; argues that many Japanese do not identify themselves primarily according to their sexuality and that Western categories of in and out of the closet do not apply.

621. Van Wijk, Christine. "Bringing Gender into Development Theatre: Five Cases in India." *Media Asia*. 24:1 (1997), pp. 23-29, 56.

Concludes a different type of theater is needed in water and sanitation programs in India; "a gender perspective....is needed consistently to avoid a situation whereby performing arts confirm and reinforce existing gender inequalities."

622. Wang, Lay-Kim. "Gender and the New Communication Technology in Malaysia." *Sojourn*. October 1994, pp. 213-225.

Discusses implications of satellite broadcasting and other new information technology on society, and women, in particular, in Malaysia; feels new technologies can exacerbate images of women perpetuated.

623. Wang, Shujen. "The Construction of Femininity and Gender Relations in Asian Music Videos: The More Things Change, The More They Stay The Same." Paper presented at "The Consoling Passions: Television, Video, and Feminism" Annual Conference, 1995.

624.   Wee, Chow-Hou, Mei-Lan Choong, and Siok-Kuan Tambyah. "Sex Role Portrayal in Television Advertising." *International Marketing Review.* 12:1 (1995), pp. 49-64.

Compares portrayal of both sexes in television advertising from Singapore's SBC 5 and Malaysia's RTM 1 and TV 3; finds that characters in both countries' advertisements were stereotyped.

625.   Wei, Yanmei. "Music and Femininity in Zhang Yimou's Family Melodrama." *CineAction.* No.42, 1997, pp. 18-27.

Concludes that from "Red Sorghum" to "Raise the Red Lantern," Chinese director Zhang Yimou shifts focus from masculine to feminine, changing his films' tones from "joyous and optimistic to burdened and helpless."

626.   Wilkins, Karin G. "Gender, News Media Exposure and Political Cynicism: Public Opinion of Hong Kong's Feature Transition." *International Journal of Public Opinion.* Fall 1995, pp. 253-281.

Predicts that women in Hong Kong, marginalized from the center of power, may be particularly vulnerable after the transfer to China; reports that women are less likely to be susceptible to press coverage about the issue.

627.   "Woman Outlaws: Hands Up." *Economist.* November 12, 1994, pp. 116-117.

Reports that India's most famous woman outlaw, Phoolan Devi, complained that film based on her misdeeds violated her privacy and distorted facts about her life.

628.   "Workshop on 'Women's Issues, Development and Media.'" *Asian Mass Communication Bulletin.* January-February 1995, p. 2.

629.   Xie Xiahang. "The Myth of New Women: The Masters of Their Own Destiny -- Comment on Female Figures in 1995's TV Plays." *Contemporary Cinema.* September 1996.

630.   Xu Xiaoqun. "The Discourse on Love, Marriage, and Sexuality in post-Mao China: A Reading of the Journalistic Literature on Women." *positions.* Fall 1996, pp. 381-414.

Concludes that journalistic literature is playing an important role in the discourse about women, because in the post-Mao era, the official ideology has failed to do this.

631.   Yau, Esther. "Is China the End of Hermeneutics? Or, Political and Cultural Usage of Non-Han Women in Mainland Chinese Films." *Discourse.* 11:2 (1989), pp. 115-136.

632.   Zhang, Yingjin. *The City in Modern Chinese Literature and Film. Configurations of Space, Time, and Gender.* Palo Alto, California: Stanford University Press, 1996. 390 pp.

Includes the gender perspective in his efforts to trace the literary and filmic configurations of the city in modern China.

633. Zhou He. "Pornography, Perception of Sex, and Sexual Callousness in China."
      Paper presented at Association for Education in Journalism and Mass
      Communication, Anaheim, California, August 1996. 30 pp.
          Examines "empirically" pornography's impact on Chinese public's
      perception of sexuality, sensitivity to women, and dispositions toward sex; student
      respondents had high exposure to pornography, but this did not affect their
      perceptions of sexuality, although the exposure did have significant impact on
      their sensitivity to women.

Women as Audience

634. Asian Cultural Centre for UNESCO, et al. *Development of Audio-Visual Literacy
      Materials for Women in Rural Areas. Final Report of the Regional Workshop on
      the Preparation of Literacy Follow-up Materials in Asia and the Pacific* (8th,
      Pattaya, Thailand, October 9-20, 1990). Tokyo: Asian Cultural Centre for
      UNESCO, Ministry of Education (Thailand), UNESCO (Bangkok), 1991. 119 pp.
          Includes Varsha Das, "How to Develop and Utilize Literacy Materials for
      Women"; Nalince Sitasuwan, "How to Develop Video Literacy Material";
      Somsak Kanha, "How to Develop Materials Using Folk Media Such as Puppets";
      T. M. Sakya, "Literacy and Continuing Education for Women"; "AACU (Asian
      Cultural Centre UNESCO) Report," and country reports from Bhutan, China,
      India, Indonesia, Laos, Malaysia, Nepal, Pakistan, Papua New Guinea,
      Philippines, and Thailand.

635. Asian Mass Communication Research and Information Centre. *AMIC Seminar on
      New Communication Technologies. Women and Democracy, Bangkok, October
      19-21, 1995.* Singapore: Asian Mass Communication Research and Information
      Centre, 1995. Various pagings.
          Reports on seminar dealing with impact of new communication
      technologies on women in Asia; examines relationship between the technology
      and democracy.

636. Bajaj, S. S. and Ishwar Banchare. "Research in Agricultural Communication: A
      Neglected Area -- Farm Women." In *Communication and Indian Agriculture*,
      edited by Ronald E. Ostman, pp. 271-276. New Delhi: Sage, 1992.
          Claims that women's participation in Indian media is very limited; that
      very few research projects have been implemented, especially for farm women.

637. Behera, Sunil K. "Advertisements and the Cultural Construction of Femininity."
      Available from AMIC, Singapore. 25 pp.
          Looks at how women in India have been exploited in the advertising
      medium.

638. Bhagat, Rekh and P. N. Mathur. *Mass Media and Farm Women.* New Delhi:
      Intellectual, 1989.
          Reviews film, TV, print media and their use by farm women in villages
      near Delhi.

639.   Bhasin, Kamla. "Some Thoughts on Development and Sustainable Development." *Women in Action*. 4/92 & 1/93, 1992/1993, pp. 10-18.

640.   Bhasin, Kamla. "The Why and How of Literacy for Women: Some Thoughts in the Indian Context." *Convergence*. No. 17, 1984, pp. 37-43.

641.   Brown, William J. and Michael J. Cody. "Effects of Prosocial Television Soap Opera in Promoting Women's Studies." *Human Communication Research*. September 1991, pp. 114-142.
        Uses questionnaire data from 1,170 respondents in India to examine the degree to which viewers' awareness and involvement mediated the effects of exposure to India's successful soap opera, "Hum Log."

642.   Chan, Kara K. W. "Creating Advertising That Appeals to Chinese Women." *Asian Journal of Communication*. 7:1 (1997), pp. 43-57.
        Examines Chinese women as a target audience group for television commercials and their perception of differing advertising strategies; employs an adjective survey adopted from Aaker and Bruzzone (1982) to gauge respondents' opinions of informative and emotional advertising techniques; finds that women like emotional advertising, that there was a consistency across Western and Chinese cultures that bodes well for international marketers of global advertising targeting women.

643.   Donald, Stephanie. "Women Reading Chinese Films: Between Orientalism and Silence." *Screen*. 36:4 (1995), pp. 325-340.

644.   Dua, M. R. and V. S. Gupta, eds. *Media and Development: Themes in Communication and Extension*. Singapore: AMIC, and New Delhi: Har-Anand Publications, 1994.
        Includes Meena Gupta and Shella Nagar, "Social Impact of Television Viewing on Rural Women," pp. 114-123; Parveen Batra and Indu Grover, "Magazine Circulation and Reading Habits of Rural Women," pp. 124-131.

645.   Dumrisomkul, Chaliya. "Educative Values of Television Programmes for Housewives." Masters thesis, Chulalongkorn University, Bangkok, 1971. 101 pp. In Thai.

646.   Faridah Ibrahim. "Wartawan Wanita Dalam Pengurusan Bilik Berita: Matlamat dan Pencapaian." *Jurnal Komunikasi*. Vol. 6 (1990), pp. 43-50.
        In Malaysia.

647.   Gomez, Ely D., Ma Rowena, and M. Baltazar. *Filipino Rural Women's Participation in Development and in Communication: An Abstract / Bibliography*. Laguna: University of Los Baños, Institute of Development Communication, 1994. 53 pp.
        Provides in bibliography form information on the many roles rural women play in Philippine development efforts; shares belief that through their participation in development broadcasting, the women will be mobilized as active contributors to development.

648.   Hart, Dennis. "Advertising and the New Feminine Ideal: The Ideology of Consumption in South Korea." *Korea Journal*. August 1990, pp. 18-26.
       Examples provided of advertising to promote consumerism among women in Korea.

649.   Intodia, S. L. and Rekha Upadhyay. "Effectiveness of Modern and Traditional Media Among Women of Tribal Areas of Rajasthan." *Interaction*. 8:2 (1990), pp. 107-112.
       Surveys 1,277 Indian women in four tribal districts on modern and traditional media effectiveness; finds that women exposed to radio, puppet show, and folk drama gained the most knowledge, that puppetry was most conducive to knowledge gain.

650.   Kaushik, Sushma and Sudershan Mehta. "Extent of Exposure and Attitude of Women Towards Mass Media." *Interaction*. 8:2 (1990), pp. 87-97.
       Measures exposure to and attitudes towards mass media of 100 women of Haryana State, India; despite their low exposure, rural women exhibited positive attitudes toward mass media.

651.   Kerwin, Ann M. "Japan's Largest Daily Offers Scratch-and-Sniff ROP Ads." *Editor & Publisher*. October 24, 1992, pp. 31-32.
       Reports on how *Yomiuri Shimbun* attempted to attract young, working, single women by mixing a scent with its printing inks.

652.   Khor, Martin. "Women, Environment and Development." *Issues in Gender and Development*. September 1992, pp. 1-4.

653.   Kim, Kyung Min. "A Study on the Uses of the Media by Korean Women: Concerning the Uses and Gratification Theory." Master's thesis, Hanyang University (Seoul), 1980. 250 pp.

654.   Kim, U-Ryong, In-Suk Chung, and Cheong-Yi Park. "Running Head: Newscaster Gender and Viewing Satisfaction -- The Effects of Audience's Gender-based Expectations About Newscasters on News Viewing Satisfaction in a Collective Culture: South Korea." Paper presented at Association for Education in Journalism and Mass Communication, Chicago, Illinois, July 31-August 2, 1997.
       Focuses on effects of audience's gender-based expectations about newscasters; tested by a nationwide survey in Korea; finds that audiences expected female newscasters to be both journalists and entertainers but male newscasters to be journalists rather than entertainers.

655.   Lee, Minu and Chong Heup Cho. "Women Watching Together: An Ethnographic Study of Korean Soap Opera Fans in the US." *Cultural Studies*. January 1990, pp. 30-44.
       Concerns the question, "Why is it that some Korean housewives in America prefer Korean soap operas to American ones?"; hones in on Korean series "Sand Castle."

656. Mahajan, Kamlesh. *Television and Women's Development*. New Delhi: Classical, 1990. 284 pp.
      Evaluates sample of college girls of Meerut City and their changes of orientation because of televiewing and watching films.

657. Medel-Añonuevo, Carolyn, ed. *Women Reading the World. Policies and Practices of Literacy in Asia*. Paris: UNESCO, 1996. 134 pp.
      Discusses history and strategies of literacy campaigns for women in Vietnam, Philippines, India, Bangladesh, and Nepal; includes contents of literacy primers, detailed checklist of elements in such campaigns.

658. Nishino, Yoshimi and Michael Schunck. "Single Thai Women's Interpersonal Communication and Mass Media Reception on AIDS." *AIDS Education and Prevention*. April 1997, pp. 181-200.
      Examines young, unmarried, Thai women's ways of talking about AIDS, AIDS prevention, and its relationship to mass media AIDS messages.

659. Park, Seung Hyun and Ho-Kyu Lee. "The Consumption of Korean Television Programs in U.S.A.: Television Viewing, Gender, and Power." Paper presented at Association for Education in Journalism and Mass Communication, Chicago, Illinois, July 31-August 2, 1997.
      Looks at Koreans living in small U.S. town; explores relationship of gender to domestic power revealed in TV viewing.

660. Pathak, M. and A. Shah. "Effectiveness of Puppetry in the Education of Rural Adult Women." *Indian Journal of Adult Education*. 45:9 (1984), pp. 32-35.

661. Puri, Jyoti. "Reading Romance Novels in Postcolonial India." *Gender and Society*. August 1997, pp. 434-452.
      Examines role of romance novels in the lives of 101 16-22-year-old females in India; explores influence of novels on women's expectations of marital sexuality and gender role, limitations of novels in dealing with Indian women's social uncertainties, and anxieties faced by women in trying to match sociocultural setting to novel content.

662. Quraishi, S. Y. *Role of Communication and Social Marketing in the Development of Women and Children in Northern and Western India*. New Delhi: Jamia Millia Islamia, 1992. 16 pp.

663. Saito, Kenji. "Katei Fujinoto Terebi Shicho: Shokugyobetsu Hikaku o Chushin ni" (Housewives and Television Ratings in a Comparative Perspective with Other Professions). *Bunken Geppo*. December 1975, pp. 10-15.

664. Schaffter, Sharada. "Sri Lankan Women Seek Justice Through Media Awareness." *Action*. March 1993, p. 3.

665. Sood, A. K. and B. N. Nagla. "Factors Affecting the Adoption of Simple Maternal and Child Health Interventions by Women." *Indian Journal of Social Work*. October 1996, pp. 605-613.

Describes level of adoption of maternal and child health interventions by 162 rural Indian mothers; observes correlation between adoption tendencies and women's educational levels and exposures to mass media.

666. "S'pore Women Top Internet Surfing Survey." *Asian Mass Communication Bulletin.* May / June 1997, p. 4.

667. Tai, S. H. C. and J. L. M. Tam. "A Lifestyle Analysis of Female Consumers in Greater China." *Psychology and Marketing.* May 1997, pp. 287-307.
    Compares lifestyles of female consumers in Hong Kong, Taiwan, and China; finds that the women differed in women's role and perception, family orientation, home cleanliness, brand consciousness, price consciousness, self-confidence, addiction to work, health consciousness, and environment consciousness, that Hong Kong women favored a modern view of women more than those in China and Taiwan.

668. Thakur, B. S. and Binod C. Agrawal, eds. *Media Utilisation for the Development of Women and Children.* New Delhi: Concept Publishing Co., 1989. 169 pp.
    Collects papers presented at 1984 seminar in India to evaluate the contribution of television in promoting the well-being of women and children.

669. Wilcox, G. B., M. Tharp, and K.-T Yang. "Cigarette Advertising and Consumption in South Korea, 1988-1992." *Journal of Advertising.* 13:4 (1994), pp. 333-346.

Women Practitioners

670. "Akemi Negishi." *Kaiju Review.* 1:8 (1995), pp. 20-21.
    Profiles Japanese horror and monster film actress, Akemi Negishi.

671. "Akiko Wakabayashi." *Kaiju Review.* 1:8 (1995), pp. 24-25.
    Features Japanese actress for Toho Studios.

672. Allott, Anna J. "Prose Writing and Publishing in Burma: Government Policy and Popular Practice." In *Essays on Literature and Society in Southeast Asia,* edited by Tham Seong Chee. Singapore: Singapore University Press, 1981.

673. "Anita Yuen." *Kung-fu Girl.* Summer 1995, p. 13-15.
    Describes career of Hong Kong film actress, Anita Yuen.

674. Asian Mass Communication Research and Information Centre. *AMIC Workshop on Editorial Management for Women Journalists, Singapore, May 24-31, 1995.* Singapore: Asian Mass Communication Research and Information Centre, 1995. Various pagings.
    Reports on workshop of 20 Asian women journalists who dealt with investigative journalism, newsroom management techniques, printing technology, development journalism, writing techniques, newspaper design, layout, publics, and editorial writing.

675.   "Asia's Most Powerful Women." *Asiaweek*. September 1, 1995, pp. 50-53.
        Includes Taiwan magazine publisher Diane Ying Yun-peng and Hong Kong newspaper publisher Aw Sian.

676.   Athale, Gouri Agtey. "Indian Nightingale." *Far Eastern Economic Review*. June 1, 1995, p. 53.
        Reviews Raju Bharatan's biography of Lata Mangeshkar, India's queen of film music.

677.   "Bangkok Seminar Examines Relationship Between NCT, Women and Democracy." *Asian Mass Communication Bulletin*. November-December 1995, p. 24.

678.   "Bangladesh Women Journalists Struggle for Their Role." *Asian Mass Communication Bulletin*. November-December 1990, p. 4.

679.   Baum, Julian. "Profile: Diane Ying -- A Magazine Publisher Committed to Taiwan." *Far Eastern Economic Review*. April 1, 1993, p. 90.
        Profiles Diane Ying, founder of *Commonwealth* magazine in Taiwan; she is credited with making it an analytical periodical on social, economic, and political trends.

680.   Bennett, Milly. *On Her Own. Journalistic Adventures from San Francisco to the Chinese Revolution, 1917-1927*. Armonk, New York: M. E. Sharpe, 1993.
        Emphasizes her journalistic work in China, including her stint helping to produce a propaganda newspaper for the Cantonese Nationalists.

681.   Berfield, Susan. "The Next Mogul: How to Build an Asian Entertainment Empire -- with Hollywood's Help." *Asiaweek*. September 20, 1996, pp. 52-54, 56.
        Reports on efforts of Korean Miky Lee and her company, Cheil, to build an entertainment empire. Lee invested in Dreamworks and linked with Raymond Chow's Golden Harvest in Hong Kong.

682.   Berry, Chris. "Pauline Chan." *Cinemaya*. Autumn / Winter 1994-1995, pp. 65-67.
        Interviews Asian-Australian filmmaker, Pauline Chan, especially about "Traps," set in her homeland of Vietnam.

683.   Bhardwaj, Neelam and B. Kumar. "Women in Newspapers: A Study of Four Leading Indian Dailies." *Interaction*. 5:2/3 (1987), pp. 41-48.

684.   Bhimani, Harish. *In Search of Lata Mangeshkar*. New Delhi: Indus, 1997.
        Profiles life and career of one of India's most famous screen singers; includes early life and development as an artist.

685.   Bisplinghoff, Gretchen D. and Carol J. Slingo. "Eve in Calcutta: The Indianization of a Movie Madwoman." *Asian Cinema*. Fall 1997, pp. 99-111.
        Analyzes Indian actress Nargis' role in "The Three Faces of Eve," her farewell cinematic appearance.

686. Bose, Sudhir. "The Contemporaries." *Cinemaya*. Autumn / Winter 1994-1995, pp. 20-23.

    Discusses Indian women film directors from the 1960s to the present, including Arundhati Mukherjee, Sai Paranjpye, Aparna Sen, Prema Karanth, Vijaya Mehta, Pamela Rooks, and Kalpana Lajmi.

687. "Breaking New Ground for Women in Japan." *Action*. August / September 1990, p. 8.

    In advertising.

688. Caldwell, John. "Picturing the Other / Expressing the Self: *Women's Movements*." *Asian Cinema*. 5:2 (1990), pp. 2-5.

    Analyzes Annette Barbier's video production from India, "Women's Movements," in light of theoretical battles in ethnography and visual anthropology.

689. Chandiram, Jai. "Women in Television in India." *Combroad*. No. 80, 1988, pp. 11-14.

690. "Changes in Women's Life and Policy-making Varied." *Gender and Mass Media Newsletter*. November 1991, p. 28.

    Reprints from *Korean Women Today* (Summer 1991) the data from a *White Paper on Women*, some of which focuses on women's roles in various mass media; reports that in 1990, 3,530 (11.3 percent of total media work force) women worked in all aspects of media and most female producers / reporters were assigned to life, culture, and art.

691. Chatterjee, Partha. "Over the Years." *Cinemaya*. Autumn / Winter 1994-1995, pp. 18-19.

    Traces roles of women film directors in India to the 1930s; provides examples of directors such as Jaddan Bai, Fatima Begum, Protima Dasgupta, Bhanumathi Ramakrishna, Shobhana Samarth, Asha Dutta, Aruna Raje, and Hema Malini.

692. Chatterji, Shoma A. "Defining Her Space." In *100 Years of Cinema*, edited by Prabodh Maitra. Calcutta: Nandan, 1995.

693. Chatterji, Shoma A. "Women Directors in India in Fictional and Documentary Films." In *Relocating Indian Cinema*, edited by Malti Sahay and Wimal Dissanayake. Np: np, 1996.

694. Chen, N. and H. M. Culbertson. "Guest Relations: A Demanding but Constrained Role for Lady Public Relations Practitioners in Mainland China." *Public Relations Review*. Fall 1996, pp. 279-296.

    Surveys 43 female PR practitioners in China; finds that women have made substantial advances in the field, but their progress has been hampered by stereotyping by males and their jobs have been limited mainly to guest relations.

695.   Cheng, Scarlet. "007's New Knockout." *Far Eastern Economic Review*. December 25, 1997-January 1, 1998, pp. 104-105.
        Profiles Hong Kong star, Michelle Yeoh, and her James Bond film role.

696.   *China Screen.*
        3, 1990 -- Two-page part on "Woman Directors" includes LiLi, "Woman Director Wang Haowei" and Li Wei, "The Strong-Willed Women of Dong Kena," both on page 8; Li Zang, "The 'Woman's Film' Director Bao Zhifang" and Li Gan, "A Sketch of Female Film Director Shi Shijun," both on page 9.

697.   "Chingmy Yau." *Kung-fu Girl*. Winter 1994, pp. 27-30.
        Profiles Hong Kong actress Chingmy Yau.

698.   *Cinemaya.*
        Autumn/Winter 1994-1995 -- Thematic double issue on "Asian Women Directors" includes Paul Clark, "Chronicles of Chinese Life," pp. 4-8; Stephen Teo, "Wenyi Madonna," p. 7; Berenice Reynaud, "Li Shaohong," pp. 8-9; Krishna Sen, "Women Directors, But Whose Films," pp. 10-13; Yves Thoraval, "Jocelyne Saab's Beirut: A World in Microcosm," pp. 14-16; Partha Chatterjee, "Over the Years," pp. 18-19; Sudhir Bose, "The Contemporaries," pp. 20-23; Mohini Kent, "Gurinder Chadha, a Woman's Eye," pp. 24-25; Manjula Negi, "Mira Nair," pp. 26-27; Berenice Reynaud, "At the Edge: Trinh T. Minh-Ha," pp. 28-29; Ken'ichi Okubo, "Islands in the Mist," pp. 30-32; Max Tessier, "Tanaka's Tales of Love and History," pp. 33-35; Noushabeh Amiri, "Daughters of the Revolution," pp. 36-40; "Directory of Women Directors," p. 41; Noushabeh Amiri, "Rakhshan Bani'etemad," pp. 42-43; "To Be Asian American: Renee Tajima," pp. 44-45; Stephen Teo, "The Silken Screen," pp. 46-49; "Sylvia Chang," p. 49; See Kam Tan, Justin Clemens, and Eleanor Hogan, "Clara Law: Seeking an Audience Outside Hong Kong," pp. 50-54; Atilla Dorsay, "Before Tomorrow After Yesterday," pp. 56-58; Atilla Dorsay, "The Stubborn Ambition of Bilge Olgaç," pp. 59-60; Gönül Dönmez-Colin, "Sema Poyraz: Contending with an Alien Land," pp. 60-61; Stephen Teo, "Traps," pp. 62-64; Chris Berry, "Pauline Chan," pp. 65-67; Aruna Vasudev, "A Good Place To Be: Deepa Mehta," pp. 68-71; Marra P. L. Lanot, "In a Macho Society, Gender Makes a Difference," pp. 72-77; Ashley Ratnavibhushana, "Sumitra Peries: The Lone Voice from Sri Lanka," pp. 78-80; Berenice Reynaud, "Fresh Kill," p. 85; Latika Padgaonkar, "The Bandit Queen," p. 86; "Traps," p. 98; "Sishi Buho," p. 99; "Digeh Che Khabar?" p. 100; "Winds of God," p. 101; "Kanya ya ma Kan, Beyrouth," p. 102; "Toorog," p. 103; "Loku Duwa," p. 104; "Peony Birds," p. 105; "Yaz Yagmuru," p. 106; "Bhaji on the Beach," p. 107, and "Vremya Jholtoi Travy," p. 108.

699.   Clark, Paul. "Chronicles of Chinese Life." *Cinemaya*. Autumn/Winter 1994-1995, pp. 4-6, 8.
        States that although women were prominent in Chinese cinema from its beginnings in the 1910s, it was in the 1980s that women began to explore a feminist voice in the medium; discusses female directors such as Wang Ping, Wang Haowei, Shi Shujun, Zhang Nuanxin, Huang Shuqin, Hu Wei, Peng Xiaolian, Li Shaohong, and Ning Ying.

700. Dai Jinhua and Mayfair Yang. "A Coversation with Huang Shuqing." *positions: east asia cultures critique*. Winter 1995, pp. 790-805.
    Interviews famous film director, Huang Shuqing, of China.

701. Davin, Delia. "China: A High Risk Business." *Index on Censorship*. October 1990, pp. 23, 26.
    Discusses women and censorship in China.

702. Deshpande, Suneeta. *And Pine for What Is Not*. Delhi: Disha, 1995.
    Explores life of prominent Indian feminist, politician, and actress -- sensitive and personal.

703. "Dhaka Workshop Calls for Enhancement of Women Journalists' Skills." *Asian Mass Communication Bulletin*. May-June 1997, p. 2.

704. *Directory of Philippine American Women and Artists*. Norwalk, California: 1994. 26 pp.
    Includes filmmakers and writers.

705. Do Rosario, Louise. "The Perfect Woman." *Far Eastern Economic Review*. February 10, 1994, p. 62.
    Profiles Japanese film star, Sayuri Yoshinaga, who, in the eyes of many Japanese men, is the perfect woman -- gentle on the surface, supportive of her man above all else.

706. Doyo, Ma. Ceres P. *Journalist in Her Country: Articles, Essays and Photographs*. Manila: Anvil Publishing, 1993. 244 pp.
    Collects 300 feature articles, 1980-1992, by Filipina Doyo, who claims martial law stimulated her to write.

707. Eashwer, Lalita. "Impact of New Communication Technology on Women As Users and Producers of the Means of Communication." *Media Asia*. 21:1 (1994), pp. 32-38.
    Based on surveys in Madras, India.

708. "Etsuko Shiomi." *Kung-fu Girl*. Summer 1995, p. 33.
    Profiles Japanese film actress, Etsuko Shiomi.

709. "Focus on Asian Women Directors, International Film Festival of India, 1995." *Cinemaya*. Autumn/Winter 1994-1995, pp. 97-108.
    Includes short sketches on "Traps," Pauline Chan (Australia); "Sisho Buho," Li Shaohong (China); "Digeh Che Khabar?," Tahmineh Milani (Iran); "Winds of God," Yoko Narahashi (Japan); "Once Upon a Time, Beirut," Jocelyne Saab (Lebanon); "Toorog," Yondonbaliin Tserendolgor (Mongolia); "Luku Duwa," Sumitra Peries (Sri Lanka); "Peony Birds," Huang Yu-shan (Taiwan); "Yaz Yagmuru," Tomris Giritlioglu (Turkey); "Bhaji on the Beach," Gurinder Chadha (UK); "Vremya Jholtoi Travy," Mairame Yusupova (Tadjkistan); "Asian Woman Directors: India."

710.   Gentry, Clyde III. "Actress Spotlight: Anita Mui." *Hong Kong Film Connection.*
        November 1993, pp. 2-3.
            Profiles Hong Kong actress and pop singer, Anita Mui, who has acted in
        more than a dozen films.

711.   Ghadially, Rehana, ed. *Women in Indian Society.* New Delhi: Sage Publications,
        1988.
            Contains 20 essays on women in Indian tradition, media, stereotypes, etc.

712.   Graham, Miyoko. "Anime Expo'97: Anecdotes from Ms. Miho Shimogasa."
        Protoculture Addicts. September-October 1997, p. 44.
            Discusses career of Japanese animator Miho Shimogasa.

713.   Grays, Kevin. "Power Women: Appreciating the Female Stars of Japanese Live
        Action Television." *Kaiju Review.* 1:8 (1995), pp. 32-39.

714.   Heger, Kyle. "A Tale of Two Lucys." *Communication World.* January 1989, pp.
        32-35.
            Profiles Lucy Siegel and Lucy Hobgood-Brown, both of whom worked as
        communications professionals in Asia.

715.   Hermano, Teresita. "Asian Women To Advocate Gender & Communication
        Policy." *Action.* September 1997, p. 3.
            Reports Asian Conference on Gender and Communication Policy, held in
        Antipolo, Philippines, July 29-August 2; claims there is a "continued lack of
        women's representation, access to expression and desicion-making in the Asian
        media."

716.   Hermelin, Francine G. "Multimedia Impresario: From Tunes to Toons." *Working
        Woman.* July 1994, p. 39.
            Relates career of Shanghai concert pianist, Yee-Ping Wu, who with her
        husband, Philip Lui, founded Music Pen, a multi-media firm.

717.   "HKJA's Daisy Lion Press Freedom: A Banned Article." *On the Record.* January
        1994, pp. 20-21.

718.   Hong Kong Film Archive. *Archive Treasures: 50 Years of Stardom -- A Tribute to
        Hung Sin-nui.* Hong Kong: Hong Kong Film Archive, 1998. 36 pp. Chinese,
        English.
            Exhibition program of film works of Hung Sin-nui, January-February
        1998, includes Hung Sin-nui, "Greetings, Hong Kong," p. 7; Law Kar, "Strength
        and Sensitivity: Crossing the Red Thread," pp. 10-13; Sek Kei, Hung Sin-nui, "A
        Legendary Woman," pp. 14-15; "A Mother's Tears," p. 16; "Soul of Jade Pear," p.
        17; "Autumn," p. 18; "The Judge Goes to Pieces," p. 19; "Mutual Understanding,"
        p. 20; "Humanity," p. 21; "It So Happens to a Woman," p. 22; "The Pretty
        Tigress," p. 23; "Wilderness," p. 24; "The Legend of Lee Heung Kwan," p. 25;
        "Filmography of Hung Sin-nui," pp. 32-36.

719. Howe, Russell W. *The Hunt for "Tokyo Rose."* Lanham, Maryland: University Press of America, 1990, 352 pp.

Exposes a miscarriage of justice carried out against Iva Toguri, tried as propagandist for the Japanese during World War II; contends that at least 27 Japanese-American "radio girls" were forced to broadcast anti-U.S. programs during the war.

720. Hsieh Shu-Fen. "The First 'Superwoman' of Chinese Film: Tung Yue-Chuan." *Sinorama.* May 1993, pp. 49-51.

721. Huang Weijun. *Ruan Lingyu Zhuan* (Biography of Ruan Lingyu). Changchun: Beifang Funü Ertong Chubanshe, 1986.

Profiles famous Chinese actress, Ruan Yingyu (1910-1935).

722. "An Interview with Peggy Chiao -- Films on Both Sides of the Taiwan Straits." *China Screen.* 3/1994, pp. 32-33.

Interviews Taiwanese film critic, Peggy Chiao.

723. Jaehne, Karen. "Boat People: An Interview with Ann Hui." *Cineaste.* 13:2 (1984), pp. 16-19.

About Hong Kong director, whose works included "Boat People," "The Boy from Vietnam," "Love in a Fallen City," and about a half dozen other works.

724. "Japan: A Petition Advocating Equality for Women and Men in Broadcasting." *Gender and Mass Media Newsletter.* March 1991, pp. 27-28.

Carries petition sent to all Japanese broadcasting stations in November 1989 by the group The Mass Media and Human Rights Network.

725. The Japan Foundation Asia Center. *Asian Cartoon Exhibition -- The Women of Asia Seen Through Cartoons.* Tokyo: The Japan Foundation Asia Center and The Japan Cartoonists Association, 1995.

Includes cartoons and profiles of cartoonists in the exhibition; among cartoonists profiled were Tito Ma. Coll Milambiling of the Philippines, Poh Yih Chwen of Singapore, and Imahase Harumi, Satonaka Machiko, and Mitsuhashi Chikako, all of Japan.

726. Jia Ming. "A Series Introducing Well-Known Chinese Actors. Part 10 -- Shu Xiuwen." *China Screen.* 4, 1990, pp. 34-35.

727. Jia Ming. "A Series Introducing Well-Known Chinese Actors. Part 14: Wu Yin." *China Screen.* No. 4, 1991, pp. 32-33.

Profiles actress Wu Yin of China.

728. Johnston, Heidi. "Top Female Journalist Stresses Self-Confidence." *Free China Journal.* September 25, 1991, p. 5.

Interviews Alice H. E. Kao, deputy chief editor of Taiwan's largest daily, *United Daily News*, on her career, philosophy, and interaction with male staff members.

729.   Joshi, Ila. "When Will This Be Considered 'Work'? 'Invisible Work' on ETV: A Formative Study." Paper presented at International Association for Mass Communication Research, Bled, Yugoslavia, August 26-31, 1990.
        In India.

730.   Joshi, Ila. *Women Dimension on Television: Policy, Personnel and Programme.* New Delhi: Concept Publishing Company, 1991. 167 pp.
        Aims to discover discrimination and exploitation of women in Indian television, a medium that is government owned and in a developing stage.

731.   Kakuchi, Suvendrini. "Mirror, Mirror: Best-Selling Author Appeals to Modern Women Who See Themselves in Her Characters." *Far Eastern Economic Review.* December 4, 1997, p. 98.
        Profiles Japanese author Banana Yoshimoto.

732.   "Kathmandu Workshop Upgrades Skills of Women Journalists." *Asian Mass Communication Bulletin.* January-February 1995, p. 3.
        Includes recommendations of workshop.

733.   Keller, Chris. "Megumi Hayashibara." *V. Max.* No. 8, pp. 8-9, 32.
        Discusses Japanese animation musician, Megumi Hayashibara.

734.   Kent, Mohini. "Gurinder Chadha: A Woman's Eye." *Cinemaya.* Autumn/Winter 1994-1995, pp. 24-25.
        Relates philosophy and style of filmmaking by Indian director Gurinder Chadha.

735.   Kishwar, Madhu. "Learning To Take Women Seriously." *Index on Censorship.* October 1990, pp. 21-22.
        Experiences of activist doing investigative work for Indian women's magazine, *Manushi.*

736.   Kodama, Miiko. *Women in Modern Journalism* (Jaanarizumu No Joseikan). Tokyo: Gakubunsha, 1991. 45 pp.
        In Japan.

737.   Kumar, K. Naresh. *Indian Cinema: Ebbs and Tides.* New Delhi: Har-Anand Publications, 1995. 168 pp.
        Includes "Women in Indian Cinema -- Marginalised and Exploited." pp. 33-49; "Stars and Starlets Criss-Cross Territories," pp. 50-82.

738.   "Lahore Workshop Helps Upgrade Skills of Senior Women Journalists." *Asian Mass Communication Bulletin.* January-February 1994, p. 3.
        In Pakistan.

739.   Lent, John A. *The Asian Film Industry.* Austin: University of Texas Press, 1990. 310 pp.

Includes references to women directors, including Ann Hui, Prema Karanth, Marilou Diaz Abaya, Devika Rani, Hu Ying Mon, Sumitra Peries, and others.

740. Lent, John A. "Womanizing Japanese Women's Comics." *WittyWorld International Cartoon Bulletin*. No. 10, 1996, p. 1.
Interviews Japanese cartoonist Machiko Satonaka on her career, and on how women's comics were changed over the years.

741. Li Erwei. "Gai Lili, a Good Actress." *China Screen*. 3, 1993, pp. 12-13.
In China.

742. Li Erwei. "Purity in the Heart -- On Golden Rooster Winner Song Xiaoying." *China Screen*. 4/1992, pp. 20-21.
Introduces Song Xiaoying, winner of a high honor for best supporting actress.

743. Li Erwei. "Siqin Gaowa, a Sincere Actress." *China Screen*. 4/1993, pp. 16-17.

744. Li Shutian. "Her Memory Lives On." *The Messenger* (Beijing). March-April 1991, p. 6.
Remembers Chinese broadcaster Li Xiaodong.

745. Li Wei. "Ning Ying Declares No More Fantasy." *China Screen*. 3/1994, p. 13.
On Chinese director.

746. Li Xuan. "Serious in Art, Honest in Life: The Career of Zheng Zhenyao." *China Screen*. 1/1993, pp. 28-29.
Profiles Chinese film actress.

747. Lin, Diana. "Stage and Screen Star Talented in Woodcuts as Well." *Free China Journal*. November 7, 1997, p. 5.
Profiles actress and singer Judy Ongg of Taiwan.

748. Luo Xueying. "Fill the World with Love, Brightness and Clarity -- Introducing Director Wang Junzheng." *China Screen*. 4/1992, pp. 16-17.
Introduces one of the few female film directors of China.

749. "Maggie Cheung." *Kung-fu Girl*. Summer 1995, pp. 17-18.
Profiles Hong Kong film actress, Maggie Cheung.

750. Maglipon, Jo-Ann Q. *Primed*. Manila: Anvil Publishing, 1993. 249 pp.
Collects articles (1972-1984) by Filipina journalist who found ways to break out of the Marcos media repression.

751. Matsumoto, Takayuki. *Yoshimoto Banana-ron: 'Futsu' to iu Muishiki* (Yoshimoto Banana: The Unconscious of the Ordinary). Tokyo: JICC Shuppankyoku, 1991.
Features Yoshimoto Banana, whose prize-winning novel, Kitchen, was very akin to comics.

752. Mendoza, Diana G. and Lou Palpal-Latoc. "Sexual Harassment in the Newsroom." *Philippine Journalism Review*. December 1992, pp. 34-38.
      Discusses Philippine case study.

753. "Michelle Yeoh." *Kung-fu Girl*. Winter 1994, pp. 12-16.
      Profiles Hong Kong film actress.

754. "Mie Hama." *Kaiju Review*. 1:8 (1995), pp. 22-23.
      Features Japanese film, TV actress, Mie Hama.

755. Mitsui, Takayuki and Koyata Washida. *Yoshimoto Banana Shinwa* (The Myths of Yoshimoto Banana). Tokyo: Aoyumisha, 1989.

756. "More Women Working on Newspapers." *NSK News Bulletin*. September 1990, pp. 5-6.
      In Japan, since passage of Equal Employment Opportunity Law in 1985.

757. Murakami, Asako. "Sexual Harassment Verdict Viewed as Landmark Ruling." *Japan Times Weekly International Edition*. May 18-24, 1992, p. 4.
      Reports that a court award to a magazine editor who said she was sexually harassed has forced companies to abandon their practice of settling such disputes at the expense of women's jobs.

758. Nair, Hema. "South Asian Films by Women: 'Making It Personal.'" *Ms.* November-December 1992, pp. 68-69.
      Reports on festival of films make by South Asian women, held in New York and sponsored by Sakhi for South Asian Women, a group to end violence against women in New York's South Asia community.

759. Negi, Manjula. "Mira Nair." *Cinemaya*. Autumn/Winter 1994-1995, pp. 26-27.
      Discusses work of Indian-born filmmaker Mira Nair, whose main credits are "Salaam Bombay!" and "Mississippi Masala."

760. Nik Naizi Husin and M. Hafez M. Soom. "Cabai. Kartunis Wanita Yang Gigih." *Sasaran*. July 1993, pp. 110-112.
      Profiles Malaysia's sole female cartoonist, Cabai.

761. Okubo, Ken'ichi. "Islands in the Mist." *Cinemaya*. Autumn/Winter 1994-1995, pp. 30-35.
      Surveys women filmmakers of Japan, starting with the first, Tazuko Sakane, in 1936; also includes analyses of works and careers of Yukiko Awaya, Yoko Narahashi, Toshie Tokieda, Sumiko Haneda, Hiroko Sekiguchi, Hiroko Kumagai, Mako Idemitsu, Shiori Kazama, Takako Sakamoto, Junko Miura, Utake Koguchi, Mai Tominaga, Kinuyo Tanaka, and others.

762. O'Neal, Jennifer. "American Film Institute Spotlights ROC Woman's More Active Screen Role." *Free China Journal*. November 19, 1991, p. 5.
      In Taiwan.

763.   Onorato, Michael P., ed. *Bessie Hackett Wilson: Memories of the Philippines.* Fullerton, California: California State University, Fullerton, Oral History Program, 1989. 21 pp.

    Interviews Bessie Hackett Wilson on her career as reporter and women's page editor of the Manila *Bulletin* before World War II.

764.   Patel, Ila. *Gender Differences in Employment Patterns of Doordarshan and All India Radio.* New Delhi: Friedrich Ebert Stiftung/Media Advocacy Group, 1994. 57 pp.

    States that representation of women in positions directly related to programming is far from satisfactory; points out absence of women in these positions implies thay have limited power in changing gender bias of media content.

765.   Ragone, August. "Kumi Mizuno." *Kaiju Review.* 1:8 (1995), pp. 26-29.

    Profiles Japanese actress with Toho Studios.

766.   Ragone, August. "Tetsuko Kobayashi Remembered." *Kaiju Review.* 1:8 (1995), p. 55.

    Obituary of Japanese actress.

767.   Rahman, M. "Hindi Films: Women Strike Back." *India Today.* July 15, 1988, pp. 80-82.

    Discusses women relative to India's short-lived new wave.

768.   Rai, Usha. "Mid-Career Blues of Media Women." *Times of India.* January 5, 1987.

769.   Rai, Usha. "What Makes the Times and Me Tick." *The Times of India.* October 18, 1988.

    Reflects on author's tenure at *The Times of India.*

770.   Rai, Usha and Urvashi Butalia. "Women, Does the Press Play Fair?" *Vidura.* September 1993, pp. 4-19.

771.   Ranawana, Arjuna. "Pride and Prejudice: Many Asian Women Directors Still Face Typecasting." *Asiaweek.* February 9, 1996, pp. 36-37.

    Features Ning Ying, Marilou Diaz Abaya, Li Shaohong, Yassamin Malek-Nasr.

772.   Rao, Maithili. "Shabana Azmi: All the World's Her Stage." *Cinemaya.* Summer 1990, pp. 48-51.

    Highlights career of Indian actress, Shabana Azmi, from her debut in 1974 film, "Ankur."

773.   Rashid, Ahmed. "Battling the Pirates." *Far Eastern Economic Review.* April 18, 1996, p. 75.

    Shows how Pakistan's Zorin Sachak Khan aggressively fights for video market niche.

774.   Rashid, Ahmed. "Hot Stuff." *Far Eastern Economic Review*. May 2, 1996, pp. 50-51.
       Shobha De's bawdy tales of Bombay ready for global distribution.

775.   Ratanarak, Chintana. "A True Pioneer in Journalism...and Life." *Bangkok Post*. August 8, 1993, p. 29.
       Deals with Thai woman journalist, Payung Isarangkun na Ayudya.

776.   Ratnavibhushana, Ashley. "Anoja Weerasinghe: Flying High, Flying Far." *Cinemaya*. Spring 1994, pp. 20-21.
       Profiles Sri Lankan actress, Anoja Weerasinghe.

777.   Ratnavibhushana, Ashley. "A Niche of One's Own: Sumitra Peries." *Cinemaya*. Summer 1990, pp. 26-29.
       Interviews Sri Lankan film director, Sumitra Peries.

778.   Ratnavibhushana, Ashley. "Sumitra Peries, the Lone Voice from Sri Lanka." *Cinemaya*. Autumn/Winter 1994-1995, pp. 78-80.
       Looks at the only woman film director in Sri Lanka, whose films deal with human (not strictly women) predicaments, and are "very personal works of art without concessions to commercialism."

779.   Reuben, Bunny. *Follywood Flashback: A Collection of Movie Memories*. New Delhi: Harper/Collins, 1993. 293 pp.
       Provides gossipy profiles of actresses, Nargis, Meena Kumari, Mumtaz, Zeenat Aman.

780.   Reynaud, Berenice. "Gong Li and the Glamour of the Chinese Star." *Sight and Sound*. 3:8 (1993), pp. 12-15.

781.   Reynaud, Berenice. "Li Shaohong." *Cinemaya*. Autumn/Winter 1994-1995, pp. 8-9.
       Profiles Chinese "Fifth Generation" filmmaker Li Shaohong, director of "Bloody Morning," "Family Portrait," and "Red Powder."

782.   Reynaud, Berenice. "Trinh T. Minh-ha, at the Edge." *Cinemaya*. Autumn/Winter 1994-1995, pp. 28-29.
       Discusses career in U.S. of Vietnam-born filmmaker Trinh T. Minh-ha.

783.   "The Role of Asian Women and Mass Media." *Asian Mass Communication Bulletin*. July-August 1990, p. 9.
       Issues of seminar on "Women and Mass Media," sponsored by AMIC, June 22-23, 1990, in Coimbatore, India.

784.   Rungachry, Santha. "Women in Journalism." *Press Forum* (Manila). July 1969, pp. 5, 9.
       Journalist of *Hindustan Times* (New Delhi) gives advice to other women on entering the field of journalism; states that, "Today the treatment of women

journalists may be more sophisticatedly polite, but the brutal fact remains that women are still not welcome on the staff especially of daily newspapers. If they begin as reporters, they end as such. And while they are there, they are deliberately restricted to assignments on 'womanly' subjects."

785. Sang Sang. "Gong Li, the Queen of Venice." *China Screen*. 1/1994, pp. 12-13.
Profiles popular Chinese actress, Gong Li.

786. Segers, Frank. "Film Biz Buries Two of Its Champions." *Variety*. September 27, 1993, p. 50.
Gives obituaries of women film promoters, Kashiko Kawakita and Kazuko Kawakita-Shibata.

787. Sen, Krishna. "Wajah Wanita dalam Filem Indonesia: Beberapa Catatan." *Prisma*. July 7, 1981, pp. 31-42.
Discusses women in leading roles in films about Indonesian revolution.

788. Sen, Krishna. "When a Woman Acts." *Cinemaya*. Winter 1990-1991, pp. 10-13.
In Indonesia.

789. Sen, Krishna. "Women Directors, But Whose Films?" *Cinemaya*. Autumn/Winter 1994-1995, pp. 10-13.
States that the sole women directors in the history of Indonesian film since 1926 were Ratna Asmara, Citra Dewi, Sofia W. D., and Ida Farida; discusses specific films of the latter two.

790. Shafer, Richard. "Women's Page Editors As Agents of Political Change in the Philippines." *Media Asia*. 21:1 (1994), pp. 21-29.
Based on interviews.

791. Shah, Amit. "A Dweller in Two Lands: Mira Nair, Filmmaker." *Cineaste*. 15:3 (1987), pp. 22-33.
Profiles Indian director who directed "India Cabaret," "Salaam Bombay!," "Mississippi Masala," and "The Perez Family," among others.

792. Shankar, Radhika. "All-American Girl." *Far Eastern Economic Review*. December 15, 1994, p. 70.
Profiles Margaret Cho, who stars in a television comedy series in the U.S. about Korean-Americans.

793. Singh, Ajay. "The Trouble with Men." *Asiaweek*. February 28, 1997, pp. 36-45.
Profiles controversial female journalist/author Shobha Dé, particularly her attitudes about men; Dé was a successful model, advertising copywriter, and the first editor of *Stardust*, as well as *Society*.

794. Siriyuvasak, Ubonrat. *Access of Thai Women to Communication Education and Work in Journalism and Communication*. Singapore: Asian Mass Communication Research and Information Centre, AMIC Research Project, 1993. 73 pp.

795.   Small, Edward S. "Teaching Film in China: An Interview with Zhu Yujun." *Journal of the University Film Association.* Fall 1981, pp. 57-60.
       Interviews woman lecturer in film production at Beijing Broadcasting College's Communication Education Department.

796.   "Sri Lankan Testimony." *Index on Censorship.* October 1990, p. 22.

797.   Stuart, Sara. "Participatory Video by Proshika in Bangladesh." In *Media Support and Development Communication in a World of Change,* edited by Manfred Oepen, pp. 118-124. Berlin: Harlemann, 1995.
       Tells how through help of NGO, Proshika introduced basics of video equipment to and trained Bangladeshi women on participatory video.

798.   Summer, Edward. "HKFC Exclusive: An Interview with Michelle Yeoh." *Hong Kong Film Connection.* 1:3 (1995), pp. 7-10.
       Hong Kong actress talks about her career, upbringing, roles.

799.   "Survey: Women Working at Newspapers." *NSK News Bulletin.* September 1992, p. 3.
       Reports "more and more" women are moving into the Japanese newsrooms; in 1991, women made up 8.06 percent of the newspapers and news agencies' workforces.

800.   "Surveys Show Number of Women in Japanese Newspaper Industry Still Low." *Asian Mass Communication Bulletin.* March/April 1993, p. 3.
       Shows 8.5 percent of newspaper, news agency employees were women; number of female reporters (1,502) at 84 companies increased.

801.   Taj, Naznin. "Women Professionals and the Media: A Case Study of Bangalore City." *ICCTR Journal.* 2:1/2 (1989), pp. 47-57.
       Levels in on the media hierarchy in which Indian women participate -- their attitudes and self-perceptions as media programmers, their role-conflicts as working journalists and homemakers, involvement in decision-making, job satisfaction, and self-portrayal in media.

802.   Tajima, Renee. "To Be Asian American." *Cinemaya.* Autumn/Winter 1994-1995, pp. 44-45.
       Discusses her career as an Asian American filmmaker; includes Tajima's filmography of 12 works.

803.   Takada, Masayuki. "Women in Broadcast Management." *Combroad.* September 1992, pp. 17-19.

804.   Tan, See Kam, Justin Clemens, and Eleanor Hogan. "Clara Law: Seeking an Audience Outside Hong Kong." *Cinemaya.* Autumn/Winter 1994-1995, pp. 50-54.
       Interviews Clara Law on the nature of her films -- motives, finances, themes.

805.   Tang Ning. "The Pure Artistic Spirit -- The Famous Director Huang Shuqin."
       China Screen. 3, 1993, pp. 16-17.

806.   Teo, Stephen. "The Silken Screen." *Cinemaya*. Autumn/Winter 1994-1995, pp.
       46-49.
              Discusses women film directors in Hong Kong, including Ann Hui, Clara
       Law, Mabel Cheung, Tang Shuxuan, and Sylvia Chang; includes sidebar on career
       of Sylvia Chang.

807.   Teo, Stephen. "Wenyi Madonna." *Cinamaya*. Autumn/Winter 1994-1995, p. 7.
              Gives brief historical account of Chinese women in cinema; states most
       women represented what she called the "Wenyi Madonna" -- "a tragic star who
       was at her best in the genre of Chinese melodramas that are known as *Wenyi pian*,
       the name for melodrama in Chinese cinema."

808.   Tessier, Max. "Tanaka's Tales of Love and History." *Cinemaya*. Autumn/Winter
       1994-1995, pp. 33-35.
              Tells how Kinuyo Tanaka, reigning star of Japanese cinema, turned film
       director in the 1950s; she directed six films between 1953 and 1992.

809.   "Toho's Fantasy Femme Fatales." *Kaiju Review*. 1:8 (1995), pp. 16-19.
              In Japanese films.

810.   "Tribute to Hung Sin-nui." *Hong Kong Film Archive Newsletter*. February 1998,
       pp. 4-5.
              Profiles Hong Kong film star Hung Sin-nui on 50th anniversary of her
       career; includes separate articles on her appraisal of her own films, on her views
       about her film style.

811.   Tsuge, Teruhiko. "Yoshimoto Banana no Sekaiteki Na Imi" (The Global
       Significance of Yoshimoto Banana). *Kaien*. 13:2 (1994), pp. 78-83.

812.   Tsuge, Teruhiko, et al. "Sekai no Naka nu Yoshimoto Banana" (Yoshimoto
       Banana Around the World). *Kokubungaku: Kaishaku to Kyⁿzai no Kenky©*. 39:3
       (1994), pp. 88-106.

813.   U Thaung. *A Journalist, a General and an Army in Burma*. Bangkok: White Lotus
       Press, 1995.

814.   Underwood, Laurie. "Four Years of Funny Stuff." *Asiaweek*. June 13, 1997, p. 46.
              Tells of praise and ire heaped on Taiwan's, and possibly Asia's, only
       regularly published female political cartoonist, Frances Ku.

815.   Vasudev, Aruna. "Deepa Mehta -- A Good Place To Be In." *Cinemaya*.
       Autumn/Winter 1994-1995, pp. 68-71.
              Interviews Indian-born Deepa Mehta, perhaps the first director to make a
       film on the Asian immigrant community in Canada.

816.   Vasudev, Aruna. "Marilou Diaz-Abaya: A Time To Live, A Time To Work." *Cinemaya*. Spring 1996, pp. 14-21.
        Profiles Philippine director of films and television programs, president of Directors Guild of the Philippines.

817.   Vasudev, Aruna. "Women Beware Men." *Index on Censorship*. March 1991, pp. 7-8.
        Says women of India walk tight rope, caught between commercial film's demands and strictures of the censor.

818.   Wang Lan. "The Inner World of Pan Hong -- An Interview with Award-Winning Actress Pan Hong." *China Screen*. 2/1994, pp. 10-11.
        In China.

819.   "Wang Tsu-Hsien (aka Joey Wang)." *Kung-fu Girl*. Winter 1994, p. 40.
        Profiles Hong Kong film actress.

820.   Watanabe, Haruko K. "UNESCO Seminar on the Role of Asian Women Journalists in Economic Reporting." *Gender and Mass Media Newsletter*. November 1991, pp. 8-9.
        Discusses background, objectives, participants, and recommendations of this conference in Manila.

821.   Watson, Paul. "The Akemi Takada Interview." *Anime UK*. December 1994/January 1995, pp. 12-13.
        Discusses Japanese animation designer.

822.   "Woman Director Liu Miaomiao." *China Screen*. 4/1993, p. 27.

823.   "Woman Director Ning Ying." *China Screen*. 2/1993, p. 29.

824.   "Woman with a Past." *Asiaweek*. April 28, 1995, p. 7.
        Features Yamaguchi Yoshiko, Japanese film and broadcasting star.

825.   "Women in Asia Fighting Same Battles with Media over Access and Influence." *Media Report to Women*. January-February 1991, pp. 7-9.

826.   "Women Journalists in Bangladesh." *Democratic Journalist*. October-November 1990, p. 30.
        States that women are underrepresented on staffs of media and as subjects.

827.   "Women's Situation Improving in Japanese Newspaper Industry." *Asian Mass Communication Bulletin*. November-December 1992, p. 14.
        Shows that more women are working in Japanese newspapers -- from 5.91 percent of workforce in 1981 to 8.06 percent in 1991.

828.   Wong, Tina. "Women in Advertising Are Marching to a New Tune." *Asian Advertising and Marketing*. March 1988, pp. 40-41.

829.   "Writing for Women's Journal." *Press Forum* (Manila). August/September 1971, p. 4.

        Claims more women in journalism in India, but most are "free-lances, mostly intelligent educated housewives with time on their hands or women in other careers either supplementing their income or indulging in a hidden talent." Most of the rest of the article is a list of do's and don't's for women journalists. Reprinted from *Vidura* of Press Institute of India.

830.   Xia Jixuan. "Women Journalists at RB." *The Messenger* (Beijing). March-April 1991, p. 5.

        Concentrates on head of Laotian Section, Liu Huijin.

831.   Yun Duo. "Liu Miaomiao -- A Fervent Director." *China Screen.* 3/1994, pp. 22-23.

        Profiles Chinese film director Liu Miaomiao.

832.   Zhang Haoyin. "A Woman Director More Manly Than Men." *China Screen.* 3/1993, pp. 20-21.

        Looks at Chinese film director Shi Shujun.

833.   Zhang Nuanxin. "A Story of Women." *China Screen.* 1/1994, p. 20.

        Film director Zhang Nuanxin discusses her work, "A Yunnan Story."

Women's Media

834.   Anderson, Erika S. "*Mississippi Masala.*" *Film Quarterly.* Summer 1993, pp. 23-26.

        Reviews film of Mira Nair; other reviews by Cecelie S. Berry in *Cineaste* (19:2-3, 1992), Samuel G. Freedman in *New York Times* (February 2, 1992), and Marie-Anne Guerin in *Cahiers du Cinema* (October 1991).

835.   "Asia: Women in Communication Asian Network." *Gender and Mass Media Newsletter.* November 1992, pp. 33-36.

        Discusses activities, recommendations, future prospects of this group.

836.   "Asian Women's Network Launches Newsletter." *Asian Mass Communication Bulletin.* September/October 1993, p. 6.

837.   Barrager, Dave. "Skin Magazines for Women?" *Mediaweek.* April 19, 1993, p. 20.

        Reports tendency in Japan for some women to express a new femininity by posing nude in magazines such as *An An.*

838.   Chanda, Ipshita. "Birthing Terrible Beauties: Feminisms and 'Women's Magazines.'" *Economic and Political Weekly.* October 26, 1991, pp. 67-70.

        In India.

839.   Chiang, W. W. *"We Two Know the Script; We Have Become Good Friends": Linguistic and Social Aspects of the Women's Script Literacy Program in*

Southern Hunan, China. Lanham, Maryland: University Press of America, 1995. 318 pp.

Relates how a group of women in China developed a written script that men could not read, a rare instance where script use is determined by gender.

840.   Dai Jinhua. "Bukejian de Nüxing: Dangdai Zhongguo Dianying Zhong de Nüxing yu Nüxing Dianying" (The Invisible Female: Women and Women's Film in Contemporary Chinese Cinema). *Dangdai Dianying* (Contemporary Cinema). 6 (1994), pp. 37-45.

841.   Dai Jinhua. "Invisible Women: Contemporary Chinese Cinema and Women's Film." *positions: east asia cultures critique.* Spring 1995, pp. 255-280.

842.   Dayal, Samir. "The Subaltern Does Not Speak: Mira Nair's *Salaam Bombay!* as a Post-Colonial Text." *Genders.* Fall 1992, pp. 16-32.

States that this 1988 Indian film, with its comments on prostitution, has postcolonialist and feminist subtexts.

843.   Fujimoto, Yukari. "A Life-Size Mirror: Women's Self-Representation in Girls' Comics." *Review of Japanese Culture and Society.* December 1991, pp. 53-57.

In Japan.

844.   Hagio, Moto and Yoshimoto Ryumei. "Jikohyogen Toshiteno Shojo Manga." (Shojo Manga As Self Representation). *Eureka.* 13:9 (1981), pp. 82-119.

Girls' comics in Japan.

845.   Hashida, Sugako. *Oshin Jinseikun: Yutaka na Jidai no "Shin no Kotoba."* (The Teachings in *Oshin*: Words from the Heart for an Affluent Age). Tokyo: Simul Press, 1984.

Deals with the TV show *Oshin*, popular with women.

846.   Honda, Masuko. "Senjika no Shojo Zasshi" (Magazines for Girls During the War). In *Shojo Zasshi Ron*, edited by Eiji Otsuka, pp. 7-43. Tokyo: Tokyoshoseki, 1991.

847.   Honda, Masuko. "Shojo Katari." *Shojoron.* Tokyo: Seikyusha, 1988, pp. 9-37.

Girls' comics in Japan.

848.   Inoue, Teruko. "Josei Zasshi ni Miru Feminizumu" (Feminism As Seen in Women's Magazines). In *Josei to Media* (Women and Media), edited by H. Kato and T. Tsuganesawa, pp. 111-119. Tokyo: Sekai Shisosha, 1992.

849.   Inoue, Teruko. *Josei Zasshi o Kaidoku-suru* (Analyses of Women's Magazines). Tokyo: Kakiuchi Shuppan, 1989.

In Japan.

850.   Johansson, Perry. "Selling the New Chinese Woman: From Hedonism to Tradition in Advertising and Women's Magazines 1985-1995." Paper presented at Association for Asian Studies, Washington, D.C., March 29, 1998.

Analyzes women's magazines, *Zhongguo Funü* and *Hunyin yu Jiating*; in mid-1980s, ads used shy-looking, amateurish models, but by mid-1990s, a new category of ads appeared, advocating the "recovery of a distinct Chinese or Oriental beauty."

851.   Kim, You Jung. "A Study on the Woman's Page on the Korean Newspapers; with Special Reference to the Content Analysis of the Woman's Page." Master's thesis, Yonsei University (Seoul), 1984. 87 pp.

852.   *Komikku Media: Yawarakai Joho Sochi to Shite no Manga* (Comic Media: Comics as a Soft Informational System). Tokyo: NTT Shuppan, Books In-Form, 1992.
Includes Kanko Akagi, "Aijo-Busoku no Kodomo-tachi: Shojo Manga ni Miru Gendai no Byori to Sono Jittai" (Loveless Children: Today's Illness and Its Reality Seen in Girls' Comics), pp. 90-117; Saeko Ishida, "'Shojo Manga' no Buntai to Sono Hogensei" (The Grammar and Its Dialecticality of Girls' Comics), pp. 54-89.

853.   Kristof, Nicholas D. "In Japan, Brutal Comics for Women." *New York Times*. November 5, 1995, p. 1.

854.   Kwok Glasser, Charlotte. "Patriarchy, Mediated Desire, and Chinese Magazine Fiction." *Journal of Communication*. Winter 1997, pp. 85-108.
Examines the relationship between mass media and social change by studying women's magazine fiction in China before and after the implementation of the Four Modernizations Policies in the late 1970s; ironically, as China moves towards relative political openness and economic modernization, old stereotypes of women as homemakers and caregivers re-emerge.

855.   Lee, Sock Hee. "An Analytical Study on the Current Status of Television Programs for Parent Education in Korea." Master's thesis, Sookmyung Women's University (Seoul), 1985. 135 pp.

856.   Lu, Sheldon H. "Chinese Soap Opera: The Transnational Politics of Visuality, Sexuality, and Masculinity." Paper presented at Association for Asian Studies, Washington, D.C., March 29, 1998.

857.   Makita, Tetsuo and Janamoto Keifuku. "*Oshin* Bomu o Saguru: Oshin to Nihonjin Chosa Kara" (Examining the *Oshin* Boom: Results from the Japanese People and Oshin Opinion Poll." *Hoso Kenkyo to Chosa*. December 1983, pp. 21-28.

858.   Miller, Laura. "'Donna Taipu?' Folk Taxonomies in Japanese Women's Magazines." Paper presented at South Atlantic Modern Language Association convention, Baltimore, Maryland, 1994.
Surveys young women's magazines and shows a rejection of homogeneity and a search for individuality.

859.   Miller, Laura. "People Types: Personality Classification in Japanese Women's Magazines." *Journal of Popular Culture*. Fall 1997, pp. 143-159.

Focuses on how personality taxonomies enunciate and dissect the Japanese women's social fabric through an analysis of Japanese women's magazines.

860.   Mitchell, Carol L. "Sisterhood Is Local: The Rise of Feminist Journals in Southeast Asia." *Bulletin of Concerned Asian Scholars*. July-December 1996, pp. 3-7.

Discusses feminist journals regionally, and then by countries of Indonesia, Malaysia, Philippines, Singapore, Thailand, and Vietnam; includes names and addresses of 23 "resources."

861.   Mitra, Ananda. "An Indian Religious Soap Opera and the Hindu Image." *Media, Culture and Society*. January 1994, pp. 149-155.

Includes the ideal Hindu woman in analysis of TV serial "Mahabharat" as shaper of Indian popular culture.

862.   Miwa, Tadashi. "Kodomotachi wa Oshin o Do Uketotta Ka" (How Did Children Relate to Oshin?) *Hoso Kenkyu to Chosa*. November 1983, pp. 14-19.

Relates to popular TV show.

863.   Nair, Mira and Sooni Taraporevala. "*India Cabaret*: Reflections and Reactions." *Discourse*. Fall-Winter 1986-1987, pp. 58-72.

Nair talks about her film "India Cabaret," which she says is a presentation of "the unshakeable inviolability of double standards, of patriarchal values, of the strong conditioning of women never to question or challenge."

864.   "Nari Tu Narayani: Report on a Television Serial on Women." *Gender and Mass Media Newsletter*. March 1991, p. 21.

Discusses "Nari Tu Narayani" (Woman, You Are Power), aired on Doordarshan Television, India, during 1983-1984.

865.   "A Newspaper for Rural Women and Women Workers." *Thai Development Newsletter*. No. 21, 1992, pp. 50-51.

866.   NHK International, ed. *International Symposium: The World's View of Japan Through Oshin*. Tokyo: NHK International, 1991.

867.   Nishiyama, Chieko. "Depictions of Sexuality in Japanese Girls' Comic Books." In *Global Perspectives on Changing Sex-Role*, translated by Martha Tocco. Tokyo: Kokuritsu Funjin Kyoiku Kaikan, 1989.

868.   *Oshin: NHK Dorama Gaido*. Tokyo: Nippon Hoso Shuppan Kyokai, 1983.

869.   Otsuka, Eiji, ed. *Shojo Zasshi Ron* (Examining Magazines for Girls). Tokyo: Tokyoshoseki, 1991.

In Japan.

870.   Ouellette, Martin. "The Movie: Studio Clamp." *Protoculture Addicts*. September-October 1997, pp. 26-27, 39.

Discusses Japanese animation studio exclusively made up of women.

871. Reid, T. R. "Comics for the Career Woman." *Mangajin*. February 1997, pp. 63-83.

Explains how career women comics hit their stride as Japanese women established a more prominent place in the workforce.

872. Sevaldsen, Line. [Ilayum Mullum]. *Media and Gender Monitor*. Spring 1998, p. 19.

Finds Indian feminist film "Ilayum Mullum" uncomfortably close to home in the West.

873. Shinoda, Hiroyuki. "Kozen no Josei Zasshi Boom Narumono no Kyomo" (Illusion of an Unprecedented Women's Magazine Boom). *The Tsukuru*. January 1990, p. 71.

In Japan.

874. "Singapore Suspends a Women's Magazine." *Asiaweek*. December 6, 1991, p. 34.

875. Singh, Ajay. "Love in the Afternoon." *Asiaweek*. February 28, 1997, p. 40.

Describes very popular Indian TV soap opera, "Swabhimaan," and how it is changing female attitudes.

876. Stuart, Sara. "Some Experiences of Video SEWA: A Grassroots Women's Video Team in Ahmedabad, India." In *The Media as a Forum for Community Building*, pp. 27-30. Washington, D. C.: Johns Hopkins University, 1992.

877. Takeshita, Toshiro, Makoto Nakata, Keiko Kodama, and Ryo Makita. "Uses and Gratifications of Women's Fashion Magazines: A Case Study of Readers of *An An* and *Non No*." *Newspaper Research*. May 1978, pp. 82-91. Japanese.

Analyzes characteristics of 208 female readers of two women's magazines, *An An* and *Non No*.

878. "Taking to the Streets." *Media and Gender Monitor*. Autumn 1997, p. 8.

Tells how theatre workshops in Sri Lanka bring down ethnic barriers between women.

879. Teo, Stephen. "Traps, a Review." *Cinemaya*. Autumn/Winter 1994-1995, pp. 62-64.

Reviews "Traps," probably the first feature film directed by an Asian-Australian, Pauline Chan.

880. Thakur, B. S. *Media Utilization for the Development of Women and Children*. New Delhi: Concept, 1989. 169 pp.

Includes 14 essays dealing with media programs for women and children of India; seminar proceedings.

881. Thorn, Matthew. "Unlikely Explorers: Alternative Narratives of Love, Sex, Gender, and Friendship in Japanese 'Girls' Comics." Paper presented at New York Conference of Asian Studies, New Paltz, New York, October 1993.

882.   Treat, John W. "Yoshimoto Banana Writes Home: Shⴖjo Culture and the Nostalgic Subject." *Journal of Japanese Studies*. 19:2 (1993), pp. 353-387.

883.   "Vol.1, No.1 of 'Asiana-Pilipina' Sets Goal of Equality in National Decision-Making." *Media Report to Women*. November 1, 1981, p. 3.
        Discusses purposes of this periodical started for and by women, dedicated to "the strong and pliant Filipina."

884.   *Women of China*.
        No.5/1991 -- Includes Bian Wen, "'Expectations,' A TV Series in 50 Episodes" and Xia Yuan," Response to the TV Series 'Expectations.'"

885.   "Women Want Trendy Mags." *Asahi Evening News*. January 22, 1993, p. 3.
        In Japan.

886.   Yamada, Tomoko. "Ladies' Comic no Han'i" (The Scope of the Ladies' Comics). *Foshiga Kenkyo*. January 20, 1998, pp. 9, 11.

AUSTRALIA AND OCEANIA

General Studies

887.   Brown, Julianne, Simon Chapman, and Deborah Lupton. "Infinitesimal Risk as Public Health Crisis: News Media Coverage at a Doctor-Patient HIV Contact Tracing Investigation." *Social Science and Medicine*. December 1996, pp. 1685-1695.
        Reviews Australian press coverage of HIV-positive hospital obstetrician and the effort by the health department to trace and test 149 women on whom he operated.

888.   Lumby, Catharine. *Bad Girls: The Media, Sex and Feminism in the 90s*. Sydney: Allen and Unwin, 1997.

889.   Moyal, Ann. "Woman and Telecommunication in Australia: Pointers to a Research Field." *Australian Journal of Communication*. 20:1 (1993), pp. 144-153.

890.   *Refractory Girl* (Australia).
        March 1991 -- Devoted to media and includes Diane Powell, "Women and Television News" and Jeannie Martin, "Aussie-Mums and Television Ads."

891.   Turnbull, Sue. "The Media: Moral Lessons and Moral Careers." *Australian Journal of Education*. August 1993, pp. 153-168.
        Challenges feminist orthodoxies being taught in media studies in Australia.

892.   "Women Organize for Media Development in Papua New Guinea." *Action*. April-May 1992, p. 8.

Historical Studies

893.   Brown, Peter. "The Containment of Women in the Australian Sporting Press from 1890-1990." *Australian Journal of Health, Physical Education and Recreation.* 1:1 (1994), pp. 4-8.

894.   Brown, Peter. "Gender, the Press and History. Coverage of Women's Sport in the *Newcastle Herald,* 1890-1990." *Media Information Australia.* February 1995, pp. 24-34.
        Looks at New South Wales (Australia) daily for 1890, 1914, 1940, 1965, and 1990 to determine coverage of women's sports; shows increase of 3.2 to 15.7 percent over century, but the gap between male and female sports coverage has widened.

895.   Kirkby, Diane. *Alice Henry: The Power of Pen and Voice.* Cambridge: Cambridge University Press, 1991. 250 pp.
        Documents career of Alice Henry, from her beginnings in Australian journalism of 1884, to her development as a progressive reformer, and eventually her move to the U.S.; for 20 years, she was heavily involved with the Women's Trade Union League as an organizer, speaker, and writer.

896.   Montgomerie, Deborah. "Reassessing Rosie: World War II, New Zealand Women and the Iconography of Femininity." *Gender and History.* April 1996, pp. 108-132.
        Explores conflict between women's wartime work and ideological definitions as femininity by analyzing visual images of New Zealand women; shows how stereotypes of women in cartoons and advertisements ridiculed women in uniforms.

Images of Women

897.   Atmore, Chris. "Brand News: Rape and the Mass Media." *Media Information Australia.* May 1994, pp. 20-31.
        Deals with various meanings of "brand news," using rape stories in the press as background, particularly a New Zealand controversy.

898.   Atmore, Chris. "Other Halves: Lesbian-Feminist Post-Structuralist Readings of Some Recent New Zealand Print Media Representations of Lesbians" Ph.D. dissertation, Victoria University of Wellington, 1992.

899.   "'Attack! Attack! Rape Is Good News': Australian Journalists Examine Coverage." *Media Report to Women.* March 1, 1979, p. 8.
        Reports on newspaper editors' feelings that rape makes good news copy.

900.   "Australia Compiles Guidelines and Recommendations To Eliminate Sexism in Media." *Media Report to Women.* August 1, 1981, p. 6.

Extracts from 138-page report, "Towards Non-Sexist Guidelines for the Media, A Compilation of Suggestions for Change in the Media's Portrayal of Women," prepared by the Office of Women's Affairs, Canberra.

901.   Australian Sports Commission and Office of the Status of Women. *Women, Sport and the Media: A Report to the Federal Government from the Working Group on Women in Sports*. Canberra: AGPS, 1985.

902.   Bertrand, Ina. "Education or Exploitation: The Exhibition of 'Social Hygiene' Films in Australia." *Continuum*. April 1998, pp. 31-46.
Traces the history of social hygiene films in Australia: those addressed primarily to women on childbirth, contraception, abortion, and white slavery, and others on venereal disease.

903.   Brown, Peter. "Changing Representations of the Female Athlete in the Australian Print Media." In *Body Matters: Leisure Images and Lifestyles*, edited by C. Brackenridge. Brighton: LSA, 1993.

904.   Brown, Peter. "Women, the Media and Equity in Sport: An Australian Perspective." In *Leisure and Tourism: Social and Environmental Change: Proceedings from the World Leisure and Recreation Congress, Sydney, 16-19 July 1991*, edited by A. Veal, P. Jonson, and G. Cushman, pp. 160-163. Sydney: UTS, 1993.

905.   Cranny-Francis, Anne. "Imaging the Writer: The Visual Semiotics of Book Reviews." *Hecate*. 17:2 (1991), pp. 43-59.
Explores the pictures and photographs which accompany reviews of books by women in the *Sydney Morning Herald* and *Australian*; states that various images used with reviews construct a patriarchal discourse disadvantageous to women.

906.   Crofts, Stephen. *Identification, Gender and Genre in Film: The Case of Shame*. Melbourne: Australian Film Institute, 1993.
Essay on film theory only loosely tied to *Shame*.

907.   "'Dykes in the Dailies': How New Zealand Newspapers Depict Lesbians." *Media Report to Women*. May/June 1990, p. 8.
Broadsheet survey found newspapers ignored lesbians, assumed all readers were heterosexual, described lesbians as criminals or child abusers.

908.   Grossman, Michele and Denise Cuthbert. "Body Shopping: Maternity and Alterity in *Mamatoto*." *Cultural Studies*. October 1996, pp. 430-448.
Focuses on The Body Shop's *Mamatoto* range as it relates to contemporary Western discursive formations of maternity, alterity, and "the vexed constructions of 'difference' and 'globalism' that emerge from them."

909.   Hafner, R. Julian. "Health Differences Between Married Men and Women: The Contribution of Sex-Role Stereotyping." *Australian and New Zealand Journal of Family Therapy*. March 1989, pp. 13-19.

Examines major health differences between married men and women relative to sex differences in mental health and mortality rates and the influence of sex-role stereotyping behavior (including by mass media) on mate selection.

910. Heaven, P. and D. Rowe. "Gender, Sport and Body Image." In *Sport and Leisure: Trends in Australian Popular Culture*, edited by D. Rowe and G. Lawrence. Sydney: Harcourt Brace Jovanovich, 1990.

911. Hindson, L. "A Newspaper Content Analysis of the *Australian*'s Treatment of Female and Male Athletes in the 1984 and 1988 Summer Olympic Games." MA thesis, University of Iowa, 1989.

912. Howe, Adrian. "'The War Against Women': Media Representations of Men's Violence Against Women in Australia." *Violence Against Women*. February 1997, pp. 59-75.
     Shows how one Australian newspaper represented men's violence against women and children in a 16-part series, "The War Against Women."

913. Huntley, Rebecca. "Slippery When Wet: The Shifting Boundaries of the Pornographic (a Class Analysis)." *Continuum*. April 1998, pp. 69-81.
     Explores various definitions of pornography and erotica with "particular reference to the opposition of elite culture and mass culture"; uses Australian examples.

914. Jeffery, Linda and Kevin Durkin. "Children's Reactions to Televised Counter-Stereotyped Male Sex Role Behaviour as a Function of Age, Sex and Perceived Power." *Gender and Mass Media Newsletter*. March 1991, pp. 24-25.
     Reports on experiment with Australian children in four age groups (5 to 14 years).

915. Jennings, Karen. *Sites of Difference: Cinematic Representations of Aboriginality and Gender*. Melbourne: Australian Film Institute, 1993.
     Offers five case studies of films from Australia, all of which touch upon the ways "white" films view Aborigines as "other," gender distinctions within and across the racial conflicts, and limitations put upon entertainment films with Aboriginal content.

916. Johnson, Lesley. "'As Housewives We Are Worms': Women, Modernity and the Home Question." *Cultural Studies*. October 1996, pp. 449-463.
     Explores the possibility of a feminist understanding of the concepts of home, using some media treatments.

917. Kiely, J. "Women, Sport and the Media: A Content Analysis of the *Australian* Newspaper, 1965-1990." M. Ed. thesis, University of Houston, 1993.

918. Liepins, Ruth. "Reading Agricultural Power: Media as Sites and Processes in the Construction of Meaning." *New Zealand Geographer*. October 1996, pp. 3-10.

Examines agricultural power as revealed in several print and electronic media of New Zealand and Australia, 1994-1996; looks at media coverage of the first International Women in Agriculture Conference, 1994.

919.   McKay, J. "Bimbos and Rambos in Sport: The Mass Media as a Barrier to Women's Participation in Sport." In *The Proceedings of the Joint Seminar on Equity for Women in Sport*, House of Representatives Standing Committee on Legal and Constitutional Affairs and the Australian Sports Commission, pp. 14-21. Canberra: AGPS, 1991.

920.   McKay, Jim and Iain Middlemiss. "'Mate Against Mate, State Against State': A Case Study of Media Constructions of Hegemonic Masculinity in Australian Sport." *Masculinities*. Fall 1995, pp. 28-45.
        Examines media construction of women and men in Queensland's rugby league.

921.   Mazzella, Carmela, Kevin Durkin, Emma Cerini, and Paul Buralli. "Sex Role Stereotyping in Australian Television Advertisements." *Sex Roles*. April 1992, pp. 243-259.
        Obtains strong evidence of differences in the presentation of male and female characters.

922.   "Media Checklist for Decoding Images in Print and Video Media." *Media Report to Women*. September-October 1990, pp. 4-5.
        Checklist for analyzing images of women in media, borrowed from Australia's Women Working in Film, Television and Video.

923.   *MediaSwitch*. Epping, Australia.
        Started in June 1989 to monitor way women are portrayed in Australian media. First issue, January 1990, included 16 pages. Box 779, Epping 2121.

924.   Menzies, H. "Women's Sport: Treatment by the Media." In *Sportswomen Towards 2000, a Celebration*, edited by K. Dyer. Adelaide: University of Adelaide, 1989.

925.   "Portrayal of Women." *Media International Australia*. August 1996, pp. 150-151.
        Reports on two studies on women's portrayals -- one in Australia that shows women are overwhelmingly shown as "dropdead gorgeous" or as housewives; the other claims advertisers of Australia do not understand women as only 10 percent of Australian copywriters and art directors are female.

926.   "The Portrayal of Women in the Media." *Media Information Australia*. November 1993, p. 96.

927.   Pringle, R. G. and A. M. Gordon. "A Feminist Analysis of the *Western Australian*'s Written Media Coverage of the 1990 Commonwealth Games." In *Sports Performance Through the Ages: Proceedings of the 27th Annual Scientific Conference of the Australian Sports Medicine Federation*, pp. 64-75. Canberra: ASMF, 1990.

928. Real, Michael R. *Exploring Media Culture*. Newbury Park, California: Sage, 1996. 405 pp.

    Includes "Gender Analysis: Patriarchy, Film Females, and *The Piano*."

929. Ross-Smith, Anne and Gael Walker. "Women and Advertising." *Media Information Australia*. May 1992, pp. 61-66.

930. Ross-Smith, Anne and Gael Walker. "Women and Advertising: An Educational Resource Package." *Gender and Mass Media Newsletter*. November 1992, pp. 36-37.

    Examines the development of an Australian educational resource package, "Women and Advertising"; includes contents of package.

931. Rowe, David and Peter Brown. "Promoting Women's Sport: Theory, Policy, and Practice." *Leisure Studies*. April 1994, pp. 97-110.

    Outlines a culture policy to reduce gender inequality in Australian sports; describes media campaign to promote teenage girls' voluntary involvement in sports.

932. Stoddart, B. *Invisible Games: A Report on the Media Coverage of Women's Sport, 1992*. Canberra: Sport and Recreation Ministers Council, 1994.

Women as Audience

933. Brook, Heather. "Big Boofy Blokes in Frocks: Feminism, Football and Sexuality." *Social Alternatives*. January 1997, pp. 5-9.

    Explores Australian TV, magazine, and news, showing how they portray football in erotic terms, presenting the sport to women as an heteroerotic spectacle.

934. Brown, Mary E. "Strategies and Tactics -- Teenagers' Readings of an Australian Soap Opera." *Women and Language*. 14:1 (1991), pp. 22-28.

935. Moyal, Ann. "The Gendered Use of the Telephone: An Australian Case Study." *Media, Culture and Society*. January 1992, pp. 51-72.

    Collects views of 200 Australian women on their use of the telephone; reveals that women's telephone communication is a major private sphere activity.

Women Practitioners

936. Agarwal, Sumegha. "Falling into Journalism -- Liz Jackson." *Reportage*. Winter 1996, p. 19.

    Australian Broadcasting Corporation journalist tells how she became a journalist.

937. Cantwell, Mary. "Jane Campion's Lunatic Women." *New York Times Magazine*. September 19, 1993, pp. 40-44, 51.

938. *Circit Newsletter*.

October 1992 -- Thematic issue on "Technology, Gender and Workplace Reform," with contributions on "New Technology and Work Organisation," by Eileen Applebaum, pp. 3-4, and "Gender and Technology at Work," by Belinda Probert, pp. 9-10.

939.   Cook, Jackie. "You Can Call Me Anytime, Darling." Paper presented at International Association for Mass Communication Research, Sydney, Australia, August 21, 1996.

Shows how radio has endured through various means, including community radio; gives examples of women's roles in radio, including unusual situations such as shows organized by wives of prisoners and by prostitutes.

940.   Cook, Jackie and Karen Jennings. "Live and Sweaty: Australian Women Re-cast Australian Sports Television." *Media Information Australia*. February 1995, pp. 5-12.

Addresses the "intervention of female sporting commentary" into the closed masculine world of sports through Australian Broadcasting Corporation's televised "Live and Sweaty," a weekly hour of sports comedy; gives vignettes from the show.

941.   Eddy, Graeme. "Women in Television New Zealand -- Management Training and Working Conditions." *Combroad*. No. 91, 1991, pp. 28-31.

942.   Kenyon, Olga. *Women Writers Talk: Interviews with Ten Women Writers*. Sydney: Allen and Unwin, 1990. 214 pp.

Interviews Anita Brookner, Margaret Drabble, Alice Thomas Ellis, Eva Figes, Nadine Gordimer, P. D. James, Iris Murdoch, Michele Roberts, Emma Tennant, and Fay Weldon.

943.   Nicolaidi, Mike. "Female Helmers Key for Kiwis." *Variety*. October 15, 1990, p. 217.

Deals with women film directors in New Zealand.

944.   Poynton, Cate. "Australian 'Opinion' Radio: Performing Gender." Paper presented at International Association for Mass Communication Research, Sydney, Australia, August 21, 1996.

States Australian talk radio is almost overwhelmingly hosted by men; women serve as the "giggle behind the male voice." Performance styles of hosts vary from expression of strong opinion, mainly male, to a strong interaction with audience where the presenter (both male and female) does not seem to have an opinion.

945.   Quart, Barbara. "The Short Films of Jane Campion." *Cineaste*. 19:1 (1992), p. 72.

The New Zealand director.

946.   Ryan, Penny and Margaret Eliot. *Women in Australian Film Production*. Sydney: Women's Film Fund, 1983.

947.   Wark, McKenzie. "Bad Girls Do It in Public." *Continuum*. April 1998, pp. 83-90.

Deals with Catharine Lumby, Australian author of *Bad Girls*; questions whether she is "fighting the good fight, bringing feminism's thinking about the media kicking and screaming into the 1980s? or is she selling feminism out to the bad guys who run the media?"

948. Wright, Andree. *Brilliant Careers*. Sydney: Pan Books, 1986.
Pieces together careers of Australian film pioneers, Lottie Lyell, who, with Raymond Longford, directed 28 movies, Paulette McDonagh, active between 1926-1933, and others.

949. Zurbrugg, Nicholas. "Linda Dement and Graham Harwood: De-Animation and Re-Animation." *Art and Design*. No. 53, 1997, pp. 82-85.
Interviews Australian computer artist on her animated story, "Cyberflesh Girlmonster."

Women's Media

950. Brunette, Peter. "Just Looking: *Proof*, the Story of a Blind Photographer." *Sight and Sound*. November 1991, pp. 10-11.
Reviews film by Australian Jocelyn Moorhouse; other reviews of "Proof" appeared in *Creative Camera* (August-September 1992, pp. 24-25), *New York Times* (November 28, 1993, p. H 13), and *Sight and Sound* (December 1991, pp. 48-49).

951. Carrington, Kerry. "Girls and Graffiti." *Cultural Studies*. January 1989, pp. 89-100.
Shows how communication by graffiti is a gendered activity; in Sydney, Australia, toilets and elsewhere, graffiti is used to reveal relationships, to seek revenge against other girls, and to nurture intimacy and genuine caring among girls.

952. Francke, Lizzie. "Dark Side -- *Crush.*" *Sight and Sound*. April 1993, pp. 18-19.
Reviews film of New Zealand filmmaker, Alison MacLean; in the same issue (p. 44) is Verina Glaessner's review.

953. Hurley, Michael. *A Guide to Gay and Lesbian Writing in Australia*. St. Leonards: Allen and Unwin / Australian Lesbian and Gay Archives, 1996. 298 pp.
Lists relevant journals, magazines, academic books, writers, academics, and activists.

954. Lawson, Olive. *The First Voice of Australian Feminism: Excerpts from Louise Lawson's The Dawn, 1888-1895*. Brookvale: Simon and Schuster / New Endeavour Press, 1990. 363 pp.

955. Lumby, Catharine. "Feminism and the Media: The Biggest Fantasy of All." *Media Information Australia*. May 1994, pp. 49-54.
Talks about feminizing of Australian newspaper formats, refocusing of magazines on formerly tabloid grounds, and various women's critiques of media.

956.   Saywell, Cherise and Jeffery Pittam. "The Discourse of HIV and AIDS in Women's Magazines: Feature Articles in Australian *Cleo* and *Cosmopolitan.*" *Australian Journal of Communication.* 23:1 (1996), pp. 46-63.

Looks at sexuality assumptions and discourses in discussion of HIV/AIDS in *Cleo* and *Cosmopolitan*; one conclusion -- the magazines devalue women's sexual choice making.

CHAPTER 4

Europe

GENERAL STUDIES

957. "Recommendations for the Promotion of Equal Opportunities." *Gender and Mass Media Newsletter*. November 1991, pp. 34-36.
    Summarizes recommendations of the Steering Committee for Equal Opportunities in Broadcasting, initiated by the European Commission.

958. Renault, Monique. "Questions from Michaela, Joanna, Monique to Michaela, Joanna, Monique." *ASIFA News*. 10:2 (1997), pp. 4-9.
    Interviews with animators Michaela Pavlátova, Joanna Priestley, and Monique Renault on a number of subjects, including films made by women.

959. Theune, Kornelia. "Blick von Unten: Zehn Jahre Frauenfilmfestival in Créteil." *Medium*. 18:2 (1988), pp. 6-8.
    On a woman's film festival.

960. Thoveron, Gabriel. *How Women Are Represented in Television Programmes in the EEC. Part I: Images of Women in News, Advertising, and Series and Serials.* Luxembourg: Commission of the European Communities, 1977.

EASTERN AND CENTRAL EUROPE

General Studies

961. Lester, Elli. "Without the Wall: Women's Communication in Berlin." In *Revolution for Freedom: The Mass Media in Eastern and Central Europe*, edited by Al Hester and L. Earle Reybold, pp. 121-135. Athens: University of Georgia, 1991, 1993.

962.   Papic, Zarana. "Nationalism, Patriarchy and War in Ex-Yugoslavia." *Women's History Review*. March 1994, pp. 115-117.

    Feels that media war propaganda developed between each warring nation of Yugoslavia and that the resulting aggressive, barbaric actions victimized women who had no voice in political decision-making.

Historical Studies

963.   Attwood, Lynn. *Red Women on the Silver Screen: Soviet Women and Cinema from the Beginning to the End of the Communist Era*. London: Pandora, 1993

    Includes women such as Dinara Asanova, Lana Gogoberidze, and others.

964.   Goscilo, Helena and Beth Holmgren, eds. *Russia. Women. Culture*. Bloomington: Indiana University Press, 1996. 400 pp.

    Looks at areas of cultural production that have offered Russian women new freedoms since the 19th century; analyzes women's creativity of all types.

965.   Jogan, Maca. "Social Construction of Gender Identity in Slovenia." *Gender and Mass Media Newsletter*. November 1991, p. 24.

    States that author has begun a research project, "Social Construction of Gender Identity from the End of 19th Century to the End of 20th Century in Slovenia."

Images of Women

966.   Dolby, Laura M. "Pornography in Hungary: Ambiguity of the Female Image in a Time of Change." *Journal of Popular Culture*. Fall 1995, pp. 119-127.

    States that pornography flourishes in Hungary, that the "new democracy has created a state of ambiguity for the female body, since domestic labor has been devalued and familial well-being left up to a new and increasingly privatized economy"; asks if Hungary can "create a democracy that includes women rather than one that uses the female body as an erotic and domestic commodity?"

967.   Corcoran, Farrel and Paschal Preston, eds. *Democracy and Communication in the New Europe: Change and Continuity in East and West*. Cresskill, New Jersey: Hampton Press, 1995. 320 pp.

    Investigates theoretical and empirical factors of change in Western, Central, and Eastern Europe in the 1990s; includes Anna Reading, "The President's Men: Television, Gender, and the Public Sphere in Eastern-Central Europe."

968.   Frumasi, Roventa. "Images of Women in the Post-Communist Society and Media- - Romania." *Gender and Communication Section International Association for Mass Communication Research Newsletter*. November 1995, p. 6.

969.   Kravchenko, Elena I. "Man and Woman: The View Through Advertising [The Sociological Mosaic of Erving Goffman]." *Sotsiologicheskie Issledovaniya*. 20:2

(1993), pp. 117-119.

Provides a Russian translation of an excerpt from Erving Goffman's *Gender Advertisement* (1979).

970. Marinescu, Valentina. "Does Indeed Angela Walk Along? Women and Media: The Romanian Case." *Gender and Communication Section International Association for Mass Communication Research Newsletter.* November 1995, p.3.

Reports that image of Romanian women in media of 1995 is not much different from that of the Communist era.

971. Mayne, Judith. *Kino and the Woman Question: Feminism and Soviet Silent Film.* Columbus: Ohio State University Press, 1989.

Analyzes Soviet silent pictures in terms of their complex and contradictory positioning of women in a socialist society.

972. Meznaric, Silva. "The Rapists' Progress: Ethnicity, Gender and Violence." *Revija za Sociologiju.* July-December 1993, pp. 119-129.

Claims that rape and its reportage helped define Serbian ethnicity during the violence and war in the former Yugoslavia.

973. Salzmann, Z. "Portrayal of Gender Relations in Contemporary Czech Mass Media." *East European Quarterly.* January 1990, pp. 399-407.

Studies *Vlasta*, an illustrated women's weekly; finds the magazine and other popular weeklies shied away from discussion of gender equality.

974. Versa, Dorotea. "Gender Portraying on Slovene Television." *Gender and Mass Media Newsletter.* November 1992, pp. 25-26.

Analyzes week of Slovenian national television programming; shows that women were underrepresented overall and in eight of ten thematic groups author used.

Women as Audience

975. Rondeli, L. D. "'Movie Menu' of School Children; 'Kinomenyu' Shkol'nikov." *Sotsiologicheskie Issledovaniya.* 22:3 (1995), pp. 92-94.

Surveys 1,000 Moscow students on favorite movies; among findings was that women were depicted primarily for their sexual attractiveness.

Women Practitioners

976. Alder, Otto. "Oksana Cherkassowa." In *Fantoche*, pp. 47-49. Baden: Buag, 1997.

Relates life and work of Russian animator.

977. Brunette, Peter. "Lessons from the Past: An Interview with Agnieszka Holland." *Cineaste.* 15:1 (1986), pp. 15-17.

Polish filmmaker.

978. Buchan, Suzanne. "Vera Neubauer." In *Fantoche*, pp. 44-46. Baden: Buag, 1997.

Features Czech-born animator now residing in Germany.

979.   Clark, Rhonda L. "Forgotten Voices: Women in Periodical Publishing of Late Imperial Russia, 1860-1905." Ph.D. dissertation, University of Minnesota, 1996.

980.   "Discrimination Against Women Journalists in the FRG." *Democratic Journalist.* September 1990, p. 27.

981.   Dovzhenko, Alexander. *The Poet as Filmmaker: Selected Writings.* Edited and translated by Marco Carynnyk. Cambridge, Massachusetts: MIT Press, 1973.
        Includes Soviet film collaboration with Dovzhenko's wife, Julia Solntseva.

982.   Enzenberger, Masha. "Dziga Vertov." *Screen.* 13:4 (1972-1973), pp. 90-107.
        Profiles film career of Soviet director Dziga Vertov, whose chief collaborator was his wife, Elizaveta Svilova.

983.   Gizycki, Marcin. "Splendid Artists: Central and East European Women Animators." *Animation World.* May 1996, 4 pp.
        Discusses Vera Ermolaeva (USSR), Vera Muchina (USSR), Franciszka Themerson (Poland), Halina Bielinska (Poland), Ewa Bibanska (Poland), Hermina Tyrlova (Czech Republic), and others; explains that Commmunist propaganda about the role of women in and out of animation in USSR, Poland, and Czechoslovakia did not always coincide with reality.

984.   Holloway, Ronald. "Larissa Shepitko: Her Life and Films." *Cinema India-International.* 2, 1990, pp. 12-16.
        Profiles Soviet filmmaker of post "thaw" period of 1960s and 1970s.

985.   Insdorf, Annette. "Childhood Loss Shapes a Director's Life and Art." *New York Times.* October 28, 1984, pp. H 21, H 26.
        Deals with Hungarian director Márta Mészáros.

986.   Kakurina, Nadia. "The Oppressive Power of Pity: Russian Women and Self-Censorship." *Index on Censorship.* October 1990, pp. 28-29.

987.   Korejwo, Aleksandra. "My Small Animation World." *Animation World.* May 1996, 6 pp.
        Polish animator Aleksandra Korejwo reminisces about her career and her way of working.

988.   Malyukova, Larissa. "Mairam Yusupova." *Cinemaya.* Spring 1995, p. 15.
        Features film director of Tadjikistan. Appeared first in *Iskusstvo Kino*, No. 8, 1994.

989.   Marsh, Rosalind. "Women, Politics and Society in Post-Communist Russia and the Former Soviet Union." *Europe.* 2:2 (1995), pp. 65-73.
        Argues that women have lost power in political, social, and economic realms in Gorbachev and Yeltsin Russia; states that nationalist propaganda picture women as mothers and housewives; discusses increased instances of rape and says

that mass media still tend to put the blame on female victims.

990. Martineau, Barbara H. "The Films of Márta Mészáros, the Importance of Being Banal." *Film Quarterly*. 34:1 (1980), pp. 21-27.
    Discusses work of one of the few Eastern European directors with a substantial number of films, and until the 1990s, the only Hungarian director dealing almost solely with women's issues.

991. Perkovi, Nevenka. "The Participation of Men in Comparison with Women in Belgrade Television News." Paper presented at International Association for Mass Communication Research, Bled, Yugoslavia, August 26-30, 1990.
    Presents results of content analysis of Belgrade Television programs that shows that women as journalists and as experts were "overwhelming" underrepresented; shows that even among citizens interviewed outside the studio, women were only one-quarter of those approached.

992. Petric, Vlada. "Esther Shub: Film as a Historical Discourse." In *"Show Us Life": Toward a History of Aesthetics of the Committed Documentary*, edited by Thomas Waugh, pp. 21-46. Metuchen, New Jersey: Scarecrow Press, 1984.
    Relates life and career of famous Soviet documentarist who worked in film as early as the 1920s.

993. Plakhov, Andrei. "Women Directors in the Republics." *Cinemaya*. Spring 1995, pp. 12-14.
    Discusses number of women film directors in Kirgizia, Georgia, Kazakhstan, Tadjikistan.

994. Portuges, Catherine. *Screen Memories. The Hungarian Cinema of Márta Mészáros*. Bloomington: Indiana University Press, 1993. 200 pp.
    Explores Eastern European post-Stalinist culture through study of its foremost woman film director; interviews with Mészáros and her collaborators.

995. Quart, Barbara. "Three Central European Women Revisited." *Cineaste*. 19:4 (1992), pp. 58-61.
    Includes Czech filmmaker, Vra Chytilová.

996. Reading, Anne. "The President's Men: Television, Gender and the Public Sphere in Central and Eastern Europe." In *Democracy and Communication in the New Europe: Change and Continuity in East and West*, edited by Farrel Corcoran and Paschal Preston, pp. 175-194. Cresskill, New Jersey: Hampton Press, 1995.
    Addresses the neglected research area of problems associated with the domination of men and marginalization of women in and by media of Eastern Europe; focuses on gender and public service television in the Visegard Group -- Hungary, Poland, Slovakia, and the Czech Republic.

997. Rosenberg, Karen. "Helke Misselwitz -- Women into Film in East Germany." *Women's Review of Books*. July 1990, pp. 6-7.
    Interview.

998. Shub, Esfir (Esther). *Zhizn Moya -- Kinematogra* (My Life -- Cinema). Moscow: Iskusstvo, 1972.

Relates her life as Soviet filmmaker, pioneering the second documentary in 1932, working exclusively as an editor in the 1940s-1950s.

999. Tolstaya, Tatyana and Irena Maryniak. "The Human Spirit Is Androgynous." *Index on Censorship.* October 1990, pp. 29-30.

In Soviet Union.

1000. Vertov, Dziga. *Statii, Dnevniki, Zamysly.* Moscow: Iskusstvo, 1966.

Relates filmmaking of leading Soviet director Dziga Vertov, whose main collaborator was his wife, Elizaveta Svilova.

1001. Vronskaya, Jeanne. *Young Soviet Film Makers.* London: Allen and Unwin, 1972.

Includes women, Larissa Shepitko among them.

1002. Wasielewska, Edyta. "Magister od Komiksów." *D/C Magazyn.* No. 15 (77), 1996, pp. 10-14.

Interviews Polish comics artist, Alexandra Czubek, who prefers a very artistic style.

1003. "Wywiadownia: Komiks Trzeba Miec w Genach." *AQQ.* No. 7, 1995, p. 36.

Profiles Polish woman cartoonist, Aleksandra Czubek.

Women's Media

1004. Gyertyan, Ervin. "Look Back to Compassion: Mészáros: *Napló Gyermekeimnek* (Diary for My Children); Janos Xantus: *Eszkimo Asszony Fazik* (Eskimo Woman Feels Cold). "*New Hungarian Quarterly.* Winter 1984, pp. 217-222.

Analyzes one of the 17 films of Hungarian director Márta Mészáros.

1005. Nenandic, Natalie. "Yugoslav Feminists Found Newspaper." *Off Our Backs.* July 1991, pp. 10-11.

Called *Kareta.*

1006. Tonscheidt, Sabine. *Frauenzeitschriften am Ende? Ostdeutsche Frauenpresse vor und nach der Wende 1989* (Women's Magazines at the End? East German Women's Press Before and After the Changes of 1989). Munster: Lit Verlag, 1996. 416 pp.

Analyzes changes after unification of women's journal market of former German Democratic Republic; gives reason for demise of all eleven magazines.

WESTERN EUROPE

General Studies

1007. Angerer, Marie-Luise. "Prolog. Gender (Relations) Als Soziale und Denk-

Kategorie." *Medien Journal*. 16:3 (1992), pp. 116-121.

1008. Angerer, Marie-Luise. "'Über Ängstliche und Angstvolle'. Weibliche und Männliche Arbeitnehmer in der Öffentlichkeit." *Medien Journal*. 16:3 (1992), pp. 161-166.

1009. ANISS. "Projectgruppe: 'Looking Good and Feeling Great.' Methodische Anmerkungen zur Bildanalyse." *Medien Journal*. 16:3 (1992), pp. 153-156.

1010. Bernold, Monika. "'Let's Talk About Clips': Feministische Analysen von MTV. Ein Blick auf die Anglo-Amerikanische Diskussion." *Medien Journal*. 16:3 (1992), pp. 133-140.

1011. Bernold, Monika and Andrea Ellmeier. "'Zur Geschichte des Senders'. Ein Projektbericht." *Medien Journal*. 16:3 (1992), pp. 176-178.

1012. Bosshart, Louis, ed. *Femmes et Médias*. Fribourg, Switzerland: Editions Universitaires Fribourg Suisse, 1991. 200 pp.
   Deals with women and media in Switzerland with chapters by Adrienne Corboud Fumagalli, "La Situation des Femmes Journalistes en Suisse"; Jean-Charles Obergfell-Abreu, "La Presse Féminine"; Janice Ryskiewic, "Magazines Féminins"; Louis Bosshart, "Les Mass-media Jugés par les Associations Féminines Suisses"; and "Femmes et Mass-media. Prise de Position de la Commission Fédérale Pour les Féminines Questions."

1013 Bosshart, Louis, ed. *Frauen und Massenmedien in der Schweiz*. Aarau: Verlag Sauerländer, 1988. 174 pp.
   Provides information on women and mass media of Switzerland through chapters by Adrienne Corboud, "Zur Berufssituation der Schweizer Journalistinnen"; Pia Pedrazzini, "Erfolgreiche Karrieren: Top-Journalistinnen im Gespräch"; Louis Bosshart, "Massenmedien im Urteil der Frauenverbände"; Louis Bosshart, Martina Lichtsteiner, Irene Lorenz, and Beatrice Zenzünen, "Frauen in der Medienrealität des Deutschschweizerischen Fernsehens"; Louis Bosshart and Pascale Gmür, "Strukturen Männlicher und Weiblicher Werte in Partnerschaftsanzeigen und Nekrologen"; Matthias F. Steinmann and Erwin Weibel, "Frauen als Rezipientinnen. Eine Studie des SRG-Forschungsdienstes"; Othmar Baeriswyl, "Die Deutschschweitzerische Leserin: Typisch Weibliches Leseverhalten?" and Eidgenössische Kommission für Frauenfragen, "Frauen und Massenmedien. Eine Stellungnahme der Eidgenössischen Kommission für Frauenfragen."

1014. Briggs, Asa. "The BBC -- From Maiden Aunt to Sexy Upstart." *Media Studies Journal*. Summer 1993, pp. 113-122.

1015. Carlsson, Ulla. "Köns--och Kvinnoperspektiv i Svensk Masskommunikations-forskning." (Sex and Female Perspectives in Swedish Mass Communication Research). In *Kvinnoperspektiv Pa Masskommunikationsforskningen*. Jämfo: Delegationen för Jämställdhetsforskning, Stockholm, 1991.
   States that only two percent of all entries in Nordicom's data base for 1975-1989 relate to research on women and media.

1016. Carlsson, Ulla, ed. *Nordisk Forskning om Kvinnor och Medier*. Göteborg: Nordicom, Göteborgs Universitet, 1993.

Includes Ulla Abrahamsson, "När Kvinnor Ser Pa TV" (When Women Watch Television); Kirsten Drotner, "Media Ethnography: An Other Story"; Lisbeth R. Egsmose, "Medvind og Modvind i TV -- Karrieremuligheder for Kvindelige Medieprofessionelle; Danmark og England" (Headwinds and Tailwinds in TV: Career Opportunities for Female Media Professionals in Denmark and England); Elisabeth Eide, "Journalisme og Enkjønnet Presentasjon" (Journalism and Unisexual Presentation); Britt Hultén, "Kön, Kontext och Gestaltning -- Från 30-Tan Till 90-Tal" (Gender, Context and Representation -- From the 1930s to the 1990s); Anne Jerslev, "Tilskuerbegrebet i den Feministiske Psykosemiotik" (The Concept of Spectator in Feministic Psycho-Semiotics); Tone K. Kolbjørnsen, "Kjonn og Filmopplevelse: En Introduksjon til Psykoanalytisk og Feministisk Filmteori" (Gender and Reception of Films: An Introduction to Psychoanalytical and Feministic Film Theory); Karin Nordberg, "Bakslag och Barrikader. Historia och Kön i Medieforskningen" (Reverses and Barricades: History and Gender in Mass Media Research); Iriis Ruoho, "Gender on Television Screen and in Audience: Family Serial as a Technology of Gender"; Tytti Soila, "Suzanne Osten som Filmregissör. En Studie i Kvinnlig Subjekställning och Modernitet" (Suzanne Osten, Film Director: A Study in Female Subject Status and Modernity); Anita Werner, "Likestilling Pa Skjermen: Hva Mener Publikum?" (Equality on the Screen: What Does the Audience Think of It?).

1017. Comas i Marine, Anna, Xavier Coller i Porta, Andrés Pérez Correa, and Joseba Ruiz Montiel. *Mujer y Medios de Comunicacion en España* (Woman and Communication Media in Spain). Study conducted for the Institute of the Woman, Madrid, 1988.

1018. Coopman, Jeremy. "BBC: Now a Woman's World?" *Variety*. May 13, 1991, p. 62.

1019. D. Derman, N. Dakovic, and Ross K., eds. *Gender and Media*. Ankara: Med-Campus, 1996.

1020. Flitterman-Lewis, Sandy. *To Desire Differently: Feminism and the French Cinema*. Urbana: University of Illinois Press, 1990.

Studies French woman filmmakers Germaine Dulac (1920s), Marie Epstein (1930s), and Agnes Varda (1960s); merges historical analysis with concerns of feminist film theory. Expanded paperback edition published by Columbia University Press, 1996.

1021. Fröhlich, Romy and Christine Holtz-Bacha, with Jutte Velte. *Frauen und Medien: Eine Synopse der Deutschen Forschung* (Women and Media: A Synopsis of German Research). Opladen: Westdeutscher Verlag, 1995. 320 pp.

Summarizes recent German research in six chapters -- overview, measures to gain equal status in public broadcasting stations, education and training, media for women, representation of women in the media, differences in reception and effects between men and women.

1022. Galán Quintanilla, María Antonia. "La Mujer a Través de la Información en la Il República Española" (Woman Through the News in the Second Spanish Republic). Ph.D. dissertation, Universidad Complutense de Madrid, Facultad de Ciencias de la Información, 1980.

1023. García de León, María Antonia. "Hombres y Mujeres en la Esfera Pública, El Caso de la Participación en los Debates Televisivos" (Men and Women in the Public Sphere, The Case of Participation in Televised Debates). In *La Flotante Identidad Sexual . La Identidad del Género en la Vida Cotidiana de la Juventud*, edited by Félix Ortega, et. al., pp. 119-132. Madrid: Dirección General de la Mujer de la Comunidad de Madrid - Instituto de Investigaciones Feministas - UCM, 1993.

1024. Halonen, Irma K. "Kvinnorna och Nyhetsoffentligheten" (Women and the *Öffentlichkeit* of the News). Paper presented to the IX Conference of Nordic Mass Communication Researchers, Borgholm, Sweden, August 20-23, 1989.

1025. Hipfl, Brigitte. "'Die Frau Möge Schweigen...' Frauenrolle und Kommunikationsverhalten." *Communications*. 14:3 (1988), pp. 39-52.

 Reflects "typical" female and male notions in various fields of communication -- interpersonal, mass media, advertising; discusses consequences of images of women in mass media and women's working conditions in media, primarily in Germany.

1026. Hoffmann, Lois W. *Frauenrollen, Kommunikation und Beruf.* Munich: K.G. Saur, 1983.

1027. Holtz-Bacha, Christina, ed. "Frauen und Massenmedien" series. Bochum: Universitätsverlag Dr N. Brockmeyer, various dates.

 Includes following volumes: Romy Fröhlich, ed. *Der Andere Blick. Aktuelles zur Massenkommunikation aus Weiblicher Sicht*, 1992; Romy Fröhlich and Christina Holtz-Bacha. *Frauen und Massenkommunikation.*

1028. Horn, Imme and Christiane Nolting. *Rollenbild der Frau in Europäischen Fernschprogrammen.* Bericht über Inhaltsanalytische Untersuchungsergebnisse, ZDF. Mainz: ZDF, 1983.

1029. Kleberg, Madeleine. "En Utländsk Forknings ö Versikt Kvinnoperspektiv I Masskommunikationsforskningen" (Female Perspectives in Mass Communication Research). In *Kvinnoperspektiv Pa Masskommunikationsforskningen*. Stockholm: Delegationen för Jämställdhetsforskning, 1991.

1030. Kleberg, Madeleine. "Kvinnor och Nyheter Förenklad Teori i Praktiken" (Women and News). *Kvinnovetenskaplig Tidskript*. 9:3 (1993), pp. 40-48.

1031. Knight, Julia. *Women and the New German Cinema.* London: Verso, 1992.

1032. *Kvinner i Film, TV og Reklame*. Rapport fra et Seminar 1992. Oslo: Senter for Kvinneforskning, Universiteteti Oslo, 1992.

Includes Tone K. Kolbjørnsen, "Estetikk, Politikk og Erfaring. Om Vibeke Løkkebergs Filmer" (Aesthetics, Politics and Experience: The Films of Vibeke Løkkeberg); Marit Myrstad, "Helt og Heltinne i to Nasjonale Melodrams); Kathrine Skretting, "Sex i Filmer Vist Pa Kino i Norge" (Sex in the Films of the Sixties: Forbidden and Accepted Forms of Womanhood in the Films Shown in Norwegian Cinemas).

1033. Löfgren, Monìca. "Kvinnor i Journalistiken." In *I Kvinnoperspektiv på Masskommunikationsforskningen*, pp. 35-49. Stockholm: JAMFO, Report No. 22, 1991.

1034. Lummerding, Susanne. "A Movie without the Picture." *Medien Journal*. 16:3 (1992), pp. 157-160.

1035. *Marketing*.

A sampling of articles includes: Sean Brierley, "Motivator Caroline Marland of the Guardian," June 15, 1989, p. 32; Hashi Syedain, "Female Touch Works in the Recession," February 27, 1992, pp. 21-22; "Magazine Focus: Women's Titles -- Conde Nast Glossies Are in Vogue," p. SS8, "Magazine Focus: Women's Titles -- Marie Claire Finds Her True Niche," p. SS8, "Magazine Focus: Women's Titles -- National Magazines Religiously Follows [sic] a Branded Philosophy," p. SS8; "Magazine Focus: Women's Titles -- Bullish EMAP Discovers a New Woman," p. SS8, "Magazine Focus: Women's Titles -- New Rival Drops in To Say Hello," p. SS7, and "Magazine Focus: Women's Titles -- Leaner and Fitter IPC Uses Its Clout To Woo Clients From TV," p. SS7, all February 25, 1993; "Personnel: EMAP Promotes Executives," May 13, 1993, p. 10; "Brand Creation: Title Woos the 40-Plus Woman," June 24, 1993, p. 15; "Guess Who! To Launch," July 1, 1993, p. 12; "Guardian Joins in French Foray," p. 19, and Simon Marquis, "Media Watch: Home Truths," p. 18, both October 14, 1993; Claire Beale, "Women's Titles Get Ad Tracking," October 21, 1993, p. 21; "UK Living Finds a 'Pure' Audience," p. 31, "Competition and the Group Sale," p. 31, and Andy Fry, "Targeting Women Through Media: This Is a Woman's World," pp. 29-31, all November 25, 1993; "Media Watch: Women's Titles," March 17, 1994, p. 10; "Women's Watch: Women's Titles," June 23, 1994, p. 11; Ruth Nicholas, "Lil-lets Sponsor 'Strong Women,'" June 30, 1994, p. 6; Conor Dignam, "Ad Push for New-Look Telegraph Magazine," September 8, 1994, p. 12; "Sex Tales Fail To Arouse Interest," December 15, 1994, p. 17; "Women's Weeklies," February 23, 1995, p. 11.

1036. Miscuglio, Annabella and Rony Daopoulo, eds. *Kinomato: La Donna nel Cinema*. Bari: Dedalo Libri, 1980.

Women and cinema in Italy.

1037. Mühleisen, Wencke. *Feministisk Filmteori og Praksis* (Feminist Film Theory and Praxis). Lecture to Seminar on Gender Theory and the Public Sphere, Institutt for

Samfunnsforskning, Oslo, March 1992.

1038. Neverla, Irene. "Von der Frauenforschung zur Geschlechterforschung. Ziemlich am Rande und Nicht zu Übersehen." *Medien Journal.* 16:3 (1992), pp. 126-133.

1039. Pedersen, Vibeke. "Kvin den som Skoerm -- en Visuel Konstruktion af Køn i Klassisk Film og Moderne TV" (Woman as a Screen: A Visual Construction of Gender in Classic Film and Contemporary Television). Dissertation, University of Copenhagen, 1993.

  Treats relationship between visual media and femininity in different periods and media.

1040. Petrie, Duncan, ed. *Inside Stories.* London: British Fim Institute, 1997. 272 pp.
  Major players in British cinema look at the present state and significance of the industry; includes contributions by Katrin Cartlidge, Pam Engel, and others.

1041. Rosenberger, Sieglinde. "Feminism and Multiculturalism. Gedanken zur 'Verschiedenheit.'" *Medien Journal.* 16:3 (1992), pp. 171-176.

1042. Savolainen, Tarja and Henrika Zilliacus-Tikkanen. "Women in Finnish Broadcasting." *Gender and Mass Media Newsletter.* November 1992, p. 32.
  Combines two studies, published in a 40-page publication of the Finnish National Commission for Unesco 61.

1043. Schmerl, Christiane. *Das Frauen -- und Mädchenbild in den Medien.* Opladen: Alltag und Biografie von Mädchen, Bd. 5, 1984.

1044. Schmerl, Christiane, ed. *In Die Presse Geraten: Darstellung von Frauen in der Presse und Frauenarbeit in den Medien.* Cologne: Böhlau Verlag, 1985.
  Includes her own "Die Öffentlische Inszenierung der Geschlechter-charaktere: Berichterstattung über Frauen und Männer in der Deutschen Presse"; Dane Archer, Bonita Iritani, Debra Kimes, and Michael Barrios, "Männer-Köpfe, Frauen-Körper: Studien zur Unterschiedlichen Abbildung von Frauen und Männern auf Pressefotos," and others.

1045. Silberman, Marc. "Film and Feminism in Germany Today." *Jump Cut.* July 1982, pp. 41-53.
  One of several reports by author (all in *Jump Cut*) on status of German film and women: "German Film Women" (February 1984, pp. 49-64) and "German Women's Film Culture" (March 1985, pp. 63-69).

1046. Stacey, Jackie S. Franklin, and C. Lury. *Off Centre. Feminism and Cultural Studies.* London: Unwin Hyman, 1991. 220 pp.
  Divided into sections on "Representation and Identity," "Science and Technology," and "Thatcherism and the Enterprise Culture"; includes some chapters on media such as popular magazines and books; predominantly about England.

1047. Vallauri, Carlo. "La Politique de l'Emploi dans les Organismes des Médias et l'Égalité entre les Femmes et les Hommes." In *Actes du Séminaire sur la Contribution des Médias à la Promotion de l'Égalité entre les Femmes et les Hommes*, pp. 44-104, edited by Conseil de l'Europe. Strasbourg: Counseil de l'Europe, 1984.

1048. Van Zoonen, Liesbet. "A Professional, Unreliable, Heroic Marionette (M/F). Structure, Agency and Subjectivity in Contemporary Journalism." *European Journal of Cultural Studies*. January 1998, pp. 123-143.

        Categorizes journalism along two dimensions that pervade the field -- gender and goals; sections on gender, audience-feminine, and institutional feminine, with some emphasis on Netherlands.

1049. Van Zoonen, Liebeth. "The Women's Movement and the Media: Constructing a Public Identity." *European Journal of Cultural Studies*. December 1992, pp. 453-476.

        Explores the interaction between the media and the women's movement in the Netherlands when the movement was resurrected in the late 1960s, early 1970s.

1050. Van Zoonen, Liesbet and Wolfgang Donsbach. "Professional Values and Gender in British and German Journalism." Paper presented at International Communication Association, New Orleans, Louisiana, May 1988.

1051. Werner, Anita. "The Feminine Perspective in Nordic Media Research." *Nordicom Review*. No. 1, 1994, pp. 35-50.

        Claims research on women and media on the "ascendant"; reviews a body of literature and finds great variety in topics studied, although much of the work fails to take account of other Nordic research; discussess themes of women and news reporting, women and men as receivers of media, women and fiction in the media, historical dimension, and differences between women's roles in news and fiction.

1052. Werner, Anita. "Women and Men as Producers and Receivers of Discussion Programs on Television." *Gender and Mass Media Newsletter*. November 1992, pp. 7-8.

        Gives overview of possible changes in the types of issues in television discussion programs, 1960-1991, the editorial process in search of a relationship between gender distribution among editors/journalists and program characteristics; deals with Norwegian television.

1053. Wyss, Laure, Eva Eggli, and Verena Grendi. *Die Frau in den Massenmedien*. Bern: 1979.

        Women and mass media of Switzerland.

1054. Zilliacus-Tikkanen, Henrika. *Kvinnojournalistikens Principer, Hinder och Möjligheteren Forskningsplan* (Journalism of, by and for Women: Principles,

Obstacles and Opportunities. A Research Outline). Trondheim: Nordiska Konferensen för Masskommunikationsforskning, 1993.

Historical Studies

1055. Alberti, Johanna. "The Turn of the Tide: Sexuality and Politics, 1928-1931." *Women's History Review*. June 1994, pp. 169-190.
Examines how achievement of women's suffrage in Great Britain was constructed in the weekly newspaper, *Time & Tide*, 1928-1931.

1056. Brummett, Palmira. "Dogs, Women, Cholera and Other Menaces in the Streets: Cartoon Satire in the Ottoman Revolutionary Press, 1908-1911." *International Journal of Middle East Studies*. November 1995, pp. 433-460.
Describes the important role of satire and cartoons in the Young Turk Revolution of 1908, showing how dogs, women, and plague in the streets were drawn to represent the problems that could rise during and after the revolution.

1057. Clark, Anna. "Queen Carolina and the Sexual Politics of Popular Culture in London, 1820." *Representations*. Summer 1990, pp. 47-68.
Adopted from her book *Women's Silence, Men's Violence: Sexual Politics in England, 1770-1845* (London, 1987).

1058. De Nora, Tia. "Configuring Sex, Via Botany, Via Opera in Early Modern Europe: Media Crossover in the Cultural Elaboration of Gender, Nature, and Bourgeois Society in 1870s Vienna." Paper presented at American Sociological Association, 1995.
Shows how during the 1780s in Vienna, dictums concerning the nature of woman and the social shape of love were reinforced in a variety of cultural media, including opera.

1059. Derman, Deniz. "Türk Sinemasinda Kadin 1920-1990" (The Woman in Turkish Cinema, 1920-1990). *Historical Journal of Film, Radio and Television*. June 1996, pp. 283-285.
Reviews Fetay Soykan's book of above title. See Soykan entry.

1060. Dimitrova, Anelia K. "Constructing the Image: Gender in the 'Bundles for Britain' Public Relations Campaign, 1940-1942." Ph.D. dissertation, University of Missouri, 1996.

1061. Doy, Gen. *Women and Visual Culture in Nineteenth-Century France 1800-1852*. London: Cassell Academic, 1998. 256 pp.
Examines the relationship of gender, class, and race to visual culture in early nineteenth-century France; includes discussion of female art critics and photographers.

1062. Farwell, Beatrice. *French Popular Lithographic Imagery, 1815-1870, Volume II*. Chicago: University of Chicago Press, 1995. 72 pp.
Collects more than 300 lithographs showing women as passive, erotic objects.

1063. Flitterman-Lewis, Sandy. "Theorizing the 'Feminine,' Women as the Figure of Desire in *The Seashell and the Clergyman*." *Wide Angle*. 6:3 (1984), pp. 32-39.
       Discusses 1927 French film by Germaine Dulac.

1064. Freist, Dagmar. "The King's Crown Is the Whore of Babylon: Politics, Gender and Communication in Mid-Seventeenth Century England." *Gender and History*. November 1995, pp. 457-472.

1065. Frieden, Sandra, Richard W. McCormick, Vibeke R. Petersen, and Laurie M. Vogelsang, eds. *Gender and German Cinema: Feminist Interventions Volume II: German Film History / German History of Film*. Oxford: Berg, 1993. 362 pp.

1066. Gilman, Sander L. "'I'm Down on Whores': Race and Gender in Victorian London." In *Anatomy of Racism*, edited by David T. Goldberg, pp. 146-170. Minneapolis: University of Minnesota Press, 1990.
       Shows how London press portrayed prostitute victims of the Jack the Ripper murders.

1067. Gledhill, Christine and Gillian Swanson, eds. *Nationalising Femininity: Culture, Sexuality and Cinema in World War Two Britain*. Manchester: Manchester University Press, 1996. 288 pp.
       Explores how the war changed notions of femininity, sexual difference, and class through case studies of cinema, women's magazines, government pamphlets, broadcasting, and fashion.

1068. Goss, Maureen F. T. "Hanna Reitsch: Shaping the Image of a Third Reich Heroine." Ph.D. dissertation, Boston University, 1996.

1069. Gullace, Nicoletta F. "Women and the Ideology of War Recruitment, Propaganda, and the Mobilization of Public Opinion in Britain, 1914-1918." Ph.D. dissertation, University of California-Berkeley, 1993.

1070. Hacker, Hanna. "Mostly, a Soldier Is Not a Woman. Gender Constructions in the Military Field." *Österreichische Zeitschrift für Soziologie*. 20:2 (1995), pp. 45-63.
       Questions gender relations and the performance of gender in the Austro-Hungarian monarchy during World War I; states women's role in the war disrupted several categories relevant to warfare; contends that the military and media worked to keep women involved in the war invisible.

1071. Hayward, Susan. "A History of French Cinema: 1895-1991: Pioneering Filmmakers (Guy, Dulac, Varda) and Their Heritage." *Paragraph*. March 1992, pp. 19-37.
       Profiles French pioneers of moviemaking, Alice Guy, Germaine Dulac, and Agnes Varda.

1072. Heineman, Elizabeth. "The Hour of the Woman: Memories of Germany's 'Crisis Years' and West German National Identity." *American Historical Review*. April

1996, pp. 354-395.

Investigates portrayal of German women in German media during the post-World War II, American occupation -- from fraternizers to rebuilders of the nation and family.

1073. Hopewell, John. *Out of the Past: Spanish Cinema After Franco*. London: British Film Institute, 1986.

Includes women in film.

1074. Hunt, Felicity. "Opportunities Lost and Gained: Mechanization and Women's Work in the London Bookbinding and Printing Trades." In *Unequal Opportunities: Women's Employment in England 1800-1918*, edited by A. V. John. Oxford: Blackwell, 1986.

1075. Hunt, Lynn, ed. *The Invention of Pornography: Obscenity and the Origins of Modernity, 1500-1800*. New York: Zone, 1993. 411 pp.

Treats pornography historically through Restoration and Enlightenment England, the French Revolution, Renaissance Italy, and the Dutch Republic of the 17th and 18th centuries.

1076. Knelman, J. "She Loves Me, She Loves Me Not: Trends in the Victorian Marriage Market." *Journal of Communication Inquiry*. Winter 1994, pp. 80-94.

Uses letters to the editor of London's *Daily Telegraph* to identify psychological forces behind the falling marriage rate in England during the last half of the nineteenth century; shows that women and men seriously weighed the advantages and disadvantages of marriage.

1077. Kundanis, Rose M. "'Baby Riots' and 'Eight-Hour Orphans': A Comparison of the Images of Child Care in Britain and U.S. Popular Magazines During World War II." *Women Studies International Forum*. May-June 1996, pp. 239-251.

Discusses British magazine depictions of women marching to demand child care in "baby riots" and U.S. magazine portrayals of babies as "eight-hour orphans" in all-day centers.

1078. Lant, Antonia. "The Female Spy: Gender and Nationality in World War II British Film." In *Resisting Images: Essays on Cinema and History*, edited by Robert Sklar and Charles Musser. Philadelphia, Pennsylvania: Temple University Press, 1990. 320 pp.

1079. McCormick, Richard W. "From *Caligari* to Dietrich: Sexual, Social, and Cinematic Discourses in Weimar Film." *Signs*. Spring 1993, pp. 640-668.

States Weimar Republic was characterized by the emergence of a "new woman" who exercised unprecedented forms of sexual and social autonomy and this was reflected in cinema.

1080. Morgan, Cheryl A. "Writing Women in (to) the July Monarchy Press: Fashion, Feminism, and the *Feuilleton*." Ph.D. dissertation, Columbia University, 1993.

1081. Morrissey, Ann. *Daumier on Women: The Lithographs*. Exhibition catalogue. Los

Angeles: University Art Galleries, University of Southern California, 1982.

1082. Nordberg, Karin. "In the Beginning Was Uncle Sven: Women's Voice and the Feminine Perspective in Swedish Radio 1925-1990." *Gender and Mass Media Newsletter*. November 1991, pp. 18-20.

Focuses on Swedish radio programs explicitly intended for female audiences from the 1930s forward.

1083. Perinat, Adolfo and María Isabel Marrades. *Mujer, Prensa y Sociedad en España, 1800-1939* (Woman, Press and Society in Spain, 1800-1939). Madrid: Centro de Investigaciones Sociológicas, 1980.

1084. Pickering-lazzi, Robin. *Unspeakable Women: Selected Short Stories Written by Italian Women During Fascism*. New York: Feminist Press, 1993. 140 pp.

Culls from the cultural pages of three Italian daily newspapers of the 1920s and 1930s, 16 short stories written by women such as Grazia Deledda, Maddalena Crispolit, Ada Negri, Clarice Tartufari, and others.

1085. Pinkus, Karen. *Bodily Regimes: Italian Advertising under Fascism*. Minneapolis: University of Minnesota Press, 1995. 288 pp.

Looks at the use and manipulation of the body in advertising under Italian fascism; focuses on the intertwined relations of race, gender, and class.

1086. Powell, Kirsten and Elizabeth C. Childs. *Femmes d'Esprit: Women in Daumier's Caricature*. Hanover and London: University Press of New England, 1990. 146 pp.

Catalogue of an exhibition held at Christian A. Johnson Memorial Gallery, Middlebury College, Middlebury, Vermont, June 16 - July 15, 1990.

1087. Rentmeister, Cäcilia. "Daumier und das Hässliche Geschlecht." In *Honoré Daumier und die Ungelösten Probleme der Bürgerlichen Gesellschaft*. Exhibition catalogue. Berlin: Neue Gesellschaft für Bildende Kunst for the Schloss Charlottenburg, 1974.

1088. Roberts-Jones, Philippe. "Les Femmes dans l'Oeuvre Lithographique de Daumier." *Médecine de France*. 23 (1951), pp. 29-32.

1089. Schlüpmann, Heide. "Melodrama and Social Drama in the Early German Cinema." *Camera Obscura*. January 1990, pp. 73-90.

Analyzes melodrama and social drama in early German film; claims melodrama was seen as an attempt to meet the theatrical standards of the middle class and social drama allowed greater scope for a "female narrative perspective" encompassing "the representation of female agency...as well as narrative strategies which displaced female eroticism into certain suspense-generating mechanisms."

1090. Tidcombe, Marianne. *Women Bookbinders. 1800-1920*. New Castle and London: Oak Knoll Press and The British Library, 1996. 240 pp.

States that the number of women bookbinders increased dramatically; discusses Sarah Prideaux, Katherine Adams, Sybil Pye, as well as others.

1091. Von Ankum, Katharina, ed. *Women in the Metropolis: Gender and Modernity in Weimar Culture*. Berkeley: University of California Press, 1997. 264 pp.

Provides introduction to women's experiences of modernism and urbanization in Weimar Germany; treats classic films such as "Metropolis" and "Berlin: Symphony of a Great City" and other forms of mass culture.

1092. Winship, Janice. "Nation Before Family: *Woman*, the National Home Weekly, 1945-1953." In *Formations of Nation and People*. London: Routledge & Kegan Paul, 1984.

1093. Winship, Janice. "Woman Becomes an 'Individual' -- Femininity and Consumption in Women's Magazines 1954-69." Birmingham, England: University of Birmingham, Centre for Contemporary Cultural Studies, Stencilled Paper No. 65, 1981.

1094. Wollstein, Hans J. *Strangers in Hollywood: The History of Scandinavian Actors in American Films from 1910 to World War II*. Metuchen, New Jersey: Scarecrow Press, 1994. 420 pp.

Includes Greta Garbo, Sonja Henie, Anna Q. Nilsson, Tula Belle, and Sadie Lindblom.

Images of Women

1095. Abrahamsson, Ulla B. "Sweden: TV-Channels for Women and Men?" *Gender and Mass Media Newsletter*. November 1992, pp. 29-31.

Reports on a replicative study carried out in 1992 by the Equality Committee of Swedish Television to see how it fared in representation of women.

1096. Advertising Standards Authority. *Herself Appraised*. London: Advertising Standards Authority, 1990.

States that in the United Kingdom, three-fourths of the public agreed with the statement, "Advertising can help establish unrealistic views of the way women should look and behave."

1097. Alankus-Kural, Sevda. "The Media, Hegemony and Representation of the Other in Turkey." *Toplum ve Bilim* (Society and Science). 67 (1995), pp. 76-110.

Examines the bias of Turkish mainstream mass media in representing the "other" in Turkish society, particularly the veiled women and Kurds.

1098. Alexander, Sue. "Gender Bias in British Television Coverage of Major Athletic Championships." *Women's Studies International Forum*. November-December 1994, pp. 647-654.

Discusses the relative invisibility of women athletes on British television during the 1991 World Athletic Championships and 1992 Summer Olympic Games.

1099. Allen, Louise. *The Lesbian Idol: Martina, kd and the Consumption of Masculinity.* London: Cassell Academic, 1997. 192 pp.

Examines the consumption of lesbian idols kd lang and Martina Navratilova by their many lesbian fans; deals with how they are represented in mainstream media.

1100. Amir, Gisele. "Bodily Intimacy and Advertising Discourse; Intimite Corporelle et Discours Publicitaire." *Communications.* 56 (1993), pp. 191-206.

Analyzes advertisements for feminine hygiene products appearing in seven French women's magazines, 1975-1990; notes gradual move away from traditional negative attitudes toward menstruation in Western culture.

1101. Anderson, Karen. "Are Women Changing the Balance of the News Agenda?" *Inter Media.* August/September 1994.

1102. Andrén, Gunnar. "Kön, Kultur, Samhälle" (Gender, Culture, Society). In *Folket i TV Demografi och Social Struktur i Televisionens Innehåll.* MASS 14. Stockholms Universitet, 1989.

1103. Angerer, Marie-Luise, Irene Nierhaus, Alfred Smudits, and Judith Schöbel. "Shifts in the Representation of Female and Male Bodies on Magazine-Covers from 1955-1985." *Gender and Mass Media Newsletter.* November 1991, p. 23.

Analyzes 1,300 magazine covers of Australian and West German magazines, 1950-1985; looks at media and public, sexuality, women's movement, ways of gender-specific representation, and morality.

1104. Angerer, Marie-Luise and Karin Stockinger. "Feministische Theorien in der Medien-und Komunikationswissenschaft." *Medien Journal.* 16:3 (1992), pp. 121-125.

1105. Apfelbaum, Erika. "Women and Men in Broadcasting Equality in the 90's." *Gender and Mass Media Newsletter.* March 1991, pp. 13-15.

Reports on conference of that title, sponsored by the European Commission and European Broadcasting Union, held in Athens, Greece, November 7-10, 1990; includes keynote speech by Hedy D'Ancona, main conclusions, proposals.

1106. Arbesú, Faustino R. "Modesty Blaise Mujer Anti-007." *El Comercio* (Barcelona). February 10, 1973.

Deals with British female comic strip character.

1107. Arbesú, Faustino R. "Nuevo Tipo de Heroína en el Comic: Barbarella-Bardot." *El Comercio* (Barcelona). March 14, 1974.

Studies the heroine in comics, specifically the character, "Barbarella."

1108. Arthurs, Jane and Jean Grimshaw, eds. *Women's Bodies: Cultural Representations and Identity.* London: Cassell Academic, 1997. 256 pp.

Presents new perspectives on how women's bodies are viewed and absorbed into popular culture; includes Clarissa Smith's comparison of the soft porn magazine *For Women* with *Cosmopolitan*.

1109. Arvidsson, Adam. "From Housewife to Authentically Human: Articles and Advertisements in Vecko Revyn 1942-1994." *Sociologisk Forkning.* 33:4 (1996), pp. 16-35.

Analyzes advertising and articles on love, sexuality, and the body in the Swedish magazine for young women, *Vecko Revyn*; finds in 1940-1950s, emphasis was on preparing young women for marriage, in the 1960s and 1970s, on the need for women to express their individuality, and in the 1980s-1990s, on young women's self-discovery. Also in *Recherches Sociologiques* (27:2, 1996, pp. 99-114).

1110. Baca Lagos, Vicente. "Public Communication and Gender: Research in Spain." *Communication Research Trends.* 15:3 (1995), pp. 10-19.

Deals with the encounter between social policies for the promotion of the equality of women and communication policies in UNESCO, the European Community, and Spain; divides research into social representations of women, uses of media and their repercussions on women, feminine employment.

1111. Balaguer Callejón, María Luisa. *La Mujer y los Medios de Comunicación de Masas: el Caso de la Publicidad en Televisión* (Woman and the Mass Communication Media: The Case of Advertising on Television). Málaga: Alianza Editorial, 1985.

1112. Balla, P. and G. Martinet. "Aprirsi con Amore: Ovvero Tutto Quello Che Si Vede Sul Sesso in Formato Televisivo." *Segno Cinema.* January 1985.

In Italy.

1113. Bell, Christine and Marie Fox. "Telling Stories of Women Who Kill." *Social and Legal Studies.* December 1996, pp. 471-494.

Examines limited literature on female killers through case study of a Northern Ireland woman who murdered her lover's wife; claims media created stock stories around themes of Lady Macbeth or "Fatal Attraction" model or the shy Northern Irish virgin duped by the English soldier.

1114. Blain, N. and R. Cere. "Dangerous Television: The *TV a Luci Rosse* Phenomenon." *Media, Culture and Society.* July 1995, pp. 483-498.

Addresses confusing Italian term meaning display of female body and concerns the proposition that Italian "red light" television constitutes a "transgressive" or "radical" form.

1115. Boëthius, Gunilla. *En Vecka med Rapport och Aktuellt -- Betraktande ur Jämställdhetssynpunkt* (One Week with the News Desks of SVT1 and SVT2 -- Viewed from the Perspective of Gender Equality). Stockholm: Swedish Television, Equality Group, 1983.

1116. Bosshart, Louis, et al. "Femmes et Questions Féminines dans les Mass Media." In

La Situation de la Femme en Suisse. 4ème Partie: Politique au Féminin. Rapport de la Commission Fédérale pour les Questions Féminines. Berne: 1984.

Women and mass media of Switzerland.

1117. Bourne, Stephen. *Brief Encounters: Lesbians and Gays in British Cinema 1930-1971.* London: Cassell Academic, 1996. 288 pp.

Close reading of mid-twentieth century British films for lesbian and gay images; hones in on the groundbreaking "victim" of 1961.

1118. Broadcasting Standards Council. *Television Advertising and Sex Role Stereotyping: A Content Analysis.* London: Broadcasting Standards Council, 1990.

Analyzes 500 British television advertisements in 1990; concludes "the patterns which emerge in this study are robust and lend strong support to the concern that women exist in what is essentially a man's world."

1119. Brosius, H.-B., N. Mundorf, and J. F. Staab. "The Depiction of Sex Roles in American and German Magazine Advertisements." *International Journal of Public Opinion Research.* Winter 1991, pp. 366-383.

Provides an analysis of depicted sex roles in *Time* and *Stern*, 1969-1988; finds considerable change in explicit depictions of male and female roles but implicit presentations remained consistent during the 20 years.

1120. Brosius, H.-B., J. B. Weaver, and J. F. Staab. "Exploring the Social and Sexual 'Reality' of Contemporary Pornography." *Journal of Sex Research.* May 1993, pp. 161-170.

Analyzes 50 pornographic videotapes released in Germany, 1979-1988; shows some trends, including that of subtle shifts toward greater equity in some portrayals and themes.

1121. Chalvon-Demersay, Sabine and Liz Libbrecht. "Scenarios of Crisis: Social Construction of Intimacy Through a Thousand TV Film Projects." *Reseaux: The French Journal of Communication.* Spring 1995, pp. 93-110.

Analyzes current social trends and problems through TV film synopses (1,120) submitted in 1991 to two French public TV channels; common themes included portrayal of an ideal woman, sexuality, disintegration of the family.

1122. Christensen, Lise. *"Visst Liker vi Damer": En Studie av Mannskulturen i Norsk Dagspresse* ("Of Course, We Like the Ladies": A Study of Male Culture in Norwegian Dailies). Oslo: Magistergradsav handling i Sosiologi, Universitetet i Oslo, 1988.

1123. Christmas, Linda. "Chaps of Both Sexes?" London: Women in Journalism, 1997.

1124. Cigognetti, Luisa and Lorenza Servetti. "'On Her Side': Female Images in Italian Cinema and the Popular Press, 1945-1955." *Historical Journal of Film, Radio and Television.* October 1996, pp. 555-563.

Looks at feature films, newsreels, and weekly magazines to see how women were treated in the crucial post-World War II era in Italy; finds "women's images were contradictory, worthy in one sense, unworthy in another."

1125. Clark, Kate. "The Linguistics of Blame: Representations of Women in *The Sun*'s Reporting of Crimes of Sexual Violence." In *Language, Text and Context: Essays in Stylistics*, edited by Michael Toolan. London: Routledge, 1992.
    In England.

1126. Creekmur, Corey K. and Alexander Doty, eds. *Out in Culture: Gay, Lesbian and Queer Essays on Popular Culture*. London: Cassell Academic, 1995. 544 pp.
    Includes "'I'm Not the Sort of Person Men Marry': Monsters, Queers, and Hitchcock's *Rebecca*" and "Crossover Dreams: Lesbianism and Popular Music Since the 1970s."

1127. Crowther, Barbara. "Viewing What Comes Naturally: A Feminist Approach to Television Natural History." *Women's Studies International Forum.* 20:2 (1997), pp. 289-300.
    Uses a small, random sample of natural history films shown on British television in the early 1990s to demonstrate how the formats reproduce an ideology of the "natural" where the female is marginalized; the films have masculine focus.

1128. Drotner, Kirsten. "Media Ethnography: An Other Story?" *Nordicom Review.* No. 2, 1993, pp. 1-13.
    Traces development of media ethnography; argues for increased professional dialogue between qualitative media research and feminism; draws on recent trends in Scandinavian media ethnography.

1129. Eide, Elisabeth. *Kvinnebildet i Norsk Dagspresse Ved Inngangen Til 1990-Arene og Journalistenes Bilde* (The Image of Women in the Norwegian Daily Press at the Start of the 1990s -- And That of Journalists). Oslo: Norsk Journalistskole, 1991.
    Studies journalists' perceptions of news values, the subjects covered, criteria of professionalization, etc.

1130. Elliott, Judy and A. J. Wootton. "Some Ritual Idioms of Gender in British Television Advertising." *Sociological Review.* August 1997, pp. 437-452.
    Analyzes gender portrayals in 75 British TV commercials of chocolate products, showing that women were usually depicted as detachable from their surroundings, men as foolish and incompetent.

1131. Ellmeier, Andrea. "Special British Mix. Feminismus und Cultural Studies." *Medien Journal.* 16:3 (1992), pp. 141-146.

1132. Espina-Barrio, Angel B. "Anthropological Dimensions and Social Communication Media: Sexuality in Television Broadcasting." *RS, Cuadernos de Realidades Sociales.* January 1993, pp. 187-197.
    Codes week of programs on Spanish TV concerning sexuality; shows that

there were 3.37 episodes of sexual behavior per program and that women exhibited sexual behavior more often than men.

1133. "Ethos und Geschlecht." Special Issue. *Frauen und Film*. April 1994.

1134. Fabris, Hans Heinz and Herta Kreuzhuber. *Das Internationale Jahr der Frau 1975 und die Darstellung von Frauenthemen in den Österreichischen Massen-Medien*. Vienna: Schriftenreihe zur Sozialen und Beruflichen Stellung der Frau 6, 1976.
Depiction of 1975 Year of the Woman in the Austrian mass media.

1135. Fagoaga, Concha. "Comunicando Violencia contra las Mujeres" (Communicating Violence against Women). In *Estudios sobre el Mensaje Periodístico* (Revista del Departamento de Periodismo I, Facultad de Ciencias de la Información, Universidad Complutense de Madrid). No. 1, 1994, pp. 67-90.

1136. Fagoaga, Concha. "Género, Sexo y Elites en los Medios Informativos" (Gender, Sex and Elites in the Information Media). In *La Flotante Identidad Sexual. La Identidad del Género en la Vida Cotidiana de la Juventud* (Floating Sexual Identity: Gender Identity in the Daily Life of Youth), edited by Félix Ortega, et al., pp. 97-118. Madrid: Dirección General de la Mujer de la Comunidad de Madrid--Instituto de Investigaciones Feministas--UCM, 1993.

1137. Fagoaga, Concha and Petra María Secanella. *Umbrales de Presencia de la Mujer en la Prensa Española* (Beginnings of the Presence of the Woman in the Spanish Press). Madrid: Instituto de la Mujer, Serie Estudios No. 1, 1983.

1138. Fowler, Roger. *Language in the News: Discourse and Ideology in the British Press*. New York: Routledge, 1991. 256 pp.
Considers newspaper representations of gender, power, authority, and law and order, including stereotyping.

1139. Frias García, Carmen. "La Defensa de la Imagen de la Mujer en TV: Análisis Específico de la Publicidad Televisiva" (The Defense of the Image of the Women on TV: Specific Analysis of Televised Advertising). In *Seminario sobre "Mujer y Medios de Comunicación Social."* Valencia: RTVE, 1987.

1140. Frieden, Sandra, ed. *Gender and the German Cinema. Feminist Interventions. Volume 1: Gender and Representation in New German Cinema. Volume 2: German Film History / German History on Film*. Providence: Berg Publishers, 1994.

1141. Fröehlich, Romy. "From Virgins, Vamps, and Lack of Reality. A Content Analysis of Crime Coverage in Local Newspapers." Paper presented at International Association for Mass Communication Research, Sydney, Australia, August 20, 1996.
Reports on content analysis of coverage of crime and/or violence in three

Hannover, Germany, newspapers; finds unexpected discrepancies, e.g., female and male victims and offenders were treated differently by the media.

1142. Furnham, Adrian and Nadine Bitar. "The Stereotyped Portrayal of Men and Women in British Television Advertisements." *Sex Roles.* August 1993, pp. 297-310.

Examines portrayals of men and women in British television commercials; finds that sex role television stereotyping in Britain was more or less constant over time periods of five and ten years, but weaker than in Italy and comparable to North America.

1143. Garreta, Nuria. *Modelos Masculino y Femenino en los Textos de EGB* (Masculine and Feminine Models in the Texts of the EGB). Madrid: Instituto de la Mujer, 1987.

1144. Garrido Arilla. María Rosa. "Funciones Comunicacionales de la Mujer en la Publicidad Dirigida al Hombre -- Análisis de Tres Revistas de Información General: Blanco y Negro, La Actualidad Española y Gaceta Ilustrada (1959-1979)" (Communicational Functions of the Three Magazines of General Information: *Blanco y Negro, La Actualidad Española*, and *Gaceta Ilustrada* [1959-1979]). Ph.D. dissertation, Universidad Complutense de Madrid, Facultad de Ciencias de la Información, 1983.

1145. Geiger, Brigitte. "Feministische Öffentlichkeit. Anmerkungen zu Ihrer Theorie und Praxis aus Anlaß Einer Aktuellen Veröffentlichung." *Medien Journal.* 16:3 (1992), pp. 166-170.

1146. "Getting Through: Five Years of the NOS Gender Portrayal Department." *Media Report to Women.* Summer 1997, pp. 6-8.

Deals with the Netherlands Broadcasting Corporation's Gender Portrayal Department.

1147. Ginsberg, Terri and Kirsten M. Thompson, eds. *Perspectives on German Cinema.* New York: Prentice Hall International, 1996.

Includes essays on German cinema studies and focuses on that field's relation to issues such as gender and sexuality and feminism, among others.

1148. Gomard, Kirsten. "Kvindelige Politkere i Dansk TV. Arbejdsvilkår og Kommunikationsstrategier" (Female Politicians in Danish TV: Working Conditions and Communication Strategies). Lecture at Seminar on Gender Theory and the Public Sphere, Institutt for Samfunnstorskning, Oslo, 1992.

Finds that women politicians are under cross pressures in television shows: in the name of equality, they are encouraged to be assertive, but all the while they receive subtle messages that their views are not important.

1149. Grover, Chris and Keith Soothill. "A Murderous 'Underclass'? The Press Reporting of Sexually Motivated Murder." *Sociological Review.* August 1996, pp. 398-415.

Analyzes reports of sexually-motivated murder in nine British newspapers in 1992; men are portrayed as the main perpetrators; not an accurate statement.

1150. Gunter, Barrie. *Television and Gender Representation*. Luton: John Libbey Media, University of Luton, 1995. 184 pp.

Presents up-to-date review of research on the way the sexes are depicted on British television; discusses how this portrayal affects children and adult viewers.

1151. Halonen, Irma K. "Women and the Public Sphere." *Gender and Mass Media Newsletter*. November 1991, pp. 14-15.

Reviews various definitions of public sphere and consequences of those definitions with respect to media coverage of women and women's issues, particularly in journalism.

1152. Hargrave, Andrea M. *Sex and Sexuality in Broadcasting*. *Broadcasting Standards Council Annual Review 1992*. London: John Libbey, 1992. 152 pp.

Takes as its 1992 theme, the portrayal in broadcasting of sexual conduct; examines what part embarrassment plays in provoking protests; looks at how female and male homosexuality are treated in British broadcasting.

1153. Hayward, Philip. *Picture This: Media Representations of Visual Art and Artists*. Revised Edition. Luton: John Libbey Media, University of Luton, 1996. 256 pp.

Brings together articles on the proliferation of British films, video, and TV shows about the arts; includes how the media represents feminist art.

1154. Hayward, Susan. "Beyond the Gaze and into Femme-Film'ecriture: Agnes Varda's *Sans Toit ni Loi*." In *French Film: Texts and Contexts*, edited by Susan Hayward and Ginette Vincendeau, pp. 285-295. London: Routledge, 1990.

Discusses from feminist perspective, French film director's "Sans Toit ni Loi."

1155. Hedlin, Maria. *Jämställt Eller Fördomsfullt? En Studie av Hur Könsroller Skildras i Sveriges Televisions Barnprogram* (Gender Equality or Bigotry? A Study of How Sex Roles Are Portrayed in Children's Programmes on Swedish Television). Högskolan i Växjö: Informationsteknik. VT, 1990.

1156. Hoijer, Birgitta. "The Dilemmas of Documentary Violence in Television." *Nordicom Review*. No. 1, 1996, pp. 53-61.

Looks at increasing changes in manner of visual representations of violence on Swedish TV news; deals in part with gender, one claim being women react emotionally to scenes of violence.

1157. Hollings, Julie. "The Portrayal of Women in Romance Comic Strips 1964-1984." BA dissertation, University of Reading, 1985.

1158. Hollowood, Bernard, ed. *The Women of Punch*. London: Arthur Baker, 1961. 166 pp.

1159. Holmlund, Christine A. "Displacing Limits of Difference: Gender, Race, and Colonialism in Edward Said and Homi Bhabha's Theoretical Models and Marguerite Duras's Experimental Films." *Quarterly Review of Film and Video.* 13:1-3 (1991), pp. 1-22.

1160. Holmqvist, Tove and Madeleine Kleberg. "Draft Legislation To Prohibit Gender Discrimination in Advertising in Sweden." *Gender and Mass Media Newsletter.* March 1991, p. 16.

    Fears that proposed Swedish legislation concerning discrimination against women in advertising would "strike down on the most outrageous ads, but will let stereotyped, gender-conservative content pass without comment."

1161. Huhnke, Brigitta. *Macht, Medien und Geschlecht: Eine Fallstudie zur Berichterstattungpraxis* (Power, Media, and Gender: A Case Study of Reporting Practices). Opladen: Westdeutscher Verlag, 1996. 292 pp.

    Analyzes content of dpa (German Press Agency), alternative daily *Die Tageszeitung,* and the "prestige" weeklies *Die Zeit* and *Der Spiegel,* 1980-1995, concerning coverage of gender themes; finds an increase of factual reporting but a decrease of general interest.

1162. Imamoglu, E. Olcay, and Yesim Gültekin. "Representation of Women and Men in Turkish Newspapers." *Journal of Human Sciences.* 9:2 (1990), pp. 57-67.

    Reports the results of two studies of direct and indirect representations of stereotyped gender roles in Turkish newspapers; finds traditional gender roles, women minimally represented compared to men, and newspaper politics unrelated to gender role portrayals.

1163. Johansson, P. O. "Rapport on Kvinnor och Män i Nyhetssandningarna 1987-88" (Report on Women and Men in Newscasts 1987-88). Stockholm: Sveriges Radio, Memorandum, October 31, 1988.

1164. Keene, Judith. "Mothering Daughters: Subjectivity and History in the Work of Helma Sanders - Brahms's *Germany Pale Mother.*" *Filmhistoria* (Barcelona). 7:1 (1997).

1165. Kirkham, Pat and Janet Thumim, eds. *Me Jane. Masculinity, Movies and Women.* New York: St. Martin's Press, 1995. 256 pp.

    Britain's top female film scholars tackle issues of gender and identity on the big screen; uses various approaches, studying one film, or an individual star, or larger issues of genre and spectatorship.

1166. Krotz, Friedrich. "The Image of Men and Their Relations to Women in a German Game Show." Paper presented at International Association for Mass Communication Research, Sydney, Australia, August 21, 1996.

    Describes German game show, "Mann-o-Mann," where women impose tasks on men and then judge their performance; claims the show belies claims that it gives women their say and makes men take notice of women's needs.

1167. Kutchinsky, B. "Legalized Pornography in Denmark." In *Men Confront*

Pornography, edited by Michael Kimmel. New York: Meridian, 1991.

Also "Pornography and Its Effects in Denmark and the United States: A Rejoinder and Beyond." *Comparative Social Research*. 8 (1985).

1168.   Larsson, Lisbeth. "Another (Hi)story: On Women's Reading and Swedish Weeklies." *Nordicom Review*. No. 2, 1993, pp. 15-24.

Describes gender inscription as expressed in criticism and scholarship concerned with Swedish popular literature; provides history of Swedish weeklies, the stories told by them about women and women's lives.

1169.   Law, Sandra. "Putting Themselves in the Pictures: Images of Women in the Work of Selected Female Animators in the U.K." *Animation Journal*. Fall 1995, pp. 21-52.

1170.   Leinfellner, Christine. *Das Bild der Frau im TV*. Salzburg: 1983.

1171.   Lindau, Rebecka. "A Sexualized Image of Lesbians in Sweden." *Off Our Backs*. June 1993, pp. 10+

States portrayals of lesbians in Swedish media have been negative and degrading.

1172.   Linne, Olga and Niels-Aage Nielsen. "The Family and Its Problems: Portrayal of the Family During a Week of Danish Television." In *The Family on Television: Empirical Study by Content Analysis in Four Countries*. Munich: Stiftung Prix Jeunesse International, 1984.

1173.   Loeb, Lori A. *Consuming Angels: Advertising and Victorian Women*. New York: Oxford University Press, 1994. 240 pp.

Examines how Victorian ads shaped social values; shows how they used "hedonistic aspects of Victorian culture to sell their wares, glorified consumerism, and mythologized middle-class life" in Great Britain.

1174.   MacCurdy, Marian. "Bitch or Goddess: Polarized Images of Women in Arthurian Literature and Film." *Platte Valley Review*. Winter 1990, pp. 3-24.

1175.   Martín Serrano, M. *Las Imágenes de las Mujeres en la Publicidad y en los Programas en Vivo de la Televisión* (The Images of Women in Advertising and in Live Television Programs). Madrid: Instituto de la Mujer, 1993.

1176.   Meijer, Maaike. "Countering Textual Violence: On the Critique of Representation and the Importance of Teaching Its Methods." *Women's Studies International Forum*. July-August 1993, pp. 367-378.

Argues for a concept of discourse containing the linguistic, material, cultural, and socio-political as undivided; uses two Dutch examples of such a discourse, a newspaper text on Dutch photographer Ed van der Elsken and Thea Beckman's children's book, *Het Wonder van Frieswijck*.

1177. Meyer zum Felde, Annette. "Sexistische Zeitschriftenwerbung -- Neu Verpackt." *Medium.* 18:4 (1988), pp. 57-59.

1178. Michielsens, Magda. "Women in the Picture. The Image of Women on the BRT-Screen." *Gender and Mass Media Newsletter.* November 1991, p. 29.
    Reports on survey of 45 men and women viewers concerning the image of women on Belgian Radio and Television; published as booklet in Dutch, available from Staatssecretariaat voor Maatschappelijke Emancipatie, Queteletplein 7, B-1030 Brussels.

1179. Mitchell, Paul C. and Wendy Taylor. "Polarising Trends in Female Role Portrayals in UK Advertising." *European Journal of Marketing.* 24:5 (1990), pp. 41-49.
    Investigates female role portrayals in the 1970s and 1980s, using three British women's magazines; finds less stereotyping of women as "physical objects."

1180. Moessner, Victoria J. "*Dragon Chow*: Asylum Seekers in German Film." In *Gender and Culture in Literature and Film East and West: Issues of Perception and Interpretation*, edited by Nitaya Masavisut, George Simson, and Larry E. Smith, pp. 85-89. Honolulu: University of Hawaii and East-West Center, 1994.
    Analyzes "Dragon Chow," black and white film in Chinese, German, and Urdu.

1181. Mortensen, Elvira. "Inner Action and Interaction: Influencing Readers Through Interactive Media, A Case from Norwegian Campaigns on Health and Sex." Paper presented at International Association for Mass Communication Research, Sydney, Australia, August 20, 1996.
    Discusses Norwegian computer game, "Det Store Manndomsspranget," designed to raise consciousness of boys relative to taking responsibility for their sexual activity.

1182. Navarro, Beatriz. *La Imagen de la Mujer en TVE. 1984. Un Guión Entre lo Real y lo Imaginario* (The Image of the Woman on TVE. 1984. A Scenario Between the Real and the Imaginary). Madrid: Instituto de la Mujer, 1984.

1183. "Netherlands Group Continues To Push for Gender Equity in Broadcasting." *Media Report to Women.* Summer 1997, p. 6.

1184. Nordlund, Roland. "PM Ang Könsroller i Sveriges Radios TV-utbud" (Memorandum on Sex-role Portrayals in Swedish Television). Stockholm: Sveriges Radio memorandum, May 22, 1978.

1185. Nowak, Kjell, et al. *Folket i TV. Demografi och Social Struktur i Televisionens Innehäll* (The People on TV. Democracy and Social Structure in Television Content). MASS 14, Stockholms Universitet, 1989.

1186. O'Connell, Judith. "Sexist Images in Children's Comics and Television." B.Ed. dissertation, University of Sheffield, 1982.

Published in *University of Sheffield: Faculty of Educational Studies* (April 1982); abstracted in *Sheffield Educational Research: Current Highlights* (April 1982).

1187. Pickering, M. "Race, Gender, and Broadcast Comedy: The Case of the BBC's Kentucky Minstrels." *European Journal of Communication*. September 1994, pp. 311-333.

Tackles the questions of sexism and racism in popular humor, looking at BBC's "Kentucky Minstrels," which aired 1933-1950.

1188. Radl Philipp, Rita. "La Imagen de la Mujer en la TV: Los Programas de Debates Políticos y Sociales" (The Image of the Woman on TV: Programs of Political and Social Debates), *IV Congreso Español de Sociología*. Madrid, September 24-26, 1992. Grupo de Trabajo: Sociología del Género, 1992.

1189. Roiz, Miguel. *Espacio, Comunicación y Mujer en el Medio Tradicional Campesino* (Space, Communication and Woman in Traditional Rural Media). *Jornadas de Investigación Interdisciplinaria*. (4-1984. Madrid). Madrid: Universidad Autónoma, 1986, pp. 65-80.

1190. Rönnberg, Margareta. *Könsrollsstereotyper i Barn-TV Program* (Sex-role Stereotypes in Television Programmes for Children). Uppsala: Sociologiska Institutionen, Uppsala Universitet, 1975.

1191. Ross, Karen. "Bambi, Thumper and the One in the Dress: Press Coverage of the Labour Party's Leadership Campaign -- 1994." *Everywoman*. No. 110, 1994, pp. 12-13.

1192. Ross, Karen. "Gender and Party Politics: How the Press Reported the Labour Leadership Campaign, 1994." *Media, Culture and Society*. July 1995, pp. 499-509.

Examines impact of gender and party politics on 1994 campaign of Margaret Becker for Labor Party leader in Great Britain; shows how newspapers established a strong bias against her.

1193. Ross, Karen. "Political Women, Newspaper Men: Analysing the Intersections Between Gender, Politics and Press." In *Gender and Media*, edited by N. Dakovic, D. Derman, and K. Ross, pp. 176-187. Ankara: Med-Campus, 1996.

1194. Ross, Karen. "Skirting the Issue: Political Women and the Media." *Everywoman*. No. 199, 1995, pp. 16-17.

1195. Ross, Karen. "Women, Politics and the Media: From Fighting to Freedom and Back Again." Paper presented at International Association for Mass Communication Research, Sydney, Australia, August 20, 1996.

Uses personal interview data and draws together experiences of women politicians from the two major British political parties; argues that despite their very different political standpoints, the universal theme that binds them together is their media-ted marginalization; states that women politicians are often caught up in a contradiction between needing the media's attention but also recognizing the dangers of being marginalized by an overemphasis on their physicalities.

1196. Ross, Karen and Annabelle Sreberny-Mohammadi. "Playing House-Gender, Politics and the News Media in Britain." *Media, Culture and Society*. January 1997, pp. 101-109.
    Looks at ways mass media frame political women and how female Parliament members in Britain view such media interventions.

1197. Ross, Karen and Annabelle Sreberny-Mohammadi. "Reporting the Body Politic: Women MPs and the Media." *Parliamentary Affairs*. 49:1 (1996), pp. 103-115.

1198. Ross, Karen and Annabelle Sreberny-Mohammadi. "Women MPs and the Media: Representing the Body Politic." In *Women in Politics*, edited by J. Lovenduski and P. Norris, pp. 105-117. Oxford: Oxford University Press, 1996.

1199. Sana, Elina. "Women in News Media: Bystanders." *Gender and Communication Section International Association for Mass Communication Research Newsletter*. November 1995, p. 5.
    Reports on survey of Finnish broadcasting which showed men dominate all topic areas of newscasts; when women were reported on, usually in soft news, they were presented in stereotyped roles.

1200. Sana, Elina and Minna Aslama. "Women in News Media: Bystanders: Results of the Research 'Portrayal of Women and Men in the News' of the Finnish Broadcasting Company." Helsinki: Yleisradio, 1995. 12 pp.
    A conference paper on said subject.

1201. Sanderson, Terry, ed. *Mediawatch. The Treatment of Male and Female Homosexuality in the British Media*. London: Cassell Academic, 1995. 256 pp.
    Shows how British press and TV manipulated homosexuality and HIV/AIDS for political purposes.

1202. Savolainen, Tarja. "Feminism and the Finnish Media." *Gender and Communication Section International Association for Mass Communication Research Newsletter*. November 1995, p. 2.
    Paper at International Association for Mass Communication Research conference in Portoroz, Slovenia, looks at feminist portrayal in news and traces different categorizations of feminism in Finnish media.

1203. Savolainen, Tarja. "The Representation of Women in Finnish Broadcasting News and Current Affairs Programmes." Paper presented at International Association for Mass Communication Research, Bled, Yugoslavia, August 26-30, 1990.
    Shows that as the number of women in Finnish media increased after the 1980s, the number of stories on the women's movement or items presented from a woman's view stayed about the same.

1204. Savolainen, Tarja. "Women, News and Politics." Helsinki: University of Helsinki, Department of Communication, 1995. 6 pp.

Presents traditional divisions of feminism and their implications for feminist news criticism.

1205. *Sexist Advertising: Now It Must Go!* Vallingby, Sweden: National Swedish Board for Consumer Policies, 1989. 10 pp.

Presents findings of the board to the Swedish government concerning the extent of, and development in, sexist advertising; offers summary of how the project was carried out and includes final chapter of the Board's report along with its proposals for action.

1206. *Sexist Advertising -- What Is That? Basic for a Discussion.* Vallingby, Sweden: National Swedish Board for Consumer Policies, 1989. 37 pp.

Presents pictures from advertisements for discussion as well as some considerations from two meetings held by the Board's Criteria Group.

1207. Sherzer, Dina, ed. *Cinema, Colonialism, Postcolonialism. Perspectives from the French and Francophone Worlds.* Austin: University of Texas Press, 1996. 280 pp.

Expounds upon the role French and Francophone films play in reconstructing and imagining France's colonial past; gender, race, and geography are central themes.

1208. Short, Claire. *Dear Claire...This Is What Women Feel About Page 3.* London: Hutchinson Radius, 1991.

Member of Parliament Short recounts her campaign to make illegal the display of naked or partially naked women in sexually provocative poses in newspapers (in UK, known as "page three girls") and describes the 5,000 letters of support she received for her proposal, mainly from women.

1209. Slade, Joseph. "Bernard Natan: France's Legendary Pornographer." *Journal of Film and Video.* Summer/Fall 1993, pp. 72-90.

Analyzes Natan's clandestine porn films as subversive works to deflate middle class conventions.

1210. Snowdon, Ros. "Women Condemn Ad Mums." *Marketing.* October 12, 1995, p. 4.

Reports on nationwide survey of 1,000 women in the U.K., who felt that television advertising's portrayal of mothers is patronizing and unrealistic.

1211. Soila, Tytti. "Valborgsmässoafton: Melodrama and Gender Politics in Swedish Cinema." In *Popular European Cinema*, edited by Richard Dyer and Ginette Vincendeau, pp. 232-244. London and New York: Routledge, 1992.

1212. Soykan, Fetay. *Türk Sinemasinda Kadin 1920-1990* (The Woman in Turkish Cinema, 1920-1990). Izmir: Altindag Matbaacilik, 1993. 159 pp.

Represents first historical account of images of women in Turkish film; investigates problems faced by a Western-oriented society with Islamic roots when seeking a suitable way to represent women on the screen; states that not until 1950-1960 did stardom become a concept for women.

1213. Sreberny-Mohammadi, Annabelle. "Women Talking Politics." In *Perspectives of Women in Television*, pp. 60-80. London: Broadcasting Standards Council, Research Working Paper IX, May 1994.

1214. Sreberny-Mohammadi, Annabelle and Karen Ross. *Political Women and News Media: Issues of Representation*. Leicester: Centre for Mass Communication Research, 1995. 34 pp.

1215. Steene, Brigitta. "Ingmar Bergman in a Gender Perspective." *Gender and Mass Media Newsletter*. November 1992, pp. 8-9.
    States that Swedish filmmaker Bergman early on (1949-1955) provided portraits of women who occupied a good deal of active space in his films as speaking subjects.

1216. "Swedish Scholar Suggests New Approach to Studying Women in TV News." *Media Report to Women*. March/April 1990, p. 8.
    Madeleine Kleberg said that the theory that TV news would change as soon as more women report the news is a simplistic one. "News is news," she said.

1217. Swedish Television Equality Group. *Nyheter för Kvinnor och Män? Jämstalldhetsgruppen vid Sveriges Television Granskar Vecka 12-83* (News for Women and Men? An Examination of Newscasts in the Twelfth Week of 1983). Stockholm: Swedish Television Equality Group, 1983.

1218. Threadgold, Terry and Anne Cranny-Francis, eds. *Feminine/Masculine and Representation*. London: Unwin Hyman, 1990. 176 pp.
    Deals with debate around how gender relations are constructed, represented, and transformed by the media; includes, Michelle Royer, "Deconstructions of Masculinity and Femininity in the Films of Marguerite Duras"; Anne Cranny-Francis and Patricia Gillard, "Soap Opera as Gender Training: Teenage Girls and TV."

1219. Tonello, Elisa and Renato Mion. "The Image of Girls in an Adolescent Magazine." *Tuttogiovani Notizie*. October-December 1995, pp. 5-36.
    Analyzes *Primavera-Mondo Giovane* (Spring-The World of Youth), an Italian magazine published for adolescent girls since 1950; shows shifts in magazine's emphases.

1220. Tremblay, Sheryl W. Y. "Caricatures of National Personification in the Popular Media of Britain: A Rhetorical Study of Gender and Nationalistic Sentiment During the War with the British Colonies in America, 1764-1783." Ph.D. dissertation, University of Pittsburgh, 1994.

1221. Vincendeau, Ginette. "Feminism and French Cinema." *Screen.* Winter 1990, pp. 454-457.

1222. Werner, Anita. "The Feminine Perspective in Nordic Media Research." *Nordicom Review.* No. 1, 1994, pp. 35-37.

1223. Zimmerman, Enid. "Art Education for Women in England from 1890-1910 as Reflected in the Victorian Periodical Press and Current Feminist Histories of Art Education." *Studies in Art Education.* Winter 1991, pp. 105-116.
        Explores how women art students were educated and viewed in England, 1890-1910; looks at their reflection in Victorian periodical press.

1224. Zotos, Yiorgos C. and Steven Lysonski. "Gender Representations: The Case of Greek Magazine Advertisements." *Journal of Euro-marketing.* 3:2 (1994), pp. 27-47.
        Draws sample of 11 magazines of various genres and shows women are portrayed stereotypically in advertisements, although some change for the good is occurring.

Women as Audience

1225. Abrahamsson, Ulla B. "When Women Watch Television." *Communications.* 19:1 (1994), pp. 67-86.
        Compares Swedish women and men relative to TV viewing, pointing out clear differences concerning content and length of viewing time. Also published in *Nordisk Forskning om Kvinnor och Medier*, edited by Ulla Carlsson. Göteborg: Nordicom, Göteborgs Universitet, 1993.

1226. Abrahamsson, Ulla B. "When Women Watch Television...." *Nordicom Review.* No. 2, 1993, pp. 37-52.
        Deals with Swedish women viewers of well-known television serial dramas; finds identification is a factor in viewers' judgments, as are the structure of the conflict in the plot, and who and what the story is about.

1227. *Annual Review of BBC Broadcasting Research. No. XVII -- 1991.* Luton: John Libbey Media, University of Luton, 1991. 128 pp.
        Includes "Women's Viewing Patterns."

1228. Arnott, Nancy. "Is There an 800 Number?" *Sales and Marketing Management.* June 1994, p. 17.
        Reports on British magazine *Options*, which commissioned six advertising agencies to create print advertisements to sell women on men.

1229. Baxendale, Leo. "Minnie the Minx -- More Than a Match for the Boys." *Guardian.* October 13, 1982.
        Discusses British girls and comics.

1230. Beere, Samantha. "Women's Viewing Patterns." In *Annual Review of BBC Broadcasting Research Findings, 17*, pp. 51-61. London: BBC Broadcasting Research Department, John Libbey, 1991.

1231. Bergseng, Ewa O., Inger Bjørkaas, Tom Rosendal, Åshild Solberg, and Yaping Tang. *Er det en Sammenheng Mellom Type av Tema i Programmet "Antenne ti" og Seernes Kjønn?* (Is There Any Correlation Between the Themes in the Program "Antenne Ti" and the Sex of the Viewers?). Oslo: Institutt for Medier og Kommunikasjon, Universitetet i Oslo, 1991.

1232. Broadcasting Standards Council. *Perspectives of Women in Television.* London: Broadcasting Standards Council, 1994.
    Reports that women and men react differently to representations of violence in the media, that women are less likely than men to watch violence.

1233. de Andrés García, Sara. "La Mujer y la Información" (Woman and Information). Ph.D. dissertation, Universidad Complutense de Madrid, Facultad de Ciencias de la Información, 1989.

1234. Drotner, Kirsten. "Girl Meets Boy: Aesthetic Production, Reception, and Gender Identity." *Cultural Studies.* May 1989, pp. 208-225.
    Studies group of 14-17 year olds who made a video in a Danish youth school (*ungdomsskole*); concludes that everyday aesthetics may serve different needs: "for boys, the widening of aesthetic contents may be the most important challenge to traditional masculine roles," "for girls, the contexts of aesthetic production may prove the most decisive."

1235. Drotner, Kirsten. *Mediated Memories and Cultural Identities.* Copenhagen: Kobenhavns Universitet, 1995. 17 pp.
    Tells how media act as agents in a process of historical construction; uses Nordic women of three generations as subjects as they were interviewed about their everyday cultures.

1236. Hellman, Heikki. "A Toy for the Boys Only?: Reconsidering the Gender Effect of Video Technology." *European Journal of Communication.* March 1996, pp. 5-32.
    Studies video in England, Finland, and Sweden, 1984-1991, especially considering men and women viewers; finds men are interested in sports and news, women in drama and soap operas.

1237. Hjort, Anne. "Kvinderne og Dallas" (Women's Reception of Dallas). In *Analyser af TV. Mediet og Dets Modtagere*, edited by R. Pittelkow. Copenhagen: Medusa, 1985.
    Compares reactions to "Dallas" among highly educated Danish women and women with little education; the more educated group was more analytical and abstract, the less educated more concrete and personal.

1238. Hjort, Anne. "Når Kvinder Ser TV: Om Medieforskning og Reception" (Women Watching Television: On Media Studies and Reception). M.A. thesis, University of Copenhagen, 1984.

1239. Iglesias Prieto, Norma V. *Discurso, Género y Recepción Cinematográfica* (Discourse, Gender and Cinematographic Reception). Mimeographed. Madrid, 1994.

1240. Kaiser, Addy. "Videotex: A Waste of Energy." Paper presented at International Association for Mass Communication Research, Bled, Yugoslavia, August 26-31, 1990.

Presents results of an analysis focusing on gender and research about nine videotex experiments in the Netherlands; finds that female participants either were not familiar with technical details or were unaware of how these technologies were distributed.

1241. Koch, Gertrude. "Why Women Go to Men's Films." In *Feminist Aesthetics*, edited by Gisela Ecker, pp. 108-119. London: Women's Press, 1985.

1242. Liikkanen, Mirja. "Culture Consumption in Finland: Distinctive Characteristics." *Nordicom Review*. No. 1, 1996.

Includes sections on "The Finnish Gender System and Patterns of Culture Consumption" and "The Question of the Female (Art) Audience."

1243. Michielsens, Magda. "Italia Mia. Watching Television in Exile." *Gender and Mass Media Newsletter*. November 1991, pp. 28-29.

Discusses Italian television's broadcasts to Italian immigrant miners in Belgium; reports on interviews with 100 of these Italian women, focusing on their roles as TV viewers.

1244. Presvelou, C. "Women as Users of Information Technology in The Netherlands." Paper presented at Colloquium Greece - EEC on Women and Informatics, Athens, Greece, 1986.

1245. Rajalahti, Hanna. "Feminist Perspectives on Media Reception: Deconstructing Patriarchal Texts and Empowering Feminine Audiences." Unpublished manuscript, University of Helsinki, 1992.

1246. Reid, Evelyn. "Black Girls Talking." *Gender and Education*. 1:3 (1989), pp. 295-300.

Studies Afro-Caribbean women in Great Britain; examines role played by media and education in constructing the dreams, world views, and lifestyles of these young women.

1247. Ruoho, Iiris. "Television as Gender Technology. A Study of Finnish Television and Viewer Discourses: Gender Dynamics in the Finnish Television Serial *Ruusun Aika* (Time of the Rose)." *Gender and Mass Media Newsletter*. November 1992, p. 8.

Attempts to uncover possible connections between television discourse, the television viewer, and the sex/gender system relative to Finnish television.

1248. Sarkkinen, Raija. "Gender in Audience Research." *Nordicom Review*. No. 1, 1997, pp. 173-181.

Traces the history of sex in audience researches in Finland since the late 1940s, and finds there is no difference in the amount of radio listening among men and women. Differences do occur in places of listening.

1249. Sarkkinen, Raija. "Naiset ja Miehet Radionkuuntelijoina ja TV: n Katsojina" (Women and Men as Viewers of Television and Listeners to Radio). In *Radio-ja TV-Tutkimuksen Vuosikirja*, edited by Heikki Kasari, pp. 12-22. Helsinki: Finnish Broadcasting Co., 1994.

1250. Stacey, Jackie. *Star Gazing: Hollywood Cinema and Female Spectatorship*. New York: Routledge, 1994. 296 pp.

Investigates how women viewers understood Hollywood stars in the 1940s and 1950s; looks at significant stars in women's memories of wartime and post war Britain.

1251. Taschler-Pollacek, Heidrun and Helmut Lukesch. "Fear of Victimization as a Consequence of Television Viewing? A Study of Older Women." *Publizistik*. October-December 1990, pp. 443-453.

Administers questionnaire to West German women to determine impact of mass media on fear of victimizations; shows that threatening information from TV and social isolation can create anxieties about possible victimization.

1252. Thomas, Lyn. "In Love with *Inspector Morse*: Feminist Subculture and Quality Television." *Feminist Review*. Autumn 1995, pp. 1-25.

Provides textual analysis of popular British TV series, "Inspector Morse" and qualitative study of audience; looks at gender representation and feminist influences "discernible in this example of quality popular culture."

1253. van der Wal, Ineke. "Women and Public Community Information in the Netherlands: A Lost Opportunity or an Attractive Option?" Paper presented at International Association for Mass Communication Research, Bled, Yugoslavia, August 26-31, 1990.

Discusses an information system designed by a regional library in the Netherlands; although 66 percent of the users were women, their needs were not reflected in the design of and information provided through the videotex information system.

1254. Wigren, Gunnila. *Kvinnor och Män Ser På TV* (Women and Men Watch Television). Stockholm: Sveriges Radio/PUB No. 11, 1985.

1255. Winkel, Frans-Willen and Aldert Vrij. "Fear of Crime and Mass Media Crime Reports Testing Similarity Hypotheses." *International Review of Victimology*. 1:3 (1990), pp. 251-265.

Evaluates effects that mass media news on the tracking and prosecution of criminal offenses may have on audiences' fear of crime; uses sample of 267 women at an Amsterdam shopping center.

Women Practitioners

1256. Abrahamsson, Ulla B. "Are We Nearing the Top of the Hill? Notes from a Decade of Working Toward Equality in Swedish Broadcasting." Paper presented at International Association for Mass Communication Research, Bled, Yugoslavia, August 26-31, 1990. 20 pp.

Provides the frame of reference for the equality work in Swedish radio and television; analyzes the concept of equality and related phenomena such as likeness-singularity, equal opportunity-equal outcome. During decade of equality work at Swedish Broadcasting, changes occurred in personnel structure and policy; changes in content were not obvious. Published in *Medier, Människor, Samhälle*, edited by Ulla Carlsson, pp. 93-110. Göteborg: Nordicom, Göteborgs Universitet, 1991.

1257. Abrahamsson, Ulla B. "Pa Vägen Mellan Ideologi och Verklighet om TV och Jämställdheten" (On the Road from Ideology to Reality: On Television and Equality of the Sexes in Sweden). *Kvinnovetenskaplig Tidskrift.* 9:3 (1988), pp. 8-39.

1258. Abrahamsson, Ulla B. "Start for Equality Work in Finnish Media." *Gender and Mass Media Newsletter.* November 1991, pp. 19-20.

Reports on conference, Hanaholmen, Helsinki, Finland, August 31-September 1, 1991, in which women journalists and researchers from Finland and Sweden assess their work for equality.

1259. "After 50 Years on the Defensive, Still a Cinema Master." *New York Times.* March 16, 1994, p. C-20.

Reviews documentary on Leni Riefenstahl.

1260. "Alison de Vere." *Animation Journal.* Fall 1995, p. 55.

Short resumé of British animator.

1261. Allen, Isobel, Michael Fogarty, and Patricia Walters. "Stuck on the Way to the Top." *New Society.* July 9, 1981, pp. 56-58.

Details status of British women in advancing to high levels in industry, civil service, and the British Broadcasting Co.

1262. Aspinall, Sue. "Interview with Lady Gardiner." In *BFI Dossier Number 18: Gainsborough Melodrama*, edited by Sue Aspinall and Robert Murphy, pp. 63-65. London: British Film Institute, 1983.

Interviews British filmmaker Lady [Muriel Box] Gardiner.

1263. Bachy, Victor. *Alice Guy-Blaché (1873-1968), La Première Femme Cinéaste du Monde.* Perpignan: Institut Jean Vigo, 1993.

Chronicles life of one of the inventors of narrative film and a pioneer of early French and American cinema.

1264. Bargh, Liz. "Awareness Raising Through Training." *Journal of European Industrial Training.* 10:7 (1986), pp. 23-27.
Describes "Women in the Work Place" project, a British training program in the printing and related industries, implemented in 1982.

1265. Bendazzi, Giannalberto. "Claire Parker: An Appreciation." *Animation World Magazine.* May 1996.
Discusses the usually unknown role of Claire Parker in her collaboration with husband Alexandre Alexeïeff.

1266. Bendazzi, Giannalberto. "Icelandic Animation." *Animation World.* October 1996, 5 pp.
Profiles Icelandic animator Inga Lisa Middleton.

1267. Bergstrom, Janet. "The Theatre of Everyday Life: Ulrike Ottinger's China: The Arts, Everyday Life." *Camera Obscura.* September 1988, pp. 43-51.
Deals with film work, among other aspects, of Ottinger's life.

1268. Bosshart, Louis, ed. *Femmes et Medias* (Women and Media). Fribourg, Switzerland: Editions Universitaires, 1991. 194 pp.
Includes analysis of more than 400 female journalists in German-speaking Switzerland; women's periodicals in US, Germany, France, and Switzerland, and women's issues in Swiss media.

1269. Box, Muriel. *Odd Woman Out.* London: Leslie Frewin, 1974.
Provides information on author's film career.

1270. Brettle, Jane and Sally Rice, eds. *Public Bodies / Private States: New Views on Photography, Representation and Gender.* Manchester: Manchester University Press, 1994. 156 pp.
Combines visual imagery from women artists with works of leading theorists in an attempt to study the body.

1271. Bright, Susie and Jill Posener, eds. *Nothing But the Girl: The Blatant Lesbian Image: A Portfolio and Exploration of Lesbian Erotic Photography.* London: Cassell Academic, 1996. 144 pp.
Contains the landmark works of influential lesbian photographers such as Morgan Gwenwald, Della Grace, Tee A. Corinne, Jill Posener, and Honey L. Cottrell.

1272. "British Survey Shows Advertising Women Not in Top Jobs." *Media Report to Women.* March/April 1990, pp. 6-7.
British survey results: "Women hold only a tiny percentage of the top agency jobs, are typically ghettoized in areas that leave little room for advancement and often suffer significant -- if subtle-- sexual discrimination."

1273. Brückner, Jutta. "Women Behind the Camera." In *Feminist Aesthetics*, edited by Gisela Ecker, pp. 120-124. Boston: Beacon, 1986.
By German woman filmmaker.

1274. Bruno, Giuliana. *Streetwalking on a Ruined Map: Cultural Theory and the City Films of Elvira Notari*. Princeton, New Jersey: Princeton University Press, 1993. 416 pp.

Interweaves examples of Italian cinema with architecture, art history, medical discourse, photography and literature, while looking at Italy's first and most prolific filmmaker, Elvira Notari.

1275. Camera Obscura Collective. "Interview with Babette Mangolte." *Camera Obscura*. Summer 1979, pp. 198-210.

French filmmaker who moved to New York.

1276. Canby, Vincent. "The Wonderful, Horrible Life of Leni Riefenstahl." *New York Times*. October 14, 1993, p. C-15.

Reviews documentary on life of Hitler's chief filmmaker.

1277. "Candy Guard." *Animation Journal*. Fall 1995, p. 54.

Short resumé of British animator Guard.

1278. Cazals, Patrick. *Musidora: La Dixième Muse*. Paris: Editions Henry Veyrier, 1978.

Describes life and career of Musidora (Jeanne Roques), French actress who also produced and directed 10 surrealist films.

1279. Cohen, Karl. "Clare Kitson: The World's Last Great Patron of Animators." *Animato!* Summer/Fall 1997, pp. 8-9.

Discusses work of Clare Kitson, commissioning editor at Channel 4 in London; concentrates on animation.

1280. Colgan, Fiona and Frances Tomlinson. "Women in Publishing: Jobs or Careers?" *Personnel Review*. 20:5 (1991), pp. 16-26.

Survey finds that contrary to popular opinion, women do not occupy top positions in British book publishing: men are five times more likely to become directors and twice as likely to become managers despite women making up more than 60 percent of the workforce.

1281. Collis, Rose. *A Trouser-Wearing Character: The Life and Times of Nancy Spain*. London: Cassell Academic, 1997. 420 pp.

Tells how lesbian feminist Spain had become known as England's most successful all-media woman between the 1940s and her death in 1964; she wrote novels, worked as a journalist, freelanced for popular magazines, and appeared on television.

1282. Confino, Barbara. "An Interview with Agnes Varda." *Saturday Review*. August 12, 1972, p. 35.

Profiles French filmmaker Agnes Varda.

1283. Cook, Pam. "*The Gold Diggers*: An Interview with Sally Potter." *Framework*.

Spring 1984, pp. 12-30.
Interviews British filmmaker Sally Potter, concentrating on one of her six major films, "The Gold Diggers" (1983).

1284. Cottenet-Hage, Madeleine and Robert P. Kolker. "The Cinema of Duras in Search of an Image." *French Review*. October 1979, pp. 88-98.

1285. "Cristina García Rodero -- Hidden Spain." *Democratic Journalist*. August 1991, pp. 28-31.
Features Spanish photographer and her works.

1286. Dargis, Manohla. "Sally Potter: A Director Not Afraid of Virginia Woolf." *Interview*. June 1993, p. 42.
Discusses British filmmaker Sally Potter who maintains that her "roots are not academic or theoretical; they are show-business roots, albeit avant-garde ones."

1287. Dawtrey, Adam. "Femme Helmers Brighten Brit Biz." *Variety*. August 7-13, 1995, pp. 5, 8.
Claims British film producers were increasingly turning to women directors for a "fresh, female perspective," and by doing so, were injecting new life into the industry.

1288. De Luca, Gianni. "Alcune Domande a Anna Salvatore." *Comics*. October 1975, pp. 10-11.
Profiles Italian comics creator Anna Salvatore.

1289. de Mateo Perez, Rosario. "El Trabajo de la Mujer en la Empresa Periodística" (The Work of the Woman in the Periodical Press). *Jornadas de Investigación Interdisciplinaria* (Universidad de Zaragoza. April 1984), 1986, pp. 373-385.

1290. Deneroff, Harvey. "The Olympiad of Animation: An Interview with Fini Littlejohn." *Animation World*. July 1996, 5 pp.
Interviews Fini Littlejohn, born Josephine (Fini) Rudiger in Vienna, and her role in setting up the Olympiad of Animation in 1984.

1291. Dixon, Wheeler W. "Alice Guy: Forgotten Pioneer of the Narrative Cinema." *New Orleans Review*. Fall-Winter 1992, pp. 7-15.

1292. Dixon, Wheeler W. "An Interview with Wendy Toye." In *Re-Viewing British Cinema, 1900-1992: Essays and Interviews*, edited by Wheeler W. Dixon, pp. 133-142. Albany, New York: SUNY Press, 1994.
Interviews comedic filmmaker Wendy Toye about her British works, which include "Raising a Riot" (1995) and "A Life To Be Lived" (1961).

1293. Dönmez-Colin, Gönül. "Personal Stories Need Not Be Autobiographical: An Interview with Yesim Ustaoglu." *Cinemaya*. Autumn 1995, pp. 30-32.
Interviews one of the most prolific and talented women filmmakers in Turkey on her films (such as "Trace" and "Hotel"), on Turkish filmmaking, on

being a woman filmmaker.

1294. Dougary, G. *The Executive Tart and Other Myths: Media Women Talk Back.* London Virago, 1994.

1295. Duras, Marguerite. *Green Eyes.* Translated by Carol Barko. New York: Columbia University Press, 1990. 264 pp.

Includes French filmmaker Duras' observations on her own work and that of other directors.

1296. Duras, Marguerite. *Marguerite Duras.* San Francisco: City Lights, 1976.

1297. Edelman, Rob. "Travelling a Different Route: An Interview with Agnes Varda." *Cineaste.* 15:1 (1986), pp. 20-21.

Interviews French film director Varda.

1298. Egsmose, Lisbeth. "Women in the Working Environment of Television. A Comparative Study of the Situation in Denmark and England." *Gender and Mass Media Newsletter.* November 1992, pp. 14-15.

Believes that despite equal opportunities, policies, and actions, there does not seem to be much progress for women on the labor market.

1299. Ehrenstein, David. "Out of the Wilderness: An Interview with Sally Potter." *Film Quarterly.* Fall 1993, pp. 2-7.

Interviews political artist, dancer, filmmaker, musician, actor, and writer of London avant-garde.

1300. Ekhart, Jaap. "Een Onbekende Ster aan het Strip Firmament: Lian Ong." *Stripschrift.* October 1989, pp. 22-29.

Deals with Dutch illustrator, cartoonist Lian Ong and her work.

1301. Elsaesser, Thomas. "It Started with These Images -- Some Notes on Political Filmmaking after Brecht in Germany: Helke Sander and Harun Farocki." *Discourse.* Fall 1985, pp. 95-120.

Discusses Helke Sander, a major figure in the New German Cinema, feminist political activist, and co-founder of the feminist film journal, *Frauen und Film.*

1302. Elsner-Sommer, Gretchen. "Interview with Cristina Perincioli." *Jump Cut.* 29 (1984), pp. 51-53.

Deals with Swiss-born German filmmaker, described as important in the tradition of Straub, Huillet, and Fassbinder.

1303. Esaiasson, Peter and Tom Moring. "Professionella Hökar och Duvor. Manliga och Kvinnliga Journalister Frågar ut Politiker" (Professional Hawks and Doves: Men and Women Journalists Interrogate Politicians). *Nordicom Information.* 1/1993.

Finds that male journalists were more active in such interrogations than were women, but that no differences between women and men were found regarding their propensity to challenge politicians.

1304. Export, Valie. "Aspects of Feminist Actionism." *New German Critique*. Spring-Summer 1989, pp. 69-82.

Export is a German filmmaker.

1305. Forsyth, Hardy, ed. *Grierson on Documentary*. New York: Praeger, 1977.

Includes information on sisters of documentarist, John Grierson, Marion and Ruby, who were important in creating the British documentary movement.

1306. Frankfurther, P. Hans. "Bommels auf Deutsch." *Stripschrift*. December 1990, pp. 30-33.

Discusses the work of Swiss-born illustrator/cartoonist Jacqueline Crevoisier.

1307. Franquet, Rosa. "Mujer y Rutinas Producción en Radio y Televisión" (Woman and Production Routines in Radio and Television). In *La Investigación en la Comunicación. III Simposio de la Asociación de Investigadores en Comunicación del Estado Español (A.I.C.E.)*, pp. 149-157, Madrid: AICE, 1992.

1308. Fröhlich, Romy and Christina Holtz-Bacha. "From Preponderance to Underrepresentation: Female Faculty in Journalism and Mass Communication in Germany. Results of the First Study on Representation and Situation of Women in German Mass Communication and Journalism Departments." Paper presented at International Association for Mass Communication Research, Seoul, Korea, July 1994. 18 pp.

Shows that 21 percent of teachers in German communication/journalism departments were women, but only 16 percent were professors and fewer women than men felt they could follow their own interests in research and teaching or that their careers had developed adequately.

1309. Fröhlich, Romy and Christina Holtz-Bacha. *Geschlossene Gesellschaft: Zwischen Majorität und Minorität, Frauen in der Publizistik* (Private Party: Between Majority and Minority, Women in Media Research). Bochum: Brockmeyer [Frauen und Massenmedien. Vol. 6], 1995. 205 pp.

Spotlights representation of women in German academic media research; claims women make up majority in education/training but minority in university teaching and top faculty and media research positions.

1310. Fröhlich, Romy and Christina Holtz-Bacha. "Women as Faculty Members in Communication." *Gender and Mass Media Newsletter*. November 1992, p. 26.

Shows that women are underrepresented in German communication education and research, in overall numbers, in upper-level ranks, and in the scientific network.

1311. Galán Quintanilla, Maria Antonia. *La Mujer a Través de la Información en la II República Española*. Madrid: UCM, 1980.

1312. Gates, Harvey. "Alice Blaché: A Dominant Figure in Pictures." *New York Dramatic Mirror*. November 6, 1912, p. 28.

Gives early account of Blaché's pioneering work; she was 39 at the time.

1313. Gates, Harvey. *The Memoirs of Alice Guy-Blaché*. Edited by Anthony Slide. Translated by Roberta and Simone Blaché. Metuchen, New Jersey: Scarecrow Press, 1986.

Profiles French filmmaker who helped to invent narrative movies.

1314. Glassman, Deborah. *Marguerite Duras. Fascinating Vision and Narrative Cure.* Cranbury, New Jersey: Fairleigh Dickinson University Press and Associated University Presses, 1991. 152 pp.

Charts Duras' career as French novelist, playwright, and filmmaker; looks at her exploration of traumatic memories of women.

1315. Graber, Sheila. "From Tea-Trolley to Technology." In *The Animated World of Sheila Graber*. Exhibition catalogue. Durham: DLI Museum and Arts, Centre, 1985.

1316. Graber, Sheila. "Sheila Graber: Everyone's an Artist. Notes on Animating Fine Art." *Art and Design*. No. 53, 1997, pp. 54-55.

British animator explains her style/technique and relates career highlights.

1317. Grisham, Therese. "An Interview with Ulrike Ottinger." *Wide Angle*. April 1992, pp. 28-36.

German filmmaker with works mainly in 1970s and 1980s.

1318. Gudmundsen, Ursula. "I Begyndelsen Fnisede de" (In the Beginning They Were Giggling. Interview with DR's EOO Anette Steen Pedersen). *Magisterbladet*. 4/1992.

Reports on Danmarks Radio (DR) hiring of women, up 1.4 percent from 1988 to 1991; positions by women in production increased by 6 percent.

1319. Gussow, Mel. "A Filmmaker at High Tide Since France's New Wave." *New York Times*. October 2, 1997, p. E-1, E-6.

Profiles France's independent filmmaker, Agnes Varda, whose retrospective of 31 films was being celebrated at Museum of Modern Art, New York.

1320. Habord, Patricia. "Interview with Jutta Brückner." *Screen Education*. 40 (1981-1982), pp. 48-57.

Profiles German filmmaker.

1321. Halonen, Irma K. "Women and the Public Sphere." *Nordicom Review*. 1/1991, pp. 9-14.

Section on feminine journalism.

1322. Hänninen, Harto. "Girls Just Wanna Have Fun. Women Renew Finnish Comics." *Nordic Comics Revue International.* Autumn 1992, pp. 11-13.

Predicts that the 1990s would be the decade of female comic artists in Finland on the basis that women had found comics as artists and readers and had founded a women's comics magazine.

1323. Hasted, Nick. "British Market Frustrating for Women Cartoonists." *Comics Journal.* February 1992, pp. 33-36.

1324. Hill, Leslie. *Marguerite Duras: Apocalyptic Desires.* New York: Routledge, 1993. 224 pp.

Encompasses all of this French writer/filmmaker's works; includes a listing of her journalism, interviews, and media appearances.

1325. Hinton, David B. *The Films of Leni Riefenstahl.* Second Edition. Metuchen, New Jersey: Scarecrow Press, 1991. 205 pp.

During the years of Nazi Germany.

1326. Hoaas, Solrun. "Anja Breien." *Cinema Papers.* 39 (1982), pp. 320-391.

Profiles Norwegian filmmaker Breien.

1327. Hoberman, J. "Once upon a Time in Amerika: Straub/Huillet/Kafka." *Artforum.* September 1984, pp. 75-77.

Discusses French/German filmmaker team of Jean-Marie Straub and Danièle Huillet.

1328. Iivari, J. and M. Igbaria. "Determinant of User Participation: A Finnish Survey." *Behaviour and Information Technology.* March/April 1997, pp. 111-121.

Delves into user participation and information systems success in Finland; shows that gender, education, and computer training have significant effects.

1329. Indiana, Gary. "Spirits Either Sex Assume: Gary Indiana Talks with Sally Potter." *Artforum.* Summer 1993, pp. 88-91.

British avant-garde filmmaker.

1330. Insdorf, Annette. "Von Trotta: By Sisters Obsessed." *New York Times.* January 31, 1982, pp. H 19, H 22.

Discusses Margarethe von Trotta, one of Germany's best-known directors.

1331. "Ireland's Truth-Teller Silenced." *CPJ Dangerous Assignments.* Summer 1996, pp. 1-2, 10.

Tells how Veronica Guerin, Ireland's leading investigative reporter, was assassinated by motorcycle gunmen, June 26, 1996. Guerin had exposed Ireland's criminal underworld.

1332. Jackson, Lynne and Jean Rasenberger. "An Interview with Martina Attile and Isaac Julien." *Cineaste.* 14:4 (1988), pp. 23-37.

Interview with British filmmaker Attile.

1333. "Joanna Quinn." *Animation Journal*. Fall 1995, p. 53.
       Short resumé of British animator.

1334. Karakas, Berrin. "Ramize Erer: Karikatür Tamamen Hayatla Ilgili.'" *Karikatürk*.
       No. 45, 1997, pp. 566-567.
       Interview with one of Turkey's few female cartoonists, Ramize Erer, who
       said walking into the humor magazine *Girgir*'s office to work was like going to
       the male dominated coffee houses.

1335. Kindblom, Mikaela. "Feministisk Filmforskning (Feminist Filmmaking)."
       Kvinnovetenskaplig Tidskrift. 12:4 (1991), pp. 66-68.

1336. Knight, Julia. *Women and the New German Cinema*. London: Routledge, Verso,
       1992. 232 pp.
       Examines how restrictive social, economic, and institutional conditions
       compounded the neglect of female directors such as Margarethe von Trotta,
       Helma Sanders-Brahms, Ulrike Ottinger, Helke Sander, and Ula Stoeckl; explores
       principal characteristics of women's filmmaking of 1970s-1980s.

1337. Kuhn, Annette. "Encounter Between Two Cultures." *Screen*. Autumn 1987, pp.
       74-79.
       A discussion with German filmmaker Ulrike Ottinger.

1338. Lacassin, Francis. "Out of Oblivion: Alice Guy-Blaché." *Sight and Sound*.
       Summer 1971, pp. 151-154.
       Laments the lack of recognition given to French film pioneer Alice Guy-
       Blaché.

1339. Law, Sandra. "Putting Themselves in the Pictures: Images of Women in the Work
       of Joanna Quinn, Candy Guard, and Alison de Vere." In *A Reader in Animation
       Studies*, edited by Jayne Pilling, pp. 48-70. London: John Libbey and Co., 1997.
       Explores work of three British filmmakers and how all three use animation
       to depict femininity and the experience of being female.

1340. Leger, Jackie. "PRO Files: German Animator Susanne Franzel." *Animation*. June
       1997, p. 46.
       Profiles career of Susanne Franzel, German animator who has her own
       studio, Sultana Films.

1341. Levin, Tobe. "Jelinek's Radical Radio -- Deconstructing the Woman in Context."
       Women's Studies International Forum. 14:1 (1991), pp. 85-97.
       Uses Austrian-born Elfriede Jelinek to show that the French have offered
       feminists a useful methodology; discusses her radio work.

1342. Linville, Susan E. *Feminism, Film, Fascism: Women's Auto/biographical Film in
       Postwar Germany*. Austin: University of Texas Press, 1998. 208 pp.
       Analyzes five important films that reflect back on the Third Reich through

the experiences of women of different ages -- Marianne Rosenblum's "Peppermint Peace," Helma Sanders-Brahms' "Germany, Pale Mother," Jutta Brückner's "Hunger Years," Margarethe von Trotta's "Marianne and Juliane," and Jeanine Meerapfel's "Malou."

1343. Löfgren-Nilsson, Monica. *Kvinnligt, Manligt. Journalistiskt -- Journalisters Syn på Nyhetsvärdering.* Göteborg: Göteborgs Universitet, Institutionen för Journalistik och Masskommunikation, 1992.

1344. Löfgren-Nilsson, Monica. "Sweden: Female Journalists -- Journalistic Culture and Equality." *Gender and Mass Media Newsletter.* November 1992, pp. 27-28.
    Shows how Swedish women and men differ in their views of journalism: women stress "stimulating new thoughts," "bringing about experience," criticizing social justice, and are more critical to the ways of deciding what is news than men.

1345. Loiperdinger, Martin. "Halb Dokument, Halb Fälschung: Zur Inszenierung der Eröffnungsfeier in Leni Riefenstahls Olympia-Film 'Fest der Völker.'" *Medium.* 18:3 (1988), pp. 42-46.

1346. "Loving Portrait of a Director's Roots." *New York Times.* June 25, 1993, p. C-21.
    States that Agnes Varda gives life to her husband's memories.

1347. Lünenborg, Margret. *Journalistinnen in Europa: Eine International Vergleichende Analyse zum Gendering in Sozialen System Journalismus* (Women Journalists in Europe: An International Comparative Analysis of Gender in the Social System of Journalism). Opladen: Westdeutscher Verlag, 1997. 377 pp.
    Contains data on Germany, Denmark, Italy, and Spain in early 1990s, plus interviews with media managers and 32 women journalists working in feminist journalism.

1348. McFarlane, Brian, ed. *Sixty Voices: Celebrities Recall the Golden Age of British Cinema.* London: British Film Institute, 1993. 272 pp.
    Stars such as Deborah Kerr talk about their careers and the glory days of British cinema.

1349. McGreal, Jill. "Out of the Animation Ghetto: Clare Kitson and Her Muffia." *Animation World Magazine.* May 1996.
    Reports on how women will lead Channel 4 of Britain into series television, using the irreverent talents of Candy Guard and Sarah Ann Kennedy.

1350. Macnab, Geoffrey. *Searching for Stars: A Survey of Stardom and Screen Acting in British Cinema.* London: Cassell Academic, 1998. 256 pp.
    Includes chapters "Phyllis Calvert v Margaret Lockwood" and "Inside the Charm School."

1351. McRobbie, Angela. "Introduction to Interview with Ulrike Ottinger." *Screen.* Winter-Spring 1982, p. 34.
    Introduces German filmmaker Ottinger.

1352. Markham, James. "Behind *Men* Stands a Woman with a Sense of Humor." *New York Times*. July 27, 1989, pp. 11, 19.
       Discusses German filmmaker, Doris Dörrie, one of whose 13 works is "Men."

1353. Marsa Vancells, P. *La Mujer en el Periodismo* (The Woman in Journalism). Madrid: Torremozas, 1987.

1354. Maxwell, Elisabeth. *A Mind of My Own: My Life with Robert Maxwell*. New York: Harper/Collins, 1994. 536 pp.
       Widow of British publishing magnate tells about her life before and after marriage to Robert Maxwell; provides much on her role behind the scenes of the media empire.

1355. Mayne, Judith, Helen Fehervary, and Claudia Lensson. "From Hitler to Hepburn: A Discussion of Women's Film Production and Reception." *New German Critique*. Fall/Winter 1981-1982, pp. 171-185.

1356. Melin, Margareta. *Female Educators and Male Craftsman? The Professional Ideals Among Swedish Journalists*. Göteborg: Institutionen för Journalistik och Masskommunikation, Göteborgs Universitet, 1995. 20 pp.
       Discusses Swedish journalists' self images; focus on gender and education; based on 1989 questionnaire answered by about 900 journalists. See her article with same title in *Nordicom Review*, No. 1, 1996, pp. 153-169.

1357. Melin, Margareta. *Var Finns Kvinnorna? En Analys Av Manligt och Kvinnligt: Kurslitteraturen Vid Journalisthögskolan i Göteborg*. Göteborgs Universitet, Institutionen för Journalistik och Masskommunikation, 1993.

1358. Merz, Caroline. "The Tension of Genre: Wendy Toye and Muriel Box." In *Re-Viewing British Cinema, 1900-1992*, edited by Wheeler Winston Dixon, pp. 121-132. Albany: State University of New York Press, 1994.
       Discusses two important British film directors.

1359. Meyer zum Felde, Annette. "Alle nur Mütter: Die 'N.S. Frauen-Warte' und Ihre Propaganda." *Medium*. 18:3 (1988), pp. 46-48.

1360. Mievis, Jean-Marie. "Chantal de Spiegeleer. Leven aan Zee." *Stripschrift*. June 1991, pp. 20-24.
       Interviews Chantal de Spiegeleer, Belgian comics illustrator, known for strips, "Mirabelle" and "Madila Bay."

1361. Monti, Adriana. "Introduction to the Script of the Film *Scuola Senza Fine*." In *Off Screen: Women and Film in Italy*, edited by Giuliana Bruno and Maria Nadotti, pp. 80-83. London: Routledge, 1988.
       Tells how author organized a group of Italian housewives to shoot the film "Scuola Senza Fine."

1362. Moritz, William. "Lotte Reiniger." *Animation World*. June 1996, 7 pp.
Profiles German animator Lotte Reiniger, who made 70 films, including features such as "The Adventures of Prince Achmed" and "Dr. Doolittle."

1363. Mueller, Roswitha. *Valie Export / Fragments of the Imagination*. Bloomington: Indiana University Press, 1994.
On German filmmaker Valie Export.

1364. Mühlen-Achs, Gitta. *Bildersturm: Frauen in den Medien* (Iconoclasm: Women in the Media). Munich: Verlag Frauenoffensive, 1990. 219 pp.
Includes fifteen articles by German women journalists.

1365. Murphy, Kathleen. "Herstory as Her Is Harped." *Film Comment*. May-June 1994, pp. 31-34.
Deals with work of Irish filmmaker Pat Murphy, whose works were "Rituals of Memory," "Mauve," and "Anne Devlin"; the same issue has Kevin Rockett's "A Short History of Cinema in Ireland," pp. 25-30.

1366. Neverla, Irene and Gerda Kanzleiter. *Die Situation von Frauen im Journalismus; Arbeitsbedingungen, Berufswege und Beruflische Orientierung von Journalistinnen*. Schlussbericht an die Deutsche Forschungsgemeinschaft. Munich: 1982.

1367. NRKs Likestillingsutralg. "Hvem Snakker i NRK?" (Who Speaks in Norwegian Broadcasting?). Report. Oslo: NRK, 1992.
Shows that at Norwegian Broadcasting Corporation, the share of women on staff increased markedly in the period 1983-1991 -- from 27 to 39 percent, but the share of women participating in programs increased only slightly, from 27 to 30 percent.

1368. *NRKs Virksomhetsplan for Likestilling* (Progress Report of the Equality Committee at NRK). Report. Oslo: NRK, 1991.

1369. Pedersen, Vibeke. *Soap, Pin up and Burlesque: Commercialization and Femininity in Danish Television*. Copenhagen: Department of Nordic Philology, University of Copenhagen, 1993. 28 pp.
Discusses 1991-1992 Danish television when several young female hosts made breakthroughs to talk shows and entertainment programs, working solely, not alongside a mature male host. Also in *Nordisk Forskning om Kvinnor Och Medier*, edited by Ulla Carlsson. Göteborg: Nordicom, 1993; *Nordicom Review*, No. 2, 1993, pp. 25-35; *Communication*, 19:1 (1994), pp. 51-66.

1370. Perez, Gilbert. "Modernist Cinema: The *History Lessons* of Straub and Huillet." *Artforum*. October 1978, pp. 46-55.
Discusses French/German filmmaker, Danièle Huillet, who with Jean-Marie Straub, co-directed about 20 films.

1371. Pickard, Jane. "Annual Hours: A Year of Living Dangerously." *Personnel Management*. August 1991, pp. 38-43.

Reports that women with children suffered the most under the system of annualized hours at England's Independent Television News.

1372. Reiniger, Lotte. "Scissors Make Films." *Sight and Sound*. Spring 1936, pp. 13-15.
Discusses the silhouette animation form she invented, made from free-cut silhouettes that are hand-cut with scissors.

1373. Reiniger, Lotte. *Shadow Theatres and Shadow Films*. New York: Guptill, 1970.
By inventor of forms of silhouette animation.

1374. Rich, B. Ruby. "Leni Riefenstahl: The Deceptive Myth." In *Sexual Stratagems: The World of Women in Myth*, edited by Patricia Erens. New York: Horizon, 1979.
Discusses career of Nazi filmmaker who protests that she was politically naive while making "Triumph of the Will" (1934-1935) and "Olympia" (1936-1938) for Hitler.

1375. Richardson, Brenda. "An Interview with Gunvor Nelson and Dorothy Wiley." *Film Quarterly*. Fall 1971, pp. 34-39.
Interviews experimental filmmakers who worked together on "Schmeerguntz," "Fog Pumas," "Five Artists," and "Before Need."

1376. Riefenstahl, Leni. *Leni Riefenstahl: A Memoir*. New York: St. Martin's Press, 1993.
Gives account of her career, including filmmaking for Hitler, which she claims was done while she was politically naive.

1377. Romani, Cinzia. *Tainted Goddesses: Female Film Stars of the Third Reich*. New York: Sarpedon, 1992. 182 pp.
Features profiles of Henny Porten, Olga Tschechowa, Lil Dagover, Brigitte Horney, Sybille Schmitz, Zarah Leander, Kristina Söderbaum, Luise Ullrich, Heidemarie Hatheyer, Liliane Harvey, Renate Müller, Grethe Weiser, Marianne Hoppe, Ilse Werner, Paula Wessley, Käthe Von Nagy, Lida Baarova, Marika Rökk.

1378. Rose, Sarah. "Soldiering on: This Is One Journalist Who Refuses To Fade Away. Clare Hollingworth." *Far Eastern Economic Review*. November 13, 1997, p. 78.
Profiles octogenarian who scooped the story of the century (beginning of World War II) and was still writing in 1997.

1379. "Sally Artz." *Cartoonist PROfiles*. June 1980, pp. 46-51.
Interviews creator of British comic strips, "Libby" and "Our Gran."

1380. Salverda, Murk. "Annie M. G. Schmidt. Het Begon Altijd met Een Versje...." *Stripschrift*. September 1991, pp. 20-23.
Relates career and work of children's literature writer, Annie M. G. Schmidt, who worked closely with many Dutch illustrators, cartoonists, and

newspapers.

1381. Schwartz, Ronald. *Spanish Film Directors*. Metuchen, New Jersey: Scarecrow Press, 1986.
Includes women directors such as Pilar Miro.

1382. Segrave, Kerry and Linda Martin. *The Continental Actress: European Film Stars of the Postwar Era*. Jefferson, North Carolina: McFarland and Co., 1990. 320 pp.
Provides brief biographies, complete filmographies of 41 famous actresses from Italy, Greece, France, West Germany, and Scandinavia.

1383. Servais, Jan, Thomas L. Jacobson, and Shirley A. White, eds. *Participatory Communication for Social Change*. Thousand Oaks, California: Sage, 1996. 286 pp.
Broken into sections on "General Perspectives," "Methodological Perspectives," and "From Theory to Practice"; includes S. Stuart and R. Bery, "Powerful Grassroots Women Communicators: Participatory Video in Bangladesh."

1384. Silverman, Kaja. "Helke Sander and the Will To Change." *Discourse*. Fall 1983, pp. 10-30.
Discusses work of German film director, Helke Sander.

1385. Skretting, Katherine. "Women As Presenters on Television." Paper presented at International Association for Mass Communication Research, Sydney, Australia, August 21, 1996.
Examines roles that women play as television presenters, based on a study of programs screened on the main Norwegian television channels in 1995; contends that women predominated in weather and news. Youth and beauty were prerequisites; women can not give their personalities to the news.

1386. Starr, Cecile. "Lotte Reiniger's Fabulous Film Career." *Sight Lines*. Summer 1980, pp. 17-19.
In silhouette animation.

1387. Stone, James S. *Emily Faithfull: Victorian of Women's Rights*. Toronto: P.D. Meany, 1994. 336 pp.
Profiles founder and manager of the Victoria Press and editor of *Victoria Magazine* in late nineteenth century London.

1388. Street, Rita. "Sue Loughlin: An Animator's Profile." *Animation World*. July 1996, 4 pp.
Profiles British animator, Sue Loughlin, and her making of "Grand National" and "Dreaming While You Sleep."

1389. Sveriges Radio, Men and Women in Broadcasting. *Working Towards Equality at Sveriges Radio. Final Report of the Swedish Broadcasting Corporation Project on Equality of the Sexes*. Stockholm: Sveriges Radio: s förlag, 1981.

1390. Talton, Jana M. "Agnès Varda: Ahead of the Avant-garde." *Ms.* May-June 1993, pp. 78-80.

Describes French filmmaker Varda's revolutionary work and thoughts on feminism; Varda has done more than a score of features, shorts, and documentaries.

1391. Tönbekici, Mutlu. "Daha Fazla Kötü Kiz Lazim." *Hürriyet.* March 15, 1998, p. 3.

Profiles one of the few women cartoonists in Turkey, Ramize Erer.

1392. Toonder, Jan Gerhard. "Over Phiny 1912-1990." *Stripschrift.* October 1990, p. 2.

Profiles Dutch illustrator, cartoonist.

1393. Treut, Monika. "Ein Nachtrag zu Ulrike Ottinger's Film *Madame X.*" *Frauen und Film.* 28 (1981), pp. 15-21.

One filmmaker discussing the work of another German director.

1394. Tuathail, Gearoid O. "An Anti-Geopolitical Eye: Maggie O'Kane in Bosnia, 1992-1993." *Gender, Place and Culture.* July 1996, pp. 171-185.

Looks at relationship among gender, geopolitics, and the "gaze," using the Bosnian dispatches of British journalist Maggie O'Kane; claims O'Kane gave voice to victims (in particular, women and children), not politicians.

1395. Van Zoonen, Liesbet. "Pia, Hennie, Maartje en Joop -- De Opkomst van Vrouwelijke Nieuwslezer" (Pia, Hennie, Maartje and Joop -- The Rise of the Female Newsreader). *Tijdschrift voor Vrouwenstudies.* 12:4 (1991), pp. 470-482.

Draws attention to the dramatic increase in the number of female newsreaders on Dutch television since 1965.

1396. Van Zoonen, Liesbet. "A Tyranny of Intimacy? Women, Femininity and Television News." In *Communication and Citizenship: Journalism and the Public Sphere in the New Media Age*, edited by P. Dahlgren and C. Sparks, pp. 217-235. London: Routledge, 1991.

Analyzes predominance of women news readers in Dutch television through "sameness-difference" dilemma of feminist theory, i.e., should women become the same as men and thus equal or should (and can) they be different from men and still be equal?

1397. Vincendeau, Ginette. "Coline Serreau: A High Wire Act." *Sight and Sound.* March 1994, pp. 26-28.

Profiles French filmmaker who makes commercial, yet feminist, films working within the mainstream industry. See analysis of her "La Crise" (1992) in *Sight and Sound* (March 1994, pp. 37-38).

1398. Vincendeau, Ginette. "Like Eating a Lot of Madeleines: An Interview with Diane Kurys." *Monthly Film Bulletin.* March 1991, pp. 69-70.

French filmmaker; same issue (pp. 68-69) carries Jill Forbes' review of Kurys' "La Baule les Pins."

1399. Vitti, Antonio C. "The Critics 'Swept Away' by Wertmüller's Sexual Politics." *NEMLA Italian Studies*. 13-14 (1989-1990), pp. 121-131.
Discusses Italian film director Lina Wertmüller and her interests in sadomasochistic sexuality and leftist politics.

1400. Wallander, Kristina. "Women's Voices and Feminine Perspectives in the Swedish Union Press. Women's Participation in Four Union Journals." *Gender and Mass Media Newsletter*. November 1991, p. 17.
Looks at women's roles and voices in the journal of the Swedish Metalworkers' Union, 1890-1978; based on her doctoral thesis which eventually became a book.

1401. Wilkinson, Helen. "Looking Down the Road Not Taken." *Working Woman*. December 1995, pp. 45, 60.
Tells how one woman left BBC career to start a policy think tank, Demos.

1402. Wonsowitz, Petra. "Eigensinn Trägt Rote Haare; Frauenbilder im Comic." *MedienConcret*. No. 1, 1993, pp. 54-60.

1403. Zilliacus-Tikkanen, Henrika. "Jämställda Pa Manliga Villkor? Finländska Kvinnliga Journalisters Strategier i ett Nordiskt Perspektiv." In *Journalistik, Kommunikation, Utbildning* (Finnish Women Journalists and Equality). Helsingfors: Svenska Socialoch Kommunalhögskolan vid Helsinfors Universitet, 1991.
Claims many women in Finnish media appear to prefer to work in alignment with prevailing cultural precepts and hesitate to enforce "feminine priorities."

1404. Zilliacus-Tikkanen, Henrika. *Kvinnliga Journalisters Strategier. En Intervju Undersökning om Attityder Hos Kvinnliga Nyhetsjournalister inom Rund-radion* (The Strategies of Female Journalists -- Interview Research). Licentiatavhandling. Helsingfors: Helsingfors Universitet, 1990.

1405. Zilliacus-Tikkanen, Henrika. "The Strategies of Female Journalists." *Gender and Mass Media Newsletter*. November 1991, p. 24.
Interviews 37 female journalists working in six newsrooms at Finnish Broadcasting Company to describe the strategies in regard to sex roles in journalism and to discuss the criteria for a female perspective in journalism and the conditions necessary for change.

1406. Zilliacus-Tikkanen, Henrika. "Strategies of Women Broadcast Journalists -- An Interview Survey." *Gender and Mass Media Newsletter*. November 1991, p. 15-16.
Presents principal findings of author's interviews with women journalists in the news departments of Finnish Broadcasting Corporation; compares their attitudes and strategies with those of Norwegian media.

1407. Zorpette, Glenn. "Elizabeth Laverick." *IEEE Spectrum*. May 1992, pp. 40-42.
Profiles Laverick, the only woman named an IEEE Fellow from UK and

Ireland; noted for her engineering work in radio.

Women's Media

1408. *Arcade*.
September 1990 -- Thematic issue on "Théatre et Séduction," edited by Louise Pelletier includes Diane Pavlovic, "Conquérantes et Captives," pp. 42-46; Lise Vaillancourt, "Comment on Fait Ça?" pp. 55-57, and Michelle Allen, "Alice Ronfard -- La Séduction par l'Excès," pp. 72-83.

1409. Ayers, M. Kathryn. "The Only Good Woman, Isn't a Woman at All: *The Crying Game* and the Politics of Misogyny." *Women's Studies International Forum*. 20:2 (1997), pp. 329-335.
Analyzes film "The Crying Game"; claims director Neil Jordan used it in misogynistic manner as he relied on the age-old definition of female political behavior.

1410. Ballaster, Rose, Margaret Beetham, Elizabeth Frazer, and Sandra Hebron. *Women's Worlds: Ideology, Femininity, and the Women's Magazine*. Houndmills, England: Macmillan, 1991.

1411. Barker, Martin. *Comics -- Ideology, Power and the Critics*. Manchester and New York: Manchester University Press and St. Martin's Press, 1989. 320 pp.
Chapters 7 and 8 analyze teen magazine, *Jackie*, and its purported impact upon British girls.

1412. Beetham, Margaret. *A Magazine of Her Own? Domesticity and Desire in the Woman's Magazine, 1800-1914*. New York: Routledge, 1996. 256 pp.
Shows how women's magazines have shaped contemporary images of women; examines British women's periodicals 1800-1914, organized around a series of intertextual case studies.

1413. Camauër, Leonor. *Women, Identity and the Public Sphere: An Ethnographic Study of Four Women's Associations' Media Practices*. Stockholm: Stockholms Universitet, Institutionen för Journalistik, Medier och Kommunikation, 1995. 24 pp.
Deals with media practices of The Women's Front (Kvinnofronten), Fredrika Bremer Association, the Swedish Organization of Emergency Shelters for Battered Women (Riksorganisationen för Kvinnojour i Sverige), and a group of women publishing a feminist magazine.

1414. de Lanerolle, Ros. "Publishing Against the 'Other Censorship.'" *Index on Censorship*. October 1990, pp. 8-9.
Describes feminist publishing in England.

1415. Dignam, Conor. "Viva! Carves a Niche in Cut-Throat Sector." *Marketing*. July 6, 1995, p. 8.

Reports on opening of Viva!, the London radio station for women.

1416. Domínguez Juan, María Milagros. "Representación de la Mujer en las Revistas Femeninas" (Representation of the Woman in Women's Magazines). Ph.D. dissertation. Universidad Complutense de Madrid, Facultad de Ciencias Políticas y Sociología, 1988.

1417. "European Women Launch Media Network." *Action*. November-December 1990, p. 3.

1418. Ford, Charles. *Femmes Cinéastes, ou Le Triomphe de la Volonté*. Paris: Denoël/Gonthier, 1972.

1419. Foster, Gwendolyn. "Giuliana Bruno: *Streetwalking on a Ruined Map*." *Post Script*. Winter-Spring 1994, p. 54-56.
        Reviews Bruno's work on city films of Italy's Elvira Notari.

1420. Franquet, Rosa. "Evolución de la Programación Femenina en la Radiodifusión. (Los Medios Electrónicos en la Configuración del Estereotipo de la Mujer)" (Evolution of Feminine Programming in Radio Broadcasting. [The Electronic Media in the Configuration of the Stereotype of the Woman]). In *Jornadas de Investigacion Interdisciplinarias* (4-1984, Zaragoza). Zaragoza: Universidad, 1986.

1421. Frazer, Elizabeth. "Teenage Girls Reading *Jackie*." *Media, Culture and Society*. 9 (1987), pp. 407-425.
        British girls' magazine, *Jackie*.

1422. Geraghty, Christine. *Women and Soap Opera: A Study of Prime Time Soaps*. Cambridge: Polity Press, 1991. 211 pp.

1423. Hausken, Liv. *En Annen Historie. En Analyse av Anja Breien's "Hustruer"* (Another Story: An Analysis of Anja Breien's Film, Hustruer). Bergen: Hovedoppgave Institutt for Massekommunikasjon, Universitetet i Bergen, 1992.
        Analyzes Norwegian film, "Wives," with attention to the relationship between the rhetoric of the film and its thematics -- the rhetoric relating to women and the images of women the film gives.

1424. Hebron, Sandra. "*Jackie* and *Woman's Own*: Ideological Work and the Social Construction of Gender Identity." BA dissertation, Sheffield City Polytechnic, 1983.
        Publicized as *Occasional Paper*, May 1983.

1425. Hellman, Heikki. "'En Edes Tiedä Miten Sitä Laitetta Käytetään.' Videon Tekniikan ja Käytön Sukupuolirakenteista" ('I Don't Even Know How To Use the Machine Properly': The Gender Structure of Video Technology). *Naistutkimus-Kvinnoforskning*. 7:2 (1994), pp. 58-74.

1426. Hermes, Joke and Veronique Schutgens. "A Case of the Emperor's New Clothes?

Reception and Text Analysis of the Dutch Feminist Magazine 'Opzij.'" *European Journal of Communication*. September 1992, pp. 307-334.

1427. Higson, Andrew, ed. *Dissolving Views: Key Writing on British Cinema*. London: Cassell Academic, 1996. 256 pp.
    Deals with "neglected topics"; includes Justine King on women's films of the 1980s.

1428. Hinnegan, Alison. "Weathering the Storm." *Women's Review of Books*. April 1992, pp. 5-7.
    States that in year of upheaval for British publishers, feminist publishers such as Virago, Pandora, and Women's Press had their problems; some smaller presses addressing their own markets were protected.

1429. Hollinger, Karen. "Losing the Feminist Drift: Adaptations of *Les Liaisons Dangereuses*." *Literature/Film Quarterly*. 24:3 (n.d.).

1430. Jallov, B. *Women's Voices: Crossing Frontiers*. European Directory of Women's Community Radio Stations and Women's Radio Production Collectives, AMARC-Europe, 1996.

1431. Kirkup, Gill and Christine von Prummer. "Distance Education for European Women: The Threats and Opportunities of New Educational Forms and Media." *European Journal of Women's Studies*. February 1997, pp. 39-62.
    Draws on data from students in England and Germany to examine distance education for women in Europe, gender barriers to its use, and how proper use of new media can offset that discrimination.

1432. Lacey, Kate. "From *Plauderei* to Propaganda: On Women's Radio in Germany, 1924-1935." *Media, Culture and Society*. October 1994, pp. 589-607.
    Traces history of first programs for women on German radio to 1924; demonstrates that in the first decades of German radio, "the contested nature of the gendered division between the public and the private spheres provided the framework for the public discourse about the social functions of radio"; shows how this discourse fed into women's programming. Abstracted from author's doctoral thesis at University of Liverpool (1993), entitled, "Bridging the Divide: Women, Radio and the Re-negotiation of the Public and Private Spheres in Germany, 1923-1945." See also author's *Feminine Frequencies: Gender, German Radio, and the Public Sphere, 1924-1945* (Ann Arbor: University of Michigan Press, 1996. 299 pp.).

1433. Lant, Antonia. "Women's Independent Cinema: The Case of Leeds Animation Workshop." In *Fires Were Started: British Cinema and Thatcherism*, edited by Lester Friedman, pp. 161-187. Minneapolis: University of Minnesota Press, 1993.

1434. Linville, Susan E. *Feminism, Film, Fascism: Women's Auto/biographical Film in Postwar Germany*. Austin: University of Texas Press, 1998. 196 pp.

1435. McRobbie, Angela. "*Jackie*: An Ideology of Adolescent Femininity." Birmingham: Occasional Paper, Centre for Contemporary Cultural Studies, University of Birmingham, 1978.

In British girls' magazine, *Jackie*.

1436. Martinez, Amalia. "La Imagen de la Mujer en las Telenovelas: Emma Harte" (The Image of the Woman in the 'Emma Harte' Soap Operas). In *Seminario sobre "Mujer y Medios de Comunicación Social.*" Valencia: RTVE, 1987.

1437. Mayne, Judith. "Female Narration, Women's Cinema: Helke Sander's *The All-Round Reduced Personality/Redupers.*" *New German Critique.* Fall-Winter 1981-1982, pp. 155-171.

Discusses a film of German feminist political activist/director Helke Sander.

1438. Melin-Higgins, Margareta. "Female Educators and Male Craftsmen? The Professional Ideals Among Swedish Journalists." *Nordicom Review.* No. 1, 1996, pp. 153-169.

Contends that Swedish women think that a journalist ought to be a scrutinizer and critic of injustices more often than men are; claims women journalists are "bloodhounds" because they know the only way to succeed is to be better than men.

1439. Morgan, Maggie. "Jam Making, Cuthbert Rabbit and Cakes: Redefining Domestic Labour in the Women's Institute, 1915-1960." *Rural History.* October 1996, pp. 207-219.

Discusses role of the monthly magazine, *Home and Country*, in the British Women's Institute Movement of the twentieth century.

1440. O'Connell, Margaret. "Cinderella...Was an Englishwoman." *Comic Fandom's Forum.* September 1982, pp. 72-77.

Discusses girls' comics in England.

1441. O'Donnell, Hugh and Paul Mohr. *Good Times, Bad Times: The New Soap Operas in Western Europe.* London: Cassell Academic, 1997. 224 pp.

Includes soaps produced all over Europe, but also others from the U.S., Australia, South America, and elsewhere that are screened in Western Europe; includes audience analysis, plot and theme similarities and differences, scheduling and screening times, etc.; concentrates on those after 1990.

1442. O'Healy, Anie. "Reframing Desire in Lina Wertmüller's *Sotto...Sotto.*" *Spectator.* Spring 1990, pp. 45-57.

Discusses one of Italian filmmaker Wertmüller's numerous films, all of which are comic sociocultural studies of Italian machismo and sexuality.

1443. Perlmutter, Ruth. "Two New Films by Helke Sander and Ulrike Ottinger." *Film Criticism.* Winter 1984-1985, pp. 67-73.

Discusses new works by prominent German directors.

1444. Ramanathan, Geetha. "Murder as Speech: Narrative Subjectivity in Marleen Gorris' *A Question of Silence*." *Genders*. Winter 1992, pp. 58-71.
Describes Dutch filmmaker Marleen Gorris' "De Stilte Rond Christine M."

1445. Ramírez, Juan Antonio. *El Comic Femenino en España*. Madrid: Editorial Cuadernos para el Diálogo, 1975.

1446. Rentschler, Eric. "Fatal Attractions: Leni Riefenstahl's *The Blue Light*." *October*. Spring 1989, pp. 46-68.
Analyzes Nazi filmmaker Riefenstahl's 1931 film, "The Blue Light," which she wrote, produced, directed, and starred in.

1447. Rogerat, Chantal. "The Case of Elletel." *Media, Culture and Society*. January 1992, pp. 73-88.
Describes French Teletel's information and communication service designed by and for women in 1984 and initially run by Agence Femmes Information; shows how Elletel was "deeply marked" by established rituals of inter-gender communication.

1448. Rogerat, Chantal. "Mode d'Usage de la Communication: La Cas d'Elletel." Paper presented at International Association for Mass Communication Research, Bled, Yugoslavia, August 26-31, 1990.
Gives case study of an information and communication service provided for and by women through the French Teletel.

1449. Ruyters, Jann. "Something To Suit All 'Viewpoints': Feminist Magazines in the Netherlands." *Women's Studies International Forum*. July-August 1993, pp. 427-436.
Outlines history and content of various Dutch feminist magazines, which since the 1970s, played a significant role in feminist debates in Holland; describes some leading magazines.

1450. Sabine, Hake. "'Gold, Love, Adventure': The Postmodern Conspiracy of Madame X." *Discourse*. Fall-Winter 1988-1989, pp. 88-110.
Analyzes "Madame X--An Absolute Ruler," a 1977 film by German director Ulrike Ottinger.

1451. Santa Eulalia, Mary G. "La Potente Ola del Periodismo Femenino" (The Mighty Wave of Feminine Journalism). La *Mujer Española: de la Tradición a la Modernidad*, pp. 127-132, Madrid: Tecnos, 1986.

1452. Savarese, Rossella. "The 'Housewife' of 3131." *Rivista di Sociologia*. 10:1-3 (1972), pp. 195-220.
Tells how Italian radio program, "Chiamate Roma 3131," was interrupted in 1972 when criticism mounted; format was call-in, with mainly women discussing love, faithfulness, Mafia, contact with other people, spousal violence, or injustice.

1453. Smelik, Anneke. "And the Mirror Cracked: Metaphors of Violence in the Films of Marleen Gorris." *Women's Studies International Forum.* July-August 1993, pp. 349-363.

Explores the metaphors of violence in Gorris' "A Question of Silence" and "Broken Mirrors"; Gorris is a Dutch director of feminist films.

1454. Thomsen, Inger. "Kvinders Film" (Women's Films). Master's thesis, University of Copenhagen, 1981. 193 pp.

1455. Tinkler, Penny. *Constructing Girlhood: Popular Magazines for Girls Growing Up in England 1920-1950.* London: Taylor & Francis, 1995. 209 pp.

Looks at "the cultural construction of adolescent girlhood" as revealed by the form and content of British magazines; states that girls were told to construct/regulate their bodies in relation to their "potential maternity, their assumed heterosexuality, and their wage labour," warned against excessive flirting, told to maintain their femininity.

1456. Tohka, Laura. *I Suggest You Accept Everything: Woman's Own's Agony Columns in 1950, 1970, and 1990.* Tampere: University of Tampere, Research Institute for Social Sciences, 1993. 77 pp.

Looks at how women's (and some men's) problems were treated in the agony columns of Britain's *Woman's Own* magazine.

1457. Wallsgrove, Ruth. "*Spare Rib*, 1972-1993: Sweet and Sour." *Off Our Backs.* May 1993, pp. 4+.

Recounts history of British women's liberation magazine, *Spare Rib*; its heyday was the late 1970s and early 1980s when it had a readership of 100,000.

1458. Weatherall, A. "Language about Women and Men: An Example from Popular Culture." *Journal of Language and Social Psychology.* March 1996, pp. 59-75.

Explores the potential of examining conversational language through fictional dialogues taken from the British soap opera, "Coronation Street"; states that scripted interactions showed virtually no evidence of a pervasive bias against women in language.

1459. Weber, Monika. *Mädchen-Zeitungs-Welten: Lebensrealität von Mädchen und ihr Bild in Mädchenzeitschriften* (Girls-Papers-Worlds: The Reality of Girls' Life and Its Image in Girls' Magazines). Munich: Votum Verlag, 1991. 206 pp.

Content analyzes girls' magazines in Germany.

1460. Weinberger, Gabriele. *Nazi Germany and Its Aftermath in Women Directors' Autobiographical Films of the Late 1970s.* San Francisco: Mellon Research University Press, 1992.

1461. Wertmüller, Lina. *The Screenplays of Lina Wertmüller.* Translated by Steven Wagner. New York: Quadrangle, 1977.

Italian actor, director, and screenwriter.

1462. Williams, James S. *The Erotics of Passage: Pleasure, Politics and Form in the*

Later Works of Marguerite Duras. New York: St. Martin's Press, 1997. 256 pp.
    Explores Duras' "self-reflexive and erotic practice of cinematic montage; her development of a new literary style called 'ecriture courante' which engages intertextually with European and American writers and filmmakers;...her performance in the media of a personal, post-political sublime."

1463. Williams, Val. *Warworks: Women, Photography and the Iconography of War*. London: Virago, 1994. 96 pp.

1464. Winship, Janice. "Book 2 Women's Magazines" PU712. In *Women, Writing and Culture*. Milton Keynes: The Open University, 1990.

1465. Winship, Janice. "A Girl Needs To Get Street-Wise: Magazines for the 1980s." *Feminist Review*. Winter 1985.

1466. Winship, Janice. "The Impossibility of *Best*: Enterprise Meets Domesticity in the Practical Women's Magazines of the 1980s." *Cultural Studies*. May 1991, pp. 131-156.
    Studies women's magazines *Prima, Best, Chat, Bella, Hallo!, Me, Take a Break, People's Friend, Woman, Woman's Own, Woman's Weekly*, and *Essentials*, of England, Germany, and Spain.

1467. Winter, Bronwyn. "International Feminist Bookfair Held in Amsterdam." *Off Our Backs*. November 1992, p. 7.
    Criticizes the fair as Eurocentric and heterosexist and for shutting down discussion.

CHAPTER 5

Latin America and the Caribbean

GENERAL STUDIES

1468. Aguirre, María T. "Citizen Keen." *Media and Gender Monitor*. Spring 1998, pp. 1-2.
   Reports on a conference on gender and communication policy in Lima, Peru, January 1998.

1469. Alfaro, Rosa M. "Mujer Como Agente Social Comunicativo: Maternidad Social y Liderazgo." Mimeographed. Peru: Calandria, n.d.

1470. Boliches, Emilia. "Mujer y Medios de Comunicación" (Woman and Communication Media). In *Seminario sobre "Mujer y Medios de Comunicación Social*," pp. 155-220, Valencia: RTVE, 1987.

1471. Burton-Carvajal, Julianne. "Introduction: Changing Gender Perspectives in Latin American Film." *Journal of Film and Video*. Fall 1992/Winter 1993, pp. 3-7.
   Introduces thematic issue on Latin American cinema.

1472. Charles, Mercedes. "Y la Mujer Prendió la Tele." *FEM*. December 1987.

1473. *Communication Research Trends*
   15:3 (1995) -- Thematic issue on "A Latin Perspective on the Media: Gender, Law and Ethics, the Environment and Media Education," edited by William E. Biernatzki, includes Mercedes Charles Creel, "Women and Men in the Latin American Media," pp. 3-9, and Vicente Baca Lagos, "Public Communication and Gender: Research in Spain," pp. 10-20.

1474. Egaña Baraona, Ana María. "Mujer Realizadora y Proyecto Profesional." *Media Development*. 4/1995, pp. 14-17.

1475. "Gender and Communication in Latin America." *Action*. March/April 1997, p. 8.

Reports on seminar in Santiago, Chile, sponsored by World Association for Christian Communication.

1476. "Global Communications: Democratic Access for Women." *Media Development*. 2/1995, pp. 38-39.

Document presented by the women of the Agencia Latinoamericana de Información to the Regional Preparatory Meeting of Latin America and the Caribbean for the 4th World Conference on Women, Beijing, 1995; suggests to the United Nations: "1. More democratic communications with a gender focus, 2. Women's access to new communications technologies that empower their communicational capacity, 3. Ensuring that media content projects a positive and non-discriminatory image of women, and 4. Labor equality between the genders and greater presence of women in decision-making positions in the media."

1477. Hermano, Teresita. "The Significance of Lima." *Media and Gender Monitor*. Spring 1998, pp. 1, 3.

Reports on conference in Lima, where Latin American women discussed codes of ethics and legislation on gender and communication. Declaration from conference on pp. 4-5.

1478. *Journal of Film and Video*.

Fall 1992/Winter 1993 -- Thematic issue on "Latin American Cinema: Gender Perspectives," edited by Julianne Burton-Carvajal, includes Julianne Burton-Carvajal, "Introduction: Changing Gender Perspectives in Latin American Film," pp. 3-7; Adrienne L. McLean, "'I'm a Cansino': Transformation, Ethnicity, and Authenticity in the Construction of Rita Hayworth, American Love Goddess," pp. 8-26; Eduardo de la Vega Alfaro and Patricia Torres San Martin, "Adela Sequeyro, Mexican Film Pioneer," pp. 27-32; Karen Schwartzman, Harel Calderon, and Julianne Burton-Carvajal, "An Interview with Margot Benacerraf: *Reverón, Araya*, and the Institutionalization of Cinema in Venezuela," pp. 51-75; Zuzana M. Pick, "An Interview with Maria Luisa Bemberg," pp. 76-82; Sergio de la Mora, "Fascinating Machismo: Toward an Unmasking of Heterosexual Masculinity in Arturo Ripstein's *El Lugar sin Limites*," pp. 83-104; Susana Conde, "Readerly and Writerly *Letters from the Park*," pp. 105-119; S. Travis Silcox, "'Represento el Pasado': Political Melodrama and Jesus Diaz's *Lejanía*," pp. 120-139; Chris Holmlund, "'The World in a Drop of Water': The Feminist Vision of Patricia Howell," pp. 140-154.

1479. Montgomery, Louise. "The Role of Women in Latin American Mass Media." In *Communication in Latin America: Journalism, Mass Media, and Society*, edited by Richard R. Cole. Wilmington, Delaware: Scholarly Resources, 1997.

1480. "New Forum in Latin America and Caribbean Will Work for Better Gender Communication." *Action*. October-November 1994, p. 7.

1481. "Santiago Conference Reviews Cultural Barriers to Media Access for Latin

American Women."
　　Reports on conference of Latin American and U.S. women journalists who met to map out a strategy for improving the role of women in the profession.

WOMEN AS AUDIENCE

1482. Alfaro, Rosa Maria. "The Omission of Woman As Subject." *Chasqui*. October 1994, pp. 59-64.
　　Contends that studies of peasant women in Latin America are lacking, especially in communications; proposes new perspective for peasant women and communication whereby they would be involved in a dialogue and reached on their own terms.

1483. Charles Creel, Mercedes. "El Espejo de Venus: Una Mirada a la Investigación Sobre Mujeres y Medios de Comunicación" (The Mirror of Venus: A View of Research on Women and Communication Media). *Signo y Pensamiento*. 15:28 (1997), pp. 37-50.
　　Reviews diverse perspectives involved in women and communication media of Latin America; includes history of the field, main trends in women's use of the media, women's receptiveness of alternative messages.

1484. Charles Creel, Mercedes. "La Investigación de la Recepción en Públicos Femeninos: La Cara Oculta del Proceso de Comunicación." Paper presented in seminar, "Women and the Media of Communication," Colegio de Mexico, 1993.

1485. Charles Creel, Mercedes. "Medios de Comunicación y Cultura Feminina: Un Tejido de Complicidades." In *Estudios sobre las Culturas Contemporáneas*. November 1990.

1486. Charles Creel, Mercedes. "Women and Men in the Latin American Media." *Communication Research Trends*. 15:3 (1995), pp. 3-10.
　　Traces chronologically the "serious" study of the relationship between women and the mass media of Latin America from the late 1960s to the present. Initially, concentration was on the message, but, by the mid-1980s, it shifted to the receiver. Deals with three models of women's reception of television programs: individual, family, and spousal.

WOMEN PRACTITIONERS

1487. Burton, Julianne and Zuzana Pick, eds. "The Women Behind the Camera." *Heresies*. No. 16, 1983, pp. 46-50.

1488. McLean, Adrienne L. "'I'm a Cansino': Transformation, Ethnicity, and Authenticity in the Construction of Rita Hayworth, American Love Goddess." *Journal of Film and Video*. Fall 1992/Winter 1993, pp. 8-26.
　　Recounts the transformation of Margarita Carmen Cansino into Rita Hayworth; challenges other biographers' accounts and claims that ethnicity served as a guarantor of her authenticity.

1489. Montgomery, Louise. "The Role of Women in Latin American Mass Media." In *Communication in Latin America: Journalism, Mass Media, and Society*, edited by Richard R. Cole, pp. 37-49. Wilmington, Delaware: Scholarly Resources, 1996.

Explains that more women are entering journalism with some moving to the top; discusses the success stories of Sofía Montenegro, Christiana Chamorro in Nicaragua, Carolina Rossetti, Patricia Escalona of Chile, María Jimena Duzán of Colombia, Elena Poniatowska of Mexico, Nila Velázquez of Ecuador.

1490. Trelles Plazaola, Luis. *Cine y Mujer en America Latina: Directoras de Largo-Metrajes de Ficción*. Río Piedras: University of Puerto Rico Press, 1991.

Deals with Latin American women directors of fictional film; starts with era of silent movies and moves to the present; includes interviews with 12 female directors from different times and styles, including Matilde Landeta, Matilde Vera, Luisa Bemberg, and Tizuka Yamazaki.

1491. Valdivia, Cecilia Crespo. "Aymara Women Gain Power Through Media Training." *Group Media Journal*. 1990, pp. 13-17.

WOMEN'S MEDIA

1492. "Adriana Santa Cruz Begins Alternative Women's Media Unit for ILET." *Media Report to Women*. September 1, 1981, p. 1.

Announces beginning of regular clipping service of Alternative Women's Communication Unit of Latin American Institute for Transnational Studies (ILET).

1493. Alfaro, Rosa M. *Una Comunicación para Otro Desarrollo*. Peru: Asociación de Comunicadores Sociales Calandria, 1993.

States that soap opera scripts and subjects were handled more carefully in the late 1980s and early 1990s in Peru.

1494. "Fempress." *Gender and Mass Media Newsletter*. November 1992, p. 38.

Reports group's latest activities.

1495. Lozano, Elizabeth. "Rhetorical Constructions of Time: Feminine Taste, Melodramatic Hours." *Media Development*. 38:2 (1991), pp. 10-12.

Reflects on the construction of gender differences as they are articulated in the cultural appreciation of soap operas; deals mainly with Latin America. Based on author's thesis at Ohio University (1990), "The Televisual Melodrama: An Intertextual Analysis of Soap Operas as Rhetorical Discourse."

1496. Mazziotti, Nora. "Estado de las Investigaciones sobre la Telenovela Latinamericana" (The State of Studies about the Latin American Telenovela). In *Revista de Ciencias de la Información*. (Madrid). Número Extraordinario 1993, pp. 45-58.

1497. Muñoz, Sonia. "Apuntes sobre Dos Modos de Ver Telenovelas." *Estudios sobre las Culturas Contemporáneas*. February 1988.
    States that women participants in research on soap operas create their own "correct" model of the ideal woman.

1498. Santa Cruz, Adriana. "Fempress: A Communication Strategy for Women." *Gender and Development*. February 1995, pp. 51-54.
    Reviews efforts of Fempress -- a Latin American media network designed to address social injustices directed toward women -- since its 1981 beginnings.

CARIBBEAN

General Studies

1499. Chanan, Michael. *The Cuban Image: Cinema and Cultural Politics in Cuba*. Bloomington: Indiana University Press, 1985.

1500. De Bruin, Marjan. *Women and Caribbean Media*. Mona, Jamaica: Caribbean Institute of Mass Communication, University of the West Indies, 1994.

1501. Deming, Caren. "Cuba's Use of Media To Improve the Status of Women -- Dr. Caren Deming Report." *Media Report to Women*. May 1, 1981, pp. 6-7.
    Discusses history, the Revolution, women practitioners in broadcasting and film, images in novels/series, and new sex-role definitions.

Historical Studies

1502. Caraballo y Sotolongo, Francisco. "La Prensa Femenina." In *Mujeres a las Urnas y al Hogar*, pp. 141-168. Havana: Librería Cervantes, 1918.

1503. Catalá, Raquel. "La Mujer." *El Fígaro* (Havana). 38:19-20, 1921.

1504. Collado Romero, María. "La Mujer en el Periodismo." *La Mujer* (Havana). November 1935, p. 3.

1505. Collado Romero, María. " La Mujer en el Periodismo." In *Memoria del Primer Congreso Nacional de Mujeres*, pp. 253-256. Havana: Imprenta La Universal, 1924.

1506. Collado Romero, María. "Los 56 Periódicos del Aire." *La Mujer* (Havana). February 20, 1937, p. 15.

1507. Cotarelo y Mori, Emilio. *La Avellaneda y Sus Obras. Ensayo Biográfico y Crítico*. Madrid: Tipografia de Archivos, 1930.
    Discusses Avellaneda's journalism, pp. 349-351.

1508. Cotto, Cándida. "Caracteristicas del Periodismo Femenino del Siglo XIX." *Homines*. August 1989-August 1990, pp. 305-308.
    In Puerto Rico, 19th century.

1509. Duvalón, Georgina. "Presencia Femenina en la Prensa Cubana del Siglo XIX." *Mujeres* (Havana). March 1968, pp. 10-11.

1510. Garfield, Evelyn P. "La Revista Femenina en Cuba, 1860/1861: *Album Cubano de lo Bueno y lo Bello y Mujeres*." *Revista de Critica Literaria Latinoamericana.* 15:30 (1980), pp. 91-96.
       Compares two Cuban women's magazines -- the colonial *Album Cubano de lo Bueno y lo Bello* (1860) and the post-revolutionary *Mujeres* (1961).

1511. Garfield, Evelyn P. "Periodical Literature for Women in Mid-Nineteenth Century Cuba: The Case of Gertrudis Gómez de Avellaneda's *Album Cubano de lo Bueno y lo Bello*." *Studies in Latin American Popular Culture*. No. 11, 1992, pp. 13-28.
       Profiles the most famous and prolific Hispanic woman author of the mid-19th century and the magazine for women she started in 1860; Gómez de Avellaneda earlier (1845) edited a Madrid women's magazine, *La Ilustración de las Damas.*

1512. M.S.R. "Letras Güineras." *Cuba y América* (Havana). December 1909, pp. 31-32.
       Recounts story of *Letras Güineras*, published and edited exclusively by women.

1513. Otero, Ernestina. "Periodismo Femenino del Pasado y Necesidades del Presente." *Cúspide* (Central Mercedita). February 1939, pp. 14-15.

1514. Planas de Garrido, Herminia. "La Mujer en el Periodismo." In *Memoria del Primer Congreso Nacional de Mujeres Organizado por la Federación Nacional de Asociaciones Femeninas*, pp. 425-430. Havana: Imprenta La Universal, 1924.

1515. Rodríguez García, José A. *De la Avellaneda. Colección de Artículos*. Havana: Imprenta Cuba Intelectual, 1914.
       Discussion of her *Album de lo Bueno y de lo Bello.*

1516. Sagra, Ramón de la. "Carta Segunda del Señor la Sagra a la Señora Avellaneda." In *Album Cubano de lo Bueno y de lo Bello* (Havana). 1:7 (1860), pp. 231-233.

1517. Sosa de Quesada, Arístides. "Álbum Cubano de lo Bueno y de lo Bello." *Revista de la Biblioteca Nacional* (Havana). January-March 1957, pp. 103-124.

Images of Women

1518. Cooper, Carolyn. *Noises in the Blood: Orality, Gender and the "Vulgar" Body of Jamaican Popular Culture*. Durham, North Carolina: Duke University Press, 1993. 214 pp.

1519. D'Lugo, Marvin. "'Transparent Women': Gender and Nation in Cuban Cinema." In *Mediating Two Worlds: Cinematic Encounters in the Americas*, edited by John King, Ana M. López, and Manuel Alvarado, pp. 279-290. London: British Film

Institute, 1993.

1520. Francis-Brown, Suzanne. *Media, Gender and Development*. Mona, Jamaica: Caribbean Institute of Mass Communications, 1996.

1521. Miller, D. "*The Young and Restless* in Trinidad: A Case of Local and Global in Mass Consumption." In *Consuming Technologies*, edited by R. Silverstone and E. Hirsch, pp. 163-182. London: Routledge, 1992.

1522. Silcox, S. Travis. "'Represento el Pasado': Political Melodrama and Jesús Díaz's Lejanía." *Journal of Film and Video*. Fall 1992/Winter 1993, pp. 120-139.
        Traces contemporary literary analyses of melodrama and the romance, using much feminist film theory and the Cuban work, "Lejanía."

1523. Vargas, Jocelyn A. Géliga. "Expanding the Popular Culture Debates: *Puertorriqueñas*, Hollywood, and Cultural Identity." *Studies in Latin American Popular Culture*. Vol. 15, 1996, pp. 155-173.
        Presents a case study of Puerto Rican women and their relationship to products of popular culture, especially film.

1524. Virtue, Grace. "Image Overhaul: Jamaica's Media Watchers Tackle the Status of Women." *Toward Freedom*. December 1994, pp. 22, 29.
        Jamaica's Women Media Watch, a 15-member group dedicated to cleaning up image of women in media, has protested through public education, lobbying media and ad agencies, and networking with other women's groups.

Women Practitioners

1525. Arocena, Berta. "Mujeres en al Periodismo Cubano." In *Álbum del Cincuentenario de la Asociación de Reporters de la Habana*, pp. 114-116, Havana: Editorial Lex, 1952.

1526. *Cine Cubano*. No. 127 (1989).
        Articles remembering Sara Gómez by Marucha Hernández, Haydee Arteaga, José A. Lezcano, Tomás Gonzales, Peter Shumann, Gerardo Fulleda Leon, Michael Chanan, Iddia Veitia, Frank Padrón.

1527. "El Tiempo de Magaly." *Mujeres* (Havana). November 1974.
        Refers to a Cuban woman journalist.

1528. Jarret-Macauley, Delia. *The Life of Una Marson, 1905-1965*. Manchester/Kingston: Manchester University Press and Ian Randle Press, 1998. 272 pp.
        Chronicles life of one of Jamaica's pioneering journalists, poet and playwright Una Marson.

1529. Lent, John A. "Mujeres Periodistas en el Caribe." *Homines*. October 1991-December 1992, pp. 265-272.
        Interviews women editors of about dozen Caribbean islands; includes

historical background.

1530. Marsán, Gloria. "Ayer, Hoy y Mañana. Presencia Femenina en el Periodismo Cubano." *UPEC*. 5:19 (1973), pp. 36-40.

1531. Martín, Yolanda. "La Mujer Cubana en la Prensa." *Reporter* (Havana). July 1954, p. 19.

1532. Soto, Ángela. "Ana Hernández, Corresponsal Guerrillera. La Única Mujer Cubana Que Reportó en la Sierra Maestra." *Bohemia*. January 1, 1971, pp. 16-19.
"Ana Hernández" was pseudonym of Ernestina Otero.

Women's Media

1533. LeSage, Julia. "*One Way or Another*: Dialectic, Revolutionary, Feminist." *Jump Cut*. 20 (1979), pp. 20-23.
Analyzes film by Cuban director Sara Gómez.

1534. Pascual, Sara. "Luz para la Mujer Cubana." *Hoy*. May 16, 1963, p. 19.

1535. Smith, Verity. "What Are Little Girls Made of Under Socialism?: Cuba's *Mujeres* [Women] and *Muchacha* [Girl] in the Period 1980-1991." *Studies in Latin American Popular Culture*. Vol. 14, 1995, pp. 1-15.
Analyzes Cuban women's periodicals under socialism; how they treated women and their issues.

1536. Torrents, Nissa. "Cuba's *Mujeres* (Women) Magazine: The First Twenty-Five Years." *Studies in Latin American Popular Culture*. 9 (1990), pp. 223-235.

CENTRAL AMERICA

General Studies

1537. "Belize Women: Many Things to Be Learnt by Establishing Global Communication." *Media Report to Women*. November 1, 1981, p. 12.
Provides ideas for improving the situation of Belizean women; reprint of article by Cynthia M. Ellis, published in the July 1981 *NetWork, The Journal of the Belizean Women's Affairs*.

1538. López, Ana M. "Tears and Desire: Women and Melodrama in the 'Old' Mexican Cinema." In *Mediating Two Worlds: Cinematic Encounters in the Americas*, edited by John King, Ana M. López, and Manuel Alvarado, pp. 147-163. London: British Film Institute, 1993.

Images of Women

1539. Chousal, Yoloxochitl. "A Different Journalism; Periodismo Diferente." *Chasqui*.

October 1994, pp. 55-58.

Claims Mexican women are not recognized as political and social beings by media; describes efforts by CIMAC (Comunicación y Informacion de la Mujer) to direct media in portraying women's conditions to the public.

1540. Franco, Jean. "Las Hijas de Corán Tullido." *Siempre* (Mexico City). December 17, 1986.

Concentrates on advertising messages aimed chiefly at women and using stereotypes which reaffirm status quo.

1541. Franco, Jean. "¿Quiénes Quieren lo Que las Mujeres Realmente Quieren?" *Siempre* (Mexico City). December 10, 1986.

1542. García Carderón, Carola. "Imagen Femenina y Vida Cotidiana." In *Estudios de Género y Femenismo II*. Mexico: Ed. Fontamara-UNAM, 1993.

1543. Gonzales Velasco, Ana Cecilia. "La Prostituta en el Cine Mexicano" (The Prostitute in Mexican Cinema). Thesis, Universidad Iberoamericana, Departamento de Comunicación, 1979.

1544. Herschfield, Joanne. *Mexican Cinema / Mexican Woman, 1940-1950*. Tucson: University of Arizona Press, 1996. 159 pp.

1545. Rubenstein, Anne. "Leaving 'The Old Nest': Morality, Modernity, and the Mexican Comic Book at Mid-Century." *Studies in Latin American Popular Culture*. 16 (1997), pp. 115-125.

Analyzes Mexican serialized story in *Pepín* comic book of 1949, with an eye on "gender, kinship, and class"; claims gender roles followed strict patterns: women submitted passively to the whims of men, maintained a "facade of obedience" to male relatives.

1546. Warlaumont, Hazel G. "Gender Ideology in Transnational Advertising: Women, Images and Mexico." *Gender and Mass Media Newsletter*. November 1992, p. 15.

Examines advertisements placed in two major Mexican magazines by international corporations, 1989-1990; analyzes the advertisements for their portrayals of women.

Women as Audience

1547. Bustos, Olga. "Visiones y Percepciones de Mujeres y Hombres como Receptoras (es) de Telenovelas." In *La Voluntad de Ser. Mujeres en los Noventa*. Mexico City: El Colegio de México, 1992.

Discusses newer research means to study the reception of soap operas.

1548. Bustos-Romero, Olga. "Gender and Mass Media in Mexico: The Receptors of Soap Operas." *Gender and Mass Media Newsletter*. November 1992, pp. 9-10.

Contends that Mexican TV soap operas have been changed to attract an audience that is not strictly women; the new soaps feature many teenagers and relate to current problematic issues such as rape, abortion, drug addiction, extramarital relationships, and so forth.

1549. Cornelius, Diana L. "The Broadcast Media, Reproductive Preferences, and Contraceptive Knowledge and Behavior: Evidence from Guatemala." Ph.D. dissertation, University of Texas, 1997.

1550. Muñoz, Sonia. *Barrio e Identidad. Comunicación Cotidiana entre las Mujeres de un Barrio Popular* (Village and Identity: Daily Communication Among the Women of a People's Village). Mexico: Trillas, 1994.

1551. Nariman, H. N. *Soap Operas for Social Change: Toward a Methodology for Entertainment-Education Television.* Westport, Connecticut: Greenwood Press, 1993. 194 pp.
 Provides a methodology for education-entertainment campaigns to bring about social change through soap operas; examples from Mexico.

1552. Ramos-Lira, Luciana, Maria T. Saltijeral, and Gabriela Saldivar. "El Miedo a la Victimizacion y su Relacion con los Medios Masivos de Comunicacion" (The Relationship Between Types of Mass Media Exposure and Fear of Victimization). *Salud Mental.* June 1995, pp. 35-43.
 Sees whether a relationship existed between amount and kind of mass media exposure and fear of crime in Mexico; shows that among women, a relationship existed.

Women Practitioners

1553. de la Vega Alfaro, Eduardo and Patricia Torres San Martin. "Adela Sequeyro, Mexican Film Pioneer." *Journal of Film and Video.* Fall 1992/Winter 1993, pp. 27-32.
 Traces career of Adela Sequeyro as producer, director, actress, and screenwriter, from 1923 through the 1930s; discusses her journalistic career.

1554. Egan, Linda. "Feminine Perspectives on Journalism: Conversations with Eight Mexican Women." *Studies in Latin American Popular Culture.* Vol. 12, 1993, pp. 175-187.

1555. Glusker, Susannah J. *Anita Brenner: A Mind of Her Own.* Austin: University of Texas Press, 1998. 334 pp.
 Relates life of journalist, historian, art critic, anthropologist, and creative writer, Anita Brenner, one of Mexico's most discerning interpreters. Daughter tells of Brenner's intellectual growth from 1920s through the 1940s.

1556. Holmlund, Chris. "'The World in a Drop of Water': The Feminist Vision of Patricia Howell." *Journal of Film and Video.* Fall 1992/Winter 1993, pp. 140-146.
 Studies second and third films ("Dos Veces Mujer" and "Intima Raíz") of Costa Rican director Patricia Howell in light of feminism.

1557. Huaco-Nuzum, Carmen. "Matilde Landeta: An Introduction to the Work of a Pioneer Mexican Filmmaker." *Screen*. 28:4 (1987), pp. 96-106.

Recounts life and work of Landeta, director of "Lola Casanova," "La Negra Augustus," and "Trotacalles"; from 1931 until the 1990s, only 15 of Mexico's 3,200 films were by women.

1558. Tanner, Eliza. "Mexican Journalist Elena Poniatowska: 'Angel's Wings and a Smile.'" Paper presented at Association for Education in Journalism and Mass Communication, Chicago, Illinois, July 30-August 2, 1997.

States that Poniatowska writes to create a sense of belonging and to identify with women and the poor in Mexico.

Women's Media

1559. Bustos, Olga. "Género, Generación y Clase en los Modos de Ver las Telenovelas Mexicanas." In *Estudios de Género y Femenismo II*. Mexico: Ed. Fontamara-UNAM, 1993.

1560. Santa Cruz, Adriana, and Viviana Erazo. *Compropolitan: El Orden Transnacional y Su Modelo Femenino. Un Estudio de las Revistas Femeninas en América Latina* ("Compropolitan": The Transnational Order and Its Feminine Model: A Study of Women's Magazines in Latin America). 2nd Edition. Mexico: Ilet-Editorial Nueva Imagen, 1981.

Gender-linked women's magazine in Mexico and consumer behavior.

1561. Valdivia, Angharad N. "Women-Centered Media Communications within Nicaragua." *Women and Language*. Fall 1990, pp. 59-63.

Deals with publications of the government's women's office, *Amnlae*, feminist, and other periodicals.

SOUTH AMERICA

General Studies

1562. Mata, Maria C., ed. *Mujer y Radio Popular*. Quito: Asociaciòn Latinoamericana de Educación Radiofónica, 1995. 95 pp.

1563. Morgan, Michael and James Shanahan. *Television, Adolescents, and Authoritarian Tensions in Argentina*. Cresskill, New Jersey: Hampton Press, 1995. 240 pp.

Includes "Demographics and the 'Gender Problem,'" "Media Use by Gender, Age, and Class," "Sex-Role Stereotypes," and "Sexism."

1564. Parra, Amparo and Virginia Parra. "Identidad Comunicativa: Una Propuesta Alternativa para la Mujer en Cine." *Cine-Mujer* (Colombia), 1993. Mimeographed.

1565. "Women Unite in Peru." *Action*. February 1998, pp. 1, 8.

Reports on conference in Peru, January 1998, that dealt with women and communication and approved The Lima Declaration which called for full and equal access to all communication media.

Historical Studies

1566. Buitoni, Dulcilia H. S. *Mulher de Papel: a Representação da Mulher na Imprensa Feminina Brasileira.* São Paulo: Edições Loyola, 1981. 170 pp.
A history of the Brazilian women's press.

1567. Castro, Rosimeiri A. "Identity, Papers and Representations: The History of Women in Londrina." *Boletin Centro de Letras e Ciencias Humanas.* January-June 1996, pp. 53-63.
Examines newspapers and magazines published in Londrina, Brazil, 1930s-1950s, to clarify history of women.

Images of Women

1568. "Bolivia: Taking Gender Seriously." *Action.* June 1997, p. 4.
Describes efforts on the part of 25 community radio stations in Bolivia to develop more programs on gender issues.

1569. Corredorova, Milada. "Appeal from Caracas Against the Feminization of Poverty." *Democratic Journalist.* January 1991, pp. 16-18.

1570. Creel, Mercedes Charles. "Women and Men in the Latin American Media." *Communication Research Trends.* 15:3 (1995), pp. 3-10.

1571. Fadul, Anamaria, Emile McAnany, and Ofélia Torres Morales. "Telenovela and Demography in Brazil: Analysis of Family, Gender, Sexuality and Reproductive Behavior." Paper presented at International Association for Mass Communication Research, Sydney, Australia, August 21, 1996.
Pulls out a segment of a larger study on Brazilian telenovelas; looks at plots of 27 telenovelas during 1980-1995; shows that sexuality, gender, and reproductive behavior are portrayed differently from reality.

1572. "New Image for Women in Latin American Media." *Action.* February 1988, pp. 1-2.

1573. Ramsey, Cynthia. "*The Official Story*: Feminist Re-Visioning As Spectator Response." *Studies in Latin American Popular Culture.* Vol. 11, 1992, pp. 157-169.
Analyzes Argentine film, "The Official Story."

1574. Sarques, Jane. "A Discriminaçao Sexual da Telenovela: Sua Influência Sobre a Mulher Brasileira." In *Teoria e Pesquisa em Comunicaçao. Panorama Latino Americano.* Brazil: Cortez Editora-Intercom, 1983.
Claims old images eventually triumph over newer ones of independent,

less submissive women in Brazilian soap operas.

1575. Velleggia, Susana. "La Imagen de la Mujer en la Cultural Nacional." *Diá-logos de la Comunicación* (Peru). October 1987.

Claims although Latin American media depictions of women have changed since 1970s, they still proclaim male dominance and female defensiveness.

Women as Audience

1576. de Albuquerque, Maria E. V., Vera L. Rocha, and Helena C. D. de Silva. *Audiência de Telenovela: Uma Perspectiva Histórica.* São Paulo: Idart, 1981.

1577. Edwards, Paula. "La TV de la Mujer Pobladora." In *Visiones y Ambiciones del Televidente.* Santiago, Chile: CENECA, 1989.

States that in Chile, the interaction between media and all aspects of the receiver's life is necessary in research; that television integrates and structures other communication media in women's lives.

1578. Hermosilla, Ma. Elena. "Mujer, Comunicación Social y Desarrollo." In *Comunicación para el Desarrollo en Chile. Experiencias y Reflexiones.* Santiago, Chile: Secretaria de Comunicación y Cultura, 1994.

Finds that for some Chilean women, the biggest value of media contents is to gain useful information to exercise their rights and better their lives.

1579. Macassi, Sandro. "Recepción Radial y Apropiación de la Palabra. Peru." In *Identidad Comunicativia y Propuesta Alternativa para la Mujer.* Memoria de Seminario Taller. Peru: CEEAL-Calandria, 1993.

Finds that in Peru, only 10 percent of women watched or listened to news, compared to 97 percent of the men.

1580. Quiroga, Cecilia. "Participación de la Mujer en el Video Informativo." In *Identidad Comunicativia y Propuesta Alternativa para la Mujer.* Memoria de Seminario Taller. Peru: CEEAL-Calandria, 1993.

Finds denunciatory reporting had no appeal to Aymara women of Bolivia, even though they were impressed at seeing Aymara women on television.

1581. Tufte, Thomas. "Living with the Rubbish Queen: A Media Ethnography About Telenovelas in Everyday Life of Brazilian Women." Ph.D. dissertation, University of Copenhagen, 1995. 442 pp.

Women Practitioners

1582. Barnard, Timothy and Peter Rist. *South American Cinema: A Critical Filmography, 1915-1994.* New York: Garland, 1996.

Women in South American film industry, pp. 11-12, 16, 61-63, 164, 183-184, 192, 194, 207, 211-216, 249-250, 263-264, 309-311, 324-326.

1583. Castellón, Lucía and Alejandro Guillier. "Chile -- The Emerging Influence of

Women in Journalism." *Media Studies Journal*. Winter/Spring 1993, pp. 231-240.

States that in a society such as Chile, where males dominate, women have found journalism as a means of expanding their horizons.

1584. "Exhibition Focuses on Opportunities for Women in the Media." *Action*. July 1994, pp. 1-2.

In Argentina.

1585. Fusco, Coco. "Dreaming Melodramas: An Interview with Valeria Sarmiento." *Afterimage*. December 1991, pp. 10-11.

Interviews leading Chilean film director, Valeria Sarmiento, exiled to France because of the 1973 political events; Sarmiento made seven films, primarily in documentary genre.

1586. Gersh, Debra. "Colombian Journalist Sues U.S. Government." *Editor & Publisher*. October 31, 1987, pp. 16-17, 41.

Reports on Patricia Lara, denied entry to U.S. in 1986 because of alleged Communist ties. Also see: "Colombian Journalist Denied Entrance into U.S.," *Editor & Publisher*, October 25, 1986, p. 15, and Debra Gersh, "Colombian Journalist Finally Gets Visa," *Editor & Publisher*, February 9, 1991, p. 38.

1587. Girven, Tim. "When Memory Speaks." *Index on Censorship*. March 1991, p. 34.

Argentine filmmaker Jeanine Meerapfel and her difficulties in chronicling the country's "dirty war."

1588. Gonzalez, Juan A. "Detrás de las Cámaras: Fina Torres Nos Habla de Mecánicas Celestes." *Encuadre*. April/June 1996, pp. 39-46.

Discusses work of Latin American filmmaker.

1589. Hartog, Susan. "A Conversation with Ana Carolina." *Framework*. 28 (1985), pp. 64-69.

Brazilian filmmaker.

1590. Kruger, Barbara. "Ana Carolina, *Mar de Rosas*: Museum of Contemporary Hispanic Art." *Artforum*. April 1987, pp. 129-130.

Brazilian filmmaker.

1591. Munerato, Elice and Maria E. Darcy de Oliveira. "When Women Film." In *Brazilian Cinema*, edited by Randal Johnson and Robert Stam, pp. 34-44. Rutherford, New Jersey: Fairleigh Dickinson University Press, 1982.

1592. Ostrower, Fayga and Eli Diniz. "Leila's Sensual Beauty and the Vitality of Matisse." *Estudios Feministas*. 2:2 (1994), pp. 463-469.

Uses interview of Brazilian actress Leila Diniz (1945-1972) to show that she became famous without an artificial image constructed of her by the media; compares her to the painter Henri Matisse in terms of her zest for life.

1593. Pick, Zuzana M. "An Interview with Maria Luisa Bemberg." *Journal of Film and Video.* Fall 1992/Winter 1993, pp. 76-82.

Interviews Bemberg, considered Argentina's most important female filmmaker, on her career and work, and especially her most important films "Camila" and "I, the Worst Woman of All."

1594. Pick, Zuzana M. "Chilean Cinema in Exile." *Framework.* 34 (1987), pp. 39-57.

Includes Chilean women filmmakers, such as Marilu Mallet.

1595. Schwartzman, Karen. "A Descriptive Chronology of Films by Women in Venezuela, 1952-1992." *Journal of Film and Video.* Fall 1992/Winter 1993, pp. 33-50.

Pulls together a list of women directors who made about 100 films, starting with Margot Benacerraf in 1952 and proceeding by decade to the present; charts films by alphabetical and chronological listings; includes translations of titles.

1596. Schwartzman, Karen, with Harel Calderon and Julianne Burton-Carvajal. "An Interview with Margot Benacerraf: *Reverón, Araya,* and the Institutionalization of Cinema in Venezuela." *Journal of Film and Video.* Fall 1992/Winter 1993, pp. 51-75.

Interviews Venezuela's first successful woman director, Margot Benacerraf, on her education, early career, studies with Erwin Piscator in New York and at IDHEC in Paris, making of *Reverón* and *Araya,* her founding of the Cinemateca, and what she sees as the future of Venezuelan film.

1597. Yeager, Gertrude M. "Women and the Intellectual Life of Nineteenth Century Lima." *Revista Interamericana de Bibliografía.* 40:3 (1990), pp. 360-393.

Includes journalistic works; lists women writers and their bibliographies.

Women's Media

1598. "Armida Testino: *La Tortuga* Offers Women in Peru Open Communication on Issues." *Media Report to Women.* September-October 1983, p. 17.

Backgrounds women and media situation in Peru, with emphasis on *La Tortuga,* a magazine Testino edits for women.

1599. Buitoni, Dulcilia H. S. *Imprensa Feminina.* São Paulo: Ática, 1990. 98 pp.

An introduction to women's press of Brazil.

1600. Buitoni, Dulcilia H. S. "Sex and AIDS According to a Brazilian Girls' Magazine: Pedagogy Without Fear." Paper presented at International Association for Mass Communication Research, Sydney, Australia, August 21, 1996.

Looks at Brazilian girls' magazine, *Capricho,* and its emphasis on sexual lifestyles, AIDS prevention, and use of condoms; concludes Brazilian women's press is researching a new language on sex and AIDS, that *Capricho* promotes a pedagogy without fear, takes into account social, cultural, and regional differences, and serves as a model of appropriated communication directed to children.

1601.   de Melo, José M. *As Telenovelas da Globo*. São Paulo: Summus, 1988.

1602.   Edwards, Paula, Soledad Cortes, and Ma. Elena Hermosilla. *Mujer TV*. Santiago, Chile: CENECA, 1987.

1603.   Fadul, Anamaria. "La Telenovela Brasileña y la Búsqueda de las Identidades Nacionales." In *El Espectáculo de la Pasión: Las Telenovelas Latinoamericanas*, edited by Nora Mazziotti, pp. 133-152.

1604.   Fadul, Anamaria, ed. *Serial Fiction in TV: The Latin American Telenovelas*. São Paulo: ECA-USP, 1993.
         Includes Anamaria Fadul and Vera A. F. de Moraes, "Bibliografia Anotada da Telenovelas Brasileira," pp. 169-233; Emile McAnany, "The Telenovela and Social Change: Popular Culture, Public Policy and Communication Theory," pp. 135-147, and Arvind Singhal, Everett M. Rogers, and William Brown, "Entertainment Telenovelas for Development: Lessons Learned," pp. 149-165.

1605.   Fernandes, Ismael. *Telenovela Brasileira: Memória*. 3rd Edition. São Paulo: Brasiliense, 1994. 402 pp.

1606.   Hippolyte, Nelson E. "Senora Culebra: The 'Telenovela' in Venezuela, 1953-1992." Ph.D. dissertation, University of Pittsburgh, 1996.

1607.   Hopkinson, Amanda. "Expanding the Airwaves." *Index on Censorship*. June 1992, pp. 20-21.
         States Radio Tierra in Chile provides women a voice they had not had for decades under dictatorship and machismo society.

1608.   Manhães Prado, Rosane. *Mulher de Novela e Mulher de Verdade: Estudo Sobre Cidade Pequena, Mulher e Telenovela*. Rio de Janeiro: Museu Nacional da Universidade Federal do Rio de Janeiro, 1987.
         Based on author's dissertation.

1609.   Monteiro, Dulce V. F. "Personagens Femininas de Telenovela e Suas Relações com o Trabalho." Dissertation, Universidade Federal do Rio de Janeiro, 1976. 182 pp.

1610.   Ortiz, Renato, Sílvia Borelli, and José R. Ortiz. *Telenovela: História e Produção*. 2nd Edition. São Paulo: Brasiliense, 1991. 197 pp.

1611.   Riedlberger, Irmela. "Development Communication and Participation in a Women's Radio Project in Peru." In *Media Support and Development Communication in a World of Change*, edited by Manfred Oepen, pp. 115-117. Berlin: Horlemann, 1995.
         Describes a radio program produced by a women's center and an NGO for women of Cuzco in southern Peru.

1612. Rodriguez, Clemencia and Patricia Tellez. *La Telenovela en Colombia. Mucho Más Que Amor y Lágrimas*. CINEP. Controversia no. 155. Bogota: 1989.

1613. Sayagues, Mercedes. "La Experiencia de Fempress: Comunicacion Alternativa." *Homines*. August 1989-August 1990, pp. 322-324.

1614. Vink, Nico. *The Telenovela and Emancipation: A Study on TV and Social Change in Brazil*. Amsterdam: Royal Tropical Institute, 1988. 287 pp.

1615. "'When Women Film.'" In *Brazilian Cinema*, edited by Randal Johnson and Robert Stam, pp. 340-350. Austin: University of Texas Press, 1982.

CHAPTER 6

North America

GENERAL STUDIES

1616. Finn, Geraldine. "Taking Gender into Account in the 'Theater of Terror': Violence, Media, and the Maintenance of Male Dominance." *Canadian Journal of Women and the Law*. 3:2 (1989-1990), pp. 375-394.
    Deals also with terror waged against women and children.

1617. Seajay, Carol. "Twenty Years of Feminist Bookstores." *Ms*. July-August 1992, pp. 60-65.
    Provides overview of the success of feminist bookstores in the U.S.; includes lists of feminist bookstores in U.S. and Canada. In same issue, Barbara Findlen lists various feminist newspapers, magazines, and journals in "Feminist Print Media: Our Fourth Estate," pp. 32-37.

CANADA

General Studies

1618. Robinson, Gertrude. "Broadcast Regulations and Sex Role Stereotyping: In Canada and the United States." Paper presented at International Association for Mass Communication Research, Bled, Yugoslavia, August 26-31, 1990.
    Describes ways used in Canada and U.S. to alter the off-balanced portrayal and employment of women in media organizations; suggests broadcast media are just catching up with print.

1619. Tuer, Dot. "Scenes of Resistance: Feminism and Video Art." *Canadian Woman Studies/Les Cahiers de la Femme*. Spring 1990, pp. 73-74.

Historical Studies

1620. Freeman, Barbara M. "Mother and Son: Gender, Class and War Propaganda in Canada, 1939-1945." *American Journalism.* Summer 1995, pp. 260-275.

1621. Martel, Joane. "Battered Woman and 'Batterer' Husband: A Mediative Reconstruction in *La Presse* in the Nineteenth Century." *Criminologie.* 27:1 (1994), pp. 117-134.

Shows that Quebec daily *La Presse* tended to expose cases of wife battering openly in nineteenth century.

1622. Martin, Michèle. *"Hello, Central?"* Gender, Technology and Culture in the Formation of Telephone System. Montréal and Kingston: McGill-Queen's University Press, 1991. 219 pp.

Attempts to explain the historical impact of a new technology on cultural practices, especially on social relations among women; deals with feminization of the telephone operator labor force of Canada, the training of these women.

Images of Women

1623. Bertrand, Marie A. and Colette Guillaumin. "6 December 1989: A Look Back." *Sociologie et Societes.* April 1990, pp. 193-213.

Comments on killing of 14 female students of the Montréal Polytechnic, December 6, 1989; inadequate reporting, emphasizing a superficial and oversimplified treatment of the event.

1624. Boyle, Christine. "Publication of Identifying Information about Sexual Assault Survivors: R. v. Canadian Newspapers Co. Ltd." *Canadian Journal of Women and the Law.* 3:2 1989-1990, pp. 602-614.

Focuses on the challenge to the constitutionality of subsections of the Criminal Code of Canada which grant survivors of sexual assault the right to insist on non-publication of their names.

1625. "Canada's MediaWatch Sounds Alarm over Sexism on Unregulated Game Channel." *Media Report to Women.* Spring 1995, pp. 1-2.

Tells how MediaWatch protested violence and sexism on Canadian television, reacting to lack of government regulation.

1626. "Canadian Broadcasters Must Follow Guidelines on Sex Stereotyping." *Broadcasting.* January 19, 1987, pp. 220, 224.

1627. Coutts, L. Block and D. H. Berg. "The Portrayal of the Menstruating Woman in Menstrual Product Advertisements." *Health Care for Women International.* March-April 1993, pp. 179-191.

Comparatively analyzes menstrual product advertisements from two Canadian and one US women's magazines; concludes portrayed women try to keep others from knowing about their menstruation.

1628. DeYoung, S. and F. G. Crane. "Females' Attitudes Toward the Portrayal of Women in Advertising: A Canadian Study." *International Journal of Advertising.* 11:3 (1992), pp. 249-256.

1629. Freeman, Barbara M. "The Media and the Royal Commission on the Status of Women in Canada, 1966-1972: Research in Progress." *Resources for Feminist Research.* Fall 1994, pp. 3-9.
       Looks at research in progress on the relation between professional media practices and cultural attitudes about gender issues in Canada, with emphasis on media coverage of the Royal Commission on the Status of Women.

1630. Harris, Debbie W. "Colonizing Mohawk Women--Representation of Women in the Mainstream Media." *Resources for Feminist Research.* Spring-Summer 1991, pp. 15-20.
       Analyzes pertinent articles in *Toronto Star* and *The Globe and Mail*, July-October 1990, concerning Canadian native women found in newspaper coverage of a two-month stand-off between Mohawk people and the Quebec provincial police.

1631. Lacombe, Dany. *Blue Politics: Pornography and the Law in the Age of Feminism.* Toronto: University of Toronto, 1994. 229 pp.
       Documents the major role played by feminist readings of pornography and grassroots activism in landmark law reform in Canada.

1632. Los, Maria and Sharon E. Chamard. "Selling Newspapers or Educating the Public? Sexual Violence in the Media." *Canadian Journal of Criminology.* July 1997, pp. 294-328.
       Examines 325 articles from two Canadian newspapers, 1980-1984, concerning representation of rape/sexual assault and the processes of the media reconstruction of women and the feminist movement.

1633. MacGregor, Robert M. "The Distorted Mirror: Images of Visible Minority Women in Canadian Print Advertising." *Atlantis.* 15:1 (1989), pp. 137-143.

1634. McShane, Steven L. "Occupational, Gender, and Geographic Representation of Information Sources in U.S. and Canadian Business Magazines." *Journalism and Mass Communication Quarterly.* Spring 1995, pp. 190-204.
       Evaluates occupational, gender, and geographic representation of 1,404 information sources in a sample of four U.S. and Canadian business magazines; determines that female sources were significantly underrepresented in most occupational groups.

1635. MediaWatch. *Response to the CRTC Report on Self-Regulation by the Broadcasting and Advertising Industries for the Elimination of Sex-Role Stereotyping in the Broadcast Media.* Vancouver: MediaWatch, March 1986.

1636. MediaWatch. "Two Years of Sexism in Canadian Newspapers: A Study of 15

Newspapers." *Resources for Feminist Research*. Spring-Summer 1991, pp. 21-22.
Reports women receive fewer bylines, are referred to less often, and are reported unequally.

1637. Nett, Emily M. "Is There Life After Fifty? Images of Middle Age for Women in *Chatelaine* Magazine, 1984." *Journal of Women and Aging.* 3:1 (1991), pp. 93-115.
Studies Canadian English-language magazine *Chatelaine*; reports that women over 50 years old are underrepresented in proportion to the population and the magazine's readers.

1638. Rohde, Stephen F. "We Have Seen a Land of Censorship, and It Is Canada." *Gauntlet*. No. 14, 1997, pp. 81-84.
Deals with *Butler v. The Queen*, a decision holding that sexually explicit media which portray women in a "subordinating" or "degrading" manner violated Canadian obscenity laws.

1639. Sansfacon, Daniel, Joseph J. Levy, and Jean-Marc Samson. "Sexual Relations and Violence Against Women: A Social Reconstruction of the Meaning of the Ecole Polytechnic Tragedy." *Revue Sexologique*. Autumn 1994, pp. 107-128.
Demonstrates how print media socially constructed the meaning of the murder of female students at Quebec's Ecole Polytechnic in December 1989.

1640. "Societal Diversity in TV Ontario Programming." *Gender and Mass Media Newsletter*. November 1991, pp. 21-22.
Reports on study by George Spears and Kaisa Seydegart with the title of this article, that discusses work by TV Ontario to eliminate stereotyping.

1641. Stone, Sharon D. "Feminists and the Toronto Press." Ph.D. dissertation, York University, 1992.

1642. Strutt, Suzanne and Lynne Hissey. "Feminisms and Balance." *Canadian Journal of Communication*. 17 (1992), pp. 61-74.
Deals with feminist perspectives on balance in broadcasting; claims that in Canada, it takes forms of "bad balance" or "balance as usual."

1643. Trimble, Linda. "Coming Soon to a Station Near You?: The CRTC Policy on Sex-Role Stereotyping." *Canadian Public Policy*. September 1990, pp. 326-338.
Examines and evaluates goals of the Canadian federal government's sex-role stereotyping policy in addressing portrayals of women in broadcast media; states it is not working. Based on author's Ph.D. dissertation at Queen's University (1990), "Coming Soon to a Station Near You: The Process and Impact of the CRTC's Involvement in Sex-Role Stereotyping."

1644. Wilgosh, Lorraine. "The Underachievement of Girls: A Societal Rather Than a Gender Issue." *Education Canada*. Spring 1994, pp. 18-23.
Samples articles dealing with women in newspapers; claims 50 percent rate of negativity toward women.

1645. Wyckham, R. G. "Self-Regulation of Sex-Role Stereotyping in Advertising: The Canadian Experience." *Journal of Public Policy Marketing.* 6 (1987), pp. 76-92.
    Discusses efforts in 1970s to inventory female stereotypes in Canadian advertising, outcries by politicians, newspaper columnists, and women's groups, and advertising industry's response.

1646. Zhou, N. and M. Y. T. Chen. "A Content Analysis of Men and Women in Canadian Consumer Magazine Advertising: Today's Portrayal, Yesterday's Image." *Journal of Business Ethics.* April 1997, pp. 485-495.
    Claims Canadian consumer magazine's portrayal of women was more positive than before.

Women Practitioners

1647. Alemany-Galway, Mary. "Lea Pool's *Anne Trister*." *Cinema Canada.* April 1986, p. 22.
    Deals with one of eight films directed by French Canadian Lea Pool between 1979 and 1994.

1648. Ayscough, Suzan. "Figures Fib: Too Few Canadian Women Get Top Pic, TV Jobs." *Variety.* June 24, 1991, p. 39.

1649. Berger, Sally. "American Indians: The Films of a Native Daughter." *Interview.* April 1993, p. 113.
    About Canadian Native American film director Loretta Todd.

1650. Bissel, Mary E. "Women Workers in the Toronto Printing Trades, 1880-1900." Ph.D. dissertation, University of Toronto, 1995.

1651. Blondeau, Dominique. "Jaqueline Barrette -- Entre le Rose et le Noir." *Arcade.* August 1990, pp. 70-83.
    Discusses Barrette's writing for film, radio, television, and theater.

1652. Boily, Lise. "Femmes, Médias et Réalités Organisationnelles." *Canadian Journal of Communication.* 17 (1992), pp. 403-413.

1653. *Canadian Journal of Communication.* Fall 1989 -- Thematic issue on "Women's Voices in Media Research."

1654. Cobb, Chris. "Women in Radio." Ottawa *Citizen.* July 12, 1992, p. 2.

1655. Dascher, Helge. "Mémoire, Reconnaissance: Entrevue avec Michelle Desaulniers et Diane Trépanière" (Memory, Recognition: Interview with Michelle Desaulniers and Diane Trépanière). *Canadian Woman Studies/Les Cahiers de la Femme.* Spring 1990, pp. 75-77.

1656. Denault, Jocelyne. "Cinquante Ans de Cinéma des Femmes au Québec -- Une

Recherche Difficile." *Canadian Woman Studies/Les Cahiers de la Femme.* Spring 1991, pp. 41-44.

Claims women have always been engaged in films in supporting positions, but that many brilliant filmmakers are in the limelight now in Quebec.

1657. Dorland, Michael. "Micheline Lanctôt's *Sonatine.*" *Cinema Canada.* 110 (1984), p. 11.

Review of Canadian filmmaker's work; accompanied by Connie Tadros' "*Sonatine*: 'Film Maudit,' A Conversation with Director Micheline Lanctôt" (pp. 7-11).

1658. Faulder, Lianne. "The Lonely World of Women on Morning Radio." *Edmonton Journal.* March 23, 1992, pp. 42-43.

1659. Global Media Monitoring Project. *Women's Participation in the News.* Vancouver: MediaWatch, 1995.

1660. Jenish, D'Arcy. "Turning Homespun Ideas into Truth on the Screen." *Maclean's.* December 25, 1989, p. 24.

Discusses Canadian film director Anne Wheeler. See reviews of her "Bye Bye Blues" in *Maclean's* (September 11, 1989, p. 72) and her "The Diviners" in *Variety* (January 11, 1993, p. 68).

1661. Lavut, Karen and Frances Beer, "Earth Is Our Root -- An Interview with Patricia Beatty." *Canadian Woman Studies/Les Cahiers de la Femme.* Spring 1990, pp. 104-105.

Interviews choreographer Beatty.

1662. Logan, Donna. "Women in Media Thus Far and Not Much Further: A CBC Women's View." *Combroad.* March 1993, pp. 15-17.

1663. "Public Policy Seen Improving Gender Balance of Canadian TV Anchors." *Media Report to Women.* May/June 1990, p. 7.

Claims government pressure improved the ratio of women on the air.

1664. Reid, Alison. *Canadian Women Film Makers.* Ottawa: Canadian Film Institute, 1972.

1665. Robinson, Gertrude J. *Female Print Journalists in Canada and the United States: A Professional Profile and Comparison.* Working Papers in Communications. Montréal: McGill University, 1981.

1666. Robinson, Gertrude J. and Armande Saint-Jean. "Canadian Women Journalists: The 'Other Half' of the Equation." In *The Global Journalist: News People Around the World*, edited by David H. Weaver. Creskill, New Jersey: Hampton Press, 1998. 512 pp.

Deals with demographics, education, socialization, professionalization, and working conditions.

1667. Rule, Jane. "Lesbian Literature Needs Readers." *Index on Censorship*. October 1990, p. 10.

Claims the rule is that lesbian writers experience censorship in Canada because of gender and sexual preference.

1668. Toronto Women in Film and Video. *A Statistical Profile of Women in the Canadian Film and Television Industry*. Toronto: Toronto Women in Film and Video, 1990.

1669. Tufts, Heather. "Filmmakers Robin J. Hood and Penny Joy." *Canadian Woman Studies/Les Cahiers de la Femme*. Spring 1990, pp. 94-96.

Women's Media

1670. Armitage, Kay. "The Feminine Body: Joyce Wieland's *Water Sark*." *Canadian Woman Studies*. Spring 1987, pp. 84-88.

Discusses one of about two dozen films of Canadian avant-garde filmmaker Joyce Wieland.

1671. Bredin, Marian. "Feminist Cultural Politics -- Women in Community Radio in Canada." *Resources for Feminist Research*. Spring-Summer 1991, pp. 36-41.

Examines theoretical questions on cultural politics and how they bear on some Canadian feminist media, on current status of women in community radio, and some of the specific communication strategies of women programmers at Montréal's CKUT.

1672. Coffey, Mary A. "Feminist Print Media in Canada: Reports to the Secretary of State Women's Program, by Eleanor Wachtel, 1982 and 1985." *Resources for Feminist Research*. Spring-Summer 1991, pp. 25-26.

Extols contributions of feminist print media in Canada based on reports in 1982 and 1985 by Wachtel to the Women's Program of the Federal Department of the Secretary of State.

1673. deRosa, Suzanne and Jeanne Maranda. "La Presse Féministe Est Différente" (The Feminist Press Is Different). *Canadian Woman Studies/Les Cahiers de la Femme*. Spring 1991, pp. 65-66.

Discusses favorable ethic to be found in feminist press.

1674. Freedman, Adele. "Joyce Wieland's Re-Emergence: The Arctic Light at the End of *The Far Shore*." *Toronto Life*. June 1980, pp. 184-185.

Reviews one of films of Canadian experimental director Wieland. Also reviewed by Barbara H. Martineau in *Cinema Canada* (April 1976, pp. 20-23).

1675. Gronou, Anna. "Avant-garde Film by Women: To Conceive a New Language of Desire." In *The Event Horizon: Essays on Hope, Sexuality, Social Space and Media(tion) in Art*, edited by Lorne Falk and Barbara Fischer, pp. 159-176. Toronto: Loach House Press, 1987.

1676. Masters, Philinda. "A Word from the Press -- A Brief Survey of Feminist Publishing." *Resources for Feminist Research.* Spring-Summer 1991, pp. 27-35.
Claims there are 44 feminist periodicals in Canada.

1677. Watson, Patricia. "Cynthia Scott and *The Company of Strangers.*" *Canadian Woman Studies.* Winter 1992, pp. 109-113.
Reviews Scott's award-winning film.

UNITED STATES

General Studies

1678. Adams, Edward E. and John V. Bodle. "Research Presented at Conventions: How Well Are Women Doing?" *Journalism and Mass Communication Educator.* Summer 1995, pp. 14-22.
Finds that between 1987 and 1993, all 16 divisions of the Association for Education in Journalism and Mass Communication experienced an increase in the percentage of scholarship by women.

1679. Allen, Donna. "Women News." *Quill.* May 1991, pp. 36-37.
Lists eight characteristics of women-owned-and-run media and five categories of essential women's news not reported in mass media.

1680. Allen, Martha L. "The Development of Communications Networks Among Women, 1963-1983." Ph.D. dissertation, Howard University, 1988.

1681. Allen, Martha L., ed. *1989 Directory of Women's Media.* Washington, D.C.: Women's Institute for Freedom of the Press, 1989.

1682. American Sociological Association Conference, 1996.
Includes Isabel C. Pinedo, "And Then She Killed Him: Women and Violence in the Slasher Film"; Melissa A. Milkie, "The Limits of Audience Power: Magazine Editors Account for the Persistence of Unrealistic Beauty Images Despite Criticism"; Christine M. Lenko, "On a Sliding Scale: Weighing the Cost of Eating Disorders for the Middle and Upper Classes."

1683. Andrews, P. H. "Sex and Gender Differences in Group Communication: Impact on the Facilitation Process." *Small Group Research.* February 1992, pp. 74-94.

1684. Association for Education in Journalism and Mass Communication. Annual Meeting, San Antonio, Texas, August 1-4, 1987.
Includes Elizabeth L. Flocke, "The 'Special' Way: Mary Paxton and Her Journalism Degree," and Larissa S. Grunig, "Shattering the 'Glass Ceiling' in Journalism Education: Sex Discrimination in Promotion and Tenure."

1685. Association for Education in Journalism and Mass Communication. Annual Meeting, Washington, D.C., August 10-13, 1989.
Includes Beverly G. Merrick, "Two Case Histories, Ishbel Ross and Emma Bugbee: Women Journalists Ride the Rail with the Suffragettes,"; Diane E.

Loupe, "Storming and Defending the Color Barrier at the University of Missouri School of Journalism: The Lucile Bluford Case,"; Carolyn M. Byerly, "Resistance to Violent Pornography: The Question of Feminist Praxis"; and Linda Lazier-Smith, "Demographics vs. Demigoddesses: A New 'Generation' of Advertising Images to Women."

1686.   Bate, B. and J. Bowker. *Communication and the Sexes*. Prospect Heights: Waveland Press, 1996. 415 pp.

Includes chapters on defining sex, gender, and communication, getting to theory, language and nonverbal messages, intimacy, family, education, organizations and employment, mass media and mediated communication, and contemporary issues about sex, gender, and communication.

1687.   Biagi, Shirley and Marilyn Kern-Foxworth. *Facing Difference: Race, Gender and Mass Media*. Thousand Oaks, California: Pine Forge Press, 1997. 284 pp.

Includes these articles of particular relevance: Jessica Hagadorn, "Asian Women in Film: No Joy, No Luck"; Lisa Schwartzbaum, "We're Gonna Make It After All"; Jean G. Wilson, "Sexism, Racism and Other -isms"; M. Junior Bridges, "Slipping from the Scene: News Coverage of Females Drops"; Jan Whitt, "Regression or Progression? *The Chicago Tribune* and 'Womanews'"; Vernon Stone, "Women Gain, Minorities Lose in TV News"; Kim Walsh-Childer, Jean Chance, and Kristin Herzog, "Outing Sexual Harassment of Women Journalists"; Judith A. Cramer, "A Woman's Place Is on the Air"; Cyndee Miller, "Study Dispels '80s Stereotypes of Women"; Fara Warner, "Imperfect Picture: Advertisers Have Long Struggled To Adjust to Women's Changing Roles at Work and Home; They Still Often Miss"; Kris Jensen, "Woman's Place? In Cyberspace"; Billy Altman, "Women in Music: Country Just Ain't What It Used to Be."

1688.   Bird, Elizabeth. "CJ's Revenge: Media, Folklore, and the Cultural Construction of AIDS." *Critical Studies in Mass Communication*. March 1996, pp. 44-58.

Examines how the story of a Dallas, Texas woman who claimed to intentionally infect men with AIDS was transformed from oral folklore to news.

1689.   Bloom, M. M. "Sex Differences in Ethical Systems: A Useful Framework for Interpreting Communication Research." *Communication Quarterly*. Summer 1990, pp. 244-254.

1690.   Borden, Diane L. and Kerric Harvey, eds. *The Electronic Grapevine: Rumor, Reputation, and Reporting in the New On-Line Environment*. Mahwah, New Jersey: Lawrence Erlbaum, 1997. 208 pp.

Shows how using virtual sources and publishing on-line is changing journalism; includes Harvey's own "Going On Line with the U.S. Constitution: Gender Discussions in the Cultural Context of the First Amendment."

1691.   Borisoff, D. and D. Hahn. "From Research to Pedagogy: Teaching Gender and Communication." *Communication Quarterly*. Fall 1995, pp. 381-393.

Explores pedagogical issues related to the teaching of gender and communication with suggestions on how to get to a stage where gender behaviors are no longer differentiated.

1692. Burston, Paul and Colin Richardson, eds. *A Queer Romance: Lesbians, Gay Men and Popular Culture*. New York: Routledge, 1995. 256 pp.

Revisits debates about the gaze; looks at texts coded as queer and gay cultural production, such as the work of Monika Treut or pornography "by women, for women, and about women."

1693. Cook, Susan C. and Judy S. Tsou. *Cecilia Reclaimed: Feminist Perspectives on Gender and Music*. Champaign: University of Illinois Press, 1994. 241 pp.

Collects 10 wide-ranging essays, including Bonny H. Miller's on women composers in U.S. magazines and Venise T. Berry's on female images in rap music.

1694. Cowan, Karen M., James R. Wilcox, and Nick Nykodym. "A Comparative Analysis of Female-Male Communication Style as a Function of Organizational Level." *Communications*. 15:3 (1990), pp. 291-308.

Investigates the relationship between styles of communication, the sex of the communicator, and the level of the communicator in the organization; finds that sex and level within the company have effect on communication style.

1695. Creedon, Pamela J., ed. *Women in Mass Communication*. Second Edition. Thousand Oaks, California: Sage, 1993. 408 pp.

Includes sections on "Perspectives on Re-Visioning Gender Values in Mass Communication Industries," and "Perspectives on the Mass Communication Classroom."

1696. Curran, James and Michael Gurevitch, eds. *Mass Media and Society*. 2nd ed. London: Arnold, 1996. 378 pp.

Includes Liesbet van Zoonen, "Feminist Perspectives on the Media," pp. 31-52; Ien Ang and Joke Hermes, "Gender and/in Media Consumption," pp. 325-347.

1697. Denton, Robert E., Jr. and Rachel L. Holloway, eds. *The Clinton Presidency: Images, Issues, and Communication Strategies*. Westport, Connecticut: Praeger, 1996. 288 pp.

Includes Janette K. Muir and Lisa M. Benitez, "Redefining the Role of the First Lady: The Rhetorical Style of Hillary Rodham Clinton."

1698. Diliberto, J. J. "A Communication Study of Possible Relationships Between Psychological Sex-type and Decision-making Effectiveness." *Small Group Research*. August 1992, pp. 379-407.

1699. Dines, Gail, Robert Jensen, and Ann Russo. *Pornography: The Production and Consumption of Inequality*. New York: Routledge, 1997. 224 pp.

Engages in empirical investigation of pornography industry; looks at politics, production, content, and consumption of mass market heterosexual pornography.

1700. Duggan, Lisa and Nan D. Hunter. *Sex Wars. Sexual Dissent and Political Culture.* New York: Routledge, 1995. 288 pp.
Seeks to clarify complex issues such as regulation/censorship of pornography.

1701. Ehrlich, Howard J. "The Politics of News Media Control." *Insurgent Sociologist.* Summer 1974, pp. 31-43.
Claims a contradictory relationship exists between news media and government and business; states that media control women by limiting the number of women journalists and by controlling the news about women.

1702. Elson, John. "Passions over Pornography." *Time.* March 30, 1992, pp. 52-53.
Deals with controversial issue of free speech vs. civil rights of abused women.

1703. *Extra!* March/April 1991. 16 pp.
Thematic issue on "Missing Voices: Women and the Media" includes Susan J. Douglas, "The Representation of Women in the News Media"; Laura Flanders, "Rape Coverage: Shifting the Blame"; Tiffany Devitt, "Abortion Coverage Leaves Women out of the Picture"; Karin Schwartz, "Lesbian Invisibility in the Media"; Jean Kilbourne, "Smoking as Liberation: The Tobacco Industry Targets Women"; Laura Fraser, "All the Women Fit to Print: A Day in the Life of the *New York Times*"; Margaret C. Duncan, "Gender Bias in Televised Sports"; Elizabeth Larsen, "Teen Magazines: Selling Lip Gloss, Sex and Anorexia"; Felicia Kornbluh, "*Newsweek* vs. Feminism"; Toni L. Kamins, "Women in Radio: Shut Up, Shut Out"; Judy Southworth, "Is There Life After Advertising: *Ms.* Magazine's Publishing Gamble," and Judy Southworth, "Women Media Workers: No Room at the Top."

1704. Ferguson, Marjorie. "Images of Power and the Feminist Fallacy." *Critical Studies in Mass Communication.* September 1990, pp. 215-230.
Issues a challenge to the popular consensus about women's images in contemporary media content and their professional status in media groups.

1705. Fine, M. G. "New Voices in Organizational Communication: A Feminist Commentary and Critique." In *Transforming Visions: Feminist Critiques in Communication Studies*, edited by S. P. Bowen and N. Wyatt. pp. 125-166, Cresskill, New Jersey: Hampton, 1993.

1706. Fineman, Martha A. and Martha T. McCluskey, eds. *Feminism, Media, and the Law.* New York: Oxford University Press, 1997. 336 pp.
Draws on legal theory, cultural studies, journalism, political science, sociology, and communications to present a collection of essays exploring how

media represent and construct gender, law, and feminism. Includes Deborah L. Rhode, "Media Images/Feminist Issues"; Patricia J. Williams, "Hate Radio: Why We Need to Tune in to Limbaugh and Stern"; Laurel Leff, "The Making of a 'Quota Queen': News Media and the Bias of Objectivity"; Mary Coombs, "The Real Real Anita Hill, or the Making of a Backlash Bestseller"; Martha T. McCluskey, "Fear of Feminism: Media Stories of Feminist Victims and Victims of Feminism on College Campuses"; Julia E. Hanigsberg, "Glamour Law: Feminism Through the Looking Glass of Popular Women's Magazines"; Elayne Rapping, "The Movie of the Week: Law, Narrativity, and Gender on Prime Time"; Dianne L. Brooks, "Rape on Soaps: The Legal Angle"; Isabel Karpin, "Pop Justice: TV, Motherhood, and the Law"; Margaret M. Russell, "Law and Racial Reelism: Black Women as Celluloid 'Legal' Heroines"; Cynthia Lucia, "Women on Trial: The Female Lawyer in the Hollywood Courtroom"; Tracy E. Higgins and Deborah L. Tolman, "Law, Cultural Media[tion], and Desire in the Lives of Adolescent Girls"; E. Ann Kaplan, "The Politics of Surrogacy Narratives"; Marie Ashe, "'Bad Mothers' and Welfare Reform in Massachusetts: The Case of Claribel Ventura"; Kristin Bumiller, "Spectacles of the Strange: Envisioning Violence in the Central Park Jogger Trial"; Lynn S. Chancer, "The Seens and Unseens of Popular Cultural Representation"; Kathleen Daly and Amy L. Chasteen, "Crime News, Crime Fear, and Women's Everyday Lives"; Ann Russo, "Lesbians, Prostitutes, and Murder: Media Constructs Violence Constructs Power"; Helen Benedict, "Blindfolded: Rape and the Press's Fear of Feminism"; Lisa C. Ikemoto, "Race Under Construction: The Master Narrative of White Supremacy in the Media Representation of African American/Korean American Conflict."

1707. Fish, S. L. "Preparation for the Year 2000: One Corporation's Attempt to Address the Issues of Gender and Race." *Howard Journal of Communications.* Summer/Fall 1991, pp. 61-72.

Investigates a *Fortune 500* company's efforts to diversify its managerial ranks, incorporating more women and minorities; focuses on communication strategies used.

1708. Fiske, John. *Media Matters. Race and Gender in U.S. Politics.* Revised Edition. Minneapolis: University of Minnesota Press, 1996. 320 pp.

Looks at how the battle over cultural meaning is played out in U.S. politics; how the line between "real" and "media" events has been eroded; includes chapters on "Murphy Brown, Dan Quayle, and the Family Row of the Year," "Hearing Anita Hill (and Viewing Bill Cosby)," "Los Angeles: A Tale of Three Videos," "Backstream Knowledge: Genocide," and "Techno-struggles."

1709. Flanders, Judy. "On the Fields of Macho." *Washington Journalism Review.* January-February 1990.

1710. Flayhan, Donna, chair. "Mass Media, Miss America and Mutilated Images: Images of Grit, Glamour, Girls, and Gays in America." Panel at Eastern Communication Association, Baltimore, Maryland, April 12, 1997.

Includes Nancy Abramson, "Cosmetics in Popular Culture: Selling to Women's Psyches"; Toni Kempler, "Teen Magazine's Promotion of the Thin Ideal."

1711. Folkerts, Jean, Stephen Lacy, and Lucinda Davenport. *The Media in Your Life: An Introduction to Mass Communication.* Boston: Allyn and Bacon, 1998. 558 pp.
Includes women as book buyers, p. 99; in fiction, p. 84; in journalism, pp. 136-137, 508; in magazine industry, p. 164; in media organizations, p. 360; as movie consumers, p. 201; in movies, pp. 190-191; as online users, p. 328; political publications and, pp. 55, 63; in printing, pp. 49-50; in public relations, pp. 445-446.

1712. *Forbes*
A sampling of articles includes: Dyan Machan, "Never Look Down," July 24, 1989, pp. 270, 272; Joshua Levine, "Marketing: Fantasy, Not Flesh," January 22, 1990, pp. 118-120; Joshua Levine, "In Your Face," November 22, 1993, pp. 164-167; Matt Walsh, "The G Word Again," April 25, 1994, p. 44; Joseph R. Garber, "Little People Steal the Show," July 3, 1995, p. 84; Marla Matzer, "An Ear for Music," December 18, 1995, pp. 138-140.

1713. Frierson, Elizabeth B. "Unimagined Communities: State, Press and Gender in the Hamidian Era." Ph.D. dissertation, Princeton University, 1996.

1714. "Gender and Communication." *Gender and Mass Media Newsletter.* November 1992, pp. 6-7.
Report on workshop at 1992 International Association for Mass Communication Research meeting.

1715. "Gender and Communication." Special Section. *Howard Journal of Communication.* 7:1 (1996), pp. 1-52.
Includes Catherine A. Dobris, "Maya Angelou: Writing the 'Black Voice' for the Multicultural Community," pp. 1-12; Robert Jensen, "The Politics and Ethics of Lesbian and Gay 'Wedding' Announcements in Newspapers," pp. 13-29; Robert L. Hertzog and Joseph N. Scudder, "Influence of Persuader Gender Versus Gender of Target on the Selection of Compliance-Gaining Strategies," pp. 29-34; Debra Reece, "Covering and Communication: The Symbolism of Dress Among Muslim Women," pp. 35-52.

1716. "Gender, Public Space and the Medium." *Gender and Mass Media Newsletter.* November 1992, pp. 12-13.
Abstracts of International Association for Mass Communication Research papers on gender and media in U.S.

1717. Gorham, Joan, ed. *Annual Editions: Mass Media 97/98.* Fourth Edition. Highstown, New Jersey: Dushkin/McGraw-Hill, 1997. 256 pp.
Includes Jane D. Brown and Jeanne R. Steele, "Sexuality and the Mass Media: An Overview"; Julia T. Wood, "Gendered Media: The Influence of Media

on Views of Gender"; Gloria Steinem, "Sex, Lies, and Advertising."

1718. Gray, Elizabeth D. "Beauty and the Beast: A Parable for Our Time." In *Women Respond to the Men's Movement: A Feminist Collection,* edited by Kay Leigh Hagan, pp. 159-168. San Francisco: Pandora, 1992.

1719. Hanson, Mary E. *Go! Fight! Win! Cheerleading in American Culture.* Bowling Green, Ohio: Popular Press, 1995. 196 pp.
   Includes cheerleading's relation to mass media entertainment and advertising.

1720. Hiebert, Ray E. *Impact of Mass Media: Current Issues.* Third Edition. White Plains, New York: Longman, 1995.
   Includes section "Women, Men, and Children," with articles by Kay Mills, "We've Come a Long Way, Maybe" and Junior Bridges, "No News Is Women's News."

1721. Humm, Maggie. *Feminism and Film.* Bloomington: Indiana University Press, 1997. 246 pp.
   Explains feminist issues and offers film analyses; topics include reproduction, "the personal is political," black feminism, and others.

1722. Iyengar, Shanto and Richard Reeves, eds. *Do the Media Govern? Politicians, Voters, and Reporters in America.* Thousand Oaks, California: Sage, 1997. 463 pp.
   Includes K. F. Khan and E. N. Goldenberg, "The Media: Obstacle or Ally of Feminists?"; C. Lake, L. DiVall, and S. Iyengar, "Women as Political Candidates: Was 1992 the Year of the Woman?"

1723. Kent, Thomas. "Gender and Professional Communication." Special issue of *Journal of Business and Technical Communication.* October 1991.
   Examines gender bias, gender-influenced job performance, and application of feminist theory to the professional world; explores topics such as the feminization of technical communication, a gender-balanced view of business and technology, modes of collaboration and gender influence, perpetuating sexual stereotypes in textbooks, and gender bias in work teams.

1724. Kramer, J. and C. Kramarae. "Gendered Ethics on the Internet." In *Communication Ethics in the Age of Diversity,* edited by R. C. Arnett, pp. 226-243. Champaign-Urbana: University of Illinois Press, 1997.
   Focuses on how a system of communication ethics might help improve the situation for women and girls on the Internet; looks at emerging Internet ethics.

1725. Leavy, Jane. *Squeeze Play.* New York: Doubleday, 1990. 369 pp.
   Takes aim at the myths of baseball and the press box "jocks" who cover it, in fiction form.

1726. Lont, Cynthia M. "Feminist Critique of Mass Communication Research." In *Transforming Visions: Feminist Critiques in Communication Studies,* edited by S.

P. Bowen and N. Wyatt, pp. 231-248. Cresskill, New Jersey: Hampton Press, 1993.

1727. Lont, Cynthia M., ed. *Women and Media: Content, Careers, Criticism*. Belmont, California: Wadsworth, 1995. 415 pp.

Uses perspectives of women as news, women as newsmakers, and portrayal of women to examine women's roles and impacts in media; explores newspapers, women's magazines, advertising, television entertainment and news, film, and rock music, and under each of these, includes an overview, a content analysis that quantifies the role(s) of women in that medium, a descriptive history of a specific woman or women's media group that has affected the medium, and a critical essay that challenges readers to think about women and media in different ways.

1728. Luthra, R. "International Communication Instruction with a Focus on Women." *Journalism and Mass Communication Educator*. Winter 1996, pp. 42-51.

Suggests ways "women in development" content and feminist pedagogies can be brought into international and development courses.

1729. McLaughlin, Lisa. "Feminism, the Public Sphere, Media and Democracy." *Media, Culture and Society*. 15 (1993), pp. 599-620.

1730. McLaughlin, Lisa. "Feminist Communication Scholarship and 'The Woman Question' in the Academy." *Communication Theory*. May 1995, pp. 144-161.

Claims feminist studies in communication remain largely unrecognized by field of communication, the academy, and even other feminist scholarships.

1731. McLaughlin, Lisa. "From Excess to Access: Feminist Political Agency in the Public Sphere." *The Public Javnost*. 2:4 (1995), pp. 37-50.

1732. Mahoney, Eileen. "Women, Equality and the Media: An Appraisal for the 1990's." *Intercom: Revista Brasileira de Comunicação*. January-June 1992, pp. 80-97.

1733. Makau, J. M. and R. C. Arnett, eds. *Communication Ethics in an Age of Diversity*. Champaign-Urbana: University of Illinois Press, 1997. 270 pp.

Discusses many issues, including language as a mechanism of sabotage in the equity process, ethical consideration and sexual orientation, and gender-oriented ethics on the Internet.

1734. Manning, Flance. "The Cyber-Sex Explosion: Cumming to a Computer Terminal Near YOU!" *Gauntlet*. No. 14, 1997, pp. 66-68.

1735. Marshall, J. "Viewing Organizational Communication from a Feminist Perspective: A Critique and Some Offerings." In *Communication Yearbook 16*, edited by S. A. Deetz, pp. 122-141. Newbury Park, California: Sage Publications, 1993.

1736. *Mediaweek*

A sampling of articles includes: Dave Martin, "Lunch with Dave Martin: How One Exec Found Success by Planning for Change," November 23, 1992, p. 10; Mary Huhn, "Woman at Her Best?" March 22, 1993, p. 16; W. F. Gloede, "For Whom the Mall Calls," March 28, 1994, p. 19; Laureen Miles, "A 3 p.m. News for Women," June 26, 1995, p. 14; Michael Freeman, "Late-Night Lady," August 21, 1995, pp. 14-16; Mark Adams, "Conde Nast Mulls Women's Sports Book," November 6, 1995, pp. 6-7.

1737. Mills, Carol A. "Women in Communication: Annotated Bibliography." Annandale, Virginia: Speech Communication Association, 1992. 11 pp.

Centers on who are and who were the women who worked in communications; includes 56 annotations, 1949-1990.

1738. Modleski, Tania. *Feminism Without Women: Culture and Criticism in a "Postfeminist" Age*. New York: Routlege, 1991. 160 pp.

Scrutinizes feminist and post-structuralist positions and shows how women are once again relegated to the margins of discourse and society; reveals what she considers are the "patriarchal anxieties that underlie the modern male's accommodation to feminists around him."

1739. Monsma, J. W. "Her Talk / His Talk: Addressing Some Key Issues in Gender Communication." Paper presented at the Western Social Science Association Annual Meeting, Albuquerque, New Mexico, 1994.

1740. Mumby, D. K. "Feminism and the Critique of Organizational Communication Studies." *Communication Yearbook 16*, edited by S. A. Deetz, pp. 155-166. Newbury Park, California: Sage Publications, 1993.

1741. Page, Benjamin I. and Jason Tannenbaum. "Populistic Deliberation and Talk Radio." *Journal of Communication*. Spring 1996, pp. 33-53.

Analyzes 1993 withdrawal of Zoe Baird as nominee for U.S. attorney general and how most mainstream media supported her and predicted her confirmation; but, an outpouring of public outrage turned the tide against her.

1742. Pearson, J. C., L. H. Turner, and T. Todd-Mancillas. *Gender and Communication*. Dubuque, Iowa: Wm. C. Brown, 1991.

1743. Perry, L. A. M., L. H. Turner, and H. M. Sterk, eds. *Constructing and Reconstructing Gender: The Links Among Communication, Language, and Gender*. Albany: State University of New York Press, 1992, 310 pp.

1744. Przybylowicz, Donna. "Toward a Feminist Cultural Criticism: Hegemony and Modes of Social Division." *Cultural Critique*. Winter 1989-1990, pp. 259-301.

Explores the way in which hegemonic formation is maintained by a woman's consent to and internalization of cultural values as presented in mass media and elsewhere.

1745. Radner, Hilary. *Shopping Around: Feminine Culture and the Pursuit of Pleasure.* New York: Routledge, 1995. 224 pp.

Investigates issues of contemporary popular narrative, feminine pleasure, and consumer culture; uses media products such as the TV series "Moonlighting," self-help books, novels, etc.

1746. Rakow, Lana F. *Women Making Meaning: New Feminist Directions in Communication.* New York: Harper & Row, 1992.

1747. Real, Michael R. *Exploring Media Culture: A Guide.* Thousand Oaks, California: Sage Publications, 1996. 405 pp.

Expands earlier version of this work; examines interplay of mass media and popular culture; includes "Reception Theory: Sex, Violence, and (Ms.) Interpreting Madonna" and "Gender Analysis: Patriarchy, Film Females, and *The Piano.*"

1748. Reinhard, J. C. "The 52 Percent Minority." In *Small Voices and Great Trumpets: Minorities and the Media,* edited by B. Rubin, pp. 169-246. New York: Praeger, 1980.

1749. "Research Roundup: Media and Women Remain Hot Topics." *Media Report to Women.* Summer 1997, pp. 8-13.

Abstracts papers dealing with media and women presented at conference of Association for Education in Journalism and Mass Communication, August 1997.

1750. Reynolds, Simon and Joy Press. *The Sex Revolts: Gender, Rebellion, and Rock 'n' Roll.* Cambridge, Massachusetts: Harvard University Press, 1996.

Blends music criticism, cultural studies, and gender theory to discern the distaff side of pop music and to read rock through the lens of gender.

1751. Romaine, Suzanne. *Communicating Gender.* Mahwah, New Jersey: Lawrence Erlbaum, 1998. 256 pp.

Shows how language and discourse play key roles in understanding and communicating gender; includes "Advertizing Gender."

1752. Rosen, Ruth. "Not Pornography!" *Dissent.* Summer 1994, pp. 343-345.

Argues that media's making pornography the number one women's issue today diverts attention from truly pressing problems.

1753. Rosenberg, R. S. "Free Speech, Pornography, Sexual Harassment, and Electronic Networks." *Information Society.* October-December 1993, pp. 285-331.

Discusses Internet and its use of pornographic materials in light of issues of free speech, sexual harassment, and censorship.

1754. Salwen, Michael B. and Don W. Stacks, eds. *An Integrated Approach to Communication Theory and Research.* Mahwah, New Jersey: Lawrence Erlbaum,

1996. 616 pp.

Mixes theory and research on a large number of topics including R. R. Rush and A. Grubb-Swetnam's "Feminist Approaches to Communication."

1755. Saunders, D. K. "A Multi-Stage Analysis of the Communication of African American Women in a Public Transit Setting." Ph.D. dissertation, Howard University, 1995.

1756. Schaninger, C. M., M. C. Nelson, and W. D. Danko. "An Empirical Evaluation of the Bartos Model of Wife's Work Involvement." *Journal of Advertising Research.* May/June 1993, pp. 49-63.

Compares alternative models of wives' work involvement and the body of research linking this involvement to consumption behavior.

1757. Schmidt, Karen and Colleen Collins. "Showdown at the Gender Gap." *American Journalism Review.* July/August 1993, pp. 39-42.

1758. *Sex Roles.*

3/4 (1985) -- Special issue on "Women, Girls and Computers," pp. 113-251.

1759. Sloan, William D. *American Journalism History: An Annotated Bibliography.* New York: Greenwood Press, 1989.

Includes 77 books and articles in section labelled "Women."

1760. Smythe, M.- J. "Gender and Communication Behaviors: A Review of Research." In *Progress in Communication Sciences, Vol.10,* edited by Brenda Dervin, pp. 173-215. Norwood, New Jersey: Ablex, 1991.

Examines gender differences in production of language, perceptions of language, gestures, and self-presentation.

1761. Society for the Study of Social Problems. Annual Conference, 1994.

Includes Don Sabo, Philip M. Gray, and Linda A. Moore, "Televised Sport and Woman Battering: The Social Construction of Violent Masculinity"; Gray Cavender and Nancy C. Jurik, "Jane Tennison and the Feminist Police Procedural"; Shelley K. Kowalski, "Watching 'Working Girl': Images of Gender and Class in Media Portrayals of Working Women."

1762. Spigel, Lynn. "U.S. Feminist Criticism: The Next Generation." *Medien Journal.* 18:1 (1994), pp. 10-19.

1763. Steiner, Linda. "Feminist Theorizing and Communication Ethics." *Communication.* 12:3 (1991), pp. 157-173.

Believes a feminist ethic challenges media institutions to include news about people oppressed, or ignored, and does so at the risk of lowering profits and alienating power brokers.

1764. Stires, Lloyd K. "Is It Time to Overturn the Miller Standard?" *Gauntlet.* No.14, 1997, pp. 85-89.

In pornography.

1765.   Sunlove, Kat and Layne Winklebleck. "Harm to Whom??" *Gauntlet*. No.14, 1997, pp. 61-65.
        Discusses court decisions on pornography.

1766.   Taylor, Anita and Judi B. Millers, eds. *Conflict and Gender*. Cresskill, New Jersey: Hampton Press, 1994. 352 pp.
        Deals with interpersonal communication; examines ways in which conflict resolution and feminist theories might be integrated to enhance understanding and management of conflicts, especially between men and women.

1767.   Taylor, H. Jeanie, Cheris Kramarae, and Maureen Ebben. *Women, Information Technology, and Scholarship*. Urbana: Woman, Information Technology and Scholarship Colloquium, Center for Advanced Study, University of Illinois, 1993.

1768.   Terry, Jennifer and Melodie Calvert, eds. *Processed Lives: Gender and Technology in Everyday Lives*. New York: Routledge, 1997. 256 pp.
        Asks the question, who actually benefits from technology; comments on the ambivalence women experience relative to machines; includes topics such as the virtual female, networking women, the sexuality of computers, the emancipation of Barbie, etc.

1769.   Todd-Mancillas, William R. and Linda Krug. *Communication and Gender: Annotated Bibliography*. Annandale, Virginia: Speech Communication Association, 1986. 6 pp.
        Focuses on differences/similarities in men's and women's verbal and non-verbal communications; contains 33 items.

1770.   Valdivia, A. N., ed. *Feminism, Multiculturalism, and the Media*. Thousand Oaks, California: Sage Publications, 1995.

1771.   Vance, Carole. "Porn in the U.S.A.: The Meese Commission on the Road." *The Nation*. August 2-9, 1986, pp. 65, 76-82.

1772.   Warner, Charles, ed. *Media Management Review*. Mahwah, New Jersey: Lawrence Erlbaum, 1997. 208 pp.
        Deals with current media management issues, including: M.D. Bunker, "Sexual Harassment and Vicarious Liability of Media Organizations"; V. Whitehouse and C. Cooper, "Should Rape Victims Be Identified in News Stories?"

1773.   Wiseman, Diane. "The Underwood Beat." *Westways*. 72 (1980), pp. 28-32.

1774.   "Women, Men and Media Center Endowed by Gannett Foundation." *Media Report to Women*. May/June 1990, p. 1.
        Project to monitor gender-related issues in the media.

1775. "Women on the Internet." *Gender and Communication Section International Association for Mass Communication Research Newsletter.* November 1995, p. 5. Sources of information for journalists on women's issues.

1776. Wood, Julia T. "Enlarging Conceptual Boundaries: A Critique of Research in Interpersonal Communication." In *Transforming Visions: Feminist Critiques in Communication Studies,* edited by S. P. Bowen and N. Wyatt, pp. 19-50. Cresskill, New Jersey: Hampton Press, 1993.

1777. Wood, Julia T. *Gendered Lives: Communication, Gender, and Culture.* Belmont, California: Wadsworth, 1994. 384 pp.
    Includes chapters on "The Study of Communication, Gender, and Culture," "Gendered Verbal Communication," "Gendered Nonverbal Communication," "Gendered Close Relationships," "Gendered Education: Communication in School Settings," "Mediated Gender: The Influence of Media on Views of Gender," "Gendered Organizational Communication."

1778. Wyatt, N. "Organizing and Relating: Feminist Critique of Small Group Communication." In *Transforming Visions: Feminist Critiques in Communication Studies,* edited by S. Bowen and N. Wyatt, pp. 51-86. Cresskill, New Jersey: Hampton Press, 1993.

Advertising, Public Relations

1779. *Advertising Age.*
    A sampling of articles includes: Ira Teinowitz, "'First' Shock Wave: Strong Start Has Some Rival Titles Reeling," August 21, 1989, pp. 1, 66; Peter S. Green, "Fashion Colonialism: French Export 'Marie Claire' Makes In-Roads," p. 18; Laura Loro, "Media Experts Pick Hot, Cold Niches," pp. S12, S14, and Joseph M. Winski, "Solidly Ensconced, Lear Builds Franchise," pp. S2, S20, all October 23, 1989; Pat Sloan, "Burns Reshaping Lauder," November 26, 1990, pp. 26, 60; Scott Donaton, "Conde Nast May Have Right 'Allure,'" December 3, 1990, p. 16; Pat Sloan, "New Maybelline Line Targets Blacks," December 17, 1990, pp. 1, 36; Melanie Rigney, "Shortcuts To Score with Niche Readers," August 12, 1991, p. S-4; Therese Kauchak, "Dominant Color? Try Red: Once Full of Fiction, 'Redbook' Puts Service First," October 6, 1991, p. 40; Gary Levin, "How Industry Views Harassment," p. 55, and Pat Sloan, "I Don't See It as Pervasive," both October 21, 1991, pp. 54-55; John P. Cortez and Ira Teinowitz, "More Trouble Brews for Stroh Bikini Team," December 9, 1991, p. 45; Joe Mandese and Scott Donaton, "CBS Entering Media Deal with *New York Times* Titles," January 27, 1992, pp. 1, 47; Phyllis Furman, "Kenar Is Finally Clothed in Media Attention," June 8, 1992, pp. 44; Julie Steenhuysen, "Reborn Seven Sisters Rediscover Tradition," October 19, 1992, pp. S2, S10; J. Clinton Brown, "Which Black Is Beautiful?" February 1, 1993, p. 19; Pat Sloan, "Numbers Tell Pretty Story for 'Allure,'" March 1, 1993, pp. S2, S10; Scott Donaton, "AmEx May Open Database with 'Style,'" April 5, 1993, pp. 3, 46; Ted Charron, "Story Behind Controversial 'Working Woman' Ad," September 13, 1993, p. 26; Adrienne W. Fawcett, "Narrowcast in Past, Women Earn Revised Role in Advertising," October 4, 1993, pp. S1, S10; Kate Fitzgerald, "In Line for Integrated Hall of Fame," November 8,

1993, p. S-12; Adrienne W. Fawcett, "Ad Department Turnover Can't Slow 'Allure' Gains," pp. S6, S10; Scott Donaton, "'Playboy' Makes Interactive Sales Pitch," p. 20, and June Weir, "Tilberis Takes Offensive on War on Cancer," pp. 3, S-8+, all March 7, 1994; Leah Rickard, "Consumers Would Rather Skip Feminine Hygiene Ads," March 14, 1994, p. 29; Emily DeNitto, "Citrus Exits Limbaugh, Now Sees Still More Ad Villains," July 25, 1994, p. 1; June Weir, "Taking Her Show on the Road," August 22, 1994, p. 25; Michael Wilke, "Women Take Up New Facet to Radio," April 10, 1995, p. 32; Keith J. Kelly, "'Cosmo's' New Girl Readies for Battle," August 28, 1995, p. 13; Adrienne W. Fawcett, "'Aspire' Aims To Succeed in Secular World," November 6, 1995, p. S22; Jane Hodges, "Cybermags Coming to 'Net Near You,'" November 27, 1995, p. 33; Keith J. Kelly, "Hearst Turns to Black for New Style," December 4, 1995, pp. 1, 4.

1780. *Adweek.*

A sampling of articles includes: Mark Schone, "The Year That Wasn't" [Eastern Ed.], November 2, 1992, p. 28; Judith Newman, "Year of the Woman" [Eastern Ed.], March 1, 1993, pp. CM12-CM15; Kathy Tyrer, "'Dragon': A Kung Fu Flick That Won't Kiss Off Women," April 26, 1993, p. 2; Richard Morgan, "Women vs. 'Old Boys' in Advertising" [Eastern Ed.], May 10, 1993, p. 50; Lisa Paikowski, "Fuelling Interest: Exxon Test Ad from McCann/Houston Aims To Bring Women to the Pump" [Southwest Ed.], August 2, 1993, p. 4; Debra Goldman, "Doin' It for Themselves" [Eastern Ed.], August 2, 1993, p. 16; Kathy Thacker, "NRA Tests Personal-Safety Program for Women" [Southwest Ed.], September 6, 1993, p. 2; "Actresses vs. Models" [Eastern Ed.], May 23, 1994, p. 17; "It's Not Easy Being a Woman, Especially If You're the Lead of a TV Movie" [Eastern Ed.], October 10, 1994, p. 20; Michele Martin, "Sexy 'Eva' Wins Women's Hearts" [Eastern Ed.], October 10, 1994, p. 14; "Women Confess: They Listen to Talk Radio, Too" [Eastern Ed.], May 8, 1995, p. 26; Ellen R. Martin, "Lee Apparel Gets Foxy Via 'Melrose Place'" [Southeast Ed.], June 26, 1995, p. 61.

1781. Edelstein, Alex S. *Total Propaganda: From Mass Culture to Popular Culture.* Mahwah, New Jersey: Lawrence Erlbaum, 1997. 376 pp.

Includes "Genderprop: Women in Midpassage."

1782. Garvey, Ellen G. "Reframing the Bicycle: Advertising-Supported Magazines and Scorching Women." *American Quarterly.* March 1995, pp. 66-101.

1783. Green, Alison. "Male/Female Behavioural Differences in an Advertising Sales Environment." *Industrial and Commercial Training.* 24:4 (1992), pp. 33-34.

Claims no discernible sex bias exists in the advertisement business, in media campaign planning, account management, or media sales.

1784. Ibarra, H. "Homophily and Differential Returns: Sex Differences in Network Structure and Access in an Advertising Firm." *Administrative Science Quarterly.* September 1992, pp. 422-447.

1785. *Marketing News.*
   A sampling of articles includes: Howard Schlossberg, "Jane and the Gang Track Trends with Public Domain Research," June 10, 1991, pp. 1, 21; Carrie Goerne, "Women's Magazines Shock 'Em or Teach 'Em in Bid for Advertisers," March 16, 1992, p. 8; Howard Schlossberg, "Playboy, That Bastion of Maleness, Adapts Feature of Women's Magazines," March 16, 1992, pp. 8, 16; Cyndee Miller, "Liberation for Women in Ads," August 17, 1992, pp. 1-2, 18; Carrie Goerne, "Gun Companies Target Women; Foes Call It 'Marketing by Fear,'" August 31, 1992, pp. 1-2; "Publisher Launches Mass-Market Cosmetic Line," February 15, 1993, p. 27; Tim Triplett, "Automakers Recognizing Value of Women's Market," April 11, 1994, pp. 1-2; Cyndee Miller, "'The Ultimate Taboo,'" August 14, 1995, pp. 1, 18; Cyndee Miller, "CD Helps Women's Foundation," November 20, 1995, p. 18.

1786. Rakow, Lana F. "From the Feminization of Public Relations to the Promise of Feminism." In *Beyond the Velvet Ghetto*, edited by E. L. Toth and C. G. Cline, pp. 287-298. San Francisco, California: International Association of Business Communicators, 1989.

1787. Rakow, Lana F. "Public Relations: Masculine or Feminine Talk?" Paper presented at the International Communication Association, Miami, Florida, May 1992.

1788. Wright, Donald K., Larissa A. Grunig, Jeffery K. Springston, and Elizabeth L. Toth. *Under the Glass Ceiling: An Analysis of Gender Issues in American Public Relations.* New York: PRSA Foundation, 1991.

Broadcasting

1789. *Broadcasting* (later *Broadcasting & Cable*)
   A sampling of articles includes: "Disagreement over Minority Grant," December 6, 1982, p. 72; "FCC Imperils Minority Preference Policy," September 22, 1986, pp. 42-46; "Court Sends 'Steele' Back to FCC," October 13, 1986, p. 44; "In Brief [FCC Minority and Women's Preferences]," April 20, 1987, p. 96; "Congress's Christmas Present to Women, Minorities," December 28, 1987, p. 38; Harry A. Jessell, "Court Overturns FCC Gender Preference," February 24, 1992, p. 16; "Mary Frost," August 31, 1992, p. 63; "Sally Hollingsworth Forman," May 17, 1993, p. 75; Peter Viles, "First for Mets, WFAN: A Woman in the Booth," June 14, 1993, p. 61; Peter Viles, "Three Stations, Two Responses to Rap," December 13, 1993, p. 90; Elizabeth A. Rathbun, "AWRT Looks Ahead To Take Place on Superhighway," May 30, 1994, p. 47; Donna Petrozzello, "Breaking the Talk Radio Sound Barrier," August 22, 1994, pp. 27-28; Christopher Stern, "FCC Says EEO Efforts Above Average," p. 58, and Donna Petrozzello, "Hundt to Radio Show: Truth in Broadcasting," p. 11, both October 17, 1994; Steve Coe, "Mixed Results for CBS Moves, Shakes," January 9, 1995, p. 18; Cynthia Littleton, "Talk's Veterans Hang Tough," December 11, 1995, pp. 50-56.

1790. Castonguay, J. "Masquerades of Massacre: Gender, Genre, and the Gulf War TV Star System." *The Velvet Light Trap.* Spring 1997, pp. 5-23.

Contends that scholars missed the hegemonizing process that took place through televised fictional forms during the Persian Gulf War; that they also did not analyze the predominantly masculine stars of television during the war.

1791. Castor, Laura. "Did She or Didn't She?: The Discourse of Scandal in the 1988 U.S. Presidential Campaign." *Genders*. December 1991, pp. 62-76.
        Discusses an interview between talk show hostess Barbara Walters and Donna Rice (who allegedly had an affair with 1988 presidential candidate Gary Hart) relative to public and private spheres.

1792. Crisp, Jane. "Women's Stake in the 'Politics of the Popular.'" *Hecate*. 17:2 (1991), pp. 110-126.
        Reviews indepth Mary E. Brown's *Television and Women's Culture: The Politics of the Popular*.

1793. Epstein, Debbie and Deborah L. Steinberg. "All Het Up! Rescuing Heterosexuality on the *Oprah Winfrey Show*." *Feminist Review*. Autumn 1996, pp. 88-115.
        Shows how "Oprah Winfrey Show" both "problemizes and yet normalizes the boundaries of heterosexuality."

1794. Gray, Ann. *Video Playtime: The Gendering of a Leisure Technology*. London: Routledge, 1992.

1795. Livingstone, Sonia and P. K. Lunt. "Women's Voices in the Public Sphere: Gendered Television and the Citizen-Viewer." *Réseaux*. 63 (1994), pp. 59-74.

1796. Mellencamp, Patricia. *High Anxiety: Catastrophe, Scandal, Age, and Comedy*. Bloomington: Indiana University Press, 1992. 432 pp.
        Critiques the temporality of U.S. television; includes subjects such as "I Love Lucy," Anita Hill, and "Oprah."

1797. Moreau, Louise R. "The Feminine Touch in Telecommunications." *AWA Review*. 4 (1989), pp. 70-83.

1798. Smith, Ruth B. "Absolute Talk on the Radio." *Media Studies Journal*. Spring-Summer 1998, pp. 72-79.
        Discusses talk radio hosts, concentrating on Dr. Laura Schlessinger, no-nonsense, tough-love advocate, Howard Stern, and Rush Limbaugh.

1799. U.S. Commission on Civil Rights. *Window Dressing on the Set: Women and Minorities in Television*. Washington, DC, 1977. *An Update*, 1979.

1800. White, Garland F., Janet Katz, and Kathryn E. Scarborough. "The Impact of Professional Football Games Upon Violent Assaults on Women." *Violence and Victims*. Summer 1992, pp. 157-171.
        Explores possible relationship between presentations of media violence

and subsequent violent behavior by viewers of pro football; hypothesizes that having a favorite team win may trigger assault behavior in some males. Also see Katz and White's "Engaging the Media: A Case Study of the Politics of Crime and the Media," *Social Justice* (Fall-Winter 1993, pp. 57-68).

1801. Wright, L. "Minority and Gender Enhancements: A Necessary and Valid Means to Achieve Diversity in the Broadcast Marketplace." *Federal Communications Law Journal*. 40 (1988), pp. 89-113.

Film

1802. Addison, Erin. "Saving Other Women from Other Men: Disney's *Aladdin*." *Camera Obscura*. January-May 1993, pp. 5-26.

1803. Becker, Edith, Michelle Citron, Julia Lesage, and B. Ruby Rich. "Lesbians and Film: Introduction." *Jump Cut*. March 1981, pp. 17-21.

1804. Carpenter, Lynette. "Guilty Pleasures -- Women and the Weepies." *Ms*. May-June 1991, pp. 74-76.

1805. *Cinema Journal*. Winter 1997.
    Includes Catherine Williamson, "Draped Crusaders: Disrobing Gender in *The Mark of Zorro*"; Maria Pramaggiore, "Performance and Persona in the US Avant Garde: The Case of Maya Deren"; Eric Schaefer, "The Obscene Seen: Spectacle and Transgression in Postwar Burlesque Films," and Jennifer Hammett, "The Ideological Impediment: Feminism and Film History."

1806. Denzin, Norman K. *The Cinematic Society: The Voyeur's Gaze*. Thousand Oaks, California: Sage Publications, 1995. 224 pp.
    Includes "Flawed Visions: The Obsessive Male Gaze" and "Fatal Female Visions."

1807. Doane, Mary Ann. *Femmes Fatales*. New York: Routledge, 1991. 320 pp.
    Examines questions of sexual difference and knowledge in cinematic, theoretical, and psychoanalytical discourse; ranges over issues such as Freud, the female body, female spectator, meaning of the close-up, and nature of stardom; "interrogates cinematic and theoretical claims to truth about women which rely to a striking extent on judgements about visions and its stability or instability."

1808. Doane, Mary Ann. "Technology's Body: Cinematic Vision in Modernity." *Differences*. Summer 1993, pp. 1-23.
    Traces consequences of the language of failure that surrounded early speculation about cinema.

1809. Erens, Patricia, ed. *Sexual Stratagems: The World of Women in Film*. New York: Horizon Press, 1979.
    Deals with images of women in film and women filmmakers.

1810. Giroux, Henry A. "Beyond the Politics of Innocence: Memory and Pedagogy in the 'Wonderful World of Disney.'" *Socialist Review*. 23:2 (1993), pp. 79-107.

Analyzes "Pretty Woman," the 1990 film, to expose Disney's "politics of innocence."

1811. Grant, Michael. "Psychoanalysis and the Horror Film." *Free Associations*. 5:4 (1995), pp. 483-491.

Discusses Barbara Creed's article on film "Alien" to offer another approach to questions raised by the relation between popular culture and psychoanalysis.

1812. Hart, Lynda and Peggy Phelan, eds. *Acting Out: Feminist Performance*. Ann Arbor: University of Michigan Press, 1993.

Includes articles on film.

1813. *Literature / Film Quarterly*.

23:3 (1995) -- Includes Jack Boozer, "Seduction and Betrayal in the Heartland: *Thelma and Louise*"; Bernard F. Dick, "Columbia's Dark Ladies and the Femmes Fatales of Film Noir"; Russell Cousins, "Sanitizing Zola: Dorothy Arzner's Problematic Nana."

1814. McCreadie, Marsha. *The Casting Couch and Other Front Row Seats: Women in Films of the 1970s and 1980s*. New York: Praeger, 1990. 208 pp.

Includes author's reviews from the *Arizona Republic*, a random selection of interviews with female stars, and other articles reprinted from a variety of places; shows that most important movies of the 1970s and 1980s were about women and these films seemed to reflect the major changes women were going through in society.

1815. Morrison, Susan. "Girls on Film: Fantasy, Desire and Desperation." *CineAction!* Fall 1985, pp. 2-6.

1816. Penley, Constance, Elizabeth Lyon, Lynn Spigel, and Janet Bergstrom, eds. *Close Encounters: Film, Feminism, and Science Fiction*. Minneapolis: University of Minnesota Press, 1990. 312 pp.

Gives critical approaches to science fiction as represented in film, TV, fan culture, and other non-literary media; addresses the way conventional notions of sexual difference are reworked by science fiction film. Includes: Vivian Sobchack, "Child/Alien/Father: Patriarchal Crisis and Generic Exchange"; Janet Bergstrom, "Androids and Androgyny"; Constance Penley, "Time Travel, Primal Scene, and the Critical Dystopia"; Harvey R. Greenberg, "Reimagining the Gargoyle: Psychoanalytic Notes on *Alien*"; Raymond Bellour, "Ideal Hadaly (on Villiers's *The Future Eve*)"; Roger Dadoun, "*Metropolis*: Mother-City -- "Mittler" -- Hitler"; Enno Patalas, "*Metropolis*, Scene 103"; Henry Jenkins III, "*Star Trek* Rerun, Reread, Rewritten: Fan Writing as Textual Poaching"; Lynn Spigel, "From Domestic Space to Outer Space: The 1960s Fantastic Family Sit-com"; Peter Wollen, "*Friendship's Death* (complete film script)."

1817. Rich, B. Ruby. "The Crisis of Naming in Feminist Film Criticism." *Jump Cut.*
December 1978, pp. 9-12.

1818. Saxton, Christine. "Feminist Intervention -- Film Practice and Theory." *NWSA
Journal.* Summer 1989, pp. 697-712.
Reviews six books on women and film.

1819. Trails, Wes. "Why I Prefer Amateur Porn: One Writer's Video Trip in the Realm
of Real Sex!" *Gauntlet.* No.14, 1997, pp. 36-40.
Claims amateur porn videos are "feisty, liberty-loving perseverance."

1820. *Velvet Light Trap, The.*
March 1990 -- Issue on "Exhibition/Conditions of Reception" includes:
Jane Gaines, "From Elephants to Lux Soap: The Programming and 'Flow' of Early
Motion Picture Exploitation" and Susan Ohmer, "Female Spectatorship and
Women's Magazines: Hollywood, *Good Housekeeping* and World War II."
Fall 1996 -- Frank P. Tomasulo, "Masculine/Feminine: The 'New
Masculinity' in *Tootsie* (1982)" and Jeff Yanc, "'More Than a Woman': Music,
Masculinity and Male Spectacle in *Saturday Night Fever* and *Staying Alive*."
Spring 1997 -- James Castonguay, "Masquerades of Massacre: Gender,
Genre, and the Gulf War TV Star System"; Taylor Harrison, "Trying Hard to Hear
You: Jean Arthur and the Problematics of Presence"; Karen O. Vared, "White and
Black in Black and White: Management of Race and Sexuality in the Coupling of
Child Star Shirley Temple and Bill Robinson," and Walter Metz, "'Another Being
We Have Created Called Us': Point-of-View, Melancholia, and the Joking
Unconscious in *The Bridges of Madison County*."

1821. Warner, Marina. "Beauty and the Beasts." *Sight and Sound.* October 1992, pp. 6-
11.

1822. Williams, Linda. "Film Bodies: Gender, Genre, and Excess." *Film Quarterly.*
Summer 1991, pp. 2-13.

Print Media

1823. Abrahamson, D., ed. *The American Magazine: Research Perspectives and
Prospects.* Ames: Iowa State University Press, 1995.
Includes L. McKinnon, "*Ms*.ing the Free Press: The Advertising and
Editorial Content of *Ms. Magazine*, 1972-1992," pp. 98-108, and C. A. Bonard,
"The Women's Movement in the 1920s: American Magazines Document the
Health and Progress of Feminism," pp. 231-240.

1824. American Sociological Association Conference, 1997.
Includes Tawnya J. Adkins-Covert, "Mobilization Propaganda:
Advertisements in Women's Magazines During World War II"; Anthony J.
Vigorito and Timothy J. Curry, "Marketing Masculinity: The Effects of Audience
Composition on Gender Depictions in Popular Magazines."

1825. Coderre, Cécile. "Acted Accusation Retiré -- Petite Histoire d'un Témoignage Contra un Distributeur de Matériel Pornographique" (Accusation Withdrawn -- An Account of Testifying Against a Distributor of Pornography). *Recherches Féministes*. 4:2 (1991), pp. 147-156.

Deals with 1985 lawsuit against a distributor of an issue of *Penthouse*; shows how some women felt trial had to take place.

1826. *Editor & Publisher*.

A sampling of articles includes: "7 Women Named to WICI's Chairs of Achievement," January 26, 1980, p. 28; Carla M. Rupp, "Three Women Who Handle the News," May 17, 1980, pp. 16, 20, 34; Carla M. Rupp, "Woman Production Exec at Dow Jones," June 14, 1980, pp. 39, 44; "Gannett Names First Woman Production Dir.," September 6, 1980, p. 32; George Wilt, "Women Readers, and Radio Topics at Promotion Meeting," pp. 20, 22, and Carla M. Rupp, "Improvements Are Sought in Covering Women's News," pp. 38-39, both October 18, 1980; "Women To Gain More Jobs on *Washington Post*," December 6, 1980, p. 15; "Women-Oriented Supp Service Offered by King," December 13, 1980, p. 28; "Newsday Women Settle for Cash and Better Job Opportunities," March 13, 1982, p. 41; "Knight-Ridder Names First Woman Publisher," March 20, 1982, p. 34; B. H. Liebes and Samantha Stevens, "Women Editors Feel Less Discrimination," September 11, 1982, p. 48; "Study of Women in Mass Media Jobs," November 6, 1982, p. 30; Celeste Huenergard, "Preliminary Report Aired on Women in the Media," November 20, 1982, pp. 15, 33; James E. Roper, "Press Clubs Merge," pp. 12-13, and Roy Whitcomb, "Sex-Discrimination Battle," pp. 30, 33, both June 22, 1985; James E. Roper, "'Pink-Collar Ghettos?'" November 2, 1985, pp. 34-35; Kathy Gurchiek, "Feminists Hope To Develop Women's News Service," November 9, 1985, p. 37; James E. Roper, "A Fascinating History of Female Journalists," pp. 44, 25, and James E. Roper, "Battering Down the Barriers," p. 30, both November 30, 1985; Maurine H. Beasley, "In Defense of 'Women in Journalism' Study," December 14, 1985, pp. 44, 33; Debra Gersh, "Advice to Women Journalists," February 22, 1986, pp. 16-17, 44; Debra Gersh, "There Are More Women in Public Relations, but Inequality Still Exists," April 19, 1986, p. 78; "Press Women in New Mexico," June 21, 1986, p. 80; James E. Roper, "Guild Says *Washington Post* Pays Blacks, Women Less," September 27, 1986, p. 17; Jim Haughton, "Women Sportswriters," December 20, 1986, pp. 12-13; Don Sarvey, "Thoughts from a Foreign Correspondent," March 14, 1987, p. 50; David Astor, "She Shops for Both Groceries and Gags," May 9, 1987, pp. 38-39; Carole Rich, "A Close-Up Look at Women Journalists," September 5, 1987, pp. 56, 45; Mark Fitzgerald, "Many Women Leaving Newspapers," October 17, 1987, p. 9; Fran Matera, "Feminists and the Funnies," October 24, 1987, pp. 68, 52; "Papers Provide Few Benefits to Keep Female Staffers," December 12, 1987, p. 30; Michele McCormick, "Helen Helps U.S. and Japanese Readers," December 19, 1987, pp. 32-33; Herm Albright, "Betty Weesner, *The Republican*, Danville, Ind.," July 25, 1987, p. 19; Maria Braden, "Knight-Ridder's 'Sounding Board,'" January 26, 1991, pp. 20-21; M. L. Stein, "Women's Sports Coverage Shortchanged," February 16, 1991, pp. 18, 51; M. L. Stein, "Journalist or Participant?" March 30, 1991, pp. 7, 40; Chris Lamb, "An Editorial Cartoonist and a Columnist," April 6, 1991, pp. 44-46; Debra Gersh, "75th Annual Pulitzer Prize Winners" (11 were women), April 13, 1991, pp. 7-9, 32-35, 44; Tony Case, "*N.Y. Times* Criticized for Printing Victim's Name," April 27, 1991, pp. 11, 39; Jack Kammer, "She Said, She Said -- Newspapers Must Begin Dealing with the Gender-Based Concerns of Men," May 4, 1991, pp. 120, 108-109; "Cathleen Black Replaces Friedheim at ANPA," May 11, 1991, pp. 13, 41; P. J. Corso, "Sexist Language in the Press," October 12, 1991, pp. 48, 40; M. L. Stein, "Female Sportswriters and Sexual Harassment," October 26, 1991, pp. 8, 40; David Astor, "Where She Came From to Get Syndicated," November 23, 1991, pp. 38-41; Mike Land, "Newspaper Woman Still Working at 91," December 28, 1991, pp. 26-27; Lawrence R. Levin, "Media Companies Not Immune from Sexual Harassment Charges," January 18, 1992, pp. 24, 45; M. L. Stein and Mark Fitzgerald, "'The Only Way We Could'; Anonymous Source Debate Begins Anew," March 14, 1992, pp. 10-11, 36; Debra Gersh, "Crime Victims and the Media," September 26, 1992, pp. 12, 36; Debra Gersh, "Promulgating Polarization," October 10, 1992, pp. 30-31, 48; Hugh Morgan, "Women Readers," October 31, 1992, p. 13; M. L. Stein, "Scooped," December 19, 1992, pp. 11, 43; Debra Gersh, "Women Still Underrepresented," May 15, 1993, pp. 20-21; David Astor, "Can Columns Bring in Women Readers?", pp. 26-27; Karen Kemp, "Three Women Start Florida Weekly to Fill a Void," pp. 20-21+, both in July 10, 1993; M. L. Stein, "Unwelcome Gender Politics," September 11, 1993, pp. 13, 50; Mark Fitzgerald, "Is It a Man's Newspaper?" January 15, 1994, pp. 19, 45; David Astor, "Wit Feature Has a Female Perspective," March 12, 1994, p. 42; Debra Gersh Hernandez, "Good and the Bad About Women's News in Newspapers," May 21, 1994, pp. 17, 41; Dorothy Giobbe, "War of Words Continues," August 6, 1994, pp. 18, 35; Chris Lamb, "A 'Capital' Decision for Ann C. Telnaes," October 8, 1994, pp. 44-45; "How Many Women Are Doing Comics?" January 28, 1995, p. 36; Tony Case, "The Women's Voice," May 13, 1995, pp. 9-11, 25; George Garneau, "Women Bump Corporate Ceiling," June 24, 1995, p. 101; Tony Case, "Reaching Out to the Female Market," November 4, 1995, pp. 15, 36; M. L. Stein, "New Spanish-Language to Appeal to Middle-Class Women," November 18, 1995, p. 21; Tony Case, "Guild's New Leader Speaks Out," February 10, 1996, pp. 14-15.

1827. Espitia, R. "Sex Bias and Bylines: Does Gender Affect the Evaluation of a News Story?" Master's thesis, University of Texas, 1983.

Does not see a divergence between men and women in how they evaluate news stories.

1828. *Folio: The Magazine for Magazine Management.*

A sampling of articles includes: Jan Jaban, "Is Mirabella Coming Back in Vogue?" February 1989, pp. 62, 64; Ron Scott, "Challenging Conventional Wisdom," March 1989, pp. 161-162; Michael Garry, "Two Women's Titles Better Than One," August 1989, pp. 53-54; Susan Hovey, "A Radical Vows to Take *Ms.* Back to Its Roots," March 1990, pp. 41-42; Susan Hovey, "Magazine People: A Sense That Transcends Trends," July 1990, pp. 33-34; Lisa I. Fried, "No Trouble Empathizing with Readers," September 1, 1990, pp. 62-64; Susan Hovey, "Good Sports," June 1, 1991, pp. 46-49; Lorraine Calvacca, "Still Editing After All These Years," February 15, 1993, pp. 41-42+; Erika Isler, "The Search for the

Ultimate Playmate," June 1, 1993, pp. 66-67; Martha Thomas, "Revolution from Within," September 15, 1993, pp. 48-50; Iris C. Selinger, "Designing Woman," September 15, 1993, p. 24; "The Women's Room," October 15, 1993, p. 62; Lorne Manly, "Coffee Talk," October 15, 1993, p. 26; Samir Husni, "A Tale of Two Women's Magazines," p. 62; Lorne Manly, "Women's Fitness Titles Pump Up in Shrinking Market," p. 22, both November 15, 1993; Lorraine Calvacca, "Sticking It to (Women and) Guns," February 1, 1994, p. 25; Lorraine Calvacca, "The Shape of Things at WSF," March 1, 1994, p. 31; "Curtain Draws on Lear's Final Act," April 1, 1994, p. 13; Iris C. Selinger, "*Women First* with First Lady," p. 33, and Phillip M. Perry, "Assault on the Workplace," pp. 41-43, both in May 1, 1994; Lorraine Calvacca, "Sisterhood Is Evolving," pp. 63-65, and "A Half-Baked Trend," p. 37, both in May 15, 1994; Lori Marden, "The World of Women Entrepreneurs," June 1, 1994, p. 71; "The Cult of Celebrity Style," July 1, 1994, p. 29; Leah Rosch, "Heart & Soul Shows Healthy Symptoms," November 1, 1994, p. 30; Lori Marden, "Sugar and Spice...," December 15, 1994, p. 74; Lori Marden, "Redesigning Women, Inc.," May 1, 1995, p. 65; Barbara Love, "*Mademoiselle* Grows Up," pp. 46-47+, and Lorraine Calvacca, "Public Pictures, Private Lives," p. 23, both May 15, 1995; Grace Mirabella, "Grace Under Pressure," pp. 58-60, and Cris Beam, "Christian Titles Cross into Mainstream," p. 30, both September 15, 1995; Lorraine Calvacca, "*New Woman*'s New Woman," October 1, 1995, pp. 45-46; Lambeth Hochwald, "A Women's Gym Without Walls," November 1, 1995, p. 34; Lorraine Calvacca, "General Media's Forum Undergoes Sex Change," November 15, 1995, pp. 30-31.

1829.   Ledbetter, James. "Man at His Most Embarrassing." *Mother Jones*. September-October 1990, p. 9.

Discusses *Esquire* magazine's treatment of women under editor Lee Eisenberg.

1830.   Sloan, William D., Shirley Carter, William Gonzenbach, and James G. Stovall, eds. *Mass Communication in the Information Age*. Northport, Alabama: Vision Press, 1996.

Includes "Women Readers Boost New Periodicals," pp. 185-186; "Women Writers and Magazines," p. 188.

1831.   Somers, Paul P., Jr. *Editorial Cartooning and Caricature: A Reference Guide*. Westport, Connecticut: Greenwood Press, 1998. 224 pp.

Includes sections describing the literature available on cartoons about suffrage, p. 16; women, pp. 23-24; counterculture, women, and ethnic, pp. 55-57; and women, p. 89.

1832.   Sullivan, Larry E. and Lydia C. Schurman. *Pioneers, Passionate Ladies, and Private Eyes: Dime Novels, Series Books, and Paperbacks*. Binghamton, New York: Haworth Press, 1997. 306 pp.

Deals with use women made of these books (as escape from hard lives of suppression in the nineteenth century), Louisa May Alcott's authorship of three dime novels, and effects of mass market fiction on young girls.

1833. Warren, Rosalind, ed. *Kitty Libber: Cat Cartoons by Women*. Freedom, California: Crossing Press, 1992.

1834. Wolseley, Roland E. and Isabel Wolseley. *The Journalist's Bookshelf: An Annotated and Selected Bibliography of United States Print Journalism*. Indianapolis, Indiana: R. J. Berg, 1986.

    Includes many references to women and journalism, including one-fourth of the 115 autobiographies of journalists listed.

Historical Studies

1835. Allen, R. C. *Horrible Prettiness: Burlesque and American Culture*. Chapel Hill: University of North Carolina Press, 1991. 350 pp.

    Deals with history of burlesque with a gender perspective; shows how the first burlesque in the U.S. was in the late 1860s with the appearance of Lydia Thompson and her "British Blondes"; tells how they were vilified by many groups, including women's rights campaigners.

1836. American Journalism Historians Association Conference, Roanoke, Virginia, October 6-8, 1994.

    Includes Janice Hume, "Defining the American Heroine Women of Godey's 'Lady's Book'"; Elizabeth V. Burt, "The General Circulation Press as a Tool for Propaganda: The Wisconsin Suffrage Movement, 1910-1919"; Karla K. Gower, "Women in the News: A Look at the Presentation of American Women in News Magazines from 1945 to 1963"; Mei-ling Yang, "Women's Pages or People's Pages: The Production of News for Women in the 'Washington Post' in the 1950s"; Linda Lumsden, "'The Suffragist': The National Woman's Party Wields the Power of the Press."

1837. Beasley, Maurine H. and Paul Belgrade. "Media Coverage of a Silent Partner: Mamie Eisenhower as First Lady." *American Journalism*. 1 (1986), pp. 39-49.

    Uses a framework that involves the symbiotic relationship between a woman newsmaker and the reporters who covered her and the "journalistic conventions of the day that tended to confine coverage of a woman to patriarchal stereotypes about a women's supportive role and value to her husband in performing traditional domestic duties."

1838. Beasley, Maurine H., ed. *The White House Conferences of Eleanor Roosevelt*. New York: Garland, 1983.

1839. Blewett, Mary. "Women in American History: A History Through Film Approach." *Film and History*. 4:4 (1974), pp. 12-16.

1840. Boisseau, T. J. "'They Called Me Bebe Bwana': A Critical Cultural Study of an Imperialist Feminist." *Signs*. Autumn 1995, pp. 116-146.

    States that May French-Sheldon's promotion as an American heroine of the nineteenth century, through her self-presentation as Bebe Bwana (a "woman master") and U.S. media's celebration of her as a modern liberated women, reveal the "imperialist feminist" to be an important part of feminism in U.S. popular culture.

1841. Endres, Kathleen L. "The Symbiotic Relationship of Eleanor Roosevelt and the Press: The Pre-War Years." *Midwest Communications Research Journal*. 2 (1979), pp. 57-65.

1842. Jansen, S. C. "The Future Is Not What It Used to Be: Gender, History, and Communication Studies." *Communication Theory*. 3:2 (1993), pp. 136-148.

1843. Parker, Alison M. "Purifying America: The Women's Moral Reform Movement and Pro-Censorship Activism, 1883-1993." Ph.D. dissertation, Johns Hopkins University, 1994.

Advertising, Public Relations

1844. Altman, Karen E. "Consuming Ideology: The Better Homes in America Campaign." *Critical Studies in Mass Communication*. September 1990, pp. 286-307.
Analyzes media practices of the Better Homes in America reform campaign of the 1920s.

1845. Creedon, Pamela J. "Public Relations History Misses 'Her Story.'" *Journalism Educator*. Fall 1989, pp. 26-30.
Analyzes coverage of women in 10 public relations textbooks; argues that history of public relations should include more women.

1846. Dirks, Jacqueline K. "Righteous Goods: Women's Production, Reform Publicity, and the National Consumers' League, 1891-1919." Ph.D. dissertation, Yale University, 1996.

1847. Fox, Bonnie J. "Selling the Mechanized Household: 70 Years of Ads in *Ladies' Home Journal*." *Gender and Society*. March 1990, pp. 25-40.
Reports an analysis of advertisements for household goods in *Ladies' Home Journal*, 1909-1910 and 1980; claims advertisers, in order to sell household appliances, promoted an ideology about housework that reinforced women's dedication to it.

1848. Jowett, Garth S. and Victoria O'Donnell. *Propaganda and Persuasion*. Second Edition. Thousand Oaks, California: Sage Publications, 1992. 296 pp.
Includes case study of women's work during World War II.

1849. Mathis, Susan. "Propaganda To Mobilize Women for World War II." *Social Education*. February 1994, pp. 94-96.
Describes government's efforts in this regard; relates need for women's participation and problems confronted when they joined the wartime labor force.

Broadcasting

1850. Altman, Karen E. "Television As Gendered Technology: Advertising the American Television Set." *Journal of Popular Film and Television.* Summer 1989, pp. 46-56.

Aims to place television set advertising into a longer history of home technology advertising and to locate gendering of TV sets with respect to earlier gendering of radio receivers.

1851. Boddy, William. "The Amateur, the Housewife, and the Salesroom Floor: Promoting Postwar US Television." *International Journal of Cultural Studies.* April 1998, pp. 129-142.

States that the viability of commercial television within the trade and financial presses of the late 1940s was often framed by the discursive figures of the male electronics hobbyist and the female homemaker-viewer.

Film

1852. Acker, Ally. *Reel Women: Pioneers of the Cinema, 1896 to the Present.* New York: Continuum, 1993. 374 pp.

1853. Basinger, Jeanine. *A Woman's View. How Hollywood Spoke to Women, 1930-1960.* Hanover, New Hampshire: University Press of New England, 1995. 542 pp.

Surveys Hollywood's view of women, showing examples of "woman's film," some rebellious long before "Thelma and Louise."

1854. Beasley, Maurine H. and Sheila Gibbons. *Taking Their Place: A Documentary History of Women.* Lanham, Maryland: University Press of America, 1993. 374 pp.

Tells stories of women trying to take their place in journalism from colonial to present times, in magazines, newspapers, and broadcasting; expanded version of a book published in 1977.

1855. Beauchamp, Cari. *Without Lying Down: Frances Marion and the Powerful Women of Early Hollywood.* Berkeley: University of California Press, 1998. 475 pp.

"Combines with a social and cultural history of filmmaking from 1916 to 1946." Marion was Hollywood's highest paid screenwriter for nearly three decades and the first woman to twice win the Academy Award for screenwriting.

1856. Berenstein, Rhona. *Attack of the Leading Ladies: Gender, Sexuality, and Spectatorship in Classic Horror Cinema.* New York: Columbia University Press, 1996. 274 pp.

Focuses on classic chillers produced by U.S. studios and some independents between 1929-1936; chapters deal with subgenres such as hypnosis, mad doctor, and jungle films; reveals a low incidence of human characters with rigidly assigned gender traits.

1857. Bowser, Eileen. *The Transformation of Cinema 1907-1915.* New York: Scribner's, 1990.
> Includes women pioneers.

1858. Deutsch, James I. "Piercing the Penelope Syndrome: The Depiction of World War II Veterans' Wives in 1940s Hollywood Films." *Humboldt Journal of Social Relations.* 16:1 (1990), pp. 31-42.
> Analyzes depictions of unfaithful wives in Hollywood films of the late 1940s; claims their prevalence resulted from an anti-feminist backlash against women's advances in the labor market and a male corporate structure seeking control.

1859. Fishbein, Leslie. "The Fallen Woman As Victim in Early American Film: Soma Versus Psyche." *Film and History.* 17:3 (1987), pp. 50-61.

1860. Mahar, Karen W. "Women, Filmmaking and Gendering of the American Film Industry, 1896-1928." Ph.D. dissertation, University of Southern California, 1995.

Print Media

1861. Abramowitz, Jack. "Whatever Happened to Superwoman?" *Comics Buyer's Guide.* January 24, 1997, p. 48.
> Details Lois Lane's "Superwoman" role beginning in 1946, and all subsequent "Superwoman" characters in the comics.

1862. American Journalism Historians Association Conference, Lawrence, Kansas, October 1-3, 1992.
> Includes Rodger Streitmatter, "Maria W. Stewart: An African-American Woman Who Raised a Fiery Voice in the Abolitionist Movement" and Bernell E. Tripp, "Abolitionist, Emigrationist, Feminist: Mary Ann Shadd Cary, First Female Editor of the Black Press."

1863. "Annual Meeting of the Illinois Women's Press Association." *Journalist.* December 18, 1886, p. 14; February 4, 1891, p. 10.

1864. Ashton, Carry M. "The Illinois Women's Press Association." *Journalist.* January 24, 1891, p. 12.

1865. Baker, Mark. "The Voice of the Deserted Jewish Woman, 1867-1870." *Jewish Social Studies.* Fall 1995, pp. 98-123.

1866. Baron, A. "Questions of Gender: Deskilling and Demasculinization in the U.S. Printing Industry, 1830-1915." *Gender and History.* Summer 1989, pp. 178-199.

1867. Beasley, Maurine H. "Women and Journalism in World War II: Discrimination and Progress." *American Journalism.* Summer 1995, pp. 321-333.

1868. Bennion, Sherilyn C. "Early Western Publications Expose Women's Suffrage Cries." *Matrix*. 64 (1979), pp. 6-9.

1869. Brislin, Tom. "EXTRA! The Comic Book Journalist Survives the Censors of 1955." *Journalism History*. Autumn 1995, pp. 122-130.
Discusses women reporters in 1955 EC Comics' *EXTRA!*; most are shown outwitting male journalists in getting stories.

1870. Brown, Elspeth. "Gender and Identity in Rural Maine: Women and the *Maine Farmer*, 1870-1875." *Maine Historical Society Quarterly*. Fall 1993, pp. 120-135.

1871. Burt, Elizabeth V. "A Bid for Legitimacy: The Woman's Press Club Movement, 1881-1900." *Journalism History*. Summer 1997, pp. 72-84.
Discusses women journalists' efforts to gain a legitimate place in journalism in the latter nineteenth century as more than 700 joined women's press organizations in more than 17 states.

1872. Cairns, Kathleen A. "Working in Fire: Culture and Feminism in American Front-Page Journalism, 1920-1945." Ph.D. dissertation, University of California-Davis, 1995.

1873. Clar, Reba. "Women in the *Weekly Gleaner*." *Western States Jewish History*. Part 1, July 1985, pp. 333-346. Part 2, October 1985, pp. 44-57.

1874. "The Club Women." *Fourth Estate*. December 10, 1898, p. 5.

1875. De Puy, E. Cora. "Organization of the Michigan Woman's Press Association." *Journalist*. August 2, 1890, p. 11.

1876. De Puy, E. Cora. "Southern Michigan." *Journalist*. July 5, 1890, p. 5, May 13, 1899, p. 264.
Relates activities of Southern Michigan women's press group.

1877. "Draws the Color Line Closely." *Fourth Estate*. March 21, 1895, p. 3.
Points out that in 1895, Georgia Woman's Press Club withdrew from General Federation of Women's Club because it had admitted to membership three African-American women's press clubs.

1878. Egan, Kathryn S. "A Constructivist's View of an Earthquake: Edith Irvine Photographs San Francisco 1906." *Journalism History*. Summer 1994, pp. 66-73.

1879. Forman, Allan. "Hardly Gallant." *Journalist*. January 23, 1892, p. 8.
Welcomes women's press clubs into journalism.

1880. Karetzky, Joanne L. *The Mustering of Support for World War I by the Ladies' Home Journal*. Lewiston, New York: Edwin Mellen Press, 1997. 160 pp.
Tells how *Ladies' Home Journal* provided the American public with propagandistic justifications for U.S. involvement in World War I and helped promote conservation on the home front.

1881. Kitch, Carolyn L. "The American Woman Series: Gender and Class in a Turn-of-the-Century Mass Circulation Magazine." Paper presented at American Journalism Historians Association, Mobile, Alabama, October 1997.
    Discusses six full-page illustrations collectively called "The American Woman" in *Ladies' Home Journal*, 1897.

1882. O'Sullivan, Judith. *The Great American Comic Strip: One Hundred Years of Cartoon Art*. Boston: Little, Brown and Co., 1990.
    Chapter 9, "Enter the Women," pp. 115-134.

1883. Patterson, Ada. *By the Stage Door*. New York: Grafton, 1902.
    Accounts of "sob sister" journalism of latter nineteenth century.

1884. Smith, Lucy W. "Woman's Number." *Journalist*. January 26, 1889.

1885. Yamane, Nancy A. "Women, Power and the Press: The Case of San Francisco, 1868-1896." Ph.D. dissertation, University of California-Los Angeles, 1995.

Images of Women

1886. Akintunde, Omowale. "Light Skinned with Good Hair: The Role of the Media and Christianity in the Maintenance of Self-Hatred in African Americans." Paper presented at Conference of the International Visual Literacy Association, Cheyenne, Wyoming, October 1996. 9 pp.
    Explores how feelings of self-hatred in African Americans are perpetuated through mass media; states that film and music videos show white females as more desirable and that African American comedy on television is self-deprecating.

1887. American Alliance for Health, Physical Education, Recreation and Dance. Annual Meeting, Indianapolis, Indiana, April 1992.
    Includes Karen H. Weiller and Catriona T. Higgs, "Images of Illusion, Images of Reality: Gender Differentials in Televised Sport -- the 1980's and Beyond"; Margaret C. Duncan, "Beyond Stereotyping: An Understanding of Sport Media As Sites of Struggle."

1888. "Baby Boom Women Say Midlife Stereotypes Are Not the Norm." *Media Report to Women*. Spring 1997, p. 5.
    Says baby boomer women consider midlife to be a happy and satisfying period in their lives despite media portrayals.

1889. Becker, Judith and Meg S. Kaplan. "Rape Victims: Issues, Theories, and Treatment." *Annual Review of Sex Research*. 2, 1991, pp. 267-292.
    Shows that media attention to rape has increased sharply; argues that society (and media?) must address the problem of preventing sexual assault.

1890. Bennetts, Leslie. "Myths That Men (and the Media) Live By." *Columbia*

Journalism Review. January-February 1992, pp. 53-55.
Reviews sympathetically Susan Faludi's *Backlash: The Undeclared War Against American Women.*

1891. Berger, Ronald J., Patricia Searles, and Charles E. Cottle. "Ideological Contours of the Contemporary Pornography Debate -- Divisions and Alliances." *Frontiers.* 11:2/3 (1990), pp. 30-38.
Attempts to clarify ideological links between anti-pornography feminism and religious conservatism and between anti-censorship feminism and civil libertarianism.

1892. Berkowitz, Dan, ed. *Social Meanings of News. A Text-Reader.* Thousand Oaks, California: Sage Publications, 1997. 535 pp.
Tries to determine what constitutes news through readings, such as, G. L. Bleske, "Ms. Gates Takes Over" and M. Meyers, "News of Battering."

1893. Bernstein, Nell. "Women Soldiers: Mothers or Amazons?" *Propaganda Review.* Fall 1991, pp. 16-17, 53.
Critiques media portrayals of women soldiers in the Gulf War; claims media regularly portray the woman soldiers as mothers, which the majority of active duty women are not, and proclaim that women should never become prisoners of war.

1894. Binns, Jane C. and Robert C. Branch. "Gender Stereotyped Computer Clip-Art Images as an Implicit Influence in Instructional Message Design." Paper presented at International Visual Literacy Association, Tempe, Arizona, October 12-16, 1994.

1895. Birch, Helen, ed. *Moving Targets: Women, Murder, and Representation.* Berkeley: University of California Press, 1994. 307 pp.
Looks at human fascination with women who murder, represented in fictional and real-life accounts in media.

1896. Bowen, Sheryl P. and Nancy Wyatt, eds. *Transforming Visions: Feminist Critiques in Communication Studies.* Cresskill, New Jersey: Hampton Press, 1993. 312 pp.
Includes: Sheryl Perlmutter Bowen and Nancy Wyatt, "Visions of Synthesis, Visions of Critique"; Julia T. Wood, "Enlarging Conceptual Boundaries: A Critique of Research in Interpersonal Communication"; Nancy Wyatt, "Organizing and Relating: Feminist Critique of Small Group Communication"; Kristin M. Langellier, Kathryn Carter, and Darlene Hantzis, "Performing Differences: Feminism and Performance Studies"; Marlene G. Fine, "New Voices in Organizational Communication: A Feminist Commentary and Critique"; Patti P. Gillespie, "Aristotle and Arimneste ('Nicador's Mother'): Theatre Studies and Feminism"; Celeste Michelle Condit, "Opposites in an Oppositional Practice: Rhetorical Criticism and Feminism"; Cynthia M. Lont, "Feminist Critique of Mass Communication Research"; Alberto Gonzalez and Tarla Rai Peterson, "Feminism and Intercultural Communication Inquiry: Extending the Critique."

1897. Bradby, Barbara. "Like a Virgin Mother?: Materialism and Maternalism in the Songs of Madonna." *Cultural Studies*. January 1992, pp. 73-96.

Analyzes Madonna's song, "Material Girl," from which author concludes Madonna represents a new discourse of sexual control for young women.

1898. Brott, Armin. "The Lace Curtain: Gender Bias in the Media." *Nieman Reports*. Winter 1994, p. 35.

1899. Burleson, Brant, ed. *Communication Yearbook, 19*. Thousand Oaks, California: Sage Publications, 1995. 458 pp.

Includes "Sexual Communication in Interpersonal Contexts: A Script-Based Approach," "Sexual Harassment: A Multidisciplinary Synthesis and Critique," and "Television Programming and Sex Stereotyping: A Meta-Analysis."

1900. Bybee, Carl R. "Constructing Women as Authorities: Local Journalism and the Microphysics of Power." *Critical Studies in Mass Communication*. September 1990, pp. 197-214.

Integrates the power/knowledge perspective into the ideological conception of news work; illustrates how women are constructed or deconstructed as legitimate authorities in local news reporting.

1901. Calia, Georgina N. "An Historical Analysis of the Impact of Title IX on Student Media Presentation of Women as Athletes." *Dissertation Abstracts International*. October 1993, p. 1546-A.

1902. Canary, D. J. and K. S. Hause. "Is There Any Reason to Research Sex Difference in Communication?" *Communication Quarterly*. Spring 1993, pp. 129-144.

Claims much incongruity on sex differences in communication because of reliance on stereotypes, polarization of sexes, lack of a valid measure of gender, and dearth of theory.

1903. Caputi, Jane. "One Size Does Not Fit All: Being Beautiful, Thin and Female in America." In *The Popular Culture Reader*, 3rd Ed., edited by Christopher D. Geist, and Jack Nachbar, pp. 186-204. Bowling Green, Ohio: Popular Press, 1983.

1904. Cardiff, D. "Virtual Prostitution: New Technologies and the World's Oldest Profession." *Comm/Ent: Hastings Communications and Entertainment Law Journal*. Summer 1996, pp. 869-900.

Explores capabilities of new technologies relative to pornographic communications, in the contexts of the traditional nuisance-based jurisprudence and the various news laws, including the Communications Decency Act of 1996.

1905. Chang, Chingching and Jacqueline Hitchon. "Mass Media Impact on Voter Response to Women Candidates: Theoretical Development." *Communication Theory*. February 1997, pp. 29-52.

Reviews cross-disciplinary literature concerning political representations by women, and includes impact of mass media.

1906. Clark, Ann K. "The Girl: A Rhetoric of Desire." *Cultural Studies*. May 1987, pp. 195-203.

Explains that "The Girl" is author's name for "one among many diverse threads in the representations of women by late twentieth-century corporate heads."

1907. Coleman, Barbara J. "Fitting Pretty: Media Construction of Teenage Girls in the 1950s." Ph.D. dissertation, University of Minnesota, 1995.

1908. Corne, Shawn, John Briere, and Lillian M. Esses. "Women's Attitudes and Fantasies About Rape as a Function of Early Exposure to Pornography." *Journal of Interpersonal Violence*. December 1992, pp. 454-461.

Determines from sample of 187 female university students that their early exposure to pornography related to subsequent rape fantasies and attitudes supportive of sexual violence against women.

1909. Cornell, Drucilla. *The Imaginary Domain. Abortion, Pornography and Sexual Harassment*. New York: Routledge, 1996.

1910. "Coverage of Women's Sports Debated; Media Performance So-So, Panelists Say." *Media Report to Women*. Fall 1997, pp. 4-11.

Reports on American University panel, November 3, 1997, on women's sports and media coverage; media did not receive high marks.

1911. Cowen, Gloria and R. R. Campbell. "Racism and Sexism in Interracial Pornography." *Psychology of Women Quarterly*. 1994, pp. 323-338.

1912. Crane, Jonathan L. "Rereading Pornography." *Journal of Communication*. Spring 1996, pp. 158-162.

Reviews six books published in 1993-1994 on pornography.

1913. Creedon, Pamela J. "Framing Feminism--A Feminist Primer for the Mass Media." *Media Studies Journal*. Winter/Spring 1993, pp. 69-80.

1914. Creedon, Pamela J., ed. *Women, Media, and Sport: Challenging Gender Values*. Thousand Oaks, California: Sage Publications, 1994. 368 pp.

Links feminist, sport, and media theory; provides a practical look at models of sport, media effects, and the construction of the sportswoman and women's sport. Includes: P. J. Creedon, "Women, Media, and Sport: Creating and Reflecting Gender Values"; M. J. Kane and S. L. Greendorfer, "The Media's Role in Accommodating and Resisting Stereotyped Images of Women in Sport"; L. D. Williams, "Sportswomen in Black and White: Sports History from an Afro-American Perspective"; P. J. Creedon, "Women in Toyland: A Look at Women in American Newspaper Sports Journalism"; P. J. Creedon, "From Whalebone to Spandex: Women and Sports Journalism in American Magazines, Photography, and Broadcasting"; J. A. Cramer, "Conversations with Women Sports Journalists"; J. A. Cramer and E. H. Granitz, "Pandering or Empowering?

Economics and Promotion of Women's Sports"; S. Birrell and C. L. Cole, "Double Fault: Renée Richards and the Construction and Naturalization of Difference"; K. Ferrante, "Baseball and the Social Construction of Gender"; A Cooper-Chen, "Global Games, Entertainment, and Leisure: Women as TV Spectators"; P. J. Creedon, "From the Feminine Mystique to the Female Physique: Uncovering the Archetype of Artemis in Sport"; M. Merryman, "Gazing at Artemis: The Active Female Archetype in Popular Film"; P. S. Highlen, "Reawakening to the Co-Essence Model of Sport: Stanford's Tara VanDerveer Leads the Way."

1915. *Critical Matrix: The Princeton Journal of Women, Gender, and Culture.* 7:2 (1993).

Thematic issue on "Feminism and Cultural Studies" includes Joanne Gottlieb and Gayle Wald, "Smells Like Teen Spirit: Riot Grrrls, Revolution, and Women in Independent Rock," pp. 11-44; David Hawk, "Interview: Tricia Rose on Hip-Hop," pp. 45-58; David Lewis, "A Home for Murphy Brown's Son(s)," pp. 59-68.

1916. *Critical Studies in Mass Communication.* September 1990.

Thematic issue on "Gender and Empowerment" includes: Carl Bybee, "Constructing Women as Authorities: Local Journalism and the Microphysics of Power," pp. 197-214; Marjorie Ferguson, "Images of Power and the Feminist Fallacy," pp. 215-230; Robert Hanke, "Hegemonic Masculinity in *thirtysomething*," pp. 231-248; Jane Connelly Loeb, "Rhetorical and Ideological Conservatism in *thirtysomething*," pp. 249-260; Bonnie J. Dow, "Hegemony, Feminist Criticism and *The Mary Tyler Moore Show*," pp. 261-274; Muriel G. Cantor, "Primetime Fathers: A Study in Continuity and Change," pp. 275-285; Karen E. Altman, "Consuming Ideology: The Better Homes in America Campaign," pp. 286-307.

1917. Daughton, S. M. "Women's Issues, Women's Place: Gender-Related Problems in Presidential Campaigns." *Communication Quarterly.* Spring 1994, pp. 106-119.

Examines 39 speeches from Democratic and Republican National Conventions (1972-1992) for discussion of women's issues, roles.

1918. Dee, Catherine. *The Girls' Guide to Life: How to Take Charge of the Issues That Affect YOU.* Boston: Little, Brown and Co., 1997. 106 pp.

Chapter 10, "Media Darling," details distorted media images of women and girls and how to counteract them.

1919. Devitt, Tiffany. "Reporting on Depo-Provera Puts Women at Risk." *Extra!* January-February 1993, pp. 15-16.

Media enthusiasm over contraceptive, Depo-Provera, failed to report findings that the drug increases likelihood that women under 35 years of age will develop breast cancer.

1920. Devitt, Tiffany and Jennifer Downey. "Battered Women Take a Beating from the

Media." *Extra!* May/June 1991, pp. 10-12.

1921. Devitt, Tiffany and Janine Jackson. "Women Candidates in '92 Election Coverage." *Extra!* September 1992, pp. 13-15.

Claims that most stories of women in politics focus on narrowly-defined "women's issues" and make wrong assumptions about women's positions; rarely do articles discuss the obstacles women candidates continue to face in raising money and securing endorsements. Sidebar on coverage of New York senatorial race between Geraldine Ferraro and Elizabeth Holtzman.

1922. Dines, Gail. "Pornography and the Media: Cultural Representations of Violence Against Women." *Family Violence and Sexual Assault Bulletin.* Fall 1992, pp. 17-20.

Explores relationship between commercially produced images of violence against women and real life violence; recommends going beyond traditional paradigms in communication to theories recently developed within sociology and cultural studies for a better understanding of the issue.

1923. Dines, Gail and Jean M. Humez, eds. *Gender, Race and Class in Media: A Text-Reader.* Thousand Oaks, California: Sage Publications, 1995. 672 pp.

Analyzes various genres to show how gender, race, and class are "structural and experimental categories that inform the production, construction, and consumption of media representation."

1924. Douglas, Susan J. "The Media on Thin Ice." *The Progressive.* March 1994, p. 12+.

States that the story about figure skaters Tanya Harding and Nancy Kerrigan was reported irresponsibly: Harding was described as white trash, vulgar, unfeminine; Kerrigan as a beautiful, deserving star.

1925. Douglas, Susan J. *Where the Girls Are: Growing Up Female with the Mass Media.* New York: Times Books, 1994. 352 pp.

Looks at mass media for previous four decades to analyze the relationship between feminism and popular culture; treats "Shirelles," "Charlie's Angels," "Roseanne," "Fatal Attraction," and others.

1926. Drucker, Susan J. and Robert S. Cathcart, eds. *American Heroes in a Media Age.* Cresskill, New Jersey: Hampton Press, 1994.

Explores relationship of the hero with the celebrity; includes Joan Fayer, "Are Heroes Always Men?"; Karin J. Billions, "Phyllis Schlafly: Great Mother, Heroine, and Villain"; Florence Rogers and Michael Real, "Theorizing Postmodern Stars: George Michael and Madonna."

1927. Ellis, Kate. "Fatal Attraction, or the Postmodern Prometheus." *Journal of Sex Research.* February 1990, pp. 111-121.

Studies impact of feminist movement on representation of women in the mass media through analyses of recent advertisements and the film, "Fatal Attraction."

1928. Ellis, Kate, Barbara O'Dair, and Abby Tallmer, eds. *Caught Looking: Feminism, Pornography and Censorship*. New York: Caught Looking, Inc., 1986.
Discourages censorship and encourages women's appropriation of pornographic materials; uses many pornographic images in historical perspective on the premise that women have been excluded from the consumption and production of sexual images.

1929. Epstein, Cynthia F. "A New Attack on Feminism." *Dissent*. Winter 1993, pp. 123-124.
Reviews books by Susan Faludi, Carol Tavris, and Nancy Caraway.

1930. *Extra!* January/February 1994.
Includes "Women ARE the News," p. 6 and "A FAIR Forum on Coverage of Women's Stories," p. 7, both by Laura Flanders.

1931. Faludi, Susan. *Backlash: The Undeclared War Against American Women*. New York: Bantam, 1991. 460 pp.
Relates media myths about women.

1932. Farina, Fatima. "The Image of Women in the Gulf War" (L'Immagine della Donna nella Guerra del Golfo). *Sociologia e Ricerca Sociale*. December 1992, pp. 133-151.
Shows how the image of an all-male military is being broken down; gives special attention to U.S. media coverage of the women involved in the Gulf War.

1933. Fisher, Glenn. "Mass Media Effects on Sex Role Attitudes of Incarcerated Men." *Sex Roles*. February 1989, pp. 191-203.
Explores impact of mass media on sex role attitudes of men in a maximum security prison; suggests that media socialization regarding sex roles may help prisoners' reentry into society by making them realize women's achievements.

1934. Fisher, W. A. and G. Grenier. "Violent Pornography, Antiwoman Thought, and Antiwoman Acts: In Search of Reliable Effect." *Journal of Sex Research*. 31:1 (1994), pp. 23-38.
Uses experimental techniques to assess effects of violent pornography; demonstrates that exposure to such pornography was not a reliable cause of anti-woman thoughts, attitudes, or acts.

1935. Flanders, Laura. "Military Women and the Media." *New Directions for Women*. November-December 1990, p. 1+.

1936. Flanders, Laura. "Mothers and Other Soldiers: The Media's 'Woman Warrior.'" *Extra!* November-December 1990, pp. 6-7.
Shows use by U.S. media to propagandize for war with Iraq by playing up role of U.S. woman soldiers.

1937. Flanders, Laura. "With Jobs at Stake, Women Are Ignored." *Extra!* January-

February 1993, p. 12.

States women's view not evident in media discussion of North American Free Trade Agreement, which disproportionately affected them.

1938. Fraser, Laura. "Posing Questions: A Critic Looks at Pornography from the Inside." *Extra!* July/August 1993, pp. 19-21.

1939. Frueh, Joanna. *Erotic Faculties.* Berkeley: University of California Press, 1996. 227 pp.

Addresses how beauty, aging, women's bodies, and sexual practices and experiences have influenced contemporary art.

1940. Garber, Marjorie, Jann Matlock, and Rebecca Walkowitz, eds. *Media Spectacles.* New York: Routledge, 1993. 288 pp.

Confronts and analyzes news media events and how they become spectacles; includes the Anita Hill/Clarence Thomas hearings and the Mike Tyson and William Kennedy Smith rape trials.

1941. Gibson, Pamela C. and Roma Gibson, eds. *Dirty Looks: Women, Pornography, Power.* Bloomington: Indiana University Press, 1993. 248 pp.

Takes stand against fundamentalist right and anti-pornography feminists; includes essays by Lynne Segal and Linda Williams and two articles on porn star Annie Sprinkle.

1942. Glascock, J. and R. LaRose. "Dial-A-Porn Recordings: The Role of the Female Participant in Male Sexual Fantasies." *Journal of Broadcasting & Electronic Media.* Summer 1993, pp. 313-324.

Reveals that typically, dial-a-porn recordings consisted of a female voice guiding a male through sexual activities that are imagined to be performed by both parties; males were seldom heard, females were present exclusively in 94 percent of fantasies.

1943. Goodman, Marcene. "Culture, Cohort, and Cosmetic Surgery." *Journal of Women and Aging.* 8:2 (1996), pp. 55-73.

Tries to draw parallel between media's idealized images of women and mainstreaming of cosmetic surgery; uses images of women in film, TV, advertising since 1940.

1944. Gordon, A. D., Michael Kittross, and Carol Reuss. *Controversies in Media Ethics.* White Plains, New York: Longman, 1996. 301 pp.

Examines 13 sets of arguments, including "The Ethics of 'Correctness' and 'Inclusiveness': Culture, Race, and Gender in the Mass Media" and "Violence and Sexual Pornography."

1945. Gorham, Joan, ed. *Annual Editions: Mass Media 98/99, Fifth Edition.* Guilford, Connecticut: Dushkin/McGraw-Hill, 1998. 240 pp.

Includes Julia T. Wood, "Gendered Media: The Influence of Media on Views of Gender," which contends that media exert a powerful influence on how we view men and women, and Ginia Bellafante, "Bewitching Teen Heroines," which states that TV does include programming that provides smart, self-possessed role models for pre-teen and teenage girls.

1946. Greenberg, Bradley S., Jane D. Brown, and Nancy Buerkel-Rothfuss. *Media, Sex and the Adolescent*. Cresskill, New Jersey: Hampton Press, 1993. 376 pp.

Presents a body of research relating media sexual content and the adolescent response to that content; analyzes gender and its use of sexual content; includes "Adolescents' Acceptance of Sex-Role Stereotypes and Television Viewing," "Gender Differences in Adolescents' Media Use, Exposure to Sexual Content and Parental Mediation," "Disinterest, Intrigue, Resistance: Early Adolescent Girls' Use of Sexual Media Content," "The Effects of Race, Gender, and Fandom on Audience Interpretation of Madonna's Music Videos."

1947. Grodin, Debra and Thomas R. Lindlof. *Constructing the Self in a Mediated World*. Newbury Park, California: Sage Publications, 1996. 230 pp.

Includes W. Simonds, "All-Consuming Selves: Self-Help Literature and Women's Identities"; S. D. Walters, "Terms of Endearment: The Social Construction of Mother/Daughter Relationships."

1948. Gruner, Elliott. "Forgetting the Gulf War POW." *Journal of American Culture*. Spring 1994, pp. 47-51.

Explores media images of 1991 Gulf War prisoners of war, with special attention to the treatment of women by the Iraqi captors and the press.

1949. Gubar, Susan and Joan Hoff, eds. *For Adult Users Only: The Dilemmas of Violent Pornography*. Bloomington and London: Indiana University Press and British Film Institute, 1989. 256 pp.

Portrays the complexity of the legal and philosophical debates women engage in over the issue of pornography and its effects.

1950. Gunther, Albert C. "Overrating the X-rating: The Third-Person Perception and Support for Censorship of Pornography." *Journal of Communication*. Winter 1995, pp. 27-38.

Uses survey approach to gauge 648 persons' exposure to X-rated material, their perceptions of the effects of such materials, and the attitudes of men in general toward women and women in general toward men.

1951. Hammonds, Evelynn. "Missing Persons: African American Women, AIDS, and the History of Disease." *Radical America*. April-June 1990, pp. 7-23.

Gives factors for the low visibility of African American women with AIDS, one of which was media reinforcement of African American women as immoral and promiscuous.

1952. Hanson, Jarice and Alison Alexander, eds. *Taking Sides: Clashing Views on Controversial Issues in Mass Media and Society*. Guilford, Connecticut: The Dushkin Publishing Group, 1990. 348 pp.

Are media messages about women improving? Diana M. Meehan said yes;

Elayne Rapping responded no.

1953. Harrison, T. M. et al. "Images Versus Issues in the 1984 Presidential Election: Differences Between Men and Women." *Human Communication Research.* December 1991, pp. 209-227.

Explores the relative importance of respondents' images of the candidates and respondents' political positions.

1954. Hartley, Nina. "Pornography at the Millennium: Some Thoughts." *Gauntlet.* No. 14, 1997, pp. 20-24.

Points out her beliefs that open sexuality, orgasms, and pornography are good for society.

1955. Healy, Lynne M. "Women in Animation: A Historical Survey of the Female Animated Character in American Film and Television." *Animatrix.* No. 9, 1995/1996, pp. 20-25.

Finds the female animated characters discussed represented stereotypes of sex symbol, jealous and greedy, the domestic.

1956. Hecht, Michael L. *Communicating Prejudice.* Thousand Oaks, California: Sage Publications, 1998. 440 pp.

Analyzes the communication of prejudice in a variety of spheres such as sexism, classism, ageism, racism, and homophobia; includes a series of personal narratives to illustrate types and instances of prejudice.

1957. Heins, Marjorie. "Portrait of a Much Abused Lady." *Index on Censorship.* 1/1993, pp. 9-10.

Analyzes the controversy over limits on artistic expression in terms of sexual politics and anti-feminist impulses.

1958. Henderson-King, Eaaron and Donna Henderson-King. "Media Effects on Women's Body Esteem: Social and Individual Difference Factors." *Journal of Applied Social Psychology.* March 1997, pp. 399-417.

Finds that media images do not similarly affect all women's body esteem.

1959. Henley, Nancy M., Michelle Miller, and Jo-Anne Beazley. "Syntax, Semantics, and Sexual Violence: Agency and the Passive Voice." *Journal of Language and Social Psychology.* March 1995, pp. 60-84.

Reports results of two studies that test the hypothesis that news media report violence against women in passive voice, leading readers to be more accepting of the violence.

1960. Holmberg, Carl B. *Sexualities and Popular Culture.* Thousand Oaks, California: Sage Publications, 1998. 230 pp.

Looks at evolving portrayal of human sexuality; gathers evidence from the "popular" inherent in all aspects of U.S. culture, such as books, films, magazines, television, sports, etc.

1961. "Images of Power and the Feminist Fallacy." *Gender and Mass Media Newsletter.* November 1991, pp. 29-30.
     Reports on article by this title, authored by Marjorie Ferguson, published in *Critical Studies in Mass Communication,* No. 7, 1990.

1962. Jennings, Karen. "Women, Media and Sport." *Media, Culture and Society.* October 1996, pp. 683-686.
     Reviews in essay form a book by the same name, edited by Pamela J. Creedon.

1963. Jensen, Robert. "Pornographic Lives." *Violence Against Women.* March 1995, pp. 32-54.
     Takes feminist anti-pornography stance.

1964. Johnson, Eithne, ed. "Pornography and Sexual Representation." Special issue of *Journal of Film and Video.* Summer/Fall 1993, pp. 3-90.
     Includes five essays on sexual representation (two specifically on pornography): Eithne Johnson, "Introduction"; Linda Mizejewski, "Picturing the Female Dick: *The Silence of the Lambs* and *Blue Steel*"; Chris Straayer, "Lesbian Narratives and Queer Characters in Monika Treut's *Virgin Machine*"; Eithne Johnson and Eric Schaefer, "Soft Core/Hard Gore: *Snuff* as a Crisis in Meaning"; Jane Banks and Patricia R. Zimmermann, "Dr. Ruth Westheimer: Talking Sex as a Technology of Power"; Joseph W. Slade, "Bernard Natan: France's Legendary Pornographer."

1965. Johnson, P. "Pornography Drives Technology: Why Not to Censor the Internet." *Federal Communications Law Journal.* November 1996, pp. 217-226.
     Claims no one has proven the extent or harm of cyberpornography and, therefore, it should be left alone.

1966. *Journal of Communication Inquiry.*
     January 1998 -- Kathleen M. Torrens, "I Can Get Any Job and Feel Like a Butterfly! Symbolic Violence in the TV Advertising of Jenny Craig"; Lisa L. Duke and Peggy J. Kreshel, "Negotiating Femininity: Girls in Early Adolescence Read Teen Magazines."

1967. Kahn, Kim F. and E. N. Goldenberg. "The Media: Obstacle or Ally of Feminists?" *Annals of the American Academy of Political and Social Science.* May 1991, pp. 104-113.
     Examines news coverage of women's movement, women candidates, and gender gap in voting behavior.

1968. Kaid, Linda L. and Diane Bystrom, eds. *The Electronic Election: Perspectives on the 1996 Campaign Communication.* Mahwah, New Jersey: Lawrence Erlbaum, 1998. 432 pp.
     Includes D. Bystrom, L. M. McKinnon, and Carol Chaney, "First Ladies and the Fourth Estate: Media Coverage of Hillary Clinton and Elizabeth Dole in

the 1996 Presidential Campaign"; K. L. DeRosa and D. Bystrom, "The Voice of and for Women in the 1996 Presidential Campaign: Style and Substance of the Convention Speeches"; D. Bystrom and J. Miller, "Gendered Communication Styles and Strategies in Campaign 1996: The Videostyles of Women and Men Candidates."

1969. Kalbfleisch, Pamela J. and Michael J. Cody, eds. *Gender, Power, and Communication in Human Relationships*. Hillsdale, New Jersey: Lawrence Erlbaum Associates, 1995. 366 pp.
Includes 14 papers on changing interpretations of sex and gender in the U.S.; shows relationship to human communication.

1970. Kane, M. J. "The Post Title IX Female Athlete in the Media: Things Are Changing, But How Much?" *Journal of Physical Education, Recreation and Dance*. 60:3 (1989), pp. 58-62.

1971. Kane, M. J. and J. Parks. "Mass Media Images as a Reflector of Historical Social Change: The Portrayal of Female Athletes Before, During, and After Title IX." In *Psychology and Sociology of Sport: Current Selected Research*, Vol. 2, edited by L. Veldon and J. Humphrey. New York: AMS Press, 1990.

1972. Kaplan, E. Ann. *Motherhood and Representation*. New York: Routledge, 1992. 272 pp.
Explores portrayal and ideological coding of motherhood in U.S. culture, 1830 to present; looks at motherhood in nineteenth century writing and twentieth century cinema. Among the latter were "Imitation of Life," "Stella Dallas," "Christopher Strong," "Now Voyager," "Marnie," "Three Men and a Baby," "The Good Mother," "The Handmaid's Tale."

1973. Keller, Gary D. *Chicano Film*. Binghamton, Washington: Bilingual Review/Press, 1985.
Includes Cordelia Candelaria, "Social Equity in Film Criticism," Sylvia Morales, "Chicano-Produced Celluloid Mujeres," and Carlos E. Cortés, "Chicanas in Film: History of an Image."

1974. Kelly, Peggy. "Pornography -- A Feminist-Existentialist Analysis." *Atlantis*. Fall-Winter 1991, pp. 129-135.

1975. Kipnis, Laura. *Ecstasy Unlimited: On Sex, Capital, Gender, and Aesthetics*. Minneapolis: University of Minnesota Press, 1993. 336 pp.
Collects author's essays on popular culture, politics, aesthetics, postmodernism, and feminism, with wide range of practical and theoretical study of film and video.

1976. Kirkham, Pat, ed. *The Gendered Object*. Manchester: Manchester University Press, 1996. 226 pp.
Treats many everyday objects from the perspective of identity with gender; includes Judy Attfield, "Barbie and Action Man: Adult Toys for Girls and Boys, 1959-93"; Anne Wales, "Jackets: Engendering the Object in *Desperately*

Seeking Susan"; Paul Wells, "Tom and Jerry: Cat Suits and Mouse-Taken Identities."

1977. Kitch, Carolyn L. "Changing Theoretical Perspectives on Women's Media Images: The Emergence of Patterns in a New Area of Historical Scholarship." *Journalism and Mass Communication Quarterly*. Autumn 1997, pp. 477-489.
Surveys the past 25 years of historical research on images of women in American mass media; places work in categories of stereotypes approach, search for alternative images, examination of imagery as ideology, and reading of images as polysemic texts; reveals that the range of content is less significant than "the array of theoretical models...that point to important concerns underlying all media history scholarship."

1978. Kozol, Wendy. "Fracturing Domesticity: Media, Nationalism, and the Question of Feminist Influence." *Signs*. Spring 1995, pp. 646-667.
Discusses media's continual rediscovery of the problem of domestic violence; an examination of news coverage and popular representation on TV and in movies from late 1970s to the present finds that mainstream media protect male power rather than challenge it.

1979. Kraus, Barbara. "Speech, Equality, and Harm: Feminist Legal Perspectives on Pornography and Hate Propaganda." *Off Our Backs*. April 1993, pp. 4-5+.
Deals with speeches given at a conference of the same name, held at the University of Chicago Law School, March 5-7, 1993.

1980. Kray, Susan. "Orientalization of an 'Almost White' Woman: The Interlocking Effects of Race, Class, Gender, and Ethnicity in American Mass Media." *Critical Studies in Mass Communication*. December 1993, pp. 349-366.
Examines the "missing" Jewish woman in U.S. mass media; provides a multidisciplinary approach for considering 'doubly' and 'triply' oppressed minority women at the hands of society and their own minority group.

1981. Lackman, Ron. *Women of the Western Frontier in Fact, Fiction and Film*. Jefferson, North Carolina: McFarland, 1997. 272 pp.
Provides factual accounts of women of the frontier West contrasted to their depictions in film and fiction.

1982. Lalvani, S. "Consuming the Exotic Other." *Critical Studies in Mass Communication*. September 1995, pp. 263-286.
Explores the multiple and heterogenous deployment of the "other" within discourses that intersect and contest each other.

1983. Leibman, Nina. "Leave Mother Out: The Fifties Family in American Film and Television." *Wide Angle*. 10:4 (1988), pp. 24-41.

1984. Leong, Wai-Teng. "The Pornography 'Problem': Disciplining Women and Young Girls." *Media, Culture and Society*. January 1991, pp. 91-117.

Looks at radical feminist movement against pornography in visual media and the parental concern in audio media.

1985. Lester, Paul M. *Images That Injure: Pictorial Stereotypes in the Media.* Westport, Connecticut: Praeger, 1996. 282 pp.

Reviews in 34 essays how various groups (including gender) have been stereotyped in newspapers, magazines, television, and movies; includes Bonnie Drewniany, "Women in Advertising"; Patsy Watkins, "Working Woman"; Dona Schwartz, "Women as Mothers"; Kim Walsh-Childers, "Women as Sex Partners."

1986. Levinson, Nan, ed. "Sex and Violence, Women and Censorship in the USA." *Index on Censorship.* 1/1993, pp. 3-12.

Includes Marcia Pally, "Out of Sight and Out of Harm's Way"; Nadine Strossen, "Freedoms in Conflict"; Marjorie Heins, "Portrait of a Much Abused Lady"; Patti Britton, "Education Through Ignorance."

1987. Lowney, Kathleen S. and Joel Best. "Stalking Strangers and Lovers: Changing Media Typifications of a New Crime Problem." In *Images of Issues: Typifying Contemporary Social Problems,* Second Edition, edited by Joel Best, pp. 33-57. Hawthorne, New York: Aldine de Gruyter, 1995.

Looks at media coverage of stalking, a crime that victimizes many women.

1988. McKay, Jim and Debbie Huber. "Anchoring Media Images of Technology and Sport." *Women's Studies International Forum.* 15:2 (1992), pp. 205-218.

Uses sport of sailing as an example of how mass media naturalize sport and technology in gender-specific ways that promote male superiority and marginalize visions of women.

1989. McLaughlin, Lisa. "Discourses of Prostitution/Discourses of Sexuality." *Critical Studies in Mass Communication.* September 1991, pp. 249-272.

Addresses issue of representation of prostitutes as "others" through discourses of sexuality in media; challenges the belief that the media image of prostitutes has shifted from disordered, deviant person to working woman.

1990. Maher, Michelle R. "Men Do and Women Are: Sixth Grade Girls, Media Messages and Identity." Paper presented at Center for the Study of Communication's Mainstream(s) and Margins Conference, Amherst, Massachusetts, April 3, 1992.

Shows how, through media messages, sixth grade girls see gender roles.

1991. Marchetti, Gina. "Readings on Women and Pornography: An Annotated Working Bibliography." *Jump Cut.* December 1981, pp. 56-60.

1992. Marks, Patricia. *Bicycles, Bangs, and Bloomers.* Lexington: The University Press of Kentucky, 1990. 222 pp.

Collects humorous periodical articles concerning the nineteenth century frame of mind about women; includes: "Women and Marriage," "Women's Work," "Women's Education," "Women's Clubs," "Women's Fashions," and "Women's Athletics."

1993. "Media and the Message of Beauty." Special Issue, *Connect Magazine* (Los Angeles). Summer 1997.

Deals with media images of women and girls.

1994. "Media Reinforce Some Stereotypes, Break Others." *Media Report to Women.* Spring 1997, pp. 1, 3.

Reports on study by Nancy Signorielli that reveals across a range of media, women are depicted as concerned with romance and dating, then work or school, and their appearance, but also shown as using intelligence and exerting independence.

1995. "Media Stereotypes of Noncustodial Moms: They Don't Have a Heart." *Media Report to Women.* Summer 1997, pp. 1, 3-4.

Reports on study in *Part Time Mom* (June 1997) that shows mothers whose children do not live with them full time are stereotyped.

1996. Meyers, Marian. *News Coverage of Violence Against Women: Engendering Blame.* Thousand Oaks, California: Sage Publications, 1996. 138 pp.

Presents findings from author's research project that included content, textual, and discursive analyses of the news, as well as interviews with journalists and advocates for women; claims news coverage perpetuates the status quo, which is based on a patriarchal society; women are cast in "good girl/bad girl" mode, and stories contain irrelevant information that puts the blame on the victims of crime.

1997. Meyers, Marian. "News of Battering." *Journal of Communication.* Spring 1994, pp. 47-63.

Looks at coverage of the 1990 murder of a Georgia woman by her husband; claims media distort the realities of battering when they focus on individual and family pathologies.

1998. "Military Women in Film, TV, Media: Invisible, Sexually Stereotyped." *Media Report to Women.* May/June 1990, pp. 6-7.

Shown as temporary diversions, sexual mascots, or in the way.

1999. Minkowitz, Donna. "Journalists on the Women's Movement: No Lesbians Need Apply." *Extra!* September 1992, p. 7.

Discusses media coverage of the women's movement; asks "Why do media outlets take such pains to emphasize that certified feminist leaders are heterosexual while expressing 'concern' that lesbians will take over the movement."

2000. Mullin, Charles, Dorothy J. Imrich, and Daniel Linz. "The Impact of Acquaintance Rape Stories and Case-Specific Pretrial Publicity on Juror Decision Making." *Communication Research.* February 1996, pp. 100-135.

Investigates effect on jury selection of exposure to publicity about the defendant and stories about acquaintance rape portraying men as sexual predators.

2001. "Naming the Rape Victim: Poll Says Most People Opposed." *Media Report to Women*. May/June 1990, p. 6.

    USA Today/Gannett News Service poll found that 84 percent said rape victims should decide themselves whether their names become public.

2002. Nehring, Neil. *Popular Music, Gender, and Postmodernism: Anger Is an Energy*. Thousand Oaks, California: Sage Publications, 1997. 203 pp.

    Includes "Emotional Rescue: Feminist Philosophy on Anger."

2003. Norris, Pippa, ed. *Women, Media, and Politics*. New York: Oxford University Press, 1994. 269 pp.

    Collects original essays by 21 academics and journalists on the impact of media on women's power in the U.S. Includes David H. Weaver, "Women as Journalists"; Kay Mills, "What Difference Do Women Journalists Make?"; Kim Fridkin Kahn and Ann Gordon, "How Women Campaign For the U.S. Senate"; Shanto Iyengar, Nicholas A. Valentino, Stephen Ansolabehere, and Adam F. Simon, "Running As a Woman: Gender Stereotyping in Women's Campaigns"; Montague Kern and Marion Just, "A Gender Gap Among Viewers?"; Everett Carll Ladd, "Media Framing of The Gender Gap"; Susan J. Carroll and Ronnee Schreiber, "Media Coverage of Women in the 103rd Congress"; Pippa Norris, "Women Leaders Worldwide: A Splash of Color in the Photo Op"; Betty Houchin Winfield, "The First Lady, Political Power, and the Media: Who Elected Her Anyway"; Leonie Huddy, "Feminists and Feminism in the News"; Anne N. Costain, Richard Braunstein, and Heidi Berggren, "Framing the Women's Movement"; Andrew Kohut and Kimberly Parker, "Talk Radio and Gender Politics"; Maurine H. Beasley, "How Can Media Coverage of Women Be Improved?"

2004. O'Brien Hallstein, D. L. "Feminist Assessment of Emancipatory Potential and Madonna's Contradictory Gender Practices." *Quarterly Journal of Speech*. May 1996, pp. 125-141.

    Applies a feminist-schizoanalytic perspective to Madonna Ciccione's "The Immaculate Collection."

2005. Ordman, Virginia L. and Dolf Zillmann. "Women Sports Reporters: Have They Caught Up?" *Journal of Sport and Social Issues*. February 1994, pp. 66-75.

    Experiments with southeast university undergraduates and finds a reporter's perceived competence was significantly influenced by gender; the female was rated less competent than the male.

2006. Pally, Marcia. "Ban Sexism, Not Pornography." *The Nation*. June 29, 1985, pp. 794-797.

2007. Pally, Marcia. "Out of Sight and Out of Harm's Way." *Index on Censorship*. January 1993, pp. 4-7.

    Documents the resilience of the idea that women must be protected from offensive images and language, despite contrary evidence.

2008. Perry, Ruth. "I Brake for Feminists: Debates and Divisions Within Women's Studies." *Transformations*. Spring 1996, pp. 1-14.
Critiques media distortion of terms "feminism" and "women's studies."

2009. "Porn in the USA 2." *Gauntlet*. No. 14, 1997. 124 pp.
Includes articles, interviews, and reviews about pornography; deals with feminism, child pornography, erotica, cyberspeech, American sexual culture.

2010. Queen, Carol. "The Cult of Conservative Feminism." *Gauntlet*. No. 14, 1997, pp. 56-60.
Relates history of the feminists' moves against pornography and sexuality.

2011. "Race and Gender." Special Issue. *Literature/Film Quarterly*. 24:1 (1996).

2012. Rapping, Elayne. *Media-tions, Forays into the Culture and Gender Wars*. Boston: South End Press, 1994. 250 pp.
Argues that the drama of the feminist struggle unfolds with uneven influence in the mass media, but in ever-widening areas; challenges "backlash" theory by showing how mass media's gender representations have been "increasingly complicated by feminist interventions."

2013. Raymond, Diane, ed. *Sexual Politics and Popular Culture*. Bowling Green, Ohio: Bowling Green State University Popular Press, 1990. 249 pp.
Employs categories of theoretical perspectives, desire and sexuality and the family, sexuality and images of women, and sexuality and politics; examines pulp publications, sitcom characters, Stephen King's films, language, pop music, and black American literature.

2014. Reading, Anna. "Representing Women: Myths of Femininity in the Popular Media." *Media, Culture and Society*. October 1996, pp. 687-690.

2015. Renov, Michael. "Leave Her to Heaven: The Double Bind of the Post-War Woman." *Journal of the University Film and Video Association*. Winter 1983, pp. 28-36.
Claims that by 1946, a process of double binding relative to women had occurred in the U.S., where injunctions of government appeal, advertising, and popular culture had undermined the stability of the female self-image; pursues this line of thinking by textual analyses of public utterances of the time and of the film, "Leave Her to Heaven."

2016. Rhode, Deborah L. "Media Images, Feminist Issues." *Signs*. Spring 1995, pp. 685-710.
Follows the development of how media deal with and reconstruct feminist issues; includes limitations of media in this regard.

2017. Roach, Colleen. "Sexism and Militarism." Paper presented at International Association for Mass Communication Research, Istanbul, Turkey, June 19-20,

1991.

States that both sexism and militarism depend on violence and the more militarized a culture is, the more likely it has a higher degree of violence towards women.

2018. Rogers, B. "Giving the Lie to Pornography." *The Guardian*. April 25, 1992.

2019. Rollins, Peter C. and Susan Rollins. *Gender in Popular Culture: Images of Men and Women in Literature, Visual Media, and Material Culture*. Cleveland, Oklahoma: Ridgemont Press, 1995.

Collects 11 essays on how gender is expressed in literature (comic books, teen romances, and detective novels), visual media (film, theater and sports), and material culture (dress, image); particularly relevant are Misty Anderson, "Justify My Desire: Madonna and the Representation of Sexual Pleasure"; Denise Heinze, "Angels in the Ballpark: Women in Baseball Films"; Amy K. Nyberg, "Comic Books and Women Readers: Trespassing in Masculine Territory?"

2020. Ross, Karen. "Political Women and the Newsboys." *Gender and Communication Section International Association for Mass Communication Research Newsletter*. November 1995, p. 2.

Looks at way news media frame women politicians in their discourse, language used, imagery invoked, sentiments expressed, and access provided women politicians.

2021. Rubart, Lisa. "Twenty Years After Title IX: Women in Sports Media." *Journal of Physical Education, Recreation and Dance*. March 1992, pp. 53-55.

Claims situation is better for women in sports media, but Title IX of the Education Amendments has barely affected their ability to successfully enter into men's sports reporting.

2022. Russell, Diana E. H. *Making Violence Sexy: Feminist Views on Pornography*. New York: Teacher College Press, Columbia University, 1993.

2023. Sacks, Valerie. "Women and AIDS: An Analysis of Media Misrepresentations." *Social Science and Medicine*. January 1995, pp. 59-73.

Claims depictions of HIV-positive women often stigmatize.

2024. Scheurer, Timothy E. "Goddesses and Golddiggers: Images of Women in Popular Music of the 1930s." *Journal of Popular Culture*. Summer 1990, pp. 23-38.

Contends that the 1930s did not alter dramatically the traditional image of the ideal woman perpetuated in popular song; in some rare cases, the woman is very much the goddess.

2025. Schrift, Melissa. "Icons of Femininity in Studio Cards: Women, Communication and Identity." *Journal of Popular Culture*. Summer 1994, pp. 111-122.

Studies humorous greeting cards whose purchase is 90 percent by women; claims the cards thrive on patriarchal language and imagery.

2026. Schwartz, Martin D. and Walter S. DeKeseredy. "The Return of the 'Battered Husband' Syndrome Through the Typification of Women as Violent." *Crime, Law and Social Change*. October 1993, pp. 249-265.

Examines premise of Murray Straus and Richard Gelles that women are as violent as men; argues that newsmaking criminology must be employed to provide media with alternative feminist views.

2027. Schwartz, N. and E. Kurz. "What's in a Picture? The Impact of Face-ism on Trait Attribution." *European Journal of Social Psychology*. July/August 1989, pp. 311-316.

Experiments with the concept of face-ism, whereby media represent men with their faces, women with larger parts of their bodies.

2028. Scodari, Christine. "Possession, Attraction and the Thrill of the Chase: Gendered Myth-Making in Film and TV Comedy of the Sexes." *Critical Studies in Mass Communication*. March 1995, pp. 23-39.

Examines "articulations of 'egalitarian' courtship in romantic comedy films of the 1930s and 1940s" and recent TV series reviving their conventions.

2029. "Sex Role Attitudes and Sex Role Stereotyping: Recent Literature." *New Jersey Research Bulletin*. Spring 1996. 6 pp.

Profiles 17 publications on these topics in annotated bibliography form.

2030. Shepard, Alicia C. "A No-Win Situation: Newspapers Have Difficulty Reporting on P.C. Jones' Harassment Charges Against B. Clinton." *American Journalism Review*. July/August 1994, pp. 26-29.

Claims the press was in a no-win situation: if it played prominently Paula Jones' harassment charges, it would be accused of sleaze journalism; if it played down what she said, it would be labelled pro-Clinton.

2031. "Should Marv Albert's Accuser Have Been Named from Outset." *Media Report to Women*. Fall 1997, p. 16.

In sexual assault trial of sportscaster Marv Albert: Yes, writers answered, because this was not a rape case.

2032. Siegel, Paul, ed. *Outsiders Looking In: A Communication Perspective on the Hill/Thomas Hearings*. Cresskill, New Jersey: Hampton Press, 1996. 304 pp.

Examines Hill/Thomas hearings as a "rhetorical artifact" to determine message sent to viewers.

2033. Simonds, W. "All Consuming Selves: Self-Help Literature and Women's Identities." In *Constructing the Self in a Mediated World*, edited by D. Grodin and T. R. Lindlof, pp. 15-29. Thousand Oaks, California: Sage Publications, 1996.

Examines notions of self represented in various forms of mass-mediated popular culture; looks at media content centered on women's lives and experiences, reviewing self-help books aimed at women.

2034. Smith, K. B. "When All's Fair: Signs of Parity in Media Coverage of Female Candidates." *Political Communication*. January-March 1997, pp. 71-82.
Claims recent portrayals of female candidates by the media have been more positive.

2035. Speech Communication Association. Annual Meeting, New Orleans, Louisiana, November 19-22, 1994.
Includes Karen E. Strother, "Like Invisible Black Dots Just Visible Enough For Us To Be Invisible: African American Women's Interpretation of 90210"; Peggy Y. Byers and Laura Eikenmeyer, "A Content Analysis of Women in Local and College Newspapers During the Year of the Woman."

2036. Steenland, Sally. "Women: First Ladies Convey Feminine Independence." *Media and Values*. Summer-Fall 1988.

2037. Stephens, Leigh F. *The Image of Women in Television and Newspapers: April 1974 Revisited April 1991*. Sacramento: California State University, Journalism Department, 1992. 97 pp.

2038. Sullivan, Patricia A. "Women's Discourse and Political Communication: A Case Study of Congressperson Patricia Schroeder." *Western Journal of Communication*. Fall 1993, pp. 530-545.
Argues that Congresswoman Patricia Schroeder's political discourse reflects a gender-based approach to decision-making; claims Schroeder's voice has been muted because she does not reflect male culture.

2039. Tseëlon, Efrat. *The Masque of Femininity: The Presentation of Woman in Everyday Life*. Thousand Oaks, California: Sage Publications, 1995. 152 pp.

2040. "2 Live Crew Lyrics Raise Problem of Censorship vs. Obscenity." *Media Report to Women*. July/August 1990, p. 1.
Accused, acquitted of performing lyrics degrading to women.

2041. Ullman, Sharon. *Sex Seen: The Emergence of Modern Sexuality in America*. Berkeley: University of California Press, 1988. 200 pp.
Provides a complex account of the changes that have taken place in the social construction of sexuality during the past century. Focusing on Sacramento, California, demonstrates how attitudes that emerged in the public discourse -- about gender, sexuality, female desire, prostitution -- often found complex and contradictory expression in the courts.

2042. Vanderford, Marsha L. and David H. Smith. *The Silicone Breast Implant Story: Communication and Uncertainty*. Mahwah, New Jersey: Lawrence Erlbaum, 1996. 232 pp.
Examines the health issue of breast implants across a series of contexts often considered separate -- media coverage, doctor-patient interaction, doctor-doctor communication, support group dialogues, public relations campaigns; provides a narrative of how communication shapes the individual perception of health, government, and social policy concerning health care.

2043. Vasil, Latika and Hannelore Wass. "Portrayal of the Elderly in the Media: A Literature Review and Implications for Educational Gerontologists." *Educational Gerontology*. January-February 1993, pp. 71-85.

Points out that the elderly, especially women, were widely underrepresented in the mass media -- not proportionate to their ratio of population and generally depicted negatively.

2044. Violanti, M. T. "Hooked on Expectations: An Analysis of Influence and Relationships in the Tailhook Reports." *Journal of Applied Communication Research*. May 1996, pp. 69-82.

Includes discussion of media coverage of the U.S. Navy's Tailhook sexual harassment scandal of 1991.

2045. Waller, Glenn, Julia Shaw, Kate Hamilton, Gillian Baldwin, et al. "Beauty Is in the Eye of the Beholder: Media Influences on the Psychopathology of Eating Problems." *Appetite*. December 1994, pp. 287 +.

Reviews whether media portrayals of slim models cause symptoms related to eating problems among women who read fashion magazines.

2046. Walters, Suzanna D. "Terms of Enmeshment: The Cultural Construction of the Mother-Daughter Realtionship." In *Constructing the Self in a Mediated World*, edited by D. Grodin and T. R. Lindlof, pp. 30-52. Thousand Oaks, California: Sage Publications, 1996.

Explores representations of the mother-daughter relationship in film, television, and magazines; believes society, through the mechanisms of mass media, compresses this relationship into a narrow vision of psychology.

2047. Walters, Suzanna D. *Lives Together/Worlds Apart. Mothers and Daughters in Popular Culture*. Berkeley: University of California Press, 1994. 308 pp.

Looks at how mothers and daughters are depicted in print, film, and television; concludes that all show never-ending conflict, anti-feminism, and "ideology of separation"; finds few positive examples ("Maude" in TV, "Since You Went Away" in film).

2048. Walters, Suzanna D. "Material Girls: Feminism and Cultural Studies." *Current Perspectives in Social Theory*. 12 (1992), pp. 59-96.

Debates two different approaches to the study of the representation of women in mass media and popular culture.

2049. Wanda, Wayne and Dawn Leggett. "Gender Stereotyping in Wire Service Sports Photos." *Newspaper Research Journal*. 10:3 (1988/89), pp. 105-114.

2050. White, Jane H. "Women and Eating Disorders, Part I: Significance and Sociocultural Risk Factors." *Health Care for Women International*. October-December 1992, pp. 351-362.

Determines risk factors common to eating disorders of Western women, including sociocultural values of a thin physique and perfection, the norm of dieting, the influence of media on these values, and profession choice.

2051. Whitely, Sheila, ed. *Sexing the Groove: Popular Music and Gender*. New York: Routledge, 1997. 400 pp.

Explores ways gender and sexuality make popular music; two of the four sections are on women and popular music and music, image, and identity.

2052. Winkel, Mark. "Autonomic Differentiation of Temporal Components of Sexist Humor." *Humor*. 6:1 (1993), pp. 27-42.

2053. Witham-Levinstein, Kathleen. "Women and Sado-Masochistic Tension in Film and Primetime Television Melodrama: An Application of Psychoanalytic Film Theory to Television." *Dissertation Abstracts International, A: The Humanities and Social Sciences*. March 1995, p. 2995-A.

2054. Wolf, Naomi. *Promiscuities: The Secret Struggle for Womanhood*. New York: Random House, 1997.

Media effects woven through this account of the path from girlhood to womanhood.

2055. Wood, Julia T. "Gendered Media: The Influence of Media on Views of Gender." In *Mass Media 96-97*, edited by Joan Gorham, pp. 23-32. Guilford, Connecticut: Dushkin Publishing, 1996.

Deals with underrepresentation of women, stereotypical portrayals of women and men, stereotypical portrayals of women, stereotypical images of relationships between men and women, women as victims and sex objects/men as aggressors, pathologizing the human body, normalizing violence against women.

2056. Woodward, Kathleen, ed. *Figuring Age: Women, Bodies, Generations*. Bloomington: Indiana University Press, 1998.

Shows how women are aged by culture and how older women are visualized in societies dominated by images of youth.

2057. Yoder, Sharon L. "Woman Under Fire: An Executive's News Coverage and the White Male and Female Systems." Paper presented at Speech Communication Association, Atlanta, Georgia, October 31-November 3, 1991.

Explores use of a male and female systems model to analyze news coverage of a woman university executive mired in controversy.

Advertising, Public Relations

2058. Belknap, Penny and Wilbert M. Leonard. "A Conceptual Replication and Extension of Erving Goffman's Study of Gender Advertisements." *Sex Roles*. August 1991, pp. 103-118.

Analyzes six magazines' advertisements using Goffman's theoretical underpinning; claims feminine touch and ritualization of subordination were often discovered.

2059. Blair, M. E. and E. M. Hyatt. "The Marketing of Guns to Women: Factors Influencing Gun-Related Attitudes and Gun Ownership by Women." *Journal of Public Policy and Marketing*. Spring 1995, pp. 117-127.

Looks at promotion of guns to women in light of the safety factor; relates two studies by the authors -- effects of gun-related advertisements on women's and men's attitudes toward owning guns, influences of social and personal experiences on women's attitudes toward guns.

2060. Burleson, Brant, ed. *Communication Yearbook, 20*. Thousand Oaks, California: Sage Publications, 1996. 712 pp.

Includes V.R. Shields, "Selling the Sex That Sells: Mapping the Evolution of Gender Advertising Research Across Three Decades."

2061. Busby, Linda J. and Greg Leichty. "Feminism and Advertising in Traditional and Nontraditional Women's Magazines 1950s-1980s." *Journalism Quarterly*. Summer 1993, pp. 247-265.

Analyzes advertising images in traditional and nontraditional women's magazines in 1959, 1969, 1979, and 1989 to determine impact of feminist movement on consumer imagery; shows women were less frequently shown in home settings, more frequently without men.

2062. Callcott, M. F. and W.- N. Lee. "A Content Analysis of Animation and Animated Spokes-characters in Television Commercials." *Journal of Advertising*. December 1994, pp. 1-12.

2063. Craig, R. Stephen. "The Effect of Television Day Part on Gender Portrayals in Television Commercials: A Content Analysis." *Sex Roles*. March 1992, pp. 197-211.

Looks at gender portrayals in 2,209 network TV commercials during daytime, evening primetime, and weekend afternoon sportscasts; shows large differences in how men and women are portrayed in these different time slots.

2064. Craig, R. Stephen. "Women as Home Caregivers: Gender Portrayal in OTC Drug Commercials." *Journal of Drug Education*. 22:4 (1992), pp. 303-312.

Determines that women were significantly more likely than men to be portrayed in primetime network TV advertisements for drugs than for other products.

2065. Creedon, Pamela J. "Public Relations and 'Women's Work': Toward a Feminist Analysis of Public Relations Roles." In *Public Relations Research Annual, Vol. 3*, edited by L. A. Grunig and J. E. Grunig, pp. 61-84. Hillsdale, New Jersey: Lawrence Erlbaum Associates, 1991.

Stimulates discourse about societal values and assumptions supporting attempts to construct the meaning of feminization in public relations; claims an effect has been trivialization of the technician's role where most women in public relations are employed.

2066. Cross, Mary, ed. *Advertising and Culture: Theoretical Perspectives*. Westport, Connecticut: Greenwood Press, 1996. 152 pp.

Presents wide variety of views on advertising's methods, language, and cultural effects, and includes Judith Waters and George Ellis, "The Selling of Gender Identity."

2067. "Debate: First Amendment vs. Responsible Advertising Images." *Media Report to Women*. Winter 1997, p. 8.

Debates advertising's depiction of women.

2068. Duker, Bob and Lewis Tucker. "Women's Lib-ers Versus Independent Women: A Study of Preferences for Women's Roles in Advertising." *Journal of Marketing Research*. 14:4 (1977), pp. 469-475.

2069. Duquin, Mary E. "Fashion and Fitness: Images in Women's Magazine Advertisements." *ARENA Review*. 13:2 (1989), pp. 97-109.

2070. Eden, Dawn, Joe Ayres, and Tim Hopf. "An Analysis of the Mythical Function of Reproductive Advertisements." *Women's Studies in Communication*. Fall 1989, pp. 77-90.

Studies pre-natal/antinatal and Enhance/Prevent/Predict pregnancy ads in *Ladies' Home Journal*, *Women's Day*, and *Cosmopolitan*, contrasted to that in *Ms.*, *Working Woman*, and *Essence*.

2071. Fahy, J. et al. "Advertising Sensitive Products." *International Journal of Advertising*. 14:3 (1995), pp. 231-243.

Presents results of two nationwide opinion studies on the advertising of sensitive products in the United States; indicates that the acceptance of such advertising is higher than previously believed.

2072. Ferguson, Jill H., Peggy J. Kreshel, and Spencer F. Tinkham. "In the Pages of Ms.: Sex Roles Portrayals of Women in Advertising." *Journal of Advertising*. 19:1 (1990), pp. 40-51.

Codes 628 advertisements, 1973-1987, from *Ms.* magazine; reports that in some cases, *Ms.* advertising practice differed from the magazine's policies and mission; harmful products and sexist messages and portrayals were frequently found in *Ms.* advertising.

2073. Flanders, Laura. "Beware: P. R. Implants in News Coverage." *Extra!* January/February 1996, pp. 8-11.

Reports that the silicone breast implants story revealing the ill effects caused was covered up as newspapers and broadcasting preferred corporation handouts to the reality of what was happening in courtrooms.

2074. Ford, J. B. and M. S. LaTour. "Differing Reactions to Female Role Portrayals in Advertising." *Journal of Advertising Research*. September/October 1993, pp. 43-52.

Looks at perceptions of women from different interest groups; finds that the National Organization for Women (NOW) and League of Women Voters respondents were significantly more critical of the way women are portrayed in advertising than general sample respondents.

2075. Frith, Katherine T., ed. *Undressing the Ad: Reading Culture in Advertising*. New York: Peter Lang, 1997. 250 pp.

Uses a "critical" approach to get at what advertisements mean; includes Ernest M. Mayes, "As Soft as Straight Gets: African American Women and Mainstream Beauty Standards in Haircare Advertising," pp. 85-108; Angharad N. Valdivia, "The Secret of My Desire: Gender, Class, and Sexuality in Lingerie Catalogs," pp. 225-250.

2076. Funderburk, Jane A. U. "The Development of Women's Ready-to-Wear, 1865 to 1914: Based on the New York Times' Advertisements." Ph.D. dissertation, University of Maryland, 1994.

2077. Gagnard, Alice. "From Feast to Famine: Depiction of Ideal Body Type in Magazine Advertising: 1950-1984." In *Proceedings of the Nineteen Eighty-Six Conference of the American Academy of Advertising*, edited by Ernest F. Larkin, pp. R46-R50. Charleston, South Carolina: American Academy of Advertising, 1986.

2078. Goldman, Robert, Deborah Health, and Sharon L. Smith. "Commodity Feminism." *Critical Studies in Mass Communication*. September 1991, pp. 333-351.

Concerns women's images in magazine advertisements, their responses to those depictions, and advertisers' managing of the responses.

2079. Gould, S. J. "Sexuality and Ethics in Advertising: A Research Agenda and Policy Guidelines Perspective." *Journal of Advertising*. September 1994, pp. 73-80.

Considers types, uses, gratifications, targets, and possible effects of sexual appeals and relates them to ethical concerns.

2080. Griggers, Cathy. "A Certain Tension in the Visual/Cultural Field -- Helmut Newton, Deborah Turbeville, and the VOGUE Fashion Layout." *Differences*. Summer 1990, pp. 76-104.

Details fashion photography as it charts "woman" images and the literal bodies of women who pose.

2081. Halgren, Jennifer N. "Women in Magazine Advertisements: A Scale for Sexism Re-examined." Master's thesis, University of Minnesota, 1991.

2082. Heinberg, Leslie J. and J. Kevin Thompson. "Body Image and Televised Images of Thinness and Attractiveness: A Controlled Laboratory Investigation." *Journal of Social and Clinical Psychology*. Winter 1995, pp. 325-338.

Looks at impacts of TV commercials containing appearance-related or non-appearance-related depictions of body image satisfaction on 138 undergraduate women.

2083. Henthome, T. L. and M. S. LaTour. "A Model to Explore the Ethics of Erotic Stimuli in Print Advertising." *Journal of Business Ethics.* June 1995, pp. 561-569.

Discusses a test of a hypothetical model of the perceived ethical feelings about the use of female nudity/erotic stimuli in print advertising; such use may not be seen as morally right or culturally acceptable.

2084. Hitchon, Jacqueline C. and Chingching Chang. "Effects of Gender Schematic Processing on the Reception of Political Commercials for Men and Women Candidates." *Communication Research.* August 1995, pp. 430-458.

Tests hypotheses in the context of political television commercials for men and women gubernatorial candidates; finds enhanced recall of content about family and appearance in the case of women, and content about campaign activities in the case of men candidates.

2085. Hitchon, Jacqueline C., Chingching Chang, and R. Harris. "Should Women Emote? Perceptual Bias and Opinion Change in Response to Political Ads for Candidates of Different Genders." *Political Communication.* January-March 1997, pp. 49-69.

Finds that neutral advertisements for candidates are thought to be more socially desirable.

2086. "Images of Women in Ads Improve Little Between 1973 and 1986." *Media Report to Women.* March/April 1990, p. 5.

Report of Linda Lazier-Smith, *Demographics vs. Demogoddesses: A New Generation of Advertising Images to Women.* Ads coded in *Ms., Playboy, Time,* and *Newsweek,* 1973 and 1986.

2087. International Communication Association Conference. Dublin, Ireland, June 24-28, 1990.

Includes Anne B. White, "Inequality in Symbolism: Cultural Barriers to Female Candidates in Political Advertising"; Michael D. Basil and Caroline Schooler, "How Cigarettes Are Sold in Magazines: Special Messages for Special Market."

2088. Jackson, Linda A. and Kelly S. Ervin. "The Frequency and Portrayal of Black Females in Fashion Advertisements." *Journal of Black Psychology.* 18:1 (1991), pp. 67-70.

2089. Jaffe, L. J. "The Unique Predictive Ability of Sex-Role Identity in Explaining Women's Response to Advertising." *Psychology and Marketing.* September/October 1994, pp. 467-482.

Compares separate contributions of masculinity, femininity, and androgyny in effort to explain women's responses to modern and traditional sex role portrayals in print media.

2090. Jaffe, L. J. and P. D. Berger. "The Effect of Modern Female Sex Role Portrayals on Advertising Effectiveness." *Journal of Advertising Research.* July/August 1994, pp. 32-42.

Looks at effects of modern female role portrayals (superwoman image, egalitarian image) on advertising effectiveness.

2091. Kahn, Kim F. "Gender Differences in Campaign Messages: The Political Advertisements of Men and Women Candidates for U.S. Senate (1984-1986)." *Political Research Quarterly.* September 1993, pp. 481-502.

2092. Kane, K. "The Ideology of Freshness in Feminine Hygiene Commercials." *Journal of Communication Inquiry.* Winter 1990, pp. 82-92.

Investigates how U.S. television commercials for feminine hygiene products "define the female body, construe its polluting effect, and prescribe rituals of purification."

2093. Kern-Foxworth, Marilyn. "Plantation Kitchen to American Icon: Aunt Jemima." *Public Relations Review.* Fall 1990, pp. 55-67.

2094. Kilbourne, Jean. "Beauty and the Beast of Advertising." In *Reading Culture: Contexts for Critical Reading and Writing*, edited by Diana George and John Trimbur. New York: Harper Collins, 1995.

2095. Kilbourne, Jean. "Deadly Persuasion: The Case Against Advertising of 'Legal' Drugs." *Propaganda Review.* Fall 1992, pp. 29-33.

Examines advertising of tobacco and alcohol; claims contrary to ads, the only equality smoking has given women is that they are afflicted with lung cancer at the same rate as men.

2096. Klassen, Michael L., Cynthia R. Jasper, and Anne M. Schwartz. "Men and Women: Images of Their Relationships in Magazine Advertisements." *Journal of Advertising Research.* March/April 1993, pp. 30-39.

Looks at advertisements in *Ms., Playboy,* and *Newsweek* to determine how women and men, when pictured together, are portrayed; finds women in "traditional" roles.

2097. Klassen, Michael L., Suzanne M. Wauer, and Sheila Cassel. "Increases in Health and Weight Loss Claims in Food Advertising in the Eighties." *Journal of Advertising Research.* December 1990-January 1991, pp. 32-37.

Finds significant increases in the percentage of claims from the 1960s to the 1980s.

2098. Kolbe, R. H. "Gender Roles in Children's Television Advertising: A Longitudinal Content Analysis." In *Current Issues and Research in Advertising 1990*, edited by J. H. Leigh and C. R. Martin, Jr., pp. 197-206. Ann Arbor: Graduate School of Business Administration, University of Michigan, 1990.

Analyzes children's Saturday morning television advertising, 1973-1988; shows males remain the dominant presence in advertising, and females have increased their presence in product user roles, voiceovers, and major roles.

2099. Kolbe, R. H. and D. Muehling. "Gender Roles and Children's Television Advertising." *Journal of Current Issues and Research in Advertising.* Spring 1995, pp. 49-64.

> Investigates whether children are aware of gender roles when exposed to advertisements containing either stereotyped or counterstereotyped role portrayals.

2100. Kramer, Kevin M. and Nancy N. Knupfer. "Gender Equity in Advertising on the World-Wide Web: Can It Be Found?" Paper presented at Association for Educational Communications and Technology, Albuquerque, New Mexico, February 14-18, 1997. 13 pp.

> Shows that women in Web advertising are a reflection of current trends in other media: they are in supportive or subordinate roles.

2101. Kurtz, Jan. "Dream Girls: Women in Advertising." *USA Today.* January 1, 1997, p. 70.

> States the obvious, that no matter in which roles women are portrayed, they are there to sell products.

2102. Lafky, Sue A., Margaret Duffy, Mary Steinmaus, and Dan Berkowitz. "Looking Through Gendered Lenses: Female Stereotyping in Advertisements and Gender Role Expectations." *Journalism and Mass Communication Quarterly.* Summer 1996, pp. 379-388.

> Conducts experiment with high school students, and although results were not dramatic, they provide evidence that even brief exposure to stereotypical ads plays a role in reinforcing stereotypes about gender roles and that gendered lenses lead to differences in how men and women process visual ads.

2103. Laird, Pamela W. "Progress in Separate Spheres: Selling Nineteenth-Century Technologies." *Knowledge and Society.* No. 10, 1996, pp. 19-49.

> Tells how with evolution of 19th century advertising, there were highly gendered expectations of women and men; states that advertisers continued to increase the demands on women's time.

2104. Lazier-Smith, Linda. "The Effect of Changes in Women's Social Status in Images of Women in Magazine Advertising: The Pingree-Hawkins Sexism Scale Reapplied, Goffman Reconsidered, Kilbourne Revisited." Ph.D. dissertation, Indiana University, 1988.

2105. Lewis, Charles and John Neville. "Images of Rosie: A Content Analysis of Women Workers in American Magazine Advertising, 1940-1946." *Journalism and Mass Communication Quarterly.* Spring 1995, pp. 216-227.

> Attempts to better explain the relationship between the advertising industry, the reality of working women, and sociocultural constructions of female gender identity before, during, and after World War II.

2106. Lovdal, Lynn T. "Sex Role Messages in Television Commercials: An Update." *Sex Roles.* December 1989, pp. 715-724.

Determines if changes occurred in the portrayal of sex roles of television commercials during 1980s; shows that men were shown in three times the variety of occupations and roles as were women.

2107. Mamay, Michelle A. and Richard L. Simpson. "Three Female Roles in Television Commercials." *Sex Roles*. 7:12 (1981), pp. 1223-1232.

2108. Manca, Luigi and Alessandra. *Gender and Utopia in Advertising: A Critical Reader*. Lisle, Illinois: Procopian Press of Illinois Benedictine College, 1994. 168 pp.

Looks at images of women, men, and society in advertising through 10 essays; includes Margaret E. Duffy, "Body of Evidence: Studying Women in Advertising"; Marian MacCurdy, "The Four Women of the Apocalypse: Polarized Feminine Images in Magazine Advertisements"; Veleda J. Boyd and Marilyn M. Robitaille, "Scent and Femininity: Strategies of Contemporary Perfume Ads"; Shelley Budgeon, "Female Magazine Advertising: Constructing Femininity in the Postfeminist Era," and Melissa E. Barth, "Made to Order: Backlash in the Catalogues."

2109. Maxcy, David J. "Advertising the Gender System: Changing Configurations of Femininity and Masculinity in Early Advertising in the United States." Ph.D. dissertation, University of Massachusetts, 1994.

2110. Mayes, Ernest M. "Images of Black Women in Print Advertisements in Relation to Dominant Cultural Standards of Beauty." Master's thesis, Pennsylvania State University, 1996.

2111. Morris, Raymond N. "Gender Advertisements and Political Cartoons." *Maieutics*. 2:1 (1985), pp. 149-171.

2112. "No End to Use of Sex in Ads as Long as Products Sell." *Media Report to Women*. March/April 1990, pp. 5-6.

Transcript of portion of "Good Morning America" show on advertising and sex.

2113. Perimenis, Louisa. "The Ritual of Anorexia Nervosa in Cultural Context." *Journal of American Culture*. Winter 1991, pp. 49-59.

Reviews ways media advertising reinforces stereotypes of women as service-oriented, unentitled, and overly concerned with their bodies; analyzes 201 TV commercials in 1990.

2114. Prakash, V. "Sex Roles and Advertising Preferences." *Journal of Advertising Research*. May/June 1992, pp. 43-52.

2115. Pratt, C. A., et al. "Do Popular Magazines Promote Weight-Control Messages? Implications of Weight-Control Advertisements for the Health of African American Women." *Howard Journal of Communications*. October-December

1996, pp. 349-364.
Examines trends in advertisements on weight control in *Essence* and *Ladies' Home Journal*, 1984-1993.

2116. Procter, David E., Roger C. Aden and Phyllis Japp. "Gender/Issue Interaction in Political Identity Making: Nebraska's Woman vs. Woman Gubernatorial Campaign." *Central States Speech Journal*. Fall-Winter 1988, pp. 190-203.
Studies TV campaign advertising by two candidates for governor of Nebraska in 1986; finds that gender perceptions combined with positions on issues influence outcome.

2117. Procter, David E., W. J. Schenck-Hamlin, and K. A. Haase. "Exploring the Role of Gender in the Development of Negative Political Advertisements." *Women and Politics*. 14:2 (1994), pp. 1-22.
Analyzes 99 negative advertisements produced in 1990 campaigns; finds women's campaigns make choices similar to men's concerning the agent who presents the attack.

2118. Pumphrey, Martin. "The Flapper, the Housewife and the Making of Modernity." *Cultural Studies*. May 1987, pp. 179-194.
Looks at 1920s' advertising images concerning the American woman through the perspective of women's history.

2119. Radner, Hilary. "'This Time's for Me': Making Up and Feminine Practice." *Cultural Studies*. October 1989, pp. 301-322.
Clouds an essay on women, advertising, and cosmetics with much academese; states the most marked transition in the "representation of women in advertising was from the domestically oriented woman to a woman who sought to please herself."

2120. Rajecki, D. W., et al. "Gender Casting in Television Toy Advertisements: Distributions, Message Content Analysis, and Evaluations." *Journal of Consumer Psychology*. 2:3 (1993), pp. 307-327.
Finds that all-boy ads were characterized by a practical subtext, boy-and-girl ads by a traditional thrust, and all-girls by emotional tone; that evaluators thought ads were suitable only for the gender for which they were created.

2121. Rakow, Lana F. "'Don't Hate Me Because I'm Beautiful': Feminist Resistance to Advertising's 'Irresistible Meanings.'" *Southern Communication Journal*. Winter 1992, pp. 132-141.

2122. Riffe, Daniel, Patricia C. Place, and Charles M. Mayo. "Game Time, Soap Time and Prime Time Television Advertisements: Treatment of Women in Sunday Football and Rest-of Week Advertising." *Journalism Quarterly*. Summer 1993, pp. 437-446.
Finds that male characters were more common in ads for sports; that there was no support for the hypothesis that there would be more provocatively dressed women in ads for sports than in soap or prime time.

2123. Rudman, William J. and Akiko F. Hagiwara. "Sexual Exploitation in Advertising Health and Wellness Products." *Women and Health.* 18:4 (1992), pp. 77-89.

Analyzes how media portray women in photographs advertising health and wellness products; finds that a high percentage of the advertisements place women in submissive positions and unnatural poses, emphasize body dismemberment, and focus on sexuality, not wellness.

2124. Rudman, William J. and Verdi Patty. "Exploitation: Comparing Sexual and Violent Imagery of Females and Males in Advertising." *Women & Health.* 20:4 (1993), pp. 1-14.

Examines the manner in which female and male models are portrayed in magazine advertisements; shows that females are more likely than males to be placed in submissive positions, sexually displayed, and to be subjects of violent imagery.

2125. Rummel, Amy, Mary Goodwin, and Mike Shepherd. "Self-Efficacy and Stereotyping in Advertising: Should Consumers Want to Change?" *International Journal of Advertising.* 9:4 (1990), pp. 308-316.

Finds that contrary to expectations, females had higher confidence in their purchase decisions after viewing stereotypical television advertisements.

2126. Russo, Nancy F., Lynn Feller, and Patrick H. DeLeon. "Sex-Role Stereotypes in Television Advertising: Strategies for Change in the 80s." *Academic Psychology Bulletin.* 4 (1982), pp. 117-135.

2127. Sheperd, Juanita M. "The Portrayal of Black Women in the Ads of Popular Magazines." *Western Journal of Black Studies.* 4 (1980), pp. 179-182.

2128. Shields, V. R. "Advertising Visual Images: Gendered Ways of Seeing and Looking." *Journal of Communication Inquiry.* Summer 1990, pp. 25-39.

Looks at meaning communicated by print advertising images, and particularly highly-stylized fashion advertising.

2129. Shields, V. R. "Selling the Sex that Sells: Mapping the Evolution of Gender Advertising Research Across Three Decades." In *Communication Yearbook*, Volume 20, edited by B. R. Burleson, pp. 71-109. Thousand Oaks, California: Sage Publications, 1996.

Provides history of gender advertising research during preceding three decades and reflects its relationship to feminist politics.

2130. Slatton, Y. L. "The Role of Women in Sport as Depicted Through Advertising in Selected Magazines, 1900-1968." Ph.D. dissertation. University Microfilms No. 71-5824.

2131. Slovenko, Ralph. "People Seeking People: Commentary." *Journal of Psychiatry and Law.* Summer 1995, pp. 333-343.

Analyzes romantic personal advertisements in newspapers and magazines;

in such ads, women list physical qualities they think are appealing to men, but they also look at financial aspects.

2132. Stephenson, Theresa, William J. Stover, and Mike Villamor. "Sell Me Some Prestige! The Portrayal of Women in Business-Related Ads." *Journal of Popular Culture*. Spring 1997, pp. 255-271.
    Analyzes 709 business-related ads in 144 magazines from 1962 through 1992, at ten-year intervals; finds sex inequality in the workplace continues to exist in business-related ads.

2133. "Tobacco Industry Criticized for Targeting Women in Its Advertising." *Media Report to Women*. January-February 1991, p. 10.

2134. Walker, Sherry J. "Gender Ideology and Drinking Norms: Content Analysis of Alcohol Advertisements in Selected Magazines, 1973 to 1988." Ph.D. dissertation, University of Tennessee, 1992.

2135. Woodruff, Katie. "Alcohol Advertising and Violence Against Women: A Media Advocacy Case Study." *Health Education Quarterly*. August 1996, pp. 330-345.
    Describes the Dangerous Promises Campaign, based on view that sexist advertising images contribute to an environment conducive to violence against women.

2136. Yamasaki, Joan M. "Only If It's Good: Teaching a Demand Reduction Campaign and a Bibliography on Women and Advertising." *Feminist Teacher*. Spring 1993, pp. 37-41.
    Identifies cigarette advertising as an example of marketing harmful products using harmful images; includes a bibliography on women and advertising.

2137. Yanni, Denise. "The Social Construction of Women as Mediated by Advertising." *Journal of Communication Inquiry*. Winter 1990, pp. 71-81.
    Addresses theories on the structure of representation, concept of commodities, nature of fetishism, and power of advertising to show that the "modern" mediation of the person-object relationship perpetuates an old system of meaning patriarchy.

Broadcasting

2138. Acland, Charles. "The 'Space' Behind the Dialogue -- The Gender-Coding of Space on Cheers." *Women & Language*. Fall 1990, pp. 38-40.
    On popular situation comedy, "Cheers."

2139. Allan, Kenneth and Scott Coltrane. "Gender Displaying Television Commercials: A Comparative Study of Television Commercials in the 1950s and 1980s." *Sex Roles*. August 1996, pp. 185-203.
    Compares 1950s and 1980s and finds that there have been changes in how women have been portrayed, but not men.

2140.   Atkin, D. J. "The Evolution of Television Series Addressing Single Women, 1966-1990." *Journal of Broadcasting and Electronic Media.* Fall 1991, pp. 517-523.
Traces development of serial programming devoted to single working women; finds of 102 programs of this type between 1966-1990, 69.8 percent were situation comedies.

2141.   Atkin, D. J. and Marilyn Fife. "The Role of Race and Gender as Determinants of Local TV News Coverage." *Howard Journal of Communications.* Winter 1994, pp. 123-137.
Compares the frequency and nature of appearances in the news of different racial or gender groups to test the theory that white women have been making progress at the expense of minorities; finds being white and female results in significant underrepresentation.

2142.   Atkin, D. J., J. Moorman, and C. A. Lin. "Ready for Prime Time: Network Series Devoted to Working Women in the 1980s." *Sex Roles.* December 1991, pp. 677-685.
Addresses trends in network series featuring working female leads during the 1980s, assessing economic factors responsible for those depictions.

2143.   Benoit, W. L. and K. K. Anderson. "Blending Politics and Entertainment: Dan Quayle versus *Murphy Brown.*" *Southern Communication Journal.* Fall 1996, pp. 73-85.
Analyzes the exchange between Vice President Quayle and television character Murphy Brown (Candice Bergen) about single parenting.

2144.   Brinson, Susan L. "TV Fights: Women and Men in Interpersonal Arguments on Prime-time Television Dramas." *Argumentation and Advocacy.* Fall 1992, pp. 89-104.
Analyzes conflicts in week (1991) of 15 primetime, network TV dramas; suggests that a weak link exists between actual argument behaviors and those on TV.

2145.   Brinson, Susan L. "TV Rape -- Television's Communication of Cultural Attitudes Toward Rape." *Women's Studies in Communication.* Fall 1989, pp. 23-36.
Discusses 1988 episode of "Cagney and Lacey."

2146.   Brinson, Susan L. "The Use and Opposition of Rape Myths in Prime-time Television Dramas." *Sex Roles.* October 1992, pp. 359-375.
Focuses on use of, and opposition to, rape myths in primetime television dramas and discusses their implications.

2147.   "Broadcasters See Ebbing of Sexism, More Clout for Women in News." *Media Report to Women.* May/June 1990, pp. 8-9.
Says that sexist practices in U.S. broadcasting waning, but women continued to lack managerial clout.

2148. Brooks, Dianne L. "Television and Legal Identity in Prime Suspect." *Studies in Law, Politics, and Society.* 14 (1994), pp. 89-104.

Discusses TV feminist age through analysis of PBS show "Prime Suspect," aired in 1992-1993; claims these shows failed in their attempts to challenge conventional representations of gender and race.

2149. Bryant, Anne. "Saturday Morning TV: No Girls Allowed." *Extra!* September-October 1991, p. 10.

2150. Butsch, Richard. "Class and Gender in Four Decades of Television Situation Comedy: Plus Ça Change..." *Critical Studies in Mass Communication.* December 1992, pp. 387-399.

States that "for four decades, the few working-class families portrayed in domestic situation comedies have inverted the gender roles of fathers and mothers, with the men failing as men and the wives filling the vacuum; series with middle-class families, by contrast, depict fathers as easily meeting the standard of masculinity. "

2151. Cantor, Muriel G. "Prime-time Fathers: A Study in Continuity and Change." *Critical Studies in Mass Communication.* September 1990, pp. 275-285.

Concentrates on how "women, and especially men," act as parents and spouses in domestic comedies on television.

2152. Coltrane, Scott and Michele Adams. "Work-Family Imagery and Gender Stereotypes: Television and the Reproduction of Difference." *Journal of Vocational Behavior.* April 1997, pp. 323-347.

Analyzes 1,699 TV commercials, 1992-1994; shows women were less prevalent, were more likely to be shown in families, less likely to hold jobs, less likely to exercise authority, and more likely to be depicted as sex objects.

2153. Columbia Broadcasting Service Television Network. "Changes in Women's Roles on Television. Special Issue: Television as a Social Issue." *Applied Social Psychology Annual.* 8 (1988), pp. 113-117.

Traces development of women's roles on TV through dialogues from many shows.

2154. Curry, Ramona. "Madonna from Marilyn to Marlene -- Pastiche and/or Parody?" *Journal of Film and Video.* Summer 1990, pp. 16-30.

Casts her analysis of the parodic potential of Madonna music videos relative to the star's composite image.

2155. D'Acci, Julie. *Defining Women: Television and the Case of Cagney and Lacey.* Chapel Hill: University of North Carolina Press, 1994. 380 pp.

Explores the social and cultural construction of gender as it was negotiated in the TV series, "Cagney and Lacey"; reveals how on-screen issues of definition of women were played out off-screen in debates about casting, writing, production, and advertising.

2156. Dates, J. "Gimme a Break? African American Women in Prime Time Television." In *Mass Media and Society*, edited by Alan Wells. Lexington, Massachusetts: D. C. Heath/Lexington, 1987.

2157. Davis, Donald M. "Portrayals of Women in Prime-time Network Television: Some Demographic Characteristics." *Sex Roles*. September 1990, pp. 325-332.
    Examines demographic variables to obtain a partial picture of portrayals of women on network television; finds that few changes had been made in portrayals from 1970s to 1980s.

2158. Detman, Linda A. "Negotiating the Woman of Broadcast News." *Studies in Symbolic Interaction*. 15 (1993), pp. 3-14.
    Examines the film, "Broadcast News," from a feminist perspective; looks at film's ideological message that white professional women must make a choice between a career or a personal life, and choosing a career makes them less a woman in the traditional sense.

2159. Dow, Bonnie J. "Femininity and Feminism in 'Murphy Brown.'" *Southern Communication Journal*. Winter 1992, pp. 143-155.
    American TV sitcom starring Candice Bergen.

2160. Dow, Bonnie J. "Hegemony, Feminist Criticism and *The Mary Tyler Moore Show*." *Critical Studies in Mass Communication*. September 1990, pp. 261-274.
    Says the feminist perspective of this television show is contradicted by the "patriarchal relationships and role definitions developed within its narrative."

2161. Dow, Bonnie J. *Prime-Time Feminism: Television, Media Culture, and the Women's Movement Since 1970*. Philadelphia: University of Pennsylvania Press, 1996. 240 pp.
    Focuses primarily on television sitcoms, with chapters on "The Mary Tyler Moore Show," "One Day at a Time," "Designing Women," and "Murphy Brown"; points out that TV's model of television is strictly for white, heterosexual, middle-class women.

2162. Duncan, M. C. and C. A. Hasbrook. "Denial of Power in Televised Women's Sports." *Sociology of Sport Journal*. 5 (1988), pp. 1-21.

2163. Duncan, Margaret C., M. Messner, and L. Williams. *Gender Stereotyping in Televised Sports*. Los Angeles, California: Athletic Foundation of Los Angeles, 1990.

2164. Eaton, B. Carol. "Prime-Time Stereotyping on the New Television Networks." *Journalism and Mass Communication Quarterly*. Winter 1997, pp. 859-872.
    Examines portrayals of women on ABC, CBS, NBC, FOX, and UPN in 1995; shows women were underrepresented in all promotional announcements.

2165. Fairchild, Halford H. "Creating Positive Television Images. Special Issue:

Television as a Social Issue." *Applied Social Psychology Annual.* 8 (1988), pp. 270-280.

    Describes concept for an educational TV program that would address concerns emerging from research on effects of media violence, including portrayals of women in the media.

2166. Galperin, W. "Sliding off the Stereotype: Gender Difference in the Future of Television." In *Postmodernism and Its Discontents*, edited by E. Ann.Kaplan, pp. 146-162. London: Verso, 1988.

2167. Gerbner, George. "Women and Minorities on TV: A Study in Casting and Fate." *Media Development.* 41:2 (1994), pp. 38-44.

    Reports on his studies of 1,371 U.S. television programs of the 1980s-1990s; states that women comprise one-third of the characters in all samples except daytime serials (45.5 percent) and game shows (55.3 percent); smallest percentages in news (27.8 percent) and children's programs (23.4 percent).

2168. Golden, Mickey. "Fighting Back Like a Man: The Morality of 'Murphy Brown.'" Paper presented at Speech Communication Association, San Francisco, California, November 18-21, 1989.

    Analyzes TV character "Murphy Brown."

2169. Goodstein, Ethel S. "Southern Belles and Southern Buildings: The Built Environment As Text and Context in 'Designing Women.'" *Critical Studies in Mass Communication.* 9:2 (1992), pp. 170-185.

2170. Gow, Joe. "Reconsidering Gender Roles on MTV: Depictions in the Most Popular Music Videos of the Early 1990s." *Communication Reports.* Summer 1996, pp. 151-161.

    Studies MTV's top 100 of the 1990s and concludes that the music videos continued to underrepresent women and to present them in a way to emphasize their physical appearance, rather than their musical ability.

2171. Hall, Christine C. and Matthew J. Crum. "Women and 'Body-isms' in Television Beer Commercials." *Sex Roles.* September 1994, pp. 329-337.

    Shows that in television beer commercials, female bodies and body parts appear more often than those of males, whose faces are usually shown.

2172. Hallingby, Leigh. "Sesame Street Still No Kid Treat: After Five Years, the Numbers Are Still Overwhelmingly Male." *New Directions for Women.* January-February 1993, p. 13.

    Shows three-fourths of all characters on "Sesame Street" were male in 1987; explains that puppet and animated characters take years to create and therefore, to change them or to introduce new ones is a long process.

2173. Hamamoto, Darrell Y. *Monitored Peril: Asian Americans and the Politics of TV Representation.* Minneapolis: University of Minnesota Press, 1994. 311 pp.

    Claims representation of Asian-American women on television carries sexist overtones -- exotic looks, tradition, compliant behavior.

2174. Hanke, Robert. "Hegemonic Masculinity in *thirtysomething.*" *Critical Studies in Mass Communication.* September 1990, pp. 231-248.

Claims television show, *thirtysomething,* is able to contain elements of "liberal feminist ideology while remaining complicit with dominant gender ideology."

2175. Hanson, Cynthia A. "The Women of China Beach." *Journal of Popular Film and Television.* Winter 1990, pp. 154-163.

Tells how women are depicted in the telefilm, "China Beach."

2176. Hanson, Elizabeth. "Reaching Out to Gifted Girls Through Television." *Gifted Child Today Magazine.* May-June 1995, pp. 8-9.

Solicits opinions of gifted female students at a southern high school on how women, especially southern women, are shown on TV.

2177. Heide, Margaret J. "Mothering Ambivalence -- The Treatment of Women's Gender Role Conflicts over Work and Family on 'thirtysomething.'" *Women's Studies.* 21:1 (1992), pp. 103-117.

Tells how the TV show re-evaluates women's gender roles and looks at problems baby-boomer women have concerning work and family.

2178. Henderson, Mary. "Professional Women in *Star Trek,* 1964-1969." *Film and History.* 24:1/2 (1994), pp. 47-59.

2179. Herrett-Skjellum, J. and M. Allen. "Television Programming and Sex Stereotyping: A Meta-Analysis." In *Communication Yearbook, 19,* edited by B. R. Burleson, pp. 156-185. Thousand Oaks, California: Sage Publications, 1995.

Indicates that television programming has many sexual stereotypes and that exposure to televised material increases acceptance of those stereotypes.

2180. "Image of Women on Entertainment TV Remains Distorted, Study Says." *Media Report to Women.* January-February 1991, p. 1.

2181. Japp, P. M. "Gender and Work in the 1980s: Television's Working Women as Displaced Persons." *Women's Studies in Communication.* Spring 1991, pp. 49-74.

Points out that television's working woman of the 1980s was a woman who just happened to be a worker rather than the other way around; blames TV for not being able to rise above the cliché in depicting women as workers.

2182. Keightley, Keir. "'Turn It Down!' She Shrieked: Gender, Domestic Space, and High Fidelity, 1948-59." *Popular Music.* May 1996, pp. 149-177.

2183. Kiester, Edwin, Jr. "Decked Out in a Silver Go-Go Skirt, Toting a Pistol or Trashing Motherhood." *TV Guide.* December 6, 1986, pp. 51-56.

Presents Delta Burke character of "Designing Women" as taboo breaker.

2184. Kircher, Cassie. "The Disruption of Glamour: Gender and MTV." *Platte Valley*

Review. Winter 1990, pp. 40-47.

2185. Korzeniowska, Victoria B. "Engaging with Gender: Star Trek's 'Next Generation.'" *Journal of Gender Studies.* March 1996, pp. 19-25.

Examines women's roles in TV series "Star Trek: The Next Generation" to determine if women's roles have improved in the 24th century.

2186. Kubey, R. et al. "Demographic Diversity on Cable: Have the New Cable Channels Made a Difference in the Presentation of Gender, Race, and Age?" *Journal of Broadcasting and Electronic Media.* Fall 1995, pp. 459-471.

Focuses on whether growth in channels has changed the representative diversity of those who appear on TV in terms of race, gender, and age; finds underrepresentation of women continues -- males are 2.5 times more likely than women to appear.

2187. Lamm, Bob. "*The Nurses*: Television's Forgotten Gems." *Journal of Popular Film and Television.* Summer 1995, pp. 72-79.

Demonstrates that "The Nurses," an early 1960s' television show, was far ahead of its time because of its portrayal of the feminist view of the lives of professional women and its treatment of sensitive ethical and political issues.

2188. Larson, Stephanie G. "Black Women on *All My Children*." *Journal of Popular Film and Television.* Spring 1994, pp. 44-48.

Examines black women on soap opera, "All My Children"; claims that although the show demonstrates an advancement for black women, a closer look at pivotal character Angie reveals that "the show embraced a familiar stereotype of black females, that of matriarch."

2189. Lee, Janet. "Subversive Sitcoms -- *Roseanne* as Inspiration for Feminist Resistance." *Women's Studies.* 21:1 (1992), pp. 87-101.

States the TV show ignores many issues (race, class, violence against women, reproductive rights, etc.) but the program portrays and problemizes the realities of women's domestic and pink collar working class existence.

2190. Lengermann, Patricia M. and Jill Niebrugge. "Flirting with Equality: A Feminist Social Commentary on the Opposition to Civil Equality for Lesbians and Gays." *NWSA Journal.* Spring 1995, pp. 30-53.

Analyzes six primetime TV portrayals, 1986-1994, of flirtations between a heterosexual and a lesbian or bisexual woman.

2191. Lichter, Robert, Linda Lichter, and S. Rothman. "From Lucy to Lacey: TV's Dream Girls." *Public Opinion.* 9:3 (1986), pp. 16-19.

2192. Livingstone, Sonia and Tamar Liebes. "Where Have All the Mothers Gone? Soap Opera's Replaying of the Oedipal Story." *Critical Studies in Mass Communication.* June 1995, pp. 155-175.

Argues that U.S. daytime soap operas represent a traditional conception of women's psychological development; explores soap operas parallel to fairy tales and therapy; emphasizes the "repressive over the liberating aspects of the soap opera."

2193. Loeb, Jane C. "Rhetorical and Ideological Conservatism in *thirtysomething*." *Critical Studies in Mass Communication*. September 1990, pp. 249-260.

Examines television show, *thirtysomething*, and shows affirmation of traditional views of patriarchy, gender, and family roles on television.

2194. Martin, Nina K. "*Red Shoe Diaries*: Sexual Fantasy and the Construction of the (Hetero)sexual Woman." *Journal of Film and Video*. Summer 1994, pp. 44-57.

Analyzes sexual fantasy in the "Red Shoe Diaries" series prepared for the cable network Showtime.

2195. Mellencamp, Patricia. "Situation Comedy, Feminism, and Freud: Discourses of Gracie and Lucy." In *Star Texts: Image and Performance in Film and Television*, edited by Jeremy G. Butler, pp. 316-332. Detroit, Michigan: Wayne State University Press, 1991.

Argues that Gracie Allen in "The George Burns and Gracie Allen Show" seemed to be beyond men's control, despite being burdened by all the clichés applied to women.

2196. Messner, Michael A., Margaret C. Duncan, and Kerry Jensen. "Separating the Men from the Girls: The Gendered Language of Televised Sports." *Gender & Society*. March 1993, pp. 121-137.

Compares verbal commentary of televised coverage of two women's and men's athletic events; claims sports commentary contributes to the construction of gender hierarchies by marking women's sports and athletes as "other."

2197. Miner, Madonne M. "'Like a Natural Woman': Nature, Technology, and Birthing Bodies in *Murphy Brown*." *Frontiers*. 16:1 1996, pp. 1-18.

2198. Mumford, Laura S. "Plotting Paternity -- Looking for Dad on the Daytime Soaps." *Genders*. Winter 1991, pp. 45-61.

Deals with pregnancy, miscarriage, abortion, and other issues as seen in daytime televised soap operas.

2199. Myers, Philip N., Jr. and Frank A. Biocca. "The Elastic Body Image: The Effect of Television Advertising and Programming on Body Image Distortions in Young Women." *Journal of Communication*. Summer 1992, pp. 108-133.

Suggests that watching even 30 minutes of television programming and advertising can alter a woman's perception of the shape of her body.

2200. Ogletree, S. M., et al. "Female Attractiveness and Eating Disorders: Do Children's Television Commercials Play A Role?" *Sex Roles*. June 1990, pp. 791-797.

Tests commercials from Saturday morning TV cartoon programs to determine if they contribute to the greater emphasis on physical attractiveness for girls compared to boys; answers that they do.

2201. Peirce, Kate. "Sex-Role Stereotyping of Children on Television: A Content Analysis of the Roles and Attributes of Child Characters." *Sociological Spectrum.* 9:3 (1989), pp. 321-328.

    Analyzes week of primetime television on ABC, CBS, NBC; finds that boy and girl characters did not differ significantly on 13 attribute scales used, but there were four attributes that separated the boys from the girls.

2202. Radner, Hilary. "Quality Television and Feminine Narcissism -- The Shrew and the Covergirl." *Genders.* Summer 1990, pp. 110-128.

    Concentrates on actress Cybil Shepherd, in dual roles as fashion model and star of a TV series "Moonlighting," as illustrative of conflicting issues of feminine representation and representation of the feminine.

2203. Rakow, Lana F. and Kimberlie Kranich. "Woman as Sign in Television News." *Journal of Communication.* Winter 1991, pp. 8-23.

    Claims that when women appear as sources or subjects in TV news, they represent "women in a ritualized role."

2204. Rasmussen, Karen. "*China Beach* and American Mythology of War." *Women's Studies in Communication.* Fall 1992, pp. 22-50.

    Discusses ABC TV series "China Beach," especially the second phase which situated women in the Vietnam War.

2205. Reep, Diana C. "Lasting Images of TV Parents." *Family Perspective.* Vol. 24 (1990), pp. 121-128.

    Reports on study of college students asked to name the first TV father or mother that came to mind and rate their parenting effectiveness; viewers were more impressed by parenting done by TV fathers than that done by TV mothers.

2206. Remafedi, G. "Study Group Report on the Impact of Television Portrayals of Gender Roles on Youth." *Journal of Adolescent Health Care.* 11 (1990), pp. 59-61.

2207. Rhodes, Jane. "Television's 'Realist' Portrayal of African American Women: The Case of L.A. Law." *Women and Language.* 14 (1991), pp. 29-33.

2208. Robinson, J. D. and T. Skill. "The Invisible Generation: Portrayals of the Elderly on Prime-Time Television." *Communication Reports.* Summer 1995, pp. 111-119.

    Finds very few (2.8 percent) of adult speaking characters are 65 or older; of those, the number of males has decreased, the number of females increased since 1975.

2209. Scrocco, Phyllis A. "A Ritual Analysis of Women and Work in Selected Situation Comedies, 1963-1973." Ph.D. dissertation, Bowling Green State University, 1992.

2210. Seidman, Steven A. "An Investigation of Sex-Role Stereotyping in Music Videos." *Journal of Broadcasting and Electronic Media.* Spring 1992, pp. 209-216.

Samples 182 MTV music videos in February 1987; reveals about two-thirds of characters were male and that portrayals of occupational roles stayed at a traditional, stereotyped level.

2211. Shillinglaw, Ann. "Mister Ed Was A Sexist Pig." *Journal of Popular Culture*. Spring 1997, pp. 245-254.

Discusses television show "Mister Ed," 1961-1967, and its sexist reinforcement about the female.

2212. Signorielli, Nancy. "Children, Television, and Gender Roles." *Journal of Adolescent Health Care*. January 1990, pp. 50-58.

Reviews literature on daytime serials, children's shows, and commercials that reveals that women are underrepresented on TV and are presented in stereotypically traditional roles.

2213. Signorielli, Nancy. "Television and Conceptions about Sex Roles: Maintaining Conventionality and the Status Quo." *Sex Roles*. September 1989, pp. 341-360.

Examines image of men and women in annual samples of primetime network dramatic television programming; finds sex role images have been stable, traditional, conventional, and supportive of the status quo during the previous 10-15 years.

2214. Signorielli, Nancy, Douglas McLeod, and Elaine Healy. "Gender Stereotypes in MTV Commercials: The Beat Goes On." *Journal of Broadcasting and Electronic Media*. Winter 1994, pp. 91-101.

Examines gender portrayals and stereotyping in a sample of MTV commercials; finds that the demographic makeup of characters in MTV commercials almost duplicated the distribution of characters in music videos.

2215. Sommers-Flanagan, Rita, John Sommers-Flanagan, and Britta Davis. "What's Happening on Music Television? A Gender Role Content Analysis." *Sex Roles*. June 1993, pp. 745-753.

Shows that males appeared nearly twice as frequently as females during music videos.

2216. Stapleton, Lara. "MTV: Flesh, Flash and Fantasy." *New Directions for Women*. September-October 1991, p. 12.

2217. Steenland, Sally. *Unequal Picture: Black, Hispanic, Asian and Native American Characters on Television*. Washington, D. C.: National Commission on Working Women of Wider Opportunities for Women, 1989. 50 pp.

Monitors more than 150 episodes of TV shows to see how minorities (including women) are portrayed.

2218. Steenland, Sally. *What's Wrong with This Picture? The Status of Women on Screen and Behind the Camera in Entertainment TV*. Washington, D.C.: National Commission on Working Women of Wider Opportunities for Women, 1990. 81 pp.

Analyzes 555 characters, 238 of whom were women, appearing on 80 entertainment series of the major networks in 1990; women continue to fare poorly on TV despite some gains and breakthroughs.

2219. Steenland, Sally. "Women: Dose of Reality Spices TV Lives." *Media and Values.* Spring 1988.

2220. Steinke, Jocelyn and Marilee Long. "A Lab of Her Own? Portrayals of Female Characters on Children's Educational Science Programs." Paper presented at International Communication Association, Albuquerque, New Mexico, May 25-29, 1995.
    Examines televised portrayals of female characters on five episodes of each of four children's educational science programs; finds men outnumber women three to one and that of 82 female characters shown, 69 were in secondary roles.

2221. Stroman, C. "From 'Julia' To 'Gimme A Break': The Portrayal of Black Womanhood on Television." Paper presented at the Middle Atlantic Writers Association Fourth Annual Conference, Washington, D.C., November, 1983.

2222. Sullivan, Patricia A. "The 1984 Vice-Presidential Debate: A Case Study of Female and Male Framing in Political Campaigns." *Communication Quarterly.* Fall 1989, pp. 329-343.
    Analyzes performances of Geraldine Ferraro and George Bush in the nationally-televised vice-presidential debate of 1984; states that Ferraro's candidacy was a challenge to frameworks based on masculine constructs.

2223. "TV Portrayal of the Childless Black Female: Superficial, Unskilled, Dependent." *Media Report to Women.* March-April 1990, p. 4.
    Claims "crippling stereotyping" of childless black woman.

2224. Vande Berg, Leah R. "'China Beach,' Prime Time War in the Postfeminist Age: An Example of Patriarchy in a Different Voice." *Western Journal of Communication.* Summer 1993, pp. 349-366.
    Examines gender ideology in primetime TV series, "China Beach"; states that the show's chief problematic is its normalization of war and feminization of violence and militarism.

2225. Vande Berg, Leah R. and Diane Streckfuss. "Prime-time Television's Portrayal of Women and the World of Work: A Demographic Profile." *Journal of Broadcasting and Electronic Media.* Spring 1992, pp. 195-208.
    Analyzes 116 primetime television shows on three major networks in 1986-1987; indicates that although there had been an increase in the representation of women and the variety of their occupational portrayals, women still were underrepresented and limited in their settings.

2226. Vartanian, Carolyn R. "Women Next Door to War: *China Beach.*" In *Inventing Vietnam: The War in Film and Television*, edited by Michael Anderegg. Philadelphia, Pennsylvania: Temple University Press, 1991. 295 pp.

2227. Vernon, JoEtta A., J. Allen Williams, Terri Phillips, and Janet Wilson. "Media Stereotyping -- A Comparison of the Way Elderly Women and Men Are Portrayed on Prime-Time Television." *Journal of Women and Aging*. 2:4 (1990), pp. 55-68.

    Finds in content analysis of 139 programs that females and the elderly continue to be underrepresented, that elderly men tend to be depicted positively while elderly women, negatively.

2228. Vest, David. "Prime-Time Pilots: A Content Analysis of Changes in Gender Representation." *Journal of Broadcasting and Electronic Media*. Winter 1992, pp. 25-43.

2229. Wells, Alan and Ernest A. Hakanen. *Mass Media and Society*. Greenwich, Connecticut: Ablex, 1997. 580 pp.

    Includes Jannette L. Dates, "From 'Beulah' to 'Under One Roof': African-American Women on Prime Time Commercial Television"; Tina Pieraccini, "Women and the Media," and Nancy Signorielli, Douglas McLeod, and Elaine Healy, "Gender Stereotypes in MTV Commercials: The Beat Goes On."

2230. White, Sylvia E. "A Content Analytic Technique for Measuring the Sexiness of Women's Business Attire in Media Presentations." *Communication Research Reports*. Fall 1995, pp. 178-185.

    Compares TV soap opera presentations of women's business attire with real world; finds former much more provocative.

Film

2231. "At Odds Over *Thelma and Louise*." *New Directions for Women*. September-October 1991, p. 16.

    Provides film reviews by Elizabeth Pincus and Judith Trojan.

2232. Badley, Linda. *Film, Horror, and the Body Fantastic*. Westport, Connecticut: Greenwood Press, 1995. 208 pp.

    Relates horror film to recent interpretations of the body and the self, drawing largely from feminist film theory and gender studies; analyzes films of Tim Burton, Tobe Hooper, George Romero, Ridley Scott, Brian De Palma, David Lynch, David Cronenberg, Jonathan Demme, and Clive Barker. Badley's sequel was *Writing Horror and the Body: The Fiction of Stephen King, Clive Barker, and Anne Rice* (Greenwood, 1996).

2233. Bakøy, Eva. "Feminism and Images of Children in Film." *Nordicom Review*. No.2, 1990, pp. 11-16.

    Looks at "Film History and Images of Children," "The Child Character, Nature and Truth," "The Child as Rhetorical Weapon in Hollywood Movies."

2234. Bakøy, Eva. *Feminist Film Theory and Criticism and the Childcharacter in Alice Doesn't Live Here Anymore and Kramer Versus Kramer*. University of

Trondheim, 1988.

2235. Bean, Jennifer M. *"Couching Resistance: Women, Film, and Psychoanalytic Psychiatry." The Velvet Light Trap.* Spring 1995, pp. 84-87.
Reviews Janet Walker's book of that title.

2236. Bell, Elizabeth, Lynda Haas, and Laura Sells, eds. *From Mouse to Mermaid: The Politics of Film, Gender, and Culture.* Bloomington: Indiana University Press, 1995. 264 pp.
Addresses Disney film legacy from feminist, Marxist, poststructuralist, and cultural studies perspectives.

2237. Bell-Metereau, Rebecca. *Hollywood Androgyny.* New York: Columbia University Press, 1985. 260 pp.
Discusses transvestism and sex-role exchange in Hollywood movies.

2238. Berckmans, Christine. "Communication: Myth and Seduction in Marilyn Monroe." Paper presented at International Sociological Association, 1994.
Highlights ambiguity of Marilyn Monroe and the images of her: traditional seductive, middle-class woman or modern woman.

2239. Bondebjerg, Ib. "Public Discourse/Private Fascination: Hybridization in 'True-Life-Story' Genres." *Media, Culture and Society.* January 1996, pp. 27-45.
Includes section on "'Soft Items' in Female Discourse and Verité Style Documentary."

2240. Boswell, Parley A. "The Thelma Ritter Syndrome: The (Wise)-Cracking Girl's Best Friend." In *Beyond the Stars: Stock Characters in American Popular Film,* edited by Paul Loukides and Linda K. Fuller, pp. 190-200. Bowling Green, Ohio: Popular Press, 1990.

2241. Bruzzi, Stella. *Undressing Cinema: Clothing and Identities in the Movies.* New York: Routledge, 1997. 248 pp.
Contends that clothing is a key element in the construction of cinematic identities; explores new film noir, the gangster movie, and new black cinema to find assumptions about femininity and masculinity; examines relationship between gender and dress and drag in films.

2242. Byars, Jackie. *All That Hollywood Allows: Re-reading Gender in 1950s Melodrama.* Chapel Hill: University of North Carolina Press, 1991. 326 pp.
Examines the issue of gender, using the 25 top-grossing films of the 1950s; reviews feminist film theory, cultural studies, psychoanalysis, and Marxist theory.

2243. Campbell, Marilyn. "RKO's Fallen Women 1930-33." *The Velvet Light Trap.* Fall 1973, pp. 13-16.
Claims fallen women -- adultress, courtesan, femme fatale, vamp, moll, prostitute, or betrayed farmer's daughter -- dominated the screen.

2244. Cochran, David. "Violence, Feminism, and the Counter-culture in Henry Fonda's *The Hired Hand.*" *Film and History.* 24:3/4 (1994), pp. 84-99.

2245. Collins, Jim, Hilary Radner, and Ava Preacher Collins, eds. *Film Theory Goes to the Movies.* New York: Routledge (AFI Film Reader), 1993. 297 pp.
Uses gender and ethnicity as recurring themes, with two chapters on "Thelma and Louise" (Sharon Willis and Cathy Criggers) and one on female agency and bodily mutilation in "The Little Mermaid" (Susan White).

2246. Cortés, Carlos E. "Who Is Maria? What Is Juan? Dilemmas of Analyzing the Chicano Image in U.S. Feature Films." In *Chicanos and Film,* edited by Chon A. Noriega, pp. 84-85. Minneapolis: University of Minnesota Press, 1992.

2247. Côté, Sylvie. "Les Représentations de la   Prostituée dans le Cinéma Contemporain" (Representation of Prostitutes in Contemporary Film). *Canadian Woman Studies.* Summer 1991, pp. 56-59.
Describes women's roles in "Dressed to Kill" and other films dealing with prostitutes.

2248. Cowan, Gloria and Margaret O'Brien. "Gender and Survival vs. Death in Slasher Films: A Content Analysis." *Sex Roles.* August 1990, pp. 187-196.
Looks at slasher films; claims female and male victims were portrayed equally frequently.

2249. Cowie, Elizabeth. *Representing the Woman. Cinema and Psychoanalysis.* Minneapolis: University of Minnesota Press, 1996. 416 pp.
Draws on psychoanalytic theories of Freud and Lacan to discuss cinematic desire that shows the interrelationship of fantasy, subjectivity, voyeurism, fetishism, and identification in the making of feminine and masculine spectators.

2250. Creed, Barbara. *The Monstrous-Feminine: Film, Feminism, Psychoanalysis.* New York: Routledge, 1993. 208 pp.
Examines the role of women in horror films; argues that when a woman is constructed as monstrous, it is almost in conjunction with reproduction and mothering functions; uses American movies such as "Carrie," "Psycho," "Alien," and "The Exorcist" for analysis.

2251. Dick, Bernard F. "Columbia's Dark Ladies and the Femmes Fatales of Film Noir." *Literature/Film Quarterly.* 23:3 (1995).

2252. Dittmar, Linda. "Beyond Gender and Within It: The Social Construction of Female Desire." *Wide Angle.* September 1986, pp. 79-90.

2253. Donaldson, Peter S. *Shakespearean Films/Shakespearean Directors.* New York: Harper/Collins, 1990. 240 pp.
Deals with gender and subjectivity regarding seven Shakespearean films.

2254. Downey, Sharon D. and Karen Rasmussen. "The Irony of *Sophie's Choice*." *Women's Studies in Communication*. Fall 1991, pp. 1-23.
   Shows how film "Sophie's Choice" dramatizes a woman's powerlessness and empowerment; says the film is important because of its portrayal of the irony surrounding Sophie's struggle to free herself of the past.

2255. Dribben, Melissa. "The Skinny on Cartoon Women." *Philadelphia Inquirer*. December 1, 1997, p. R-3.
   Comments on the thinness of cartoon women in "Anastasia."

2256. Eaklor, Vicki L. "'Seeing' Lesbians in Film and History." *Historical Reflections*. Summer 1994, pp. 321-333.

2257. Edge, Sarah. "'Women Are Trouble, Did You Know That Fergus?' Neil Jordan's *The Crying Game*." *Feminist Review*. Summer 1995, pp. 173-186.
   Analyzes how Jude the IRA woman was represented in "The Crying Game"; claims she represented both "national and international anxieties concerning contemporary masculine and feminine subject positions."

2258. Ferguson, Susan J. "The Old Maid Stereotype in American Film, 1938 to 1965." *Film and History*. 21:4 (1991), pp. 131-144.

2259. Flinn, Caryl. *Strains of Utopia. Gender, Nostalgia, and Hollywood Film Music*. Princeton, New Jersey: Princeton University Press, 1992. 195 pp.

2260. Franklin, Pamela. "Teen Flicks Since 50s: Girls Still Chicks and Boys Must Get Laid." *New Directions for Women*. September-October 1991, p. 13.

2261. Fregoso, Rosa L. "The Mother-motif in *La Bamba* and *Boulevard Nights*." In *Building with Our Hands: Issues in Chicana Studies*, edited by Beatriz Pesquera and Adela De La Torre. Berkeley: University of California Press, forthcoming.

2262. Freydberg, Elizabeth H. "Sapphires, Spitfires, Sluts, and Superbitches: Aframericans and Latinas in Contemporary American Film." In *Black Women in America*, edited by K. M. Vaz. Thousand Oaks, California: Sage Publications, 1995.

2263. Fuchs, Cindy. "Virulent Machismo Rampant in Vietnam War Films." *New Directions for Women*. January-February 1990, p. 10.

2264. Fuller, Linda K. "From Servile to Sassy: A Look at Hollywood's 'Maids.'" In *Beyond the Stars: Stock Characters in American Popular Film*, edited by Paul Loukides and Linda K. Fuller, pp. 110-119. Bowling Green, Ohio: Popular Press, 1990.

2265. Ganguly, Keya. "The 'Other' Woman in *A Passage to India* -- Film as Colonialist Discourse." *Women and Language*. Winter 1988, pp. 11-14.

2266. Graham, Louise E. and Geraldine Maschio. "A False Public Sentiment: Narrative and Visual Images of Women Lawyers in Film." *Kentucky Law Journal*. 84:4 (1995-1996), pp. 1027-1073.

Looks at depictions of women lawyers in "Adam's Rib" (1949), "The Accused" (1988), "The Music Box" (1989), "Class Action" (1991), and "The Client" (1994); claims women lawyers surrender power to a male or lose the power because of their emotional state.

2267. Grant, Barry K., ed. *The Dread of Difference. Gender and the Horror Film.* Austin: University of Texas Press, 1996. 496 pp.

Posits that horror is always rooted in gender, "particularly in anxieties about sex difference and gender politics"; explores the history of the genre, the work of horror auteurs, and the importance of gender relative to horror marketing and reception.

2268. Griffin, Sean. "The Illusion of 'Identity': Gender and Racial Representation in *Aladdin.*" *Animation Journal*. Fall 1994, pp. 64-73.

2269. Hardcastle, Valerie G. "Changing Perspectives of Motherhood: Images from the *Aliens Trilogy.*" *Film and Philosophy*. Vol. III, 1996.

2270. Harwood, Sarah. *Family Fictions: Representations of the Family in 1980s Hollywood Cinema.* New York: St. Martin's Press, 1997.

Claims the 1980s' Hollywood nuclear family reflected tensions in real-life families; fathers often were the problem to be resolved and mothers had background roles. States "Anxieties over the role of the father served to displace the mother at the center of the narrative."

2271. Hawkins, Harriett. "Maidens and Monsters in Modern Popular Culture: *The Silence of the Lambs* and *Beauty and the Beast.*" *Textual Practice*. Summer 1993, pp. 258-266.

2272. Heung, Marina. "Abortion Grist for Movie Mill." *New Directions for Women*. September-October 1989, p. 11.

2273. Higashi, Sumiko. "Ethnicity, Class, and Gender in Film: DeMille's *The Cheat.*" In *Unspeakable Images: Ethnicity and the American Cinema*, edited by Lester Friedman, pp. 112-139. Urbana: University of Illinois Press, 1991.

2274. Holmlund, Christine A. "Visible Difference and Flex Appeal: The Body, Sex, Sexuality, and Race in the Pumping Iron Films." *Cinema Journal*. Summer 1989, pp. 38-51.

2275. hooks, bell. "Male Heroes and Female Sex Objects: Sexism in Spike Lee's *Malcolm X.*" *Cineaste*. 29:4 (1993), pp. 13-15.

2276. hooks, bell. *Reel to Real. Race, Sex, and Class at the Movies.* New York:

Routledge, 1997. 256 pp.

Collects author's essays on films such as "Paris Is Burning," "She's Gotta Have It," "Waiting to Exhale," or "Pulp Fiction"; examines world of independent filmmaking, all through depictions of race, sex, and class.

2277. Hunt, Jean and Howard R. Pollio. "What Audience Members Are Aware of When Listening to the Comedy of Whoopi Goldberg." *Humor*. 8:2 (1995), pp. 135-154.

Concludes undergraduates tested focused on "here-and-now of present experiences emphasized by non-narrative routines" and on "imaginary contexts emphasized by the unfolding storyline characteristic of narrative routines."

2278. Inness, Sherrie A. "The Feminine Engendering of Film Consumption and Film Technology in Popular Girls' Serial Novels, 1914-1931." *Journal of Popular Culture*. Winter 1995, pp. 169-182.

Discusses characters in girls' serial fiction lured into producing movies, such as Alice B. Emerson's Ruth Fielding novels and Laura Lee Hope's Moving Picture Girl stories.

2279. Jacobs, Lea. *The Wages of Sin: Censorship and the Fallen Woman Film, 1928-1942*. Berkeley: University of California Press, 1997. 220 pp.

Explores the story of the fallen woman, a staple of film melodrama of 1920s, 1930s; looks at evolution of the rules governing representations of sexuality.

2280. James, Caryn. "The Woman in 'True Lies,' A Mouse That Roared." *New York Times*. July 17, 1994, p. II-13.

Deals with character, "Helen," in film, "True Lies," and director James Cameron, known for putting women at the center of action.

2281. James, Caryn. "Women: Swap 'Em or Sell 'Em." *New York Times*. April 11, 1993, p. II-11.

Critiques film, "Indecent Proposal."

2282. James, Caryn. "The Year of the Woman? Not in Movies." *New York Times*. January 10, 1993, p. II-11.

Claims it was difficult to come up with five roles "meaty enough to fill Oscar's best-actress category."

2283. Jansma, L. L. et al. "Men's Interactions with Women After Viewing Sexually Explicit Films: Does Degradation Make a Difference?" *Communication Monographs*. March 1997, pp. 1-24.

States that short-term exposure to nonviolent sexual media stimuli can change men's attitudes toward women.

2284. Johnson, Angela. "From Molly Ringwald to Cher -- Hollywood's Portrayal of Working Class Women." *Off Our Backs*. October 1989, pp. 18+.

Reports on workshop at NWSA conference at Towson State University.

2285. Johnson, Eithne and Eric Schaefer. "Soft Core/Hard Gore: *Snuff* as a Crisis in Meaning." *Journal of Film and Video*. Summer/Fall 1993, pp. 40-59.

Explores *Snuff* (1976); points out public pressure mounted to monitor *Snuff* and its audience.

2286. Jones, Sonny. "Linda Hamilton Gets Tough in *Terminator 2*: *Judgement Day*." *Women and Guns*. October 1991, pp. 12-15.

Justifies women as gun carriers via this film.

2287. Jones, Sonny. "*Thelma and Louise*: Reality Meets Movie Myth." *Women and Guns*. September 1991, pp. 12-16.

Uses film to justify women's purchase of guns.

2288. *Journal of Popular Culture*.

Winter 1992 -- Thematic section on "*Fatal Attraction*, Feminist Readings," edited by Liahna Babener, includes Liahna Babener, "Introduction," pp. 1-4; Joyce Thompson, "From *Diversion* to *Fatal Attraction*: The Transformation of a Morality Play into a Hollywood Hit," pp. 5-16; Susan Bromley and Pamela Hewitt, "*Fatal Attraction*: The Sinister Side of Women's Conflict About Career and Family," pp. 17-24; Liahna Babener, "Patriarchal Politics in *Fatal Attraction*," pp. 25-34; Elaine Berland and Marilyn Wechter, "Fatal/Fetal Attraction: Psychological Aspects of Imagining Female Identity in Contemporary Film," pp. 35-46; Kathe Davis, "The Allure of the Predatory Woman in *Fatal Attraction* and Other Current American Movies," pp. 47-58; Sandra R. Joshel, "Fatal Liaisons and Dangerous Attraction: The Destruction of Feminist Voices," pp. 59-70; Jim Hala, "*Fatal Attraction* and the Attraction of Fables: A Morphological Analysis," pp. 71-82; John Rohrkemper, "*Fatal Attraction*: The Politics of Terror," pp. 83-90.

2289. Juhasz, Alexandra. "The Contained Threat: Women in Mainstream AIDS Documentary." *Journal of Sex Research*. February 1990, pp. 25-46.

Examines four mainstream documentaries addressing AIDS; shows women characters in the films characterized into sexual practice types such as middle-class yuppie, single, the unmarried procreating low income woman of color, the teenager forced to say no, the promiscuous prostitute, the procreating white wife, and the unsexed and lesbian.

2290. Kaplan, E. Ann. "The Couch Affair: Gender and Race in Hollywood Transference." *American Imago*. 50:4 (1993).

2291. Kaplan, E. Ann. *Looking for the Other. Feminism, Film, and the Imperial Gaze*. New York: Routledge, 1997. 256 pp.

Employs Hollywood films about colonial or exotic travel, and those by women filmmakers of color, to take stock of how "looking relations" are determined by history, power hierarchies, and political economy.

2292. Kaplan, E. Ann. *Women in Film Noir*. Expanded Edition. Bloomington: Indiana

University Press, 1998. 256 pp.

Includes new readings on "neo-noir," postmodernism, and other recent trends, with contributions by Pam Cook, Richard Dyer, Christine Gledhill, Sylvia Harvey, Claire Johnston, E. Ann Kaplan, Angela Martin, Janey Place, Kate Stables, Chris Straayer, and Patricia White.

2293. Kirkham, Pat and Janet Thumim, eds. *Me Jane: Masculinity, Movies and Women.* New York: St. Martin's Press, 1995. 296 pp.

2294. Klinger, Barbara. "Much Ado About Excess: Genre, Mise-en-scène, and the Woman in *Written on the Wind*," *Wide Angle.* October 1989, pp. 4-22.

2295. Kreps, Gary L., ed. *Sexual Harassment: Communication Implications.* Cresskill, New Jersey: Hampton Press, 1993. 368 pp.

Provides indepth analyses of the influences of communication on sexual harassment; includes Jill Axelrod, "Sexual Harassment in the Movies and Its Affect [sic] on the Audience."

2296. Kristin, Jack. "The Many Faces of Eve/The Changing Image of the Sex Goddess." *American Film.* April 1989, pp. 39-41.

2297. Lawrence, Amy. *Echo and Narcissus: Women's Voices in Classical Hollywood Cinema.* Berkeley: University of California Press, 1991. 218 pp.

2298. Lentz, Kirste M. "The Popular Pleasures of Female Revenge (or Rage Bursting in a Blaze of Gunfire)." *Cultural Studies.* October 1993, pp. 374-405.

Looks at women as subjects of violence, seekers of revenge, carriers of guns, analyzing films such as "Thelma and Louise," "Blue Steel," "V.I. Warshawski," and "Eve of Destruction" and the magazine *Women and Guns.*

2299. Levine, Nancy J. "'I've Always Suffered from Sirens': The Cinema Vamp and Djuna Barnes' *Nightwood.*" *Women's Studies.* 16:3/4, 1989, pp. 271-281.

2300. Levitin, Jacqueline. "Guidelines for Feminist Criticism." *Jump Cut.* No. 29, 1984, pp. 29-30.

2301. Lindsey, Shelley S. "Horror, Femininity, and Carrie's Monstrous Puberty." *Journal of Film and Video.* Winter 1991, pp. 33-44.

Suggests, through rereading of film "Carrie," ways in which "horrific family dramas might be opened up to considerations of gender by investigating the mix of horror, melodrama, and the supernatural that they engage."

2302. Luce, Leilani N. "'...We Don't Live in That Kind of World, Thelma.'" *Film and Philosophy.* Vol. III, 1996.

2303. Lucia, Cynthia. "Redefining Female Sexuality in the Cinema." *Cineaste.* 19:2-3 (1992), pp. 6-19.

2304. Lupack, Barbara T., ed. *Vision/Re-Vision: Adapting Contemporary American Fiction by Women to Film*. Bowling Green, Ohio: Popular Press, 1997. 175 pp.
Assesses many films adapted from novels by American women, and finds that representing the female point of view continues to be a problem.

2305. McCormick, Richard W. "Politics and the Psyche: Feminism, Psychoanalysis, and Film Theory." *Signs*. August 1992, pp. 173-187.
Reviews eight books on feminism and film, art, and cultural studies.

2306. Macklem, Ann J. "The Popular Pleasures of Film: Feminist Perspectives." Masters thesis, Simon Fraser University, 1992.
Suggests that an inversion of gender roles in film does not challenge male authority.

2307. McMullen, W. J. "Reconstruction of the Frontier Myth in *Witness*." *Southern Communication Journal*. Fall 1996, pp. 31-41.
Examines film "Witness" relative to the frontier myth; concludes that the myth is still patriarchal where women are dominated by men.

2308. McPhail, Mark L. "Race and Sex in Black and White: Essence and Ideology in the Spike Lee Discourse." *The Howard Journal of Communications*. April-June 1996, pp. 127-138.
Analyzes the critical consideration of race and gender in Spike Lee films that feature depictions of women and interracial relationships; argues that Lee's films subscribe to assumptions and practices that undermine representation of race and gender in mainstream media.

2309. Maio, Kathi. "Mr. Right Is a Beast: Disney's Dangerous Fantasy." *Visions Magazine*. Summer 1992, pp. 44-45.
Expresses negative feminist response to "Beauty and the Beast."

2310. Maio, Kathi. "Women Who Murder for the Man." *Ms*. November-December 1991, pp. 82-84.
Deals with women portrayed in film.

2311. Malveaux, Julianne. "Spike's Spite -- Women at the Periphery." *Ms*. September-October 1991, pp. 78-80.
States that women in Spike Lee films are very marginalized or they are portrayed demeaningly and stereotypically.

2312. Manchel, Frank. *Film Study: An Analytical Bibliography*. Cranbury, New Jersey: Fairleigh Dickinson University, 1990. 4 vols.
Volume 1 of 976 pages includes portrayals of women in film.

2313. Marchetti, Gina. "*The Crimson Kimono*: Hollywood, Interracial Sexuality, and the Asian American Image." *Aamplitude*. Autumn 1989, pp. 9-10.

2314. Marchetti, Gina. "*Karma* -- Fatalism or Feminism?" In *The Tenth Asian American Film Festival* (catalogue), pp. 17-19. Washington, D.C.: Asian American Arts and Media, 1991.
Excerpted from *Genders*, Spring 1991, pp. 47-74.

2315. Maslin, Janet. "Sex and Terror: The Male View of the She-Boss." *New York Times*. January 14, 1994, p. C-1.
In "Mrs. Doubtfire," "Disclosure."

2316. Mayne, Judith. *The Woman at the Keyhole: Feminism and Women's Cinema.* Bloomington: Indiana University Press, 1990. 270 pp.

2317. Mellencamp, Patricia. "Female Bodies and Women's Past-times, 1890-1920." *East-West Film Journal.* January 1992, pp. 17-65.

2318. Mellencamp, Patricia. *Indiscretions: Avant-Garde Film, Video, and Feminism.* Bloomington: Indiana University Press, 1990. 254 pp.

2319. Merck, Mandy, ed. *The Sexual Subject. Screen Reader in Sexuality.* New York: Routledge, 1992. 320 pp.
Brings together writing on sexuality appearing in *Screen* from 1970s to early 1990s; deals with questions of sexuality and signification in cinema; explores arguments around pornography and the representation of the body, representation of femininity and masculinity, the female spectator.

2320. Mintz, Steven. "Foundation of Independent Video and Film: The Cinematic Treatment of Age, Ethnicity, Gender, Region, Religion, and Sexuality." *Film and History.* 25: 1-2 (1995).

2321. Mizejewski, Linda. "Picturing the Female Dick: *The Silence of the Lambs* and *Blue Steel.*" *Journal of Film and Video.* Summer/Fall 1993, pp. 6-23.
Examines the recent emergence in crime films of the gun-carrying female on the side of the law.

2322. Murray, Timothy. *Drama Trauma: Specters of Race and Sexuality in Performance, Video and Art.* New York: Routledge, 1997. 320 pp.
Examines artistic struggle over traumatic fantasies of race, sexuality, gender, and power; among topics, includes feminist interventions in video.

2323. Negra, Diane. "Coveting the Feminine: Victor Frankenstein, Norman Bates, and Buffalo Bill." *Literature/Film Quarterly.* 24:2 (n.d.).

2324. Paige, Linda R. "Wearing the Red Shoes: Dorothy and the Power of the Female Imagination in *The Wizard of Oz.*" *Journal of Popular Film and Television.* Winter 1996, pp. 146-153.
Analyzes Dorothy's wearing of the red shoes in "The Wizard of Oz" and contends, "Though wearing the red shoes hints of rebellion, it simultaneously presents a visible reminder of the penalty for women's insurrection."

2325. Parry-Giles, S. J. and T. Parry-Giles. "Gendering Politics and Presidential Image Construction: A Reassessment of the 'Feminine Style.'" *Communication Monographs*. December 1996, pp. 337-353.

Analyzes five presidential campaign films; reveals "feminist style" in these films; claims the films offer a portrayal of women that marginalizes their status in the political process.

2326. Penley, Constance. *The Future of an Illusion: Film, Feminism, and Psychoanalysis*. Minneapolis: University of Minnesota Press, 1989. 208 pp.

Deals with sexual politics of representation, film, and feminist theory.

2327. Powers, Stephen P., David J. Rothman, and Stanley Rothman. "Transformation of Gender Roles in Hollywood Movies: 1946-1990." *Political Communication*. July-September 1993, pp. 259-283.

Explores shifts of gender roles in Hollywood movies: many of the earlier types of representations were modified or tossed out; despite beliefs to the contrary, the 1980s did not represent a reactionary trend in portrayals of women.

2328. Press, Andrea L. "Ideologies of Femininity: Film and Popular Consciousness in the Post-War Era." In *Media, Audience and Social Structure*, edited by Muriel Cantor and Sandra Ball-Rokeach, pp. 313-323. Beverly Hills, California: Sage Publications, 1986.

2329. Prince, Stephen and Paul Messaris. "The Question of a Sexuality of Abuse in Pornographic Films." In *Communication and Culture: Language, Performance, Technology and the Media*, edited by Sari Thomas and William A. Evans, pp. 281-284. Norwood, New Jersey: Ablex, 1990.

Studies 29 top-selling films, 1972-1985, according to characters, sex scenes, and violent acts; slightly more than one half of the characters were male and the mean number of sex scenes per film was eight.

2330. Rakøy, Eva. "Feminism and Images of Children in Film." *Nordicom Review*. No. 2, 1990, pp. 11-16.

Shows how feminist movement has not been very concerned with children; reviews works by a few feminists who analyzed children's images in American film; reflects upon the image of the child as a rhetorical weapon.

2331. Robards, Brooks. "Newshounds and Sob Sisters: The Journalist Goes to Hollywood." In *Beyond the Stars: Stock Characters in American Popular Film*, edited by Paul Loukides and Linda K. Fuller, pp. 131-145. Bowling Green, Ohio: Popular Press, 1990.

2332. Roberts, Robin. *Ladies First: Women in Music Videos*. Jackson: University Press of Mississippi, 1996. 184 pp.

Shows how the world of the video has thrust feminism to the forefront, despite the criticism that videos degrade women.

2333. Rollyson, Carl E., Jr. "More Than a Popcorn Venus: Contemporary Women Reshape the Myth of Marilyn Monroe." *Journal of American Culture*. 10 (1987), pp. 19-25.

2334. Ruyters, Jann. "Horror-Heldinnen: Een Feministische Interpretatie van *The Silence of the Lambs*" (Horror Heroines: A Feminist Interpretation of *The Silence of the Lambs*). *Tidjschrift voor Vrowenstudies*. 13:4 (1992), pp. 461-476.
    Places horror film "The Silence of the Lambs" in tradition of Hollywood "slasher" films.

2335. Sander, H. "Feminism and Film." *Jump Cut*. 27 (1982), pp. 49-50.
    Describes role of women in film as passive objects to be viewed by active male spectators.

2336. Schrage, Laurie. "Feminist Film Aesthetics: A Contextual Approach." *Hypatia*. Summer 1990, pp. 137-148.
    Considers problems with text-centered psychoanalytic and semiotic approaches to film that have dominated feminist film criticism; develops alternative approach.

2337. Selig, Michael. "Hollywood Melodrama, Douglas Sirk, and the Repression of the Female Subject." *Genders*. Fall 1990, pp. 35-48.
    Deals with "Magnificent Obsession."

2338. Silverman, Sheldon. "Hollywood's Murdering Mothers: The Rationalization of Psychotic Mother-Love." In *Beyond the Stars: Stock Characters in American Popular Film*, edited by Paul Loukides and Linda K. Fuller, pp. 234-242. Bowling Green, Ohio: Popular Press, 1990.

2339. Staiger, Janet. *Bad Women. Regulating Sexuality in Early American Cinema*. Minneapolis: University of Minnesota Press, 1995. 248 pp.
    Shows how film in early part of twentieth century gave women and women's sexuality images useful to the new consumer culture developing at the time.

2340. Stubbs, F. M. and E. H. Freydberg. "Black Women in American Films." In *Multiple Voices in Feminist Film Criticism*, edited by D. Carson, L. Dittmar, and J. A. Welsh, pp. 481-491. Minneapolis: University of Minnesota Press, 1994.

2341. Sturma, Michael. "Women, the *Bounty*, the Movies." *Journal of Popular Film and Television*. Summer 1995, pp. 88-93.
    States that the "Mutiny on the Bounty" movies conform to a pattern in which males assume the active role of advancing the storyline, while women's bodies provide "exotic spectacle."

2342. Swedberg, Deborah. "What Do We See When We See Woman/Woman Sex in Pornographic Movies." *NWSA Journal*. Summer 1989, pp. 602-616.

2343. Ta, Anh. "Female Subjectivity in Animated Narrative Film." *Animatrix*. No. 9, 1995/1996, pp. 15-19.
> Looks at "Who Framed Roger Rabbit?" and "Cool World."

2344. Tasker, Yvonne. *Working Girls: Gender and Sexuality in Popular Cinema*. New York: Routledge, 1998. 240 pp.
> Investigates thematic concerns of contemporary Hollywood cinema and its "ambivalent articulation of women as both active, and defined by sexual performance."

2345. Thompson, Teresa L. and Eugenia Zerbinos. "Gender Roles in Animated Cartoons: Has the Picture Changed in 20 Years?" *Sex Roles*. 32:9/10 (1995), pp. 651-673.
> Updates 1970s' research on gender representation in children's cartoons by analyzing 175 episodes of 41 animated shows; finds that both male and female characters were portrayed stereotypically, but males were depicted more frequently, given more prominence, and were involved in more of almost all of the noted behaviors.

2346. Traube, Elizabeth G. *Dreaming Identities: Class, Gender, and Generation in 1980s Hollywood Movies*. Boulder, Colorado: Westview Press, 1992. 207 pp.
> Exposes how certain movies of the Reagan era "pointed toward contradictory tendencies in the larger society" -- on the one hand, proposing to restore an idealized (but white male-dominated) past; on the other hand, envisioning a world free of gender domination.

2347. Traube, Elizabeth G. "Transforming Heroes: Hollywood and the Demonization of Women." *Public Culture*. Spring 1991, pp. 1-28.

2348. Viegener, Matias. "The Only Haircut That Makes Sense Anymore: Queer Subculture and Gay Resistance." In *Queer Looks: Perspectives on Lesbian and Gay Film and Video*, edited by Martha Gever, John Gregson, and Pratibha Parmar, pp. 116-133. New York: Routledge, 1993.

2349. Walker, Janet. *Couching Resistance: Women, Film, and Psychoanalytic Psychiatry*. Minneapolis: University of Minnesota Press, 1993. 248 pp.
> Explores how American psychoanalytic psychiatry and Hollywood film between World War II and the mid-1960s "negotiated women psychosexuality and life experience."

2350. Walsh, Andrea. "Films of Suspicion and Distrust: Undercurrents of Female Consciousness in the 1940's." *Film and History*. 8:1 (1978), pp. 1-9.

2351. Weaver, James B., Jr. "The Impact of Exposure to Horror Film Violence on Perceptions of Women: Is It the Violence or an Artifact?" In *Current Research in Film: Audiences, Economics, and Law*, edited by Bruce A. Austin. Norwood, New Jersey: Ablex, 1990.

2352. Wee, Valerie Su-Lin. "The Most Poetic Subject in the World: Observations on Death, (Beautiful) Women and Representation in *Blade Runner*." *Kinema*. Spring 1997, pp. 57-72.

Analyzes and discusses how traditional notions of death and femininity are treated in science-fiction film, "Blade Runner."

2353. Weiss, Andrea. *Vampires and Violets: Lesbians in Film*. New York: Penguin, 1993.

2354. White, Mimi. "Representing Romance: Reading/Writing/Fantasy and the 'Liberated' Heroine of Recent Hollywood Films." *Cinema Journal*. Spring 1989, pp. 41+.

2355. Wilkerson, Isabel. "Hollywood Shuffle: With White Men Calling the Shots, Black Women Have No Reel Power." *Essence*. March 1997.

Says the world, according to a dozen black actresses and directors, has yet to figure out what to make of black women on the screen and how to present full and accurate portrayals.

2356. Willis, Sharon. *High Contrast: Race and Gender in Contemporary Hollywood Films*. Durham, North Carolina: Duke University Press, 1997. 304 pp.

Examines the dynamic relationships between racial and sexual difference in Hollywood film, 1980s-1990s; argues that race, gender, and sexuality, as they are "figured in the fantasy of popular film, do not function separately, but rather they inform and determine each other's meaning."

2357. Willis, Sharon. "'Lynching' As Entertainment: Race and Gender in David Lynch's *Wild at Heart*." *East-West Film Journal*. July 1991, pp. 93-114.

2358. Young, Elizabeth. "Here Comes the Bride -- Wedding Gender and Race in *Bride of Frankenstein*." *Feminist Studies*. Fall 1991, pp. 403-437.

In James Whale's 1935 film.

2359. Young, Lola. *Fear of the Dark. "Race," Gender and Sexuality in the Cinema*. New York: Routledge, 1995. 232 pp.

Examines a number of films to develop a "critical perspective" on film portrayals of female African-American sexuality; questions the extent that African-American filmmakers have challenged the stereotypical images.

2360. Zucker, Carole, ed. *Making Visible the Invisible: An Anthology of Original Essays on Film Acting*. Metuchen, New Jersey: Scarecrow Press, 1993. 458 pp.

Includes feminist reading of role playing in Bergman's "Persona" and Mai Zetterling's "The Girls" and theatricality and authorship in the collaborations of Josef von Sternberg and Marlene Dietrich.

Print Media

2361. Adams, Kathryn T. "Paper Lesbians: Alternative Publishing and the Politics of Lesbian Representation in the United States, 1950-1990." Ph.D. dissertation, University of Texas, 1994.

2362. Astor, David. "A Ms-story About Gender in Comics." *Editor & Publisher.* October 5, 1996, p. 34.
    States that there are many male cartoonists who create female characters, but few female cartoonists who create male characters; a survey of cartoonists provided different opinions for this; claims the few female cartoonists may feel obliged to represent their gender and thus, do not produce male characters.

2363. Atkinson, Diane. *Funny Girls: Cartooning for Equality.* New York: Penguin Books, 1997. 105 pp.

2364. Bailey, Gina. "Body Politics and Missing Themes of Women in American News." *Media Development.* No. 1, 1995, pp. 31-34.
    Seeks to reveal the meta-discourses which surround women in the news by asking: How are women portrayed in American news? What women's activities merit front page coverage? Who constructs these narratives and how does this discourse support or not support gender equality? Identifies two main meta-discourses: Women are identified by their bodies, body parts, and physical relations to others; women are primarily passive and agents to be acted upon.

2365. Baughman, Linda. "A Psychoanalytic Reading of a Female Comic Book Hero -- *Elektra: Assassin.*" *Women & Language.* Fall 1990, pp. 27-30.

2366. Benedict, Linda F. "Coverage of Rape in Women's Magazines from 1960 to 1990: An Index of Social Change." Ph.D. dissertation, University of Missouri, 1994.

2367. Berg, Dale H. and LaDawn B. Coutts. "Extracted Image Analysis: A Technique for Deciphering Mediated Portrayals." *Health Care for Women International.* March-April 1995, pp. 179-189.
    Discusses extracted image analysis, a technique for analyzing print media, developed in response to interest in the portrayal of women in menstrual product advertising.

2368. Blix, Jacqueline. "Which Family? A Case Study of Family and Gender in the Mass Media of the 1890s and the 1950s." *Dissertation Abstracts.* 56, 11, 4188-A.

2369. Bogaert, A. F., D. A. Turkovich, and C. L. Hafer. "A Content Analysis of *Playboy* Centerfolds from 1953 through 1990: Changes in Explicitness, Objectification, and Model's Age." *Journal of Sex Research.* May 1993, pp. 135-140.
    Analyzes 430 issues of *Playboy*, 1953-1990, to determine explicitness of pose, objectification (face not visible), age, race, hair color, etc. of centerfold models.

2370. Bramlett-Solomon, S. "Civil Rights Vanguard in the Deep South: Newspaper Portrayal of Fannie Lou Hamer, 1964-1977." *Journalism Quarterly.* Fall 1991, pp. 515-521.

Reveals through analysis of five major U.S. newspapers, that there was very little recognition of the civil rights activities of Hamer until her death in 1977.

2371. Brandt, Pamela R. "Infiltrating the Comics." *Ms.* July-August 1991, pp. 90-92.

2372. Burkhart, Ford N. and Carol K. Sigelman. "Byline Bias? Effects of Gender on News Article Evaluations." *Journalism Quarterly.* Autumn 1990, pp. 492-500.

Reports on two experiments using college students; finds that audiences judged stories similarly regardless of gender of byline.

2373. Burt, Elizabeth V. "An Arena for Debate: Woman Suffrage, the Brewing Industry and the Press, Wisconsin 1910-19." Ph.D. dissertation, University of Wisconsin-Madison, 1994.

Examines the coverage of woman suffrage by the temperance and prohibition press, the anti-suffrage press, and publications of the liquor and brewing industries.

2374. Burt, Elizabeth V. "The Wisconsin Press and Woman Suffrage, 1911-1919: An Analysis of Factors Affecting Coverage of Ten Diverse Newspapers." *Journalism and Mass Communication Quarterly.* Autumn 1996, pp. 620-634.

Analyzes ten Wisconsin papers during six week-long periods in which a major woman suffrage event took place; found that these examples of mainstream press represented a diversity of voices.

2375. Byerly, Carolyn M. "An Agenda for Teaching News Coverage of Rape." *Journalism Educator.* Spring 1994, pp. 59-69.

Explores issues related to news reports of rape and sexual assault; reviews current journalism texts/resources, and offers an approach for journalism teachers to prepare students to cover these issues.

2376. Capezzi, Rita A. "Reading Domesticity in the 'Harper's Bazaar.'" Paper presented at Conference on College Composition and Communication, Milwaukee, Wisconsin, March 27-30, 1996. 6 pp.

Shows how this periodical historically instructed women on the mysteries of domesticity.

2377. Chmaj, Betty E. "Fantasizing Women's Lib -- Stereotypes of Women in Comic Books." In *Image, Myth and Beyond*, edited by Betty E. Chmaj, pp. 311-312. Pittsburgh, Pennsylvania: KNOW, Inc., 1972.

2378. Chrisler, J. C. and K. B. Levy. "The Media Construct a Menstrual Monster: A Content Analysis of PMS Articles in the Popular Press." *Women and Health.* 16:2 (1990), pp. 89-104.

2379. Christ, William G. and Sammye Johnson. "From Ethel Merman to Barbara Bush: 50 Years of Women's Images Through *Time*." *Southwestern Mass Communication Journal*. 9:1 (1993), pp. 1-17.

2380. Cohen, Gloria T. "Journalists' Treatment of Female Candidates for the United States Senate, 1976-1986: Eight Case Studies." Ph.D. dissertation, Temple University, 1994.

2381. *Comics Buyer's Guide*.
       May 22, 1998 -- Issue devoted to girls' comics includes, Craig Shutt, "A Pop Quiz on Wonder Woman's Duds," pp. 34-35; T. M. Lowe, "How Heroines Stole the Stage in DC's *Girlfrenzy*!" p. 36; Mark Evanier, "Point of View," p. 42.

2382. "Comics Heroines Lauded in *Ms*." *Comics Journal*. September 1991, p. 7.

2383. Daddario, G. "Swimming Against the Tide: *Sports Illustrated*'s Imagery of Female Athletes in a Swimsuit World." *Women's Studies in Communication*. Spring 1992, pp. 49-64.

2384. Damon-Moore, Helen. *Magazines for the Millions: Gender and Commerce in the Ladies Home Journal and the Saturday Evening Post, 1880-1910*. Albany: State University of New York Press, 1994. 263 pp.
       Discusses how the two Curtis Publishing magazines "constructed public and private spheres for men and women and thereby created an interdependent relationship between gender and commerce."

2385. Davis, Laurel R. *The Swimsuit Issue and Sport. Hegemonic Masculinity in Sports Illustrated*. Albany: State University of New York Press, 1997. 224 pp.
       Reveals how sexism, racism, heterosexism, and Western ethnocentrism are interwoven in the cultural fabric of men's sports; analyzes all *Sports Illustrated* swimsuit issues from first in 1964 to those of the 1990s, concluding that the issue secures a large male audience while trampling women, gays, lesbians, and people of color.

2386. Davis, Richard A. "Working Women and the Popular Print Media: A Changing View of Motherhood." *Free Inquiry in Creative Sociology*. May 1990, pp. 43-47.
       Tests the assumption that popular print media provide women with timely advice on coping with norms of the working woman.

2387. Dean, Michael. "Twisted Sisters." *Comics Buyer's Guide*. August 22, 1997, p. 22.
       In comics world, the "distaff side" is divided into "daughters of satan" or "pistol-packing nuns."

2388. Derks, P. "Category and Ratio Scaling of Sexual and Innocent Cartoons." *Humor*. 5:4 (1992), pp. 319-330.

2389. Dodd, D., B. Foerch, and H. Anderson. "Content Analysis of Women and Racial

Minorities As New Magazine Cover Persons." *Journal of Social Behavior and Personality.* 3:3 (1988), pp. 231-236.

2390. Duffy, Margaret and J. Michael Gotcher. "Crucial Advice on How To Get the Guy: The Rhetorical Vision of Power and Seduction in the Teen Magazine *YM.*" *Journal of Communication Inquiry.* Spring 1996, pp. 32-48.

Claims *YM* provides young women a world view void of occupational opportunities (other than modeling), educational opportunities, and intrinsic motivators -- a world view where success is determined by meeting male needs/expectations.

2391. Duggan, Lisa. "The Trials of Alice Mitchell: Sensationalism, Sexology, and the Lesbian Subject in Turn-of-the-Century America." *Signs.* Summer 1993, pp. 791-814.

Tells about sensationalistic media coverage of trials of Mitchell, a 19-year-old from Memphis, Tennessee, charged with the murder of her female lover.

2392. Duncan, Margaret C. "Sports Photographs and Sexual Difference: Image of Women and Men in the 1984 and 1988 Olympic Games." *Sociology of Sport Journal.* 7 (1990), pp. 22-43.

2393. Duncan, Margaret C., M. Messner, and L. Williams. *Coverage of Women's Sports in Four Daily Newspapers.* Los Angeles, California: Amateur Athletic Foundation of Los Angeles, 1991.

2394. Duncan, Margaret C. and Amoun Sayaovong. "Photographic Images and Gender in *Sports Illustrated for Kids.*" *Play and Culture.* 3 (1990), pp. 91-116.

Examines sports photographs in six issues of *Sports Illustrated for Kids*; reveals both quantitative and qualitative differences in depictions of male and female athletes.

2395. Duran, R. L. and D. T. Prusnak. "Relational Themes in Men's and Women's Popular Nonfiction Magazine Articles." *Journal of Social and Personal Relationships.* April 1997, pp. 165-189.

Explores differences and similarities in relational issues and the ways they are discussed in men's (*Playboy, Penthouse, GQ*) and women's (*Self, Cosmopolitan, Glamour*) magazines; finds they were similar in relationship types and issues discussed, different in portrayal of relationships and advice discussed.

2396. Eisner, Will. "Women as They Are Portrayed in Comics." *Comics Collector.* Spring 1985, pp. 32+.

2397. Evans, Ellis D. "Content Analysis of Contemporary Teen Magazines for Adolescent Females." *Youth and Society.* September 1991, pp. 99-120.

Analyzes three adolescent commercial magazines (*Sassy, Seventeen, Young Miss*) concerning identity development and cultural pluralism; a major theme was how women attract men through fashion and personal beautification.

2398. Fairstein, Linda. "Virgins, Vamps and the Tabloid Mentality." *Media Studies Journal*. Winter 1998, pp. 92-99.
    Interviews prosecutor Fairstein who contends that rape makes news, the press offers titillation, not education.

2399. Farr, Moira. "Revenge Becomes Her." *This Magazine*. October 1992, p. 20.
    Discusses women and comics.

2400. Ferre, John P. "Home, Religion and Equality: How Wedding Announcements Have Changed." Paper presented at American Journalism Historians Association, Mobile, Alabama, October 1997.
    Analyzes wedding announcements in Louisville (Ky.) *Courier-Journal*, 1868 to present; changes were that weddings were no longer solely women's events, women gained status, ministers disappeared, and social standing gave way to inclusiveness.

2401. Fisher, Jennifer. "The Comic Mirror -- Domestic Surveillance in *Mary Worth*." *Canadian Woman Studies/Les Cahiers de la Femme*. Spring 1990, pp. 60-61.
    The comic strip.

2402. Flamiano, Dolores L. "The Birth of a Notion: Early Media Coverage of Contraception in America, 1915-1917." Paper presented at American Journalism Historians Association, Mobile, Alabama, October 1977.
    Says that early media coverage of birth control emphasized its social utility and played down controversial issues of gender, sexuality, and power.

2403. Flanders, Laura. "Compassion Rationed: Scapegoated Women Disappear from Coverage." *Extra!* November/December 1996, p. 9.
    Shows how debate about "welfare" in early 1990s targeted poor women as the source of the nation's problems; claims the scapegoating worked to the extent that when the Senate passed the 1996 welfare bill, "it was so acceptable to starve and impoverish women" that virtually no editors opposed the president's signing of the bill.

2404. Foreit, K. G., T. Agor, J. Byers, J. Larue, H. Lokey, M. Palazzini, M. Patterson, and L. Smith. "Sex Bias in the Newspaper Treatment of Male-Centered and Female-Centered News Stories." *Sex Roles*. 6 (1980), pp. 475-480.

2405. Franckenstein, Frauke. "Making Up Cher -- A Media Analysis of the Politics of the Female Body." *European Journal of Women's Studies*. February 1997, pp. 7-22.
    Examines media representation of pop singer Cher, a woman who underwent much cosmetic surgery, in German-language newspapers and magazines; shows how cosmetic surgery objectifies the body and allows women entry into the public sphere so long as men define, create, and control their bodies.

2406. Franzen, Monika and Nancy Ethiel. *Make Way! 200 Years of American Women in*

Cartoons. Chicago, Illinois: Chicago Review Press, 1988.

2407. Geigel, Jennifer. "'Manya' and AIDS: A Departure for Comics." *The Progressive*. May 1997, p. 13.

Tells how Milwaukee writer Jen Benka and Chicago illustrator Kris Dresen, reacting to what they saw as a shortage of realistic female comic characters, created "Manya," a woman grieving the loss of her friend to AIDS.

2408. Gold, E. R. and R. Speicher. "Marilyn Quayle Meets the Press: Marilyn Loses." *Southern Communication Journal*. Winter 1995, pp. 93-103.

Analyzes 40 articles about Marilyn Quayle in major daily newspapers; reports she was portrayed in a critical and traditional way and that only after Quayle apologized for her negative statements of the press did she obtain more balanced coverage.

2409. Goulart, Ron. "The History of Good Girl Art (Part I)." *Comics History Magazine*. Spring 1997, pp. 6-9.

Claims that good girl art ("good drawings of pretty young women") was featured in comic books almost from their beginnings in the 1930s. This part deals with these comics in 1930s' period.

2410. Goulart, Ron. "The History of Good Girl Art: Part III." *Comics History Magazine*. Fall/Winter 1997, pp. 6-9.

Describes the history of portrayals of women in comic books, early 1940s.

2411. Goulart, Ron. "The History of Good Girl Art: [Part IV]." *Comics History Magazine*. Winter 1997, pp. 1-4.

Gives early history of comic books with female characters, early 1940s.

2412. Goulart, Ron. "The Many Lives of Dixie Dugan (Part Two)." *Comics History Magazine*. Spring 1997, pp. 15-17.

Details career of comic strip character, "Dixie Dugan," from her debut in 1928 *Liberty* magazine.

2413. Greenwald, Marilyn S. "Gender Representation in Newspaper Business Sections." *Newspaper Research Journal*. 11:1 (1990), pp. 68-79.

2414. Hicks, Donald W. and Rita P. Hull. "Gender Based Language in Accounting and Business Journals." *Woman CPA*. Summer 1991, pp. 4-7.

Indicates that sexist language still continues in both academic and non-academic journals, despite the editorial review process.

2415. Hilliard, D. C. "Media Images of Male and Female Professional Athletes. An Interpretive Analysis of Magazine Articles." *Sociology of Sport Journal*. 1 (1984), pp. 251-262.

2416. Hoffert, Sylvia D. "New York City's Penny Press and the Issue of Women's Rights, 1848-1860." *Journalism Quarterly*. Autumn 1993, pp. 656-665.

Finds that *New York Daily Herald, New York Daily Tribune,* and *New York Daily Times* gave woman's rights movement considerable attention in antebellum period.

2417. Honey, Maureen. *Breaking the Ties That Bind: Popular Stories of the New Woman, 1915-1930.* Norman: University of Oklahoma Press, 1992. 336 pp.

Reminds readers that in early Amarican magazines, fiction spoke louder than ads; from reading more than 700 stories, finds that the content addressed young women's personal concerns and concerned independent, career-oriented women achieving in a man's world.

2418. Howell, Richard. "Women in Terry and the Pirates." *Comics Feature.* October 1980, pp. 70-76.

Describes images, roles of women in Milton Caniff's comic strip, "Terry and the Pirates."

2419. Hume, Janice. "Defining the Historic American Heroine: Changing Characteristics of Heroic Women in Nineteenth-Century Media." *Journal of Popular Culture.* Summer 1997, pp. 1-21.

Looks at how *Godey's Lady's Book* depicted women in fictional stories for 1837-1838 and 1857-1858, 10 years before and 10 after the Seneca Falls Women's Rights Convention.

2420. Iacobucci, Christine. "Women As Alternative: An Analysis of Sex Role Stereotypes in Clip Art." Paper presented at Eastern Communication Association, Baltimore, Maryland, April 11, 1997.

2421. Illouz, Eva. *Consuming the Romantic Utopia: Love and the Cultural Contradictions of Capitalism.* Berkeley: University of California Press, 1997. 371 pp.

Argues that modern ideas of romantic love are related to capitalism; states that women's magazines encourage women to view romantic love through frames of consumption and production.

2422. Illouz, Eva. "Reason Without Passion: Love in Women's Magazines." *Critical Studies in Mass Communication.* September 1991, pp. 231-248.

Analyzes "how a seemingly private emotion such as romantic love is shaped by the public discourses of late capitalism" and the roles media play in the "modern" construction of romantic love, through women's magazines.

2423. "The Invisible Majority: News Magazines Still Ignoring Women." *Gender and Mass Media Newsletter.* November 1992, p. 32.

Finds for third year in a row, that *Time, Newsweek,* and *U.S. News and World Report* provided extraordinarily low coverage of women.

2424. Jensen, Robert. "Pornographic Novels and the Ideology of Male Supremacy." *Howard Journal of Communications.* Fall 1993/Winter 1994, pp. 92-107.

Looks at 20 pornographic novels, searching for common themes, types, and plots.

2425. Jolliffe, Lee and Terri Catlett. "Women Editors at the 'Seven Sisters' Magazines, 1965-1985: Did They Make a Difference?" *Journalism Quarterly*. Winter 1994, pp. 800-808.

Answers not much; the presence of women editors did not reduce stereotypical portrayals but did increase positive depictions of women.

2426. Kahn, Kim F. and E. N. Goldenberg. "Women Candidates in the News: An Examination of Gender Differences in U.S. Senate Campaign Coverage." *Public Opinion Quarterly*. Summer 1991, pp. 180-199.

Assesses possible differences in newspaper coverage of sample of male and female U.S. Senate candidates in elections, 1982-1986; shows women receive less coverage and what they do receive is more on their viability and less on their issue positions.

2427. Kaite, Berkeley. *Pornography and Difference*. Bloomington: Indiana University Press, 1995. 208 pp.

Studies pornographic magazine photographs of all types to determine the visual codes of these images and raise questions about masculinity.

2428. Kamalipour, Yahya R., ed. *The U.S. Media and the Middle East*. Westport, Connecticut: Praeger, 1997.

Includes Karin G. Wilkins, "Middle Eastern Women in Western Eyes: A Study of U.S. Press Photographs of Middle Eastern Women."

2429. Keller, Kathryn. *Mothers and Work in Popular American Magazines*. Westport, Connecticut: Greenwood Press, 1994. 208 pp.

2430. Keller, Kathryn. "Nurture and Work in the Middle Class - Imagery from Women's Magazines." *International Journal of Politics, Culture and Society*. Summer 1992, pp. 577-600.

Documents changes in gender-based divisions of labor in the home and workplace as seen in women's magazines; finds that explanations for working outside the home moved from excuses to justifications, although the latter were tied to the powerful image of the good mother.

2431. Kessler, Lauren. "The Ideas of Woman Suffrage and the Mainstream Press." *Oregon Historical Quarterly*. Autumn 1983, pp. 257-275.

2432. Kidd, Viriginia. "Happily Ever After and Other Relationship Styles: Advice on Interpersonal Relations in Popular Magazines, 1951-1973." *Quarterly Journal of Speech*. 61 (1975), pp. 31-39.

2433. King, Donna. "'Prostitutes as Pariah in the Age of AIDS' -- A Content Analysis of Coverage of Women Prostitutes in *The New York Times* and *The Washington Post* September 1985-April 1988." *Women and Health*. 16:3-4 (1990), pp. 155-176.

Finds these dailies showed little concern for the health of prostitutes at risk for AIDS, but rather for their role as possible disease vectors.

2434. Kitch, Carolyn L. "The Flapper in the Art of John Held, Jr.: Modernity, Post-Feminism, and the Meaning of Women's Bodies in 1920s Magazine Cover Illustration." Paper presented at Association for Education in Journalism and Mass Communication, Chicago, Illinois, July-August 1997.

States that in the 1920s, the "Flapper" was associated with the magazine illustration of Held; claims an analysis of this imagery "considers women's representation as primary site for the intersection of early twentieth-century feminism, modernism, and consumerism."

2435. Kitch, Carolyn L. "'The Girl on the Magazine Cover': Gender, Class, and Representation in the First Mass Media, 1895-1930." Ph.D. dissertation, Temple University, 1998.

2436. Klein, Sheri. "Breaking the Mold with Humor: Images of Women in the Visual Media." In *Working Papers in Art Education* No.10, edited by Marilyn Zurmuehlen. Iowa City. University of Iowa, School of Art and Art History, 1991.

Addresses three issues related to the comics: images of women in comics, conflicting and fragmented images of women in comics, and differences in content, message, and humor between mainstream and feminist comics.

2437. Kramer, Dale. "Those Hokinson Women." *Saturday Evening Post*. April 1951, p. 98.

Describes cartoons of Helen Hokinson.

2438. Lake, J. B. "Of Crime and Consequence: Should Newspapers Report Rape Complaints' Names?" *Journal of Mass Media Ethics*. 6:2 (1991), pp. 106-118.

Examines cases for concealment and disclosure in rape and other sexual assault crimes; debates alternatives editors have.

2439. Larew, Karl G. "Planet Women: The Image of Women in Planet Comics, 1940-1953." *Historian*. Spring 1997, pp. 591-612.

Shows how women portrayed in *Planet Comics* were drawn to be beautiful and lascivious; states women often were strong lead characters, other times, villains and victims.

2440. Ledesma, Irene. "Texas Newspapers and Chicana Workers' Activism, 1919-1974." *Western Historical Quarterly*. Autumn 1995, pp. 309-331.

2441. List, Karen K. "Realities and Possibilities: The Lives of Women in Periodicals of the New Republic." *American Journalism*. Winter 1994, pp. 20-38.

Presents the way in which the "realities and possibilities" of American women were portrayed in Philadelphia newspapers and magazines during the post-Revolutionary period; claims the portrayal ignored the lives women led, condemned and trivialized women-to-women relationships, and assigned them to a male-defined "women's sphere."

2442. List, Karen K. "Two Party Papers' Coverage of Women in the New Republic." *Critical Studies in Mass Communication*. 2 (1985), pp. 152-165.

2443. "Little Improvement Noted in Women's Page One Status." *Media Report to Women*. May/June 1990, pp. 3-4.
    In page one photos, women as sources, and female bylines.

2444. Lumpkin, Angela and Linda D. Williams. "An Analysis of Sports Illustrated Feature Articles, 1954-1987." *Sociology of Sport Journal*. March 1991, pp. 16-32.
    Studies all *Sports Illustrated* feature articles, 1954-1987, to determine how the magazine portrays women and blacks in sports; finds many more were about males than females and those about men were longer.

2445. MacDonald, Heidi. "Archetype Meets Angst." *Comics Journal*. July 1982, pp. 35-39.
    Reviews comic books and images of women through analysis of "Marada, the She-Wolf."

2446. McDonald, S. M. "Sex Bias in the Representation of Male and Female Characters in Children's Picture Books." *Journal of Genetic Psychology*. December 1989, pp. 389-401.
    Analyzes 41 children's picture books published 1976-1987; male characters were overrepresented and had much broader range of roles.

2447. Maguire, Mariangela. "Sexual Identity/Identification in Communicative Practices: A Semiological Analysis of Newspaper Coverage of Sports." Paper presented at International Communication Association, Chicago, Illinois, May 23-27, 1991.

2448. Manning-Miller, Carmen L. "Media Discourse and the Feminization of Poverty." *Explorations in Ethnic Studies*. January 1994, pp. 79-88.
    Looks at articles on poverty or welfare in five major U.S. dailies, 1988-1992, and finds portrayals of poor people, particularly women and people of color, have not changed.

2449. Markens, Susan. "The Problematic of 'Experience': A Political and Cultural Critique of PMS." *Gender and Society*. February 1996, pp. 42-58.
    Analyzes a select sample of popular magazines and self-help books, 1981-1994, to determine how premenstrual syndrome (PMS) was constructed as a legitimate disease worthy of medical consideration.

2450. Miller, Penny M. "Teaching Women in the News: Exposing the 'Invisible Majority.'" *PS: Political Science and Politics*. September 1996, pp. 513-517.
    Investigates the representation of women in national and regional newspapers; claims stories about women consistently focus on victimization and gender oddities.

2451. Miller, R. E. "Women's Sports Coverage in Six Daily Texas Newspapers." Master's thesis, Texas Tech University, 1983.

2452. Mooney, Linda A. "The Portrayal of Boys and Girls in Six Nationally-Syndicated Comic Strips." *Sociology and Social Research*. January 1990, pp. 118-126.
Studies six nationally syndicated Sunday comic strips for portrayals of boys and girls, their activities, and their parental interaction.

2453. Moyer, A., et al. "Accuracy of Health Research Reported in the Popular Press: Breast Cancer and Mammography." *Health Communication*. 7:2 (1995), pp. 147-161.
Finds in a two-year sample of newspapers and magazines, 116 articles, in which there were 113 citations to a scientific study; of the 60 traceable to an original source, 43 content-based inaccuracies were found.

2454. Obbink, Laura J. A. "'The Most Heroic Figure of All History': The Construction of Woman in 'Youth's Companion' Serials Set in the West, 1880-1910." Ph.D. dissertation, University of Iowa, 1994.

2455. O'Connell, Margaret. "Do You Have What It Takes to Be a Claremont Woman?" *Bem*. No. 36, 1982, p. 59.
Shows women's portrayal by comic book artist, Chris Claremont.

2456. O'Connell, Margaret. "Jean Grey in the Storeroom of Sad Thought Balloons." *Comics Feature*. February 1982, pp. 36-43.
Describes comic book superheroines.

2457. O'Connell, Margaret. "The Super-Heroine as Chaos-Bringer: Women and Power." *Comics Feature*. September-October 1981, pp. 77-81.

2458. O'Connell, Margaret. "Women and Power IV: Dark Phoenix and the Prime-Time Vixens." *Comics Feature*. June 1982, pp. 58-63.
Features women in comic books.

2459. Olson, Valerie V. "Garry Trudeau's Treatment of Women's Liberation in 'Doonesbury.'" Masters thesis, Michigan State University, 1979.

2460. Ono, Kent A. and John M. Sloop. "The Critique of Vernacular Discourse." *Communication Monographs*. March 1995, pp. 19-46.
Includes brief study of vernacular discourse through World War II representations of women in a Japanese-American newspaper, *Pacific Citizen*.

2461. Patthey-Chavez, G. G., L. Clare, and M. Youmans. "Watery Passion: The Struggle Between Hegemony and Sexual Liberation in Erotic Fiction for Women." *Discourse & Society*. January 1996, pp. 77-106.
Analyzes sexual experiences in 16 romances representing a North American sample; finds the romances present a unique erotic style.

2462. Peirce, Kate. "A Feminist Theoretical Perspective on the Socialization of Teenage Girls Through *Seventeen* Magazine." *Sex Roles*. November 1990, pp. 491-500.

Analyzes *Seventeen* for 1961, 1972, and 1985; finds concerns of teenage girls are primarily with their appearance, household activities, and romance/dating and that feminist movement of late 1960s had no permanent effect.

2463. Peirce, Kate. "Socialization of Teenage Girls Through Teen-Magazine Fiction: The Making of a New Woman or an Old Lady." *Sex Roles*. July 1993, pp. 59-68.

Analyzes all fiction stories in *Seventeen* and *Teen* magazines, 1987-1991; finds that in 62 percent of stories, the main character depended on someone else to solve problems, in 43 percent of stories, the girls' conflicts had to do with boys.

2464. Phillips, Kimberly. "How *Seventeen* Undermines Young Women." *Extra!* January-February 1993, p. 14.

Contends *Seventeen* magazine "reinforces the cultural expectations that an adolescent woman should be more concerned with her appearance, her relations with other people and her ability to win approval from men than with her ideas or her expectations for herself."

2465. Powers, A., S. Serini, and S. Johnson. "How Gender and Ethnicity Affected Primary Coverage." *Newspaper Research Journal*. Winter-Spring 1996, pp. 105-112.

Explores whether gender and ethnic background of political candidates affected newspaper coverage; answers in affirmative as the female candidate (in the 1994 Illinois Democratic gubernatorial primary) received the greatest and most positive coverage.

2466. Prusnak, D. T., R. L. Duran, and D. A. Deliott. "Interpersonal Relationships in Women's Magazines: Dating and Relating in the 1970s and 1980s." *Journal of Social and Personal Relationships*. August 1993, pp. 307-320.

Analyzes eight women's magazines and shows that relationship types were consistent with the theme that a woman's role is to be wife and mother, that the largest number of articles dealt with some form of conflict.

2467. Purcell, Piper and Lara Stewart. "Dick and Jane in 1989." *Sex Roles*. February 1990, pp. 177-185.

Replicates 1972 study, *Dick and Jane as Victims*; determines that over the 17 intervening years between the studies, the differences in the rate of portrayal for males and females were not as pronounced in 1989.

2468. Rich, Melissa K. and Thomas F. Cash. "The American Image of Beauty: Media Representations of Hair Color for Four Decades." *Sex Roles*. July 1993, pp. 113-124.

Shows that blond hair dominated in *Ladies' Home Journal* and *Vogue* and in *Playboy* centerfolds.

2469. Schanes, Steve. "Broadway Brings Female Perspective to Pin-up Projects." *Comics Buyer's Guide*. May 3, 1996, p. 60.

Describes Broadway Comics' attempt to "break away from the stereotypical pin-up stuff in comics."

2470. Schrader, Stuart M. "Images of Women in Post World War I Health Campaigns: The Rhetoric of the 'Bad Woman.'" Paper presented at Eastern Communication Association, Baltimore, Maryland, April 11, 1997.

2471. Sealander, J. "Antebellum Black Press Images of Women." *Western Journal of Black Studies*. 1982, pp. 159-165.

2472. Sena, John R. "A Picture Is Worth a Thousand Votes: Geraldine Ferraro and the Editorial Cartoonists." *Journal of American Culture*. 8 (1985), pp. 2-12.

2473. Shanks-Meile, Stephanie and Betty A. Dobratz. "'Sick' Feminists or Helpless Victims: Images of Women in Ku Klux Klan and American Nazi Party Literature." *Humanity and Society*. February 1991, pp. 72-93.
Analyzes stories from 1980s' newspapers of the Ku Klux Klan and American Nazi Party to examine fascist images of women.

2474. Smith, Ellen Hart. "Kind Hearted, Immortal Hokinson Ladies." *New York Herald Tribune Book Review*. October 26, 1952, pp. 7+.
Describes Helen Hokinson cartoon subjects.

2475. Spencer, Gary. "An Analysis of JAP-Baiting Humor on the College Campus." *Humor*. 2:4 (1989), pp. 329-348.
Researches stereotype of the Jewish American Princess (JAP) used on college campuses, through interviews and analyses of college newspapers.

2476. Steiner, Linda. "Construction of Gender in News Reporting Textbooks, 1890-1990." *Journalism Monographs*. October 1992, 47 pp.

2477. "Study of Newspaper Business Sections: Still a Male Domain." *Media Report to Women*. May/June 1990, p. 3.

2478. Teitelbaum, Richard S. "Rabbit Redux: Playboy Flunks Feminist Fund Trust." *Fortune*. November 29, 1993, p. 30.
Shows how Women's Equity Mutual Fund screened out *Playboy* as an investment possibility because of its pornographic proclivities.

2479. Thompson, Julie M. "Incarcerated Souls: Women as Individuals in Margaret Fuller's 'Woman in the Nineteenth Century.'" *Communication Quarterly*. Winter 1995, pp. 53-63.
Examines journalist/essayist Fuller's treatise in which she uses transcendentalist philosophy to show how women lacked a sense of "self."

2480. "Twin Cities Newspaper Study: Women Only 21% of Names in the News." *Media Report to Women*. Summer 1997, pp. 4-6.

Reports on Minnesota Women's Press survey of women's names in the news in May 1997.

2481. Tyler, Pamela. "The Ideal Southern Woman as Seen by the *Progressive Farmer* in the 1930s." *Southern Studies*. Fall/Winter 1991, pp. 315-333.

2482. Urbanski, Marie M. O. *Margaret Fuller's Woman in the Nineteenth Century: A Literary Study of Form and Content, of Sources and Influence*. Westport, Connecticut: Greenwood Press, 1980.

2483. Walter, Gerry and Suzanne Wilson. "Silent Partners: Women in Farm Magazine Success Stories, 1934-1991." *Rural Sociology*. Summer 1996, pp. 227-248.
Examines depictions of women's roles as contributors to farm work; magazines showed women as spouses or farm helpers, but not as producers or planners.

2484. Weaver, Leah. "Cartoon Images of Women in *The New Yorker*." *Inks*. November 1994, pp. 8-17.

2485. Williams, J. A., Jr., J. A. Vernon, M. C. Williams, and K. Malecha. "Sex-Role Socialization in Picture Books: An Update." *Social Science Quarterly*. 68 (1987), pp. 148-159.

2486. Williams, J. P. "All's Fair in Love and Journalism: Female Rivalry in *Superman*." *Journal of Popular Culture*. Fall 1990, pp. 103-112.

2487. Winick, Charles. "A Content Analysis of Sexually-Explicit Magazines Sold in an Adult Bookstore." *Journal of Sex Research*. 21 (1985), pp. 206-210.

2488. Women on Words and Images. *Dick and Jane as Victims: Sex Stereotyping in Children's Readers*. Princeton, New Jersey: Women on Words and Images, 1974. 58 pp.
Gives many examples of sexism that have appeared in *Dick and Jane* and other children's books.

2489. Wright, Richard A. "Women as 'Victims' and as 'Resisters': Depictions of the Oppression of Women in Criminology Textbooks." *Teaching Sociology*. April 1995, pp. 111-121.
Analyzes 54 introductory criminology textbooks; finds that although recent textbooks have made gains in discussing women as victims of oppression, they have not said much about women's ability to resist their oppression.

Women as Audience

2490. Anderson, Rebecca C. and David L. Larson. "Reconstruction and Augmentation Patients' Reaction to the Media Coverage of Silicone Gel-filled Implants: Anxiety Evaluated." *Psychological Reports*. June 1995, pp. 1323-1330.

Questions 53 breast reconstruction and 25 breast augmentation patients concerning extensive media coverage regarding silicone gel-filled implants; media coverage influenced these women.

2491. Beasley, Maurine H. "Women Audiences." In *Handbook on Mass Media in the United States: The Industry and Its Audience*, edited by E. K. Thomas and B. H. Carpenter, pp. 207-230. Westport, Connecticut: Greenwood Press, 1994.

Argues that women as a media audience is tied to women's political, social, and economic place in society.

2492. Bhatia, Azra S. and Roger J. Desmond. "Emotion, Romantic Involvement, and Loneliness: Gender Differences Among Inner States and Choice of Entertainment." *Sex Roles*. June 1993, pp. 655-665.

Gives results of survey of 404 Northeastern undergraduates; finds that for females, the state of a love relationship and loneliness feelings are related to choice of media entertainment, but affect is not.

2493. Chatman, Elfreda A. "Channels to a Larger Social World: Older Women Staying in Contact with the Great Society." *Library and Information Science Research*. July-September 1991, pp. 281-300.

Describes information and recreational needs of 55 elderly women living alone in a retirement community; finds that the women watched "quality programs" and listened to "good music" but preferred print media.

2494. D'Acci, Julie. "Looking at the Female Spectator." *Media Information Australia*. August 1990, pp. 52-56.

Reviews E. Deidre Pribram's *Female Spectators: Looking at Film and Television*; Lorraine Gamman and Margaret Marshment's *The Female Gaze: Women as Viewers of Popular Culture*, and Constance Penley's *Feminism and Film Theory*, all 1988 imprints.

2495. Forman, Murray. "Media Form and Cultural Space: Negotiating Rap 'Fanzines.'" *Journal of Popular Culture*. Fall 1995, pp. 171-188.

Includes sections, "Rap Fanzines and the Female Reader: Pleasure...," "...Or Power?"

2496. Funk, J. B. and D. D. Buchman. "Playing Violent Video and Computer Games and Adolescent Self Concept." *Journal of Communication*. Spring 1996, pp. 19-32.

States that for girls, more time playing violent video and computer games is associated with lower scores on six sub-scales of the Harter Self-Perception Profile for Adolescents.

2497. Johnson, J. David and Hendrika Meischke. "Cancer Information: Women's Source and Content Preferences." *Journal of Health Care Marketing*. March 1991, pp. 37-44.

Examines preferences for particular types of information from specific sources by women who have undergone mammography.

2498. Johnson, J. David, Hendrika Meischke, Jennifer Grau, and Sally Johnson. "Cancer-Related Channel Selection." *Health Communication.* 4:3 (1992), pp. 183-196.
Interviews 395 women regarding information-seeking patterns about breast cancer; media among four channels analyzed. Also see J. D. Johnson and Hendrika Meischke's "Mass Media Channels: Women's Evaluations for Cancer-related Information" in *Newspaper Research Journal* (Winter/Spring 1992, pp. 146-159); "Cancer-Related Channel Selection: An Extension for a Sample of Women Who Have Had a Mammogram" in *Women and Health* (20:2 1993, pp. 31-44), and "Differences in the Evaluations of Communication Sources by Women Who Have Had a Mammogram" in *Journal of Psychosocial Oncology* (11:1 1993, pp. 83-101).

2499. Lee, J. S. and W. R. Davie. "Audience Recall of AIDS PSAs Among U.S. and International College Students." *Journalism and Mass Communication Quarterly.* Spring 1997, pp. 7-22.
Finds that audience recall of AIDS public service announcements was related to gender, message appeal types, and cultural identity: college women recall more of the AIDS messages, especially emotional ones, than men.

2500. Malamuth, Neil M. "Sexually Explicit Media, Gender Differences, and Evolutionary Theory." *Journal of Communication.* Summer 1996, pp. 8-31.
States that research on gender differences in response to sexually-explicit media can be explained by evolutionary psychology-derived theory, but media scholars resist this approach because of two problems: "an overly simplistic view of evolutionary models" and "a distrust of ideological implications."

2501. Martin, C. R. "The Naturalized Gender Roles of Rock and Roll." *Journal of Communication Inquiry.* Spring 1995, pp. 53-74.
Looks at the social order of gender in the 1950s and how young, white, middle-class, teenage females transgressed the "normal" gender order as rock and roll fans.

2502. "Media Glorification of Thin Celebs Influences Eating Disorders, Study Says." *Media Report to Women.* Fall 1997, pp. 1-3.
Surveys 232 female students at University of Wisconsin; claims 15 percent met criteria for disordered eating; that these women were affected by media's representation of thin celebrities.

2503. Moore, Suzanne. "Here's Looking at You Kid!" In *The Female Gaze: Women as Viewers of Popular Culture*, edited by I. L. Gamman and M. Marshment, pp. 44-59. Seattle, Washington: Red Comet, 1989.

2504. Owen, Diana and Jack Dennis. "Sex Differences in Politicization: The Influence of Mass Media." *Women and Politics.* 12:4 (1992), pp. 19-41.
Examines relationship between sex roles, mass media use, and preadult politicization, using data from a study of ten to seventeen-year olds in Wisconsin.

2505. Press, Andrea L. and Elizabeth R. Cole. "Reconciling Faith and Fact: Pro-Life Women Discuss Media, Science and the Abortion Debate." *Critical Studies in Mass Communication.* December 1995, pp. 380-402.

Uses focus group interviews with 41 non-activist, pro-life women, 1989-1993; determines that pro-life women search for information on abortion by "wading through much that is presented in mainstream society as unbiased information."

2506. Rakow, Lana F. *Gender on the Line: Women, the Telephone, and Community Life.* Urbana: University of Illinois Press, 1992. 165 pp.

Presents results of 1985 ethnographic study of role of telephone in a small midwestern town; shows that women's use of the telephone remains largely confined to a private sphere.

2507. Rakow, Lana F. and V. Navarro. "Remote Mothering and the Parallel Shift: Women Meet the Cellular Telephone." *Critical Studies in Mass Communication.* June 1993, pp. 144-157.

Reveals from survey data that women were most likely to use their cellular telephones for domestic responsibilities or personal reasons than business purposes.

2508. Reid, Penny and Gillian Finchilescu. "The Disempowering Effects of Media Violence Against Women on College Women." *Psychology of Women Quarterly.* September 1995, pp. 397-411.

Investigates disempowering effect of exposure to media violence against women on female students; claims a result of heightened feelings of disempowerment.

2509. Rios, D. I. and S. O. Gaines, Jr. "Impact of Gender and Ethnic Subgroup Membership on Mexican Americans' Use of Mass Media for Cultural Maintenance." *Howard Journal of Communications.* April-June 1997, pp. 197-216.

Finds that three Mexican-American subgroups (predominantly Mexican heritage, bicultural, and low Mexican heritage) differed significantly in mass media use for cultural maintenance; concludes that gender alone was not important as a predictor of purposive use of media.

2510. Ruiz, Monica S., Gary Marks, and Jean L. Richardson. "Language Acculturation and Screening Practices of Elderly Hispanic Women: The Role of Exposure to Health-Related Information from the Media." *Journal of Aging and Health.* May 1992, pp. 268-281.

Finds that language acculturation predicted media exposure, which, in turn, predicted screening and symptom knowledge.

2511. St. Lawrence, J. S. and D. J. Joyner. "The Effects of Sexually Violent Rock Music on Males' Acceptance of Violence Against Women." *Psychology of Women Quarterly.* March 1991, pp. 49-63.

Evaluates effects of sexually violent rock music on attitudes of undergraduate males toward women, acceptance of violence against women, and sexual arousal; finds exposure to this music increased males' sex-role stereotyping and negative attitutes toward women.

2512. Sarch, A. "Making the Connection: Single Women's Use of the Telephone in Dating Relationships with Men." *Journal of Communication.* Spring 1993, pp. 128-144.

Claims women in study had two levels of telephone use -- actual and expected, reflecting behavior men expect of them and behavior they expect of themselves.

2513. Senn, Charlene Y. "Women's Multiple Perspectives and Experiences with Pornography." *Psychology of Women Quarterly.* September 1993, pp. 319-341.

Uses Q methodology to gauge the spectrum of women's experiences with and attitudes toward pornography.

2514. Shani, David, Dennis M. Sandler, and Mary M. Long. "Courting Women Using Sports Marketing: A Content Analysis of the US Open." *International Journal of Advertising.* 11:4 (1992), pp. 377-392.

Finds that to a large extent, marketers were not taking advantage of sports marketing targeted to women.

2515. Shoos, Diane. "The Female Subject of Popular Culture." *Hypatia.* Spring 1992, pp. 215-226.

Discusses place of popular culture in theories of female subjectivity; examines two books on popular culture and women: Lorraine Gamman and Margaret Marshment's *The Female Gaze: Women as Viewers of Popular Culture* (Seattle: Real Comet Press, 1989) and Andrea L. Press's *Women Watching Television: Gender, Class, and Generation in the American Television Experience* (Philadelphia: University of Pennsylvania Press, 1991).

2516. "The Spectatrix." Special issue of *Camera Obscura.* May/September 1989.

Surveys "research on and theories of the female spectator in film and television studies."

2517. Steeves, H. Leslie, Samuel L. Becker, and Hyeon C. Choi. "The Context of Employed Women's Media Use." *Women's Studies in Communication.* Fall 1988, pp. 21-46.

Shows that employed women usually do other things while using mass media, usually related to family and home care.

2518. Stern, Barbara B. "Media Use and Gender Differences: Retailing Strategies for Bank Marketers." *International Journal of Bank Marketing.* 6:2 (1988), pp. 20-30.

Considers current state of knowledge about male/female financial media usage.

2519. Stern, Barbara B., Usha Rao, and Stephen J. Gould. "Business Media Segmentation for Services Marketers; Education and the Gender Gap." *Service Industries Journal*. July 1990, pp. 549-561.

Uses questionnaire to find out the effects of education on female and male business media use to ascertain whether education has leveled sex differences.

2520. Thompson, Margaret E., Steven H. Chaffee, and Hayg H. Oshagan. "Regulating Pornography: A Public Dilemma." *Journal of Communication.* Summer 1990, pp. 73-83.

Examines predictors of opinion toward pornography controls, exposure and reactions to pornography, and other issues in Wisconsin telephone interview study.

2521. Valenti, Joann M. and Daniel A. Stout. "Diversity from Within: An Analysis of the Impact of Religious Culture on Media Use and Effective Communication to Women." In *Religion and Mass Media: Audiences and Adaptations*, edited by Daniel A. Stout and Judith M. Buddenbaum, pp. 183-196. Thousand Oaks, California: Sage Publications, 1996.

Surveys religious affiliation and media consumption among 966 Mormon women.

2522. Wallston, Barbara S., Kathleen V. Hoover-Dempsey, Jane S. Brissie, and Patricia Rozee-Koker. "Gatekeeping Transactions: Women's Resource Acquisition and Mental Health in the Workplace." *Psychology of Women Quarterly*. June 1989, pp. 205-222.

Studies women in three occupational fields (media/communication is one of them) as to their gatekeeping transactions (seeking access to resources) and their effects on mental health.

2523. Widgery, Robin and Jack McGaugh. "Vehicle Message Appeals and the New Generation Woman." *Journal of Advertising Research*. September/October 1993, pp. 36-42.

Samples five markets nationally to measure the importance of various message appeals; finds that females generally consider more seriously the purchase of a vehicle than males.

2524. Widgery, Robin, M. D. Angure, and R. Nataraajan. "The Impact of Employment Status on Married Women's Perceptions of Advertising Message Appeals." *Journal of Advertising Research*. January-February 1997, pp. 54-62.

Compares employed and unemployed wives on the importance given to aspects of automobile advertising message appeals; finds that employment status of a wife makes a significant difference and that the married women market is not homogeneous.

Advertising, Public Relations

2525. Bellizzi, J. A. and L. Milner. "Gender Positioning of a Traditionally Male-

Dominant Product." *Journal of Advertising Research.* June/July 1991, pp. 72-79.
Observes how men and women reacted to a gender-related position (brand name, copy, voiceover) for a traditionally male-dominant product on radio.

2526. Burns, A. C. and E. R. Foxman. "Some Determinants of the Use of Advertising by Married Working Women." *Journal of Advertising Research.* October/November 1989, pp. 57-63.
Develops hypotheses concerning married working women's reliance on advertising as an information source.

2527. Ernster, Virginia. "Mixed Messages for Women: A Social History of Cigarette Smoking and Advertising." *New York State Journal of Medicine.* 85 (1985), pp. 335-340.

2528. Jaffee, L. J. "Impact of Positioning and Sex-Role Identity on Women's Responses to Advertising." *Journal of Advertising Research.* June/July 1991, pp. 57-64.
Tests 200 adult women exposed to "carefully-prepared" print advertisements; finds modern positioning enhances advertising response to a greater extent than traditional positioning.

2529. Laczniak, N., D. D. Muehling, and L. Carlson. "Mothers' Attitutes Toward 900-Number Advertising Directed at Children." *Journal of Public Policy and Marketing.* Spring 1995, pp. 108-116.
Finds that mothers are extremely negative toward advertisers' use of 900-numbers in children's advertising, more so than any other controversial promotional gimmicks directed at children.

2530. LaTour, Michael S. "Female Nudity in Print Advertising: An Analysis of Gender Differences in Arousal and Ad Response." *Psychology and Marketing.* Spring 1990, pp. 65-81.
Reports on an experiment where arousal was manipulated through three versions of a print advertisement with varying degrees of female nudity; men were aroused, women were made tense and fatigued.

2531. LaTour, Michael S. and T. L. Henthorne. "Female Nudity: Attitudes Toward the Ad and the Brand, and Implications for Advertising Strategy." *Journal of Consumer Marketing.* 10:3 (1993), pp. 25-32.
Experiments with sample of 202 participants concerning their comfort levels with advertisements showing women in different degrees of exposure; finds that nude ads, though considered most erotic, caused the most negative tension.

2532. Meyers-Levy, J. and D. Maheswaran. "Exploring Differences in Males' and Females' Processing Strategies." *Journal of Consumer Research.* June 1991, pp. 63-70.

2533. Moog, Carol. *Are They Selling Her Lips? Advertising and Identity.* New York: Morrow, 1990.
Discusses contemporary advertising and its psychological effect on consumers.

2534. Moss, G. "Sex--The Misunderstood Variable." *Journal of Brand Management.* April 1996, pp. 296 +.

Contends that women's behavior as consumers may be distinctive and considers implications of this factor for the design of goods for women.

2535. Riddle, Judith S. "Mining the Non-White Markets." *Brandweek.* April 12, 1993, pp. 29-32.

Reports Maybelline Inc. was making efforts to court minority women for its "Shades of You" cosmetics line.

2536. Worth, L. T., J. Smith, and D. M. Mackie. "Gender Schematicity and Preference for Gender-typed Products." *Psychology & Marketing.* January 1992, pp. 17-30.

Broadcasting

2537. Anderson, Daniel R. et al. "Stressful Life Events and Television Viewing." *Communication Research.* June 1996, pp. 243-260.

Finds that life events stress was not related to time spent viewing TV but, for women, was positively related to television "addiction."

2538. Bacon-Smith, Camille. *Enterprising Women: Television Fandom and the Creation of Popular Myth.* Philadelphia: University of Pennsylvania Press, 1992. 338 pp.

Concerns "women who produce a massive body of literature, art, and criticism about their favorite television and movie characters"; they are the fans of programs who "steal" characters, plots, and settings off home and movie screens and from them create new characters.

2539. Brown, J. D., Kenneth Campbell, and L. Fisher. "American Adolescents and Music Videos: Why Do They Watch?" *Gazette.* 37 (1986), pp. 9-32.

2540. Dittmar, M. L. "Relations Among Depression, Gender, and Television Viewing of College Students," *Journal of Social Behavior and Personality.* 9:2 (1994), pp. 199-218.

Shows that women watched more television than men and depressed women watched more than any other group; that depressed women viewed more soap operas than any group.

2541. Frueh, T. and P. E. McGhee. "Traditional Sex Role Development and Amount of Time Spent Watching Television." *Development Psychology.* 11 (1975), p. 109 +.

2542. Gantz, Walter and Lawrence A. Wenner. "Men, Women, and Sports: Audience Experiences and Effects." *Journal of Broadcasting and Electronic Media.* Spring 1991, pp. 233-243.

Examines gender differences in the audience experience with televised sports; uses telephone interviews with Los Angeles and Indianapolis samples; shows that more than women, men responded like fans.

2543. Grabarek, Brooke. "Ladies, Don't Touch That Dial." *Financial World.* February 14, 1995, pp. 98-102.
Uses example of figure skating to show how women are being drawn to televised sports.

2544. Heide, Margaret J. *Television Culture and Women's Lives: thirtysomething and the Contradictions of Gender.* Philadelphia: University of Pennsylvania Press, 1995.
Compares characters in the television series (1987-1991) with audience members; discusses role of the program, its socio-historical context, storylines, women's responses to gender conflicts in the series, women tell their stories, etc.

2545. Johnson, Melissa A. "Latinas and Television in the United States: Relationships Among Genre Identification, Acculturation, and Acculturation Stress." *Howard Journal of Communications.* October-December 1996, pp. 289-313.
Investigates relationship between television use by Hispanic women in the U.S. and the process of acculturation; finds women who identified most with talk shows endured the lowest level of acculturation stress, those who identified with comedies, the most.

2546. Joyrich, Lynne. *Re-Viewing Reception: Television, Gender, and Postmodern Culture.* Bloomington: Indiana University Press, 1996. 288 pp.
Focuses on U.S. television of the 1980s; explores how gender affects the reception of television; traces how the medium has been characterized as "feminine."

2547. Kapadia, Reshma. "Men, Women Differ in CATV Services." *Telephony.* October 2, 1995, p. 17.
Surveys 676 cable TV customers and 329 non-customers; finds women want the basics in service and are more likely to switch than men.

2548. Livingstone, Sonia. "Watching Talk Shows: Gender and Engagement in the Viewing of Audience Discussion Programs." *Media, Culture and Society.* July 1994, pp. 429-447.
Focuses on relations between gender and genre in audience responses to audience discussion programs on TV.

2549. Lottes, Ilsa, Martin Weinberg, and Inge Weller. "Reactions to Television on a College Campus: For or Against." *Sex Roles.* July 1993, pp. 69-89.
Surveys predominantly Caucasian sample of students in Midwest; shows that women, more religious respondents, less sexually active individuals, and those who never saw pornographic images were more negative toward them.

2550. Press, Andrea L. *Women Watching Television: Gender, Class and Generation in the American Television Experience.* Philadelphia: University of Pennsylvania Press, 1991. 186 pp.
Looks at two generations and two classes of women interacting with television images; uses both British feminist critiques of cultural studies and

American feminism. Author's Ph.D. dissertation at University of California-Berkeley.

2551. Press, Andrea L. "Working-Class Women in a Middle-Class World: The Impact of Television on Modes of Reasoning about Abortion." *Critical Studies in Mass Communication*. December 1991, pp. 421-441.

Investigates how focus groups of working-class and middle-class women discuss abortion before and after viewing a television show that treats the issue; groups' speech becomes more similar after television viewing.

2552. Press, Andrea L. and Elizabeth R. Cole. "Women Like Us: Working-Class Women Respond to Television Representations of Abortion." In *Reading, Viewing, Listening: Audiences and Cultural Reception*, edited by J. Cruz and J. Lewis, pp. 55-80. Boulder, Colorado: Westview Press, 1994.

2553. Renn, J. A. and S. L. Calvert. "The Relation Between Gender Schemas and Adults' Recall of Stereotyped and Counter Stereotyped Televised Information." *Sex Roles*. April 1993, pp. 449-459.

Indicates that there was no relation between a person's gender and his/her masculinity and femininity scores when viewing a television program that presented two plots -- one gender stereotyped, the other counter stereotyped.

2554. Riggs, K. E. "The Case of the Mysterious Ritual: Murder Dramas and Older Women Viewers." *Critical Studies in Mass Communication*. December 1996, pp. 309-323.

Compares television shows "Murder, She Wrote" and "Perry Mason"; cites literature linking the genre to elderly women viewers.

2555. Scott, R. K. "Effect of Sex on Excitation Transfer and Recall of Television News." *Psychological Reports*. April 1990, pp. 435-441.

Examines effects of transferred arousal from a prior television show in relation to gender of subjects and their recall of television news.

2556. Slater, M. D., et al. "Adolescent Responses to TV Beer Ads and Sports Content/Context: Gender and Ethnic Differences." *Journalism and Mass Communication Quarterly*. Spring 1997, pp. 108-122.

Examines gender and ethnic differences in adolescent responses to television beer advertising in sports and entertainment programming; finds that females responded less positively than males.

2557. Spigel, Lynn. "The Domestic Economy of Television Viewing in Postwar America." *Critical Studies in Mass Communication*. December 1989, pp. 337-354.

Analyzes postwar media, especially women's magazines, to show how TV was introduced to housewives and how they dealt with it.

2558. Spigel, Lynn and Denise Mann, eds. *Private Screenings: Television and the*

Female Consumer. Minneapolis: University of Minnesota Press, 1992. 294 pp.
Analyzes how television delivers definitions of femininity to its female audiences; includes a source guide for television shows, 1946-1970.

2559. Stafford, M. R. and T. F. Stafford. "Mechanical Commercial Avoidance: A Uses and Gratifications Perspective." *Journal of Current Issues and Research in Advertising*. Fall 1996, pp. 15-38.
Finds that males and females differ in their motivations for engaging in mechanical commercial avoidance (zapping, zipping).

2560. Tucker, L. A. and M. Bagwell. "Television Viewing and Obesity in Adult Females." *American Journal of Public Health*. July 1991, pp. 908-911.
Reports on study of 4,771 females, where those watching three to four hours of television daily were twice as likely to be obese than those viewing less than one hour daily.

2561. Weaver, James B., III, and Elizabeth A. Laird. "Mood Management During the Menstrual Cycle Through Selective Exposure to Television." *Journalism Quarterly*. Spring 1995, pp. 139-146.
Claims "women in different phases of the menstrual cycle reported their preferences for various genres of television programs, along with ratings of their affective disposition."

Film

2562. Angel, Maria and Zoë Sofia. "Cooking Up: Intestinal Economics and the Aesthetics of Specular Orality." *Cultural Studies*. October 1996, pp. 464-482.
Aims to make a psychoanalytical contribution to a cultural studies understanding of the logics of commodity consumption in the visual culture of capitalism, through an analysis of two films on themes of food and money -- Adrian Lynne's "9 1/2 Weeks" and Peter Greenaway's "The Cook, the Thief, His Wife and Her Lover."

2563. Bobo, J. "Articulation and Hegemony: Black Women's Response to the Film 'The Color Purple.'" Ph.D. dissertation, University of Oregon, Eugene, 1988.

2564. Butler, Cheryl B. "The Color Purple Controversy: Black Woman Spectatorship." *Wide Angle*. 13:3/4 (1991), pp. 62-69.

2565. Clover, Carol J. *Men, Women and Chain Saws: Gender in the Modern Horror Film*. Princeton, New Jersey: Princeton University Press, 1992. 260 pp.
Looks at audience for horror films; the book is divided into slasher films, possession films, and rape-revenge films, with a final chapter on the theoretical/feminist literature pertaining to cinema spectatorship.

2566. Corry, Shauna and Jo-Ann A. Thompson. "Popular Film Media and Viewers' Preference for Interior Design Characteristics: Is There a Relationship?" *Journal of Interior Design*. 19:2 (1993), pp. 27-33.

Finds that gender, age, and community size affect influences of popular film media on viewer's preference of interior design characteristics, especially among women aged 23-30.

2567. Doane, Mary Ann. "Building the Feminine: Feminist Film Theory and Female Spectatorship." *Continuum*. 4:2 (1991), pp. 206-217.

2568. Hollinger, Karen. "Theorizing Mainstream Female Spectatorship: The Case of the Popular Lesbian Film." *Cinema Journal*. Winter 1998, pp. 3-17.

2569. Jenkins, Henry III. "'It's Not a Fairy Tale Anymore': Gender, Genre, *Beauty and the Beast*." *Journal of Film and Video*. Spring-Summer 1991, pp. 90-110.
Interviews members of a Boston area "Beauty and the Beast" fan club to see the ways the program was received; finds that fans liked the show because they felt a compatibility with its world view.

2570. Jerslev, Anne. "American Fan Magazines in the 30s and the Glamorous Construction of Femininity." *The Nordicom Review*. No.1, 1996, pp. 195-209.
Summarizes that there were "different constructions of the relation between fan and star, at every reader's disposal," and suggests that it was because of stars' "stylized, de-personalized stagings," that they could serve as a "surface on which the female fans could project their fantasies and desires."

2571. Koch, G. "Why Women Go to the Movies." *Jump Cut*. 27 (1982), p. 51.
Makes the point that narcissistic females do not challenge the male gaze and find themselves attempting to attract that gaze.

2572. Kowalski, Shelley K. "Watching 'Working Girl': Images of Gender and Class in Media Portrayals of Working Women." Paper presented at Society for the Study of Social Problems, 1996.
Surveys university students on their impressions of 1980s movie "Working Girl."

2573. Lindsey, Shelley S. "'Eighty Million Women Want -- ?' Women's Suffrage, Female Viewers and the Body Politics." *Quarterly Review of Film and Video*. 16:1 (1996), pp. 1-22.

2574. Lindsey, Shelley S. "Is Any Girl Safe? Female Spectators at the White Slave Films." *Screen*. Spring 1996, pp. 1-15.

2575. Linz, Daniel, I. A. Fusion, and E. Donnerstein. "Mitigating the Negative Effects of Sexually Violent Mass Communications Through Preexposure Briefings." *Communication Research*. October 1990, pp. 641-674.
Studies effects of preexposure briefings upon male students viewing films portraying violence against women; concludes the briefings help males sympathize with female victims.

2576. Meischke, Hendrika. "Implicit Sexual Portrayals in the Movies: Interpretations of Young Women." *Journal of Sex Research*. 32:1 (1995), pp. 29-36.

Investigates college women's inferences from an implicit sex scene and how they arrived at them.

2577. Mosher, D. L. and P. Maclan. "College Men and Women Respond to X-Rated Videos Intended for Male or Female Audiences: Gender and Sexual Scripts." *Journal of Sex Research*. 31:2 (1994), pp. 99-114.

Assesses psychosexual responses to X-rated video intended for male and female audiences; finds women reported more sexual arousal, more absorption, and more frequent sexual intercourse after viewing videos designed for women compared to those intended for men.

2578. Mundorf, Norbert, James Weaver, and Dolf Zillmann. "Effects of Gender Roles and Self Perceptions on Affective Reactions to Horror Films." *Sex Roles*. June 1989, pp. 655-673.

Looks at the impact of individuals' self-perceived gender role and other personality characteristics on affective responses to horror.

2579. Padgett, V. R., J. A. Brislin-Slutz, and J. A. Neal. "Pornography, Erotica, and Attitudes Toward Women: The Effects of Repeated Exposure." *Journal of Sex Research*. November 1989, pp. 479-491.

Tests samples of university psychology students and patrons of an adult theater; finds that the latter who viewed more pornography had more favorable attitudes toward women than male or female students.

2580. Rapping, Elayne. *The Movie of the Week. Private Stories/Public Events*. Minneapolis: University of Minnesota Press, 1992. 208 pp.

Shows how women audiences can and do find voices and points of views in the products of a patriarchal industry.

2581. Sparks, G. G. "The Relationship Between Distress and Delight in Males' and Females' Relations to Frightening Films." *Human Communication Research*. June 1991, pp. 625-637.

Analyzes two secondary studies on sex differences and viewing of horror films.

2582. Taylor, Helen. *Scarlett's Women. Gone with the Wind and Its Female Fans*. New Brunswick, New Jersey: Rutgers University Press, 1989. 275 pp.

2583. Williams, J. P. "'A Bond Stronger Than Friendship or Love': Female Psychological Development and *Beauty and the Beast*." *NWSA Journal*. Spring 1992, pp. 59-72.

Claims the primary attraction of this program for female fans is the character Vincent and his relationship with the female protagonist Catherine Chandler.

2584. Williamson, Catherine. "'You'll See It Just as I Saw It': Voyeurism, Fetishism, and the Female Spectator in *Lady in the Lake*." *Journal of Film and Video*. Fall 1996, pp. 17-29.

Explores "how a simple experiment with the classic structure of looking -- the conflation of the look of the camera with that of the protagonist through the extended first-person campaign technique -- manages to dismantle conventional voyeuristic visual pleasure, how this experiment affects the representation / fetishization of women in the film 'Lady in the Lake.'"

Print Media

2585. Alcalay, R. and R. A. Bell. "Ethnicity and Health Knowledge Gaps: Impact of the California *Wellness Guide* on Poor African American, Hispanic, and Non-Hispanic White Women." *Health Communication*. 8:4 (1996), pp. 303-329.

Examines impact of *Wellness Guide*, a booklet containing information about health and well-being.

2586. Aronson, Amy B. "Understanding Equals: Audience and Articulation in the Early American Women's Magazine." Ph.D. dissertation, Columbia University, 1996.

2587. Bird, Elizabeth. "Understanding the Ethnographic Encounter: The Need for Flexibility in Feminist Reception Studies." *Women and Languages*. Fall 1995, pp. 22-26.

Argues from research on tabloid newspaper readers that a consideration of methodology in audience studies should take from, while enriching, feminist theorizing on communication styles.

2588. Breazeale, Kenon. "In Spite of Women: *Esquire* Magazine and the Construction of the Male Consumer." *Signs*. Autumn 1994, pp. 1-22.

2589. Britt, Theron. "Reversing the Romance: Class and Gender in the Supermarket Tabloids." *Prospects*. 21 (1996), pp. 435-451.

Argues that the mass appeal of supermarket tabloids to working-class women makes them an important force in mass culture.

2590. "Comics for Women and Girls: Impossible Market or Untapped Riches." *Comics Journal*. May 1996, pp. 11-12.

Reports on panel at Pro/Con conference in Oakland, California: not much reading material for girls in modern comics.

2591. Fannin, Rebecca. "The Growing Sisterhood." *Marketing and Media Decisions*. October 1989, pp. 38-44.

Claims a new emphasis on home and family narrowed the gap between homemakers and "modern women," giving the editors of mass-market women's service magazines a new sense of purpose.

2592. Fuss, Diana. "Fashion and the Homospectatorial Look." *Critical Inquiry*. Summer

1992, pp. 713-737.

Examines the fascination that commercial fashion photography has for women through an analysis of fashion magazines; concludes that the fashion industry is one of the few areas where women are encouraged to consume the images of other women.

2593. Hansen, Susan. "Reconcilable Differences?" *News Inc.* September 1992, pp. 22-28.

States women newspaper readers are leaving in droves and lip service alone won't get them back; shows what is needed and how women would rewrite stories.

2594. Herzog, Thomas R. and Andrew J. Hager. "The Prediction of Preference for Sexual Cartoons." *Humor.* 8:4 (1995), pp. 385-405.

Concludes that sexually liberal females tended to dislike cartoons rated highly demeaning to women; sexually liberal members of both sexes tended to dislike cartoons rated highly demeaning to men.

2595. Holt, Marilyn I. "Farm Women, Domestic Economy, and South Dakota's Agrarian Press." *South Dakota History.* Summer 1994, pp. 77-98.

2596. Kelley, Caitlin. "The Great Paper Chase: Losing Women's Readers, the Dailies Try to Win Us Back." *Ms.* May-June 1993, pp. 34-35.

States that daily newspapers run mostly by male executives have tried to lure women readers back with special sections and features, but not to much avail.

2597. Krafft, Susan. "Window on a Woman's Mind." *American Demographics.* December 1991, pp. 44-50.

Claims demographic profiles of women's-magazine readers are often similar.

2598. "Newspapers Searching for Ways to Increase Readership by Women." *Media Report to Women.* January-February 1991, p. 1.

2599. Nyberg, Amy K. "Comic Books and Women Readers: Trespassers in Masculine Territory?" In *Gender and Popular Culture: Images of Men and Women in Literature, Visual Media, and Material Culture*, edited by Peter C. Rollins and Susan W. Rollins, pp. 205-226. Cleveland, Oklahoma: Ridgemont Press, 1995.

2600. Palazzi, Lynne. "*True Love* Lasts Forever: Confession Mags Have Evergreen Appeal for Women." *Magazine Week.* February 8, 1993, pp. 20-21, 33.

Provides some demographic data on industry; presents views on what they do for or to women.

2601. White, H. A. and J. L. Andsager. "Newspaper Column Readers' Gender Bias: Perceived Interest and Credibility." *Journalism Quarterly.* Winter 1991, pp. 709-718.

Uses laboratory experiment and finds that readers more highly evaluate same-gender journalists and their writing than they evaluate opposite-gender journalists; females found columns they believed women wrote to be more interesting than those they thought men had written.

2602. Zboray, Ronald J. and Mary Saracino Zboray. "Political News and Political Readership in Antebellum Boston and Its Region." *Journalism History*. Spring 1996, pp. 2-14.
    Concludes that women were devoted readers of newspapers and savvy consumers of political culture in antebellum Boston; attributes this to high literacy rates in region; states "gender, politics, and print in antebellum America interact in a manner more complex than can be deduced from an unqualified consideration of the women's sphere."

Women Practitioners

2603. "Age Bias in Media Industry Complicating Career Paths." *Media Report to Women*. September-October 1990, pp. 3-4.
    Report of Women, Men, and Media of University of Southern California.

2604. Becker, Audrey. "New Lyrics by Women: A Feminist Alternative." *Journal of Popular Culture*. Summer 1990, pp. 1-22.
    Reviews the role of women song writers Tracey Thorn, Natalie Merchant, and Suzanne Vega.

2605. Bermar, Amy. "Women in Communications." *Network World*. June 10, 1991, pp. 32-34, 50.
    Cites traits of women in top communications positions (empathy high among them), as well as their problems and support systems.

2606. Brislin, Tom and N. Williams. "Beyond Diversity: Expanding the Canon in Journalism Ethics." *Journal of Mass Media Ethics*. 11:1 (1996), pp. 16-27.
    Shows how American newspapers and broadcast stations strive to staff their newsrooms with more women and minorities; claims newsroom culture will change as these new journalists bring different backgrounds and values to the news mix.

2607. Chow, Clement, et al. "Gaining on the Goals? Affirmative Action Policies, Practices, and Outcomes in Media Communication Education." Paper presented at Broadcast Education Association, Las Vegas, Nevada, April 12-15, 1996. 52 pp.
    Finds that despite their sizes, small media departments also find women to hire, that more women are hired because of a perceived need for them and the absence of sexist and racist attitudes of faculty.

2608. Devitt, Tiffany. "Women and the Media: Big Lies....and the Truth." *New Directions for Women*. November-December 1992, pp. 3-4.
    Discusses how the underrepresentation of women as editors and reporters, media's partiality toward corporate and government sources, and cultural biases maintain the gap between the reporting and reality of women's lives.

2609. Dobbs, G. Michael. "Women in Animation." *Animato!* Winter 1995, pp. 32-34.
First of a series profiles Linda Simensky, Vanessa Coffey, and Mary Harrington.

2610. Dowd, Maureen. "Requiem for the Boys on the Bus." *Media Studies Journal.* Winter 1995, pp. 44-48.
Rebuts claim women have taken fun out of political campaign reporting. Reprinted from same periodical (Winter/Spring 1993, pp. 99-104).

2611. Dragga, S. "Women and the Profession of Technical Writing: Social and Economic Influences and Implications." *Journal of Business and Technical Communication.* July 1993, pp. 312-321.
States that in U.S., most technical writers and technical writing teachers are women; advises professional associations to equip technical writers and their teachers with information about satisfactory salaries and working conditions to prevent these women from being exploited.

2612. Dupagne, Michel, W. James Potter, and Roger Cooper. "A Content Analysis of Women's Published Mass Communication Research, 1965-1989." *Journalism Quarterly.* Winter 1993, pp. 815-823.
Shows that the amount of research by females has grown dramatically and that few major differences exist between female and male scholars in research methods.

2613. Eastman, Beva. "Women, Computers, and Social Change." *Computers in Human Services.* 8:1 (1991), pp. 41-53.
Presents models for the feminist use of computers; includes an organizational resource list.

2614. Elmore, Garland C. and Michael E. Balmert. "A Profile of College and University Faculty: Minorities and Women in Advertising, Communication, Journalism, Media Studies, Public Relations, and Related Fields." *Journal of the Association for Communication Administration.* May 1995, pp. 66-81.
Finds that with continuing shifts toward more non-traditional students, college administrators will be prompted to recruit, hire, and retain more female faculty members.

2615. Fearnow, Mark. *Clare Booth Luce: A Research and Production Sourcebook.* Westport, Connecticut: Greenwood Press, 1995. 208 pp.
Looks at dramatic works written by Luce; provides treatment of her published and unpublished writings and annotated bibliography of reviews and criticism.

2616. Flanders, Laura. *Real Majority, Media Minority: The Cost of Sidelining Women in Reporting.* Monroe, Maine: Common Courage Press, 1997. 300 pp.
Recounts Flanders' views over 10 year period; she feels it is not enough to count how many women are moving up in the ranks of journalism, but whether their views are being expressed.

2617. Flanders, Laura. "Sex Panicked: Women Unheard in Sexuality Debates." *Extra!* March/April 1998, pp. 9-11.
Claims that women have not been given a role in media's increasing discussion of sexuality.

2618. Fleischman, Doris E. "Women in Business." *Ladies' Home Journal.* January 1930, p. 6 +, and March 1930, p. 229 +.
Includes mass media.

2619. Golden, Cassie. "Women Flood into Journalism, Media Fields." *Iowa Journalist.* Spring 1996, pp. 12-13.
Claims influx of women in journalism schools since the 1970s.

2620. Hickson, M. III, D. W. Stacks, and J. H. Amsbary. "Active Prolific Female Scholars in Communication: An Analysis of Research Productivity II." *Communication Quarterly.* Fall 1992, pp. 350-356.

2621. Hine, Darlene C., Elsa B. Brown, and Rosalyn Terborg-Penn, eds. *Black Women in America: An Historical Encyclopedia.* Bloomington: Indiana University Press, 1994. Vol. I, A-L, 764 pp.; Vol. II, M-Z, 808 pp.
Includes many black women journalists, media personalities, and entertainers among the 604 biographical entries.

2622. Hunter-Gault, Charlayne. *In My Place.* New York: Farrar Straus Giroux, 1992.
Relates her career as African American newswoman.

2623. Jackson, Carlton. *Hattie: The Life of Hattie McDaniel.* Lanham, Maryland: Madison Books, 1989. 256 pp.
Depicts life of stage, screen, and radio personality Hattie McDaniel, winner of an Academy Award in 1939; talks about impact her success had upon African-Americans.

2624. Kaufman, Susan J. "Developing Administrative Leadership Among Women in Journalism and Mass Communication Education Programs: A Conceptual Model." Ph.D. dissertation, Indiana State University, 1992.

2625. Kent, Letitia. "They Were Behind the Scenes of Between the Lines." *New York Times.* June 12, 1977, p. H15.
Discusses work of Joan Micklin Silver.

2626. Klein-Häss, Michelle. "Faces Behind the Voice: June Foray -- The Queen of Cartoons." *Animato!* Fall 1994, pp. 18-20.
Interviews June Foray, actress who provided the voices for scores of film and TV animation characters.

2627. Knupfer, Nancy N. and William J. Rust. "Technology, Mass Media, Society, and Gender." Paper presented at Association for Educational Communications and

Technology, Albuquerque, New Mexico, February 14-18, 1997. 8 pp.

Claims women are not well represented in the new generation of high technology occupations.

2628. Kynell, Teresa. "Wives, Mothers, and Scholars: What Women Write About." *Teaching English in the Two-Year College.* February 1992, pp. 55-60.

Discusses the need for knowledge about what women write about in magazines, newspapers, and other media.

2629. Lafky, Sue A. "The Women of American Journalism." Ph.D. dissertation, Indiana University, 1990.

2630. Langer, Mark. "Mancia Musings." *Animation World Magazine.* January 1997, 4 pp.

Museum of Modern Art's Adrienne Mancia reminisces about her efforts in animation programming and on the state of animation as a profession.

2631. Leger, Jackie. "Susan Pitt: An Animator's Journey." *Animation World Magazine.* February 1997.

Explores the visions of painter, designer, and animation filmmaker, Susan Pitt.

2632. Lipartito, Kenneth. "When Women Were Switches: Technology, Work and Gender in the Telephone Industry, 1890-1920." *American Historical Review.* October 1994, pp. 1074-1111.

2633. Logie, Iona R. *Careers for Women in Journalism: A Composite Picture of 881 Salaried Women Writers at Work in Journalism, Advertising, Publicity and Promotion.* Scranton, Pennsylvania: International Textbook, 1938.

2634. Miller, Phyllis and Randy Miller. "The Invisible Woman: Female Sports Journalists in the Workplace." *Journalism and Mass Communication Quarterly.* Winter 1995, pp. 883-889.

Explores experiences of women sports journalists, focussing on condescension in the workplace, equal opportunity, perceived performance, and job satisfaction; finds more women in sports journalism but they feel they are invisible to male colleagues. Also by Miller, "Female Journalists as Sports Reporters." *Southwest Journal of Minorities and Media* (Fall/Winter 1990, pp. 56-60).

2635. Moore, Molly. *A Woman at War: Storming Kuwait with the U.S. Marines.* New York: Charles Scribner's Sons, 1993. 336 pp.

Relates views of servicemen about the Gulf War which Moore covered as a correspondent.

2636. Morton, L. P. "Minority and Female Representation Plans at Accredited Schools." *Journalism Educator.* Spring 1993, pp. 28-36.

Studies journalism education plans relative to representation of minority and female members; claims the greatest consistency was found in student recruitment section.

2637. Palmer, Linda G. "Perceptions of Women About Their Roles and Experiences as Communications Faculty in a Southern Land-Grant University, 1947-1992." Ph.D. dissertation, University of Tennessee, 1994.

2638. Polk, Mary L. "Marlene Sanders: Words of Wisdom." *College Media Review.* Fall 1994, pp. 18-19.
Reports on talk by Sanders in which she related her pioneering work as a newsperson in a male-dominated industry.

2639. Rohlfing, Mary E. "'Don't Say Nothin' Bad About My Baby': A Re-evaluation of Women's Roles in the Brill Building Era of Early Rock 'n' Roll." *Critical Studies in Mass Communication.* June 1996, pp. 93-114.
Argues that the "Brill Building" era (1960-1964) marked the massive entry of women into rock and roll, "providing Anglo Americans with their first taste of a female youth culture focused on sexuality and their first exposure in popular rock 'n' roll to the voices and vernacular of young, African American women."

2640. Rowe, Kathleen K. *The Unruly Woman: Gender and the Genres of Laughter.* Austin: University of Texas Press, 1995.
Examines development of comedic roles for actresses, showing how unruly women "made spectacles of themselves to generate humor and undermine patriarchal norms and authority."

2641. Rush, Ramona. "Being All That We Can Be: Harassment Barriers Prevent Progress." *Journalism Educator.* 48:1 (1993), pp. 71-79.

2642. Sandler, Bernice R. "Women Faculty at Work in the Classroom or, Why It Still Hurts To Be a Woman in Labor." *Communication Education.* January 1991, pp. 6-15.
Reviews research on different ways in which male and female students communicate with men and women faculty.

2643. Schneider, Rebecca. *The Explicit Body in Performance.* New York: Routledge, 1997. 256 pp.
Examines the controversial issues which surround the female body in performance art; discusses many artists, such as Karen Finley, Spiderwoman Theatre, Carolee Schneeman, and Annie Sprinkle.

2644. Seger, Linda. *When Women Call the Shots: The Developing Power and Influence of Women in Television and Film.* New York: Holt, 1996. 304 pp.
Interviews key industry personnel such as Sherry Lansing, Gillian Armstrong, Marlo Thomas, Nora Ephron, Liv Ullman, and Loretta Young; provides insights about how important a woman's influence is on what we see on

the screen.

2645. Signorielli, Nancy, ed. *Women in Communications: A Biographical Source Book.* Westport, Connecticut: Greenwood Press, 1996. 528 pp.

Gives biographical information and critical evaluations of the work of 48 women, including Mary Clemmer Ames, Sarah Hale, Ida Tarbell, Ida Wells-Barnett, Connie Chung, Barbara Walters, Dorothy Day, Peggy Charen, Anne Royall, etc.

2646. Steiner, Linda. "Gender at Work: Early Accounts by Women Journalists." *Journalism History.* Spring 1997, pp. 2-12.

Analyzes careers of women journalists through their autobiographies; among those included are Florence Finch Kelly, Elizabeth Jordan, Elizabeth Banks, Joan Lowell, Frances Davis, Mary Margaret McBride.

2647. Street, Rita. "Rose Bond: An Animator's Profile." *Animation World Magazine.* May 1996, 4 pp.

Explores philosophy, methodology, and foray into computed-assisted animation of independent animator Rose Bond.

2648. Strossen, Nadine. "Freedoms in Conflict." *Index on Censorship.* 1/1993, pp. 7-9.

Examines tension between women's right to employment equality and freedom from harassment at work with the right to free speech.

2649. "Study Finds Nearly 70 % of Denver Women Journalists See Sexism at Work." *Media Report to Women.* March/April 1990, pp. 4-5.

2650. Sullivan, Patricia A. and Lynn H. Turner. *From the Margins to the Center: Contemporary Women and Political Communication.* Westport, Connecticut: Praeger, 1996.

Examines the patterns of women as political communicators in the United States; uses case studies of Patricia Schroeder, Lani Guinier, Hillary R. Clinton, and Janet Reno.

2651. "Three Reports on Women and News in the USA." *Gender and Mass Media Newsletter.* March 1991, pp. 23-24.

Includes "Women Gain as Broadcast News Directors in New RTNDA Study," "ANPA Issues 1990 Report on Women and Minority Employment at Newspapers," "RTNDA Survey Shows Little Change for Women in Newsrooms."

2652. Walsh-Childers, K., J. Chance, and K. Herzog. "Sexual Harassment of Women Journalists." *Journalism and Mass Communication Quarterly.* Autumn 1996, pp. 559-581.

Surveys 227 women journalists, 60 percent of whom believed sexual harassment is a problem of the profession; news sources were most frequent harassers.

2653. "Washington Reporters' Experiences and Perceptions: Does Gender Matter?" *Media Report to Women.* Spring 1997, pp. 7-8.

States a survey showed women and men journalists covering Washington, D. C., are much more alike than different. Also: women are more likely to perceive the effects of gender in their careers; women are more likely to perceive that men hold advantages; women are more likely to be lower paid.

2654. "WICI Survey Finds Media Salaries for Women Depressed Throughout Careers." *Media Report to Women.* May/June 1990, pp. 5-6.

Surveys 2,500 women writers and reporters; shows their salaries remained low throughout their careers.

2655. "Women Business Communicators Still Behind in Compensation, Study Says." *Media Report to Women.* March/April 1990, p. 1.

Study by International Association of Business Communicators Research Foundation.

2656. *Working Woman.*

A sampling of articles includes: Eileen Prescott, "How a One-Woman Show Becomes a Big-Bucks Business," March 1989, pp. 51-56; Mary Rowland, "The Mastermind of a Media Empire," November 1989, pp. 114-120; Ronni Sandroff, "The Manager Who Never Says Never," December 1989, pp. 90-94, 124; Renee Edelman, "When Little Sister Means Business," February 1990, pp. 82-88; Mark Stevens, "How to Take a Good Business and Make It Better," March 1990, pp. 38-46; Sara Nelson, "What's the Big Idea?" July 1990, pp. 96-98, 108; Jennet Conant, "Broadcast Networking," August 1990, pp. 58-61; Elizabeth Perle, "Creating the Perfect Staff (for Fun and Profit)," November 1990, pp. 73-76, 171; Karen Stabiner, "Where Does Murphy Brown Get Her Big Mouth? Ask Diane English," December 1990, pp. 62-65; Conan Putnam, "Why Would a Smart Woman Work for Playboy?" January 1991, pp. 76-79, 102, 108; Valerie Salembier, "Brainy Broad Gets Boot (and Spills Beans)," February 1991, pp. 58-61; Ellen Hopkins, "The Media Murder of Karen Valenstein's Career," March 1991, pp. 70-73, 120-122; Jennifer Lawson, "Persuading Staffers to Get with the Program," April 1991, pp. 57-60; Joshua Hammer, "The Chance of a Lifetime," May 1991, pp. 78-81; Sue Woodward, "Victoria Reigns ... Again," p. 77; and Lynn Povich, "Did Meredith Vieira Expect Too Much?" pp. 40-47, both September 1991; John McCormick, "Making Women's Issues Front-Page News," October 1991, pp. 78-81, 106, 108; Fred Goodman, "Madonna and Oprah: The Companies They Keep," December 1991, pp. 52-55, 84; Carol Pogash, "The Brains Behind 'Backlash,'" April 1992, pp. 64-67, 104; Nikki Finke, "Insanity T.V.," October 1993, pp. 42-45 +; Marilyn A. Moore, "Cristina: The Hispanic Oprah," October 1993, p. 16; Charles E. Cohen, "Tied to Your Company's Benefits," pp. 71-73; and Robin Kamen, "She Can Get It for You Wholesale," p. 19, both December 1993; "Hollywood '93 - '94: Reel Women Make Headway," April 1994, p. 20; Meredith Berkman, "The Fabulous Sports Babe Tells All," May 1995, p. 22; Lisa Schwarzbaum, "We're Gonna Make It After All," pp. 30-36, Alan Mirabella, "Linda Ellerbee, One Lucky Duck," p. 16, and Maura Sheehy, "Broad Appeal on Late-Night TV," pp. 11-12, all October 1995; Anna Quindlen, "Why I Quit," pp. 30-33, Hagar Scher, "Hail Mary. And Frida. And Lucy," p. 14;

Helaine Olen, "The Handywoman's Special," p. 12, all December 1995; John Solomon, "Media-Savvy Conservative ...Women," February 1996, p. 17; Stephanie Mansfield, "Barbara Walters," November-December 1996, pp. 80-83.

Advertising, Public Relations

2657. Applegate, Edd, ed. *The Ad Men and Women: A Biographical Dictionary of Advertising.* Westport, Connecticut: Greenwood Press, 1994. 424 pp.
Provides extended profiles of 46 men and eight women who shaped advertising from 19th century to present; includes copywriters, theorists, empire builders.

2658. Bernays, Doris Fleischman. *A Wife Is Many Women.* New York: Crown, 1955.
Discusses some of her pioneering work in public relations alongside her husband, Edward L. Bernays.

2659. "Doris Fleischman Bernays, Public Relations Pioneer, 88." *Boston Globe.* July 12, 1980, Business Section, p. 15.
Obituary of Doris Fleischman Bernays.

2660. Fannin, Rebecca. "1989 Media All-Star -- Media Director: Felice Kincannon." *Marketing and Media Decisions.* December 1989, pp. 36-44.
Profiles advertising executive Felice Kincannon, one of a handful of women who run good-sized media departments.

2661. Fleischman, Doris E. "Key to a Public Relations Career." *Independent Woman.* November 1941, pp. 340 +.

2662. Fleischman, Doris E. "Notes of a Retiring Feminist." *American Mercury.* February 1949, p. 161.

2663. Fleischman, Doris E. "Public Relations -- A New Field for Women." *Independent Woman.* February 1931, p. 58 +.

2664. Gallick, Karen. "Janice Mayo: Talent That Travels." *Direct Marketing.* August 1990, pp. 77, 95.
Profiles Mayo, marketing official of the world's largest video dating service.

2665. "Gender Gap in Public Relations Extends Beyond Compensation." *Media Report to Women.* January-February 1991, p. 9.

2666. "Gender Gap Persists in Compensation for Public Relations Professionals." *Media Report to Women.* July-August 1990, p. 5.
Finds that a record number of women are entering public relations; yet, at each job title level, median salary of women lower than that of men.

2667. Henry, Susan J. "Anonymous in Her Own Name: Public Relations Pioneer Doris E. Fleischman." *Journalism History.* Summer 1997, pp. 50-62.

Examines Doris Fleischman's pioneering work alongside her famous husband, Edward L. Bernays, focusing on their personal and professional partnership. Her work in media and public relations spanned more than 50 years.

2668. Henry, Susan J. "Dissonant Notes of a Retiring Feminist: The Later Life of Doris E. Fleischman." *Journal of Public Relations Research.* Fall 1997.
Describes life of public relations pioneer, Doris Fleischman, her professional life, marriage to Edward L. Bernays, and name.

2669. Kern-Foxworth, Marilyn. "Public Relations Books Fail To Show Women in Context." *Journalism Educator.* August 1989, pp. 31-36.

2670. Kern-Foxworth, Marilyn, Oscar Gandy, B. Hines, and D. Miller. "Assessing the Managerial Roles of Black Public Relations Practitioners Using Individual and Organizational Discriminants." *Journal of Black Studies.* 1994, pp. 416-434.

2671. Lariscy, R. A. W., L. Sallot, and G. T. Cameron. "Justice and Gender: An Instrumental and Symbolic Explication." *Journal of Public Relations Research.* 8:2 (1996), pp. 107-121.
Sheds light from a nationwide survey of public relations practitioners on gender equity, ethical guidelines for client relations, and salaries; reveals that many of the differences existing between men and women in public relations can be explained by inherent differences between symbolic and instrumental beliefs about the issues.

2672. Larson, Keith A., comp. *Public Relations, the Edward L. Bernayses and the American Scene: A Bibliography.* Westwood, Massachusetts: F. W. Faxon Co., 1978.
Includes items on Doris Fleischman (Bernays).

2673. Lauzen, Martha. "Effects of Gender on Professional Encroachment in Public Relations." *Journalism Quarterly.* Spring 1992, pp. 173-180.

2674. Paul, Neena. "Larger Percentages of Women PR Pros Mean Altered Responsibilities." *Iowa Journalist.* Spring 1996, p. 15.
Questions why there are so few women in journalism jobs, while in public relations, the number grows.

2675. "PRSA Adopts Policy Statement Affirming Equal Opportunity for Women." *Media Report to Women.* March/April 1990, pp. 1-2.
Reprints Public Relations Society of America policy statement on women employees.

2676. Serini, S. A., et al. "Watch for Falling Glass ... Women, Men, and Job Satisfaction in Public Relations: A Preliminary Analysis." *Journal of Public Relations Research.* 9:2 (1997), pp. 99-118.
States that important differences in levels of job satisfaction among

women and men working in public relations occurred between 1990 and 1995.

2677. Toth, Elizabeth L. "Whose Freedom and Equity in Public Relations? The Gender Balance Argument." *Mass Communication Review.* 16:1/2 (1989), pp. 70-76.

2678. Toth, Elizabeth L. and Carolyn G. Cline. "Public Relations Practitioner Attitudes Toward Gender Issues: A Benchmark Study." *Public Relations Review.* Summer 1991, pp. 161-174.
Analyzes 443 questionnaires returned by public relations practitioners; finds that a marked salary disparity existed between women and men, that women face special problems in moving up to management levels and are victims of sexual bias.

2679. Toth, Elizabeth L. and Carolyn G. Cline, eds. *Beyond the Velvet Ghetto.* San Francisco, California: IABC Research Foundation, 1989.
Includes Wilma Mathews, "Killing the Messenger," pp. 1-6; Lana F. Rakow, "From the Feminization of Public Relations to the Promise of Feminism," pp. 287-298.

2680. Versh, Bonita. "Making the Cel: A Profile of Women's Commercials." *Variety.* May 1997, 4 pp.
Deals with a number of women makers of television commercials.

2681. Voelker, Judy. "Doris Bernays '13: She Wanted to Major in Penology." *Barnard Bulletin.* April 1974, p. 3 +.
Profiles public relations pioneer Doris Fleischman Bernays as an alumna.

2682. Zoch, Lynn M. and Maria P. Russell. "Women in PR Education: An Academic 'Velvet Ghetto'?" *Journalism Educator.* 46:3 (1991), pp. 25-35.

Broadcasting

2683. Abalos, Marilyn. "Her Station in Life." *Filipinas.* March 1998, pp. 34-36.
Profiles New York, Filipino-American TV journalist Ernabel Demillo.

2684. "ABC Has Poorest Network Showing of On-Air Women Correspondents." *Media Report to Women.* July/August 1990, p. 1.

2685. American Women in Radio and Television, Inc., Women's Bureau. *Women on the Job: Careers in the Electronic Media.* Washington, D.C.: 1990. 26 pp.
Introduces career possibilities in broadcasting and cable; discusses education, training, suggestions for beginning a career.

2686. Banks, Jane and Patricia Zimmermann. "Dr. Ruth Westheimer: Talking Sex as a Technology of Power." *Journal of Film and Video.* Summer/Fall 1993, pp. 60-71.
Investigates media personality who has made sex safe for television discussion; argues that Dr. Ruth's delimitation of sexual representation through her medicalized dialogue reduces sex to a set of techniques practiced off screen by anonymous, individual bodies.

2687. Baugh, Elaine. "Fostering Opportunities." *Communications*. March 1994, p. 6.
       Editorial stressing qualifications and importance of women in wireless communications.

2688. Beasley, Maurine H. "Mary Marvin Breckinridge Patterson: Case Study of One of 'Murrow's Boys.'" *Journalism History*. Spring 1994, pp. 25-35.
       Profiles early radio news reporter.

2689. Bly, Nellie. *Oprah: Up Close and Down Home*. New York: Zebra Books, 1993. 383 pp.
       Discusses career of film and TV personality Oprah Winfrey.

2690. Brownlow, S. and L. A. Zebrowitz. "Facial Appearance, Gender, and Credibility in Television Commercials." *Journal of Nonverbal Behavior*. Spring 1990, pp. 51-60.
       Samples 150 commercials from three major networks; reports that actors' facial maturity and gender influenced the type of commercials they were chosen to do.

2691. Bugbee, Emma. "Mary Margaret McBride Is Back on Air Tomorrow." *New York Herald Tribune*. July 10, 1960, p. 9.

2692. Burks, Kimberly K. and Vernon A. Stone. "Career-Related Characteristics of Male and Female News Directors." *Journalism Quarterly*. Autumn 1993, pp. 542-549.
       Assesses variables related to career progress by men and women in broadcast news management nationwide; men and women expressed similarities in job satisfaction, management styles, and career optimism but differences in career goals and forms of discrimination encountered.

2693. "But On-Camera Visibility for Top Women Reporters Declines." *Media Report to Women*. March-April 1990, p. 3.
       Reports that number of female reporters making list of 50 most visible reporters on evening newscasts of top three networks down in 1989, from 1988 level.

2694. Chason, Daniel J. *On the Air: The King Broadcasting Story*. Anacortes, Washington: Island Publishers, 1996. 249 pp.
       Spends considerable space on Dorothy Bullitt, the founder of King, one of the nation's premier broadcasting networks.

2695. Clements, Cynthia. *George Burns and Gracie Allen*. Westport, Connecticut: Greenwood Press, 1996. 444 pp.
       Summarizes the lives and achievements of the Burns/Allen team from vaudeville to television.

2696. Cloud, Dana L. "Hegemony or Concordance? The Rhetoric of Tokenism in

'Oprah' Winfrey's Rags-to-Riches Biography." *Critical Studies in Mass Communication.* June 1996, pp. 115-137.

   Examines television and print biographies of talk show host/producer Oprah Winfrey and challenges redefinitions of hegemony as happy "concordance."

2697. Cloud, Stanley and Lynne Olson. *The Murrow Boys: Pioneers on the Front Lines of Broadcast Journalism.* Boston: Houghton Mifflin, 1996. 445 pp.

   Tells story of people Edward R. Murrow hired during World War II who shaped radio news; Mary Marvin Breckinridge among the "boys."

2698. Craft, Christine. *Too Old, Too Ugly, and Not Deferential to Men: An Anchorwoman's Courageous Battle Against Sex Discrimination.* Rockland, California: Prima, 1988.

   Tells story of her firing by Metromedia, Inc. and its Kansas City TV station because she was "too old, too unattractive and not deferential enough to men."

2699. "Curtis Mitchell Recalls Early Work of Mary Margaret." *Mexico* (Missouri) *Ledger.* May 20, 1976, p. 2.

   Recalls early career of radio star Mary Margaret McBride.

2700. Deneroff, Harvey. "Jim and Stephanie Graziano." *Animation World Magazine.* May 1996, 4 pp.

   Interviews husband-wife team chosen to head DreamWork's new television animation division.

2701. Dworkin, Susan. "Joy in the Morning -- Reconteur [Joy Behar] Raises Hackles with Humor." *New Directions for Women.* January-February 1992, p. 7.

   On New York City's WABC morning show, in comedy clubs, on cable TV, and ABC late night TV.

2702. Dworkin, Susan. "Roseanne Barr: The Disgruntled Housewife as Stand-up Comedian." *Ms.* July-August 1987, pp. 106-108, 205-206.

   Champions TV comedian within the feminist discourse.

2703. Eberly, Carole M. "The Life and Times of Frances Alvord Harris: Michigan's First Woman Newscaster." Ph.D. dissertation, Michigan State University, 1996.

2704. "EEOC Files Suit for Anchorwoman." *Media Report to Women.* January-February 1991, p. 4.

2705. Egan, Kathryn S. "New Teaching Approaches for Teaching Female Students in Broadcasting." *Journalism Educator.* Fall 1991, pp. 36-43.

   Reports on how women in broadcasting view themselves and the industry, their perceptions of formal education as preparation for their career.

2706. Egan, Kathryn S. "Women Who Succeed in Broadcast Communications Academe: A Feminist Success Story." *Journalism Quarterly.* Winter 1994, pp. 960-972.

Evaluates women as "constructivists--viewing knowledge as contextual and experiencing themselves as creators of knowledge--and proceduralists-- seeking gratification in pleasing others and applying objective procedures to obtain knowledge--in relationship to success as academics in broadcast communications."

2707. Egan, Kathryn S. "Women's Career Construction: The Contribution of Epistemology to Career Satisfaction in the Broadcast Industry." *Mass Communication Review.* 18:3 (1991), pp. 38-47.

Survey of American Women in Radio and Television reveals that constructivist self-efficacy orientation contributes to career success.

2708. Findlen, Barbara. "'Women Aloud': Reinventing the Talk Show." *Ms.* January- February 1993, pp. 66-67.

Discusses feminist Mo Gaffney, host to the show on cable channel "Comedy Central."

2709. Fulton, Eileen, with Desmond Atholl and Michael Cherkinian. *As My World Still Turns: The Uncensored Memoirs of America's Soap Opera Queen.* New York: Birch Lane Press, 1995. 243 pp.

2710. Furniss, Maureen. "What's So Funny About Cheese? and Other Dilemmas: The Nickelodeon Television Network and Its (Female) Animation Producers." *Animation Journal.* Spring 1994, pp. 5-22.

Claims women's voice in animation has become stronger in recent years; praises Nickelodeon Television Network for promoting female employees; discusses work of Linda Simensky, Mary Harrington, and Vanessa Coffey.

2711. Gauger, T. R. "The Constitutionality of the FCC's Use of Race and Sex in the Granting of Broadcast Licenses." *Northwestern University Law Review.* Spring 1989, pp. 665-728.

Traces history and rationale of FCC's comparative merit policies, questioning their constitutionality.

2712. Geertsema, Tobie. "Goodbye, Mary Margaret." *Freeman* (Kingston, New York). April 11, 1976, pp. 4-5.

Obituary of radio pioneer Mary Margaret McBride.

2713. Godfrey, Donald G. and Alf Pratte. "Elma 'Pem' Gardner Farnsworth: The Pioneering of Television." *Journalism History.* Summer 1994, pp. 74-79.

Claims wife of television pioneer Philo Farnsworth also played role in medium's development.

2714. Haley, Delphine. *Dorothy Stimson Bullitt: An Uncommon Life.* Seattle,

Washington: Sasquatch Books, 1995. 344 pp.

Describes how Dorothy Stimson Bullitt founded KING-TV after her husband's death and made it into a hometown-centered station that garnered large audiences and many awards.

2715. Heggie, Barbara. "Mary Margaret's Miracle." *Woman's Home Companion.* April 1949, p. 83.

Radio news personality Mary Margaret McBride.

2716. Hill, George H., Lorraine Raglin, and Chas. Floyd Johnson. *Black Women on Television. An Illustrative History and Bibliography.* New York: Garland, 1990. 192 pp.

Highlights black actresses, singers, directors, writers, producers in Hollywood, 1939-1989; bibliography, appendices listing Oscar, Emmy, NAACP Image award nominees and winners.

2717. Hunter, Catherine E. "The Ultimate Achiever." *Drug and Cosmetic Industry.* February 1994, pp. 19-20.

Discusses Diane Von Furstenberg, star of QVC, the US's largest cable television shopping network.

2718. Jerome, Jim. "Roseanne Unchained." *People Weekly.* October 9, 1989, pp. 84-86+.

About Roseanne Barr of TV sitcom.

2719. Kagan, Daryn. "Live from the Locker Room." *Stanford Magazine.* March-April 1997.

Relates trials of being CNN morning sports anchor.

2720. King, N. *Everybody Loves Oprah.* New York: William Morrow and Co., 1987.

Discusses life and career of television talk show hostess, Oprah Winfrey. Other biographies appeared in *Good Housekeeping* (August 1986), *Ms.* (August 1986, January-February 1989), *Ladies' Home Journal* (August 1991, December 1988, February 1994), *Cosmopolitan* (February 1989), *Reader's Digest* (February 1989), *Essence* (October 1986), *Working Woman* (December 1991), New York *Times Magazine* (June 11, 1989), *Genders* (Fall 1991), *Ebony* (April 1985, October 1993), *People Weekly* (January 12, 1987), *Redbook* (September 1993), *McCall's* (August 1987), *Time* (August 8, 1988).

2721. Kleiman, H. "Content Diversity and the FCC's Minority and Gender Licensing Policies." *Journal of Broadcasting and Electronic Media.* Fall 1991, pp. 411-429.

Discusses FCC minority and gender preference policies; points out that after a decade of the policies, only 2.5 to 3.5 percent of broadcast stations are owned by minorities.

2722. Lavin, Marilyn. "Creating Consumers in the 1930s: Irna Phillips and the Radio Soap Opera." *Journal of Consumer Research.* June 1995, pp. 75-89.

Tells how Phillips developed a program format that appealed to American housewives -- adjusting storylines to appeal to sponsors' needs, using soap opera characters to do testimonials, and designing program promotions to augment product sales.

2723. Lieberman, Philip A. *Radio's Morning Show Personalities: Early Hour Broadcasts and Deejays from the 1920s to the 1990s*. Jefferson, North Carolina: McFarland, 1996. 213 pp.
        Some women in list of over 200 "lesser known" personalities.

2724. Lipschultz, Jeremy H. "Craft Versus Metromedia, Inc. and Its Social-Legal Progeny." *Communications and the Law*. March 1994, pp. 45-74.
        Tells how the case, *Craft vs. Metromedia, Inc.*, dealt with a number of issues besides sex discrimination in the newsroom.

2725. Lont, Cynthia M. "The Roles Assigned to Females and Males in Non-Music Radio Programming." *Sex Roles*. May 1990, pp. 661-668.
        Summarizes non-music programming of two Top 40 radio stations; shows males dominate as Djs, newscasters, voiceovers in advertising, sportscasters, and weathercasters.

2726. McBride, Mary Margaret. *America for Me*. New York: Macmillan, 1941.
        Gives some details of McBride's career in radio broadcasting.

2727. McBride, Mary Margaret. *Out of the Air*. New York: Doubleday, 1960.
        Provides some information on McBride's radio career.

2728. McKeon, Kelley. "Stone Study: Radio Gender Gap Grows Wider, with Women on the Short End." *Iowa Journalist*. Spring 1996, p. 16.
        Contends that women occupy less than one-third of radio news positions in the United States.

2729. Maddox, Kate. "Women in Cable Changes with the Times." *Communications Week*. November 14, 1994, p. PNU 7.
        Interviews president of Women in Cable and Telecommunications on organization's primary objectives.

2730. Mair, George. *Oprah Winfrey: The Real Story*. New York: Birch Lane Press, 1994. 376 pp.
        Profiles film and television personality.

2731. Merrick, Beverly. "Mary Margaret McBride: At Home in the Hudson Valley." *Journalism History*. Autumn 1996, pp. 110-118.
        Relates broadcasting career of Mary Margaret McBride, especially her talk show, "Your Hudson Valley Neighbor," broadcast from her country home.

2732. Miller, Joy. "Radio's 1st Lady." *Columbia Missourian*. January 6, 1961, p. 5.
        Mary Margaret McBride.

2733. Moore, Mary Tyler. *After All*. New York: G.P. Putnam's Sons, 1996.
Relates life story of TV sitcom star, with candid discussions about her tragedies, fears, insecurities.

2734. Morgenthau, Henry. "Dona Quixote: The Adventures of Frieda Hennock." *Television Quarterly*. 26:4 (1993), pp. 61-73.
Reports on the first woman member of the Federal Communications Commission (1948) and her campaign for noncommercial educational television.

2735. Neuman, Linda. "Diverse Stories and Voices: Women and Radio." *Voices*. 3:3 (1995), pp. 35-36, 47.

2736. O'Dell, Cary. *Women Pioneers in Television: Biographies of Fifteen Industry Leaders*. Jefferson, North Carolina: McFarland, 1997. 264 pp.
Focuses on television work of Mildred Freed Alberg, Lucille Ball, Gertrude Bergs, Peggy Charran, Joan Ganz Cooney, Faye Emerson, Pauline Frederick, Dorothy Fuldheim, Betty Furness, Frieda Hennock, Lucy Jarris, Ida Lupino, Irna Phillips, Judith Waller, and Betty White.

2737. Pomerantz, A. P. "No Film at 11: The Inadequacy of Legal Protection and Relief for Sexually Harassed Broadcast Journalists." *Cardoza Arts and Entertainment Law Journal*. 8:1 (1989), pp. 137-166.
Discusses the case of *Meritor Savings Bank FSB v. Vinson* and its impact on women in broadcasting relative to sexual harassment.

2738. Prato, Lou. "The News Director Proves Her Mettle." *Washington Journalism Review*. January-February 1992, pp. 24-28.
Discusses women directors in major TV markets.

2739. Ramsey, Shirley. "Gender Competency in TV-News Spokespersons." Paper presented at International Association for Mass Communication Research, Sydney, Australia, August 20, 1996.

2740. Rappaport, Jennifer. "Women Talkshow Hosts: An Endangered Species?" *Extra!* July-August 1990, p. 15.

2741. Rowe, Kathleen K. "Roseanne: Unruly Woman as Domestic Goddess." *Screen*. Winter 1990, pp. 408-419.
Claims Roseanne Barr em*bodies*, literally, "the unruly qualities of *excess* and *looseness*," but sees the unruly woman as "prototype of woman as subject -- transgressive above all when she lays claim to her own desire."

2742. "RTNDA Survey Shows Little Change for Women in Newsrooms." *Media Report to Women*. September/October 1990, p.1.
Reports on latest Vernon Stone survey, for 1989.

2743. St. John, Jacqueline D. "Sex Role Stereotyping in Early Broadcast History: The Career of Mary Margaret McBride." *Frontiers*. Fall 1978, pp. 31-38.

Examines broadcast activities of Mary Margaret McBride; concludes prejudice against women broadcasters for psychological, not physical and mechanical reasons.

2744. Sanders, Marlene. "The Face of the News Is Male." *Television Quarterly*. 26:1 (1992), pp. 57-60.

Relates surveys that show men reported 86 percent of the broadcast news stories and were sources 79 percent of the time; concludes that if networks and stations' newscasts do not better represent the diversity of the marketplace, they may lose viewers to the competition.

2745. Seiter, Ellen. "'To Teach and to Sell': Irna Phillips and Her Sponsors, 1930-1954." *Journal of Film and Video*. Spring 1989, pp. 21-35.

Shows how scriptwriter Irna Phillips was the most important person in soap opera production from the 1930s through the 1960s; tells how Phillips depicted women, her relationships with men she worked for, and her characterization of her audiences.

2746. Simensky, Linda. "Women in the Animation Industry -- Some Thoughts." *Animation World*. May 1996, 3 pp.

Cartoon Network's director of programming discusses some bright spots for women in animation, but wishes for "female show creators, more female directors, and a funny cartoon with a female lead character."

2747. Smith, Betsy C. *Breakthrough: Women in Television*. New York: Walker and Co., 1981.

2748. Steenland, Sally. "Women and Television in the Eighties." *Television Quarterly*. 24:3 (1990), pp. 53-60.

Contends that 1980s did not live up to expectations that women would fare better on TV; states, "By 1989, women hadn't cracked any of the industry's decision-making jobs in significant number, nor were female images on the screen devoid of titillation and stereotype."

2749. Stilson, Janet. "Stuck on the Ground Floor: Men and Women Climb Different, Unequal Ladders in TV News: It's Likely to Stay That 'Way." *Channels*. September 24, 1990, pp. 20-26.

2750. Stix, Harriet. "Sincerity Is 'Secret' Behind Her Success." *New York Herald Tribune*. November 28, 1960, p. 14.

On Mary Margaret McBride, radio broadcaster.

2751. Stone, Vernon A. "Little Change for Minorities and Women." *RTNDA Communicator*. August 1992, pp. 26-27.

States roles of women in broadcast news did not change much in recent years.

2752. Stone, Vernon A. "Minority Men Shoot ENG; Women Take Advancement Tracks." *RTNDA Communicator*. August 1988, pp. 10-14.
   In broadcast news.

2753. Stone, Vernon A. "Pipelines and Dead Ends: Jobs Held by Minorities and Women in Broadcast News." *Mass Communication Review*. 15:2/3 (1988), pp. 10-19.

2754. Stone, Vernon A. "Surveys Show Younger Women Becoming News Directors." *RTNDA Communicator*. October 1976, pp. 10-12.

2755. Stone, Vernon A. "Women Gain, Black Men Lose Ground in Newsrooms." *RTNDA Communicator*. August 1987, pp. 9-11.

2756. Stone, Vernon A. "Women Gaining as News Directors." *RTNDA Communicator*. October 1988, pp. 20-21.

2757. Stone, Vernon A. and Barbara Dell. "More Women in News Broadcasting According to RTNDA Survey." *RTNDA Communicator*. August 1972, p. 4.

2758. "Survey Finds Women in Cable Earn 15% Less Than Male Counterparts." *Media Report to Women*. Fall 1997, pp. 1-2.
   Claims the gap is not closing.

2759. Torre, Marie. *Don't Quote Me*. Garden City, New York: Doubleday & Company, 1965.
   Covers Torre's career as a writer about radio and television and her chief claim to fame when in 1959, she was jailed for 10 days for refusing to reveal a source.

2760. "TV Network News Changing; News Assignment Altered for Women, Men." *Media Report to Women*. Spring 1997, pp. 1-2.
   Shows new domestic focus of TV network newscasts has done little to expand the journalistic beats that women work.

2761. Unger, Arthur. "Barbara Walters: 'I Can Ask Them But I Can't Answer Them.'" *Television Quarterly*. 24:3 (1990), pp. 5-17.
   Interviews newswoman Barbara Walters, host of "The Barbara Walters Special" and co-host of "The Today Show."

2762. Unger, Arthur. "Diane Sawyer: The Warm Ice Maiden." *Television Quarterly*. 26:1 (1992), pp. 39-54.
   Interviews "Primetime Live" co-host Diane Sawyer of ABC about her years in TV news and her work with Richard Nixon.

2763. Unger, Arthur. "Kay Koplovitz of USA Network: 'I Remember the Future.'" *Television Quarterly*. 28:2 (1996), pp. 20-33.
   Interviews chief executive officer of USA Network, cable empire which includes the Sci-Fi Channel; discusses her network.

2764. "Women Broadcasting Men's Sports." *Media Report to Women*. January-February 1991, p. 4.

2765. "Women Could Dominate News Director Positions Early in 21st Century." *Media Report to Women*. March/April 1990, pp. 2-3.
    If 1980s' growth rate holds, women will become majority of U.S. news directors by 21st century.

2766. "Women Gaining As TV News Directors, Could Be One Third of Them by 2001." *Media Report to Women*. Winter 1997, p. 10.
    Shows how women increased their share of TV news directorships from two or three of 630 total in 1972 to 205 of 805 in 1996.

2767. "Women in Broadcasting Going It Alone, Magazine Says." *Media Report to Women*. September-October 1990, pp. 1-2.
    States that women in TV superstar ranks are without the support given to males. Excerpted from Jennet Conant's article in *Working Woman*, August 1990.

2768. "Women in Management." *RadioActive*. June 1987, pp. 7-22.

2769. Yakir, Dan. "Eastern Star." *Philip Morris Magazine*. November/December 1990, pp. 19-20.
    Discusses career of television producer Yue-Sai Kan.

2770. Ziegler, Dhyana and Alisa White. "Women and Minorities on Network Television News: An Examination of Correspondents and Newsmakers." *Journal of Broadcasting and Electronic Media*. Spring 1990, pp. 215-223.
    Examines race and gender of correspondents on network newscasts, topics they covered and role of newsmakers presented in the news: few changes after 20 years.

Film

2771. Acker, Ally. "Women Behind the Camera." *Ms*. March-April 1992, pp. 64-67.
    Reports an important increase in the number of women film directors; although far behind Europe in output, they are discussing taboo subjects, creating realistic, well-developed characters, and bringing women's perspective into cinema.

2772. Allan, Robin. "Mary Blair: An Indelible Imprint." *Animation*. July 1995, pp. 58-61.
    Profiles Mary Blair, a Disney animator known for her styling and expressionistic flair.

2773. Allan, Robin. "Sylvia Holland: Disney Artist." *Animation Journal*. Spring 1994, pp. 32-41.
    Profiles Sylvia Holland, Disney animator who worked on important

segments of "Fantasia," "Bambi," and "Make Mine Music"; highlights her "indomitable" spirit.

2774. Allyson, June, with Frances S. Leighton. *June Allyson*. New York: G.P. Putnam's Sons, 1982.
Autobiography of Hollywood star.

2775. Andersen, Christopher. *Citizen Jane: The Turbulent Life of Jane Fonda*. New York: Henry Holt, 1990.
Exposes movie star, occasional political activist, and home video fitness promoter.

2776. *Animation Journal*.
Spring 1994 -- Thematic issue on women in animation, edited by Maureen Furniss, includes Maureen Furniss, "What's So Funny about Cheese? and Other Dilemmas: The Nickelodeon Television Network and Its (Female) Animation Producers," pp. 4-22; Joanna Priestley, "Creating a Healing Mythology: The Art of Faith Hubley," pp. 23-31; Mary Beams, "Subverting Time: A Woman's Perspective," pp. 42-53; Atom Klein, "La Verne Harding: Hollywood's First Woman Animator," pp. 54-67.

2777. Anthology Film Archives. *The Legend of Maya Deren*. New York: Anthology Film Archives, 1988.

2778. Astor, Mary. *My Story: An Autobiography*. New York: Doubleday, 1959. 332 pp.
Deals with this actress's lifelong lack of self-worth, alcoholism, promiscuity; discusses her roles in films "Red Dust," "Hurricane," "Tonight at 8:30," and "The Great Lie," among others.

2779. Aufderheide, Patricia. "Desert Hearts: An Interview with Donna Deitch." *Cineaste*. 15:1 (1986), pp. 18-19.

2780. Bacall, Lauren. *By Myself*. New York: Knopf, 1978.
Autobiography of actress Bacall.

2781. Baisley, Sarah. "Phyllis Craig 1929-1997." *Animation Magazine*. July 1997, p. 2.
Recounts life of early woman animator at Disney, and later at Hanna-Barbera.

2782. Baker, Carroll. *Baby Doll: An Autobiography*. New York: Arbor House, 1983.
Autobiography of Hollywood actress; title emphasizes her sole important role.

2783. Barbagallo, Ron. "Cel Art Pioneer: Discovering Helen." *Animation Magazine*. August 1997, pp. 37-39.
Introduces Helen Nerbovig, an early animator who worked on "Snow White and the Seven Dwarfs" and other Disney features from the 1930s on.

2784. Barranger, Milly S. *Jessica Tandy: A Bio-Bibliography*. Westport, Connecticut: Greenwood, 1991. 168 pp.

Features a biographical sketch, a chronology, chapters documenting Tandy's career in theater, film, television, and recordings, a listing of awards (including 1989 Oscar for best actress), and an annotated bibliography.

2785. Baty, S. Paige. *American Monroe: The Making of a Body Politic*. Berkeley: University of California Press, 1995. 185 pp.

Discusses actress Marilyn Monroe in context of American culture.

2786. Beams, Mary. "Subverting Time: A Woman's Perspective." *Animation Journal*. Spring 1994, pp. 42-53.

Discusses use (and extension) of time in doing animation, including topics such as "Power and Loss," tools, "Touching Time," technology and financing's influences on time, and deadlines; tells of tribulations of trying to animate while also parenting; includes bio sketch and filmography.

2787. Beauvais, Yann. "Interview with Barbara Hammer." *Spiral*. January 1986, pp. 33-38.

Profiles lesbian filmmaker Hammer.

2788. Beeman, Marsha L. *Joan Fontaine: A Bio-Bibliography*. Westport, Connecticut: Greenwood Press, 1994. 360 pp.

Discusses varied and successful career of Fontaine, winner of the 1941 Academy Award for best actress; biographical sketch, filmography, bibliography.

2789. Bendazzi, Giannalberto. "Claire Parker, an Appreciation." *Animation World*. May 1996, 3 pp.

Gives a brief account of the working relationship between animator Claire Parker and her artist husband, Alexandre Alexeïeff.

2790. Benzel, Kathryn N. "The Body as Art: Still Photographs of Marilyn Monroe." *Journal of Popular Culture*. Fall 1991, pp. 1-29.

2791. Bergan, Ronald. *Katharine Hepburn: An Independent Woman*. New York: Arcade Publications, 1996.

Charts a career that has spanned seven decades and produced four Oscars; touches on all her films and relationships.

2792. Bergman, Ingrid and Alan Burgess. *Ingrid Bergman: My Story*. New York: Delacorte Press, 1980.

Autobiography of controversial actress Bergman.

2793. Billips, Connie J. *Janet Gaynor: A Bio-Bibliography*. Westport, Connecticut: Greenwood Press, 1992. 184 pp.

Profiles actress Gaynor in biographical sketch, filmography, and bibliography.

2794. Billips, Connie J. *Maureen O'Sullivan: A Bio-Bibliography*. Westport, Connecticut: Greenwood Press, 1990. 224 pp.

Traces 60-year career of O'Sullivan; includes biography, career chronology, separate sections on the actress's film, stage, TV, and radio appearances, bibliography, and two short stories written by O'Sullivan for *Ladies' Home Journal*.

2795. Billman, Larry. *Betty Grable: A Bio-Bibliography*. Westport, Connecticut, Greenwood Press, 1993. 328 pp.

Describes Grable's film career in biographical sketch, filmography, and bibliography.

2796. Black, Shirley Temple. *Child Star: An Autobiography*. New York: McGraw-Hill, 1988.

Describes life of Shirley Temple, from child star to ambassador.

2797. Bodeen, De Witt. "Frances Marion." *Films in Review*. February 1969, pp. 71-91.

Part II in March 1969 issue, pp. 129-152.

2798. Bogle, D. *Brown Sugar: Eighty Years of America's Black Female Superstars*. New York: Continuum, 1988.

2799. Bond, Rose. "Joanna Priestley: A Continuing Dialogue." *Animation World Magazine*. September 1997, 4 pp.

Profiles independent animator Joanna Priestley, creator of "Utopia Parkway," "After the Fall," "Grown Up," "Hand Held," "All My Relations" and described as "a leading light" in animation.

2800. Boseman, Keith. "Ayoka Chenzira: Sharing the Empowerment of Women." *Black Film Review*. Summer 1986, p. 18.

Black filmmaker.

2801. Britton, Andrew. *Katharine Hepburn: Star as Feminist*. New York: Continuum, 1995. 256 pp.

Argues through feminist theory that Hepburn's persona raises problems about female sexuality, class, and women's rights, which "strain to the limits the conventions of a cinematic establishment that was (and still is) thoroughly committed to the reassertion of bourgeois gender roles."

2802. Brown, Catherine H. *Letters to Mary: The Story of Helen Hayes*. New York: Random House, 1940. 343 pp.

Deals with theater, Hollywood, mother-daughter interrelationships; written by Helen Hayes' mother.

2803. Brunette, Peter. "Imagin(in)ing Pictures: An Interview with Holly Fisher." *Film Quarterly*. Winter 1993-1994, pp. 2-7.

Fisher is a film director.

2804. Bryan, George B. *Ethel Merman: A Bio-Bibliography*. Westport, Connecticut: Greenwood Press, 1992. 320 pp.
> Details Merman's 55-year career that encompassed cabaret, vaudeville, film, recordings, radio, television, and concert stage; divided into biographical essay, chronology, filmography, stage appearances, radio-TV appearances. discography, bibliography, and subject index.

2805. Burchill, Julie. *Girls on Film*. New York: Pantheon Books, 1986. 192 pp.
> Reviews the history of women in film, mainly "sex kittens," in popular, overwritten, gossipy style; from earliest days of silent movies to 1980s.

2806. Burke, Billie, with Cameron Shipp. *With Powder on My Nose*. New York: Coward-McCann, 1959. 249 pp.
> Deals largely with her feelings as an aging but active woman and actress; focuses also on beauty tips and exercise.

2807. Butler, Judith. "Lana's 'Imitation' -- Melodramatic Repetition and the Gender Performative." *Genders*. Fall 1990, pp. 1-18.
> Concerns actress Lana Turner in "Imitation of Life."

2808. Calvet, Corrine. *Has Corrine Been a Good Girl?* New York: St. Martin's Press, 1983.
> Autobiography of film actress Calvet.

2809. Campbell, Loretta. "Reinventing Our Image: Eleven Black Women Filmmakers." *Heresies*. No.16, 1983, pp. 58-62.

2810. Canemaker, John. *Before the Animation Begins: The Art and Lives of Disney Inspirational Sketches*. New York: Hyperion, 1996. 210 pp.
> Chapter 3, "Inspired Women," includes profiles of female animators Bianca Majolie, Sylvia Moberly-Holland, and Mary Blair.

2811. Carey, Gary. *Doug and Mary: A Biography of Douglas Fairbanks and Mary Pickford*. New York: E. P. Dutton, 1977.

2812. Carrier, Jeffrey L. *Tallulah Bankhead. A Bio-Bibliography*. Westport, Connecticut: Greenwood, 1991. 288 pp.
> Documents Tallulah Bankhead's 19 films, 56 stage plays, 167 radio appearances, and 56 TV appearances, listing other professional work, awards, tributes. Includes biographical sketch, chronology, annotated bibliography, and photographs.

2813. Castle, Ted. "Carolee Schneemann: The Woman Who Uses Her Body as Her Art." *Artforum*. November 1980, pp. 64-70.
> Explores filmmaking of Schneemann, whose "Fuses" (1968) is a major avant-garde work incorporating the director's vision of her own identity as a sexual human being and woman in love.

2814. Charisse, Cyd and Tony Martin, as told to Dick Kleiner. *The Two of Us*. New York: Mason/Charter, 1976.
Autobiography of dance and film star Charisse.

2815. "Chic, Mlle." (pseud.). "The Dual Personality of Cleo Madison." *Moving Picture Weekly*. July 1, 1910, pp. 24-25, 34.
Deals with life of actress, producer, and director Madison, whose 19 films were done in 1915-1916.

2816. Chin, Daryl. "Walking on Thin Ice: The Films of Yoko Ono." *Independent*. April 1989, pp. 19-23.
Discusses some of the 20 experimental films of Ono; "Walking on Thin Ice" (1981) was the title of a video she made.

2817. Cohen, Karl. "Lucille Bliss: From Crusader Rabbit to Smurfette." *Animato!* Spring 1994, pp. 30-31, 61.
Recounts career of voice actress Lucille Bliss of animation fame.

2818. Coleman, Emily R. *The Complete Judy Garland: The Ultimate Guide to Her Career in Films, Records, Concerts, Radio, and Television, 1935-1969*. New York: Harper & Row, 1990. 440 pp.
Stands as a comprehensive guide, with bibliography, indices by song and name, and more than 100 photographs.

2819. Conway, Michael and Mark Ricci. *The Films of Jean Harlow*. New York: Bonanza, 1965.

2820. Cooper, Karen. "Shirley Clarke's Videos." *Filmmakers Newsletter*. June 1972, pp. 35-38.
U.S. filmmaker.

2821. Corr, Casey O. *KING: The Bullitts of Seattle and Their Communications Empire*. Seattle: University of Washington Press, 1996. 306 pp.
Provides history of KING-TV of Seattle and the role of its owners, the Bullitt family, particularly Dorothy Stimson Bullitt.

2822. Curcio, Vincent. *Suicide Blonde: The Life of Gloria Grahame*. New York: William Morrow, 1989.
Tells how Grahame's career as Hollywood actress was underrated.

2823. Curry, Ramona. *Too Much of a Good Thing. Mae West as Cultural Icon*. Minneapolis: University of Minnesota Press, 1996. 288 pp.
Looks at impact of American film star Mae West through her films, attitude, and aphorisms; examines interplay between West's "bawdy, worldly persona and twentieth-century gender and media politics"; examines how a star image emerges and spreads through a culture; reexamines West's role in the development of film censorship of the 1930s, and uses the actress to address existing theories about sexual representation.

2824.   Danielson, Sarah P. *Katharine Hepburn: A Hollywood Portrait*. Smithmark Publishing Inc., 1993. 111 pp.
        Chronicles long career of film actress Hepburn, famous for her independent nature and indomitable spirit; includes more than 100 photographs, filmography.

2825.   Davidson, Bill. *Jane Fonda: An Intimate Biography*. New York: E.P. Dutton, 1990.

2826.   Davis, Bette. *The Lonely Life*. New York: G.P. Putnam's Sons, 1962. 254 pp.
        Famous film actress shares her views on Hollywood, movies, marriage, life, etc.

2827.   Davis, Bette, with Michael Herskowitz. *This 'n' That*. New York: Putnam, 1987.
        Sequel to Davis' earlier *The Lonely Life: An Autobiography*.

2828.   Davis, Zeinabu Irene. "An Interview with Julie Dash." *Wide Angle*. 13:3/4 (1991), pp. 110-118.
        Talks about one of the most prolific black woman independent filmmakers. Reprinted from *Black Film Review*. 6:1 (1990), pp. 12-17, 20-21.

2829.   DeCarlo, Yvonne, with Doug Warren. *Yvonne*. New York: St. Martin's Press, 1987.
        Autobiography of Hollywood star.

2830.   de Hirsch, Storm and Shirley Clarke. "A Conversation." *Film Quarterly*. Autumn 1967, pp. 44-54.
        Between filmmakers.

2831.   De Mille, Agnes. *Dance to the Piper*. Boston: Little, Brown, 1952. 256 pp.
        Provides candid autobiography of American ballet dancer and choreographer of "Oklahoma!" and other works.

2832.   Deneroff, Harvey. "Animated Women." *Animation Magazine*. July 1995, pp. 44-45, 66.
        A television series of four animated films by Independent Television Service created by Faith Hubley, Joanna Priestley, Ruth Peyser, and Lynn Smith.

2833.   Dickens, Homer. *The Films of Katharine Hepburn*. New York: Citadel Press, 1971.

2834.   Dittus, Erick. "Mississippi Triangle: An Interview with Christine Choy, Worth Long, and Allan Siegel." *Cineaste*. 14:2 (1985), pp. 38-40.
        U.S. filmmaker Christine Choy.

2835.   Dixon, Wheeler W. "Gender Approaches to Directing the Horror Film: Women Filmmakers and the Mechanisms of the Gothic." *Popular Culture Review*.

February 1996, pp. 121-134.

Argues that women directors of horror films bring a different vision to their work; claims "By choosing forms of representations in their horror films that deviate from the patriarchal models of the Gothic narrative these filmmakers have given us a fresh and exhilarating vision of the uncanny that undercuts and questions much that recently has been created by men."

2836. Dorf, Shel. "June Foray." *Comics Interview*. No. 54 (1988), pp. 52-59.

Interviews animation voice actress June Foray.

2837. Dunning, Jennifer. "A Woman Film Maker in the Coal Mines." *New York Times*. October 15, 1976, p. 8.

Discusses Barbara Kopple, Academy Award-winning documentarist and her "Harlan County U.S.A."

2838. Elfman, Danny. "Penelope Spheeris and Danny Elfman." *American Film*. February 1991, pp. 42-45.

Relates work of filmmaker Spheeris.

2839. Ellis, Robert. "Ida Lupino Brings New Hope to Hollywood." *Negro Digest*. August 1950, pp. 47-49.

Hollywood director/actress.

2840. Eyman, Scott. *Mary Pickford: America's Sweetheart*. New York: Donald I. Fine, 1990.

Deals with silent screen star and government bonds saleswoman.

2841. Faris, Jocelyn. *Jayne Mansfield: A Bio-Bibliography*. Westport, Connecticut: Greenwood, 1994. 304 pp.

Explains that though she starred in only three American movies and a few low-budget European films, Mansfield, a master of publicity, gave the false impression she was a major star.

2842. Farrow, Mia. *What Falls Away*. Garden City, New York: Doubleday, 1997. 370 pp.

Tells of movie and TV acting career, but also her marriages to Frank Sinatra, Andre Previn, and Woody Allen, her 14 children (10 adopted), and Allen's affair with one of her adopted daughters.

2843. Ferrer, Esteban. "Emotional Roles Fire Up Actress's Career." *Variety*. March 12, 1998, pp. A10, A14.

Profiles actress Joan Allen, star of "Nixon," "The Ice Storm," and "Face/Off."

2844. Filemyr, Ann. "Zeinabu Irene Davis: Filmmaker, Teacher with a Powerful Mission." *Angles: Women Working in Film and Video*. Winter 1992, pp. 6-9, 22.

2845. Fisher, Carrie and Penny Marshall. "Rappin' with Penny and Carrie." *People* (Special edition, "Inside Hollywood: Women, Sex and Power"). Spring 1991, pp. 95-97.

> Concentrates on career of Marshall, woman who has lasted the longest as a mainstream director.

2846. Fontaine, Joan. *No Bed of Roses: An Autobiography*. New York: William Morrow, 1978.

> Hollywood actress's life story.

2847. Foreman, Alexa L. *Women in Motion*. Bowling Green, Ohio: Bowling Green Popular Press, 1983. 248 pp.

> Lists representative women in U.S. film by independent and avant-garde filmmakers, directors, editors, and screenwriters. Includes selected filmographies.

2848. Fowler, Karin. *Anne Baxter. A Bio-Bibliography*. Westport, Connecticut: Greenwood, 1991. 288 pp.

> Describes life and career of Academy Award winning actress Anne Baxter, providing full credits, synopses, and review sources for her films and plays, as well as a bibliography.

2849. Fowler, Karin. *Ava Gardner: A Bio-Bibliography*. Westport, Connecticut: Greenwood, 1990. 256 pp.

> Deals with Gardner's five-decade actress career; highlights her marriages and her dozens of classic roles in a comprehensive filmography.

2850. Francke, Lizzie. *Script Girls: Women Screenwriters in Hollywood*. London and Bloomington: British Film Institute and Indiana University Press, 1994. 184 pp.

> Traces history of Hollywood screenwriters -- from Gene Gauntier's version of "Ben Hur" to Callie Khoun's "Thelma and Louise"; looks at lives and careers of women who wrote for film; includes interviews with Khoun, Nora Ephron, Caroline Thompson, and others.

2851. Friedberg, Anne. "An Interview with Filmmaker Lizzie Borden." *Women and Performance*. 1:2 (1984), pp. 37-45.

2852. Fuller, Graham. "Ida Lupino." *Interview*. October 1991, p. 118.

> Interviews the only woman director who managed to work in Hollywood in the repressive 1950s.

2853. Gauntier, Gene. "Blazing the Trail." *Women's Home Companion*. October 1928, p. 6.

> Gauntier was a pioneering filmmaker in the serial genre.

2854. Genini, Ronald. *Theda Bara: A Biography of the Silent Screen Vamp, with a Filmography*. Jefferson, North Carolina: McFarland, 1996. 168 pp.

> Uses contemporary newspaper stories, reviews, interviews, and other

sources to document the life and times of one of Hollywood's first female stars.

2855. Gibson-Hudson, Gloria J. "African American Literary Criticism as a Model for the Analysis of Films by African American Women." *Wide Angle*. 13:3/4 (1991), pp. 44-54.
Concludes that African-American women produce films that are diverse, not monolithic.

2856. Gill, Glenda E. "'Her Voice Was Ever Soft, Gentle, and Low, an Excellent Thing' in Ruby Dee." *Journal of Popular Culture*. Summer 1994, pp. 61-72.
Profiles half-century acting career of African-American Ruby Dee, who performed consistently and seldom, if ever, in servant or slut parts.

2857. Gish, Lillian and Ann Pinchot. *The Movies, Mr. Griffith, and Me*. Englewood Cliffs, New Jersey: Prentice-Hall, 1969.
Recounts part of the long movie career of Lillian Gish.

2858. Goldman, Herbert G. *Fanny Brice: The Original Funny Girl*. New York: Oxford University Press, 1992. 336 pp.
Combines biography with theater history; illuminates Brice's stage and radio career, including her long run as "Baby Snooks."

2859. Grattan, Virginia L. *American Women Songwriters. A Biographical Dictionary*. Westport, Connecticut: Greenwood Press, 1993. 294 pp.
Profiles 181 women who have written popular and motion picture songs, musicals, country, blues, jazz, folk, gospel, hymns, and 19th century songs.

2860. Green, Shelley. *Radical Juxtaposition: The Films of Yvonne Rainer*. Metuchen, New Jersey: Scarecrow Press, 1994. 174 pp.
Highlights Rainer's avant-garde filmmaking; investigates her "complex and disjunctive use of language, speech, repetition, interpolated texts, fragmentation, self-conscious camera movement, autobiography, and the formulation of alternative narrative codes."

2861. Gross, Barry. "No Victim, She: Barbra Streisand and the Movie Jew." *Journal of Ethnic Studies*. Spring 1975, pp. 28-40.
Discusses ethnicity and actress (later director) Barbra Streisand.

2862. Grossman, Barbara. *Funny Woman: The Life and Times of Fanny Brice*. Bloomington: Indiana University Press, 1991. 304 pp.
Portrays stage and radio star Fanny Brice.

2863. Haller, Robert. "Rolling in the Maelstrom: A Conversation Between Carolee and Robert Haller." *Idiolects*. Spring 1984, pp. 50-55.
Carolee (Schneeman) is a feminist filmmaker.

2864. Hamilton, Marybeth. *"When I'm Bad, I'm Better": Mae West, Sex, and American Entertainment*. Berkeley: University of California Press, 1998. 317 pp.

"Combines elements of biography, cultural analysis, and social history to unmask Mae West and reveal her commercial savvy, will-power, and truly shocking theatrical transgressions."

2865. Hayes, Helen, with Katherine Hatch. *My Life in Three Acts*. New York: Harcourt Brace Jovanovich, 1990. 266 pp.
On famous actress, Helen Hayes.

2866. Hayes, Richard K. *Kate Smith: A Biography, with a Discography, Filmography and List of Stage Appearances*. Jefferson, North Carolina: McFarland, 1995. 336 pp.
Uses singer's correspondence, interviews, etc.

2867. Henry, William M. "Cleo, the Craftswoman." *Photoplay*. January 1916, p. 108.
On filmmaker Cleo Madison.

2868. Henshaw, Richard. "Women Directors: 150 Filmographies." *Film Comment*. November-December 1972, pp. 33-45.

2869. Hobart, Rose. *A Steady Digression to a Fixed Point*. Metuchen, New Jersey: Scarecrow Press, 1994. 186 pp.
Provides autobiographical account of Hobart's careers on stage in the 1920s and on screen in 1930s-1940s, and her blacklisting later.

2870. "Hollywood Hype and Hope: The Latest on Prospects for Actresses, Directors." *Media Report to Women*. Spring 1997, pp. 6-7.
Discusses women's prospects in the film industry as related in three articles.

2871. Holston, Kim. *Starlet: Biographies, Filmographies, TV Credits and Photos of 54 Famous and Not So Famous Leading Ladies of the Sixties*. Jefferson, North Carolina: McFarland, 1988. 320 pp.
Includes photographs, filmographies, bibliography.

2872. Horn, Barbara L. *Colleen Dewhurst: A Bio-Bibliography*. Westport, Connecticut: Greenwood Press, 1992. 192 pp.

2873. Hotchner, A. S. *Doris Day: Her Own Story*. New York: William Morrow, 1976.
Combines biography/autobiography in presenting story of singing and film star Day.

2874. Houston, Beverle. "Missing in Action: Notes on Dorothy Arzner." *Wide Angle*. 6:3 (1984), pp. 24-31.

2875. Howe, Joyce. "My Heroine...A Chinese American Woman Undertakes Her First Screenplay." In *The 1987 Asian American International Film Festival*, pp. 35-36. New York: Asian Cine Vision, 1987.

2876. *Independent Film and Video Monthly.* July 1990.
Issue devoted to women in film with features on women producers and directors, historical treatment of women in film, works by women of color.

2877. Jackson, Elizabeth. "Barbara McCullough: Independent Filmmaker." *Jump Cut.* 36 (1990), pp. 94-97.
McCullough directed four films in 1979-1980.

2878. Jackson, Lynne. "Labor Relations: An Interview with Lizzie Borden." *Cineaste.* 15:3 (1987), pp. 4-17.

2879. Jackson, Lynne and Karen Jaehne. "Eavesdropping on Female Voices: A Who's Who of Contemporary Women Filmmakers." *Cineaste.* 16:1-2 (1988), pp. 38-43.

2880. Jackson, Wendy. "Cecile Starr: A Pioneer's Pioneer." *Animation Journal.* Spring 1995, pp. 40-43.

2881. Jackson, Wendy. "Yvonne Anderson: Profile of a Pioneer." *Animation World.* March 1997, 5 pp.
Profiles Yvonne Anderson, teacher of animation and director of children's animation workshops.

2882. Jarrell, Joe. "Talkin' to Poor White Trash: Penelope Spheeris Speaks Her Mind." *High Performance.* September 1991, pp. 24-25.
Talks about her life, beliefs, filmmaking; Spheeris directed "Hollywood Vice Squad" (1986), "Wayne's World" (1992), "The Beverly Hillbillies" (1993), and "The Little Rascals" (1994). See Jamie Diamond's review of "Wayne's World" in *New York Times* (April 12, 1992, pp. H11, H20).

2883. Jayamanne, Laleen, Leslie Thornton, and Trinh T. Minh-ha. "If Upon Leaving What We Have To Say We Speak: A Conversation Piece." In *Discourses: Conversations in Postmodern Art and Culture,* edited by Russell Ferguson, William Olander, Marcia Tucker, and Karen Fiss, pp. 44-66. Cambridge: MIT Press, 1990.
Includes thoughts of Vietnam-born American filmmaker Trinh T. Minh-ha.

2884. "Jodie Foster." In *The Media in Your Life: An Introduction to Mass Communication,* edited by Jean Folkerts, Stephen Lacy, and Lucinda Davenport, p. 191. Boston: Allyn and Bacon, 1998.
Briefly describes Foster's acting career.

2885. Jones, Linda. "Through the Looking-Cel...er, Glass." *Animation World.* December 1996, 4 pp.
Describes her career selling animation cels. Linda Jones is the daughter of renowned animator Chuck Jones.

2886. Jordan, Orma. "Kentucky Babe." *Photoplay.* October 1916, p. 41.

Profiles Margery Wilson, a Kentuckian actress who starred in D. W. Griffith's "Intolerance" (1916).

2887. Kafi-Akua, Afua. "Ayoka Chenzira: Filmmaker." *SAGE: A Scholarly Journal on Black Women.* Spring 1987, pp. 69-72.

2888. Kear, Lynn. *Agnes Moorehead: A Bio-Bibliography.* Westport, Connecticut: Greenwood Press, 1992. 320 pp.
       Discusses life and career of actress Moorehead; includes biography, listings of her work, synopses, casts and credits, review excerpts, miscellaneous information.

2889. Kennedy, Madge. *A Darling of the Twenties: The Autobiographies of Madge Kennedy.* Vestal, New York: Vestal Press, 1990.
       Tells story of an "unknown" actress of the silent and early sound screen, with filmography, correspondence, many photographs.

2890. Keyes, Evelyn. *Scarlett O'Hara's Younger Sister: My Lively Life in and Out of Hollywood.* Secaurus, New Jersey: Lyle Stuart, 1977.
       Autobiography of Hollywood actress Keyes.

2891. Klein, Atom. "La Verne Harding: Hollywood's First Woman Animator." *Animation Journal.* Spring 1994, pp. 54-67.
       Describes career of Harding, who in 1932, became the first female animator in Hollywood with Walter Lantz at Universal Studios; tells about Harding's newspaper comic strip, "Cynical Susie."

2892. Kobal, John. *Rita Hayworth: The Time, the Place and the Woman.* New York: W.W. Norton, 1977.
       Profiles Hollywood movie star of the World War II era.

2893. Kotlarz, Irene. "Imagery of Desire." *Sight and Sound.* October 1992, p. 27.
       On women animators.

2894. Krasilovsky, Alexis. *Women Behind the Camera: Conversations with Camerawomen.* Westport, Connecticut: Praeger Publishers, 1997.
       Shows how the number of Hollywood camerawomen quadrupled in previous 15 years; presents interviews with 23 of them, most of whom were pioneers: Brianne Murphy, Juliana Wang, Estelle Kirsh, Emiko Omori, Judy Irola, etc.

2895. Kuhn, Annette, ed. *Queen of the 'B's: Ida Lupino Behind the Camera.* Westport, Connecticut: Greenwood Press, 1995. 208 pp.
       Profiles Ida Lupino, actress who in the late 1940s, turned writer, producer, and director in her own independent production company; her films took uncompromising stands on controversial subject matter.

2896. Lacayo, Richard. "Women in Hollywood." *People*. Spring 1991, pp. 35-43.

2897. Lamour, Dorothy, as told to Dick McInnes. *My Side of the Road*. Englewood Cliffs, New Jersey: Prentice-Hall, 1980.
       Autobiography of actress Lamour.

2898. Leaming, Barbara. *If This Was Happiness: A Biography of Rita Hayworth*. New York: Viking, 1989.

2899. Leigh, Janet. *There Really Was a Hollywood*. Garden City, New York: Doubleday, 1984.
       Autobiography of Hollywood star.

2900. Loy, Myrna and James Kotsilibus-Davis. *Myrna Loy: Being and Becoming*. New York: Knopf, 1987.
       Autobiography of Hollywood star Loy.

2901. McCreadie, Marsha. *The American Movie Goddess*. New York: Wiley, 1973.

2902. McCreadie, Marsha. *The Women Who Write the Movies: From Frances Marion to Nora Ephron*. New York: Birch Lane Press, 1994. 241 pp.
       Points out that there are 1,500 male and only 33 women screenwriters; gives history with background on silent era writers Adela Rogers St. Johns, Jeannie Macpherson, June Mathis, and Frances Marion, through golden era (Catherine Turney, Dorothy Parker, Anita Loos) and contemporary times (Callis Khouri, Nora Ephron, Leslie Dixon); provides examples of scripts.

2903. McCready, Sam. *Lucille Lortel: A Bio Bibliography*. Westport, Connecticut: Greenwood Press, 1993. 304 pp.

2904. MacDonald, Scott. *A Critical Cinema: Interviews with Independent Filmmakers*. Berkeley: University of California Press, 1988. 448 pp.
       Includes Carolee Schneeman, Beth B, Vivienne Dick, Babette Mangolte, and Diana Barrie.

2905. MacDonald, Scott. *A Critical Cinema 2: Interviews With Independent Filmmakers*. Berkeley: University of California Press, 1992.

2906. MacDonald, Scott. "*Damned If You Don't*: An Interview with Su Friedrich." *Afterimage*. May 1988, pp. 6-10.
       Interviews filmmaker who directed ten films from 1978-1991.

2907. MacDonald, Scott. "Interview with Lizzie Borden." *Feminist Studies*. Summer 1989, pp. 327-345.
       Uses film "Working Girls" as catalyst for a discussion of issues relating to the sex industry.

2908. MacDonald, Scott. "Yoko Ono: Ideas on Film (Interview/Scripts)." *Film Quarterly*. Fall 1989, pp. 2-23.

Interviews Ono about her experimental filmmaking.

2909. McEvilley, Thomas. "Carolee Schneeman." *Artforum*. April 1985, p. 92.
Controversial filmmaker.

2910. McGilligan, Pat. *Backstory 1: Interviews with Screenwriters of Hollywood's Golden Age*. Berkeley: University of California Press, 1986. 390 pp.
Includes Frances Goodrich.

2911. McGilligan, Pat. *Backstory 2: Interviews with Screenwriters of the 1940s and 1950s*. Berkeley: University of California Press, 1991. 356 pp.
Includes Betty Comden.

2912. McGilligan, Pat. *Backstory 3: Interviews with Screenwriters of the 1960s*. Berkeley: University of California Press, 1997. 464 pp.
Chronicles lives of famous Hollywood screenwriters, including Harriet Frank, Terry Southern, etc.

2913. McHenry, S. "Odd Couplings: Sex, Smiles and Savvy from Two Young Filmmakers." *Ms.* October 1986, pp. 14-16.

2914. Machiorlatti, J. "Julie Dash as a Postmodern Griot: The Theory of an Integrative and Mobile Aesthetic." Paper presented at Speech Communication Association, Miami, Florida, November 1994.
Deals with African American filmmaker.

2915. Macnamara, Paul. *Those Were The Days, My Friend: My Life in Hollywood with David O. Selznick and Others*. Metuchen, New Jersey: Scarecrow Press, 1993. 207 pp.
Tells of this writer, editor, and television producer's work in Hollywood with Selznick, but also Jennifer Jones and Shirley Temple.

2916. Marchetti, Gina and Keith Tishken. "An Interview with Beth and Scott B." *Millennium Film Journal*. Fall/Winter 1981-1982, pp. 158-167.

2917. Margold, William. "The Legends of Erotica." *Gauntlet*. No. 14, 1997, pp. 25-28.
Surveys "people I trusted" to come up with a list of the 25 greatest porn stars, to celebrate the 25th anniversary of the blue industry in 1997.

2918. Markson, Elizabeth W. and Carol A. Taylor. "Real Versus Reel World: Older Women and the Academy Awards." *Women and Therapy*. 14:1-2 (1993), pp. 57-72.
Looks at 1,169 actresses and actors nominated for Oscars, 1927-1928 through 1990; finds women over 39 accounted for only 27 percent of all winners for Best Actress, whereas men in the same age category won Best Actor 67 percent of the time.

2919. Martineau, Barbara H. "Women and Cartoon Animation, or Why Women Don't Make Cartoons, or Do They?" In *The American Animated Cartoon: A Critical Anthology*, edited by Gerald and Danny Pearcy. New York: Dutton, 1980.

2920. Maslin, Janet. "Audrey Hepburn: Farewell to the Swan." *New York Times*. January 31, 1993, p. II-11.
    A perspective on actress who died January 20, 1993.

2921. Maslin, Janet. "Nell." *New York Times*. December 14, 1994, p. C-15.
    Reviews first film from Jodie Foster's company, Egg.

2922. Mayne, Judith. *Directed by Dorothy Arzner*. Bloomington: Indiana University Press, 1995. 240 pp.
    Billed as the first major study of "the only woman film director who survived and flourished in Hollywood of the 1930s and 1940s."

2923. Michelson, Annette. "Yvonne Rainer, Part One: The Dancer and the Dance." *Artforum*. 12:5 (1974), pp. 57-63.
    Deals with filmmaker who regularly questions the boundaries of political and mainstream representation, using autobiographical accounts, and deals with issues in women's lives.

2924. Millsapps, Jan L. "Maya Deren, Imagist." *Literature/Film Quarterly*. 14:1 (1986), pp. 22-31.

2925. Modleski, Tania. "The Films of Diana Barrie." *Wide Angle*. 7:1-2 (1985), pp. 62-67.

2926. Modleski, Tania. "Our Heroes Have Sometimes Been Cowgirls -- An Interview with Maggie Greenwals." *Film Quarterly*. Winter 1995-1996.

2927. Molt, Cynthia M. *Vivien Leigh: A Bio-Bibliography*. Westport, Connecticut: Greenwood Press, 1992. 352 pp.
    Gives biographical information on actress Vivien Leigh's life and career; listings of performances, discography, filmography, and chronology.

2928. Monet, Melissa. "Phallic Fallacies and Ball Blunders." *Gauntlet*. No. 14, 1997, pp. 10-12.
    Adult performer and pornographer Melissa Monet talks about the myths surrounding adult performances.

2929. Morella, Joe and Edward Z. Epstein. *Rita: The Life of Rita Hayworth*. New York: Delacorte, 1983.

2930. Moritz, William. "Mary Ellen Bute: Seeing Sound." *Animation World*. May 1996, 5 pp.
    Profiles career of Mary Ellen Bute, pioneer animator who made 11 abstract films between 1934-1959.

2931. Moss, Robert. *The Films of Carol Reed*. New York: Columbia University Press, 1987. 312 pp.
    Film director Carol Reed.

2932. *Movieline*. April 1997.
    Special issue on Hollywood women with list of 100 best female film characters, interviews and profiles with "Hollywood darlings."

2933. Myers, Louis B. "Marie Menken Herself." *Film Culture*. Summer 1967, pp. 37-39.
    Profiles underground filmmaker who was at the center of the New York avant-garde film colony.

2934. "Nancy Beiman." *Cartoonist PROfiles*. June 1982, pp. 53-58.
    Features animator at Zanders Animation Parlour.

2935. Nardini, Gloria. "Is It True Love? Or Not? Patterns of Ethnicity and Gender in Nancy Savoca." *VIA: Voices in Italian Americana*. Spring 1991, pp. 9-17.
    Discusses work of Nancy Savoca, women-identified, Italian-American-centered, personal filmmaker. See analysis of one of her films in Dale Kutzera's "In *Dogfight*, Cruel Wager Leads to Love," *American Cinematographer* (September 1991, pp. 26-28).

2936. Neal, Patricia. *As I Am: An Autobiography*. New York: Simon & Schuster, 1988.
    Hollywood actress Neal.

2937. Nicholson, David. "Conflict and Complexity: Filmmaker Kathleen Collins." *Black Film Review*. Summer 1986, pp. 11-17.

2938. Ono, Yoko. "On Yoko Ono." *Film Culture*. Winter/Spring 1970, pp. 32-33.
    Reflects on her experimental filmmaking, started well before she met John Lennon.

2939. Paris, Barry. *Audrey Hepburn*. New York: G.P. Putnam's Sons, 1996. 464 pp.
    Portrays life of Hollywood star Audrey Hepburn -- her underground activities as a child courier for the Dutch Resistance, chorus line work in post-war London, Broadway success in "Gigi" and first movie, "Roman Holiday," work with UNICEF, death from cancer at age 63.

2940. Parish, James R. and Vincent Terrace. *The Complete Actors' Television Credits, 1948-1988, 2nd Ed. Volume 2: Actresses*. Metuchen, New Jersey: Scarecrow Press, 1990. 447 pp.
    Chronicles the individual performances of 1,739 actresses from January 1948 to August 1989, in network, syndicated, and cable programming.

2941. Park, Ida May. "The Motion Picture Director." In *Careers for Women*, edited by Catherine Filene, pp. 335-337. Boston: Houghton Mifflin, 1924.

By a pioneering woman director in the 1910s and 1920s.

2942. Patterson, Wendy. "Far from Documentary: An Interview with Jill Godmilow." *Afterimage*. February 1986, pp. 4-7.
Interviews director of about a dozen films, including "Far from Poland."

2943. Pederson, Lucille M. *Katherine Cornell: A Bio-Bibliography*. Westport, Connecticut: Greenwood Press, 1993. 264 pp.
Summarizes life and career of actress Cornell, known mainly for stage performances, although she also appeared on radio, television, and in films; including credits, casts, synopses, brief histories, commentaries, and reviews.

2944. Penley, Constance. "Documentary/Documentation." *Camera Obscura*. Spring/Summer 1985, pp. 85-161.
Includes women, such as Academy Award winner Barbara Kopple, and others.

2945. Penley, Constance and Andrew Ross. "Interview with Trinh T. Minh-ha." *Camera Obscura*. Spring-Summer 1985, pp. 86-111.
Discusses Trinh T. Minh-ha's life (born in Vietnam in 1970, studied in U.S. and Senegal) and filmmaking.

2946. Pierce, Arthur and Douglas Swarthout. *Jean Arthur: A Bio-Bibliography*. Westport, Connecticut: Greenwood, 1990. 288 pp.
Profiles actress Arthur's career in biography, filmography, and bibliography; Arthur was a major star of the 1930s with a list of hits to her credit.

2947. Powell, Jane. *The Girl Next Door...and How She Grew*. New York: William Morrow, 1988.
Autobiography of Hollywood star Powell.

2948. *Prevue*.
No. 55 -- *All-Woman Issue* includes material on Brooke Shields, Jessica Lange, Jane Seymour, Jennifer Jason Leigh, Cynthia Sikes, Tanya Roberts, and Jamie Lee Curtis.
No. 63 -- *All-Woman Issue* with interviews and profiles on Meryl Streep, Kathleen Turner, Wendy O. Williams, Caroline Munro, Glenn Close, Mariel Hemingway, and Sylvia Kristel.
No. 69 -- *All-Woman Issue* includes "The Witches of Eastwick," Madonna, Mariel Hemingway, Nancy Allen, Diane Lane, Phoebe Cates, Kim Basinger, Elizabeth Taylor, Valerie Perrine, Ann-Margaret, Ally Sheedy, Lisa Bonet, and Meg Ryan.
No. 75 -- *Superwoman of Cinema* special includes Alison Doody, Julia Roberts, Jane Fonda, etc.
No. 79 -- *All-Woman Extravaganza* includes material on Brinke Stevens, Jane Fonda, Kathleen Turner, Sally Kirkland, Phoebe Cates, Theresa Russell, Traci Lords, Glenn Close, Kelly McGillis, Jodie Foster, Meryl Streep, Shirley MacLaine, and Nancy Allen.

No. 83 -- Pin-Up, *All-Woman Issue* on Traci Lords, Julia Roberts, Demi Moore, Glenn Close, Suzie Owens, Sherily Fenn, Kathy Ireland, and Teri Garr.

No. 87 -- *All-Woman Issue* includes Christina Applegate, Traci Lords, Jodie Foster, Bobbie Bresee, Whitney Houston, Michelle Pfeiffer, Cynthia Rothrock, Kim Basinger, Winona Ryder, and Rebecca DeMornay.

No. 90 -- *All-Woman Issue* includes Traci Lords, Michelle Pfeiffer, Geena Davis, Kathleen Turner, Sharon Stone, Bridget Fonda, Suzanne Ager, Jessica Lange, Mary Stuart Masterson, and Betty Page.

No. 91 -- *Pin-Up Special 1* includes glamour girls and their creators Rhonda Shear, Olivia DeBerardinis, Ginger Lynn Allen, Rene Russo, and Tia Carrere.

No. 92 -- *Pin-Up Special 2* includes "Sheena," She-Cats of the pulps, Tempest Storm, Holly Hunter, Traci Lords, Maria Ford, and Michelle Pfeiffer.

2949. Priestley, Joanna. "Creating a Healing Mythology: The Art of Faith Hubley." *Animation Journal*. Spring 1994, pp. 23-31.

Profiles Hubley, who with her husband John and singly since his death in 1977, has produced and directed 37 animated films; includes a list of her works.

2950. Province, John. "The Virginia Davis Interview." *Hogan's Alley*. No. 2, 1995, pp. 106-113.

Interviews star of Walt Disney's *Alice in Cartoonland* series of the 1920s.

2951. Rainey, Buck. *Sweethearts of the Sage: Biographies and Filmographies of 258 Actresses Appearing in Western Movies*. Jefferson, North Carolina: McFarland, 1992. 652 pp.

Includes any actress who appeared in at least eight "Western" films; divided by "Path Finders," before 1920; "Trail Blazers," 1920s; "Pioneers," 1930s, 1940s; and "Homesteaders," post-1940.

2952. Rebello, Stephen. "Jodie Foster: Nice Girls Do Finish First." *Cosmopolitan*. April 1996, p. 176.

2953. Regester, Charlene. "Hazel Scott and Lena Horne: African-American Divas, Feminists, and Political Activists." *Popular Culture Review*. February 1996, pp. 81-95.

Shows how Scott and Horne would not compromise their views on prejudice.

2954. Reynaud, Berenice. "Chris Choy et Renee Tajma." *Cahiers du Cinéma*. June 1990, p. 61.

2955. Reynolds, Debbie, with David P. Columbia. *Debbie: My Life*. New York: William Morrow, 1988.

Autobiography of Hollywood star Reynolds.

2956. Rice, Susan. "Shirley Clarke: Image and Images." *Take One*. 3:2 (1972), pp. 20-

21.
American filmmaker.

2957. Ringgold, Gene. *The Films of Rita Hayworth.* Secaucus, New Jersey: Citadel, 1974.

2958. Riva, Maria. *Marlene Dietrich.* 2 Volumes. New York: Random House, 1993. 1,441 pp.
Dietrich's daughter chronicles her mother's life and Hollywood in its heyday; Dietrich's travels, relationships, alcoholism, performances, etc.

2959. Rivadue, Barry. *Lee Remick: A Bio-Bibliography.* Westport, Connecticut: Greenwood Press, 1995. 248 pp.
Chronicles actress Remick's early successes in films ("Anatomy of a Murder," "Days of Wine and Roses") and later rewarding opportunities in television; includes entries for all her performances.

2960. Rivadue, Barry. *Mary Martin: A Bio-Bibliography.* Westport, Connecticut: Greenwood Press, 1991. 256 pp.
Includes biographical information on Mary Martin's career in screen, stage, broadcasting, and recordings; chronology; listing of awards; annotated bibliography, and archival information.

2961. Robertson, Pamela. "'The Kinda Comedy That Imitates Me': Mae West's Identification with the Feminist Camp." *Cinema Journal.* Winter 1993, pp. 57-72.

2962. Robinson, Alice M. *Betty Comden and Adolph Green: A Bio-Bibliography.* Westport, Connecticut: Greenwood Press, 1993. 384 pp.
Deals with this team, who for more than 50 years, collaborated on skits, musicals, revues, and films; includes biography, chronology, cast lists, plot summaries, reviews, and commentaries.

2963. Royce, Brenda S. *Donna Reed: A Bio-Bibliography.* Westport, Connecticut: Greenwood Press, 1990. 192 pp.
Details life and career of actress called "America's favorite mother"; contains brief biography, detailed examination of her work, listing of reviews of her films, awards and nominations, chronology, and annotated bibliography.

2964. Royce, Brenda S. *Lauren Bacall: A Bio-Bibliography.* Westport, Connecticut: Greenwood Press, 1992. 312 pp.
Provides critical guide to actress Bacall's career, beginning with "To Have and Have Not" in 1944; includes biographical sketch, cast and production credits, plot synopses, review excerpts of all radio, film, and stage appearances, annotated bibliography.

2965. Russell, Jane. *Jane Russell, My Path and My Detours: An Autobiography.* New York: F. Watts, 1985.
Provides glimpses of her Hollywood career.

2966. Russell, Rosalind and Chris Chase. *Life Is a Banquet*. New York: Random House, 1977.
>   Autobiography of Hollywood actress.

2967. Sanders, Richard, ed. "Kathryn Bigelow -- Director." *People* (Special issue: "Women, Sex and Power"). Spring 1991, p. 85.
>   About filmmaker.

2968. Sargeant, Winthrop. "The Cult of the Love Goddess in America." *Life*. November 10, 1947, pp. 80-96.

2969. Schultz, Margie. *Irene Dunne. A Bio-Bibliography*. Westport, Connecticut: Greenwood, 1991. 336 pp.
>   Describes varied career of "First Lady of Hollywood," who excelled in dramas, comedies, and musicals on screen, TV, stage, radio, and recordings and was alternate delegate to the United Nations. Includes biographical overview, annotated bibliography, and photographs.

2970. Schwichtenberg, Cathy. "Madonna's Postmodern Feminism: Bringing the Margins to the Center." *Southern Communication Journal*. Winter 1992, pp. 120-131.

2971. Segal, Steve. "The Surreal World of Sally Cruikshank." *Animato!* Winter 1992, pp. 23-27.
>   Discusses movie titles, animation industry, her career as animator.

2972. Segrave, Kerry and Linda Martin. *The Post-Feminist Hollywood Actress: Biographies and Filmographies of Stars Born After 1939*. Jefferson, North Carolina: McFarland, 1990. 300 pp.
>   Contains profiles of 50 actresses of contemporary Hollywood, each entry containing a brief biography, detailed filmography, and a list of popular magazine sources on the actress at hand.

2973. Shirkani, K. D. "Serving in Silence: Many Talented Femme DPs Not Reflected in ASC's Ranks." *Daily Variety*. March 6, 1998, pp. A2, A10.
>   Discusses women film directors; states only 2 percent of members of American Society of Cinematographers are women.

2974. Sigall, Martha. "Phyllis Craig: A Woman of Many Colors (1929-1997)." *Animation World Magazine*. July 1997, pp. 87-90.
>   Profiles animation pioneer.

2975. Silver, Joan M. "Independent Charts Her Success." *American Film*. May 1989, pp. 22-27.
>   Recounts Silver's success in filmmaking with hits such as "Hester Street" (1975), "Between the Lines" (1977), "Crossing Delancey" (1988). See Grace Lichtenstein's review of "Hester Street" in *New York Times* (October 15, 1975, p. 34).

2976. Simon, Libby. "Women Who Made Animation History." *Animation Magazine.* May 1996, pp. 55, 60.
Relates experiences and observations after recording 18 histories -- starting with Martha Sigall -- that are to be archived at UCLA Special Arts Library. Undertaken by Women in Animation, the project is meant to record the oral histories of important women in animation.

2977. Singer, Marilyn. "The Originals: Women in Art." *Film Library Quarterly.* 11:3 (1978), pp. 17-26.

2978. Singer, Michael. "From the Director's Chair: An Interview with Amy Heckerling." In *Film Directors: A Complete Guide*, edited by Michael Singer, pp. 23-33. Beverly Hills, California: Lone Eagle, 1987.
Discusses Hollywood writer and filmmaker, Amy Heckerling, whose credits include "Look Who's Talking" and "Clueless."

2979. Singer, Michael. "Interview with Martha Coolidge." In *Film Directors: A Complete Guide*, edited by Michael Singer, pp. 6-9. Beverly Hills, California: Lone Eagle Press, 1984.

2980. Sischy, Ingrid. "Interview with Jodie Foster." *Interview.* October 1991, pp. 79-84.
Hollywood actress and director.

2981. Slide, Anthony. *Lois Weber. The Director Who Lost Her Way in History.* Westport, Connecticut: Greenwood Press, 1996. 192 pp.
Documents career of Lois Weber as a film director from 1908 through 1934; points out the all-but-ignored Weber was a genuine auteur, directing, writing, and starring in films. Weber often used film to give her views on topics such as abortion, birth control, racial intolerance, or capital punishment.

2982. Smelik, Anneke. "Uit de Doos van Pandora -- Interview met Laura Mulvey" (Out of Pandora's Box -- Interview with Laura Mulvey). *Tijdschrift voor Vrouwenstudies.* 12:4 (1991), pp. 531-536.

2983. Smith, Sharon. *Women Who Make Movies.* New York: Hopkinson and Blake, 1975.
Includes historical and contemporary (to 1970s) assessments.

2984. Smith, Valerie. "The Black Woman Independent: Representing Race and Gender." *The New American Filmmaker Series 34.* New York: Whitney Museum of American Art, December 1986.

2985. Smith, Valerie. "Reconstituting the Image: The Emergent Black Woman Director." *Callaloo.* Fall 1988, pp. 709-719.

2986. Souhami, Diana. *Greta and Cecil.* New York: HarperCollins, 1994. 271 pp.
Relates "extraordinary" relationship between actress Greta Garbo and Cecil Beaton, the Hollywood photographer who immortalized her image.

2987. Spada, James. *More Than a Woman: An Intimate Biography of Bette Davis*. New York: Bantam Books, 1994. 514 pp.
    Reveals her self doubts about her Hollywood career, extramarital affairs, insecure family background.

2988. Springer, Gregory. "Barbara Hammer: The Leading Lesbian Behind the Lens." *Advocate*. February 7, 1980, pp. 29, 35.

2989. Starr, Cecile. "Claudia Weill: From Shoestring to Studio." *New York Times*. August 6, 1978, p. 11.
    Discusses film work of Claudia Weill, who has directed films ("The Other Half of the Sky," 1974; "Girlfriends," 1978, "It's My Turn," 1980, etc.) and television series ("thirtysomething").

2990. Steinem, Gloria. "Women in the Dark -- Of Sex Goddesses, Abuse, and Dreams." *Ms.* January-February 1991, pp. 35-37.
    Tells how Rita Hayworth and other sex symbols were sexually abused as children.

2991. Tierney, Gene, with Mickey Herskowitz. *Self-Portrait*. New York: Wyden Books, 1978.
    Autobiography of film star Gene Tierney.

2992. Tucker, Sophie. *Some of These Days: The Autobiography of Sophie Tucker*. Garden City, New York: Doubleday, 1946.
    On famous actress, Sophie Tucker.

2993. Turner, Lana. *Lana: The Lady, the Legend, the Truth*. New York: E.P. Dutton, 1982.
    Autobiography of Hollywood actress Turner.

2994. Unterbrink, Mary. *Funny Women: American Comediennes, 1860-1985*. Jefferson, North Carolina: McFarland, 1987. 283 pp.

2995. Van Doren, Mamie, with Art Aveilhe. *Playing the Field*. New York: G.P. Putnam's Sons, 1987.
    Autobiography of Hollywood actress Van Doren.

2996. Vaughan, Don. "From Reel to Real: A Conversation with Annie Sprinkle." *Gauntlet*. No. 14, 1997, pp. 13-19.
    Interviews adult film actress/stripper/prostitute, Annie Sprinkle, on sex films, Andrea Dworkin, censorship.

2997. Vaughan, Don. "Words That Arouse: An Interview with Cathy Tavel." *Gauntlet*. No. 14, 1997, pp. 41-47.
    Writer of more than 100 adult movie scripts tells how she became involved in pornography business.

2998. Weber, Lois. "How I Became a Motion Picture Director." *Static Flashes*. April 24, 1915, p. 8.
    Gives personal account of how she became one of the very first women film directors.

2999. Whitney Museum of American Art. *Yoko Ono: Objects, Films*. New York: Whitney Museum of American Art, 1989.

3000. Wilson, Margery. *I Found My Way: An Autobiography*. Philadelphia, Pennsylvania: J. B. Lippincott, 1956.
    Recounts her career as film actress in the 1910s, and producer, director, and actress in her own films of the 1920s.

3001. Winters, Shelley. *Shelley, Also Known as Shirley*. New York: William Morrow, 1980.
    Autobiography of Hollywood star Winters.

3002. "Women Filmmakers." In *1990 Asian American International Film Festival*. New York, June 28-July 3, 1990. New York: Asia Cine Vision, pp. 14-15, 28-31; i-xxvii.

3003. "Women in Int'l Sales: Survey." *Variety*. May 6-12, 1996, pp. C-10-C-16.
    Series of articles on women in international film sales; includes Beverly Walker, "Femmes Click in Sales Shtick," pp. C-11, C-14.

3004. Woods, Jeannie M. *Maureen Stapleton: A Bio-Bibliography*. Westport, Connecticut: Greenwood Press, 1992. 192 pp.
    Profiles life and career of Academy Award actress Stapleton with biographical narrative, chronology, filmography, summaries of stage and television appearances, annotated bibliography, appendix of awards, and index.

Print Media

3005. Abernathy, Barbara T. and Mary Trimble. *Rose O'Neill*. N.p.: Privately printed, 1968.
    Story of early cartoonist who created "Kewpie Dolls."

3006. Abramson, Phyllis L. *Sob Sister Journalism*. Westport, Connecticut: Greenwood Press, 1990. 144 pp.
    Analyzes and profiles women journalists of the post-yellow journalism era who engaged in tear-producing, emotional reportage: Winifred Black, Dorothy Dix, Nixola Greeley-Smith, Ada Patterson, Evelyn Nesbit.

3007. "Alice Dunnigan, Noted News Woman, Dies at 77." *Jet*. May 23, 1983, p. 42.

3008. Alley, Patricia W. "Hokinson and Hollander: Female Cartoonists and American Culture." In *Women's Comic Visions*, edited by June Sochen, pp. 115-138. Detroit, Michigan: Wayne State University, 1991.

3009. Andsager, Julie L. "Perceptions of Credibility of Male and Female Syndicated Political Columnists." *Journalism Quarterly*. Autumn 1990, pp. 485-491.
    Uses college students in experiment; shows there was little prejudice against female versus male bylines in political interpretative columns.

3010. "ANPA Issues 1990 Report on Women and Minority Employment at Newspapers." *Media Report to Women*. July-August 1990, pp. 3-4.

3011. Applegate, Roberta. "Homemakers: This Editor Likes You." *Miami Herald*. March 10, 1964, p. C-1.
    Concerns Margaret Cousins, magazine editor.

3012. Arfuso, Dawn. "Diversity Keeps Newspaper up with the Times." *Personnel Journal*. July 1995, pp. 30-41.
    Shows how the Seattle Times Co.'s commitment to diversity is reflected in a workforce comprised of 33 percent women.

3013. Armitage, Shelley. *Kewpies and Beyond: The World of Rosie O'Neill*. Jackson: University of Mississippi Press, 1994. 227 pp.
    Biography of very successful illustrator and cartoonist who created the "Kewpies" and titans.

3014. "ASNE Report: Gay, Lesbian Journalists Concerned over Newsroom Roles, Coverage." *Media Report to Women*. July-August 1990, pp. 4-5.
    Reports on survey of 205 newspaper people.

3015. Astor, David. "A Director of Comic Art Looks at Her Job." *Editor and Publisher*. May 10, 1986, pp. 32-33.
    Sarah Gillespie of United Media.

3016. Austin, Mary. *Earth Horizon*. Boston: Houghton Mifflin, 1928.
    Gives information on her journalistic work, including on women's magazines.

3017. Bagge, Peter. "Aline Kominsky-Crumb." *Comics Journal*. December 1990, pp. 50-73.
    Profiles underground comics artist.

3018. Barlow, Marjorie D. *Notes on Woman Printers in Colonial America and the United States, 1639-1975*. New York: The Hroswitha Club, 1976. 89 pp.
    Lists alphabetically state by state. From the introduction: "In addition to the many women who owned and published newspapers, others were employed as printers, largely because they were deft, sober, and reliable, and their labor was cheap.... By 1889, the typographical union in New York boasted a membership of 200 women printers."

3019. Barnes, Kathleen. *Trial by Fire: A Woman Correspondent's Journey to the*

Frontline. New York: Thunder's Mouth Press, 1990. 230 pp.
Autobiography of former freelancer who covered Rome and war-torn Belfast and, as an ABC News correspondent, the Philippines.

3020. Baumgold, Julie. "Charlotte, Super Reporter." *New York*. October 6, 1969, p. 41.
On Charlotte Curtis.

3021. Baxandall, Rosalyn F. *Words on Fire: The Life and Writing of Elizabeth Gurley Flynn*. New Brunswick, New Jersey: Rutgers University Press, 1987. 320 pp.
Profiles defender of free speech, an organizer of the American Civil Liberties Union, chair of the Communist Party of America Elizabeth Gurley Flynn; includes examples of her writings, including columns for the *Daily Worker*.

3022. Beasley, Maurine H. "Historiographical Essay, Women in Journalism: Contributors to Male Experience or Voices of Feminine Expression?" *American Journalism*. Winter 1990, pp. 39-54.
Reviews literature on history of women in journalism to see where it fits in the framework of the journalism historiography set forth by David Sloan.

3023. Beasley, Maurine H. "Mary Clemmer Ames: A Victorian Woman Journalist." *Hayes Historical Journal*. Spring 1978, pp. 57-63.

3024. Bederman, Gail. "'Civilization,' the Decline of Middle-Class Manliness, and Ida B. Wells' Antilynching Campaign (1892-94)." *Radical History Review*. Winter 1992.
Provides Wells' critique of mainstream ideas about "civilization."

3025. Bennion, Sherilyn C. *Equal to the Occasion: Women Editors of the Nineteenth Century West*. Reno: University of Nevada Press, 1990. 225 pp.
Profiles two dozen pioneer women editors of the West, beginning with Sarah M. Clarke and her *Contra Costa*, established in Oakland, California, in 1854; appendix lists the 230 women editors of the West, 1854-1900.

3026. Bilgore, Ellen. "Charlotte Curtis: She Did It Her Way." *Harper's Bazaar*. March 1981, p. 72.
Profiles *New York Times* journalist Curtis.

3027. Blankenhorn, Heber. "The Grandma of the Muckrakers." *American Mercury*. 12 (1927), pp. 87-93.
Credits Anne Royall, a Washington editor-publisher from 1832-1854, as early investigative reporter.

3028. Booker, Edna L. *News Is My Job: A Correspondent in War-Torn China*. New York: Macmillan Co., 1940.

3029. Boycott, Rosie. "Sex and Feminism." *Daily Mail* (London). April 20, 1996, p. 36.
On Gloria Steinem.

3030. Boyd, Robert. "Shary Flenniken." *Comics Journal*. November 1991, pp. 54-78, 81-83.

Profiles cartoonist of "Trots and Bonnie" published in *National Lampoon*.

3031. Boyd, Robert. "State of Minicomics, Part Three." *Comics Journal*. September 1996, pp. 39-44.

Interviews young underground comix publisher/artist, Jessica Abel.

3032. Braden, Maria. *She Said What? Interviews with Women Newspaper Columnists*. Lexington: University Press of Kentucky, 1993. 208 pp.

Includes interviews with Erma Bombeck, Jane Brody, Mona Charen, Merlene Davis, Georgia A. Geyer, Dorothy Gilliam, Ellen Goodman, Molly Ivins, Mary McGrory, Judith Martin (Miss Manners), Joyce Maynard, Anna Quindlen, and Jane B. Quinn.

3033. Bradley, Patricia. "Media Leaders and Personal Ideology: Margaret Cousins and the Women's Service Magazines." *Journalism History*. Summer 1995, pp. 79-83.

Biographical sketch of Margaret Cousins, former managing editor of *McCall's*, fiction editor of *Ladies' Home Journal*, and editor at Doubleday.

3034. Brandon, Barbara. "'Where I'm Coming From.'" *Cartoonist PROfiles*. December 1992, pp. 10-17.

Interviews cartoonist Barbara Brandon about her strip, "Where I'm Coming From."

3035. Brantley, Will, ed. *Conversations with Pauline Kael*. Jackson: University Press of Mississippi, 1996. 216 pp.

Brings together roughly half of film critic Kael's published interviews; provides perspectives on her aesthetics, politics, and perceptions of critiquing.

3036. "Brenda Starr. A Pretty Nose for News." *The World of Comic Art*. Fall 1966, pp. 20-23.

Describes creator of "Brenda Starr" comic strip, Dale Messick.

3037. Brogan, Madeline. "The First Lady." *Cartoonist PROfiles*. December 1993, pp. 28-35.

Self-profile by Brogan, creator of comic strip, "The First Lady."

3038. Brown, John Mason. "Helen Hokinson." *Saturday Review*. December 10, 1949, pp. 81+.

Briefly sketches career of gag cartoonist Hokinson.

3039. Bruere, Martha B. and Mary R. Beard. *Laughing Their Way: Women's Humor in America*. New York: Macmillan, 1934.

Includes women humorists such as Dorothy Parker, Anita Loos, and Margaret Widdemer, and cartoonists Lou Rogers, Rose O'Neill, Helen Hokinson, and Nina Allender.

3040. Buranelli, Vincent. "The Myth of Anna Zenger." *William and Mary Quarterly.* 3rd series, 13 (1956), pp. 160-169.

Challenges Kent Cooper's book on Anna Zenger; claims she was merely a courageous wife who ran her husband's paper, *New York Weekly Journal,* while he was in jail.

3041. Burbey, Mark. "The Fine Art of Comics -- Carol Tyler Interview." *Comics Journal.* June 1991, pp. 90-102.

3042. Burt, Elizabeth V. "Rediscovering Zona Gale, Journalist." *American Journalism.* Fall 1995, pp. 444-461.

3043. Capper, Charles. *Margaret Fuller: An American Romantic Life. Vol. 1: The Private Years.* New York: Oxford University Press, 1993. 456 pp.

Deals with American pioneer journalist.

3044. Capper, Charles. "Margaret Fuller as Cultural Reformer: The Conversations in Boston." *American Quarterly.* 39 (1987), pp. 509-528.

3045. Carpenter, Liz. *Getting Better All the Time.* New York: Simon and Schuster, 1987. 304 pp.

Details her life as Texas journalist and later press secretary to Lady Bird Johnson.

3046. Carpenter, Liz. *Ruffles and Flourishes: The Warm and Tender Story of a Simple Girl Who Found Adventure in the White House.* Garden City, New York: Doubleday, 1970. 341 pp.

On Lady Bird Johnson's press secretary.

3047. "Cathy." *Cartoonist PROfiles.* June 1977, pp. 34-36.

Profiles Cathy Guisewite, creator of "Cathy" comic strip.

3048. Chase, Michelle. "Visiting *Times* Columnist Wade Pays Price for Gender Warfare." *Iowa Journalist.* Spring 1996, p. 19.

Betsy Wade, one of seven plaintiffs in a 1970s' class action discrimination lawsuit against *The New York Times,* claims she is "in exile" at the *Times* because of her action.

3049. Childers, Kim W., Jean Chance, and Kristin Herzog. "Sexual Harassment of Women Journalists." *Journalism and Mass Communication Quarterly.* Autumn 1996, pp. 559-581.

Reports that in a survey of 227 women newspaper journalists, more than 60 percent believed sexual harassment is "at least somewhat a problem" for women journalists; more than one-third said it was a problem for them.

3050. Clark, Anne B. "My Dear Mrs. Ames: A Study of the Life of Suffragist Cartoonist and Birth Control Reformer Blanche Ames, 1879-1969." Ph.D. dissertation, University of Massachusetts, 1996.

3051. Coburn, Marcia F. "On the Draw." *Chicago*. August 1984, p. 147+.
       Short biographies of women cartoonists.

3052. Cooper, Kent. *Anna Zenger, Mother of Freedom*. New York: Farrar, Strauss,
       1946.
       Uses quasi-novel approach to depict Anna Zenger as spirit behind
       husband, John Peter Zenger; author was manager of Associated Press.

3053. Craig, Robert L. "The Journalism of Josephine Herbst." *American Journalism*.
       Spring 1994, pp. 116-138.

3054. Crouchett, Lorraine J. "Delilah Beasley, Trail Blazer." *Oakland Heritage Alliance
       News*. Winter 1988-1989, pp. 1-6.
       Discusses African-American journalist Beasley.

3055. Crouchett, Lorraine J. "Delilah Leontium Beasley." In *Black Women in America:
       An Historical Encyclopedia*, Vol. 1, edited by Darlene C. Hine, pp. 98-99. New
       York: Carlson, 1993.

3056. Crouchett, Lorraine J. *Delilah Leontium Beasley: Oakland's Crusading
       Journalist*. El Cerrito, California: Downey Place, 1990.

3057. Daly, Dorothea. "The Flower of American Caricature." *Art News*. March 1940,
       pp. 18+.
       On cartoonist Helen Hokinson.

3058. Dana, Marjorie. *Notes on Woman Printers in Colonial America and The United
       States 1639-1975*. New York: The Hroswitha Club, 1976.
       Biographical sketches and a list of sources.

3059. Dann, Martin E. "Women as Journalists." In *The Black Press 1827-1890: The
       Quest for National Identity*, pp. 61-67. New York: G. P. Putnam's Sons, 1971.

3060. David, Frances. *A Fearful Innocence*. Kent, Ohio: Kent State University Press,
       1981.
       Describes the socialist, utopian community where Frances David lived, her
       efforts to become a foreign correspondent, and her journalistic efforts during
       Spain's Civil War.

3061. David, Elizabeth L. *Lifting as They Climb*. Washington, D.C.: National
       Association of Colored Women, 1933.
       Includes sketches of black women journalists such as Delilah L. Beasley.

3062. Davis, Simone W. "The 'Weak Race' and the Winchester: Political Voices in the
       Pamphlets of Ida B. Wells-Barnett." *Legacy*. 1:2 (1995), pp. 77-97.

3063. Dearborn, Mary. *Queen of Bohemia: The Life of Louise Bryant*. Boston: Houghlin

Mifflin, 1996. 365 pp.

Shows that Louise Bryant was an important journalist apart from her collaboration with John Reed; details her tumultuous life that led to an early death.

3064. Demeter, Richard L. *Printer, Presses and Composing Sticks: Women Printers of the Colonial Period*. New York: Exposition Press, 1979.

3065. Dickey, Jerry. *Sophie Treadwell: A Research and Production Sourcebook*. Westport, Connecticut: Greenwood Press, 1997. 304 pp.

Details career of dramatist and journalist Treadwell who used her works to explore women's personal and social struggles for independence and equality.

3066. Donovan, Katie. "Feminist Enigma." *The Irish Times*. April 9, 1996, Section News Features, p. 9.

Profiles Gloria Steinem.

3067. Dorr, Rheta Childe. *A Woman of Fifty*. New York: Funk & Wagnalls Company, 1924.

Deals with Dorr's work on the *New York Evening Post* and *New York Evening Mail* and her writings on feminism, labor, socialism, and suffrage in *Hampton's*; highlights conflicts between romantic life, work, and domestic responsibilities in context of sexism.

3068. "Dorothy Ahle." *Cartoonist PROfiles*. March 1984, pp. 26-31.

Profiles political cartoonist and caricaturist Dorothy Ahle.

3069. Drewry, John E., ed. *More Post Biographies of Famous Journalists*. Athens: University of Georgia Press, 1947.

Includes Stanley Frank and Paul Sann's "Paper Dolls," pp. 206-217.

3070. Dunnigan, Alice A. *A Black Woman's Experience--From Schoolhouse to White House*. Philadelphia: Dorrance & Company, 1974. 673 pp.

Details her move up from a government clerk to head of the Associated Negro Press Washington bureau in 1947; Dunnigan was the first African-American woman accredited in the capital press corps.

3071. Ebener, Charlotte. *No Facilities for Women*. New York: Alfred Knopf, 1955.

Recounts adventures as a foreign correspondent, especially during China's Civil War; also worked in Europe and other parts of Asia.

3072. Eisele, James. "From 'Justice League' to 'Castle Waiting': An Interview with Linda Medley." *Comics Buyer's Guide*. February 20, 1998, pp. 52, 58.

Interviews comic book story creator, Linda Medley, on how she gets ideas for stories and her career achievements.

3073. Emery, Michael. *On the Front Lines: Following America's Foreign Correspondents Across the Twentieth Century*. Lanham, Maryland: University Press of America, 1995. 356 pp.

Details the story of foreign correspondents, including women such as Marguerite Higgins.

3074. Entrikin, Isabelle W. *Sarah Josepha Hale and Godey's Lady's Book*. Philadelphia: Lancaster Press, 1946.

3075. "Etta Hulme." *Cartoonist PROfiles*. September 1980, pp. 74-79.
Describes political cartoonist for *Fort Worth* (Texas) *Star-Telegram*, Etta Hulme.

3076. Fiedelholtz, Sara. "Editor in Chief Susan Taylor Turns Mirror on Face of Essence." *Magazine Week*. April 20, 1992, pp. 15-16, 18.
Interviews Taylor on what it is like editing a magazine for African-American women.

3077. Flanders, Laura. "The Pundit Spectrum: How Many Women -- and Which Ones?" *Extra!* September/October 1995, p. 6.
Concludes that getting a "hard-hitting, outspoken feminist ... into the front ranks of columnists will not be easy."

3078. Flatow, Gail. "Sexual Harassment in Indiana Daily Newspapers." *Newspaper Research Journal*. Summer 1994, pp. 32-45.
Finds that 68 percent of women in Indiana dailies' newsrooms experienced sexual harassment, usually of a verbal type.

3079. Foote, Joe S. "Women Correspondents' Visibility on the Network Evening News." *Mass Communication Review*. 19:1/2 (1992), pp. 36-40.

3080. Forbes, Thomas. "Fine Line Distinction." *News Inc*. October 1990, p. 59.
Discusses role Nell Brinkley, the illustrator, played on *Denver Post* and *New York Journal*.

3081. Fox, Jo. "Lise Connell -- The Grass Is Greener." *Cartoonist PROfiles*. March 1985, pp. 58-61.
Profiles strip cartoonist Connell.

3082. Freely, Maureen. "Glory and Me." *The Guardian*. April 18, 1996, Section Features, p. 6.
On Gloria Steinem.

3083. Fried, Lisa I. "Ruth Whitney: 25 Years of Pure *Glamour*." *Magazine Week*. February 8, 1993, p. 9.
Fetes *Glamour* Editor-in-Chief Whitney on her 25 years service to the magazine.

3084. Fry, S. D. "Newspaper Woman." *Journalist*. November 19, 1892, p. 10.

3085. "Funny Femmes -- Saluting Women Cartoonists." *Cartoonist PROfiles*. June 1984, pp. 64-71.
Cartoons paying tribute to women cartoonists.

3086. Gale, Zona. "Editors of the Younger Generation." *The Critic*. April 1904, p. 320+.
Mentions women hired by media to attract a female readership.

3087. Garrison, Dee. *Mary Heaton Vorse: The Life of an American Insurgent*. Philadelphia, Pennsylvania: Temple University Press, 1989. 400 pp.
Vorse was called the "foremost pioneer of labor journalism in the U.S."; she edited the *Masses* in the early 1900s.

3088. "Gay, Lesbian Journalists Rate Climate, Coverage in Their Newsrooms." *Media Report to Women*. May/June 1990, pp. 2-3.
Shows that newspapers were "largely hospitable" to gay and lesbian journalists; undercurrent of bias remained in newsrooms.

3089. "Gertrude Battles Lane, Noted Editor Dies." *New York Times*. September 26, 1941, p. 23.

3090. "Gertrude Lane As Publisher Secure in 'Higher Brackets.'" *New York Times*. February 13, 1939, p. D5.

3091. Gibbons, Robert H. *Sweet Monsters: The Secret Art of Rose O'Neill*. N.p.: Privately published, 1980.
Early twentieth century cartoonist and illustrator.

3092. Gibbons, Sheila. "'Woodhull Here. And How Are You?'" *Media Report to Women*. Spring 1997, p. 16.
Gives brief account of career and characteristics of Nancy Woodhull, a founder of *USA Today*, who died April 1, 1997.

3093. Glazer, Penina M. and Miriam Slater. *Unequal Colleagues: The Entrance of Women into the Professions, 1890-1940*. New Brunswick, New Jersey: Rutgers University Press, 1987.
Includes information on journalism.

3094. "Gloria Steinem." In *The Media in Your Life: An Introduction to Mass Communication*, edited by Jean Folkerts, Stephen Lacy, and Lucinda Davenport, p. 162. Boston: Allyn and Bacon, 1998.
Gives a brief profile of *Ms. Magazine* founder and her contributions to journalism.

3095. Goldsmith, Barbara. *Other Powers -- The Age of Suffrage, Spiritualism and the Scandalous Victoria Woodhull*. New York: Alfred A. Knopf, 1998.
Gives biographical details of life of Victoria Woodhull, publisher of *Woodhull's Weekly* in 1870s, candidate for U.S. presidency, friend of Cornelius Vanderbilt.

3096. Goldsmith, Barbara. "The Woman Who Set America on Its Ear." *Parade Magazine*. March 8, 1998, pp. 14-15.
Discusses Victoria Woodhull, 19th century publisher/editor; mainly a promo for Goldsmith's new book.

3097. Goodman, Helen. *The Art of Rose O'Neill*. Chadds Ford, Pennsylvania: Brandywine River Museum, 1989.
Exhibition catalogue of works of cartoonist O'Neill.

3098. Goodman, Susan. "She Lost It at the Movies." *Modern Maturity*. March-April 1998, pp. 48-52, 80.
Profiles veteran film critic Pauline Kael; gives her views on the movies and film criticism.

3099. Goodwin, Lavinia S. "Magnetic Journalism." *Journalist*. July 27, 1889, p. 4.
Argues that women could be trained in journalism better under proper supervision than by learning on the job.

3100. Gordon, Lynn D. "Why Dorothy Thompson Lost Her Job: Political Columnists and the Press Wars of the 1930s and 1940s." *History of Education Quarterly*. Fall 1994, pp. 281-304.

3101. Gorney, Cynthia. "Gloria." *Mother Jones*. November/December 1995, pp. 22-24, 26-27.
Ms. founder Gloria Steinem talks about politics, aging, and her future activist roles, but not about *Ms.*

3102. Gottlieb, Agnes H. "Women Journalists and the Municipal Housekeeping Movement." Ph.D. dissertation, University of Maryland, 1992.

3103. Graham, Katharine. *Personal History*. New York: Alfred A. Knopf, 1997. 625 pp.
Recounts history of *Washington Post*, at the same time that she chronicles her own family, friends, and career. Tells both the successes and blemishes of *Post* journalism and her family's roles: both her father and husband preceded her as head of the company.

3104. Greenwald, Marilyn S. "'All Brides Are Not Beautiful': The Rise of Charlotte Curtis at the *New York Times*." *Journalism History*. Autumn 1996, pp. 100-109.
Tells story of *New York Times*' society reporter, women's page editor, associate editor, and columnist, Charlotte Curtis, 1961-1987.

3105. Grey, L. C. "McCormick of the Times." *Current History*. 50 (1939), p. 27.
Profiles Anna O'Hare McCormick, Pulitzer Prize-winning foreign correspondent of *New York Times*.

3106. Griffin, C. L. "Women As Communicators: Mary Daly's Hagiography As Rhetoric." *Communication Monographs*. June 1993, pp. 158-177.

Contends that work of Mary Daly can be used to understand the concept of women as communicators; Daly's writings suggested the existence of rhetorical foreground which silences women and rhetorical background where women act as communicators.

3107. Griggs, Catherine M. "Beyond Boundaries: The Adventurous Life of Marguerite Harrison." Ph.D. dissertation, George Washington University, 1996.

3108. Hamm, Margherita A. "Among the Newspaper Women." *Journalist*. May 28, 1892, p. 6; September 3, 1892, p. 10.

3109. Hamm, Margherita A. "The Journalist's Birthday." *Journalist*. April 1898, p. 9.
Discusses the 4,000 women working in U.S. journalism at the time.

3110. Hardesty, Carolyn. "Carrie Chapman Catt and Woman Suffrage." *Goldfinch*. September 1989, 33 pp.
Devotes most of issue to Catt, early Iowa suffragette who also worked as a journalist.

3111. Hardin, Marie M. "The Journey of a Southern Woman's Career in Journalism During the 1920s: Julia Collier Harris at the Columbus (Georgia) *Enquirer-Sun*." Paper presented at American Journalism Historians Association, Mobile, Alabama, October 1997.
Explores why Harris remained an obscure figure in journalism.

3112. Harlan, Christi. "Role Models in Transition." *The Quill*. July/August 1995, pp. 39-40.
Claims that women's success in journalism is no longer predicated on the departure of individuals, because women are no longer the exception in the newsroom.

3113. Harvey, R. C. "At Swords' Point -- Humor As Weapon." *Cartoonist PROfiles*. December 1996, pp. 48-57.
Interviews gag cartoonist Betty Swords on her career, philosophy, and techniques.

3114. Hayes, Ruth. "Review / A Century of Women Cartoonists." *Animation Journal*. Spring 1994, pp. 80-82.

3115. Heintjes, Tom. "A Good Cartoonist Is Hard To Find. Flannery O'Connor: Cartoonist." *Hogan's Alley*. No. 2, 1995, pp. 116-123.
Documents cartooning interest and work of author Flannery O'Connor.

3116. "Helen E. Hokinson." *New Yorker*. November 1949, p. 160+.
Briefly profiles gag cartoonist.

3117. "Helen Wilmans of Woman's World." *Journalist*. May 29, 1886, p. 7.

3118. Hemingway, Mary W. *How It Was*. New York: Alfred A. Knopf, 1976.

Deals mostly with her life as wife and widow of Ernest Hemingway, but also with her stints as reporter and war correspondent with the *Chicago Daily News*, *London Daily Express*, *Time*, and *Life*.

3119. Henry, Susan J. "Ann Franklin: Rhode Island's Woman Printer." In *Colonial Newsletters and Newspapers: Eighteenth-Century Journalism*, edited by Donovan H. Bond and W. Reynolds McLeod. Morgantown, West Virginia: School of Journalism, West Virginia University, 1977.

3120. Henry, Susan J. "Near-Sightedness and Blind Spots in Studying the History of Women in Journalism." Paper presented to American Journalism Historians Association, Coeur d'Alene, Idaho, October 1990.

3121. Henry, Susan J. "Notes Toward the Liberation of Journalism History: A Study of Five Women Printers in Colonial America." Ph.D. dissertation, Syracuse University, 1976.

3122. "Hispanic Women Journalists Dissatisfied with Their Status." *Media Report to Women*. Summer 1997, p. 16.

3123. Hoffman, Betty H. "Gertrude Battles Lane." In *Notable American Women*, edited by Edward T. James, Vol. II, p. 364. Cambridge: Belknap Press of Harvard University, 1921.
    Profiles longtime editor of *Woman's Home Companion*.

3124. Horine, Maude M. *Memories of Rose O'Neill: Creator of the Kewpie Doll*. N.p.: Privately published, 1950.
    Profiles early twentieth century cartoonist.

3125. "How the Ladies Got Out the Journal." *Atlanta Journal*. February 18, 1895, p. 3.

3126. Howard, Jane. "Charlotte Curtis, First Lady of the *New York Times*." *Cosmopolitan*. January 1975, p. 158.

3127. Howard, Justice. "PornArtraphy." *Gauntlet*. No. 14, 1997, pp. 48-55.
    Photographer of porn stars relates anecdotes about her photo sessions.

3128. Hull, Gloria T. "Alice Dunbar-Nelson: Delaware Writer and Woman of Affairs." *Delaware History*. 17 (1976), pp. 87-103.

3129. Hurt, Elizabeth. "Just Ask Penelope: The Role of Sallie Joy White in Promoting the Professionalism of Journalists in the 19th Century." Paper presented at American Journalism Historians Association, Mobile, Alabama, October 1997.
    Profiles career of first fulltime newswoman for a Boston newspaper in 1870.

3130. Ingall, Marjorie. "Supergirls." *Sassy*. November 1994, pp. 68-69.

Discusses female cartoonists.

3131. "It Does Happen Here." *News Inc.* December 1991, pp. 27-31.
Sexual harassment rates are twice as high in newsrooms as other workplaces.

3132. Jackson, Florence. "Chances for Women in Journalism." *Harper's Weekly.* September 12, 1903, p. 1493.
Claims women were paid much better on newspapers than on magazines.

3133. Jackson, George. *Uncommon Scold: The Story of Anne Royall.* Boston: Bruce Humphries, 1937.

3134. Johns, Robert L. "Alice Dunnigan." In *Notable Black American Women,* edited by Jessie C. Smith, pp. 301-303. Detroit, Michigan: Gale Research, 1992.

3135. Jones, Douglas C. "Teresa Dean: Lady Correspondent Among the Sioux Indians." *Journalism Quarterly.* 49 (1972), pp. 656-662.

3136. Jones, Margaret C. *Heretics and Hellraisers: Women Contributors to* The Masses, *1911-1917.* Austin: University of Texas Press, 1993. 224 pp.
Explores women contributers to *The Masses,* left-wing magazine of the early twentieth century; individuals such as Mary H. Vorse, Dorothy Day, Louise Bryant, Elsie C. Parsons, or Inez H. Gillmore; looks at their perspectives on patriarchy, birth control, woman suffrage, pacifism, ethnicity; includes examples of work, biographies, and bibliographies.

3137. Jones, Robert and Louis K. Falk. "Caro Brown and the Duke of Duval: The Story of the First Woman to Win the Pulitzer Prize for Reporting." *American Journalism.* Winter 1997, pp. 40-53.

3138. Kalish, Carol. "An Interview with Mary Jo Duffy." *Comics Feature.* February 1982, pp. 20-34.
Comic book writer.

3139. Kane, Harnett T. *Dear Dorothy Dix: The Story of a Compassionate Woman.* Garden City, New York: Doubleday, 1952.

3140. Katz, Esther. "The Editor as Public Authority: Interpreting Margaret Sanger." *Public Historian.* Winter 1995, pp. 41-50.

3141. Keener, Polly. "Kate Salley Palmer." *Cartoonist PROfiles.* June 1985, pp. 22-27.
Profiles South Carolina political cartoonist.

3142. Kelley, Mary, ed. *The Portable Margaret Fuller.* New York: Penguin; 1994. 528 pp.
Collects work of this 19th century editor, literary critic, poet; includes her reportage for Greeley's *Tribune,* criticism, essays, correspondence, etc.

3143. Kennedy, Martha A. "Nebraska's Women Photographers." *Nebraska History.* Summer 1991, pp. 62-77.

Claims more than 140 during 19th and early 20th centuries; contains many photographs, including Native American and rancher subject matter.

3144. Kenney, Anne R. "'She Got to Berlin': Virginia Irwin, *St. Louis Post-Dispatch* War Correspondent." *Missouri Historical Review.* 79 (1985), pp. 456-479.

3145. Kerr, Sophie. "Gertrude B. Lane, A Biographical Sketch." Personal memoir in possession of Mary E. Zuckerman, January 13, 1985.

Looks at career of longtime women's magazine editor.

3146. Kilmer, Paulette D. "Flying Around the World in 1889 -- In Search of the Archetypical Wanderer." Paper presented at American Journalism Historians Association, Mobile, Alabama, October 1997.

Analyzes significance of two rival women journalists' race to beat the around-the-round travel time in Jules Verne's novel.

3147. Kitch, Carolyn L. "'The Courage to Call Things by Their Right Names': Fanny Fern, Feminine Sympathy, and Feminist Issues in Nineteenth-Century American Journalism." *American Journalism.* Summer 1996, pp. 286-303.

3148. Kitch, Carolyn L. "Domestic Images in the Age of the Girl: The Work of Jessie Willcox Smith and Other Women Artists in Early-Twentieth-Century Magazine Illustration." Paper presented at Association for Education in Journalism and Mass Communication, Anaheim, California, August 1996.

Describes career of magazine illustrator Jessie Willcox Smith in context of the women's art community.

3149. Klejment, Anne and Nancy L. Roberts, eds. *American Catholic Pacifism: The Influence of Dorothy Day and the Catholic Worker Movement.* Westport, Connecticut: Greenwood Press, 1996. 224 pp.

Deals with Day's socialist/spiritual Catholic Worker Movement; includes scattered mentions of her newspaper, *Catholic Worker.*

3150. Knight, Denise D. "Charlotte Perkins Gilman, William Randolph Hearst and the Practice of Ethical Journalism." *American Journalism.* Fall 1994, pp. 336-347.

3151. Kochersberger, Robert C., Jr. *More Than a Muckraker: Ida Tarbell's Lifetime in Journalism.* Knoxville: University of Tennessee Press, 1994. 296 pp.

Brings together the best of Tarbell's articles, book chapters, speeches, and unpublished work; re-examines her role as journalist, biographer, and social commentator.

3152. Konner, Joan. "Women in the Marketplace." *Vital Speeches.* September 15, 1990, pp. 726-728.

Talks about the impact in media by women in journalism.

3153. Kossan, Pat. "Sexual Harassment in the Newsroom and on the Job." *APME News*. April-May 1992, pp. 1-11.

3154. Kraft, David A. "Adrienne Roy." *Comics Interview*. March 1984, pp. 74-77. Comic book colorist.

3155. Kroeger, Brooke. *Nellie Bly: Daredevil, Reporter, Feminist*. New York: Times Books, 1994. 631 pp.
Profiles investigative journalist/"sob sister" Nellie Bly, her self-invention, gimmicks, and stunts to cover events in the nineteenth century; notes that she practiced a style of advocacy journalism that is considered unethical today, that she initially failed as a columnist, that she was highly litigious, suing both her mother and brother, and that much that previously had been written about her was highly exaggerated in her favor. Also by Kroeger, "Nellie Bly: She Did It All." *Prologue* (Spring 1996, pp. 7-15).

3156. Kurth, Peter. *American Cassandra: The Life of Dorothy Thompson*. Boston: Little, Brown, 1990. 587 pp.
Details personal and professional lives of columnist, correspondent, and journalist Dorothy Thompson.

3157. Kusner, Trucia D. "People You Should Know: Charlotte Curtis." *Viva*. March 1974, p. 52.
Of the *New York Times*.

3158. Lafky, Sue A. "Women Journalists." In *The American Journalist: A Portrait of U.S. News People and Their Work*. Second Edition, edited by David H. Weaver and G. Cleveland Wilhoit, pp. 160-181. Bloomington: Indiana University Press, 1991.

3159. Larson, Arthur J., ed. *Crusader and Feminist: Letters of Jane Grey Swisshelm 1855-1865*. St. Paul: Minnesota Historical Society, 1934.

3160. Levenson, Roger. *Women in Printing: Northern California, 1857-1890*. Santa Barbara, California: Capra Press, 1994. 272 pp.
Story of the 300 or more women who worked in printing in San Francisco and environs.

3161. Linfield, Susie. "Martha Gellhorn, Journalist." *The Nation*. April 13, 1998, pp. 10, 36.
Relates foreign correspondent role Martha Gellhorn played, especially in the 1930s and 1940s; the news peg was on her death at 89.

3162. Loeb, Sophie I. "Women in the Realm of Journalism." *American Suffragette*. June 1909, p. 4.

3163. "Looking at Things Differently: Women and Men Photojournalists." *Media Report to Women*. Winter 1997, pp. 10-11.

3164. Loomis, Amy W. "Kodak Women: Domestic Contexts and the Commercial Culture of Photography, 1880s-1980s." Ph.D. dissertation, University of Massachusetts, 1994.

3165. Loupe, Diane E. "Storming and Defending the Color Barrier at the University of Missouri School of Journalism: The Lucile Bluford Case." *Journalism History.* Spring/Summer 1989, pp. 20-31.
   Lucile Bluford's attempt to enroll in University of Missouri School of Journalism in 1939 denied because of segregation.

3166. Lowe, T. M. "Donna Barr." *Comics Journal.* September 1996, pp. 100-108.
   Interviews comics artist Donna Barr, creator of "Desert Peach" and "Stinz."

3167. Lubkeman, Lynn M. "Anna Louise Strong and the Stalinist Era." Ph.D. dissertation, University of Wisconsin, 1995.

3168. Luckett, Margie, ed. *Maryland Women*, Vol. 1. Baltimore: n.p., 1931.
   Mentions colonial printer Mary Katherine Goddard, p. 169.

3169. Lumsden, Linda. "'You're a Tough Guy, Mary -- And a First-Rate Newspaperman': Gender and Women Journalists in the 1920s and 1930s." *Journalism and Mass Communication Quarterly.* Winter 1995, pp. 913-921.
   Analyzes how gender-based polarities affected 10 "front-page gals" between 1920 and 1940; demonstrates how women had to abandon their feminine selves to succeed in male-dominated cityrooms.

3170. Lyons, Sarah. "Daughter of the Revolution." *South China Morning Post.* July 6, 1996, Section Books, p. 8.
   Profiles Gloria Steinem.

3171. McBride, Genevieve G. *On Wisconsin Women: Working for Their Rights from Settlement to Suffrage.* Madison: University of Wisconsin Press, 1994. 352 pp.
   Discusses role of women in Wisconsin's reform press of nineteenth and early twentieth centuries and women journalists' marshaling of the press in the suffrage fight.

3172. McCanse, Ralph A. *Titans and Kewpies: The Life and Art of Rose O'Neill.* New York: Vantage Press, 1968.
   Cartoonist, illustrator.

3173. MacDonald, Heidi. "You Guys Need to Get Laid." *Comics Journal.* December 1997, pp. 90-97.
   Illuminates the slowly evolving role women have carved in comic book production by discussing fandom and her own life in/with comics; at the time of writing, she was comics editor for *Disney Adventures*.

3174. McFadden, Robert. "Charlotte Curtis, a Columnist for the Times Is Dead at 58." *New York Times*. April 17, 1987, p. B-6.

3175. McGlashan, Zena B. "The Evolving Status of Newspaperwomen." Ph.D. dissertation, University of Iowa, 1978.

3176. McGrath, Kristen. "Women and Newspapers." *Newspaper Research Journal*. 14:2 (1993), pp. 95-109.

3177. McKee, Alice. "A Girl Cartoonist of the West, Miss Alice McKee." *Cartoons*. March 1913, p. 140.

3178. McLean, Albert F., Jr. "Hokinson, Helen Elna." In *Notable American Women, 1607-1950: A Biographical Dictionary*, edited by Edward T. James. Cambridge, Massachusetts: Harvard University Press, 1971.

3179. "Magazine Cartoonist Margaret Blanchard." *Cartoonist PROfiles*. Fall 1969, pp. 40-45.

3180. Manning, Marie. *Ladies Now and Then*. New York: E.P. Dutton, 1944.
        Describes her work on Pulitzer and Hearst newspapers, her invention of the "Beatrice Fairfax" lovelorn advice column, and her philosophy about the latter.

3181. Marchalonis, Shirley. *The Worlds of Lucy Larcom, 1824-1893*. Athens: University of Georgia Press, 1989. 336 pp.
        Portrays 19th century writer Larcom whose "verses" and moral essays regularly appeared in prominent magazines and weekly literary newspapers; Larcom became an editor of *Our Young Folks* magazine in the 1860s.

3182. Marek, Jayne E. *Women Editing Modernism: "Little" Magazines and Literary History*. Lexington: University Press of Kentucky, 1995. 252 pp.
        Examines seven women editors whose work in *Poetry*, *The Little Review*, *The Dial*, and *Close Up*, was not given due attention: Harriet Monroe, Alice Corbin Henderson, Margaret Anderson, Jane Heap, H. D. Bryher, and Marianne Moore.

3183. "Mary Katherine Goddard." In *The Media in Your Life: An Introduction to Mass Communication*, edited by Jean Folkerts, Stephen Lacy, and Lucinda Davenport, p. 50. Boston: Allyn and Bacon, 1998.

3184. Masterson, Kate. "Small Beginnings in Journalism." *Journalist*. December 1, 1894, p. 5.
        Argues that practical experience and common sense helped women in journalism more than college education.

3185. Maurice, Arthur B. "Feminine Humorists." *Good Housekeeping*. January 1910, pp. 35-40.

3186. May, Antoinette. *Witness to War: A Biography of Marguerite Higgins*. New York: Beaufort, 1983.

    Profiles correspondent particularly famous for her Korean War reporting.

3187. Mitchell, Catherine C. "Bibliography. Scholarship on Women Working in Journalism. Categorized by Gerda Lerner's Stages of History." *American Journalism*. Winter 1990, pp. 33-38.

    Includes sections on compensatory journalism, contribution history, and transitional history.

3188. Mitchell, Catherine C. "Horace Greeley's Star: Margaret Fuller's New York Tribune Journalism, 1844-1846." Ph.D. dissertation, University of Tennessee, Knoxville, 1987.

3189. Mitchell, Catherine C. "The Place of Biography in the History of News Women: The Careers of Women Journalists Remain an Important Topic for Historical Research." *American Journalism*. Winter 1990, pp. 23-32.

    Describes Gerda Lerner's four stages in the conceptualization of women's history and uses them to categorize the historical research on women working in journalism; argues that more "contribution history" is needed in history of women working in journalism.

3190. Mitchell, Catherine C., ed. *Margaret Fuller's New York Journalism: A Biographical Essay and Key Writings*. Knoxville: University of Tennessee Press, 1995. 240 pp.

    Fills the gap in knowledge about Fuller's journalistic career; concentrates on the more journalistic, rather than literary, essays and articles she wrote while on the *New York Tribune*, 1844-1846.

3191. Mitchell, Ed. "Emmy Lou." *Cartoonist PROfiles*. March 1977, pp. 50-55.

    Interviews Marty Links, creator of comic strip, "Emmy Lou."

3192. Montgomery, Ruth. *Hail to the Chiefs: My Life and Times with Six Presidents*. New York: Coward-McCann, 1970.

    Provides story of Montgomery's 25-year career in political journalism, most of which as Washington correspondent for the New York *Daily News*.

3193. Mossell, Gertrude B. "Our Women in Journalism." In *The Work of the Afro-American Woman*, pp. 98-103. New York: Oxford University Press, 1988. Originally published in 1894.

3194. Moutoussamy-Ashe, Jeanne. *Viewfinders: Black Women Photographers*. New York: Dodd, Mead, 1986.

3195. Munce, Howard. "Nurit Karlin." *Cartoonist PROfiles*. June 1996, pp. 82-87.

Profiles New York cartoonist who does captionless cartoons.

3196. Myerson, Joel. *Margaret Fuller: A Descriptive Bibliography.* Pittsburgh, Pennsylvania: University of Pittsburgh Press, 1978. 178 pp.
On nineteenth century foreign correspondent for *New York Tribune.*

3197. "Narrow Definition of Women's Roles Handicapped Her, Kate Graham Says." *Media Report to Women.* Winter 1997, pp. 7-8.

3198. Nekola, Charlotte and Paula Rabinowitz. *Writing Red: An Anthology of American Women Writers, 1930-1940.* New York: Feminist Press, 1987. 368 pp.
Includes short biographical sketches and representative works from nearly 50 women writers, active in the 1930s-1940s; 20 were journalists such as Agnes Smedley, Anna L. Strong, Josephine Herbst, Tillie Olsen, Mary H. Vorse, Dorothy Day, Meridel LeSueur, Ella Ford, Ruth Gruber, Vivian Dahl, Elaine Ellis, Grace Hutchins, or Mary G. Lear.

3199. Nelson, Jill. *My Authentic Negro Experience.* Chicago, Illinois: Noble Press, 1993. 243 pp.
Relates caustically and negatively her experiences as a black woman journalist at the *Washington Post* in the 1980s.

3200. "NFPW Study: Women Grossly Underrepresented in Newspaper Content, Editorial Decisions." *Media Report to Women.* July/August 1990, pp. 2-3.
Shows that women made up 7.3 percent of U.S. newspaper publishers, 16.5 percent of directing editors in 1989.

3201. Ohrn, Karen B. "What You See Is What You Get: Dorothea Lange and Ansel Adams at Manzanar." *Journalism History.* 4 (1977), pp. 14-22.
Relates experiences of two famous photographers at Japanese-American concentration camp.

3202. Okker, Patricia. *Our Sister Editors: Sarah J. Hale and the Tradition of Nineteenth-Century American Women Editors.* Athens: University of Georgia Press, 1995. 280 pp.
Relates career of Hale as editor of *Ladies' Magazine*, 1828-1836, and *Godey's Lady's Book*, 1837-1877; also provides an overview of the large and diverse group of nineteenth-century women editors. Appendix highlights contributions of more than 600 women editors during this period.

3203. O'Neill, Patrick D. "Ann Nocenti." *Comics Interview.* No. 39 (1986), pp. 58-59.
Profiles comic book editor.

3204. Ostroff, Roberta. *Fire in the Wind: The Life of Dickey Chapelle.* New York: Ballantine, 1992. 408 pp.
About foreign correspondent-photojournalist killed in Vietnam, November 4, 1965.

3205. "Pages for Women." *Time*. May 19, 1967, p. 55.
On Charlotte Curtis of *New York Times*.

3206. Palmquist, Peter E. "Pioneer Women Photographers in Nineteenth Century California." *California History*. Spring 1991, pp. 110-127.

3207. Parker, Dorothy. *The Portable Dorothy Parker*. Introduction by Brendan Gill. New York: Penguin, 1994. 640 pp.
Includes stories, poems, reviews, articles from *Esquire* and *The New Yorker*, and *Constant Reader*, her collection of book reviews from *The New Yorker*.

3208. Payne, Ethel L. "Loneliness in the Capital: The Black National Correspondent." In *Perspectives of the Black Press*, edited by Henry G. LaBrie III, pp. 153-161. Kennebunkport, Maine: Mercer House Press, 1974.
Tells author's experiences working for *Chicago Defender*.

3209. Peaselee, Maude S. "Here's Hopin." *Journalist*. January 1891, p. 12.

3210. Pekar, Harvey. "Two Women to Watch Out For." *Comics Journal*. October 1990, pp. 129-132.
Cartoonists Holly Tuttle and Alison Bechdel.

3211. Penn, Garland. *The Afro-American Press and Its Editors*. Springfield, Massachusetts: Wiley, 1891.
Includes chapter, "Afro-American Women in Journalism," pp. 367-427, which provides sketches of 20 women.

3212. Pierson, Michael D. "Between Antislavery and Abolition: The Politics and Rhetoric of Jane Grey Swisshelm." *Pennsylvania History*. 60 (1993), pp. 305-321.
Early nineteenth century journalist.

3213. Pini, Wendy. "Women, Comics, and Elfquest." *Comics Collector*. Fall 1985, pp. 17-20, 22-24.
Cartoonist Wendy Pini, co-creator of "Elfquest," talks about women in comic art and her comics character.

3214. Pinkham, Jeremy. "Diane Noomin." *Comics Journal*. October 1993, pp. 67-77.
Interviews cartoonist who has drawn "DiDi Glitz," an alter ego who "jumps the suburban rut for adventures of sexual exploitation, hard-boiled mystery, and immodest, honest autobiography."

3215. Plunkett, Wilma M. "Edith Irvine: Her Life and Photography." Masters thesis, Brigham Young University, 1989.
Details life and career of photographer, who covered among major stories,

the San Francisco earthquake.

3216. Pompper, Donnalyn. "The Empress of Publishing: The Other Frank Leslie." *Media History Digest*. Spring/Summer 1993, pp. 2-10.
Relates the personal life and journalist career of Mariam Folline Squires Leslie, before and after her marriage to Frank Leslie, the magazine publisher; after his death in 1880, she assumed his publishing empire and name, becoming Frank Leslie.

3217. Porter, Jack N. "Rosa Sonneschein and *The American Jewess*: New Historical Information of an Early American Zionist and Jewish Feminist." *American Jewish Archives*. November 1980, p. 20.

3218. Porter, Sarah H. *The Life and Times of Anne Royall*. Cedar Rapids, Iowa: Torch Press, 1909.
Describes career of colonial printer, editor.

3219. Pratte, Alf. "'A Tortuous Route Growing Up': The Rise of Women in the American Society of Newspaper Editors." *Journal of Women's History*. Spring 1994, pp. 51-66.

3220. Preece, Charles. *E. W. and Ellen Browning Scripps: An Unmatched Pair*. Chelsea, Michigan: Bookcrafters, 1990. 199 pp.
Profiles E.W. Scripps, founder of Scripps-Howard chain and United Press, and sister Ellen B. Scripps, columnist and foreign correspondent.

3221. Pry, Pauline. "The 'New Woman.'" *Journalist*. October 23, 1890, p. 12.

3222. "PT Interview: A Woman for the Times: Anna Quindlen." *Psychology Today*. September 1994, p. 26 +.
Profiles one of the major American columnists who represents a new type of journalism that obliterates the differences between what happens at home and in the world of politics and business.

3223. "Quota of None." *Extra!* September-October 1995, p. 6.
Says that op-ed pages lost their leading feminist voice when Anna Quindlen quit her *New York Times* post in 1994.

3224. Ragland, Ruth A. "Publisher Daisy Bates: Arkansas Crusader for School Integration, 1954-59." *Southwestern Mass Communication Journal*. 9:1 (1993), pp. 72-91.

3225. Read, Phyllis J. and Bernard L. Witlieb. "Mary Katherine Goddard." In *The Book of Women's Firsts*, pp. 177-178. New York: Random House, 1992.

3226. Reed, Barbara S. "Trude Weiss-Rosmarin: Rebel with a Cause." *New Jersey Journal of Communication*. Spring 1995, pp. 58-76.

Profiles Weiss-Rosmarin, who, in 1935, published an independent magazine of Jewish ideas; notes that the periodical focused on Jewish survival in an assimilationist milieu and on the role of Jewish women.

3227. Reinhard, Beth. "Anna Quindlen." *The Quill.* July-August 1991, pp. 18-21.
Of *New York Times.*

3228. "Reporter Alice Allison Dunnigan Dies." *Washington Post.* May 8, 1983, p. C-7.

3229. Rhodes, Jane. "Breaking the Editorial Ice: Mary Ann Shadd Cary and the 'Provincial Freeman.'" Ph.D. dissertation, University of North Carolina, 1992.

3230. Rhodes, Jane. "Mary Ann Shadd and the Legacy of African-American Women Journalists." In *Women Making Meaning: New Feminist Directions in Communication,* edited by Lana K. Rakow. New York: Routledge Kegan Paul, 1992.

3231. Ricchiardi, Sherry. "'Giving Great War.'" *American Journalism Review.* September 1996, pp. 30-31.
Discusses Christiane Amanpour, a CNN correspondent, and her experiences covering war in Bosnia, which she calls "my Vietnam."

3232. Ricchiardi, Sherry and Virginia Young. *Women on Deadline: A Collection of America's Best.* Ames: Iowa State University Press, 1991. 224 pp.
Focuses on nine women emerging as stalwart American journalists with biographical interviews and work samples: Lucy Morgan, Jacqui Banaszynski, Alice Sternbach, Bella Stumbo, Cynthia Gorney, Anna Quindlen, Molly Ivins, Christine Brennan, and Sara Terry.

3233. Rinehart, Mary R. *My Story: A New Edition and Seventeen New Years.* New York: Rinehart & Company, 1948.
Adds to the 1931 edition with information on Rinehart's careers as novelist, playwright, and war correspondent during World War I.

3234. Ripley, Wendy L. "Women Working at Writing: Achieving Professional Status in Nineteenth-Century America." Ph.D. dissertation, George Washington University, 1996.

3235. Robbins, Trina. "Artist Ruth Atkinson Ford Dies June 1." *Comics Buyer's Guide.* July 4, 1997, pp. 6, 8.
Profiles cartoonist who drew "Millie the Model" and "'Patsy Walker" in the 1940s.

3236. Robbins, Trina. *A Century of Women Cartoonists.* Northampton, Massachusetts: Kitchen Sink Press, 1993. 180 pp.
Historical overview of women cartoonists with vignettes and much artwork. Second half rather preachy.

3237. Robbins, Trina. "Hidden Treasure: Jackie Ormes Brought to Light." *Comics Journal*. July 1993, pp. 47-50.
> Drew "Torchy Smith" strip.

3238. Roberts, Nora R. "Josephine Herbst and the Journalistic Novel." In *The Eye of the Reporter: Literature's Heritage in the Press*, edited by Deckle McLean and Bill Knight, pp. 56-68. Macomb, Illinois: Western Illinois University Press, 1996.

3239. Roberts, Nora R. *Three Radical Women Writers: Class and Gender in Meridel Le Sueur, Tillie Olsen, and Josephine Herbst*. New York: Garland, 1996.
> Shows relationships of these writers and the radical press of their time.

3240. Robertson, Nan. *The Girls in the Balcony: Women, Men and "The New York Times."* New York: Random House, 1992. 274 pp.
> Sketches *Times* women from the 1850s to those of the present day, pointing out the paucity of female staff members at times; Adolph Ochs was unyieldingly against women on the staff from 1896 til his death in 1935. Robertson was one of the plaintiffs in a discrimination suit against the paper in the 1970s.

3241. Rodman, Larry. "A Serious Film About *Funny Ladies*: A Portrait of Women Cartoonists." *Comics Journal*. September 1991, pp. 39-42.
> Discusses Dale Messick, Cathy Guisewite, Nicole Hollander, and Lynda Barry.

3242. Rogers, Sherbrooke. *Sarah Josepha Hale: A New England Pioneer, 1788-1879.* Grantham, New Hampshire: Thompson and Rutter, 1985.

3243. Rollin, Lucy. "Kate Salley Palmer: A Profile." *Inks*. February 1997, pp. 29-34.
> Profiles South Carolina political cartoonist who left her newspaper position in the 1980s because of the political topics she dealt with.

3244. Rollyson, Carl E., Jr. *Nothing Ever Happens to the Brave: The Story of Martha Gellhorn*. New York: St. Martin's Press, 1990. 398 pp.
> Describes longtime foreign correspondent and novelist Martha Gellhorn, always resentful that she was known instead for being Ernest Hemingway's third wife.

3245. Rubenstein, Anne. "Mary Fleener." *Comics Journal*. February 1994, pp. 106-117.
> Interviews comic book artist.

3246. Rubenstein, Anne. "Roberta Gregory: Cartooning on the Cultural Zeitgeist." *Comics Journal*. May 1994, pp. 56-74.
> Interviews underground cartoonist, Roberta Gregory.

3247. St. Johns, Adela Rogers. *The Honeycomb*. Garden City, New York: Doubleday,

1969.
>Rehashes her career as a journalist, mostly with the Hearst chain; her *Final Verdict* (1962) includes some material about her early reporting experiences.

3248. Salicrup, Jim. "Fabulous Flo Steinberg." *Comics Interview*. November 1984, pp. 59-75.

3249. Sangster, Margaret E. "Editorship as a Profession for Women." *The Forum*. September 1895-February 1896, pp. 445-486.
>Represents a contemporary view of women in journalism at turn of century.

3250. Schuler, Marjorie, Ruth A. Knight, and Muriel Fuller. *Lady Editor*. New York: E.P. Dutton, 1941.

3251. Schweitzer, J.C. and J. Miller. "What Do Newswomen Cover? A First Attempt to Uncover Subtle Discrimination." *Newspaper Research Journal*. Spring 1991, pp. 72-80.
>Surveys four largest Texas dailies; shows that there were no clear differences in the kinds of news stories assigned to newswomen as compared to their male colleagues.

3252. Scott, Matthew S. "New Era at Oakland Trib." *Black Enterprise*. February 1993, p. 40.
>Discusses appointment of Pearl Stewart as editor of *Oakland Tribune*, making her the first black woman to head a metropolitan daily newspaper.

3253. Sebba, Anne. *Battling for News: The Rise of the Woman Reporter*. London: Hodder and Stoughton, 1994. 301 pp.

3254. Sheppard, Alice. "There Were Ladies Present: American Women Cartoonists and Comic Artists in the Early Twentieth Century." *Journal of American Culture*. Fall 1984, pp. 38+.

3255. "Sketchbook: Jill Thompson." *Comics Journal*. February 1994, pp. 119-123.
>Comic book artist.

3256. Smedley, Agnes. *China Correspondent*. London: Pandora Press, 1984.
>Originally published as *Battle Hymn of China* (1943), relating author's important career covering China.

3257. Smith, Harold L. "The Beauteous Jennie June: Pioneer Woman Journalist." *Journalism Quarterly*. 40 (1963), pp. 169-174.

3258. Smith, Joan. "The Unexplained Feminist." *Financial Times*. May 4, 1996, Section Books, p. 11.

Profiles Gloria Steinem.

3259. Snorgrass, J. William. "Pioneer Black Women Journalists from the 1850s to the 1950s." *Western Journal of Black Studies.* Fall 1982, pp. 150-158.

3260. "Sociologist on the Society Beat." *Time.* February 19, 1965, p. 51.
On Charlotte Curtis of *New York Times*.

3261. Stearns, Bertha-Monica. "Reform Periodicals and Female Reformers 1830-1860." *American Historical Review.* 37 (1932), pp. 678-699.
Trivializes purposes and concerns of female reformist editors of period.

3262. Steiner, Linda. "Autobiographies by Women Journalists: An Annotated Bibliography." *Journalism History.* Spring 1997, pp. 13-15.
Includes 29 abstracts of autobiographies on women who established their reporting careers before 1960.

3263. Stephens, Paula S. "Christie Hefner Kept Re-engineering of Playboy All in the Family." *National Real Estate Investor.* April 1995, p. 58.
Tells how Christie Hefner has changed *Playboy*, including how to make it acceptable to women.

3264. Stevens, John. "Edna Ferber's Journalistic Roots." *American Journalism.* Fall 1995, pp. 497-501.
Recounts famous novelist's (*Show Boat*) journalism in Appleton, Wisconsin.

3265. Stoughton, Judith. *Proud Donkey of Schaerbeek: Ade Bethune, Catholic Worker Artist.* N.p.: North Star Press, 1988. 168 pp.
Describes Ade Bethune, who began her work as an artist for *Catholic Worker* in 1933.

3266. Streitmatter, Rodger. "African-American Women Journalists and Their Male Editors: A Tradition of Support." *Journalism Quarterly.* Summer 1993, pp. 276-286.
States that black women journalists have not been stopped by men's sexist attitudes to the degree that white women have, because African-American women have a tradition of working outside the home, black male editors had history of being racial activists, and African-American editors treated black women journalists as daughters.

3267. Streitmatter, Rodger. "Alice Allison Dunnigan: An African-American Woman Journalist Who Broke the Double Barrier." *Journalism History.* Autumn-Winter 1989, pp. 87-97.
Details life of Alice Allison Dunnigan, first black woman to receive credentials to cover the U.S. Congress, White House, Supreme Court, and State Department; in 1955, she desegregated the Women's National Press Club.

3268. Streitmatter, Rodger. "Delilah Beasley: A Black Woman Journalist Who Lifted as She Climbed." *American Journalism*. Winter 1994, pp. 61-75.

Gives account of career of Delilah Beasley, the first African-American woman to write regularly for the white press -- *Oakland Tribune*.

3269. Streitmatter, Rodger. "Economic Conditions Surrounding Nineteenth-Century African-American Women Journalists: Two Case Studies." *Journalism History*. 18, 1992, pp. 33-40.

Concerns 19th century black journalists Josephine St. Pierre Ruffin, founder of *Woman's Era*, and Delilah Leontium Beasley, column writer for the *Oakland Tribune*.

3270. Streitmatter, Rodger. "Gertrude Bustill Mosell: Guiding Voice For Newly Freed Blacks." *Howard Journal of Communications*. 2:4 (1993), pp. 317-328.

3271. Streitmatter, Rodger. "No Taste for Fluff: Ethel L. Payne, African-American Journalist." *Journalism Quarterly*. Fall 1991, pp. 528-540.

Chronicles *Chicago Defender* journalist Ethel L. Payne, who avoided "women's stories" to concentrate on coverage of civil rights, the South, war, and the Third World.

3272. Streitmatter, Rodger. *Raising Her Voice: African-American Women Journalists Who Changed History*. Lexington: University Press of Kentucky, 1994. 208 pp.

Profiles chronologically Maria W. Stewart, Mary Ann Shadd Cary, Gertrude Bustill Mossell, Ida B. Wells-Barnett, Josephine St. Pierre Ruffin, Delilah Beasley, Marvel Cooke, Charlotta A. Bass, Alice Allison Dunnigan, Ethel L. Payne, and Charlayne Hunter-Gault; includes their journalistic accomplishments, details on their personal lives, nature of their accomplishments and crusades, and their post-journalism lives.

3273. Streitmatter, Rodger and Barbara Diggs-Brown. "Marvel Cooke: An African-American Woman Journalist Who Agitated for Racial Reform." *Afro-Americans in New York Life and History*. July 1992, pp. 47-68.

3274. Suggs, Henry L., ed. *The Black Press in the Middle West, 1865-1985*. Westport, Connecticut: Greenwood Press, 1996. 416 pp.

Includes Genevieve G. McBride, "The Progress of 'Race Men' and 'Colored Women' in the Black Press in Wisconsin, 1892-1985."

3275. Sullivan, Constance. *Women Photographers*. New York: Harry Abrams, 1990. 263 pp.

Presents work by 73 artists from the mid-19th century to the present, including Julia Margaret Cameron, Gertrude Kasebier, Florence Henri, Dorothea Lange, Germaine Krull, Diana Arbus, Bernice Abbott, and others.

3276. Sutton, Terri. "Media Kids: Terri Sutton on Bad-Girl Cartoonists." *Artforum*. October 1991, pp. 23-24.

3277. Swords, Betty. "Why Women Cartoonists Are Rare, and Why That's Important." In *New Perspectives on Women and Comedy*, edited by Regina Barreca, pp. 65-84. Philadelphia, Pennsylvania: Gordon and Breach, 1992.

3278. Szabo, Joseph G. "'I Am the Same Sarcastic Bitch As I Always Was' -- The First Woman To Win the Pulitzer Prize in Editorial Cartooning, Signe Wilkinson." *WittyWorld*. Winter 1993, pp. 15-16, 18-19.
     Interviews Wilkinson of Philadelphia *Daily News* on her career and role as woman cartoonist.

3279. Thogmartin, Gwen H. and Ardis H. Anderson. *The Gazette Girls of Grundy County: Horse Trading, Hot Lead, and High Heels*. Columbia: University of Missouri Press, 1994. 168 pp.

3280. Thompson, Maggie. "Trina Robbins: Comics for Girls, Women -- Too Gentle?" *Comics Buyer's Guide*. June 10, 1994, pp. 28, 30, 34, 38.
     Robbins, author of a history of U.S. women cartoonists, discusses her career and her book.

3281. Thompson, Mildred I. *Ida B. Wells-Barnett: An Exploratory Study of an American Black Woman, 1893-1930*. Brooklyn, New York: Carlson, 1990. 328 pp.
     Profiles noted African-American editor and writer Wells and her many crusades, including that for stronger anti-lynching laws.

3282. "Three Bright Chicago Women." *Journalist*. January 26, 1889, p. 17.
     Discusses Helen M. Mott, Katherine G. Todd, and Mrs. Charles B. Smith, who founded the American Women's College of Practical Arts, with some instruction in journalism.

3283. Tinling, Marion. "Hermione Day and the Hesperian." *California History*. 59 (1980-1981), pp. 282-289.

3284. Tripp, Bernell E. "Black Women Journalists, 1825-1860." Ph.D. dissertation, University of Alabama, 1993.

3285. Tylee, Claire M. *The Great War and Women's Consciousness: Images of Militarism and Womanhood in Women's Writing*. Iowa City: University of Iowa Press, 1990. 293 pp.
     Includes a chapter on World War I women correspondents Mildred Aldrich, May Sinclair, and Mrs. St. Clair Stobart.

3286. "Upper Crust." *Newsweek*. September 28, 1964, p. 62.
     On Charlotte Curtis of *New York Times*.

3287. Upton, Kim. "The Wit Behind the Wisdom of 'Sylvia.'" *The Funnie's Paper*.

March 1984, pp. 8-10.

    Profiles Nicole Hollander, creator of the comic strip, "Sylvia." Reprinted from Berwyn (Illinois) *Sun Times*.

3288. Vaughan, Don. "Star Bright: An Interview with Susie Bright." *Gauntlet*. No. 14, 1997, pp. 30-35.

    Founding editor of *On Our Backs*, groundbreaking lesbian erotic magazine, discusses the state of pornography, Dworkin, sex movies.

3289. "Verbena -- What Becomes a Legend?" *Cartoonist PROfiles*. June 1981, pp. 10-16.

    Profiles cartoonist Perry Howze, creator of "Verbena."

3290. Vernon, Di. "What Is a Newspaper Woman?" *Journalist*. September 5, 1891, p. 7.

3291. von Mehren, Joan. *Minerva and the Muse: A Life of Margaret Fuller*. Amherst: University of Massachusetts Press, 1995. 536 pp.

    Deals with life of writer, teacher, feminist Fuller, including her editorship of the Transcendentalist *Dial*, work as first woman reporter for the *New York Tribune*, and as foreign correspondent in Europe.

3292. Vorse, Mary H. *A Footnote to Folly: The Reminisces of Mary Heaton Vorse*. New York: Farrar and Rinehart, 1935.

    Deals with her journalistic work, including with women's magazines such as *Woman's Home Companion* and *Ladies' Home Journal*.

3293. Wade, Betsy. "Surviving Being a Survivor, Or, Whatever Became of What's Her Name?" *Media Studies Journal*. Winter 1995, pp. 32-43.

    Recounts sex discrimination case, *Boylan v. Times*, of which she was a part.

3294. Wade-Gayles, Gloria. "Black Women Journalists in the South, 1880-1905: An Approach to the Study of Black Women's History." *Callaloo*. February-October 1981, pp. 138-152.

    Includes much substantive data on subject, although for limited time period. Also in D.C. Hine, ed. *Black Women in United States History* (Brooklyn, New York: Carlson, 1990).

3295. Warren, Joyce W. *Fanny Fern: An Independent Woman*. New Brunswick, New Jersey: Rutgers University Press, 1992. 380 pp.

    Profiles Fanny Fern (Sara Parton), witty columnist for the *New York Ledger* in the mid-1800s, who satirized woman's lot and male-female relationships.

3296. Watters, James. *Jean Howard's Hollywood: A Photo Memoir*. New York: Abrams, 1997. 248 pp.

By female photographer.

3297. Welch, Margaret H. "Newspaper Women." *Fourth Estate*. April 13, 1899, pp. 2, 4.

3298. Wellers, Meta. "The Press League." *Journalist*. November 26, 1892, p. 14.
    Describes club that split into Chicago Women's Press Club and Chicago Press League in 1895.

3299. Wells, Ida B. *Southern Horrors*. New York: The New York *Age* Print, 1892.
    Pamphlet providing account of the life and thought of journalist and black activist, Ida B. Wells.

3300. Wheeler, Cora S. "Mrs. M. L. Rayne." *Journalist*. February 28, 1891, pp. 1-2.
    Discusses teacher/founder of first journalism class in U.S.

3301. Wheeler, Joseph T. *The Maryland Press, 1777-1790*. Baltimore: Maryland Historical Society, 1938.
    Discusses briefly colonial printer Mary Katherine Goddard, pp. 11, 14.

3302. "When No One Listens." *News Inc.* December 1991, p. 32.
    Sexism in newsroom case study.

3303. White, Karl T. "Frontier Journalist Stakes Early Claim." *Matrix*. 65 (1980), pp. 24-27.

3304. "Who Are Newspaper Women?" *Fourth Estate*. April 4, 1895, p. 7.

3305. Williams, Sara L. "The Editor's Rib." *Matrix*. 27 (1942), p. 13.
    Focuses on contributions of editors' wives to local newspapers.

3306. Willis, Ronald G. "The Persuasion of Clare Booth Luce." Ph.D. dissertation, Indiana University, 1993.

3307. Windham, Kathryn T. *Odd-Egg Editor*. Jackson: University Press of Mississippi, 1990. 170 pp.
    Tells how Windham became a reporter for the *Alabama Journal* in 1941 when the male police reporter went into the military. Her title evolved because of her duty to interview and write about anyone who brought a freakish story to the paper.

3308. "Woman Editor Sees This As a Golden Age, Opportunity Awaits Her Sex, Gertrude Battles Lane Says." *New York Telegram*. June 9, 1929, p. 9.

3309. "Woman in Press Club." *Fourth Estate*. September 23, 1897, p. 3.

3310. "Women as News-Scoopers." *Journalist*. March 31, 1888, p. 12.
    Editor of *Somerville* (Mass.) *Journal* welcomes press bureau to provide

women work for which they would be fit.

3311. "Women in Journalism." *Fourth Estate*. March 7, 1895, p. 7.

3312. "Women in Journalism." *Journalist*. May 28, 1887, p. 8.

3313. *Women in Journalism: Oral Histories of Pioneer Journalists*. Washington, D. C.:
        Washington Press Club Foundation, 1989-1994.
        Includes 57 folders and one guide for the ridiculous price of $1,200.

3314. "Women on the Frontlines: Do They Have a Different Agenda?" *Media Report to
        Women*. Winter 1997, pp. 4-5.
        Discussion among foreign correspondents Martha Gellhorn, Fiona Murch,
        Kate Adie, Marci McGinnis, Karen Curry, Wivina Belmonte, Giselle Portenier,
        and Jane Kokan.

3315. Wooley, John. "An Interview with Wendy Pini." *Comics Collector*. Fall 1985, pp.
        24-27.
        Interviews cartoonist of "Elfquest."

3316. Yale, Kim. "Not Just John Ostrander's Wife." *Comics Buyer's Guide*. June 28,
        1996, pp. 56, 62.
        Talks about Yale's career in comics.

3317. Yglesias, Helen. "Through the Back Door." *Women's Review of Books*. March
        1994, p. 13.
        Describes author's work during the Depression and as editor of *The
        Nation*.

3318. Youngblood, Amy. "Cathy." *The Funnie's Paper*. October 1983, pp. 6-7.
        Reprints from August 21, 1981, Fort Myers, Florida, *News-Press*; profile
        of "Cathy" comic strip creator, Cathy Guisewite.

3319. Zimmerman, D. Jon. "June Brigman." *Comics Interview*. March 1984, pp. 7-12.
        Comics editor at Marvel.

3320. Zophy, Angela M. H. "For the Improvement of My Sex: Sarah Josepha Hale's
        Editorship of Godey's Lady's Book, 1837-1877." Ph.D. dissertation, Ohio State
        University, 1978.

3321. Zuckerman, Mary Ellen. "*Pathway to Success*: Gertrude Battles Lane and the
        Woman's Home Companion." *Journalism History*. Autumn/Winter 1989, pp. 64-
        75.
        Chronicles Gertrude Battles Lane's career at *Woman's Home Companion*,
        1903-1941, 30 of those years as editor-in-chief. Actually, from 1905 on, she took
        on much of the day-to-day responsibility for operating the magazine. Author said

"few other women in publishing succeeded so spectacularly."

Women's Media

3322. Barker-Plummer, Bernadette. "News As a Political Resource: Media Strategies and Political Identity in the U.S. Women's Movement, 1966-1975." *Critical Studies in Mass Communication.* September 1995, pp. 306-324.
      Shows how the two branches of the women's movement understood news differently and developed different strategies--media pragmatism and media subversion.

3323. Britton, Patti. "Education Through Ignorance." *Index on Censorship.* 1/1993, pp. 11-12.
      Finds U.S. sadly lacking in terms of access to medical care and information for women on sexual and reproductive issues.

3324. Fenton, Natalie. "Women, Communication and Theory: A Glimpse of Feminist Approaches to Media and Communication Studies." *Feminism and Psychology.* August 1995, pp. 426-431.
      Assesses processes of communication from different theoretical perspectives; outlines feminist developments in communication studies useful to feminist psychologists looking at power relationships.

3325. Flanders, Laura. "How Alternative Is It? Feminist Media Activists Take Aim at the Progressive Press." *Extra!* May/June 1996, pp. 6-7.
      Reports on gender panel at Media and Democracy Congress, San Francisco, March 1, 1996.

3326. Freeman, Alexa and Valle Jones. "Creating Feminist Communications." *Quest.* 3 (1976), pp. 3-12.

3327. Haraway, Donna. *Modest-Witness@Second Millennium. FemaleMan©-Meets-OncoMouse.™ Feminism and Technoscience.* New York: Routledge, 1997. 388 pp.

3328. Henry, Dawn, comp. *A Directory of Women's Media.* 16th Edition. New York: National Council for Research on Women, 1992. 268 pp.
      Indexes periodicals, publishers/presses, news services, radio/TV, film/video/cable, music, theatre/dance/multimedia, art, crafts/cards/T-shirts, writers' groups, speakers' bureaus, distributors, media organizations, bookstores, libraries/archives/museums, and directories/catalogues.

3329. Jasper, Laura G. and Ellen L. Terwilliger. "Advertising's Impact on Calls to a Women's Healthline." *Journal of Health Care Marketing.* September 1989, pp. 62-66.
      Studies a Wisconsin hospital's "healthline"; word-of-mouth communication and television were the most frequently used sources of

information about "healthline."

3330. Kranich, Kimberly. "Women's Media ca. 1989." *Women and Language*. Spring 1989, pp. 19-22.

3331. McElroy, Wendy. *XXX: A Woman's Right to Pornography*. New York: St. Martin's Press, 1995. 243 pp.

3332. National Council for Research on Women. *1992 Directory of Women's Media*. New York: National Council for Research on Women, 1992.

3333. Parrott, Roxanne L. and Celeste M. Condit, eds. *Evaluating Women's Health Messages: A Resource Book*. Thousand Oaks, California: Sage Publications, 1996. 450 pp.
    Explores various forms of health messages and the ways they compare with and contradict one another; includes the work of 30 contributors.

3334. Rabinowitz, Paula. *They Must Be Represented: History and the Rhetoric of Gender in American Political Documentaries*. New York: Routledge, 1995. 288 pp.
    Analyzes documentary in print, photography, television, and film, from the 1930s through the 1980s, using the lens of feminist film theory.

3335. Scott, Sandra D. "Beyond Reason: A Feminist Theory of Ethics for Journalists." *Feminist Issues*. Spring 1993, pp. 23-40.
    States that emotion can be superior to reason in ethical decision-making.

3336. Walters, Suzanna D. *Material Girls: Making Sense of Feminist Cultural Theory*. Berkeley: University of California Press, 1995. 217 pp.
    Acquaints readers with major theories, debates, and concepts of feminist cultural theory.

3337. *What Black Women Should Know About Lupus: Ideas for Community Programs*. Bethesda, Maryland: National Institute of Arthritis and Muscoloskeletal and Skin Diseases, 1993. 92 pp.
    Includes Section Two, "How to Work with the Media."

3338. Wood, Julia T. and C. C. Inman. "In a Different Mode: Masculine Styles of Communicating Closeness." *Journal of Applied Communication Research*. August 1993, pp. 279-295.
    Analyzes textbooks on gender and communication and interpersonal relationships; contends that existent is a bias that favors feminine styles of relating, characterized by verbal emotional disclosure rather than activity-focused modes more usually associated with males.

Broadcasting

3339. Balka, E. "Womantalk Goes On-Line: The Use of Computer Networks in the Context of Feminist Social Change." Ph.D. dissertation, Simon Fraser University, 1992.

3340. Banks, Jane and Jonathan Tankel. "A Tube of One's Own: *Lifetime* as an Electronic Space for Woman." *Gender and Mass Media Newsletter*. November 1992, pp. 11-12.
    Discusses "Lifetime," a cable channel overtly defined as a service that understands and meets the needs of contemporary women.

3441. Bathrick, Serafina. "*The Mary Tyler Moore Show*: Women at Home and at Work." In *MTM: "Quality Television*," edited by J. Feuer, P. Kerr, and T. Vahimagi, pp. 99-131. London: British Film Institute, 1984.
    Deals with situation comedy popular primarily in the 1970s.

3442. Brown, Mary E. *Soap Opera and Women's Talk: The Pleasure of Resistance*. Thousand Oaks, California: Sage Publications, 1994. 218 pp.
    Claims soap operas create and sustain a "social network in which talk becomes a form of resistive pleasure."

3443. Butler, Jeremy G. "Redesigning Discourse: Feminism, the Sitcom, and *Designing Women*." *Journal of Film and Video*. Spring 1993, pp. 13-26.
    Shows how television sitcom, "Designing Women" (1986), activates television's ambivalence toward women: "The characters are outspoken about issues that are important to women, but, despite the trepidations of Madison Avenue executives, 'Designing Women' is not female-dominated to the point of sexism."

3444. Ganas, Monica C. "'Queen for a Day,' the Cinderella Show: Broadcasting Women's True Stories." Ph.D. dissertation, University of Kentucky, 1995.

3445. Kalas, Andrea and Rhona J. Berenstein. "*Woman Speaks*: Representations of Working Women in Postwar America." *Journal of Film and Video*. Fall 1996, pp. 30-45.
    Discusses newsreel/television show, "Woman Speaks," created in 1945 by H. A. Spanuth, and shown mainly in the Midwest.

3446. Kaler, Anne K. "*Golden Girls*: Feminine Archetypal Patterns of the Complete Woman." *Journal of Popular Culture*. Winter 1990, pp. 49-60.

3447. Lague, Louise. "Real Women Make a TV Comeback Thanks to Susan Saint James and Jane Curtin in *Kate and Allie*." *People*. 21(18), 1984, pp. 154-157.
    A television series.

3448. Lerner, Elinor. "To Robin Roberts." *NWSA Journal*. Spring 1990, pp. 329-339.
    Reacts to Robin Roberts' article, "Sex as a Weapon: Feminist Rock Music

Videos" in *NWSA Journal* (Winter 1990, pp. 1-15); Roberts' reply, pp. 337-339.

3449. "Lifetime: A Cable Network 'For Women.'" Special Issue. *Camera Obscura*. May-September-January 1994-1995.

3450. Maibach, Edward and June A. Flora. "Symbolic Modeling and Cognitive Rehearsal: Using Video To Promote AIDS Prevention Self-Efficacy." *Communication Research*. August 1993, pp. 517-545.

3451. Masciarotte, Gloria J. "C'mon, Girl: Oprah Winfrey and the Discourse of Feminine Talk." *Genders*. Fall 1991, pp. 81-110.
     Looks at history, structure, and hegemonic importance of TV talk shows and their feminine subject.

3452. Montgomery, Kathryn C. *Target: Prime Time/Advocacy Groups and the Struggle Over Entertainment Television*. New York: Oxford University Press, 1989. 272 pp.
     Gives accounts of battles of activists and TV networks, including some involving women's groups.

3453. Mumford, Laura S. *Love and Ideology in the Afternoon. Soap Opera, Women and Television Genre*. Bloomington: Indiana University Press, 1995. 176 pp.
     Shows how soap operas reinforce dominant ideas of gender and sexuality and why soaps are so popular, even to feminists.

3454. Nochimson, Martha. *No End to Her: Soap Opera and the Female Subject*. Berkeley: University of California Press, 1993. 232 pp.
     Demonstrates how soap opera validates a feminist perspective and responds to complex issues of women's desires and power with strong, active female characters.

3455. Nochimson, Martha. "TV Soaps Counter Hollywood Image." *New Directions for Women*. January-February 1991, pp. 8-9.
     Relates to "Days of Our Lives" and "Santa Barbara."

3456. O'Reilly, Jane. "At Last! Women Worth Watching." *TV Guide*. May 27, 1989, pp. 18-21.
     Calls late 1980s, new golden age of female comedy with "Roseanne," "Murphy Brown," and "Designing Women."

3457. Robbins, Leah. "The Social Construction of Gender in the Media: Hidden Dimensions and Contradictions." Paper presented at the American Sociological Association, 1994.
     Examines gender differences regarding distribution of five types of power in soap operas: influence, connections, decisions, sexuality, and income; shows that the most powerful woman has about the same amount of power as the average

man on a show, but she usually uses sex to gain power.

3458. Sanoff, Alvin P. and Adam P. Weisman. "Television's Women of the Hour." *U.S. News & World Report*. September 22, 1986, pp. 78-80.
Discusses the number of female sitcoms appearing on television.

3459. Shattuc, Jane M. *The Talking Cure: TV Talk Shows and Women*. New York: Routledge, 1997. 272 pp.
Traces expansion of four such shows ("Donahue," "Oprah Winfrey," "Geraldo," and "Sally Jessy Raphael") and explores the terms of debate about the shows, how the industrial production process constructs femininity, and other topics.

3460. Stamps, Wickie. "They Say It Sister, On the Air." *New Directions for Women*. September-October 1989, p. 7.
Deals with "Say It Sister," Boston feminist program on Massachusetts Institute of Technology radio station.

3461. Stanback, M. H. "Feminist Theory and Black Women's Talk." *Howard Journal of Communications*. 1:4 (1988-1989), pp. 187-194.

3462. van Zoonen, Liesbet. "Sekse en Populaire Cultuur." *Tidjschrift voor Vrowenstudies*. 13:3 (1992), pp. 386-397.
Discusses why soap operas and other popular culture forms appeal to women: they are an "expression of discontent with dominant gender discourse instead of as a sign of its hegemony."

3463. Waters, Harry F. and Janet Huck. "Networking Women." *Newsweek*. March 13, 1989, pp. 48-52+.
Calls late 1980s the "feminization of television" with rash of female sitcoms.

Film

3464. Bernard, Jami. *Chick Flicks: A Movie Lover's Guide to the Movies Women Love*. Secaucus, New Jersey: Citadel Press/Carol Publishing Group, 1997. 240 pp.
Reviews 75 films that women love and qualities they find appealing -- strong female cast, subject matter they can identify with, etc.

3465. Blackman, Ann, et al. "Hell Hath No Fury." *Time*. October 7, 1996, pp. 80-85.
Describes the impact of film, "The First Wives Club," which packed theaters in the summer of 1996 with women who "recognize the plot and welcome the message: 'get even, then get over it.'"

3466. Castle, Ted and Julia Ballerini, eds. *Carolee Schneemann: Early and Recent Work*. New Paltz, New York: Documentext, 1982.
Discusses work of Carolee Schneemann, known for personal, feminist filmmaking.

3467. Cavell, Stanley. *Contesting Tears: The Hollywood Melodrama of the Unknown Woman*. Chicago: University of Chicago Press, 1997. 256 pp.

Demonstrates that a genre he calls the "melodrama of the unknown woman" exists in films such as "Letter from an Unknown Woman," "Gaslight," "Now Voyager," and "Stella Dallas."

3468. Corliss, Richard. "The Ladies Who Lunge." *Time*. October 7, 1996, pp. 86-87.

Reviews films historically where strong women were featured, starting with 1932 "Three on a Match," through 1996 blockbuster "The First Wives Club."

3469. Couzin, Sharon. "An Analysis of Susan Pitt's *Asparagus* and Joanna Priestley's *All My Relations*." In *A Reader in Animation Studies*, edited by Jayne Pilling, pp. 71-81. London: John Libbey and Co., 1997.

Chooses these two animation films because of an interest in "the iconographic qualities of animation in a field where the ruling ideologies of language, have, in many cases, reduced or limited critical discourse by narrowly inscribing meaning."

3470. Dash, Julie. *Daughter of the Dust: The Makings of an African American Woman's Film*. New York: The New Press, 1992.

3471. Dawson, Bonnie, ed. *Women's Films in Print*. San Francisco: Booklegger Press, 1975.

3472. de Lauretis, Teresa. "Cavani's *Night Porter*: A Woman's Film?" *Film Quarterly*. Winter 1976-1977, pp. 35-38.

3473. de Lauretis, Teresa. "Rethinking Women's Cinema." In *Technologies of Gender*. Bloomington: Indiana University Press, 1987.

3474. de Lauretis, Teresa. "Rethinking Women's Cinema: Aesthetics and Feminist Theory." In *Multiple Voices in Feminist Film Criticism*, edited by Diane Carson, Linda Dittmar, and Janice R. Welsch, pp. 140-161. Minneapolis: University of Minnesota Press, 1994.

Appears originally in *New German Critique*. Winter 1985, pp. 154-175.

3475. de Lauretis, Teresa. "Through the Looking Glass: Woman, Cinema and Language." *Estudos Feministas*. 1:1 (1993), pp. 96-122.

Translation of first chapter of book, *Alice Doesn't: Feminism, Semiotics, Cinema*.

3476. Del Castillo, Adelaida, Ana Nieto-Gómez, and Elizabeth Martínez. "La Chicana." In *Third World Women*, pp. 130-132. San Francisco: Third World Communications, 1972.

3477. Dittmar, Linda. "Feminist Film Scholarship." *NWSA Journal*. Fall 1992, pp. 359-

365.

> Reviews *Issues in Feminist Film Criticism* (Erens), *Now You See It: Studies on Lesbian and Gay Film* (Dyer), *The Difficulty of Difference: Psychoanalysis, Sexual Difference, and Film Theory* (Rodowick), and *The Woman at the Keyhole: Feminism and Women's Cinema* (Mayne).

3478. Dozoretz, Wendy. "The Mother's Lost Voice in *Hard, Fast and Beautiful*." *Wide Angle*. 6:3 (1984), pp. 50-57.

> Discusses film by director/actress Ida Lupino.

3479. Erens, Patricia. "U.S. Women's Documentary Filmmaking: The Personal Is Political." In *The Hawai'i International Film Festival*, pp. 79-82. Honolulu: East-West Center, 1985.

3480. Erens, Patricia, ed. *Issues in Feminist Film Criticism*. Bloomington: Indiana University Press, 1991. 320 pp.

> Covers the development of feminist film theory and criticism through the 1980s; essays by Laura Mulvey, Mary Ann Doane, Tania Modleski, Pam Cook, Claire Johnston, Jane Gaines, Jackie Stacey, Lucie Arbuthnot, Gail Seneca, and Mary C. Gentile.

3481. Fischer, Lucy. "Shall We Dance? Feminist Cinema Remakes the Musical." *Film Criticism*. Winter 1989, pp. 7-17.

3482. Fischer, Lucy. "Shot/Countershot: An Intertextual Approach to Women's Cinema." *Journal of Film and Video*. Winter 1989, pp. 3-14.

> Proposes to examine women's art work within the contexts of men to "configure it as engaged in an ongoing intertextual debate."

3483. Fishbein, Leslie. "Women on the Fringe: A Film Series." *Film and History*. 8:3 (1978), pp. 49-58.

3484. Fletcher, John. "Primal Scenes and the Female Gothic: *Rebecca* and *Gaslight*." *Screen*. Winter 1995, pp. 341-370.

> Analyzes theme through Alfred Hitchcock's "Rebecca" and George Cukor's "Gaslight," films belonging to the cycle of 1940s' women's film variously labelled "the Freudian feminist melodrama."

3485. Franke, Lizzie. "*Go Fish*." *Sight and Sound*. July 1994, p. 42.

> Reviews Rose Troche's 1994 lesbian comedy/drama "Go Fish."

3486. Fregoso, Rosa L. *The Bronze Screen: Chicana and Chicano Film Culture*. Minneapolis: University of Minnesota Press, 1993. 168 pp.

> Combines social histories, textual analyses, and film theories in survey of Chicana and Chicano film.

3487. Fregoso, Rosa L. "Chicana Film Practices: Confronting the Many-Headed Demon of Oppression." In *Chicanos and Film*, edited by Chon A. Noriega, pp. 168-182.

Minneapolis: University of Minnesota Press, 1992.

3488. Freydberg, Elizabeth H. "Women of Color: No Joy in the Seduction of Images." In *Multiple Voices in Feminist Film Criticism*, edited by Diane Carson, Linda Dittmar, and Janice Welsch, pp. 468-480. Minneapolis: University of Minnesota Press, 1994.

3489. Gaither, Laura. "Close-up and Slow Motion in Julie Dash's *Daughter of the Dust*." *The Howard Journal of Communications*. April-June 1996, pp. 103-112.
         Tells how Julie Dash (black feminist independent filmmaker) responds to mainstream cinema's marginalization of women of color with her film, "Daughter of the Dust."

3490. Gleick, Elizabeth. "Hell Hath No Fury." *Time*. October 7, 1996, pp. 80-87.
         Discusses the film "The First Wives Club" with its message to divorced women: get even, then get over it; includes Richard Corliss's "The Ladies Who Lunge," depicting the return of the strong women to movies.

3491. Goldberg, Marianne. "The Body, Discourse, and *The Man Who Envied Women*." *Women and Performance: A Journal of Feminist Theory*. 3:2 (1987-1988), pp. 97-102.
         Discusses one of Yvonne Rainer's films, "The Man Who Envied Women."

3492. Gollan, Donna. "From Weepies to Women's Flicks: We've Come a Long Way, Baby!" *Globe and Mail* (Toronto). October 23, 1993, p. C3.
         States that women's movies of the 1990s look like the old weepy varieties, but there is a difference; the earlier genre acted as a catharsis to help women to accept their lot; the modern films move women to reject the status quo.

3493. Grey, Juliann and Bronwen Hruska. "They Shoot *Bad Girls*, Don't They?: How a Low-Budget 'Feminist Western' Turned into a Big-Budget *Wild Bunch* with Women." *US Magazine*. May 1994, pp. 74, 90.

3494. Hammett, J. "The Ideological Impediment: Feminism and Film Theory." *Cinema Journal*. 36:2 (1997).

3495. Hart, Lynda. "Til Death Do Us Part: Impossible Spaces in Thelma and Louise." *Journal of the History of Sexuality*. January 1994, pp. 430-446.
         Presents a feminist/psychoanalytic reading of the film "Thelma and Louise" and its reception in the mass media.

3496. Healey, Jim. "'All This For Us': The Songs in *Thelma and Louise*." *Journal of Popular Culture*. Winter 1995, pp. 103-119.
         Analyzes about a dozen songs of this 1991 movie and concludes that they grew out of the movie's plot and "attest to the art and skill evident in the making of an effective film soundtrack."

3497. Hollinger, Karen. *In the Company of Women: Contemporary Female Friendship Films*. Minneapolis: University of Minnesota Press, 1998. 256 pp.

Discusses wave of films focusing on friendship between women since the 1970s; argues that contemporary female friendship films both critique and defend traditional female roles.

3498. Holmlund, Christine. "When Is a Lesbian Not a Lesbian: The Lesbian Continuum and the Mainstream Feminine Film." *Camera Obscura*. January-May 1991, pp. 145-178.

3499. Holmlund, Chris and Cynthia Fuchs, eds. *Between the Sheets, in the Streets. Queer, Lesbian, Gay Documentary*. Minneapolis: University of Minnesota Press, 1997. 304 pp.

Discusses gay, lesbian, queer, bisexual, and transgender films and videos, "testifying to the unavoidable connections between sexuality (the sheets) and activism (the streets) for all who identify as gay, lesbian, or queer in the 1990s."

3500. Jones, Elizabeth. "The Failure of Imagination in *Thelma and Louise*: The Crisis of Identity in the Pursuit of the Ideal." *Film and Philosophy*. Vol. III, 1996.

3501. Kaplan, Cora. "Dirty Harriet/*Blue Steel*: Feminist Theory Goes to Hollywood." *Discourse*. Fall 1993, pp. 50-70.

Discusses "Blue Steel," film by Kathryn Bigelow.

3502. Kay, Karyn. "New Films of Lust and Evil -- *Henry and June* and *The Nasty Girl*." *New Directions for Women*. January-February 1991, p. 9.

Reviews films about Anais Nin, Henry and June Miller and a woman's search for the truth about what happened in her hometown during the Holocaust.

3503. Kay, Karyn and Gerald Peary. "Dorothy Arzner's Dance, Girl, Dance." *The Velvet Light Trap*. Fall 1973, pp. 27-31.

An obscure RKO comedy of 1940 directed by Dorothy Arzner.

3504. Keller, Gary D. *Hispanics and United States Film: An Overview and Handbook*. Tempe, Arizona: Bilingual Review/Press, n.d. 256 pp. Companion Volume: *A Pictorial Handbook of Hispanics and United States Film*. 1995, 240 pp.

Both include chapters on Chicana film.

3505. Knight, Deborah. "Women, Subjectivity, and the Rhetoric of Anti-Humanism in Feminist Film Theory." *New Literary History*. 26:1 (1995), pp. 39-56.

3506. Luke, C. "Feminist Pedagogy and Critical Media Literacy." *Journal of Communication Inquiry*. Summer 1994, pp. 30-47.

Introduces cultural and media literacy, outlines aspects of contemporary social theories salient to a media and cultural studies pedagogy, links feminist pedagogy.

3507. MacDonald, Scott. "Demystifying the Female Body: Anne Severson -- *Near the*

Big Chakra, Yvonne Rainer -- *Privilege*." *Film Quarterly*. Fall 1991, pp. 18-32.
Analyzes one of Yvonne Rainer's dozen films, "Privilege."

3508. McKee, Alison L. "'L' Affair Praslin' and *All This, and Heaven Too*: Gender, Genre, and History in the 1940s Woman's Film." *The Velvet Light Trap*. Spring 1995, pp. 33-51.
Relates the murder of the Duchesse de Praslin in 1847 to the film, "All This, and Heaven Too," in 1940.

3509. Maio, Kathi. "A Screen of One's Own." *Women's Review of Books*. February 1993, pp. 10-11.
Reviews Julie Dash's *Daughter of the Dust: The Making of an African American Woman's Film.*

3510. Man, Glenn. "Gender, Genre, and Myth in *Thelma and Louise*." In *Gender and Culture in Literature and Film East and West: Issues of Perception and Interpretation*, edited by Nitaya Masavisut, George Simson, and Larry E. Smith, pp. 113-126. Honolulu: University of Hawaii and East-West Center, 1994.

3511. Marchetti, Gina. "Women Fight Back on Film: *Kiai!: Women in Self-Defense*." *Jump Cut*. March 1986, pp. 34-35.

3512. Marchetti, Gina and Carol Slingo. "Romanticism Reconsidered: The Films of Sharon Couzin." *Jump Cut*. April 1983, pp. 44-46.

3513. Margolies, Harriet. "*Blue Steel*: Progressive Feminism in the '90s?" *Post Script*. Fall 1993, pp. 67-76.
Discusses Kathryn Bigelow's film, "Blue Steel."

3514. Meyers, Ellen and Toni Armstrong, Jr. "A Visionary Woman Creating Visions: Barbara Hammer." *Hot Wire*. May 1991, pp. 42-44.
Discusses work of Hammer, who created a couple dozen films, including 1990s' "Sanctus," "Vital Signs," and "Nitrite Kisses."

3515. Morey, Anne. "'The Judge Called Me an Accessory': Women's Prison Films, 1950-1962." *Journal of Popular Film and Television*. Summer 1995, pp. 80-87.
Examines four women's prison films ("Caged," 1950, "Women's Prison," 1955, "Girls in Prison," 1956, "House of Women," 1962), in which prison is shown as an agent to return women to domesticity.

3516. Nagel, Jessie. "Women in Animation." *Animato!* Summer/Fall 1997, pp. 6-7.
The first in a regular column, looks at the association, Women in Animation, founded in 1994 by Rita Street.

3517. Natale, Richard. "Women's Pix Not Just for Women Anymore." *Variety*. February 10, 1992, pp. 5, 10.

3518. Ouellette, Laurie. "Reel Women: Feminism and Narrative Pleasure in New Women's Cinema." *The Independent*. April 1995, pp. 29-34.

Analyzes new film features directed by women: Jane Campion's "The Piano," Stacey Cochran's "My New Gun," Tamra Davis' "Guncrazy," Allison Anders' "Gas Food Lodging" and "Mi Vida Loca," Nancy Savoca's "True Love," Mina Shum's "Double Happiness," Darnell Martin's "I Like It Like That," Leslie Harris' "Just Another Girl on the IRT," Julie Dash's "Daughters of the Dust," Rose Troche's "Go Fish," Maria Maggenti's "The Incredible Adventure of Two Girls in Love," and Sally Potter's "Orlando."

3519. Parker, Alan. *The Making of Evita*. New York: HarperCollins, 1996. 128 pp.

Features an introduction by the film's star, Madonna; a behind-the-scenes account of the making of the film by its director.

3520. Phillips, Julie. "Growing up Black and Female: Leslie Harris's *Just Another Girl on the IRT*." *Cineaste*. 19:4 (1992), pp. 86-87.

Discusses her female-centered, positive hip-hop film.

3521. Pollitt, Katha. "Women and Children First." *The Nation*. March 30, 1998, p. 9.

Contends that the film "Titanic" is not just a women's film, but a feminist film as well.

3522. Poyntz, Stuart. "Hurt, Vulnerable and Sweaty: Looking in *Prince of Tides* and the Weight Room." *Reverse Shot*. January 1994, pp. 32-37.

Discusses second film (after "Yentl," 1983) directed by Barbra Streisand.

3523. Rabinowitz, Lauren. *Points of Resistance: Women, Power and Politics in the New York Avant-Garde Cinema, 1943-71*. Champaign: University of Illinois Press, 1991. 264 pp.

Discusses the works of Shirley Clarke, Joyce Wieland, Maya Deren, and Marie Manken as a "collective point of resistance" to a still male-dominated canon; argues that each woman contributed significantly to the underground film movement, but that each one's success depended upon avant-garde cinema being perceived as marginal.

3524. Reid, Mark A. "Dialogic Modes of Representing Africa(s): Womanist Film." *Black American Literature Forum*. Summer 1991, pp. 375-388.

3525. Robertson, Pamela. *Guilty Pleasures: Feminist Camp from Mae West to Madonna*. Durham, North Carolina: Duke University Press, 1996. 208 pp.

3526. Self, Robert T. "Redressing the Law in Kathryn Bigelow's *Blue Steel*." *Journal of Film and Video*. Summer 1994, pp. 31-43.

Maintains that the film "Blue Steel," about a female cop, "activates instabilities of sexual difference without containing them."

3527. Shohat, Ella. "Gender and Culture of Empire: Toward a Feminist Ethnography of the Cinema." *Quarterly Review of Film and Video*. 13:1-3 (1991), pp. 45-84.

3528. Smith, Greg M. "Silencing the New Woman: Ethnic and Social Mobility in the Melodramas of Norma Talmadge." *Journal of Film and Video.* Fall 1996, pp. 3-16.

Focuses on public discourses that provide background for Talmadge's departure from the movies when sound was introduced in the 1920s.

3529. Straayer, Chris. "Lesbian Narratives and Queer Characters in Monika Treut's *Virgin Machine." Journal of Film and Video.* Summer/Fall 1993, pp. 24-39.

Considers the limits of the lesbian "coming-out romance" film and analyzes the differences between "coming-of-age" and "coming-out" narratives and their successful recombination in Treut's film.

3530. Street, Rita. "Women in Animation -- Changing the World: Person by Person, Cel by Cel." *Animation World.* May 1996, 5 pp.

Describes the motivation behind Rita's Street's founding of Women in Animation.

3531. Waxman, Sharon. "Role Reversal: Women Become More of a Force in Film." *Washington Post.* March 4, 1997.

Claims 1996 was year when women's films were prominent and women audiences became marketing and production factor. Reason: More women executives at studios.

3532. Weiss, Julie. "Feminist Film Theory and Women's History: *Mildred Pierce* and the Twentieth Century." *Film and History.* 22:3 (1992), pp. 75-88.

3533. Welsch, Janice R. "Feminist Film Theory/Criticism in the United States." *Journal of Film and Video.* Spring 1987, pp. 66-81.

Provides ideas, philosophies, outlines, and readings for a university-level course on film theory/criticism.

3534. Whatling, Clare. *Screen Dreams: Fantasising Lesbians in Film.* New York: St. Martin's Press, 1997. 208 pp.

Argues there is no such thing as lesbian film: that films are lesbianized by audiences watching them; reinvestigates mainstream feminist and lesbian film theory.

3535. Wilton, Tamsin. *Immortal, Invisible: Lesbians and the Moving Image.* New York: Routledge, 1995. 288 pp.

Debates lesbian and queer filmmaking from the queer cinema of Monika Treut to lesbian filmmakers Andrea Weiss and Greta Schiller; explores lesbian spectatorship in Hollywood mainstream films ("Red Sonya" and "Aliens") and independent cinema ("Desert Hearts" or "She Must Be Seeing Things").

3536. Winterson, Jeanette. "Outrageous Proportions." *Sight and Sound.* October 1992, pp. 26-27.

Animated films by women.

3537. Yarbro-Bejarano, Yvonne. "De-constructing the Lesbian Body: Cherríe Moraga's *Loving in the War Years*." In *Chicana Lesbians*, edited by Carla Trujillo. Berkeley, California: Third Women Press, 1991.

3538. Zita, Jacqueline. "Counter Currencies of a Lesbian Iconography: The Films of Barbara Hammer." *Jump Cut.* 24 (1981), pp. 26-30.

Print Media

3539. Albright, Cheryl L., David G. Altman, Michael D. Slater, and Nathan Maccoby. "Cigarette Advertisements in Magazines: Evidence for a Differential Focus on Women's and Youth Magazines." *Health Education Quarterly.* 15:2 (1988), pp. 225-233.

3540. Alexander, Susan H. "Messages to Women and Men on Love and Marriage: An Analysis of Change over Time in Nonfiction Articles in Gender-Oriented Magazines." Ph.D. dissertation, American University, 1989.

3541. Beaulieu, Anne and Abby Lippman. "'Everything You Need To Know': How Women's Magazines Structure Prenatal Diagnosis for Women over 35." *Women and Health.* 23:3 (1995), pp. 59-74.
         Surveys contents of ten women's magazines to understand the context in which women age 35 or more undergo prenatal diagnostic tests.

3542. Bennion, Sherilyn C. "The Pioneer: The First Voice of Women's Suffrage in the West." *Pacific Historian.* 25 (1981), pp. 15-21.

3543. Bennion, Sherilyn C. "The Woman's Exponent: Forty-two Years of Speaking for Women." *Utah Historical Quarterly.* 44 (1976), pp. 222-239.

3544. Blanchard, Margaret. "Speaking of Plural: The Example of *Women: A Journal of Liberation*." *NWSA Journal.* September 1992, pp. 84-97.
         Describes this journal founded in Baltimore as the first publication of the second wave of the women's movement.

3545. Blix, Jacqueline. "A Place to Resist: Reevaluating Women's Magazines." *Journal of Communication Inquiry.* Winter 1992, pp. 56-71.

3546. Braden, Maria. "Women: Special Again." *Washington Journalism Review.* June 1991, pp. 30-32.
         Discusses recent revival of newspaper women's pages.

3547. Brody, Michal. *Are We There Yet? A Continuing History of Lavendar Woman, a Chicago Lesbian Newspaper, 1971-1976.* Iowa City: Aunt Lute Book Company, 1985.

3548. Burkhalter, Nancy. "Women's Magazines and the Suffrage Movement: Did They Help or Hinder the Cause?" *Journal of American Culture*. Summer 1996, pp. 13-24.

Looks at coverage of suffrage movement, 1918-1920, in *Ladies' Home Journal*, *Good Housekeeping*, *New Republic*, and *Literary Digest*; contends that the editors were concerned with minimizing the impact of woman's suffrage on the traditional and stereotypical roles of women advocated by such magazines.

3549. Colbert, Ann. "Philanthropy in the Newsroom: Women's Editions of Newspapers, 1894-1896." *Journalism History*. Autumn 1996, pp. 90-99.

Deals with special woman-edited and woman-written editions of newspapers, whereby women formed themselves into staff to sell advertising, to solicit or develop articles, to plan illustrations, and show up on the appointed day to finish production of the paper. Includes newspapers country-wide.

3550. Cox-Bennion, Sherilyn. "The *Woman's Exponent*: Forty-Two Years of Speaking for Women." *Utah Historical Quarterly*. Summer 1976, pp. 222-239.

3551. Cuklanz, Lisa M. "'Shrill Squawk' or Strategic Innovation: A Rhetorical Reassessment of Margaret Sanger's 'Woman Rebel.'" *Communication Quarterly*. Winter 1995, pp. 1-19.

Takes issue with earlier claims that Sanger's *The Woman Rebel* was a failure; contends it was a success that offered a clear description of socialist feminism through simplistic moral reasoning.

3552. Curtis, Charlotte. *The Rich and Other Atrocities*. New York: Harper & Row, 1976.

Collects Curtis's *New York Times* columns.

3553. Dean, Gabrielle N. "The 'Phallacies' of Dyke Comic Strips." *Genders*. Fall 1997, p. 199 (25).

Critically analyzes the "phallicized" dyke comic strips and the fallacies they convey; claims such strips are counterproductive to the feminine movement they supposedly represent.

3554. "Donna Allen's Comment." *Media Report to Women*. September-October 1990, p. 12.

On *Ms.* financial woes.

3555. Doughty, Frances and Charlotte Bunch. "Frances Doughty Talks to Charlotte Bunch about Women's Publishing." *Sinister Wisdom*. 13 (1980), pp. 71-77.

3556. Durham, Gigi. "The Taming of the Shrew: Women's Magazines and the Regulation of Desire." *Journal of Communication Inquiry*. Spring 1996, pp. 18-31.

Analyzes *Cosmopolitan*, *Glamour*, and *Seventeen* to find the role these women's magazines play in channeling women's sexuality in socially prescribed directions. Four main themes were evident: 1. presumption of heterosexuality, 2. goal of marriage or heterosexual monogamy, 3. oppositional tension between the imperative of free sexual expression and the need to submit to men's desires, 4. the male-centered construction of women's desire as either insatiable lack or a passion in need of strict control.

3557. Eberle, Nance. "A Review of *I'm in Training to Be Tall and Blonde*." *Chicago*. June 1979, pp. 206+.

> Nicole Hollander's cartoon strip.

3558. Endres, Kathleen L. "Eleanor Roosevelt and Her Magazine Columns: The Making of a Liberal Feminist." Paper presented at American Journalism Historians Association, Mobile, Alabama, October 1997.

> Determines from the First Lady's columns, that she did espouse liberal feminism.

3559. Endres, Kathleen L. and Therese L. Lueck. *Women's Periodicals in the United States: Consumer Magazines*. Westport, Connecticut: Greenwood Press, 1995. 528 pp.

> Provides information on 75 consumer magazines aimed at women; entries describe the social and cultural contexts of the magazines, their histories and significance. Almost one-half of the profiled publications are post-World War II, although several 18th and 19th centuries works are included.

3560. Endres, Kathleen L. and Therese L. Lueck, eds. *Women's Periodicals in the United States: Social and Political Issues*. Westport, Connecticut: Greenwood Press, 1996. 560 pp.

> Profiles more than 70 different women's magazines published in the United States during the 19th and 20th centuries; each entry includes critical narrative history, circulation figures, other information and bibliography.

3561. Evans, William. "Divining the Social Order: Class, Gender, and Magazine Astrology Columns." *Journalism and Mass Communication Quarterly*. Summer 1996, pp. 389-400.

> Compares astrological advice offered in magazines for working and middle-class women; finds "readers' social class was a far better predictor than readers' zodiac sign of the nature of astrological advice offered."

3562. Farr, Marie T. "Freedom and Control: Automobiles in American Women's Fiction of the 70s and 80s." *Journal of Popular Culture*. Fall 1995, pp. 157-169.

3563. Farrell, Amy E. "A Social Experiment in Publishing: Ms. Magazine, 1972-1989." *Human Relations*. June 1994, pp. 707-730.

> Explores attempt by *Ms.* editors to create a non-hierarchical, collective-type organization; finds that the primary transformations occurred within the editorial side.

3564. Flanders, Laura. "Conservative Women Are Right for Media: Mainstream Media

Have Finally Found Some Women To Love." *Extra!* March/April 1996, pp. 6, 27.

Independent Women's Forum, started in 1992 as an alternative to feminists, is liked by mainstream media as a source on issues.

3565. Fugua, Edward. "Is Wonder Woman Ruined?" *Comic Fandom's Forum.* December 1982, pp. 20-28.

3566. Gahr, Evan. "Uncovering the Politics of Women's Magazines." *Wall Street Journal.* August 21, 1997.

States women's magazines support many liberal programs of the federal government.

3567. Gentner, Stephen H. "Fox's Glamour Girl of Mystery: Phantom Lady." *Comic Book Marketplace.* July 1995, pp. 30-34.

Some felt this cheesecake comic book was Dr. Fredric Wertham's most hated.

3568. Glessing, Robert J. *The Underground Press in America.* Bloomington: Indiana University Press, 1970.

Includes aspects of women's periodicals published in 1960s.

3569. Gollin, Albert. "'Women's Sections' Win Back Female Readers in the US." *Panap Bulletin.* February 1993, pp. 40-42.

3570. Gordon, J. and J. McArthur. "Popular Culture, Magazines, and American Domestic Interiors, 1898-1940." *Journal of Popular Culture.* Spring 1989, pp. 35-60.

Discusses domestic interiors as presented in *Good Housekeeping, Ladies' Home Journal,* and *House Beautiful,* 1898-1940; claims *Good Housekeeping* least interested in topic.

3571. Gottlieb, Agnes H. "Networking in the Nineteenth Century of the Woman's Press Club of New York City." *Journalism History.* Winter 1995, pp. 156-163.

Details Jane C. Croly's establishment of the Woman's Press Club of New York City in 1889, as a network to communicate and maintain contact with other women writers; relies heavily on the club's minutes from 1889 to 1900.

3572. Goulart, Ron. "Female Funnies, Part I. Flyin' Jenny." *Comics Feature.* March 1987, pp. 40-42.

Describes comic strip that was female based.

3573. Goulart, Ron. "Wonder Woman and Heinrich Kley." *Ron Goulart's Comics History Magazine.* Fall 1996, pp. 18-19.

Tells how comic, "Wonder Woman," was drawn by Harry G. Peter, who, in turn, was influenced by the German artist, Heinrich Kley.

3574. Grand, Alison. "Giving Advertisers What They Want. The Economics of Women's Magazines." *Extra!* March/April 1996, pp. 26-27.
    Insists when it comes to women's magazines, women "have *not* come a long way, baby." Shows how newsletters and regional magazines tried to act as an alternative press for women.

3575. Green, Karen and Tristan Taormino, eds. *A Girls's Guide to Taking Over the World: Writings from the GirlZine Revolution.* New York: St. Martin's Griffin, 1997. 221 pp.

3576. Hammond, Joyce D. "Gender Inversion Cartoons and Feminism." *Journal of Popular Culture.* Spring 1991, pp. 145-160.

3577. "Hawk." "Boston Beanlets." *Journalist.* July 24, 1897, p. 110; January 1, 1898, p. 130.
    Ridicules New England Woman's Press Association.

3578. Heller, Janet R. "*Primavera* and *Black Maria*: Two Chicago Women's Literary Magazines." *Women's Studies.* 23 (1994), pp. 175-190.
    Started in 1960s-1970s to encourage women's studies and foster contemporary women writers.

3579. Hermes, Joke. *Reading Women's Magazines.* New York: Polity Press, 1995.
    Draws from ethnographic research in examining women's magazines through their readers' eyes; explores ways individuals use media on daily basis and interpretive repertoires they employ to make sense of media texts.

3580. Hochschild, Arlie R. and Martin Herz. "The Commercial Spirit of Intimate Life and the Exploitation of Feminism." *Argument.* September-October 1995, pp. 667-680.
    Examines best-selling women's self-help books published in US, 1970-1990, to determine popular attitudes concerning women and intimate life.

3581. Hokinson, Helen E. *The Ladies, God Bless 'Em!* New York: E.P. Dutton, 1950.
    Anthology of her gag cartoons.

3582. Hokinson, Helen E. *My Best Girls.* New York: E.P. Dutton, 1941.
    Anthology of her gag cartoons.

3583. Hokinson, Helen E. *There Are Ladies Present.* New York: E.P. Dutton, 1952.
    Anthology of her gag cartoons.

3584. Hokinson, Helen E. *When Were You Built?* New York: E.P. Dutton, 1952.
    Anthology of her gag cartoons.

3585. "The Hokinson Girls." *Time.* November 14, 1949, pp. 80-81.
    Deals with work of gag cartoonist Helen Hokinson.

3586. Hollander, Nicole. *My Weight Is Always Perfect for My Height - Which Varies.*

New York: St. Martin's Press, 1982.
   Anthology of Hollander feminist cartoons.

3587. Hollander, Nicole. *That Woman Must Be on Drugs.* New York: St. Martin's Press, 1981.
   Anthology of Hollander gag cartoons.

3588. Hollander, Nicole. *The Whole Enchilada: A Spicy Collection of Sylvia Best.* New York: St. Martin's Press, 1976.
   Hollander's gag cartoon anthology, featuring her character, "Sylvia."

3589. Hutton, Frankie. "Satire, Muses and Advice in 'The Women': Evelyn Cunningham as *Pittsburgh Courier* Columnist." Paper presented at American Journalism Historians Association, Mobile, Alabama, October 1997.
   Tells how "The Women" column gives glimpses of black middle class life in Pittsburgh and New York City during the late 1940s and 1950s.

3590. "The Illinois Woman's Press Association." *Fourth Estate.* May 23, 1895, p. 3.

3591. Ingall, Marjorie. "Paper Movies: Female Cartoonists Create Characters That Are Real, Raunchy -- and They'll Knock Your Socks Off." *Ms.* May/June 1997, pp. 40-47.
   Gives synopses of a number of comic books by and for women: Roberta Gregory's *Naughty Bits*, Ellen Forney's *Dyke Strippers*, Megan Kelso's *Girlhero*, Fiona Smyth's *Nocturnal Emissions*, Dame Darcy's *Meatcake*, Julie Doucet's *Dirty Plotte*, and others.

3592. Jesuele, Kim. "Sherrie Shepherd's Francie." *Cartoonist PROfiles.* September 1991, pp. 18-25.
   Discusses comic strip, "Francie," by Sherrie Shepherd.

3593. Johnson, Angela. "Start a Fucking Riot: Riot Grrrrl DC." *Off Our Backs.* May 1993, pp. 6-10.
   Interviews three Washington, D.C. riot grrrls; provides list with addresses of riot grrrl magazines.

3594. Johnson, Sammye. "Mary Barney's 19th Century Magazine of Politics and Purpose for Women." *Southwestern Mass Communication Journal.* 10:2 (1996), pp. 81-90.

3595. Jolliffe, Lee. "Women's Magazines in the 19th Century." *Journal of Popular Culture.* Spring 1994, pp. 125-140.
   Breaks into parts on the growth of the new medium of magazines for women and on Lucy Stone's *Women's Journal* as suffrage promoter.

3596. Kennedy, Pagan. "Alive and Sick." *Off Our Backs.* April 1992, p. 9.

Reviews Diane Noomin's edited book of women's cartoons, *Twisted Sisters: A Collection of Bad Girl Art.*

3597. Kincaid, Jean. "The New England Women's Press Association." *Journalist.* January 26, 1889, pp. 7-11.

Gives account of early female journalists' association, which flourished from 1855 on.

3598. Kranich, Kimberly. "A Bibliography of Periodicals by and about Women of Color." *Feminist Teacher.* Spring 1990, pp. 26-41.

Includes 50 such periodicals; discusses some in detail.

3599. Lavernoich, John L. "Wonder Woman: TV Star with Golden Age Roots." *Comics Buyer's Guide.* September 20, 1996, p. 23.

Claims the comic book superheroine, "Wonder Woman," which first appeared in 1941, did not make her TV debut until 1972; discusses various "Wonder Woman" television movies.

3600. Lewis, Mary J. "'Godey's Lady's Book': Contributions to the Promotion and Development of the American Fashion Magazine in Nineteenth-Century America." Ph.D. dissertation, New York University, 1996.

3601. Longstaff, Jay. "Shanna of the Jungle: A Heroine History." *Bem.* No. 36, 1982, pp. 29-33.

Describes comic book of that name.

3602. Lorber, Judith. "From the Editor." *Gender and Society.* December 1990, pp. 445-450.

Sums up *Gender and Society*'s developing feminist perspective in author's last issue as editor.

3603. Lumsden, Linda. "*Suffragist*: The Making of a Militant." *Journalism and Mass Communication Quarterly.* Autumn 1995, pp. 525-538.

Describes the *Suffragist* newspaper, founded in 1913 by the National Woman's Party, and its militant stand relative to NWP peaceful pickets at the White House (1917), and the brutal reactions of the police and mobs to the protesters. Evolved from author's Ph.D. dissertation at University of North Carolina (1994), entitled "Rampant Women: The Role of the Right to Peaceably Assemble in the Woman Suffrage Movement, 1908-1919."

3604. Luscombe, Belinda. "Do Women Want More Sex?" *Magazine Week.* March 9, 1992, pp. 7-8.

In their women's magazines.

3605. Lyvely, Chin and Joyce Farmer. "Women's Underground Comix." In *The Official Underground and Newave Comix Price Guide*, edited by Jay Kennedy, pp. 28-30. Cambridge, Massachusetts: Boatner Norton Press, 1982.

3606. McCracken, Ellen. *Decoding Women's Magazines: From* Mademoiselle *to* Ms. New York: St. Martin's Press, 1993. 341 pp.

Studies 50 glossy women's magazines from 1981-1983; claims they manipulate women through covertly-linked advertising and editorial content.

3607. McNamara, Mary. "Laughing All the Way to the Revolution -- The New Feminist Comics." *Ms.* January-February 1992, pp. 22-27.

Deals with women comedians who make unfunny women's issues hilarious.

3608. Mann, Judy. *Mann for All Seasons: Wit and Wisdom from* The Washington Post*'s* Judy Mann. New York: MasterMedia Limited, 1990. 306 pp.

Collects Judy Mann's columns written between 1986-1989; her subjects generally were women, families, and the women's revolution.

3609. Mather, Anne. "A History of Feminist Periodicals, Part III." *Journalism History.* Winter 1975, pp. 19-23, 31.

3610. Mathews, Fannie A. "The Woman's Press Club of New York City." *Cosmopolitan.* August 1892, pp. 455-461.

Stresses "unity, fellowship and cooperation" among members; profiles 22 members.

3611. *Mediascene.*

No. 8 -- Called "The Pin-Up Girls Issue," it includes art by Vargas, Petty, Moran, and Elvgren, as well as comic strip pin-ups.

No. 37 -- Called "Paper Girls! Issue"; includes comics classic pin-up girls from "Blondie" to "Torchy."

3612. "Mervyn's California Has the Young, Moms in 'View.'" *Discount Store News.* September 4, 1995, p. 13.

Discusses launching of *View,* a seasonal magazine primarily targeted to active mothers.

3613. Metzger, Kim. "Media Meanderings." *Comics Buyer's Guide.* July 25, 1997, pp. 50, 52.

Describes 1960s comic book of Archie Group, *Sabrina.*

3614. Miller, Cristanne. "Who Talks Like a Women's Magazine? Language and Gender in Popular Women's and Men's Magazines." *Journal of American Culture.* 10 (1987), pp. 1-9.

3615. Miller, Susan H. "Women's Lifestyles: A Special Report." *Scripps-Howard Editors Newsletter.* Spring 1989, p. 12.

3616. Mookerji, Rita. "A Content Analysis of Five Selected American Women's

Magazines in the Last Twenty Years." Masters thesis, University of Georgia, 1967.

3617. Morgan, Robin. "Editorial -- *Ms.* Lives!" *Ms.* July-August 1990, pp. 1-2.

3618. "Ms. Liz by Barbara Slate." *Cartoonist PROfiles.* June 1983, pp. 26-32.
        Discusses Slate's cartoon strip.

3619. Myers, Annie E. "Illinois Woman's Press Club." *Journalist.* October 15, 1887, p. 6.

3620. Nelson, Wendy. "17 Going on 50: *Seventeen* Magazine." *Media History Digest.* Spring/Summer 1994, pp. 62-64.

3621. Nelton, Sharon. "Catering to Women Readers." *Nation's Business.* October 1994, p. 19.
        Discusses Sisters Syndicate, a publishing company that targets "pink collar" women.

3622. Orenstein, Peggy. "*Ms.* Fights for Its Life." *Mother Jones.* November-December 1990, pp. 32-36, 81-83, 91.
        Claims because of threats from new magazines and bigness of media conglomerates.

3623. Phillips, Kimberly. "The *Sassy/'Teen* Merger: Invasion of the Magazine Snatchers." *Extra!* November/December 1995, pp. 21-22.
        Tells how *Sassy* changed to a more sedate magazine after its 1994 purchase by Peterson Publishing and eventual merger with *'Teen.*

3624. Porter, Jack N. "Rosa Sonneschein and *The American Jewess*: The First Independent English-Language Jewish Women's Journal in the United States." *American Jewish History.* October 1958, pp. 57-63.

3625. "Prototype Newspaper for Women Circulated at ASNE Convention." *Media Report to Women.* May/June 1990, p. 3.
        "Womenews," designed as a stand-alone paper or supplement of a daily, discussed at ASNE.

3626. Rakow, Lana F. and Cheris Kramarae, eds. *The Revolution in Words: Righting Women, 1868-1871.* New York: Routledge, 1990. 297 pp.
        Profiles the brief but change-inducing life of *The Revolution*, Elizabeth Cady Stanton and Susan B. Anthony's newspaper of the post-Civil War era.

3627. Rapoport, Ron, ed. *A Kind of Grace: A Treasury of Sportswriting by Women.* Berkeley, California: Zenobia Press, 1994. 384 pp.

3628. Redmond, Pat. "Against the Odds Welfare Mothers Publish Newspaper." *New Directions for Women.* January-February 1990, p. 8.

3629. Reed, Barbara S. "Rosa Sonneschein and *The American Jewess.*" *Journalism History.* Autumn 1990-Winter 1991, pp. 54-62.

Uses primary data to discuss role of *The American Jewess* in reflecting nineteenth century Jewish women's thought. Started in Chicago in 1895 by Rosa Sonneschein, the magazine was intended for the New Woman, providing role models and much sage advice. *The American Jewess* folded in 1899.

3630. Robbins, Trina. "When Girls Read Comics." *Comics Buyer's Guide.* July 25, 1997, pp. 28-30.

Provides history of U.S. girls' comics and shows that today, the Archie Line of comics is the only one of girls' comics.

3631. Rosenberger, Nancy. "Don't Think! There's No Time! Message of Individuality, Freedom and Status in Young Women's Magazines." Paper presented at Association for Asian Studies, New Orleans, Louisiana, March 1991.

3632. Russo, Ann and Cheris Kramarae, eds. *The Radical Women's Press of the 1850s.* New York: Routledge, 1991. 368 pp.

Reprints from periodicals and newspapers of the period; divided into sections on "Domestic Tyranny," "Working into Poverty," "Sex Differences and Inequality," "Men's Chivalry -- and All That," and "Organizing for Social Change"; deals with the works of Amelia Bloomer of *The Lily*, Elizabeth A. Aldrich of *The Genius of Liberty*, Anna W. Spencer of *The Pioneer and Woman's Advocate*, Paulina W. Davis of *The Una*, Ann McDowell of *The Woman's Advocate*, and Dr. Lydia S. Hasbrouck of *The Sibyl*.

3633. Scanlon, Jennifer. *Inarticulate Longings: The Ladies' Home Journal, Gender, and the Promises of Consumer Culture.* New York: Routledge, 1995. 288 pp.

Provides connections between publishing and advertising industries and an analysis of popular fiction written by and for women.

3634. Schiffren, Lisa. "What the Well-Dressed Woman Is Thinking." *National Review.* October 28, 1996, p. 44+.

States that fashion magazines have been regularly politically correct on all liberal issues, especially those pertaining to feminists.

3635. Seller, Maxine. "World of Our Mothers: The Women's Page of the *Jewish Daily Forward.*" *Journal of Ethnic Studies.* Spring 1989, pp. 95-118.

3636. Sellers, Susan. "How Long Has This Been Going On? 'Harpers Bazaar,' 'Funny Face,' and the Construction of the Modernist Woman." *Visible Language.* Winter 1995, pp. 12-35.

Looks at ways women understood the fashion magazine *Harper's Bazaar*.

3637. Short, Kayann. "*Sylvia* Talks Back." In *New Perspectives on Women and Comedy*, edited by Regina Barreca, pp. 57-64. Philadelphia, Pennsylvania: Gordon and

Breach, 1992.
> On Nicole Hollander's comic strip, "Sylvia."

3638. Shutt, Craig. "Introducing Miss Arrowette." *Comics Buyer's Guide*. July 25, 1997, p. 38.
> Briefly profiles 1960s' comic book featuring "Miss Arrowette."

3639. Shutt, Craig. "Thirteen: Stanley Fills the Lulu Archie Gap." *Comics Buyer's Guide*. July 25, 1997, p. 32, 34.
> Discusses Dell girls' comic book, *Thirteen*, created in 1960 by John Stanley.

3640. Shutt, Craig. "Zatanna's Magical Mystery Tour." *Comics Buyer's Guide*. February 20, 1998, p. 24-26.
> Recounts story of comic book superheroine "Zatanna," prominent during comics' Silver Era.

3641. Solomon, Martha M., ed. *A Voice of Their Own: The Woman Suffrage Press, 1840-1910*. Tuscaloosa: University of Alabama Press, 1991. 233 pp.
> Focuses on how periodicals worked to raise women's consciousness, create a sense of community, change women's images and societal roles; chapters analyze particular periodicals.

3642. Steinem, Gloria. "Sex, Lies and Advertising." In *Mass Media 96/97*, edited by Joan Gorham, pp. 157-165. Guilford, Connecticut: Dushkin Publishing Group, 1996.
> Asks question: "Suppose archaeologists of the future dug up women's magazines and used them to judge women. What would they think of us -- and what can we do about it?" Deals with the refusal of corporations to advertise in magazines that do not actively support their products. Originally in *Ms* (July-August 1990, pp. 18-28).

3643. "Steinem To Detail *Ms.* Advertiser Pressure in Re-Launch Issue in June." *Media Report to Women*. May-June 1990, p. 1.
> *Ms.* founding editor detailed advertising pressures in article, "Sex, Lies and Advertising," scheduled for publication in relaunch issue.

3644. Steiner, Linda. "The Woman's Suffrage Press, 1850-1900: A Cultural Analysis." Ph.D. dissertation, University of Illinois, 1979.

3645. Stiles, Cindy A. "Windows into Antebellum Charleston: Caroline Gilman and the *Southern Rose* Magazine." Ph.D. dissertation, University of South Carolina, 1994.

3646. "They Will Realize $7,000, Great Success of the Women's Edition of the Sentinel." *Indianapolis Sentinel*. November 29, 1895, p. 5.

3647. "U.S. Women's Magazines in Search of an Audience." *Media Report to Women*. September-October 1990, p. 5.

410 Women and Mass Communications

Declining circulation and advertising affected women's magazines.

3648. von Bergen, Jane M. "My Name Is So Out, It's in -- and on Newsstands, Everywhere." *Inquirer Magazine* (Philadelphia). December 28, 1997, pp. 14-17.

Discusses *Jane Magazine* and its name, from its editor, Jane Pratt, former editor of *Sassy* and talk show host.

3649. von Hoffman, Nicholas. "Women's Pages: An Irreverent View." *Columbia Journalism Review*. July-August 1971, pp. 52-54.

Attacks separate newspaper pages for women.

3650. Walker, Nancy A., ed. *Women's Magazines from the 1940s and 1950s*. New York: St. Martin's Press, 1998. 200 pp.

Chronicles women's domestic and public roles during 1940s and 1950s by looking at women's magazines; organized into seven topics with 60 articles and 10 advertisements from magazines.

3651. Waller, Mary Ellen. "Popular Women's Magazines, 1890-1917." Ph.D. dissertation, Columbia University, 1987.

3652. Waller-Zuckerman, Mary E. "Old Homes in a City of Perpetual Change: The Women's Magazine Industry, 1890-1917." *Business History Review*. Winter 1989, pp. 715-756.

3653. "*Wall Street Journal* Essay: Women's Magazines Have Liberal Bias." *Media Report to Women*. Fall 1997, pp. 3-4.

Reports on *Journal* article that claimed mainstream women's magazines promote a liberal agenda that recommends reliance on government programs to resolve social problems.

3654. Warner, Richard F. "Godey's Lady's Book." *American Mercury*. 2 (1924), pp. 399-405.

3655. Wechsler-Chaput, Elayne. "Hell Hath No Furies." *The Jack Kirby Collector*. July 1995, pp. 20-21.

Discusses Jack Kirby's comic book stories on "Female Furie Battalion."

3656. Willen, Janet L. "Not for Women Only." *Nation's Business*. September 1994, p. 16.

Essence magazine founders discuss how they built the magazine for black women into a diversified media corporation.

3657. Wilson, Sally B. "How Magazines Reflect Social Movements: A Case Study of the Women's Liberation Movement as Reflected in Three Women's Magazines." Masters thesis, University of Missouri, 1972.

3658. Winship, Janice. "'Options -- for the Way You Want To Live Now' or a Magazine for Superwoman." *Theory, Culture and Society.* 1:3 (1983), pp. 44-65.

3659. "Women's Editions." *Journalist.* March 7, 1895, p. 4.
Discusses these women's editions as opportunities for women journalists.

3660. "Women's Magazines Still Downplay Smoking Dangers." *Media Report to Women.* Winter 1997, p. 16.

3661. "Women's Papers." *Woman's Tribune.* March 2, 1895, p. 34.

3662. Wright, Nicky. "Cheesecake and Crime for Just a Dime a Time." *Comic Book Marketplace.* July 1995, pp. 22-29.
Discusses the "good girl" of the comics, "Phantom Lady."

3663. Yang, Mei-ling. "Women's Pages or People's Pages: The Production of News for Women in the *Washington Post* in the 1950s." *Journalism and Mass Communication Quarterly.* Summer 1996, pp. 364-378.
Examines *Washington Post* women's pages of the 1950s, edited by Marie Sauer; shows how *Post* turned down Sauer's 1952 proposal to change from traditionally women's to unisex lifestyle pages, and how women's pages were shaped by factors such as advertising, professional values, and gender beliefs.

3664. Zandy, Janet. *Calling Home: Working-Class Women's Writings: An Anthology.* New Brunswick, New Jersey: Rutgers University Press, 1990. 340 pp.
Includes more than 50 selections that represent the ethnic, racial, and geographic diversity of working class women; women journalists Agnes Smedley, and Meridel Le Sueur.

3665. Zerkel, Joanne. "From Milady to Ms. -- Changing Tastes and Techniques." *Press Woman.* April 1986, pp. 9-10.

3666. Zinkhan, George A. and Linda A. Hayes. "Changing Patterns of Other-Directedness: A Content Analysis of Women's Magazines." *Journal of Social Psychology.* December 1989, pp. 825-831.

3667. Zuckerman, Mary E. *Sources on The History of Women's Magazines, 1792-1960. An Annotated Bibliography.* Westport, Connecticut: Greenwood Press, 1991. 207 pp.
Includes more than 960 entries on categories of "Women's Magazines," "Portrayal of Women in the Media," "Studies of Content in Women's Magazines," "Individuals Working for Women's Magazines," "Advertising and Ad Agencies," "Surveys, Marketing Research Reports, and Promotional Materials," "The Business of Women's Magazines," and "Critiques of Women's Magazines."

CHAPTER 7

Addendum: Updates

GLOBAL AND COMPARATIVE PERSPECTIVES

3668. Albury, Katherine. "Spanking Stories: Writing and Reading Bad Female Heterosex." *Continuum.* April 1998, pp. 55-68.
     Feels it is self-defeating to insist that "sexual bottoms" can never be "political tops."

3669. Anand, Anita, Pat Made, Sheila Gibbons, and Rina Jimenez-David. "The Women's Page: Godsend or Ghetto?" *Media & Gender Monitor.* Summer 1998, pp. 9-11.
     Questions media practitioners from India, Africa, United States, and Philippines as to whether women's pages were places where women's issues were relegated, or spaces for empowerment and information for women.

3670. Association for Education in Journalism and Mass Communication Conference. Baltimore, Maryland, August 3-8, 1998
     Includes Chompunuch Punyapiroje, Mariea Grubbs Hoy, and Margaret Morrison, "Adver-Thai-sing Standardization: Can a U.S. Study of Sex Role Portrayals Transcend Cultural Boundaries?"; Debra Merskin, "The American Way to Menstruate: Feminine Hygiene Advertising and Adolescent Girls"; Moon Jeong Lee, "The Effects of Hypertext on Readers' Recall Based on Gender"; Julie L. Andsager, "Examining Rhetorical Structures in Competing News Frames: How Interest Groups Shaped Coverage of the Lateterm Abortion Debate"; Venhwei Lo and Anna R. Paddon, "The Third-person Perception and Support for Restriction of Pornography: Some Methodological Problems"; Patricia Bradley, "*The Feminist Mystique* and Mass Media: Implications for the Second Wave"; Elizabeth V. Burt, "Pioneering for Women Journalists: Sallie Joy White, 1870-1909"; Virginia H. Carroll and Patricia G. McNeely, "The Remarkable Timothy Women"; Mary M. Cronin, "'Those Who Toil and Spin': Female Textile Operatives' Publications and

the Response to Industrialization"; Dolores L. Flamiano, "Covering Contraception: Discourses of Gender, Motherhood, and Sexuality in Women's Magazines, 1938-1969"; Kristine L. Nowak, "Women's Historical Contribution to Journalism Education As Seen in Emery's *The Press and America*"; Marilyn S. Sarow, "At Our House: A Case Study of Grace B. Freeman, Syndicated Columnist, 1954-1964"; Rana Knio and Michael Elasmar, "Factors Influencing Gender Role Attitudes Among Lebanese Youth"; Radhika E. Parameswaran, "Popular Literature and Gender Identities: An Analysis of Young Indian Women's Anxieties About Reading Western Romances"; Helena K. Särkiö, "Finnish Women and Political Knowledge: What Do They Know and How Do They Learn It?"; Britto M. Berchmans, "Consumption of Teen Magazines by Adolescent Italian Girls: Reading Patterns and Motives"; Lisa Daigle, "The Astounding Women of *Analog*: A Content Analysis of Cover Art"; Agnes Gottlieb, "'When I Grow Up...' How Popular Magazines Portrayed Journalism as a Career for Women, 1872-1926"; Ernest C. Hynds, "Women's Magazines Used Agenda-Setting, Priming In Effort to Influence '96 Election"; Steven R. Thomsen, J. Kelly McCoy, Marleen Williams, and Robert L. Gustafson, "Beauty and Fashion Magazine Reading and Anorectic Cognitions As Predictors of Dieting Behavior in College-Age Women"; Jane R. Ballinger, "Marketing A Movement: Media Relations Strategies of the Gay and Lesbian Movement"; Joseph P. Bernt, "Poor Vision of Intelligence: The Very White, Very Male, and Very Professional World of Jeopardy!"; Martin Eichholz, "Thoughtful Self-Critique of Journalistic Cannibalism? International Press Coverage of Princess Diana's Death"; Debra Merskin, "Adolescence, Advertising, and the Menstrual Taboo"; Lisa M. Weidman, "In the Olympic Tradition: Sportscasters' Language and Female Athleticism"; Lori Bergen, "Not the Same Story: Differences in Sexual Harassment of Women Who Work as Newspaper and Television Journalists"; Melissa A. John, "Sex Without Consequence: The Sexual and Reproductive Health Content of Latino Magazines"; Patricia A. Curtin and Karen S. Miller, "Women in the Public Relations Trade Press: A Content Analysis of *Tide* and *Public Relations Journal* (1940s through 1960s)"; Susan Henry, "Learning to Swim Skillfully in Uncharted Waters: Doris E. Fleischman"; Michael A. Mitrook, Kimberly V. Wilkes, and Glen Cameron, "Dealing With The Feminization of the Field: Attitudes and Aptitudes of College Women in Public Relations"; Cindy M. Brown, "Grounded Moral Theory: A Feminist Way of Doing (Media) Ethics"; Brenda Cooper, "Hegemony and the Re-Creation of Dominant Culture: A Critique of Hollywood's Cinematic Distortion of Women of Color and Their Stories"; Fabienne Darling-Wolf, "On the Possibility of Communicating: Critical Theory, Feminism, and Social Position"; Darlene Jirikowic, "*I Love Lucy* and Ethel Mertz: An Expression of Internal Conflict and Pre-Feminist Solidarity"; Linda Steiner, "The Cable Collective as Public Space: 'New Directions for Women'"; Laura K. Smith and John W. Wright II, "Women in Television News Management: Do They Make A Difference?"; John M. King, "Who Gets Named?: Nationality, Race and Gender in *New York Times* Photograph Cutlines"; A. P. Brousseau, "Conflict Between Religion and Media Messages Aimed at Young Women"; Julie L. Andsager, "Reframing Media Coverage of Women's Health: Magazine Reports on Breast Cancer and Implants in the 1990s"; Bente Bjornsen, "Media Coverage of Women's Sports: Perspectives of Female Journalists and Athletes in the United States and Norway"; Constance Ledoux Book, "An

Examination of the Women Featured in *Broadcasting and Cable*'s 'Fifth Estater' 1992-1997"; Mia Consalvo, "News of 'Kiddle Killings': Feminist Theories of News Coverage and Violence"; Fabienne Darling-Wolf, "Gender, Beauty, and Western Influence: Negotiated Femininity in Japanese Women's Magazines"; E-K. Daufin, "Suffocating Jezebel, Sapphire and Mammy: Persistent Cross-Media Stereotypes of African-American Women in 'Waiting to Exhale'"; Erika Engstrom and Anthony J. Ferri, "Gender Differences in the Perceptions of Television News Anchors' Career Barriers"; Joe S. Foote and Cynthia Price, "Women Correspondent Visibility 1983-1997"; Dustin Harp, "Blame and Shame: Teen-aged Mothers, Ideologies and the *New York Times*"; Kim E. Karloff, "Mary, Patricia, Maxine and Cynthia: Tracking the Stories Behind the First Rape Victim Identification Debates, for Columbia S.C. 1909 to the U.S. Supreme Court 1975"; Carolyn Kitch, "Sexual Saints and Suffering Sinners: The Uneasy Feminism of *The Masses*, 1911-1917"; Myra Gregory Knight, "Listen Up: A Comparison of Male and Female Opinion on the Issue of Family Values"; Abigail S. Leafe, "Blurring the Lines: Postfeminism, Sanity and *Ally McBeal*"; Christine Martin, "War Stories: Women Correspondents Battle to Cover the Vietnam Conflict"; Katjar R. Pinkston, "Gender Roles in *Rumpelstiltskin*: The Effect of Fantasy Portrayals on Real-Life Attitudes"; Susannah R. Stern, "All I Really Needed to Know (About Beauty) I Learned by Kindergarten: A Cultivation Analysis"; Troy Tanner, "The Portrayal of Professional Beach Volleyball Players in Three Major Newspapers, 1995-1997: An Analysis of Media Coverage of Male and Female Athletes."

3671. Barrett, Jacqueline, ed. *Encyclopedia of Women's Organizations Worldwide*. Detroit, Michigan: Gale, 1993. 471 pp.
    Gives directory data for 3,400 groups, including a number on media.

3672. Capek, Mary Ellen, ed. *DWN: Directory of Women's Media*. New York: National Council for Research on Women, 1994. 205 pp.
    Compiles information on women's media in more than 50 countries. Seventeenth edition.

3673. "Clips -- A Glance Around the Globe at WACC-Funded Women's Projects." *Media and Gender Monitor*. Spring 1998, p. 7.
    Includes short articles on Malaysia, Myanmar, Kenya, Uganda, and Jamaica.

3674. *Continuum.*
    April 1998 -- Thematic issue on "Censorship and Pornography," edited by Kate Bowles, John Hartley, and Alan McKee, includes: John Hartley, "'When Your Child Grows Up Too Fast': Juvenation and the Boundaries of the Social in the News Media," pp. 9-30; Ina Bertrand, "Education of Exploitation: The Exhibition of 'Social Hygiene' Films in Australia," pp. 31-46; Catharine Lumby, "No Kidding: Paedophilia and Popular Culture," pp. 47-54; Katherine Albury, "Spanking Stories: Writing and Reading Bad Female Heterosex," pp. 55-68; Rebecca Huntley, "Slippery When Wet: The Shifting Boundaries of the

Pornographic (a Class Analysis)," pp. 69-82; McKenzie Wark, "Bad Girls Do It in Public," pp. 83-90; Stephanie Donald, "Symptoms of Alienation: The Female Body in Recent Chinese Film," pp. 91-104.

3675. De Wiest, Annie. "Lest We Forget." *Media & Gender Monitor*. Summer 1998, p. 5.

Rehashes issues of Platform J of the Fourth World Conference on Women, Beijing, March 1995.

3676. Eliasson, Dagny and Gunilla Ivarsson. *Equality in the Broadcasting*. Stockholm: Sveriges Radio, 1997. 9 pp.

Pushes for training of women journalists globally.

3677. Fallon, Helen. *WOW: Women on the Web, A Guide to Gender-Related Resources on the Internet*. Dublin: University Centre, 1997.

Questions why women are underrepresented on Internet and suggests ways this shortcoming can be solved.

3678. Furniss, Maureen. *Art in Motion: Animation Aesthetics*. Sydney: John Libbey, 1998.

Includes chapter, "Women's Voices in Animation."

3679. Hauserman, Nancy. "Comparing Conversations about Sexual Harassment in the US/Sweden: Print Media Coverage of the Case Against Astra USA." Paper presented at International Association for Media and Communication Research, Glasgow, Scotland, July 26-30, 1998.

Compares U.S. and Swedish print media coverage of a sexual harassment case.

3680. International Association for Media and Communication Research Conference. Glasgow, Scotland, July 26-30, 1998

Includes Birgette Jallov, "Women's (Community) Radio as a Feminist Public Sphere"; John W. Higgins, "Critical/Feminist Media Pedagogies in a Turkish Cypriot Context"; Changhee Park, "The Ideological Shift of Gender Representations in Korean Television Dramas"; Myoung Hye Kim, "Western Psychoanalysis Hits the Korean Television Drama"; Henrika Zilliacus Tikkanen, "Who Speaks? A Study on Men and Women in Prime Television in Five Countries Focusing on Data from Finland"; Sanna Ojajärvi, "Gendered or Generic Codes? A Study of Hosts on Finnish Television"; Anne Cooper-Chen, "Manga for the Masses: Portrayals of Women in Japanese Comics for Men"; Manisha Pande, "Projections of Today's Indian Woman's Images in Indian Commercials: A Misnomer?" Ramona R. Rush, "Natural Communications: An Unnatural Act for Mankind?" Gita Bamezai and Kiran Bansal, "The Press in India and Violence Against Women: An Advocacy or Objectivity"; Steven A. Carr, "Lewinsky's Mouth and the Fragmentation of Persuasion"; Daniel R. Nicholson, "The Peacettes: *The New York Times*' Coverage of the First International Conference for Women at The Hague in 1915"; Susannah Stern, "All I Really Needed to Know (About Beauty) I Learned by Kindergarten: A Cultivation Analysis"; Nancy Hauserman, "Comparing Conversations About Sexual Harassment in the

US/Sweden: Print Media Coverage of the Case Against Astra USA"; Ellen Riordan and Eileen Meehan, "The Intersection of Political Economy and Feminist Theory"; Ellen Balka, "Long Numbers and Wrong Numbers: New Technology and the Restructuring of Women's Work in Telecommunications in Atlantic Canada"; Amy Beer, "Periodical Pleasures: Magazines for the US Latina Market"; Ramona Curry and Anghy Valdivia, "Xuxa and Borders of Global TV"; Kate Kane, "The Post Soviet Order and Feminine Hygiene"; Stana B. Martin, "Women's Employment in the Information Sector: The Effects of Sexsegregation and Technological Unemployment"; B. Gerry Coulter, "Political Economy and Dialectical Feminism"; Alison Beale, "Beyond the Cultural Consumer: Using Feminist Scholarship To Understand Cultural Policy in the Era of Free Trade Agreements"; Carolyn M. Byerly, "Women, Media and Structure: Seeking a Feminist Macroresearch Agenda in an Era of Globalization"; Michele Martin, "Unsuitable Systems for Women? Communication as Circulation"; Karen Ross, "Sex, Politics and the Media: Selling Women (Down the River)"; Marjan de Bruin, "Gender in the Newsroom: Does It Make a Difference?" Monika Djert Pierre and Margareta M. Higgins, "Networking in Newsrooms: Journalism and Gender Cultures"; Shakuntala Rao, "'Our Borders Are Out of Control!': Media, Nationalism and the Politics of Gender"; Stacy Benjamin and Oscar H. Gandy, "Lady Luck Falls on Hard Times: Themes of Risk, Fate and Uncertainty in American Popular Music 20th Century"; Angharad N. Valdivia, "Ethnicity and Expressive Culture: Gender and Ethnic Assertion Through Dance and Music"; Tarja Savolainen, "Film Journalist Brita Wrede and Finnish Nationalism"; Irina Novikova, "Fashioning Our Minds: Women's Press in Latvia (Latvian and Russian Women's Magazines at the Crossroads of Gender, Ethnicity and Citizenship)"; Dafna Lemish, "The Whore and the Other: Images of Former USSR Female Immigrants in the Israeli Popular Press"; Elisabeth Eide, "Is the African Woman Allowed to Speak?"

3681. *The Journal of International Communication*.

      3:1 -- Special number on women includes: Ellen Balka, "Women and Computer Networking in Six Countries"; Joan R. Frankson, "Women's Global Faxnet"; Lily Ling, "Feminist International Relations: From Critique to Reconstruction"; Valentine M. Moghadam, "Feminist Networks North and South"; Annabelle Sreberny-Mohammadi, "International Feminism(s)"; Angharad N. Valdivia, "Is Modern to Male as Traditional Is to Female?"

3682. Juno, Andrea. *Dangerous Drawings*. New York: Juno Books, 1997. 224 pp.

      Interviews 14 cartoonists out of the mainstream; among them are Julie Doucet, Diane Noomin, Emiko "Carol" Shimoda, Aline Kominsky-Crumb, and Phoebe Gloeckner.

3683. Kenyon, Heather. "A Conversation with ... Chris Walker and Corky Quakenbush." *Animation World*. February 1998. 9 pp.

      Interviews animation motion-capture trailblazer Chris Walker.

3684. Krikos, Linda A. "Women and the Mass Media: Reference Works in the 1990s."

Communication Booknotes Quarterly. Summer 1998, pp. 133-144.

Discusses 26 reference titles on women and mass media published in the 1990s, with emphasis on materials that appeared after 1993; includes abstracts by categories of general women's studies sources, filmmaking, television, periodicals and publishing, journalism, orators, and the Internet.

3685. McQuillan, Libbie. "Tradition and Transgression: The Laughter of Claire Bretecher." Paper presented at International Comics and Animation Festival, Bethesda, Maryland, September 25, 1998.

3686. Martin, Michele. "Unsuitable Systems for Women? Communication as Circulation." Paper presented at International Association for Mass Communication Research, Glasgow, Scotland, July 26-30, 1998.

Critically examines recent feminist periodical literature on international systems of communication.

3687. *Media & Gender Monitor.*

Summer 1998 -- Includes "Not Enough," pp. 1, 4, 6; "Cape Town Declaration," p. 2; Teresita Hermano, "Programme Notes," p. 3; Annie De Wiest, "Lest We Forget," p. 5; "Cape Fearless," p. 7; "Net Gains," p. 8; "The Women's Page: Godsend or Ghetto?" pp. 9-11; "Clips," p. 12; "Fighting Chance," p. 13; "WACCtivities," pp. 14-15.

3688. *Media Development.*

3/1998 -- Includes four articles dealing with mass media and women: Christine Ogan and Marisca Milikowski, "Television Helps To Define 'Home' for the Turkish Women of Amsterdam," pp. 13-21; Laura Agustín, "The Plight of Migrant Women: They Speak, but Who's Listening?" pp. 24-26; Janet Bauer, "Cultural Communication, Media, and Iranian Women Refugees in Germany and Canada," pp. 27-33; and Keith Suter, "Australia, the Media and the Politics of Anger," pp. 38-40.

3689. Merino, Ana. "Two Little Girls and Their Ideological Perspectives, or: How Comics Represent Childhood: Little Orphan Annie and Conservative Discourse vs. Little Lulu, the First Feminist." Paper presented at International Comics and Animation Festival, Bethesda, Maryland, September 25, 1998.

3690. "The Monitor Forum." *Media and Gender Monitor.* Spring 1998, pp. 11, 13, 15, 17.

Discusses sex and the media globally through interviews with Gabrielle Le Roux, Margaret Gallagher, Hilary Nicholson, Samere Tansley, Urvashi Butalia, María E. Hermosilla, and Joan Ross.

3691. Pandian, Hannah. "The Debate." *Media and Gender Monitor.* Spring 1998, pp. 8-10, 12, 14, 16.

Looks at international pornography industry, with women's perspectives from around the world.

3692. Pandian, Hannah. "Not Enough." *Media & Gender Monitor*. Summer 1998, pp. 1, 4, 6.

Reports on World Association for Christian Communication's third gender and communication policy conference in Cape Town, June 1998. In same issue, see "Cape Town Declaration" and Teresita Hermano's news notes from the conference.

3693. Rosoff, Ilene, ed. *The Catalog and Review: Tools for Connecting the Community of Women*. Berkeley, California: Celestial Arts, 1995. 504 pp.

Lists many women-created books, websites, videos, periodicals, and other materials worldwide.

3694. Schubart, Rikke. "Woman with a Gun Does Not Signify Man with a Phallus: Gender and Narrative Change in the Action Movie." *Nordicom Review*. June 1998, pp. 205-214.

States that although there have been action heroines since the beginning of action cinema, the "woman with a gun does not signify a man with a phallus. She is always daughter, mother, amazon, always a fantasy, always using a fetish offered by him. And she is always at his command, at his feet and at his service."

3695. Sinclair, Heather. "Julie Doucet's *Dirty Plotte*." Paper presented at International Comics and Animation Festival, Bethesda, Maryland, September 25, 1998.

3696. Thalheimer, Anne N. "What Does a White Dyke Write Like?: Borders and Borderlands in Roberta Gregory's *Naughty Bits* and Alison Bechdel's *Dykes to Watch Out for*." Paper presented at International Comics and Animation Festival, Bethesda, Maryland, September 24, 1998.

3697. Thornham, Sue. *Passionate Detachments: An Introduction to Feminist Film Theory*. London: Arnold, 1998. 204 pp.

Starts with second-wave feminism and proceeds through first feminist film discussions in the early 1970s to lesbian and black female spectatorship.

3698. Union for Democratic Communications Conference. San Francisco, California, June 11-14, 1998.

Eileen Meehan and Ellen Riordan, "Intersections of Political Economy and Feminism"; Bernadette Barker-Plummer, "Feminist Media Strategies and News Discourse: Is Incorporation Inevitable?"; Lisa McLaughlin, "Communities, Publics, and Counterpublics: Feminist Access and the Mass-Mediated Public Sphere"; Kate Kane, "Feminine Hygiene and Post-Soviet Markets"; Virginia Keller, "Mother Trucker: Now You See Her, Now You Don't -- Women, the Labor Movement, and Democracy in Canadian and U.S. Media Images"; Jeanne Hall, "Union Maids and Union Busters: Goal Centered Characters and Class Action in Norma Rae and Matewan."

3699. Walters, Margaret. "Girls on Film." *The Listener*. February 1990, pp. 26-27.

Discusses female film directors.

3700. Wilkins, Karin G. "Gender, Power and Development." *Journal of International Communication*. December 1997, pp. 102-120.

Surveys research on subject and illustrates the changing images of women in development discourse, as well as institutional responses to these shifts.

AFRICA AND THE MIDDLE EAST

3701. Bauer, Janet. "Cultural Communication, Media, and Iranian Women Refugees in Germany and Canada." *Media Development*. 3/1998, pp. 27-33.

Illustrates the "complex nuances of refugees' rights to cultures and the requirements of their host societies to support this through various means"; uses example of Iranian women in Germany and Canada.

3702. "Cape Fearless." *Media & Gender Monitor*. Summer 1998, p. 7.

Deals with a project, "Ilita Labantu," in South Africa designed to enlighten people on women and child abuse, because "the media cover these issues insufficiently."

3703. Eide, Elisabeth. "Is the African Woman Allowed to Speak?" Paper presented at International Association for Mass Communication Research, Glasgow, Scotland, July 26-30, 1998.

Analyzes two articles where male journalists are concerned with women of Mozambique who offer sexual services for money.

3704. Lemish, Dafna. "The Whore and the Other: Images of Former USSR Female Immigrants in the Israeli Popular Press." Paper presented at International Association for Mass Communication Research, Glasgow, Scotland, July 26-30, 1998.

Suggests that female immigrants from former USSR countries appear in the Israeli press in two negative images: as suppliers of sexual services and as "not one of us."

3705. Njanji-Matetafuka. "Fighting Chance." *Media & Gender Monitor*. Summer 1998, p. 13.

Agence France Press correspondent writes about covering conflict situations in Angola and Rwanda as an African woman.

3706. Pandian, Hannah. "Women Banging the Drums in South Africa." *Action*. July 1998, p. 8.

Reports on conference on Gender and Communication Policy for Anglophone Africa, Cape Town, South Africa, June 1-4, 1998.

3707. "WACCtivities." *Media & Gender Monitor*. Summer 1998, p. 14.

Reports on Cape Town, South African youth who in a television debate, questioned politicians.

ASIA, AUSTRALIA, AND OCEANIA

3708. Bamezai, Gita and Kiran Bansal. "The Press in India and Violence Against Women: An Advocacy or Objectivity." Paper presented at International Association for Mass Communication Research, Glasgow, Scotland, July 26-30, 1998.
    Correlates through content analysis the number of violent incidences reported in the press in 1988 and 1997; in latter year, issues of violence are reported with concern and sensitivity.

3709. Blonski, Annette and Freda Frieberg. "Double Trouble: Women's Films." In *The Australian Screen*, edited by Albert Moran and Tom O'Regan. Melbourne: Penguin, 1989.

3710. Bradbury, Keith. "An Ambivalent Industry: How Australian Animation Developed." Master's thesis, University of Queensland, 1997.
    Includes "Women in Animation," pp. 136-139, and other references.

3711. Cooper-Chen, Anne. "Manga for the Masses: Portrayals of Women in Japanese Comics for Men." Paper presented at International Association for Mass Communication Research, Glasgow, Scotland, July 26-30, 1998.
    Analyzes covers and photo spreads for August-September 1997 issues of *Shukan Young Jump*, one of Japan's largest comic books.

3712. Donald, Stephanie. "Symptoms of Alienation: The Female Body in Recent Chinese Film." *Continuum*. April 1998, pp. 91-103.
    Discusses a "developing aesthetic of transnational spectatorship that revels in sexism" in Chinese cinema; uses examples of "Beijing Bastards" by Zhang Yuan and "The Days" by Wang Xiaoshuai.

3713. Fu, Winnie and Agnes Lam. "Film Personalities in the 40s." *Hong Kong Film Archive Newsletter*. May 1998, pp. 9-10.
    Discusses Wong Man-lei and Tong Sing-to.

3714. Khan, Jalal Uddin. "Reflections on the Issue of Taslima Nasreen." *Asian Thought and Society*. September-December 1998, pp. 238-243.
    Condemns writings of Bangladeshi Taslima Nasreen which call for rewriting of *Koran*.

3715. Kim, Myoung Hye. "Western Psychoanalysis Hits the Korean Television Drama." Paper presented at International Association for Mass Communication Research, Glasgow, Scotland, July 26-30, 1998.
    Takes Korean television drama "The Lover" to examine how the Western notion of gender identity formation operates.

3716. Lumby, Catherine. "No Kidding: Paedophilia and Popular Culture." *Continuum*. April 1998, pp. 47-54.

Discusses use of very young female models and paedophilia in Australia; discusses Charles Dodgson (Lewis Carroll).

3717. "A Nationwide UNDP Project Zooms in on Media Images of Women on Pakistan Television." *Media & Gender Monitor.* Spring 1998, p. 18.

Says that media sexism has come a long way -- before, stereotypes were straightforward and derogatory; now, much more subtle.

3718. "Nepal's First Women's Publishing House Focuses on Media." *Media & Gender Monitor.* Summer 1998, p. 15.

Discusses Asmita Publishing House, set up in 1988.

3719. Pande, Manisha. "Projections of Today's Indian Woman's Images in Indian Commercials: A Misnomer?" Paper presented at International Association for Mass Communication Research, Glasgow, Scotland, July 26-30, 1998.

Analyzes Indian television commercials in context of contemporary realities including the role shifts of women and men.

3720. Park, Changhee. "The Ideological Shift of Gender Representations in Korean Television Dramas." Paper presented at International Association for Mass Communication Research, Glasgow, Scotland, July 26-30, 1998.

Suggests that the Korean dramas of the 1980s differed from those of the 1990s in terms of structural encoding patterns and narrative structures.

3721. Robson, Jocelyn and Beverley Zalcock. *Girls' Own Stories: Australian and New Zealand Women's Film.* Scarlet Press, 1998. 144 pp.

Gives history, theory, and textual analysis of film of Australia and New Zealand.

3722. Suter, Keith. "Australia, the Media and the Politics of Anger." *Media Development.* 3/1998, pp. 38-40.

Tries to answer the question: What are the implications for the mass media surrounding the rise of Pauline Hanson, one of Australia's most notorious politicians?

3723. Yau, Esther C. M. "Filmic Discourses on Women in Chinese Cinema (1949-1965): Art, Ideology, and Social Relations." Ph.D. dissertation, University of California, 1990.

EUROPE

3724. Agustín, Laura. "The Plight of Migrant Women: They Speak, but Who's Listening?" *Media Development.* 3/1998, pp. 24-26.

Discusses migrant women's access to information, capacity to speak out and be heard, especially in Europe.

3725. Djert-Pierr, Monika and Margareta Melin Higgins. "Networking in Newsrooms: Journalism and Gender Cultures." Paper presented at International Association for Mass Communication Research, Glasgow, Scotland, July 26-30, 1998.

Looks at Swedish women broadcast journalists in 1960s, and British journalists in 1990s, to show how they struggle to be "one of the boys" while trying to define their own journalist culture.

3726. Forst, Birgit. "Absolventinnen der Deutschen Journalistenschule. Ergebnisse einer Befragung zum Berufsweg von Frauen im Journalismus" (Graduates of the "Deutsche Journalistenschule": Evidence on the Careers of Women in Journalism). *Publizistik.* 34:1-2, pp. 146-151.
        Claims that female journalists still find it more difficult than men to advance in the field.

3727. Ganetz, Hillevi. "Her Voices: Mediated Female Texts in a Cultural Perspective." *Nordicom Review.* June 1998, pp. 215-224.
        Deals with Swedish female rock stars Turid Lundqvist, Eva Dahlgren, and Kajsa Grytt.

3728. Harris, Warren G. *Sophia Loren: A Biography.* New York: Simon and Schuster, 1998. 399 pp.
        Discusses life and career of Italian film actress.

3729. Higgins, John W. "Critical/Feminist Media Pedagogies in a Turkish Cypriot Context." Paper presented at International Association for Mass Communication Research, Glasgow, Scotland, July 26-30, 1998.
        Discusses theories regarding critical and feminist media pedagogies and their application within the university classroom in the Turkish Republic of Northern Cyprus.

3730. Hirdman, Anja. "Male Norms and Female Forms: The Visual Representation of Men and Women in Press Images in 1925, 1955 and 1987." *Nordicom Review.* June 1998, pp. 225-254.
        Looks at commonalities and differences in the gender ideology depicted in pictures in Swedish dailies *Dagens Nyheter* and *Aftonbladet* and five magazines.

3731. Hirdman, Anja. "Veckotidningen och Damrummet" (The Weekly Magazine and the Ladies' Room). In *Medierummet,* edited by Karin Becker. Stockholm: Carlsson, 1996.

3732. Horrocks, Dylan, ed. *Nga Pakiwaituhi o Aotearoa: New Zealand Comics.* Auckland: Hicksville Press, 1998. Unpaginated.
        Includes brief profiles of New Zealand female comics artists Indira Neville, Renee Jones, Lisa Noble, and Sophie McMillan.

3733. Jääsaari, Johanna and Raija Sarkkinen. *Gender Counts? Gender in Finnish Broadcasting Audience Research.* Helsinki: Finnish Broadcasting Company, 1997. 14 pp.
        Discusses how to persuade media executives that focusing on gender is worthwhile.

3734. Jallov, Birgette. "Women's (Community) Radio as a Feminist Public Sphere." Paper presented at International Association for Mass Communication Research, Glasgow, Scotland, July 26-30, 1998.

Uses empirical data from women's radio stations and projects in different parts of Europe to explore how these stations might contribute to a feminist public sphere and work as a tool for women's empowerment.

3735. Lawson, Annie. *Biological Function.* London: Deirdre McDonald Books, 1991. 64 pp.

Includes more than 60 strip cartoons by former *Guardian* and *City Limits* cartoonist Lawson. Also see her *Brilliant Advice!* (London: Deirdre McDonald Books, 1988. 64 pp.); *Life on the Hard Shoulder* (London: Deirdre McDonald, 1991. 64 pp.); *Tortoise Woman* (London: Deirdre McDonald, 1992. 64 pp.); *More Brilliant Advice!* (London: Deirdre McDonald, 1989. 64 pp).

3736. Lent, John A. and Asli Tunç. "Women and Animation in Turkey." Paper presented at Society for Animation Studies, Orange, California, August 15, 1998.

Uses primary data to discuss women print cartoonists and animators, their breaking into the profession, problems, relationships within a patriarchal workforce.

3737. Masi, S. and E. Lancia. *Italian Movie Goddesses: Over 80 of the Greatest Women in Italian Cinema.* Gremese Editore International, 1997. 226 pp.

Discusses 80 significant Italian actresses and gives insights on the evolution of roles for women in Italian cinema.

3738. Meils, Cathy. "E. Euros Soak in Soaps." *Variety.* July 13-19, 1998, p. 33.

States that a spurt of women's channels and increasingly female-friendly programming has fueled a market for telenovelas in Eastern Europe.

3739. Mühleisen, Wencke. "Direkte Lykke! A Naivist Parody of Old-Time TV Hosted by a Transgressive Woman." *Nordicom Review.* June 1998, pp. 255-270.

Analyzes youth entertainment series "Direkte Lykke!" on Norwegian television to focus on how "femaleness" is staged among program hosts.

3740. Novikova, Irina. "Fashioning Our Minds: Women's Press in Latvia (Latvian and Russian Women's Magazines at the Crossroads of Gender, Ethnicity and Citizenship)." Paper presented at International Association for Mass Communication Research, Glasgow, Scotland, July 26-30, 1998.

Focuses on different media discursive strategies in gendering stereotypes of Latvian and Russian women after restoration of political independence in Latvia in 1991.

3741. O'Donnell, Hugh. *Good Times, Bad Times: Soap Operas and Society in Western Europe.* Leicester: Leicester University Press, 1998. 224 pp.

Claims by end of 1980s, Western Europe had a total of eight domestic soap operas; by mid-1997, the number was over 50; provides analysis of all new Western European soap operas -- in Belgium, Denmark, Finland, Germany,

Greece, Ireland, Italy, Netherlands, Norway, Portugal, Spain, Sweden, and United Kingdom.

3742. Ogan, Christine and Marisca Milikowski. "Television Helps To Define 'Home' for the Turkish Women of Amsterdam." *Media Development.* 3/1998, pp. 13-21.

Determines role of mass media in the Turkish communities, especially women living in Amsterdam; answers vary according to age and circumstance, but television is a key factor.

3743. Ojajärvi, Sanna. "Gender or Generic Codes? A Study of Hosts on Finnish Television." Paper presented at International Association for Mass Communication Research, Glasgow, Scotland, July 26-30, 1998.

Focuses on the construction of gender and gender systems in different generic types of Finnish television programs.

3744. O'Sickey, Ingeborg M. and Ingeborg von Zadow, eds. *Triangulated Visions: Women in Recent German Cinema.* Albany, New York: State University of New York Press, 1998.

Illuminates challenges faced by feminist German filmmakers; discusses narrative, documentary, "art," and essay films from West and East Germany before and after unification.

3745. Ross, Karen. "Sex, Politics and the Media: Selling Women (Down the River)." Paper presented at International Association for Mass Communication Research, Glasgow, Scotland, July 26-30, 1998.

Analyzes a week of broadcast news reporting during the 1997 British general elections; argues that once again, gender and gender issues were invisible during the campaign.

3746. Sarkkinen, Raija. "Does Gender Count in Radio?" Paper presented at International Association for Mass Communication Research, Glasgow, Scotland, July 26-30, 1998.

Says that Finnish female audiences have been "much to the fore" recently in the expansion of the country's broadcasting.

3747. Savolainen, Tarja. "Film Journalist Brita Wrede and Finnish Television." Paper presented at International Association for Mass Communication Research, Glasgow, Scotland, July 26-30, 1998.

Tells story of Finnish/Swedish filmmaker and journalist Brita Wrede (1894-1973).

3748. Winter, Kirsten. "Creating Music and Imagery Together." *Animation World.* March 1998, 3 pp.

Discusses collaboration of German animator Kirsten Winter and Russian-Australian composer Elena Kats-Chernin.

3749. Zilliacus Tikkanen, Henrika. "Who Speaks? A Study on Men and Women in

Prime Television in Five Countries, Focusing on Data from Finland." Paper presented at International Association for Mass Communication Research, Glasgow, Scotland, July 26-30, 1998.

Involves Finland, Norway, Sweden, Denmark, and the Netherlands with data concerning producers, journalists, and actors in primetime TV.

LATIN AMERICA AND THE CARIBBEAN

3750. de Bruin, Marjan. "Gender in the Newsroom: Does It Make a Difference." Paper presented at International Association for Mass Communication Research, Glasgow, Scotland, July 26-30, 1998.

Looks at various levels, and from different angles, Caribbean media organizations and their output from a gender perspective.

3751. "Feminist Radio Fortified in Costa Rica." *Action.* May/June 1998, p. 8.

Discusses Association of Interactive Feminist Radio Communications.

NORTH AMERICA

3752. Ashley, Laura and Beth Olson. "Constructing Reality: Print Media's Framing of the Women's Movement, 1966 to 1986." *Journalism and Mass Communication Quarterly.* Summer 1998, pp. 263-277.

Examines framing techniques and their use in *New York Times, Time,* and *Newsweek*'s coverage of the women's movement; studied both those who supported and deterred the movement. In coverage, neither group was considered important.

3753. Berger, Samantha A. "NYC Wonder Women." *Animation World.* July 1998, 5 pp.

Discusses comic books for girls and women.

3754. Bonfante, Jordan. "Lady Power in the Sunbelt." *Time.* March 19, 1990, pp. 21-24.

States that Helen Copley, owner of the San Diego *Union* and *Tribune* and other newspapers, was part of a "powerful troika of female leadership" in the city.

3755. Borden, Diane L. "Reputational Assault: A Critical and Historical Analysis of Gender and the Law of Defamation." *Journalism and Mass Communication Quarterly.* Spring 1998, pp. 98-111.

Looks at how the U.S. judicial system treats men and women in terms of reputational harm.

3756. Brinson, Susan L. "Frieda Hennock: FCC Activist and the Campaign for Educational Television, 1948-1951." *Historical Journal of Film, Radio and Television.* August 1998, pp. 411-429.

Uses primary documents to chronicle career of Frieda Hennock, first woman appointed to the Federal Communications Commission; she served seven years, 1948-55, during which time U.S. television was restructured.

3757. Burt, Elizabeth V. "The Ideology, Rhetoric, and Organization Structure of a Countermovement Publication: *The Remonstrance*, 1890-1920." *Journalism and Mass Communication Quarterly*. Spring 1998, pp. 69-83.

Discusses organ of the Massachusetts Association Opposed to the Further Extension of Suffrage to Women.

3758. Carter, Cynthia, Gill Branston, and Stuart Allan, eds. *News, Gender and Power*. London: Routledge, 1998. 296 pp.

Addresses questions of how gender shapes the forms, practice, institutions, and audiences of journalism; contributors are: Stuart Allan, Patricia Bradley, Gill Branston, Rod Brookes, Cynthia Carter, John Hartley, Beverley Holbrook, Patricia Holland, Jenny Kitzinger, Myra Macdonald, Lisa McLaughlin, Paula Skidmore, Linda Steiner, Janet Thumim, Liesbet van Zoonen, C. Kay Weaver, and Maggie Wykes.

3759. Chimovitz, Melissa. "Declaration of Independents: Independent Animation Is Alive and Well in New York." *Animation World*. May 1998. 10 pp.

Profiles New York City independent animators Kathy Rose, Debra Solomon, and Janie Geiser.

3760. Dean, Michael. "The Truth About 'Truths and Legends': Liar Comics' Sharon Scott Gives Birth to a New Heroine." *Comics Buyer's Guide*. July 3, 1998, pp. 40-41.

3761. Donald, Stephanie. "Landscape and Agency: *Yellow Earth* and the Demon Lover." *Theory, Culture and Society*. 14:1 (1997), pp. 97-112.

3762. Flanders, Judy. "Women War Correspondents: On the Fields of Macho." *Washington Journalism Review*. January-February 1990, pp. 38-41.

Shows the tiny group of women war correspondents exhibited nerve and stamina to obtain stories that men could not.

3763. Flowers, Amy. *The Fantasy Factory: An Insider's View of the Phone Sex Industry*. Philadelphia: University of Pennsylvania Press, 1998. 200 pp.

Explores the world of women on the other end of phone sex lines; interviews these women; relates her own experiences as an operator.

3764. Freese, Gene S. *Hollywood Stunt Performers: A Directory and Filmography of Over 600 Men and Women, 1922-1996*. Jefferson, North Carolina: McFarland, 1998. 268 pp.

Includes profiles and filmographies of stunt appearances.

3765. Goulart, Ron. "Forgotten Funnies." *Comics History Magazine*. Spring 1998, pp. 9-11.

Profiles Dale Conner Ulrey, who drew the newspaper strips "Mary Worth's Family," "Ayer Lane," and "Hugh Striver" in the 1940s.

3766. Goulart, Ron. "The History of Good Girl Art (Part Five)." *Comics History Magazine*. Spring 1998, pp. 5-8.
　　　In comic books of 1930s-1940s.

3767. Hannsberry, Karen B. *Femme Noir: Bad Girls of Film*. Jefferson, North Carolina: McFarland, 1998. 643 pp.
　　　Provides biographies of 49 women most frequently featured in *film noir*; filmography of *noir* appearances.

3768. Inness, Sherrie A. *Tough Girls: Women Warriors and Wonder Women in Popular Culture*. Philadelphia: University of Pennsylvania Press, 1998. 256 pp.
　　　Looks at tough women of popular culture -- "The Avengers," "Charlie's Angels," "Bionic Woman," "The X-Files," and "Xena: Warrior Princess."

3769. Kanfer, Stefan. "Tina Brown and the Coming Decline of Celebrity Journalism." *Columbia Journalism Review*. September-October 1998, pp. 41-45.
　　　Discusses Tina Brown's quitting the editorship of *The New Yorker* and the "bitter excoriation" that followed; claims she had no one to blame but herself because she was a "celebrity hound."

3770. Kitch, Carolyn. "The American Woman Series: Gender and Class in *The Ladies' Home Journal*, 1897." *Journalism and Mass Communication Quarterly*. Summer 1998, pp. 243-262.
　　　Analyzes six full-page illustrations drawn by Alice B. Stephens in *Ladies' Home Journal* in 1897; titled "The American Woman," the series was among the first visual commentary on gender in a national medium.

3771. Klein, Andy. "Disney's *Mulan*: A More Modern Heroine." *Animation World*. July 1998, 4 pp.
　　　Says no previous Disney animated feature has been so centrally concerned with gender roles.

3772. Landay, Lori. *Madcaps, Screwballs, and Con Women: The Female Trickster in American Culture*. Philadelphia: University of Pennsylvania Press, 1998. 272 pp.
　　　Considers fiction, film, radio, and television to determine how popular heroines used "craft and deceit to circumvent the limits of femininity."

3773. Long, John. "Women Achieving Goals: 2 Points of View." *News Photographer*. January 1990, pp. 12-14.
　　　Gives two views on whether the National Press Photographers Association should have a women's committee.

3774. Lowe, T. M. "Anina Bennett: Heartbreaker at Large." *Comics Buyer's Guide*. June 19, 1998, p. 46.
　　　Interviews comics writer who wrote "heartbreakers."

3775. McFadden, Ed. *Women's Issues*. New York: Berkley Books, 1996. 534 pp.
　　　Contains sections on film and television, the media, and performing arts.

3776. McKinley, E. Graham. *Beverly Hills, 90210: Television, Gender, and Identity.* Philadelphia: University of Pennsylvania Press, 1997. 288 pp.

Uses interviews of young women who watched the show in groups to determine its significance.

3777. Mank, Gregory W. *Women in Horror Films.* Jefferson, North Carolina: McFarland, 1998. Vol. 1 (1930s), 408 pp: Vol. 2 (1940s), 392 pp.

Gives details on lives and careers of 40 cinematic leading ladies, femmes fatales, monsters, and misfits.

3778. Nicholson, Daniel R. "The Peacettes: The New York Times' Coverage of the First International Conference for Women at The Hague in 1915." Paper presented at International Association for Mass Communication Research, Glasgow, Scotland, July 26-30, 1998.

Relates the *Times'* coverage with written accounts by some American delegates, particularly Jane Addams.

3779. Ott, Louise and Linda Russman. "The Story of Women in Communication, Inc." *Professional Communicator.* Fall 1989, pp. 7-11.

Recounts 80-year history of first association for women in journalism.

3780. Pollak, R. Robert. "From the '40s to the '90s: Dale Messick's Starr Qualities." *Comics Buyer's Guide.* June 26, 1998, p. 44.

A 1988 interview with Dale Messick, creator of "Brenda Starr" comic strip in 1940.

3781. Sandler, Kevin S. "Gendered Evasion: Bugs Bunny in Drag." In *Reading the Rabbit: Explorations in Warner Bros. Animation*, edited by Kevin S. Sandler, pp. 154-172. New Brunswick, New Jersey: Rutgers University Press, 1998.

Includes sections on "Gender Theory and Anthropomorphism," "Femininity in Warner Bros. Cartoons," "Transvestite Kiss," "Backwoods Bunny as Incidental Bivalency."

3782. Serini, Shirley A., Angela A. Powers, and Susan Johnson. "Of Horse Race and Policy Issues: A Study of Gender in Coverage of a Gubernatorial Election by Two Major Metropolitan Newspapers." *Journalism and Mass Communication Quarterly.* Spring 1998, pp. 194-204.

Shows as one of its major findings that a woman will be more successful in coverage of a gubernatorial race if she presents herself as a man.

3783. Thompson, Maggie. "Vampirella: Is She a 'Bad Girl' -- Or Just Drawn That Way?" *Comics Buyer's Guide.* July 31, 1998, pp. 26-28.

Describes vampire story in comic book form.

3784. Valiquette, Michele, comp. *Women and the Media: Resources for Analysis and Action.* Toronto: MediaWatch, 1993. 88 pp.

Emphasizes materials published in feminist and alternative presses and those by and about Canadians.

3785. Waldron, Carolyn. "'Is Feminism Dead?' Is Not the Question. Reframing Mainstream Media's Debate on the Women's Movement." *Extra!* September/October 1998, p. 14.

States a better question is: "What are today's diverse strains of feminist thought and political and social action, and how might they be affecting society?"

3786. Xing, Jun. *Asia America Through the Lens: History, Representations, and Identity.* Walnut Creek, California: AltaMira, 1998. 248 pp.

Discusses Asian American women filmmakers, especially in chapter entitled "Hybrid Cinema by Asian American Women."

3787. Zeidenberg, Leonard. "Global View of NTIA." *Broadcasting.* January 29, 1990, pp. 41-42.

Tells how head of National Telecommunications and Information Administration took a global view.

Author Index

Abalos, Marilyn, 2683
Abd-el-Kader, Soha, 281
Abd-el Rahman, Awatef, 364-365
Abella, Olga, 59
Abelman, Robert, 6
Abernathy, Barbara T., 3005
Abeyesekera, Sunila, 444
Abrahamson, David, 8, 1823
Abrahamsson, Ulla B., 34, 1016, 1095, 1225-1226, 1256-1258
Abramowitz, Jack, 1861
Abramson, Nancy, 1710
Abramson, Phyllis L., 3006
Abreo, Desmond A. D., 27
Acker, Ally, 1852, 2771
Acland, Charles, 2138
Acosta-Alzuru, Carolina, 13
Adams, Ed, 13
Adams, Edward E., 10, 1678
Adams, Kathryn T., 2361
Adams, Mark, 1736
Adams, Michelle, 2152
Addison, Erin, 20, 1802
Adeleye-Fayemi, Bisi, 282-283
Aden, Roger C., 2116
Adkins-Covert, Tawnya J., 1824
Agarwal, Sumegha, 204, 936
Agor, T., 2404
Agrawal, Binod, 668
Aguirre, Maria T., 1468
Agustin, Laura, 3688, 3724
Ahn, Byung-Sup, 445
Aikat, Debashis, 12
Aishah, Ali, 446
Akagi, Akira, 571

Akhava-Majid, Roya, 36
Akintunde, Omowale, 1886
Akpan, Emmanuel D., 284
Alankus-Kural, Sevda, 1097
Alberti, Joanna, 1055
Albright, Cheryl L., 3539
Albury, Katherine, 3668, 3674
Alcala, Pilar Riaño, 180
Alcalay, R., 2585
Alder, Otto, 976
Aldoory, Linda, 12-13
Aledia Luna, M. Juris, 411
Alemany-Galway, Mary, 1647
Alexander, Alison, 1952
Alexander, Karen, 104
Alexander, Susan H., 1098, 3540
Alfaro, Rosa M., 64, 1469, 1482, 1493
Algoe, Jennifer J., 59
Alinange, Dan, 12
Al-Khaja, M. A. W., 372
Allan, Kenneth, 2139
Allan, Robin, 2772-2773
Allan, Stuart, 3758
Allen, Donna, 1, 37, 241, 369, 1679
Allen, Isobel, 1261
Allen, Louise, 1099
Allen, M., 2179
Allen, Martha L., 1680-1681
Allen, Michelle, 1308
Allen, Robert C., 20, 242, 1835
Allen, S., 86
Alley, Patricia W., 3008
Allison, Anne, 401, 447-448
Allison, Tony, 384
Allott, Anna J., 672

Bobo, Jacqueline, 14, 206, 2563
Boddy, William, 1851
Bodeen, De Witt, 2797
Bodle, John V., 10, 13, 1678
Boëthius, Gunilla, 1115
Bogaert, A. F., 2369
Bogle, D., 2798
Boily, Lise, 1652
Boisseau, T. J., 1840
Boliches, Emilia, 1470
Bolinder, Vibeke, 18, 34
Bonard, C. A., 1823
Bond, Donovan H., 3119
Bond, Rose, 2799
Bondebjerg, Ib, 2239
Bonfante, Jordan, 3754
Book, Constance Ledoux, 3670
Booker, Edna L., 3028
Boozer, Jack, 1813
Borden, Diane L., 10, 1690, 3755
Bordo, Susan, 14
Borelli, Sílvia, 1610
Borisoff, D., 1691
Bornoff, Nicholas, 460
Bose, Sudhir, 686, 698
Boseman, Keith, 2800
Bosshart, Louis, 1012-1013, 1116, 1268
Boswell, Parley A., 2240
Botta, Renee A., 13
Bourne, Stephen, 104, 1117
Bowen, Michelle, 10
Bowen, Sheryl P., 1705, 1776, 1896
Bowker, J., 1686
Bowles, Kate, 3674
Bowser, Eileen, 1857
Boycott, Rosie, 3029
Boyd, Robert, 3030-3031
Boyd, Veleda J., 2108
Boyle, Christine, 1624
Boynton, Lois A., 12
Boyster, Melissa, 36
Box, Muriel, 1269
Brackenridge, 903
Bradbury, Keith, 3710
Bradby, Barbara, 1897
Braden, Maria, 3032, 3546
Bradley, Patricia, 3033, 3670
Brain, Mary, 13
Bramlett-Solomon, S., 2370

Branch, Robert C., 1894
Brandon, Barbara, 3034
Brandt, Brenda, 59
Brandt, Pamela R., 2371
Branston, Gill, 86, 3758
Brantley, Vanessa, 59
Brantley, Will, 3035
Braunstein, Richard, 2003
Breazeale, Kenon, 2588
Bredin, Marian, 1671
Brennen, Bonnie, 9
Brettle, Jane, 1270
Bridges, M. Junior, 1687
Briefel, Aviva, 20
Briere, John, 1908
Brierley, Sean, 1035
Briggs, Asa, 1014
Bright, Susie, 1271
Brinson, Susan L., 2144-2146, 3756
Brislin, Tom, 1869, 2606
Brislin-Slutz, J. A., 2579
Brissie, Jane S., 2522
Britt, Theron, 2589
Britton, Andrew, 2801
Britton, James, 59
Britton, Patti, 1986, 3323
Broderick, Mick, 614
Brody, Michal, 3547
Brogan, Madeline, 3037
Bronstein, Carolyn, 13, 20
Brook, Heather, 933
Brooks, Dianne L., 1706, 2148
Brooks, Stella, 104
Brosius, H.-B., 1119-1120
Brott, Armin, 1898
Brousseau, A. P., 3670
Brown, Catherine H., 2802
Brown, Cindy M., 3670
Brown, Elsa B., 2621
Brown, Elspeth, 1870
Brown, J. D., 2539
Brown, Jane D., 1717, 1946
Brown, John Mason, 3038
Brown, Julianne, 887
Brown, Mary Ellen, 19, 52, 184, 934, 3442
Brown, Peter, 893-894, 903-904, 931
Brown, William J., 641, 1604
Brownlow, S., 2690

Subject Index

106, 221, 265, 477, 534, 872, 971, 1045, 1063, 1065, 1140, 1342, 1429, 1553-1554, 1556, 1573, 1721, 1815-1818, 2233-2234, 2244, 2291, 2300, 2305-2306, 2314, 2316, 2318, 2326, 2330, 2334-2336, 2567, 2961, 2970, 3477, 3480-3481, 3493-3494, 3501, 3505-3506, 3513, 3518, 3525, 3527, 3532-3533, 3697; and media, 81-83, 148, 160, 189-190, 231, 246, 261, 264, 361, 489, 838, 848, 888, 891, 933, 954-955, 1005, 1051, 1093, 1202, 1426, 1619, 1641-1642, 1673, 1696, 1706, 1727, 1729-1730, 1872, 1913, 1967, 1978, 2016, 2587, 3258, 3339, 3576, 3729; and news, 86-87; and press, 860, 927, 1080, 1414, 1428, 1449, 1676, 3029, 3147, 3159, 3217, 3325, 3335, 3558, 3609; and radio, 1082, 3460, 3734, 3751; and technology, 84, 1797; and television, 21, 207, 1010, 1245, 2159-2161, 2189-2190, 2195-2196, 2202, 3443, 3446, 3454, 3474

Feminist International Radio Endeavor (FIRE), 260, 266

femme fatale, 142, 1807, 2251

Fempress, 1494, 1498, 1613

Fer, Fahriye Tamkan, 375

Ferber, Edna, 3264

Fern, Fanny (Sara Parton), 3147, 3295

Ferraro, Geraldine, 1921, 2222, 2472

fetishism, 2584

feuilleton, 1080

fiction, 25, 270, 440, 552, 854, 1604, 2304, 2417, 2424, 2454, 3562

Figes, Eva, 942

figure skating, 2543

film, 20, 25, 75, 99, 150, 161, 177, 405, 428-430, 442, 1031-1032, 1036-1037, 1040, 1045, 1802-1822; audiences, 189, 643, 975, 1241, 1250, 2562-2584; by women, 46, 58, 70, 103-104, 295-296; for women, 254, 257, 265, 840-842, 863, 872, 879, 959, 1409, 1418-1419, 1423, 1427, 1429, 1434, 1437, 1442-1444, 1446, 1450, 1453-1454, 1460-1462, 1533, 1615, 3464-

3538, 3709, 3721; historical studies of, 1852-1860; images of women in, 7-8, 122, 142-143, 145, 158, 167, 172, 247, 366-367, 407, 434, 443-445, 451, 454, 460, 462-463, 466-468, 470, 472, 474-475, 477-478, 480-482, 486-488, 493, 500-503, 508, 512, 514, 516, 520-521, 523, 557, 565, 572, 580-581, 584-586, 588, 590, 593, 595-596, 599, 604, 614, 617, 625, 631-633, 902, 906, 915, 928, 971, 1039, 1059, 1063, 1065, 1078-1079, 1089, 1091, 1117, 1124, 1140, 1147, 1154, 1159, 1164-1165, 1174, 1180, 1207, 1209, 1211-1212, 1215, 1221, 1471, 1478, 1518, 1522-1523, 1538, 1543-1544, 1565, 1573, 1981, 1983, 2019, 2053, 2231-2260, 3694, 3697, 3712, 3715, 3723; women directors of, 134, 371, 373-377, 381, 383, 686, 693, 699-700, 709-710, 734, 745, 771, 777-778, 781, 802, 804-807, 815, 822-823, 831-834, 943, 945, 963, 992-995, 997-998, 1071, 1078-1079, 1089, 1091, 3747; women practitioners in, 206, 208, 210-214, 221, 223-224, 227, 229, 333, 337, 341, 370, 379, 452, 671, 673, 676, 681-682, 684-686, 688, 691-692, 695-700, 702, 704-705, 708, 712, 718, 720-723,726-727, 737, 739, 741-743, 746-749, 753, 758-759, 761-762, 765-767, 772, 776, 779-780, 795, 798, 808-810, 816-819, 824, 937, 946, 948, 977, 981-982, 984-985, 988, 990, 1000-1001, 1004, 1020, 1073, 1094, 1259, 1262-1263, 1265, 1267, 1269, 1273-1276, 1278, 1281-1284, 1286-1287, 1291-1293, 1295-1297, 1299, 1301-1302, 1304-1305, 1312-1314, 1317, 1319-1320, 1324-1327, 1329-1330, 1332, 1335-1338, 1342, 1345-1346, 1348, 1350-1352, 1355, 1358, 1361, 1363, 1365, 1370, 1374-1375, 1381-1382, 1384, 1390, 1393, 1397-1399, 1487-1488, 1490, 1526, 1553, 1556-1557, 1582, 1585, 1587-1596, 1647,

About the Compiler

JOHN A. LENT is the author or editor of fifty-two books and monographs and hundreds of articles. He is founding editor of the *International Journal of Comic Art* and editor of *Asian Cinema*, and holds a professorship at Temple University. In 2000, he will hold the Rogers Distinguished Professorship at the University of Western Ontario.

ISBN 0-313-30209-X

HARDCOVER BAR CODE